Lecture Notes in Computer Science 10105

Commenced Publication in 1973
Founding and Former Series Editors:
Gerhard Goos, Juris Hartmanis, and Jan van Leeuwen

Editorial Board

More information about this series at http://www.springer.com/series/7407

Alberto Leporati · Grzegorz Rozenberg
Arto Salomaa · Claudio Zandron (Eds.)

Membrane Computing

17th International Conference, CMC 2016
Milan, Italy, July 25–29, 2016
Revised Selected Papers

 Springer

Editors
Alberto Leporati
University of Milano-Bicocca
Milan
Italy

Grzegorz Rozenberg
Leiden University
Leiden
The Netherlands

Arto Salomaa
Turku Center for Computer Science
Turku
Finland

Claudio Zandron
University of Milano-Bicocca
Milan
Italy

ISSN 0302-9743   ISSN 1611-3349   (electronic)
Lecture Notes in Computer Science
ISBN 978-3-319-54071-9   ISBN 978-3-319-54072-6   (eBook)
DOI 10.1007/978-3-319-54072-6

Library of Congress Control Number: 2017932126

LNCS Sublibrary: SL1 – Theoretical Computer Science and General Issues

Printed on acid-free paper

This Springer imprint is published by Springer Nature
The registered company is Springer International Publishing AG
The registered company address is: Gewerbestrasse 11, 6330 Cham, Switzerland

Preface

This volume contains the invited contributions and a selection of papers presented at the 17th International Conference on Membrane Computing (CMC17), held in Milan, Italy, during July 25–29, 2016 (see the website: http://cmc17.disco.unimib.it for further information) as well as two selected papers from the Asian Conference on Membrane Computing (ACMC 2016), held in Bangi, Selangor, Malaysia, during November 14–16, 2016 (website: http://2016.asiancmc.org/).

The CMC series started with three workshops organized in Curtea de Argeş, Romania, in 2000, 2001, and 2002. The workshops were then held in Tarragona, Spain (2003), Milan, Italy (2004), Vienna, Austria (2005), Leiden, The Netherlands (2006), Thessaloniki, Greece (2007), and Edinburgh, UK (2008).

The 10th edition was organized again in Curtea de Argeş, in August 2009, where it was decided to continue the series as the Conference on Membrane Computing (CMC). The following editions were held in Jena, Germany (2010), Fontainebleau, France (2011), Budapest, Hungary (2012), Chişinău, Moldova (2013), Prague, Czech Republic (2014), and Valencia, Spain (2015).

A regional version of CMC, the Asian Conference on Membrane Computing, ACMC, started in 2012 in Wuhan (China), and continued in Chengdu, China (2013), Coimbatore, India (2014), Hefei, Anhui, China (2015), and Bangi, Selangor, Malaysia (2016).

CMC17 was organized, under the auspices of the International Membrane Computing Society and the European Molecular Computing Consortium (EMCC), by the Research Group on Molecular Computing of the Department of Informatics, Systems, and Communication, at the University of Milano-Bicocca.

CMC17 consisted of three different parts. During the first day, representatives of research groups working on membrane computing presented recent research activities of their groups, the composition of the research teams, and research networks and projects that the groups are involved in. From Tuesday to Thursday the conference continued with standard sessions; invited lectures were given by Matteo Cavaliere (Edinburgh, UK), Thomas Hinze (Cottbus, Germany), Paolo Milazzo (Pisa, Italy), and Agustín Riscos-Núñez (Seville, Spain). The last day of the conference was devoted to interaction between participants, centered around open problems and new research topics. Based on the votes of the participants, one Best Paper Award and two Best Student Paper Awards were bestowed. The Best Paper Award was given to Zsolt Gazdag and Gábor Kolonits for their paper "Remarks on the Computational Power of Some Restricted Variants of P Systems with Active Membranes." The two Best Student Paper Awards were given once again to Zsolt Gazdag and Gábor Kolonits for the same paper, and to Thomas Hinze, Lea Louise Weber, and Uwe Hatnik for their paper "Walking Membranes: Grid-exploring P Systems with Artificial Evolution for Multipurpose Topological Optimisation of Cascaded Processes."

The editors are grateful to the Program Committee, the invited speakers, the authors of the papers, the reviewers, and all the participants for their contributions to the success of CMC17.

The support of the Department of Informatics, Systems, and Communication of the University of Milano-Bicocca and of Springer for funding the Prize for the Best Student Paper is gratefully acknowledged.

November 2016

Alberto Leporati
Grzegorz Rozenberg
Arto Salomaa
Claudio Zandron

Organization

Steering Committee of CMC and ACMC

Henry Adorna	University of the Philippines-Diliman, Quezon City, Philippines
Artiom Alhazov	Institute of Mathematics and Computer Science of Academy of Sciences of Moldova, Chişinău, Moldova
Bogdan Aman	A.I. Cuza University, Iaşi, Romania
Matteo Cavaliere	The University of Edinburgh, Edinburgh, UK
Erzsébet Csuhaj-Varjú	Eötvös Loránd University, Budapest, Hungary
Rudolf Freund	Technical University Vienna, Vienna, Austria
Marian Gheorghe (Honorary Member)	University of Bradford, Bradford, UK
Thomas Hinze	Brandenburg University of Technology, Cottbus, Germany
Florentin Ipate	University of Bucharest, Bucharest, Romania
Shankara N. Krishna	Indian Institute of Technology, Bombay, India
Alberto Leporati	University of Milano-Bicocca, Milan, Italy
Taishin Y. Nishida	Toyama Prefectural University, Toyama, Japan
Linqiang Pan (Co-chair)	Huazhong University of Science and Technology, Wuhan, China
Gheorghe Păun (Honorary Member)	Institute of Mathematics of the Romanian Academy, Bucharest, Romania
Mario J. Pérez-Jiménez	University of Seville, Seville, Spain
Agustín Riscos-Núñez	University of Seville, Seville, Spain
Petr Sosík	Charles University, Opava, Czech Republic
Kumbakonam Govindarajan Subramanian	University Sains Malaysia, Penang, Malaysia
György Vaszil	University of Debrecen, Debrecen, Hungary
Sergey Verlan	University Paris Est Créteil, Paris, France
Claudio Zandron (Co-chair)	University of Milano-Bicocca, Milan, Italy
Gexiang Zhang	Southwest Jiaotong University, Chengdu, China

Organizing Committee of CMC17

Alberto Leporati (Co-chair)	University of Milano-Bicocca, Milan, Italy
Luca Manzoni	University of Milano-Bicocca, Milan, Italy
Antonio E. Porreca	University of Milano-Bicocca, Milan, Italy
Claudio Zandron (Co-chair)	University of Milano-Bicocca, Milan, Italy

Program Committee of CMC17

Artiom Alhazov	Institute of Mathematics and Computer Science of Academy of Sciences of Moldova, Chişinău, Moldova
Bogdan Aman	A.I. Cuza University, Iaşi, Romania
Lucie Ciencialová	Charles University, Opava, Czech Republic
Erzsébet Csuhaj-Varjú	Eötvös Loránd University, Budapest, Hungary
Giuditta Franco	University of Verona, Verona, Italy
Rudolf Freund	Technical University Vienna, Vienna, Austria
Marian Gheorghe	University of Bradford, Bradford, UK
Thomas Hinze	Brandenburg University of Technology, Cottbus, Germany
Florentin Ipate	University of Bucharest, Bucharest, Romania
Shankara N. Krishna	Indian Institute of Technology, Bombay, India
Alberto Leporati (Co-chair)	University of Milano-Bicocca, Milan, Italy
Vincenzo Manca	University of Verona, Verona, Italy
Maurice Margenstern	University of Lorraine, Metz, France
Giancarlo Mauri	University of Milano-Bicocca, Milan, Italy
Radu Nicolescu	The University of Auckland, Auckland, New Zealand
Linqiang Pan	Huazhong University of Science and Technology, Wuhan, China
Gheorghe Păun	Institute of Mathematics of the Romanian Academy, Bucharest, Romania
Mario J. Pérez–Jiménez	University of Seville, Seville, Spain
Antonio E. Porreca	University of Milano-Bicocca, Milan, Italy
Agustín Riscos-Núñez	University of Seville, Seville, Spain
José M. Sempere	Technical University of Valencia, Valencia, Spain
Petr Sosík	Charles University, Opava, Czech Republic
György Vaszil	University of Debrecen, Debrecen, Hungary
Sergey Verlan	University Paris Est Créteil, Paris, France
Claudio Zandron (Co-chair)	University of Milano-Bicocca, Milan, Italy
Gexiang Zhang	Southwest Jiaotong University, Chengdu, China

Additional Reviewer

Luca Manzoni	University of Milano-Bicocca, Milan, Italy

Contents

Invited Papers

The Evolutionary Resilience of Distributed Cellular Computing   3
  Matteo Cavaliere and Alvaro Sanchez

Coping with Dynamical Structures for Interdisciplinary Applications
of Membrane Computing.   16
  Thomas Hinze

Applications of P Systems in Population Biology and Ecology:
The Cases of MPP and APP Systems   28
  Roberto Barbuti, Pasquale Bove, Paolo Milazzo, and Giovanni Pardini

Regular Papers

Simulating R Systems by P Systems   51
  Artiom Alhazov, Bogdan Aman, Rudolf Freund, and Sergiu Ivanov

Purely Catalytic P Systems over Integers and Their Generative Power.   67
  Artiom Alhazov, Omar Belingheri, Rudolf Freund, Sergiu Ivanov,
  Antonio E. Porreca, and Claudio Zandron

P Systems Working in Maximal Variants of the Set Derivation Mode   83
  Artiom Alhazov, Rudolf Freund, and Sergey Verlan

Computational Power of Protein Networks.   103
  Bogdan Aman and Gabriel Ciobanu

Comparative Analysis of Statistical Model Checking Tools   119
  Mehmet Emin Bakir, Marian Gheorghe, Savas Konur, and Mike Stannett

Chemical Term Reduction with Active P Systems.   136
  Péter Battyányi and György Vaszil

P Colonies with Evolving Environment   151
  Lucie Ciencialová, Luděk Cienciala, and Petr Sosík

Continuation Passing Semantics for Membrane Systems.   165
  Gabriel Ciobanu and Eneia Nicolae Todoran

Minimal Multiset Grammars for Recurrent Dynamics   177
  Alessandro Farinelli, Giuditta Franco, and Romeo Rizzi

Solution to Motif Finding Problem in Membranes.   190
   Katrina B. Gapuz, Ephraim D. Mendoza, Richelle Ann B. Juayong,
   Nestine Hope S. Hernandez, Francis George C. Cabarle,
   and Henry N. Adorna

Remarks on the Computational Power of Some Restricted Variants
of P Systems with Active Membranes   209
   Zsolt Gazdag and Gábor Kolonits

Kernel P Systems Modelling, Testing and Verification - Sorting Case Study . . .   233
   Marian Gheorghe, Rodica Ceterchi, Florentin Ipate, and Savas Konur

Walking Membranes: Grid-Exploring P Systems with Artificial Evolution
for Multi-purpose Topological Optimisation of Cascaded Processes.   251
   Thomas Hinze, Lea Louise Weber, and Uwe Hatnik

Array-Rewriting P Systems with Basic Puzzle Grammar Rules
and Permitting Features   272
   Pradeep Isawasan, Ravie Chandren Muniyandi, Ibrahim Venkat,
   and K.G. Subramanian

Agent-Based Simulation of Kernel P Systems with Division Rules
Using FLAME   286
   Raluca Lefticaru, Luis F. Macías-Ramos, Ionuţ Mihai Niculescu,
   and Laurenţiu Mierlă

Shallow Non-confluent P Systems.   307
   Alberto Leporati, Luca Manzoni, Giancarlo Mauri, Antonio E. Porreca,
   and Claudio Zandron

Revising the Membrane Computing Model for Byzantine Agreement   317
   Radu Nicolescu

Rewriting P Systems with Flat-Splicing Rules   340
   Linqiang Pan, Bosheng Song, and K.G. Subramanian

A View of P Systems from Information Theory   352
   José M. Sempere

Author Index   363

Invited Papers

The Evolutionary Resilience of Distributed Cellular Computing

Matteo Cavaliere[1](✉) and Alvaro Sanchez[2]

[1] University of Edinburgh, Edinburgh, UK
mcavali2@staffmail.ed.ac.uk
[2] Yale University, New Haven, USA
alvaro.sanchez@yale.edu

Abstract. Individual cells process environmental information relevant to their functions using biochemical processes and signalling networks that implement a flow of information from the extracellular environment, across the cell membrane to the cytoplasm in which the actual cellular computation takes place (in the form of gene expression). In many cases, the environmental information to be processed are either molecules produced by other cells or shared extracellular molecules - in this case the processing of the environmental information is a distributed, highly parallel computing process, in which cells must synchronize, coordinate and cooperate. While the ability of cells to cooperate can increase their overall computational power, it also raises an evolutionary stability issue - population of cooperating cells are at risk of cheating cells invasions, cells that do not cooperate but exploit the benefits of the population. The bridge between membrane computing (as a mathematical formalization of cellular computing) and evolutionary dynamics (as mathematical formalization of natural selection) could lead to interesting insights on the evolutionary stability of cellular computing.

1 How Much Cells Can Compute

Populations of living cells can be seen as systems that implement information processing in a distributed manner. This is a repeated motif in biology, where examples of biological systems that are distributed, process information and make decisions without a centralized coordinator occur at multiple levels of organization [10,14,16]. Several authors have tried to understand the similarities and differences between distributed computations in biological and human-designed systems (e.g., see [14] for a recent review). Distributed information processing in cellular populations is often result of the interplay between inter-cellular communication and cellular physiology. Cells can often secrete signaling molecules which, through the activation of internal signaling networks, affect other cells' behavior. This form of cellular communication endows populations of cells with the ability to synchronize their actions. In turn, the ability of single cells to synchronize their decisions may lead to populations of cells to overcome individual cellular limitations to processing environmental information [3,12,14]. A natural

© Springer International Publishing AG 2017
A. Leporati et al. (Eds.): CMC 2016, LNCS 10105, pp. 3–15, 2017.
DOI: 10.1007/978-3-319-54072-6_1

question is then how one could quantify these aspects of cellular information-processing [16].

One of the possible approaches, inspired by computer science and automata theory, is membrane computing that propose a formal mathematical framework to investigate the computing power of living cells [15]. We briefly revise here a specific membrane computing model based on agents that can process information internally or in coordination with other cells, highlighting the essential point that higher computing power can only be obtained when the cells are able to coordinate (when individual cells are sufficiently simple). However, an important aspect that is generally not considered in membrane computing (and similar biologically-inspired models of cellular computation) is that a population of cells is subject to natural selection - cells compete for resources and different cells can replicate at different rates.

This leads to a key problem. Distributed cellular computing relies on the coordination of the different cells in the population by endogenously produced shared molecules. Since these molecules are thus public goods, their production can suffer from the spreading of cheating mutants: cells that benefit from the public good (in this case the enhanced powers of information processing achieved by the population), but which do not contribute to its production [11]. Because these such non-producing cheating cells enjoy the benefits but avoid paying the metabolic costs associated to the production and secretion of the signaling molecules, they have an advantage over the producer cells and will divide faster, spreading in the population and ultimately collapsing the coordination mechanism (and the overall cellular computation). This paper briefly reviews the relevant aspects of this issue and tries to suggests that the bridge between membrane computing and evolutionary dynamics could lead to interesting insights on this problem and, more in general, on the evolutionary stability of cellular computing.

2   A Colony of Synchronizing Agents (CSA) Computational Framework of Cellular Synchronization

The issue of evolutionary resilience as described above appears independent of the specific mathematical formalism; however, to provide a simple example of how one could quantify the role of cellular synchronization (from a computational perspective) we briefly review a model of membrane computing called CSA (colony of synchronizing agents) inspired by the interactions between living cells [1] (clearly, the questions driving this paper could also be reformulated in other frameworks of biological computing and cellular decision-making [14,16]).

The model CSA abstracts intracellular and intercellular mechanisms of cellular populations in terms of multisets-rewriting (often used to analyze the computational aspects of biochemistry [22]). As several models in membrane computing, it is based on a multiset of agents (cells) in a common environment. Each agent has a local contents, stored in the form of a multiset of atomic objects, updated by multiset rewriting rules which may act on individual agents (intracellular action) or synchronize the contents of pairs of agents (intercellular action). Intercellular actions are abstractions of the process in which cells change synchronously their contents by using a shared environmental molecules (using a terminology from game theory [11], such shared molecule could constitute a public good).

A general approach to quantify the computation power of a system is to compare it with an appropriate device from formal language theory and multiset-rewriting.

In this paper we use only basic aspects of this theory - a more complete introduction can be found in the corresponding book chapter of the membrane computing handbook [15] and in the introductory book on automata theory [8].

The computational model (called CSA [1]) is based on a population/colony of *agents* (e.g., corresponding to *cells*) in a common environment, able to modify their contents and to synchronize with other agents in the same environment. Each agent has a contents represented by a multiset of atomic objects (e.g., corresponding to chemical compounds or the characteristics of individual molecules) with some of the objects classified as terminals (e.g., corresponding to properties or chemicals visible to an external observer). An agent's contents may be modified independently of other agents by means of multiset rewriting rules (called *internal rules*) which can mimic biochemistry or other types of *intracellular mechanisms*. Moreover, the agents can influence each other by synchronously changing their contents using pairwise *synchronization rules* (this represents the ability of the cells to coordinate). Rules are global, so all agents obey the same rules: the only feature which may distinguish the agents is their contents. Dynamics of CSAs are defined as sequences of transitions obtained by applying the rules to the agents (i.e., cells). These transitions thus mark the passage of the system from one configuration to another.

To evaluate its computing power, one can interpret CSAs as computational devices and can thus study CSAs by applying tools from classical fields of computer science, such as formal language and automata theory. This is usually done by defining computations of CSAs the trajectories that reach halting configurations, i.e. configurations where the contents of the agents can no longer be changed because no rules may be applied (this situation can be interpreted as a particular kind of steady state of the system). We are interested in the configuration of the colony when a halting condition is reached and we may take the precise contents of the agents as the output (the result) produced by the CSA.

The model has similarities with cellular automata (CAs) another computational formalism widely used to simulate and model cellular populations [9]. In CAs, cells exist on a regular grid, where each cell has a finite number of possible states and where cells react to or with a defined neighbourhood. In the presented model, because of the multiset-based contents and because of the arbitrary multiset rewriting rules, a cell may have infinitely distinct states and could interact with an arbitrary number of other cells.

From a computational point of view, cellular automata that use synchronous update are computational complete (i.e., equivalent to Turing machines), even when employing *simple* rules (e.g., rule 110 [9]).

In our case, to characterize the computing power of the presented CSAs and describe their dynamics we use few basic concepts from formal language theory and multisets rewriting.

We denote by $|A|$ the cardinality of set A and by $\emptyset$ the empty set. By V^* we denote the set of all strings (sequences of symbols) over V. By V^+ we denote the set of all strings over V excluding the empty string. The empty string is denoted by λ. The *length* of a string v is denoted by $|v|$. The concatenation of two strings $u, v \in V^*$ is written uv.

The number of occurrences of the symbol a in the string w is denoted by $|w|_a$. We denote by $\mathbb{N}$ the set of natural numbers and use standard set operations union, intersection and inclusion denoted by $\cup$, $\cap$ and $\subseteq$, respectively.

The Parikh vector (also called Parikh image) associated to a string x, with respect to an alphabet V, is denoted by $Ps_V(x)$. We then denote by $Ps_V(L)$ the Parikh image of L, with respect to the alphabet V.

Given a multiset M, we denote by $M(a)$ the multiplicity (i.e., number of occurrences) of the symbol a in the multiset M. We denote by $card(M)$ the cardinality of the multiset M.

For multisets M and M' we write $(M \subseteq M')$ to denote that M is included in M'. The *sum* of multisets M and M' is written as the multiset $(M + M')$ and the *difference* between M and M' is written as $(M - M')$. We denote by $\mathbb{M}(V)$ the set of all possible multisets over V and by $\mathbb{M}_m(V)$ the set all multisets over V having cardinality m.

As originally defined in [1], a *Colony of Synchronizing Agents* (CSA) of degree m is a construct $\Pi = (A, T, C, R)$ in which

- A is a finite alphabet of symbols (its elements are called *objects*). $T \subseteq A$ is the set of *terminal objects*.
- An *agent* over A is a multiset over the alphabet A (an agent can be represented by a string $w \in A^*$, since A is finite). C is the *initial configuration of Π* and it is a multiset of agents, with $card(C) = m$.
- R is a finite set of *rules* over A. We have *internal rules* of type $u \to v$, with $u \in A^+$ and $v \in A^*$, and *synchronization rules* of the type $\langle u, v \rangle \to \langle u', v' \rangle$ with $uv \in A^+$ and $u', v' \in A^*$.

An occurrence γ of an internal rule $r : u \to v$ can be applied to an agent w by taking a multiset u from w (hence, $u \subseteq w$) and *assigning* it to γ (i.e., assigning the occurrences of the objects in u to γ). The application of an occurrence of rule r to the agent w consists of removing from w the multiset u and then adding the multiset v to the resulting multiset.

An occurrence γ of a synchronization rule $r : \langle u, v \rangle \to \langle u', v' \rangle$ can be applied to the pair of agents w and w' by: (i) taking from w a multiset u (hence, $u \subseteq w$) and *assigning* it to γ; (ii) taking from w' a multiset v (hence, $v \subseteq w'$) and *assigning* it to γ. The application of an occurrence of rule r to the agents w

and w' consists of: (i) removing the multiset u from w and then adding the multiset u' to the resulting multiset; (ii) removing the multiset v from w' and then adding the multiset v' to the resulting multiset.

Adopting a simplification often used in the area of membrane computing, we assume the existence of a *global clock* which marks the passage of units of time.

A *configuration* of a CSA, Π, consists of the agents present in the colony at a given time. We denote by $\mathbb{C}(\Pi)$ the set of *all possible configurations* of Π. Therefore, using the notation introduced before, $\mathbb{C}(\Pi)$ is exactly $\mathbb{M}(H)$ with $H = \mathbb{M}(A)$.

A single *transition* of Π from an arbitrary configuration c of Π to the next one lasts exactly one time unit and is obtained by applying the rules in the set R to the agents present in c in an *asynchronous* way. This means that, for each agent w and each pair of agents w' and w'' present in c, the occurrences of the objects of w, w' and w'' are *either* assigned to occurrences of the rules, with the occurrences of the objects and the occurrences of the rules chosen in a non-deterministic way, *or* left unassigned. A single occurrence of an object may only be assigned to a single occurrence of a rule. In a transition any number of occurrences of rules (zero, one, or more) can be applied to the agents in the configuration c.

A sequence (possibly infinite) $\langle C_0, C_1, \cdots, C_i, C_{i+1}, \cdots \rangle$ of configurations of Π, where C_{i+1} is obtained from C_i, $i \geq 0$, by a transition is called a *trajectory* of Π. A trajectory of Π is said to be *halting* if it halts, that is if it is finite and the last configuration of the sequence is a *halting configuration*, i.e., a configuration containing only agents for which no occurrences of rules from R can be applied.

A trajectory of Π that is halting and that *starts with the initial configuration* of Π is called a *computation* of Π. The *result/output* of a computation is the *set of vectors of natural numbers*, one vector for each agent w present in the halting configuration with the vector describing the multiplicities of terminal objects present in w. More formally, the result of a computation which stops in the halting configuration C_h is the set of vectors of natural numbers $\{Ps_T(w) \mid w$ is an agent present in $C_h\}$.

Because of the way rules can be applied, several possible computations of Π may exist. Taking the union of all the results for all possible computations of Π, we get the *set of vectors generated* by Π, denoted by $Ps_T(\Pi)$ (that, informally, is what the colony of cells "compute").

Example 1. A CSA with degree 3 is defined by the following.

$\Pi = (A, T, C, R)$ with $A = \{a, b, c\}$, $T = \{a\}$, $C = \{(abcba, 1), (abbcc, 1), (bab, 1)\} = \{abcba, abbcc, bab\}$.

The rules $R = \{r_1 : abca \to ba, \; r_2 : \langle abc, cc \rangle \to \langle aa, cb \rangle\}$.

The application of an occurrence of internal rule r_1 to the agent $abcba$ in the configuration C is shown diagrammatically in Fig. 1(a).

The application of an occurrence of the synchronization rule r_2 to the pair of agents $abcba$ and $abbcc$ in the configuration C is shown diagrammatically in Fig. 1(b).

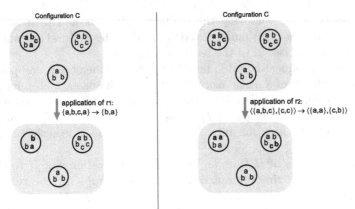

(a) Internal rule r_1 applied to C | (b) Synchronization rule r_2 applied to C

Fig. 1. Alternative application of rules r_1 and r_2 to configuration C from Example 1.

A more complex example of part of a trajectory is presented in Fig. 2(a): $\Pi' = (A', T', C', R')$ with the initial configuration $C' = \{(ac, 2), (a, 1)\}$ and rules $R' = \{ac \to aa, a \to b, \langle aa, aa \rangle \to \langle ab, ab \rangle, \langle ab, d \rangle \to \langle bb, d \rangle, b \to d\}$.

In the next Example we show how the output (result) produced by a CSA is obtained.

Example 2. Consider a CSA $\Pi = (A, T, C, R)$ with $A = \{a, b, c, d, e, f\}$, $T = \{e, f\}$, $C = \{(ab, 1), (bc, 1), (bd, 1), (a, 1)\}$. The rules in R are $\{r_1 : \langle ab, bc \rangle \to \langle eff, eff \rangle, r_2 : \langle ab, bd \rangle \to \langle eff, eff \rangle\}$.

There are *only two possible computations* of Π and these are represented diagrammatically in Fig. 2(b).

In this case, we have that the output of the system is $Ps_T(\Pi) = \{(1, 2), \overline{0}\}$. Informally, this is what the colony of cells Π computes (a set of vectors of natural numbers).

In fact, we have two possible halting configurations (for the two computations).

This outcome can be understood in the following manner. In the first halting configuration we have the agent (in two copies) eff whose associated Parikh vector (with respect to T) is $(1, 2)$ and the agents bd and a, whose associated Parikh vectors (with respect to T) are null vectors $\overline{0}$ (these agents do not contain any terminal object from T). Then the result of this computation is the set of vectors $\{(1, 2), (1, 2), \overline{0}, \overline{0}\} = \{(1, 2), \overline{0}\}$ with each vector describing the multiplicities of the terminal objects in the agents in the halting configuration.

In the second halting configuration we have the agent (in two copies) eff whose associated Parikh vector (with respect to T) is $(1, 2)$ and the agents bc and a, whose associated Parikh vectors (with respect to T) are null vectors. Then, also in this case, the result of the computation is the set of vectors $\{(1, 2), \overline{0}\}$.

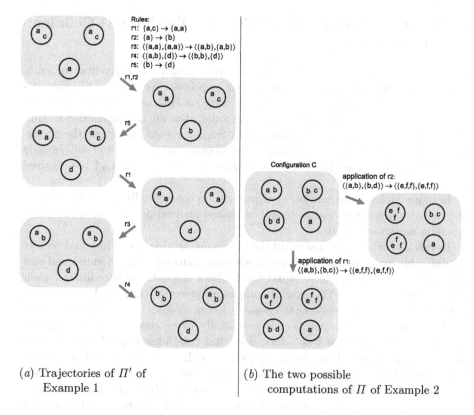

(a) Trajectories of Π' of Example 1

(b) The two possible computations of Π of Example 2

Fig. 2. Trajectories and computations.

Taking the union of the results for the (two) possible computations we get the overall output $Ps_T(\Pi) = \{(1,2),\overline{0}\} \cup \{(1,2),\overline{0}\} = \{(1,2),\overline{0}\}$.

The examples show a specific instance of a CSA but one can study the general computing power of this class of devices. How much CSAs can compute (i.e., assuming one could design/program arbitrary internal and synchronizing rules)?

As proved in [1], if the internal rules of the cells are sufficiently restricted, then the ability for the cells to coordinate (i.e., to employ synchronizing rules) is crucial to get high computational power, i.e., to simulate powerful computing devices such as register machines and Turing machines. In fact, when cells can coordinate, one can formally prove that CSAs are equivalent to a specific class of register machines (called blind [15]), i.e., they can be programmed to compute whatever blind register machines can do. On the other hand, if cells are unable to coordinate then their overall computing power is much more limited [1].

3   The Evolutionary Instability of (Distributed) Cellular Computation

Cellular populations are able to process more complex environmental information by synchronizing or coordinating their responses. As presented in the previous section, this can be formally shown using an abstract agent based model. Synchronization is a key ingredient of this model, allowing the population to simulate the computations of register machines. Similar results that stress the importance of synchronization, i.e., coordination, between a population of cells/agents can be found for other models of membrane computing [15] and bio-inspired computation [10].

In many biological scenarios, synchronization is essentially based on the possibility to communicate either trough a shared environment or using diffusible signaling molecules [11, 16].

In this last case, at least some of the cells must be able to produce and secrete the diffusible molecule. Such producers are cooperators paying an individual cost to produce a public good: a signal that allows the cells to coordinated their response to a stimulus. The overall computing power of the population is then in the hands of those cells that choose to contributing. However, the public goods nature of the computation is potentially threatened by the endogenous appearance of cheaters or free-riders, cells that take advantage of the enhanced computing power that is mediated by public good, but which do not contribute to its production, avoiding paying the costs associated to it. In situations where the cost-benefit breakdown is favorable to these cheaters, cheating cells may ultimately spread in the population disrupting the ability of the cells to properly process environmental information [11].

In summary, when the ability to perform powerful computations is based on cellular coordination, within-group competition may make cellular coordination inherently evolutionary unstable. One could then hypothesize an endogenous evolutionary cost for distributed cellular computing which would be on top of the energy cost for cellular computations [13]. Given this cost, one may then ask how cellular information-processing, and more generally cellular computing, could be distributed among cells so that it is evolutionary resilient to cheaters.

One of the possibilities is the presence of an interplay between cellular information processing and the eco-evolutionary dynamics that characterize the cellular population, as presented in recent works [2, 4]. Proper cellular information-processing could minimize the risk of cheaters spreading when coupled to specific ecological constraints. This is reminiscent of the connection between optimal decision-making and the particular environment where they are to be applied, as discussed by H.A. Simon [20].

This possibility was investigated computationally by Cavaliere and Poyatos in [2]. In this paper, the authors analyze communities of cells structured in colonies that recurrently are recreated and whose growth depends on a public good (as in the standard Hamilton's group model [21]). The emergence (by mutation) of free-riders (cheaters) that do not contribute but use the accessible public good leads to the demographic collapse of the population. The authors also found that low densities (following the spreading of cheaters and lack of public good) can facilitate the recover of cooperation (i.e., of producer cells) due to a phenomenon called Simpson's paradox [21], but on the other hand they may also lead to demographic extinctions [2]. The risk of extinction can be minimized when the cells use proper cellular information-processing, whereby the amount investment in the public good can be adjusted in response to the structure of the population, i.e. the fraction of other cooperators in it.

Results in [2] (and presented in Fig. 3) show that the optimal kinds of cellular information-processing depend on the ecological constraints (the size of the colonies) and on the efficiency of the public good. For low efficiency of the public good (and sufficiently small colony size) the optimal cellular decision-making consists in withholding production of public goods when cheaters are detected above a certain threshold (this is called positive plasticity). The reaction to cheaters invasions is interrupted as result of the feedback between the cellular decision and colonies assortment stressing how limited information processing can be efficient due to the specific ecological structure in which they are applied [20].

However, such type of decision making does not work when the cellular population is structured in large colonies. In this case, negative plasticity is a better strategy. Such strategy maintains the population in a dynamical equilibrium with the largest possible amount of non-producers that minimizes cheaters advantage but is compatible with population growth. In this case cells do not produce public good unless thy need it - population density reaches critical values.

These results were consistent with later analytical work based on the Ecological Public Goods Game (EPGG), which found that strategies akin to negative plasticity can sustain cooperation in a way that is both ecologically and evolutionary resilient [17]. In this work, Rauch et al. considered an implementation of the Ecological Public Goods Game [6,7], where cooperators were allowed to implement either fixed strategies with different investment levels, or facultative strategies where the amount of public good that cooperators produced could be tuned in response to the density of cooperators in the population. These authors found that the structure of the EPGG causes an inherent tradeoff between ecological resilience (the ability to recover from perturbations that cause a sudden increase in mortality) and evolutionary resilience (the ability to resist invasion by cheaters). Cooperators that use a (typically low) fixed investment strategy cannot avoid this tradeoff, and therefore strategies that are non-invasible by cheaters have low ecological resilience and are prone to extinction in a fluctuating environment. On the other hand, cooperators that are highly stable to such ecological stressors (by producing large amounts of the public good) were very sensitive to invasion by cheaters, which would take over the population and drive cooperators to exceedingly low frequencies.

However, cooperators that used facultative rather than fixed investments were able to circumvent this tradeoff and reach high levels of ecological resilience while remaining fully resistant to invasion by cheaters. The facultative strategies that yielded this behavior were reminiscent of the negative plasticity strategies

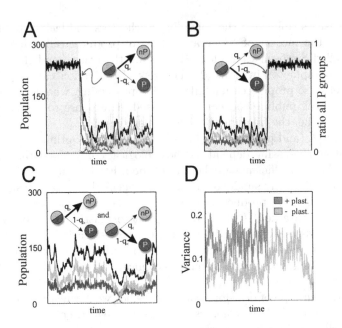

Fig. 3. Cellular decision-making can repress cheating cells. Cellular information-processing can alter the evolutionary dynamics and constrain the spreading of cheaters in communities of cells structured in colonies, i.e., Hamilton's group model [21] (Figures from [2]). Tick arrows denote the cellular decision to switch to production (P) or non production (nP) of the public good; q denotes the individual chances to switch to nP given the amount of public good received. (A) Positive plasticity consists in producing public good, stopping it as response to cheaters. This causes a fast reduction of the amount of public good and consequently of population density. After cheater invasion is stopped, the population finally evolve to the initial scenario of all cells producing (B). (C) A population of negative plastic producers is characterized by its permanent low density favored by the constant presence of non-producing cells which helps controlling cheaters invasion. (D) The success of the decision-making is coupled to the ecological constraints as it is related to the colonies heterogeneity, i.e., positive plasticity transiently modifies the inter-colonies variance to control cheaters. This contrasts with the relatively constant variance observed in a population of negative plastic producers (variances correspond to time series (B) and (C), respectively).

that Cavaliere and Poyatos found stabilized cooperation in agent based simulations. The two studies differ in the exact nature of the facultative or plastic strategies. In the EPGG-based analytical model, the amount of investment (rather than the probability to invest or not, as was the case for the computational model) was modulated in the facultative strategy. In addition, the analytical model consider infinitely large populations and produced deterministic dynamics, whereas the computational models considered finite populations, and thus stochastic dynamics. Agent based simulations with large population sizes displayed behavior that was consistent with the analytical model, thus bridging the two approaches.

Altogether, these two studies showed that if cellular information-processing is properly coupled to environmental constraints, then cheaters spreading can be minimized, public goods production can be maintained, and this may facilitate the presence of cellular coordination (hence, more complex kinds of cellular computations, as discussed above).

Beyond the realm of theoretical speculation, the basic types of cellular decision-making outlined above (negative or positive plasticity) are often found in natural scenarios [4]. Intriguingly, the types of strategies used by microbes in nature are consistent with the strategies predicted by mathematical and computational models to stabilize cooperation. Negative plasticity resembles the notion of facultative cheating, a cellular strategy implemented by different molecular mechanisms: generation of iron-scavenging pyoverdin molecules –iron being an essential public good in some environments– is reduced when enough molecules are already in the environment minimizing in this way the ability of cheaters to invade [5]. On the other hand, gene regulatory functions that are consistent with positive plasticity have also been documented in cases where eco-evolutionary modeling would predict they would maximize resistance to cheater invasion [18,19].

4   Perspective

Drawing inspirations from biology, computer science, mathematics and engineering one can understand, study and quantify the process of cellular decision-making as the ability of cells to process environmental information and take decisions (i.e., compute) in a distributed manner [10,16]. There are multiple ways to quantify how much cells can compute. Membrane computing is a computational model inspired by the principles of information-processing in living cells and focused on automata theory [15]. Several results in the area of membrane computing highlight, in various forms, a key point: The ability to encode powerful computations is generally linked to the ability of the cells to have some sort of synchronization or coordination of their responses i.e., the ability to communicate and to exchange (simple) messages [15]. This is, for instance, the case in the simple model of agents (abstracted cells) [1] that we have briefly reviewed in this paper - the ability of agents to synchronize allow the population to perform powerful computations, equivalent to a class of register machines.

One usual way to facilitate synchronization between cells is the sharing of a diffusible signaling molecule produced by cooperative (producer) cells [16]. These molecules may act as a public good, and lead to a classical evolutionary problem: cheating cells that avoid the costly production of the public good can appear by mutation and spread in the population, causing a concomitant decline in the public good [11]. In this sense, then, we could say that a corollary of this is that population of living cells find challenges to parallelize complex computations, as the need for synchronization may lead to the appearance of cheaters that would in turn lead to the collapse of the computation. From this point of view, one could even speculate that the complexity of distributed cellular computation is bounded by the ability to encode complex functions and the need to be evolutionary sustainable.

On the other hand, the ability of individual cells to process information can itself be a possible solution to the cheating problem. This is indeed the case when such information-processing is coupled to the ecological constraints in which the cellular population is embedded. This possibility discussed in [2,4], however, has not been studied in a systematic way and the area of membrane computing may be a possible framework in which one can easily combine the notion of cellular computation with evolutionary dynamics.

For instance, one could quantitatively study the potential trade-off between cellular computation, parallelism and evolutionary resilience. How can a computational process be distributed between individual cells and which is the cost to pay in terms of evolutionary resilience? Which is the best strategy to divide the computational labor between the cells to avoid the emergence of detrimental mutants?

All these types of questions may be approached by extending standard models of membrane computing. For instance, in the context of the presented model with agents, one may incorporate cell division and assume that cells may divide at different speed - cells that are simpler (in terms of the employed internal biochemistry/computational instructions) will divide faster (i.e., possibly spreading in the population, altering the balance between different types of cells). This would couple the notion of cellular fitness to that of cellular computation. Such idea could also be incorporated in classical models of membrane computing with division, known for their ability to solve efficiently (in parallel way) hard computational problems [15]. One could then study which of the obtained results with membrane systems with divisions are also evolutionary stable - i.e., they are not compromised by the fact that some cells may execute less complex instructions/biochemistry and then divide faster (remains to formulate a proper measure for the complexity of instructions).

We believe that these types of questions can help to address one of the key differences between distributed cellular computing and standard models of distributed computing - cells need to split the computational tasks with the evolutionary constraint to keep the proper balance between the different types, avoiding that some of them would outcompete the others.

Acknowledgments. M.C. acknowledges the support from the Engineering and Physical Sciences Research Council (EPSRC) grant EP/J02175X/1. Work in the Sanchez laboratory is supported by a Young Investigator grant from the Human Frontiers Science Project and a Scialog seed grant from Simons Foundation.

References

1. Cavaliere, M., Mardare, R., Sedwards, S.: A multiset-based model of synchronizing agents: computability and robustness. Theor. Comput. Sci. **391**(3), 216–238 (2008)
2. Cavaliere, M., Poyatos, J.F.: Plasticity facilitates sustainable growth in the commons. J. Roy. Soc. Inter. **10**(81), 20121006 (2013)

3. Feinerman, O., Korman, A.: Theoretical distributed computing meets biology: a review. In: Hota, C., Srimani, P.K. (eds.) ICDCIT 2013. LNCS, vol. 7753, pp. 1–18. Springer, Heidelberg (2013). doi:10.1007/978-3-642-36071-8_1

4. Harrington, K.I., Sanchez, A.: Eco-evolutionary dynamics of complex social strategies in microbial communities. Commun. Integr. Biol. **7**(1), e28230 (2014)

5. Harrison, F., Paul, J., Massey, R.C., Buckling, A.: Interspecific competition and siderophore-mediated cooperation in pseudomonas aeruginosa. ISME J. **2**(1), 49–55 (2008)

6. Hauert, C., Holmes, M., Doebeli, M.: Evolutionary games and population dynamics: maintenance of cooperation in public goods games. Proc. Roy. Soc. Lon. B: Biol. Sci. **273**(1600), 2565–2571 (2006)

7. Hauert, C., Wakano, J.Y., Doebeli, M.: Ecological public goods games: cooperation and bifurcation. Theor. Popul. Biol. **73**(2), 257–263 (2008)

8. Hopcroft, J.E., Motwani, R., Ullman, J.D.: Introduction to Automata Theory, Languages, and Computation, 3rd edn. Addison-Wesley Longman Publishing Co. Inc., Boston (2006)

9. Ilachinski, A.: Cellular Automata: A Discrete Universe. World Scientific, River Edge (2001)

10. Kari, L., Rozenberg, G.: The many facets of natural computing. Commun. ACM **51**(10), 72 (2008)

11. Levin, S.A.: Public goods in relation to competition, cooperation, and spite. Proc. Natl. Acad. Sci. **111**(Supplement_3), 10838–10845 (2014)

12. Macía, J., Posas, F., Solé, R.V.: Distributed computation: the new wave of synthetic biology devices. Trends Biotechnol. **30**(6), 342–349 (2012)

13. Mehta, P., Schwab, D.J.: Energetic costs of cellular computation. Proc. Natl. Acad. Sci. **109**(44), 17978–17982 (2012)

14. Navlakha, S., Bar-Joseph, Z.: Distributed information processing in biological and computational systems. Commun. ACM **58**(1), 94–102 (2015)

15. Paun, G., Rozenberg, G., Salomaa, A.: The Oxford Handbook of Membrane Computing. Oxford University Press Inc., Oxford (2010)

16. Perkins, T.J., Swain, P.S.: Strategies for cellular decision-making. Mol. Syst. Biol. **5**, 326 (2009)

17. Rauch, J., Kondev, J., Sanchez, A.: Cooperators trade off ecological resilience and evolutionary stability in public goods games. J. R. Soc. Interface (2017). http://dx.doi.org/10.1098/rsif.2016.0967

18. Ross-Gillespie, A., Gardner, A., Buckling, A., West, S.A., Griffin, A.S.: Density dependence and cooperation: theory and a test with bacteria. Evolution **63**(9), 2315–2325 (2009)

19. Ross-Gillespie, A., Gardner, A., West, S.A., Griffin, A.S.: Frequency dependence and cooperation: theory and a test with bacteria. Am. Nat. **170**(3), 331–342 (2007)

20. Simon, H.A.: Models of Man; Social and Rational. Wiley, New York (1957)

21. Sober, E.: The Nature of Selection: Evolutionary Theory in Philosophical Focus. University of Chicago Press, Chicago (1993)

22. Soloveichik, D., Cook, M., Winfree, E., Bruck, J.: Computation with finite stochastic chemical reaction networks. Nat. Comput. **7**(4), 615–633 (2008)

Coping with Dynamical Structures for Interdisciplinary Applications of Membrane Computing

Thomas Hinze[1,2]($\boxtimes$)

[1] Department of Bioinformatics, Friedrich Schiller University Jena,
Ernst-Abbe-Platz 2, 07743 Jena, Germany
thomas.hinze@uni-jena.de
[2] Institute of Computer Science, Brandenburg University of Technology,
Postfach 10 13 44, 03013 Cottbus, Germany

Abstract. Biological information processing and maintenance of life mainly utilise *dynamical structures* at different levels from a nanoscopic up to a macroscopic scale. Providing a high degree of reliability, reproducibility, unambiguousness, and addressability, underlying compositional processes appear as ideal candidates to perform computational tasks in a discretised manner. In this essay, we consider four levels in which dynamical structures enable an efficient handling with information: (1) the molecular level, (2) the level of reaction network modules, (3) the level of membranes, and (4) the level of higher-order organisms and populations. All of them have in common the capability of controlled memory-based state transitions and hence dedicated systems's configurations encoding behavioural patterns. Due to its discrete algebraic nature, *membrane systems* represent advantageous frameworks in order to formalise corresponding activities. This in turn paves the way towards efficient tools inspired by nature with manifold smart applications in engineering, computer science, and systems biology. We illustrate membrane system's abilities, benefits, and progress for coping with dynamical structures from an integrative perspective.

1 Introduction

Living organisms comprise astonishing capabilities of information processing resulting in complex behavioural patterns and in the presence of fascinating properties like intelligence, creativity, self-organisation, strategy, cognition, awareness, and many others. There is a widespread intuitive imagination about these phenomena but most of them still lack a comprehensive understanding based on formal methods. Over the last decades, we observe a deeper and deeper *formalisation* of natural sciences. Starting from big theories in physics and inorganic chemistry, nowadays the fine-grained nature of biochemical reactions along with detailed shaping of macromolecules becomes more and more unravelled. Underlying principles and laws have been formulated in a conclusive and consistent way. Highly productive experimental equipment, precise measurement,

© Springer International Publishing AG 2017
A. Leporati et al. (Eds.): CMC 2016, LNCS 10105, pp. 16–27, 2017.
DOI: 10.1007/978-3-319-54072-6_2

visualisation, and particle tracing at nanometre scales provide a huge amount of interwoven data. By means of statistical analysis in conjunction with data mining techniques, a growing essence of new knowledge emerges which is characterised by a strictly mathematical denotation using formal expressions and formal methods. In addition, even previously informal pure evidence-based or empirical knowledge became specified by deduced formalisms which in turn enable computer-based simulation and integration towards more holistic systems hierarchically composed of functional units. Formalisation can be seen as crucial clue for understanding and for obtaining substantiated conclusions. After physics and chemistry, formalisation is going to pervade biology and life sciences. This comes along with tremendous re-organisation and extension of the particular scientific subject. Medical, social and economic sciences represent further candidates still awaiting a rigorous formalisation of its facets as a whole. From a visionary point of view, it seems possible that complex issues – like cognition abilities or existence of a circadian clock [1] an organism is equipped with – can be defined exclusively by usage of formal methods and afterwards automatically checked using reasoning techniques. Currently, this objective is still far away to be reached soon, but it gives a strong motivation.

When considering technical principles of information processing invented in engineering, it turns out that data storage as well as data manipulation is typically organised in a strictly *discrete manner* which means that the underlying system carries out well-defined *state transitions* controlled by a program or by external signal courses. Toggling between (pre)defined states ensures a high degree of safety and diminishes the danger to loose correct data or to initiate undesired effects of processing steps on the underlying data. Discretisation of information processing comes with a certain redundancy which implies that the physical implementation of a state might slightly vary without any consequences on the encoded information. Interestingly, dynamical structures evolved in living organisms perfectly permit a discrete manner of information processing.

A *structure* in this context is a spatial or topological arrangement of physical constituents. Composition of constituents together with the shape of the resulting formation defines evaluable individuals for clear identification of *data values*. In concert with the basic concept of the *von-Neumann* computer architecture, data values can represent instructions or operators as part of a program on the one hand but also input data, operands, or final results of computations on the other. In order to distinguish whether a data element is treated as operator or as an operand, an *addressable memory* is needed which also facilitates pointing to the next instruction to execute. Within the sphere of living organisms, the positional location or inner placement of an information-encoding *structure* inside the organism's body reflects the notion of addressability. In geometrical relation to its environment, presence or absence of a certain structure might cause specific effects forming a chain or sequence of activities at different places of the organism. Thus, addressability within a biological memory can be seen as more or less associative form of storage technique due to its dependence on local characteristics of the involved structures. Completing the image of a biological

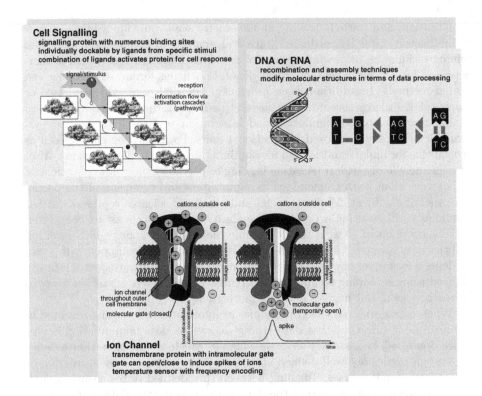

Fig. 1. Three typical examples of dynamical structures at **molecular level**: composition of molecules from monomeric constituents like strands of DNA or RNA (**upper right part**), three-dimensional shape and orientation of complex macromolecules shown by an ion channel (**lower part**), and combination of composition and shape found for instance in cell signalling by successive activation of transcription factors for stimulus-induced gene expression (**upper left part**).

computation, structures are able to modify over time. The underlying *dynamics* of the structure makes accessible dedicated changes of the represented data values. To this end, the structure undergoes controllable interactions with other structures or with the environment resulting in behavioural patterns.

The general term of a dynamical structure in living organisms subsumes many forms of occurrences and facets which makes corresponding systems complex but also extremely powerful and flexible. Having in mind that a typical biological cell is composed of 10^8 up to 10^9 interacting molecules while an adult human being consists of approximately 10^{14} cells, it becomes obvious that detection and understanding of biological information processing requires appropriate *levels of abstraction* complemented by purposive formalisation. Since membrane systems allow hierarchical composition and decomposition of algebraic elements and structures in a rule-based or functionally controlled manner, they are ideal candidates to model systems with dynamical structures even at different scales.

In the next section, we identify four corresponding levels. Section 3 assigns a membrane system for each level taken from our previous research. It stands out that the variety of membrane systems throughout all levels complements to each other in a way that structures obtained as outputs of lower-level systems can act as elementary constituents of higher-level systems finally producing a hierarchically organised meta-system. This consistently perceived modular approach encourages a subsequent setup of tools and instruments for further analysis and interdisciplinary applications like identification and classification of capabilities or detection of algorithmic strategies found in organisms. Section 4 is dedicated to this visionary topic discussing in brief some first ideas prone to attract membrane computing beyond computer science.

2   Biological Information Processing Primarily Utilises Dynamical Structures at Different Levels

Coping with *dynamical structures* turns out to be both, a challenging task but also a crucial clue in understanding, fine-grained modelling, and utilisation of biological and biologically inspired information processing [10]. Principles of molecular computing are mainly based on modifiable spatial and topological arrangements in different forms, contexts, and scales ranging from nanoscopic surface shapes up to complex macroscopic behavioural patterns. From a composition-oriented point of view, we identify at least *four levels* in which dynamical structures essentially occur:

1. The **molecular level** comprises spatial grouping of atoms by chemical bonds forming macromolecules. Figure 1 illustrates typical examples by schematic representations. Most notably, intramolecular structures of DNA, RNA, and proteins constitute their functionality as data carrier and storage medium along with a co-ordinated set of biochemical reaction schemes. *Cell signalling* gives an illustrative example. Here, external stimuli like hormones or environmental factors reach receptors at the outer face of a cell membrane. At its inner part, signalling proteins and second messengers (ligands) are released. By passing a signalling cascade, signalling proteins become activated by a specific combination of ligands residing at protein binding sites. This results in composition of a dedicated molecular structure acting as transcription factor which in turn can enter the cell nucleus and afterwards initiate a specific gene expression producing a cell response. Even without modification of chemical bonds, we can observe dynamical molecular structures in a functional context. Let us consider an *ion channel*: It mainly consists of a transmembrane protein incorporating a controllable gate. Cations accumulate close to the channel entry outside the cell. As far as enough cations are present, the gate temporarily opens for a short moment, and an amount of cations can pass the channel into the cell inducing a spiking signal. The function of the underlying gate is based on a dynamically movable side chain inside the transmembrane protein. Ion channels can for instance act as temperature sensors producing a frequency-encoded oscillatory spiking signal [8].

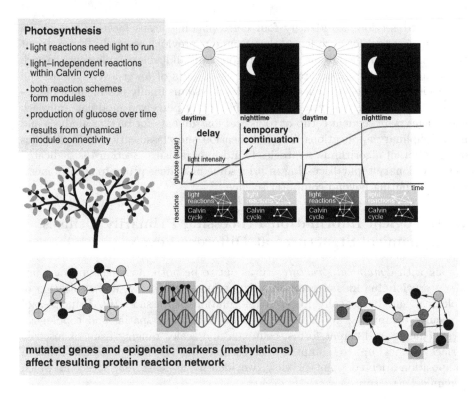

Fig. 2. Two representative examples of dynamical structures at the **level of reaction networks**: topological changes can be caused by external stimuli. Here, the processing scheme of photosynthesis varies by the intensity of brightness: light-dependent reactions dynamically join or leave in accordance with presence or absence of environmental sunlight during daytime and nighttime (**upper part**). Alternatively, changes of a reaction network structure can also result from intrinsic reasons like mutations of genomic DNA or influences of epigenetic factors (**lower part**).

2. The **level of reaction network modules** opens the next stage of dynamical structures, see Fig. 2 for an overview of case scenarios. Chemical reaction schemes, particularly those found in living organisms, apper to represent *invisible* networks. Nevertheless, they provide the driving force in information processing by conducting state transitions from one molecular configuration to another one. The topology of a chemical reaction network is commonly treated as a static structure due to its highly conserved genetic blueprint. A corresponding network of densely interwoven reactions forms a *module*, an elementary unit also called *motif*. Structural dynamics becomes visible when studying the interplay of reaction network modules over time. It turns out that several modules merge or couple to each other temporarily while modular compounds can also dissolve, re-arrange, or re-assembly. Initiated by trigger signals, by perturbances, or simply by random, network re-compositions arise.

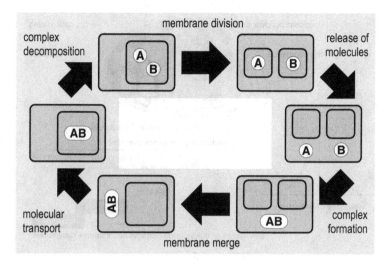

Fig. 3. Information processing at the **level of dynamical membrane structures** might also incorporate oscillatory behaviour resulting in a cycle of system's configurations. A toy example addresses a cycle composed of six stages. Let A and B symbolise molecular constituents able to form a complex which is promoted by the outer membrane. In contrast, the inner membrane(s) enhance complex decomposition. Membrane division and membrane merge complement the processing loop.

Photosynthesis is representative for that: Depending on presence or absence of light, different reaction schemes are active. Light intensity toggles between several underlying reaction network topologies composed of a set of modules. Another obvious example is given by *mutation* or *recombination* of genetic DNA which results in modified reaction network structures. Also *infection* of a cell by a virus or *bacterial gene transfer* can have similar effects. When aiming at understanding of maintenance of life, dynamics of reaction network structures is essential.

3. Increasing within the hierarchy, the **level of membranes** characterises a new quality of dynamical structures. Membranes enable a *compartmentalisation* of spatial structures in which chemical reactions and transportation processes appear. Having in mind that membranes form a physical *boundary* and they offer a selective or general *permeability* for molecules at the same time, it becomes obvious that dynamics at this level can imply powerful features [13]. *Cell division* is probably the most popular example of a dynamical membrane structure. Following this line, the formation of *tissues*, *organs*, and finally multi-cellular *organisms* exhibits an amazing capability of self-organisation [3] and self-coordination [2]. For instance, the spatial derivation of cytokines manages the progress in *cellular differentiation*. *Exocytosis* as well as *endocytosis* in conjunction with membrane creation and dissolution provides molecular containers for directed transportation. Often, membrane structures need to be assembled in an optimal way in order to achive a certain

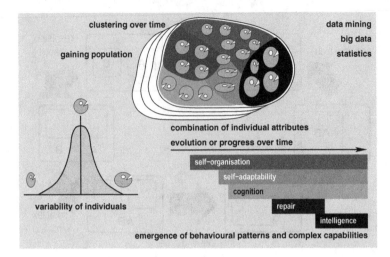

Fig. 4. Individuals within a population come with specific combinations of properties and attributes. An extensive variability among the occurrences in conjunction with a combinatorial multiplicity of potential individuals leads to an assessable population whose members can be clustered using *categorised counting* [7] for instance. Each cluster stands for a certain common capability of its members. A cluster in this context forms a structure whose emergence over time implies dynamics at the **level of organisms and populations**.

functionality at its best. *Optimal placement* of branches and junctions within capillar blood vessels for adequate supply of neighboured cells keeping low the overall need of molecular resources is a typical outcome. Even oscillatory behaviour might include circular modifications of membrane structures, see Fig. 3. More notably, using *neural plasticity* the process of (re)mapping the brain structure emerges.

4. The **higher-order organism or population level** marks the topmost instance of dynamical structures found in complex biological systems. Unequivocally, underlying rules, principles, or laws responsible for control and development of the corresponding structures are often hard to identify and sometimes prone to errors, misinterpretations, or incompleteness. State-of-the-art approaches attempt to identify the rules by comprehensive statistical analyses of huge amounts of experimentally observed data resulting from macroscopic behavioural patterns [12]. A simple example is a *predator-prey system* for instance consisting of a population of rabbits and a population of foxes sharing the same living area. Dependent on relevant parameter values like rabbit's birth rate, fox's death rate and feeding activity, the system exhibits various behavioural patterns like stable oscillation with variable periodicity, extinction of foxes, or exponential growth of involved populations. An opposite example is *symbiosis* of organisms or populations. Moreover, *swarms*, *colonies*, and *societies* create highly complex behavioural patterns

incorporating fascinating properties like cooperation, altruism, cognition, consciousness, or *intelligence*. Many of these properties still lack a formal definition based on substantiated understanding. Figure 4 sketches the general idea and principle which is based on categorised counting among individuals with a combination of attributes.

3 Membrane Systems for Explicit Formalisation of Structural Dynamics at Different Levels

Due to its discrete nature composed of algebraic elements, membrane systems appear to be an ideal candidate able to describe dynamical structures on adequate levels of abstraction [14]. Within research projects during the last years, we developed several P systems frameworks coping within dynamical structures at molecular level, at the level of reaction network modules, and at the level of membranes. Most of these descriptive frameworks come with simulation software tools employed for tackling a number of application case studies.

P systems for cell signalling modules (Π_{CSM}) act at the *molecular level* [6]. Here, each molecule is represented by a regular expression denoted as a string. The characters within the string reflect the underlying signalling protein name together with an arbitrary number of ligands which in turn can be individually present or absent in the protein structure. Unknown or irrelevant binding situations are allowed to be written by a placeholder symbol ($\star$). A multiset of strings constructed in this way defines the initial pool of molecules. The set of reaction rules is also allowed to utilise placeholder symbols when describing substrates or products. Hence, the number of reaction rules can be kept low. Execution of a reaction rule includes a matching process which identifies the affected substrate molecules. We equipped the system's specification with a discretised form of reaction kinetics estimating the selection of substrate molecules taken into account per time step for each available reaction. Based on the Π_{CSM} framework, the simulation software SRSim emerged in which SR stands for "structural rules" but also for "spatial rules" [4]. In addition to the string describing a molecule, three-dimensional cartesian coordinates together with bond length and angles can be assigned to each molecular component. In this way, a reactive calotte-like model of each molecule is obtained.

Within the *level of reaction network modules*, we introduced the P meta framework for polymorphic processes [5,9]. Here, the main focus of attention is laid to dynamical composition and decomposition of modules towards formalisation of more complex system's behaviour. We permit modifications of the module connectivity at arbitrary points in time but also subject to conditional trigger signals. This feature offers a high flexibility in formalisation of measurable system's properties which can be helpful to bring in silico-simulations closer to experimental observations. Furthermore, a compact but expressive formalism is provided to manage dynamical topologies of reaction network structures. The underlying concept resembles an *event-based programming language*: A program is built of a final set of *instructions*. Each instruction contains a specific *condition* (a boolean term based on evaluation of elapsed model time and conditional trigger signals) followed by a corresponding *action*. An action could be the connection of two dedicated modules including coupling of shared species and supply of affected signal values. Other actions incorporate disconnection of modules, coupling/decoupling of additional species, module exchange, or module reset. The sequence of instructions defines individual priorities in order to prevent ambiguities.

Aimed at exploring abilities of self-organisation by dynamical structures within the *level of membranes*, we currently elaborate the idea of grid-exploring P systems assuming an initial grid of membranes. Each membrane on its own acts in terms of a module. It can be entered, passed, and left by molecules. In some dedicated modules called processing units, molecules can be processed by reactions of different types like composition $(a + b \rightarrow c)$, incorporation $(a + b \rightarrow a)$, and unification $(a + a \rightarrow b)$. Molecules initially placed at different positions of the grid's boundary individually run through the grid visiting a sequence of designated membranes in which they become successively processed. Using artificial evolution, the arrangement of membranes within the grid becomes optimised for shortening the total time duration necessary for complete passage and processing of all molecules. We employ grid-exploring P systems for topological grid optimisation using artificial evolution which in turn cares for variation of grid elements following the metaphor of *walking membranes*.

Advantageously, the aforementioned membrane systems flanking different levels of dynamical structures can be coupled in order to interact by bridging these levels. Let us consider this feature by a case study addressing the existence of a circadian clock which generates an endogenous oscillation whose periodicity resembles the duration of one earth rotation (24 h). Furthermore, a circadian clock is able to get entrained by adaptation to external stimuli like alteration between sunlight and darkness. Organisms equipped with a circadian clock typically possess an advantage over those who do not since they can for instance better exploit the sunlight by initiation of biochemical processes accurately timed before sunrise. The Π_{CSM} framework provides appropriate instruments to model an underlying reaction scheme taking into account submolecular structures like successive protein phosphorylations and dephosphorylations or formation of protein complexes within the reaction cycle. Corresponding courses of molecular amounts express the (core) oscillatory behaviour which becomes complemented by additional influencing factors. Most of them control the oscillation and its periodicity by inhibition or by activation (amplification) of selected reactions. Since this effect strongly depends on the brightness of environmental light (for instance measured by light-sensitive substances like chlorophyll), we achieve a dynamical overall reaction scheme over time. Some reactions have been iteratively switched on or switched off, or their velocity is diminished or accelerated. Here, the P meta framework for polymorphic processes represents a sufficient tool in order to capture the entire system's description in an appropriately formalised way. Organisms in general and especially those comprising a circadian clock undergo a life cycle consisting of different phases like nutrition, growth, and reproduction. Since organisms coexist in a population embedded into a more or less heterogeneous environment, the life span of an individual can be seen as a walking tour through various places, each of them dedicated to a specific task or function. Organisms unable to reach a desired place to perform the next task in time run into serious danger to die. Grid-exploring P systems offer a descriptive formal framework for the behaviour of a resulting population. From a technical point of view, the orchestrated interplay of membrane systems at different levels of abstraction and among different levels of dynamical structures opens a strategy to cope with the complexity of biological systems.

4   Usefulness of Membrane Systems Managing Dynamical Structures

Convincing simulations and visualisations of biological and biologically inspired processes utilising dynamical structures can be seen as a first and essential step towards a beneficial toolbox of complementary membrane system instances. Beyond pure system's definition along with estimation of its computational capacity, our research is focused on identification and exploration of useful practical applications and application scenarios for membrane systems managing dynamical structures. Projects and case studies are motivated by finding hypotheses to *explain* phenomena and afterwards being able to *predict* a system's behaviour. Having this knowledge at hand, it is worth to become *adopted* and *adapted* for suitable engineering tasks in terms of bionics like construction of a girder inspired by a bone structure. Another application objective is dedicated to *optimise* a system's behaviour like the best possible topological arrangement of processing units on a grid. We believe that bringing together the descriptive advantages of membrane systems with the existence of biological phenomena under study and capabilities of data mining could be a fruitful strategy. To this end, we closely collaborate with experts of life sciences, engineering, or natural sciences in an interdisciplinary manner.

Focussing on interdisciplinarity turns out to be a fascinating driving force towards beneficial utilisation of membrane systems. It becomes still more attractive if a huge amount of raw data – for instance from experimental studies, from monitoring, from archival storage, or from direct observations – is available waiting for computational analysis and employment of deductive algorithms directed to get new insights. By following this line of research, evidence-based knowledge can be made available along with a consistent formalisation. In systems biology, it is helpful to elucidate complex behavioural capabilities obtained from specific combinations of attributes. So, the existence of a circadian clock together with its suitability for fast entrainment or for precise synchronisation could be derived automatically from the underlying parameterised low-level reaction scheme. Moreover, its evolutionary potential might be disclosed as well resulting from subsequent studies of artificial evolution. This in turn lays the foundation to indicate effective starting points for development of drugs able to restore the functionality of an impaired circadian clock system and related diseases. Using membrane systems, a comprehensive pervasion of life sciences and medicine inspired by methods from engineering and supported by approaches of high-performance computing is ahead with no doubt.

References

1. Aschoff, J.: Circadian rhythms in man. a self-sustained oscillator with an inherent frequency underlies human 24-hour periodicity. Science **148**, 1427–1432 (1965)
2. Bernardini, F., Gheorghe, M., Krasnogor, N., Giavitto, J.-L.: On self-assembly in population P systems. In: Calude, C.S., Dinneen, M.J., Păun, G., Pérez-Jímenez, M.J., Rozenberg, G. (eds.) UC 2005. LNCS, vol. 3699, pp. 46–57. Springer, Heidelberg (2005). doi:10.1007/11560319_6
3. Camazine, S., Deneubourg, J.L., Franks, N.R., Sneyd, J., Theraulaz, G., Bonabeau, E.: Self-Organization in Biological Systems. Princeton University Press, Princeton (2003)
4. Grünert, G., Ibrahim, B., Lenser, T., Lohel, M., Hinze, T., Dittrich, P.: Rule-based spatial modeling with diffusing, geometrically constrained molecules. BMC Bioinform. **11**, 307 (2010)
5. Hinze, T., Schell, B., Schumann, M., Bodenstein, C.: Maintenance of chronobiological information by P system mediated assembly of control units for oscillatory waveforms and frequency. In: Csuhaj-Varjú, E., Gheorghe, M., Rozenberg, G., Salomaa, A., Vaszil, G. (eds.) CMC 2012. LNCS, vol. 7762, pp. 208–227. Springer, Heidelberg (2013). doi:10.1007/978-3-642-36751-9_15
6. Hinze, T., Behre, J., Bodenstein, C., Escuela, G., Grünert, G., Hofstedt, P., Sauer, P., Hayat, S., Dittrich, P.: Membrane systems and tools combining dynamical structures with reaction kinetics for applications in chronobiology. In: Frisco, P., Gheorghe, M., Pérez-Jiménez, M.J. (eds.) Applications of Membrane Computing in Systems and Synthetic Biology. ECC, vol. 7, pp. 133–173. Springer, Cham (2014). doi:10.1007/978-3-319-03191-0_5
7. Hinze, T., Grützmann, K., Höckner, B., Sauer, P., Hayat, S.: Categorised counting mediated by blotting membrane systems for particle-based data mining and numerical algorithms. In: Gheorghe, M., Rozenberg, G., Salomaa, A., Sosík, P., Zandron, C. (eds.) CMC 2014. LNCS, vol. 8961, pp. 241–257. Springer, Cham (2014). doi:10.1007/978-3-319-14370-5_15
8. Hinze, T., Kirkici, K., Sauer, P., Sauer, P., Behre, J.: Membrane computing meets temperature: a thermoreceptor model as molecular slide rule with evolutionary potential. In: Rozenberg, G., Salomaa, A., Sempere, J.M., Zandron, C. (eds.) CMC 2015. LNCS, vol. 9504, pp. 215–235. Springer, Cham (2015). doi:10.1007/978-3-319-28475-0_15
9. Hinze, T., Behre, J., Kirkici, K., Sauer, P., Sauer, P., Hayat, S.: Passion to P for polymorphic processes in practice. In: Gheorghe, M., Petre, I., Perez-Jimenez, M.J., Rozenberg, G., Salomaa, A. (eds.) Multidisciplinary Creativity. Spandugino (2016)
10. Kitano, H.: Computational systems biology. Nature **420**, 206–210 (2002)
11. Martin-Vide, C., Paun, G., Pazos, J., Rodriguez-Paton, A.: Tissue P systems. Theor. Comput. Sci. **296**(2), 295–326 (2003)

12. Matsumaru, N., Lenser, T., Hinze, T., Dittrich, P.: Toward organization-oriented chemical programming: a case study with the maximal independent set problem. In: Dressler, F., Carreras, I. (eds.) Advances in Biologically Inspired Information Systems: Models, Methods, and Tools. SSCI, pp. 147–163. Springer, Heidelberg (2007)
13. Porreca, A.E., Leporati, A., Mauri, G., Zandron, C.: P systems with active membranes working in polynomial space. Int. J. Found. Comput. Sci. **22**(1), 65–73 (2011)
14. Păun, G.: Membrane Computing: An Introduction. Springer, Heidelberg (2002)

Applications of P Systems in Population Biology and Ecology: The Cases of MPP and APP Systems

Roberto Barbuti, Pasquale Bove, Paolo Milazzo[✉], and Giovanni Pardini

Dipartimento di Informatica, Università di Pisa,
Largo B. Pontecorvo 3, 56127 Pisa, Italy
{barbuti,bovepas,milazzo,pardinig}@di.unipi.it

Abstract. We describe two extensions of P systems for the modelling of populations and ecosystems. They are the Minimal Probabilistic P systems (MPP systems) and the Attributed Probabilistic P systems (APP systems). We describe also two case studies in which the two formalisms have been applied to the study of real ecological systems. The first case study deals with the causes of the stability of European hybrid populations of water frogs. The second case study deals with social interactions and the establishment of dominance hierarchies in primates.

1 Introduction

The modelling of population dynamics is quite a common task in many application domains such as, of course, population biology, but also ecology, evolutionary biology, social sciences and epidemiology. Models allow hypotheses on the causes of observed phenomena to be tested in a rigorous way, and this can contribute to the understanding of the factors governing population growth, evolution, extinction, etc. Moreover, models can be used to make predictions on the fate of a population of interest. This, for instance, can be useful to identify and evaluate threats. Finally, models can support the planning of control policies, such as reintroduction actions in an endangered population of animals [18].

Classical approaches to population modelling are mainly based on mathematical means (ODEs, recurrence equations, etc.) or individual-based modelling techniques. Mathematical modelling methods [28] have the advantages of being rigorous and of offering many analysis techniques. On the other hand, when the complexity of the population dynamics increases, they tend to become unfriendly and difficult to handle. As regards individual-based models, we have that individuals are modelled as entities whose behaviour is described by some kind of algorithm or set of rules. This approach is commonly used in particular in the context of ecological modelling [22], and it offers the advantage of a simpler way of expressing the system dynamics (that emerges from the behaviour of the individuals). Moreover, individual-based models are usually analysed by means of simulation approaches, that are often very effective in showing the trends in the dynamics of the population. On the other hand, individual-based models are

© Springer International Publishing AG 2017
A. Leporati et al. (Eds.): CMC 2016, LNCS 10105, pp. 28–48, 2017.
DOI: 10.1007/978-3-319-54072-6_3

often unformalized and ambiguous, with an impact on reproducibility of experiments. Such a problem of individual-based models required the definition of a sort of standard modelling protocol to be used as a reference in order to minimize ambiguities [23].

In the last few years, many formal notations have been proposed by computer scientists for the modelling of populations and ecosystems. Such notations aim at combining the unambiguous nature of mathematical methods with the effectiveness of individual-based models. Some of them came from the fields of concurrency theory [25,33] and agent-based modelling [20,31]. Some proposals came also from the membrane computing community, such as [2,9,12,16,34].

In this paper we describe two extensions of P systems for the modelling of populations that evolve by stages (seasons, generations, etc.). They are the *Minimal Probabilistic P systems (MPP systems)* [5,6] and the *Attributed Probabilistic P systems (APP systems)* [4]. Both MPP and APP systems aim at allowing modellers to construct concise, elegant and unambiguous population models. In particular, MPP systems include a minimal set of features useful for the modelling of stage-based populations: maximal parallelism, rule promoters and probabilistic dynamics. APP systems extend MPP systems with the possibility of enriching objects with attributes.

Simulation is the most common analysis approach for formal models of ecosystems like the ones obtained by applying MPP and APP systems. Nevertheless, the formal nature of such models allows other analysis approaches to be applied. The complexity of the modelled systems very often makes exhaustive approaches such as model checking infeasible. However, other approaches such as statistical model checking [27] and causality analysis [10,13,21] could be successfully applied. In particular, in [6] we defined a translation of MPP systems models into the input language of the PRISM model checker [26] in order to allow statistical model checking to be applied to MPP systems models.

MPP systems have been applied in [6] to investigate the mechanisms underlying the stability of European hybrid populations of water frogs [15]. APP systems have been applied in [4] to study social interactions and the establishment of dominance hierarchies in primates.

The paper is structured as follows: the definition of MPP and APP systems is recalled in Sect. 2; Sect. 3 describes the case study of water frog complexes; Sect. 4 describes the case study of social interactions in primates; and, finally, Sect. 5 briefly concludes the paper.

2   Modelling Populations with P Systems: MPP and APP Systems

P systems can provide a simple, elegant and unambiguous notation for population modelling. In particular, the objects of a P system can represent population individuals (and their different states), as well as the available natural resources (e.g. food) and the state of the environment (the current season, weather conditions, etc.). Moreover, evolution rules can represent events like birth, mating,

oviposition, growth, death, predation, transmission of diseases, fight, communication, aggression and so on.

Maximal parallelism is a feature of P systems that makes them well suited for
the modelling of populations that evolve by stages in which all the individuals are
involved in essentially the same activity (e.g. reproduction season, hibernation,
etc.). The modelling of stage-based populations can be made even more natural
by exploiting rule promoters, that allow different sets of evolution rules to be
enabled in different stages. Finally, since often population individuals can be
subject to alternative events (birth of a male or a female, to survive or not to
survive, etc.) it is important to include a form of probabilistic choice of evolution
rules in order to suitably represent the likelihood of each such event. Probabilities
have been used in many variants of P systems (e.g. in [3, 7, 8, 19, 32]). In this paper
we use probabilities of rules in conjunction with maximal parallelism.

The identification of the features of P systems that are essential for the
modelling of stage-based populations led us to the definition in [5, 6] of *Minimal Probabilistic P systems (MPP systems)*. A MPP system is essentially a flat
P system [11], namely a P systems consisting of a single membrane, in which evolution rules can have promoters and are associated with rate functions, namely
functions that give a measure of their likelihood depending on the current state
of the system.

Definition 1 (MPP system). *A* Minimal Probabilistic P system *is a tuple*
$\langle A, w_0, R \rangle$ *where:*

- *A is a possibly infinite alphabet of objects, with A^* denoting the universe of
  all multisets having A as support;*
- $w_0 \in A^*$ *is a multiset describing the initial state of the system;*
- *R is a finite set of evolution rules having the form*

$$u \xrightarrow{f} v \mid_{pr}$$

*where $u, v, pr \in A^*$, $u \neq \emptyset$, are multisets (often denoted as strings) of reac-
tants, products and promoters, respectively, and $f : A^* \mapsto \mathbb{R}^{\geq 0}$ is a rate
function.*

The semantics of MPP systems, given in [6] as a probabilistic transition
system, corresponds to a Discrete Time Markov Chain where a *state* is a multiset
of objects in A^*, and each probabilistic transition models a maximally-parallel
step. In this paper, we describe the dynamics of a MPP system by defining the
algorithm that computes a single maximally-parallel step (Algorithm 1).

Given a set of evolution rules R and the current system state w, the algorithm copies w into x, and then iteratively selects and applies applicable rules.
At each iteration, one of the applicable rules (the set of which is denoted R') is
probabilistically chosen. The probability of each rule is proportional to the rate
value obtained by applying its rate function to the current state w. Once a rule
is selected, its application consists in removing its reactants from x and adding
its products into y. The latter multiset will collect all products of all applied

---

Algorithm 1. Probabilistic maximally parallel evolution step of a MPP system

---

function MPP_STEP(R,w)

    $x = w$

    $y = \emptyset$

    while there exists $u \xrightarrow{f} v \mid_p$ in R s.t. $u \subseteq x$, $p \subseteq w$ and $f(w) > 0$ **do**

        $R' = \{u \xrightarrow{f} v \mid_p \in R \mid u \subseteq x \text{ and } p \subseteq w\}$

        choose $u' \xrightarrow{f'} v' \mid_{p'}$ from R' with a probability proportional to $f'(w)$

        $x = x \setminus u'$

        $y = y \cup v'$

    end while

    return $x \cup y$

end function

---

rules. Such products are not immediately added to x to avoid the application of a rule at the i-th iteration to consume objects produced by a rule applied in a previous iteration. Indeed, this iterative procedure simulates a parallel application of rules in which the reactions are applied all at the same time (their products are available only at the next parallel step). Once objects in x are such that no further rule in R can be applied to them, the algorithm stops iterating and returns the new state of the system $x \cup y$ (where x are the unused objects and y are the new products). Note that in order to determine (in the guard of the loop and in the definition of R') whether a rule is applicable or not, reactants are checked to be contained in x (the remaining objects) while promoters are checked to be present in w (the system state at the beginning of the iteration).

Example 1. A MPP system modelling a population of males and females that reproduce (once) during summer and are subject to natural selection during winter can be defined as $\langle A_{MF}, w_{0MF}, R_{MF} \rangle$ where $A_{MF} = \{M, F, SUM, WIN\}$, w_{0MF} contains $M\,F\,SUM$ and R_{MF} consists of the following rules:

$$M\,F \xrightarrow{f_1} M\,F\,M \mid_{SUM} \qquad M\,F \xrightarrow{f_1} M\,F\,F \mid_{SUM}$$

$$M \xrightarrow{f_{live}} M \mid_{WIN} \qquad M \xrightarrow{f_{die}} \epsilon \mid_{WIN} \qquad F \xrightarrow{f_{live}} F \mid_{WIN} \qquad F \xrightarrow{f_{die}} \epsilon \mid_{WIN}$$

$$SUM \xrightarrow{f_1} WIN \qquad WIN \xrightarrow{f_1} SUM$$

where ϵ represents the empty multiset and for all w in A_{MF}^* it holds $f_1(w) = 1$, $f_{live}(w) = cc/|w|$ and $f_{die}(w) = |w|/cc$, with cc the carrying capacity of the environment (a parameter representing the amount of environmental resources).

From the initial state w_{0MF} we have the birth of either a new male (M) or a new female (F). These two events have the same probability to happen, and in both cases the control object SUM is replaced by WIN, modelling the change of the season. In winter, each individual can either survive or die. Survival is more likely than death when the size of the population $|w|$ is smaller than the carrying capacity of the environment, and viceversa.

MPP systems use objects to represent the states of individuals. Often, the state of an individual depends on a number of parameters (age, position, colour, social role, etc.). In order to allow the state of an individual to be described with a single object, the alphabet of the MPP system has to include as many different objects as the possible combinations of values for the parameters to be considered. Moreover, evolution rules describing events that do not depend on the value of a specific parameter, have to be repeated for each object representing a different value of such a parameter. In order to avoid such an explosion of both the alphabet and the set of evolution rules, we proposed in [4] an extension of MPP systems, called *Attributed Probabilistic P systems (APP systems)*, in which objects can be enriched with attributes that can store the values of the parameters that are relevant for the modelled individual. Evolution rules can then be defined in a symbolic way, with reactants described as patterns that have to match the objects in the multiset representing the current state of the system. In this way, the same rule can be applied to objects that differ in the values of some parameters, and it is also possible to include constraints on such values and to compute the values of the parameters of the products on the basis of the values of the parameters of the reactants.

Definition 2 (APP system). *An* Attributed Probabilistic P system *is a tuple* $\langle A, arity, D_{a_1}, \ldots, D_{a_n}, w_0, R \rangle$ *where:*

- *A is an ordered finite alphabet of symbols,* $\{a_1, \ldots, a_n\}$;
- $arity : A \to \mathbb{N}$ *is a function which for each* $a_i \in A$ *gives the arity of* D_{a_i};
- *each* $D_{a_i} = I_1 \times \ldots \times I_{arity(a_i)}$ *is a set of tuples, where each* I_j *is a (possibly infinite) set of values; the set* D_{a_i} *is called the set of attributes of* a_i;
- w_0 *is a multiset of values in* $\Gamma = \{\langle a_i, d_i \rangle \mid a_i \in A, \ d_i \in D_{a_i}\}$ *describing the initial state of the system, where* Γ *is called the set of* objects *of P. In the following we will write* $w_0 \in \Gamma^*$.
- *given a set of variables V, R is a finite set of evolution rules having the form*

$$u_V \xrightarrow{f} v_V \mid_{pr_V}$$

where $u_V, pr_V \in \Gamma_V^*$ *are multisets of objects (with variables) denoting reactants and promoters, respectively;* $v_V \in \Gamma_{EV}^*$ *is a multiset of objects (with expressions) denoting products; and* $f : \Gamma^* \times \Sigma \mapsto \mathbb{R}^{\geq 0}$, *with* $\Sigma = V \mapsto \bigcup_{i=1}^{n} D_{a_i}$, *is a rate function. Precisely:*

$$\Gamma_V = \{\langle a_i, d_i \rangle \mid a_i \in A, d_i \in D_{a_i}^V\} \qquad \Gamma_{EV} = \{\langle a_i, e_i \rangle \mid a_i \in A, e_i \in E_{a_i}^V\}$$

where $D_{a_i}^V = (V \cup I_1) \times \ldots \times (V \cup I_{arity(a_i)})$; *and* $E_{a_i}^V = Exp(V, I_1) \times \ldots \times Exp(V, I_{arity(a_i)})$, *with* $Exp(V, I)$ *denoting the set of well-typed expressions built from operators, variables V, and values of I. Moreover, we have* $Vars(v_V) \subseteq Vars(u_V) \cup Vars(pr_V)$, *where* $Vars(t)$ *denotes the set of variables occurring in t. Rules without variables are called* ground rules.

In what follows we will denote an (attributed) object $\langle a, d \rangle$ as $a_{(d)}$. Moreover, we allow constraints on the instantiation of variables to be associated with a rewrite rules in order to limit its application to multisets of objects satisfying

Algorithm 2. Probabilistic maximally parallel evolution step of an APP system

```
function APP_STEP(R,w)
    x = w
    y = ∅
    while there exists u →f v |ₚ in R and σ s.t. uσ ⊆ x, pσ ⊆ w and f(w,σ) > 0 do
        R' = {uσ →k vσ | u →f v |ₚ∈ R, uσ ⊆ x, pσ ⊆ w and f(w,σ) = k}
        choose u' →k' v' from R' with a probability proportional to k'
        x = x \ u'
        y = y ∪ v'
    end while
    return x ∪ y
end function
```

some requirements. Actually, the constraints of a rule could be removed by suitably modifying the rate function in order to make it give 0 as result when the constraints are not satisfied. We will assume that such a translation is always done, and hence we will specify constraints in evolution rules although they are not present in the formal definition of APP systems.

A state (or configuration) of an APP system is a multiset of objects in Γ^*. The semantics of an APP system, defined in [4] as a probabilistic transition system, is analogous to that of an MPP system, with the only difference that rule instantiation has not only to take care of applying the rate functions to the multiset representing the current state of the system, but also to instantiate variables in the evolution rules. This results in a slightly different algorithm for computing a maximally-parallel step (Algorithm 2).

The instantiation of variables in evolution rules is done by a function $\sigma : V \mapsto \bigcup_{i=1}^{n} D_{a_i}$ that is obtained by matching the left-hand side of the rule with the objects in the current state of the system. The same instantiation is also passed to the rate function in order to instantiate variables used in the definition of the latter. We use the postfix notation $x\sigma$ to denote the application of an instantiation function σ to all the variables in a multiset of objects x.

Example 2. We enrich Example 1 by modelling also the age of individuals. We define the following APP system: $\langle A_{MFa}, arity_{MFa}, \mathbb{N}, \mathbb{N}, \emptyset, \emptyset, w_{0MFa}, R_{MFa} \rangle$ where $A_{MFa} = \{M, F, SUM, WIN\}$ and $arity_{MFa}$ gives 1 with M and F, and 0 otherwise. Moreover, w_{0MFa} contains $M_{(5)}, F_{(3)}$ and SUM. Finally, R_{MFa} consists of the following rules:

$$M_{(x)} F_{(y)} \xrightarrow{f_1} M_{(x)} F_{(y)} M_{(1)} |_{SUM} \qquad \text{if } x \geq 3 \text{ and } y \geq 3$$

$$M_{(x)} F_{(y)} \xrightarrow{f_1} M_{(x)} F_{(y)} F_{(1)} |_{SUM} \qquad \text{if } x \geq 3 \text{ and } y \geq 3$$

$$M_{(x)} \xrightarrow{f_{live}} M_{(x+1)} |_{WIN} \qquad M_{(x)} \xrightarrow{f_{die}} \epsilon |_{WIN}$$

$$F_{(x)} \xrightarrow{f_{live}} F_{(x+1)} |_{WIN} \qquad F_{(x)} \xrightarrow{f_{die}} \epsilon |_{WIN}$$

$$SUM \xrightarrow{f_1} WIN \qquad WIN \xrightarrow{f_1} SUM$$

where ϵ represents the empty multiset and for all w in A^*_{MFa} it holds $f_1(w) = 1$, $f_{live}(w) = (cc/|w|) \cdot (al/x)$ and $f_{die}(w) = (|w|/cc) \cdot (x/al)$, with cc the carrying capacity of the environment and al the average life duration of an individual.

From the initial state w_{0MFa} we have the birth of either a new male (M) or a new female (F) of age 1. These two events have the same probability to happen, but mating is possibile only if the age of both parents is at least 3. In winter, each individual can either survive or die. Survival is more likely than death when the size of the population $|w|$ is smaller than the carrying capacity of the environment, and viceversa. Moreover, survival is more likely for young individuals. When an individual survives to winter, its age is incremented.

3   Case Study 1: On the Stability of Lake Frog Complexes

Lake frog (*Pelophylax ridibundus* Pallas, 1771) and pool frog (*Pelophylax lessonae* Camerano, 1882) can mate producing the hybrid edible frog (*Pelophylax esculentus* Linneus, 1758). The edible frog can coexist with one or both of the parental species giving rise to mixed populations. Usually the genotypes of *P. ridibundus*, *P. lessonae* and *P. esculentus* are indicated by RR, LL, and LR, respectively. In Europe there are mainly mixed populations containing *P. lessonae* and *P. esculentus*, called L-E systems. Hybrids in these populations reproduce in a particular way, called *hybridogenesis*. Hybridogenesis consists in a particular gametogenetic process in which the hybrids exclude one of their parental genomes premeiotically, and transmit the other one, clonally, to eggs and sperm. This particular way of reproduction requires that hybrids live sympatrically with the parental species the genome of which is eliminated. In this way hybrids in a L-E system eliminate the L genome thus producing *P. esculentus* when mating with *P. lessonae*, and generating *P. ridibundus* when mating with other hybrids. Usually *P. ridibundus* generated in L-E complexes are inviable due to deleterious mutations accumulated in the clonally transmitted R genome. Because of inviability of *P. esculentus* × *P. esculentus* offspring, edible frog populations cannot survive alone, but they must act as a sexual parasite of one of the parental species. In L-E complexes the reproductive pattern is the one in Table 1 where the subscribed Y indicates the male sexual chromosome.

Note that the Y chromosome, determining the sex of frog males, can occur only in the L genome, due to primary hybridization which involved, for size constraints, *P. lessonae* males and *P. ridibundus* females. Table 1 shows that only one of the three possible matings resulting in viable offspring produce LL

Table 1. Reproductive pattern of water frogs

	LL	LR
L_yL	L_yL LL	L_yR LR
L_yR	LR	RR not viable

genotypes. This would give an advantage to edible frogs which could outnumber *P. lessonae* and eventually eliminate them. This situation would result in an extinction also of *P. esculentus* which cannot survive without the parental species. In addition to their relative abundance which can be promoted by the above reproductive pattern, edible frogs show, by heterosis, a greater fitness than the parental species. The sum of relative abundance and heterosis should out-compete *P. lessonae* in L-E complexes. The widespread distribution of L-E complexes reveals the existence of mechanisms which contribute to the stability of such complexes, namely to the ability of such populations to self-maintain their structure. Among such mechanisms sexual selection seems to be one of the most important: *P. esculentus* females prefer *P. lessonae* males with respect to males of their own species. Many mathematical and computational models were devoted to the study of the influence of sexual selection in the evolution of populations. The models in [24, 35] show how female preference is able to stabilize L-E complexes by counterbalancing both heterosis and reproductive advantage of edible frogs.

In [6] we used MPP systems for studying the dynamics of European water frog populations. In particular, we showed that female preferences and the inviability of *P. ridibundus* offspring can stabilize L-E complexes. Moreover, we showed how the introduction of translocated *P. ridibundus* in stable L-E complexes can lead to the collapse of the systems. The dynamics of the population in the different cases is studied both by means of stochastic simulation and by means of statistical model checking with PRISM [26]. We also published a more detailed investigation of biological properties of L-E complexes in [15].

In this section we recall the definition of the MPP systems model and of the main simulation results presented in [6].

The MPP systems model

We model a L-E complex by means of a MPP system $\langle A_{LE}, w_{0LE}, R_{LE} \rangle$ in which each individual of the population is represented by an object in the state of the system. Hence, the alphabet A_{LE} contains one object for each possible genotype of an individual. We use different objects for juveniles (immature individuals) and adults. Moreover, the alphabet includes some control objects used to realize alternation of reproduction and selection stages. As a consequence, we define $A_{LE} = A_{LEa} \cup A_{LEj} \cup A_{ctrl}$, where A_{LEa} represents adults, A_{LEj} represents juveniles and A_{ctrl} are control objects.

Since the R genome may contain a deleterious mutation or not, we use different objects for representing *P. esculentus* and *P. ridibundus* individuals carrying or not a mutation in their genotype. Thus, the alphabet representing adults is

$$A_{LEa} = \{ LL, L_yL, LR_*, L_yR_*, LR_\circ, L_yR_\circ, R_*R_\circ, R_\circ R_\circ \}$$

where y represents the Y chromosome, and $*$ and $\circ$ represent the presence and the absence of a deleterious mutation, respectively.

The alphabet representing juveniles is

$$A_{LEj} = \{\, LL^j \,,\, L_y L^j \,,\, LR_*^j \,,\, L_y R_*^j \,,\, LR_\circ^j \,,\, L_y R_\circ^j \,,\, R_* R_*^j \,,\, R_* R_\circ^j \,,\, R_\circ R_\circ^j \,\}$$

where j denotes that the individual is a juvenile, and the other notations are as before. Note that $R_* R_*^j$ is allowed although it represents non viable genotype since in our model individuals with such a genotype will be allowed to be born, but they will not be allowed to become adults.

Finally, the alphabet of control objects is

$$A_{ctrl} = \{\, REPR \,,\, SEL \,,\, 1 \,,\, 2 \,,\, 3\,\}$$

where $REPR$ and SEL represent reproduction and selection stages, respectively, and natural numbers 1, 2 and 3 will be used as counters.

The set of evolution rules R_{LE} contains reproduction, selection and control rules. Hence, we have $R_{LE} = R_{LEr} \cup R_{LEs} \cup R_{ctrl}$.

Reproduction rules R_{LEr} are of the following form:

$$x\, y \xrightarrow{f_{xy}} x\, y\, z \,|_{REPR} \qquad f_{xy}(w) = k_{mate}(x,y) \cdot |w|_x \cdot |w|_y \cdot 1/k_{o\_kind}(x,y)$$

where $x \in A_{LEa}$ is any object representing a female and $y \in A_{LEa}$ is any object representing a male. Function f_{xy} gives the rate of mating of females of type x with males of type y by taking into account the sexual preferences of x females and the quantities of individuals of types x and y. In the definition, $k_{mate}(x,y)$ is the preference of a female x for a male y, and $k_{o\_kind}(x,y)$ is the number of possible offspring kinds that can be generated by the mating of x with y. Remark that $1/k_{o\_kind}(x,y)$ distributes the rate of the mating event of x and y over the rules for this mating.

Finally, $z \in A_{LEj}$ is an object representing the newborn, and it is related with x and y as described in Table 1. For example, for $x = LL$ and $y = L_y L$ there are two rules, one with $z = L_y L^j$ and the other with $z = LL^j$. The full list of reproduction rules is described in [6].

As regards selection rules R_{LEs}, they contain two rules for each individual of the population describing its survival and its death during the selection stage, respectively. For each object $x \in A_{LEa}$ representing an adult individual we have:

$$x \xrightarrow{g_x} x \,|_{SEL} \qquad x \xrightarrow{g'_x} \epsilon \,|_{SEL} \qquad g_x(w) = \cfrac{1}{\sigma + \cfrac{|w|}{k_{fit}(x)\cdot cc}} \qquad g'_x(w) = 1 - g_x(w)$$

where ϵ represent the empty multiset and g_x and g'_x give the probability of survival and death, respectively, of an individual of type x. Function g_x takes into account the size of the population $|w|$, the carrying capacity of the environment cc, and the fitness of the individual $k_{fit}(x)$.

For each object $x^j \in (A_{LEj} \setminus \{R_* R_*^j\})$ representing a juvenile (but not $R_* R_*^j$) we have:

$$x^j \xrightarrow{g_{xj}} x \,|_{SEL} \qquad x^j \xrightarrow{g'_{xj}} \epsilon \,|_{SEL} \qquad R_* R_*^j \xrightarrow{f_1} \epsilon \,|_{SEL}$$

where $x \in A_{LE}$ is the object representing the adult of the same type of x^j, and ϵ, g_{x^j} and g'_{x^j} are as before. In the case of $R_*R_*^j$ we consider only the death rule, since such a kind of juvenile is considered too unfit to be able to grow up, and for all $w \in A^*$ it holds $f_1(w) = 1$.

Finally, as regards control rules R_{ctrl}, they are responsible for the appearance and disappearance of objects $REPR$ and SEL in order to activate alternatively reproduction and selection rules. For the sake of simplicity, we assume that the offspring of each female in each reproduction stage are exactly 3. Hence, the object $REPR$ has to be present for 3 subsequent steps, then it has to be replaced by SEL for one step, and these 4 steps should be iterated forever. This result is obtained by ensuring that $REPR$ is in the initial state of the system and by using the following control rules:

$$1 \xrightarrow{f_1} 2 \qquad 2 \xrightarrow{f_1} 3 \qquad 3\,REPR \xrightarrow{f_1} SEL \qquad SEL \xrightarrow{f_1} 1\,REPR$$

where, as before, for all $w \in A^*$ it holds $f_1(w) = 1$.

The initial state w_{0LE} of the MPP system will change in different simulations. In general, it will contain the control objects 1 and $REPR$, and one object for each individual present in the considered initial population.

Model parameters

In order to perform simulations we consider the following initial parameters (some of them will be changed later on).

– No sexual preference: for every female x and male y we have $k_{mate}(x, y) = 1$.
– 10% higher fitness for hybrids (heterosis effect), namely

$$k_{fit}(x) = \begin{cases} 0.55 & \text{if } x \in \{LyR_*, LyR_\circ, LyR_*, LyR_\circ\} \\ 0.5 & \text{if } x \in \{LL, LyL, R_\circ R_\circ, R_*R_\circ\} \\ 0.88 & \text{if } x \in \{LyR_*^j, LyR_\circ^j, LyR_*^j, LyR_\circ^j\} \\ 0.8 & \text{if } x \in \{LL^j, LyL^j, R_\circ R_\circ^j, R_*R_\circ^j\} \end{cases}$$

– The carrying capacity cc is set to 400.

Model analysis

We study the stability of L-E complexes by considering populations without deleterious mutations in the R genome of *P. esculentus*. We performed 1000 simulations with initial populations composed by *P. lessonae* frogs and a percentages of 10% of mutation-free edible frogs. The initial state of the system is hence described by the multiset w_{0LE} consisting of 90 instances of LL, 90 of L_yL, 10 of $LR_\circ$, 10 of $L_yR_\circ$ and of the control objects 1 and $REPR$.

We observe that, in all the simulations, the population evolves towards a mono-specific population of viable all-females *P. ridibundus* which eventually collapses for the absence of males (recall that the Y chromosome can occur only on the L genome). Figure 1(a) shows the outcome of a typical simulation. In the first few years (a), the population grows towards the carrying capacity of the environment. Then, when the hybrid population raise in number, the first interspecies matings happen with the appearance of $P.$ $ridibundus$ females (b). Finally, the $P.$ $ridibundus$ females act as sexual parasites (c) leading first to extinction of $P.$ $lessonae$, then of hybrids and finally of themselves (all females).

Let us now consider an initial population with the same percentages of edible frogs (10%), but in which all the $P.$ $esculentus$ individuals carry the deleterious mutations on the R genome, that is $P.$ $ridibundus$ females are not viable and they do not appear in the population. The initial state of the system is hence described by the multiset w_{0LE} consisting of 90 instances of LL, 90 of L_yL, 10 of $LR_\circ$, 10 of L_yR_* and of the control objects 1 and $REPR$.

We performed 1000 simulations. We observe that also in this case the population collapses in all simulations. In particular, in the first few years (a) the population grows towards the carrying capacity of the environment. Then, the population shows a decline (b), first of $P.$ $lessonae$ and then of $P.$ $esculentus$. Figure 1(b) shows the outcome of a typical simulation in this case.

Finally, we introduce in the population a female preference towards L_yL males. In particular, we set $k_{mate}(LL, L_yL) = 6$ and $k_{mate}(LR, L_yL) = 2$. Also in this case we performed 1000 simulations with the same initial state as before.

We observe that in almost all simulations the complex evolves towards a stable L-E complex. Figure 1(c) shows the outcome of a typical simulation in this case. We do not show the outcome of simulations in a population with female preferences but without deleterious mutations in the R genome since also in this case the population evolves towards an all-females $P.$ $ridibundus$ population.

The result we obtained with these simulations is a demonstration of the validity of the hypothesis that both the accumulation of deleterious mutations and the presence of a mechanism like sexual selection are necessary for the stability of L-E complexes. In addition to this, in [6] we investigated also the consequences of the introduction of $P.$ $ridibundus$ in a stable L-E complex. What we demonstrated in such a case is that quite surprisingly the introduction of even a small number of $P.$ $ridibundus$ individuals in a stable L-E complex leads either to the extinction of the whole population, or to the replacement of the original population by a population of only $P.$ $ridibundus$ individuals.

4 Case Study 2: Establishment of Dominance Hierarchies in Primate Societies

In this model, we describe the behaviour of male monkeys and how it changes when a female monkey enters the oestrum. The model is inspired by the social behaviour of species of prosimians as described in [17, 29, 30].

The APP model

The population is dispersed in an environment, which is modelled as a continuous 2D space, hence each individual is associated with coordinates (x, y).

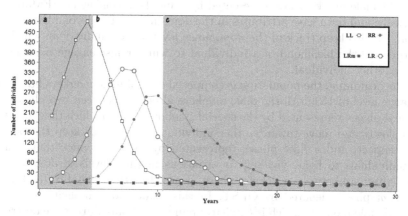

(a) No deleterious mutations, no sexual selection

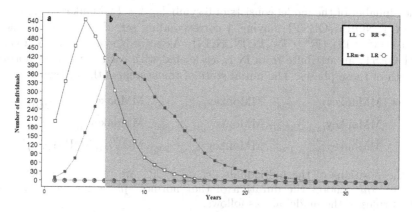

(b) Deleterious mutations, no sexual selection

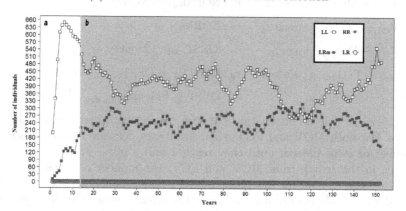

(c) Deleterious mutations and sexual selection

Fig. 1. Examples of simulation results of L-E complexes.

Male and female monkeys are represented by symbols MMonkey and FMonkey, respectively, and both have attributes in the domain $\mathbb{R}^2 \times \mathbb{N}$. Beyond the actual position, we also keep track of the *dominance* level of each individual, which is used to derive the likelihood of a individual to win (or just engage in) a fight against another individual.

At the beginning, the population is composed only of male monkeys having a dominance level of 1500. All the male monkeys alternate between two phases: a *movement* phase, represented by the special symbol MOV, in which they wander around slowly and move towards other individuals in order to keep the population compact; and a *fight* phase, represented by FGT, in which they chase other individuals to fight, yielding to variations in their levels of dominance. Females alternate between a *normal* phase, denoted by the symbol NORM, and an *oestrum* phase, denoted by OEST. In this model, for simplicity, there is only one female monkey, which is explicitly represented only during the oestrum phase.

The alphabet of the model consists of 6 symbols, $A = \{$MMonkey, FMonkey, MOV, FGT, NORM, OEST$\}$, having a corresponding set of attributes defined as $D = \{(\mathbb{R}^2 \times \mathbb{N}), (\mathbb{R}^2 \times \mathbb{N}), \mathbb{N}, \mathbb{N}, \mathbb{N}, \mathbb{N}\}$. As regards symbols MOV, FGT, NORM, OEST, an attribute from $\mathbb{N}$ is associated with each of them, denoting the length of those phases. The initial state of the system is the following:

$$w_0 = \{\text{MMonkey}_{(x_1, y_1, 1500)}, \text{MMonkey}_{(x_2, y_2, 1500)}, \text{MMonkey}_{(x_3, y_3, 1500)},$$
$$\text{MMonkey}_{(x_4, y_4, 1500)}, \text{MMonkey}_{(x_5, y_5, 1500)}, \text{MMonkey}_{(x_6, y_6, 1500)},$$
$$\text{MMonkey}_{(x_7, y_7, 1500)}, \text{MMonkey}_{(x_8, y_8, 1500)}, \text{MOV}_{(1)}, \text{NORM}_{(Snl)}\}$$

where the positions of the individuals $(x_i, y_i) \in \mathbb{R}^2$ are randomly generated. Parameter Snl denotes the duration of the "normal" phase for females. The evolution rules of the model are as follows.

$r_1 : \text{MOV}_{(n)} \xrightarrow{1} \text{MOV}_{(n-1)} \quad \forall n > 1$ $r_6 : \text{NORM}_{(n)} \xrightarrow{1} \text{NORM}_{(n-1)} \quad \forall n > 1$

$r_2 : \text{MOV}_{(1)} \xrightarrow{1} \text{FGT}_{(Nfl)} | \text{NORM}_{(n)}$ $r_7 : \text{NORM}_{(1)} \xrightarrow{1}$

$r_3 : \text{MOV}_{(1)} \xrightarrow{1} \text{FGT}_{(Ofl)} | \text{OEST}_{(n)}$ $\qquad \text{OEST}_{(Sol)}, \text{FMonkey}_{(FInitX, FInitY, FInitD)}$

$r_4 : \text{FGT}_{(n)} \xrightarrow{1} \text{FGT}_{(n-1)} \quad \forall n > 1$ $r_8 : \text{OEST}_{(n)} \xrightarrow{1} \text{OEST}_{(n-1)} \quad \forall n > 1$

$r_5 : \text{FGT}_{(1)} \xrightarrow{1} \text{MOV}_{(Msn)}$ $r_9 : \text{OEST}_{(1)}, \text{FMonkey}_{(x,y,dom)} \xrightarrow{1} \text{NORM}_{(Snl)}$

Rules $r_1 - r_5$ model the alternation between "movement" and "fight" phases for males. For both MOV and FGT, their attributes decrease to keep track of the number of steps passed, until they reach 1 and a phase switch occurs. In particular, in the switch from MOV and FGT, the number of steps that the fight phase lasts depend on the phase of the female; namely it is either Nfl or Ofl, if the female is currently either in the normal phase (NORM) or the oestrum phase (OEST), respectively. The movement phase lasts Msn steps.

Rules $r_6 - r_9$ model the alternation between "normal" and "oestrum" phases for the female monkey. The durations of the oestrum phase is modelled by parameter Sol. The initial coordinates of the female monkey are denoted by the parameters $FInitX$ and $FInitY$, while $FInitD$ denotes its initial dominance level.

$$r_{10} : \text{MMonkey}_{(x',y',dom')} \xrightarrow{f_{10}} \text{MMonkey}_{(\text{move}(x',x'',SMMA),\text{move}(y',y'',SMMA),dom')}$$

$$|\text{MOV}_{(n)},\text{NORM}_{(m)},\text{MMonkey}_{(x'',y'',dom'')}$$

$$r_{11} : \text{MMonkey}_{(x',y',dom')} \xrightarrow{f_{11}} \text{MMonkey}_{(\text{move}(x',x'',SMMA),\text{move}(y',y'',SMMA),dom')}$$

$$|\text{MOV}_{(n)},\text{OEST}_{(m)},\text{MMonkey}_{(x'',y'',dom'')}$$

Rules $r_{10} - r_{11}$ handle the movement of males during either the "normal" or "oestrum" phase for the female. In both cases, a male (in a position x', y') is allowed to move towards any other male (in position x'', y''). The resulting position of the male which moves is computed as $(\text{move}(x', x'', SMMA), \text{move}(y', y'', SMMA))$, where move is a function to move the coordinates (x', y') towards coordinates (x'', y'') with a given speed factor described by the parameter $SMMA$ (Speed Male-Male approach). Formally, this function is defined as:

$$\text{move}(a, b, \gamma) = a + (b - a)/\gamma$$

The most important difference between rules r_{10} and r_{11} lies in the rate functions, which are defined as:

$$f_{10} = \begin{cases} 1 & \text{if } SD/NT < dist((x',y'),(x'',y'')) < SD; \\ 0 & \text{otherwise;} \end{cases}$$

$$f_{11} = \begin{cases} 1 & \text{if } SD/OT < dist((x',y'),(x'',y'')) < SD; \\ 0 & \text{otherwise.} \end{cases}$$

where $dist((x', y'), (x'', y''))$ is a function giving the euclidean distance between two points, parameter SD (Spot Distance) denotes the maximum visibility distance of a monkey, and parameters NT (Normal Tolerance) and OT (Oestrum Tolerance) are used to derive the minimum distance allowed between two monkeys to enable the relative movement of one towards the other. In particular, such a minimum distance depends on the phase of the female, and it is either SD/NT during the NORM phase, and SD/OT during the OEST phase. In this manner, during the oestrum phase, males are allowed to come closer one another, hence increasing the possibility to engage in a fight.

$$r_{12} : \text{MMonkey}_{(x',y',dom')} \xrightarrow{f_{12}} \text{MMonkey}_{(\text{move}(x',x'',SMFA),\text{move}(y',y'',SMFA),dom')}$$

$$|\text{MOV}_{(n)},\text{FMonkey}_{(x'',y'',dom'')}$$

Rule r_{12} models the movement of a male monkey towards the female. In this case, the speed of the male is denoted by the parameter $SMFA$. The corresponding rate function is:

$$f_{12} = \begin{cases} PfF & \text{if } dist((x',y'),(x'',y'')) < SD \text{ and } dom' + FT > dom''; \\ 0 & \text{otherwise;} \end{cases}$$

which enables the movement only if both (i) their relative distance is less than SD, and (ii) the dominance level of the male, plus a tolerance value FT (Female Tolerance), is greater than that of the female. The actual rate used is denoted by the parameter PfF (Preference for Female).

$$r_{13} : \text{MMonkey}_{(x',y',dom')}, \text{MMonkey}_{(x'',y'',dom'')} \xrightarrow{elo\_rating(dom',dom'')}$$

$$\text{MMonkey}_{(\text{chase}(x',x'',CSN),\text{chase}(y',y'',CSN),elow(dom',dom'')),}$$

$$\text{MMonkey}_{(\text{flee}(x',x'',FSN),\text{flee}(y',y'',FSN),elol(dom'',dom'))}|\text{FGT}_{(n)},\text{NORM}_{(m)}$$

with $dom' \geq dom''$, $dist((x',y'),(x'',y'')) \leq NAD$, and $dom' - dom'' \leq AN$, where NAD (Normal Aggression Distance) and AN (Avoidance Normal) are model parameters representing the minimum distance and the maximum difference in dominance that enable an aggression when the female is in normal condition. In this rule the monkey in position (x',y') has a dominance that is higher or equal to that of the other monkey. The probability that the first monkey wins the fight is given by the standard Elo rating method, originally defined for applications to games, and then used for the modelling of social interactions. Such a method is based on a table that gives the probability of success in a fight depending on the difference of rating (or dominance) of the involved individual. The Elo rating table we consider for this model is in [1]. The function $elo\_rating(\Delta dom)$ looks in the table and gives as result the probability of the victory of the stronger monkey over the weaker one.

Function chase gives the new position of the winner of the fight; function flee gives the new position of the looser of the fight; $elow$ gives the new dominance of the winner of the fight following the Elo rating table and method; $elol$ the new dominance of the looser of the fight. These functions are defined as follows:

$$\text{chase}(a,b,\rho) = a + \rho \cdot (b-a) \qquad \text{flee}(a,b,\rho) = b + \rho \cdot (b-a)$$

$$elow(d',d'') = d' + \begin{cases} (1 - elo\_rating(\Delta dom)) \cdot steepness & \text{if } d' > d'' \\ elo\_rating(\Delta dom) \cdot steepness & \text{if } d' < d'' \end{cases}$$

$$elol(d',d'') = d' - \begin{cases} elo\_rating(\Delta dom) \cdot steepness & \text{if } d' > d'' \\ 1 - (elo\_rating(\Delta dom)) \cdot steepness & \text{if } d' < d'' \end{cases}$$

where $\Delta dom = |d'-d''|$, and $steepness$ is a parameter representing the maximum increase/decrease of dominance. The parameters CSN(Chase Speed Normal) and FSN (Flee Speed Normal) used in rule r_{13} describe how fast the monkeys move.

$$r_{14} : \text{MMonkey}_{(x',y',dom')}, \text{MMonkey}_{(x'',y'',dom'')} \xrightarrow{1-elo\_rating(dom',dom'')}$$

$$\text{MMonkey}_{(\text{flee}(x',x'',FSN),\text{flee}(y',y'',FSN),elol(dom',dom'')),}$$

$$\text{MMonkey}_{(\text{chase}(x',x'',CSN),\text{chase}(y',y'',CSN),elow(dom'',dom'))}|\text{FGT}_{(n)} \text{NORM}_{(m)}$$

with $dom' > dom''$, $dist((x',y'),(x'',y'')) \leq NAD$, and $|dom' - dom''| \leq AN$.

Rule r_{14} is analogous to rule r_{13}, but describes the case in which the winner is the weaker monkey.

$$r_{15} : \text{MMonkey}_{(x',y',dom')}, \text{MMonkey}_{(x'',y'',dom'')} \xrightarrow{elo\_rating(dom',dom'')}$$
$$\text{MMonkey}_{(\text{chase}(x',x'',CSO),\text{chase}(y',y'',CSO),elow(dom',dom'')),}$$
$$\text{MMonkey}_{(\text{flee}(x',x'',FSO),\text{flee}(y',y'',FSO),elol(dom',dom''))}\big|\text{FGT}_{(n)},\text{OEST}_{(m)}$$

with $dom' \geq dom''$, $dist((x',y'),(x'',y'')) \leq OAD$, and $dom' - dom'' \leq AO$.

$$r_{16} : \text{MMonkey}_{(x',y',dom')}, \text{MMonkey}_{(x'',y'',dom'')} \xrightarrow{1-elo\_rating(dom',dom'')}$$
$$\text{MMonkey}_{(\text{flee}(x',x'',FSO),\text{flee}(y',y'',FSO),elol(dom',dom'')),}$$
$$\text{MMonkey}_{(\text{chase}(x',x'',CSO),\text{chase}(y',y'',CSO),elow(dom'',dom'))}\big|\text{FGT}_{(n)},\text{OEST}_{(m)}$$

with $dom' > dom''$, $dist((x',y'),(x'',y'')) \leq OAD$, and $|dom' - dom''| \leq AO$.

Rules r_{15} and r_{16} are analogous to r_{13} and r_{14}, respectively, but describe the case in which the female is in oestrum state. Parameters OAD (Oestrum Aggression Distance), AO (Avoidance Oestrum), CSO (Chase Speed Oestrum) and FSO (Flee Speed Oestrum) of these rules are analogous to the corresponding ones of rules r_{13} and r_{14}, but with values that depend on the fact that the female is in oestrum state.

$$r_{17} : \text{MMonkey}_{(x',y',dom')}, \text{MMonkey}_{(x'',y'',dom'')} \xrightarrow{1}$$
$$\text{MMonkey}_{(\text{chase}(x',x'',CSN),\text{chase}(y',y'',CSN),dom'),}$$
$$\text{MMonkey}_{(\text{flee}(x',x'',FSN),\text{flee}(y',y'',FSN),dom'')}\big|\text{FGT}_{(n)},\text{NORM}_{(m)}$$

with $dom' > dom''$, $dist((x',y'),(x'',y'')) \leq NAD$ and $|dom' - dom''| > AN$.

$$r_{18} : \text{MMonkey}_{(x',y',dom')}, \text{MMonkey}_{(x'',y'',dom'')} \xrightarrow{1}$$
$$\text{MMonkey}_{(\text{chase}(x',x'',CSO),\text{chase}(y',y'',CSO),dom')}$$
$$\text{MMonkey}_{(\text{flee}(x',x'',FSO),\text{flee}(y',y'',FSO),dom'')}\big|\text{FGT}_{(n)},\text{OEST}_{(m)}$$

with $dom' > dom''$, $dist((x',y'),(x'',y'')) \leq OAD$ and $|dom' - dom''| > AO$.

Rules r_{17} and r_{18} describe the interaction between two individuals when the difference in dominance is too high to motivate a fight (greater than parameters AN and AO for the normal and oestrum cases, respectively). In these cases the monkeys move but do not fight, so there is no change in dominance levels.

Experimental results

In Figs. 2 and 3 we show the simulation results of two groups of monkeys. Figure 2 refers to a group with a low level of aggressiveness (egalitarian), while Fig. 3 describes a group with a higher level of aggressiveness (despotic). The upper part of both figures shows the dominance level of each male in the group during

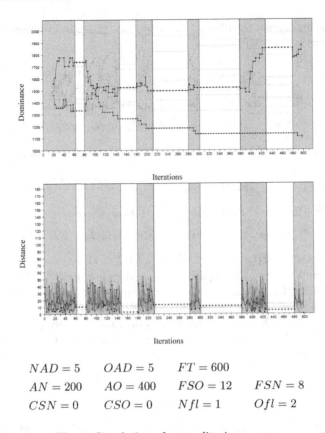

$$NAD = 5 \qquad OAD = 5 \qquad FT = 600$$
$$AN = 200 \qquad AO = 400 \qquad FSO = 12 \qquad FSN = 8$$
$$CSN = 0 \qquad CSO = 0 \qquad Nfl = 1 \qquad Ofl = 2$$

Fig. 2. Simulation of an egalitarian group.

the simulation, while the lower part shows the distance of each male either from the centre of the group or from the female (when present). In the figures we put in evidence the lines corresponding to both the monkey with highest dominance level at the end of the simulation (line marked with •) and the one with the lowest one (marked with +). The main model parameters (that are different in the two cases) are reported in the figures. The other parameters have the following values: iteration = 498, Sol = 20, Snl = 80, SMMA = 0.25, SD = 100, NT = 3, OT = 2, SMFA = 0.25, PfF = 8, Msn = 1 and Steepness = 100. The other model parameters they have been estimated from [17, 29, 30], and the results we obtain are compatible with the behaviours described in those studies.

As regards Fig. 2, initially all the males have the same dominance level. From the beginning and up to about 210 iterations, the group of monkeys struggles to define a clear dominance among individuals. Between iteration 210 and 390, the dotted line is not the dominant of the group, thus its position is not the closest neither to the group centre nor to the female. At the end of the simulation, when the monkey with dotted line becomes the most dominant (alpha male), we can observe that it gains a central position in the group.

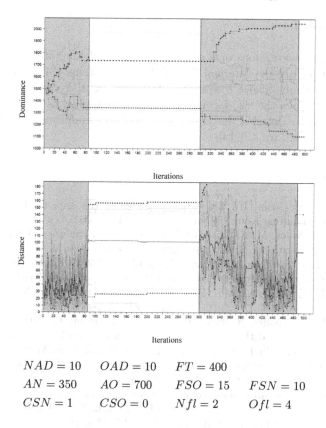

$$NAD = 10 \qquad OAD = 10 \qquad FT = 400$$
$$AN = 350 \qquad AO = 700 \qquad FSO = 15 \qquad FSN = 10$$
$$CSN = 1 \qquad CSO = 0 \qquad Nfl = 2 \qquad Ofl = 4$$

Fig. 3. Simulation of a despotic group.

Figure 3 shows the dynamics of a group with a more rigid hierarchy, due to the higher level of aggressiveness. The first phase, up to iteration 90, in which the males establish a first hierarchy, is followed by a phase in which the hierarchy becomes very stable. From iteration 320, where the monkey with the dotted line becomes the alpha male, it gains the position that is closer to the centre of the group and to the female, and it does not allow any other monkey to come close.

Normal and oestrum periods last respectively 80 and 20 iterations. In normal phase monkeys are less willing to fight and they keep a distance from each other in order to avoid unnecessary conflicts; this corresponds to the more linear parts of the graphs. In oestrum periods males have the female as the pole of attraction and they are more willing to fight. Fights can change the dominance levels of males, thus oestrum periods correspond to more struggling parts of the graphs, where, often, the ranking of dominance changes. When the dominance levels change, the topology of the group changes accordingly.

5   Conclusions

We described two extensions of P systems for the modelling of populations and ecosystems. They are the Minimal Probabilistic P systems (MPP systems) and the Attributed Probabilistic P systems (APP systems). We described also two case studies in which the two formalisms have been applied to the study of real ecological systems. Detailed descriptions of the two formalisms and of the case studies can be found in [4,6,14].

References

1. Albers, P.C., de Vries, H.: Elo-rating as a tool in the sequential estimation of dominance strengths. Anim. Behav. **61**(2), 489–495 (2001)
2. Martínez-del-Amor, M.A., et al.: DCBA: simulating population dynamics P systems with proportional object distribution. In: Csuhaj-Varjú, E., Gheorghe, M., Rozenberg, G., Salomaa, A., Vaszil, G. (eds.) CMC 2012. LNCS, vol. 7762, pp. 257–276. Springer, Heidelberg (2013). doi:10.1007/978-3-642-36751-9_18
3. Barbuti, R., Levi, F., Milazzo, P., Scatena, G.: Maximally parallel probabilistic semantics for multiset rewriting. Fundamenta Informaticae **112**(1), 1–17 (2011)
4. Barbuti, R., Bompadre, A., Bove, P., Milazzo, P., Pardini, G.: Attributed probabilistic P systems and their application to the modelling of social interactions in primates. In: Bianculli, D., Calinescu, R., Rumpe, B. (eds.) SEFM 2015. LNCS, vol. 9509, pp. 176–191. Springer, Heidelberg (2015). doi:10.1007/978-3-662-49224-6_15
5. Barbuti, R., Bove, P., Schettini, A.M., Milazzo, P., Pardini, G.: A computational formal model of the invasiveness of eastern species in european water frog populations. In: Counsell, S., Núñez, M. (eds.) SEFM 2013. LNCS, vol. 8368, pp. 329–344. Springer, Cham (2014). doi:10.1007/978-3-319-05032-4_24
6. Barbuti, R., Bove, P., Milazzo, P., Pardini, G.: Minimal probabilistic P systems for modelling ecological systems. Theor. Comput. Sci. **608**, 36–56 (2015)
7. Barbuti, R., Caravagna, G., Maggiolo–Schettini, A., Milazzo, P., Pardini, G.: The calculus of looping sequences. In: Bernardo, M., Degano, P., Zavattaro, G. (eds.) SFM 2008. LNCS, vol. 5016, pp. 387–423. Springer, Heidelberg (2008). doi:10.1007/978-3-540-68894-5_11
8. Barbuti, R., Cataudella, S., Maggiolo-Schettini, A., Milazzo, P., Troina, A.: A probabilistic model for molecular systems. Fundamenta Informaticae **67**(1), 13–27 (2005)
9. Barbuti, R., Cerone, A., Maggiolo-Schettini, A., Milazzo, P., Setiawan, S.: Modelling population dynamics using grid systems. In: Cerone, A., Persico, D., Fernandes, S., Garcia-Perez, A., Katsaros, P., Shaikh, S.A., Stamelos, I. (eds.) SEFM 2012. LNCS, vol. 7991, pp. 172–189. Springer, Heidelberg (2014). doi:10.1007/978-3-642-54338-8_14
10. Barbuti, R., Gori, R., Levi, F., Milazzo, P.: Investigating dynamic causalities in reaction systems. Theor. Comput. Sci. **623**, 114–145 (2016)
11. Barbuti, R., Maggiolo-Schettini, A., Milazzo, P., Tini, S.: A P systems flat form preserving step-by-step behaviour. Fundamenta Informaticae **87**(1), 1–34 (2008)
12. Besozzi, D., Cazzaniga, P., Pescini, D., Mauri, G.: Modelling metapopulations with stochastic membrane systems. Biosystems **91**(3), 499–514 (2008)
13. Bodei, C., Gori, R., Levi, F.: Causal static analysis for brane calculi. Theor. Comput. Sci. **587**, 73–103 (2015)

14. Bove, P.: Development of extensions of P systems for modelling and simulation of population dynamics. Ph.D. thesis, University of Pisa, October 2016

15. Bove, P., Milazzo, P., Barbuti, R.: The role of deleterious mutations in the stability of hybridogenetic water frog complexes. BMC Evol. Biol. **14**(1), 1 (2014)

16. Cardona, M., Colomer, M.A., Margalida, A., Palau, A., Pérez-Hurtado, I., Pérez-Jiménez, M.J., Sanuy, D.: A computational modelingfor real ecosystems based on P systems. Nat. Comput. **10**(1), 39–53 (2011)

17. Cavigelli, S.A., Pereira, M.E.: Mating season aggression and fecal testosterone levels in male ring-tailed lemurs (Lemur catta). Horm. Behav. **37**(3), 246–255 (2000)

18. Cerone, A., Scotti, M.: Research challenges in modelling ecosystems. In: Canal, C., Idani, A. (eds.) SEFM 2014. LNCS, vol. 8938, pp. 276–293. Springer, Cham (2015). doi:10.1007/978-3-319-15201-1_18

19. Ciobanu, G., Cornacel, L.: Probabilistic transitions for P systems. Prog. Nat. Sci. **17**(4), 432–441 (2007)

20. Nieto Coria, C.A., Tesei, L., Scarcella, G., Russo, T., Merelli, E.: Sea-scale agent-based simulator of *Solea solea* in the adriatic sea. In: Canal, C., Idani, A. (eds.) SEFM 2014. LNCS, vol. 8938, pp. 259–275. Springer, Cham (2015). doi:10.1007/978-3-319-15201-1_17

21. Gori, R., Levi, F.: Abstract interpretation based verification of temporal properties for bioambients. Inform. Comput. **208**(8), 869–921 (2010)

22. Grimm, V.: Ten years of individual-based modelling in ecology: what have we learned and what could we learn in the future? Ecol. Model. **115**(2), 129–148 (1999)

23. Grimm, V., Berger, U., Bastiansen, F., Eliassen, S., Ginot, V., Giske, J., Goss-Custard, J., Grand, T., Heinz, S.K., Huse, G., et al.: A standard protocol for describing individual-based and agent-based models. Ecol. Model. **198**(1), 115–126 (2006)

24. Hellriegel, B., Reyer, H.U.: Factors influencing the composition of mixed populations of a hemiclonal hybrid and its sexual host. J. Evol. Biol. **13**(6), 906–918 (2000)

25. Kahramanoğulları, O., Lynch, J.F., Priami, C.: Algorithmic systems ecology: experiments on multiple interaction types and patches. In: Cerone, A., Persico, D., Fernandes, S., Garcia-Perez, A., Katsaros, P., Shaikh, S.A., Stamelos, I. (eds.) SEFM 2012. LNCS, vol. 7991, pp. 154–171. Springer, Heidelberg (2014). doi:10.1007/978-3-642-54338-8_13

26. Kwiatkowska, M., Norman, G., Parker, D.: PRISM 4.0: verification of probabilistic real-time systems. In: Gopalakrishnan, G., Qadeer, S. (eds.) CAV 2011. LNCS, vol. 6806, pp. 585–591. Springer, Heidelberg (2011). doi:10.1007/978-3-642-22110-1_47

27. Legay, A., Delahaye, B., Bensalem, S.: Statistical model checking: an overview. In: Barringer, H., Falcone, Y., Finkbeiner, B., Havelund, K., Lee, I., Pace, G., Roşu, G., Sokolsky, O., Tillmann, N. (eds.) RV 2010. LNCS, vol. 6418, pp. 122–135. Springer, Heidelberg (2010). doi:10.1007/978-3-642-16612-9_11

28. Murray, J.D.: Mathematical Biology I: An Introduction. Interdisciplinary Applied Mathematics, vol. 17. Springer, New York (2002)

29. Nakamichi, M., Koyama, N.: Social relationships among ring-tailed lemurs (Lemur catta) in two free-ranging troops at berenty reserve, madagascar. Int. J. Primatol. **18**(1), 73–93 (1997)

30. Palagi, E., Paoli, T., Tarli, S.B.: Aggression and reconciliation in two captive groups of Lemur catta. Int. J. Primatol. **26**(2), 279–294 (2005)

31. Penna, P., Paoletti, N., Scarcella, G., Tesei, L., Marini, M., Merelli, E.: DISPAS: an agent-based tool for the management of fishing effort. In: Counsell, S., Núñez, M. (eds.) SEFM 2013. LNCS, vol. 8368, pp. 362–367. Springer, Cham (2014). doi:10.1007/978-3-319-05032-4_26

32. Pescini, D., Besozzi, D., Mauri, G., Zandron, C.: Dynamical probabilistic P systems. Int. J. Found. Comput. Sci. **17**(1), 183–204 (2006)

33. Philippou, A., Toro, M., Antonaki, M.: Simulation and verification in a process calculus for spatially-explicit ecological models. Sci. Ann. Comput. Sci. **23**(1), 119–167 (2013)

34. Setiawan, S., Cerone, A.: Stochastic modelling of seasonal migration using rewriting systems with spatiality. In: Counsell, S., Núñez, M. (eds.) SEFM 2013. LNCS, vol. 8368, pp. 313–328. Springer, Cham (2014). doi:10.1007/978-3-319-05032-4_23

35. Som, C., Anholt, B.R., Reyer, H.U.: The effect of assortative mating on the coexistence of a hybridogenetic waterfrog and its sexual host. Am. Nat. **156**(1), 34–46 (2000)

Regular Papers

Simulating R Systems by P Systems

Artiom Alhazov[1], Bogdan Aman[2], Rudolf Freund[3(✉)], and Sergiu Ivanov[4]

[1] Institute of Mathematics and Computer Science, Academy of Sciences of Moldova,
Str. Academiei 5, 2028 Chişinău, Moldova
`artiom@math.md`
[2] Romanian Academy, Institute of Computer Science,
Blvd. Carol I no.8, 700505 Iaşi, Romania
`bogdan.aman@gmail.com`
[3] Faculty of Informatics, TU Wien, Favoritenstraße 9–11, 1040 Vienna, Austria
`rudi@emcc.at`
[4] Université Paris Est, Paris, France
`sergiu.ivanov@u-pec.fr`

Abstract. We show multiple ways of how to simulate R systems by non-cooperative P systems with atomic control by promoters and/or inhibitors, or with matter/antimatter annihilation rules, with a slowdown by a constant factor only. The descriptional complexity of the simulating P systems is also linear with respect to that of the simulated R system. All constants depend on how general the model of R systems is, as well as on the chosen control ingredients of the P systems. Special attention is paid to the differences in the mode of rule application in these models.

1 Introduction – Differences Between P and R

Membrane systems, also called P systems (non-distributed, with symbol objects) are a formal model of (possibly controlled) multiset rewriting [8]. Reaction systems, also called R systems, also are a formal rewriting-like model of set evolution introduced in [6], see also a recent survey in [5]. Both P systems and R systems are inspired by the functioning of the living cells. It is a natural task to compare R systems, which were introduced later, to P systems, by simulation. A successful solution would allow us to use membrane computing tools for studying reaction systems. Some research comparing them was done in [10]. More exactly, the cited paper considers P systems with the no-persistence aspect of R systems, from the viewpoint of computational power. We here, however, first focus on comparing standard R systems to standard P systems by simulating the former with the latter, and then revisit the direction of bringing aspects of R systems to the P systems model, verifying how closer this can make the models.

We start with the explanation of the simplest case – triples of single objects for the rules in R systems having the form (a, b, c), which loosely corresponds to a rule $a \to c|_{\neg b}$ in P systems, i.e., the first element is the reactant (in this paper we may also call it the left side), the third element is the product (in this paper we may also call it the right side), and the second element is the inhibitor, with the following differences in the mode of application.

© Springer International Publishing AG 2017
A. Leporati et al. (Eds.): CMC 2016, LNCS 10105, pp. 51–66, 2017.
DOI: 10.1007/978-3-319-54072-6_4

The first difference is that the configuration is a set, not a multiset, and thus simultaneously producing the same symbol by multiple rules yields a single object. P systems with sets of objects instead of multisets of objects have been considered in [1], where they have been shown to be universal in the case of distributed P systems, both for the transitional model and for the model with active membranes. However, in [1] the goal of showing universality was reached without actually using this first aspect (automatic reduction of multiple copies of the same object into one copy), but rather by avoiding to ever need multiple copies of the same object (in the same region). This aspect and the one discussed below together are called the *threshold principle* in the literature. However, it is also meaningful to view these aspects individually.

The second difference is that, if multiple rules with the same a in the left side exist, if a is present in the configuration, *all* of these rules where the inhibitors are not present in the configuration are applied, simultaneously producing the corresponding products. This comes from an inspiration that either the abundance of objects a is sufficient, or the replication and, possibly, proper control take place to guarantee the application of all such rules. This second aspect is standard, for instance, in *H systems* (together with the first one), e.g., see [11]. The second aspect has already been considered in the P systems area, too, for example, see [3].

The third difference is that the objects are not persistent. This means that, even if an object does not undergo any rule, it still disappears from the configuration of the next step, unless, of course, it is (re-)produced by some rule. This third aspect is standard in time-varying distributed H systems, for example see [9,12], together with the first and the second aspect, and together they naturally relate to *TVDH1* systems, see [7].

In the general case, the elements of the triples describing the rules of R systems are *sets* of objects. Hence, the meaning of the triple (A, B, C) is: the joint presence of all the objects in A, in the case when all objects in B are absent, leads to the production of the objects in C, and, moreover, the subsequent configuration is precisely equal to the union of the right sides of applicable rules.

2 Preliminaries

The reader is assumed to be familiar with the basic notions of formal languages and membrane computing, see [13] for a comprehensive introduction and the webpage [15] of P systems.

In this paper, we only consider *simple* P systems with the trivial membrane structure only consisting of the skin membrane as its single membrane. Hence, a *simple P system* Π will be specified by

$$\Pi_0 = (O, w_1, R_1)$$

where

- O is the set of objects,
- w_1 is the initial configuration (the multiset contained in the skin membrane at the beginning of a computation), and
- R_1 is a finite set of rules.

The notation $(ncoo, pro_{k,l} + inh_{k',l'})$ describes the class of rules with non-cooperative evolution rules with at most k promoters of weight at most l and at most k' inhibitors of weight at most l', see [4,14]; the sign "+" here means both promoters and inhibitors are allowed to be used in the same rule, if it is not the case, we write a comma instead of the plus sign. If the weight of a promoter or an inhibitor is one, then it is called *atomic*.

The notation $(ncoo, antim/pri)$ stands for non-cooperative evolution rules and matter-antimatter annihilation rules, with weak priority of *all* annihilation rules over all the other rules (the most studied variant of P systems with anti-matter), see [2].

An *R system Π* is written as

$$S = (V, w_0, R)$$

where

- V is the set of objects,
- w_0 is the set of objects present at the beginning of a computation, and
- R is a finite set of rules of the form (A, B, C) with $A, B, C \subseteq V$.

3 Using Promoters and Inhibitors

In fact, in terms of intuition from P systems, A is more similar to a promoter than a reactant (and there is no difference between a set of distinct atomic promoters and a corresponding one higher-weight promoter), and B corresponds to a set of atomic inhibitors (if B were a single higher-weight inhibitor, it would disable the rule when all its elements are present, not just any of them, which would not correspond to the correct definition). However, within the traditional P systems mode, we would additionally need to restrict the rule application to only once per step.

We recall that a rule with the set of atomic inhibitors $\{a, b\}$ will be disabled in configurations in which *either* a or b is present, while a rule equipped with the higher-weight inhibitor ab will only be disabled when *both* a and b are present in the configuration.

3.1 Using Powerful Rules

Hence, an arbitrary general R system $S = (V, w_0, R)$ with an alphabet V of k symbols and R consisting of the rules (A_i, B_i, C_i), $1 \leq i \leq n$, can be written as the following P system (non-cooperative, but with powerful promoters and inhibitors), having additional objects I_1 and d_i with $1 \leq i \leq n$:

$$\Pi_0 = (O, w_1, R_1) \text{ where}$$
$$O = V \cup \{d_i \mid 1 \leq i \leq n\} \cup \{I_1\},$$
$$w_1 = w_0 I_1 \prod_{1 \leq i \leq n} d_i,$$
$$R_1 = \{I_1 \rightarrow I_1 \prod_{1 \leq i \leq n} d_i\} \cup \{d_i \rightarrow \prod_{c \in C_i} c \mid_{\{\prod_{a \in A_i} a\}, \{\neg b \mid b \in B_i\}} \mid 1 \leq i \leq n\}$$
$$\cup \{d_i \rightarrow \lambda \mid_{\neg A_i}, \; d_i \rightarrow \lambda \mid_b \mid b \in B_i, \; 1 \leq i \leq n\} \cup \{a \rightarrow \lambda \mid a \in V\}.$$

This combination of features only takes one step to simulate one step of the underlying R system, $n + k + 1$ symbols and $2n + k + 1 + \sum_{1 \leq i \leq n} |B_i|$ rules. The objects from V present in the configuration of the P system Π_0 after m steps, $m \geq 0$, are exactly the same as the objects from V present in the configuration of the R system S, but probably in several copies. Note that the first rule in the description of R_1 uses a higher-weight promoter *together* with a *set* of atomic inhibitors. Also note that in a special case when the rules of the simulated R system are triples of *single* symbols, the control used becomes atomic promoters *together* with atomic inhibitors.

In the rest of the paper we show how to achieve the same goal with P systems having more restricted rules, also discussing how to produce only *one* copy of symbols present in the simulated R system. We use promoters and inhibitors, then also considering only one kind of these features. Instead of promoters and/or inhibitors we can also use matter/antimatter annihilation rules. Finally, we discuss how much the problem is simplified if some of the aspects of R systems are assumed to be part of the P systems model, too.

3.2 Triples of Symbols

We start with the simplest case – when the elements of triples describing the rules are single elements. Consider such an R system $S = (V, w_0, R)$ with the alphabet V and the rules $\{(a_i, b_i, c_i) \mid 1 \leq i \leq n\}$. We construct a P system Π_1 simulating S, the simulation taking only 2 steps:

$$\Pi_1 = (O, w_1 = w_0, R_1 = R_{1,1} \cup R_{1,2}) \text{ where}$$
$$O = V \cup \{a' \mid a \in V\} \cup \{d_i \mid 1 \leq i \leq n\},$$
$$R_{1,1} = \{a \rightarrow a' \prod_{a_i = a, 1 \leq i \leq n} d_i \mid a \in V\},$$
$$R_{1,2} = \{d_i \rightarrow c_i \mid_{\neg (b_i)'}, \; d_i \rightarrow \lambda \mid_{(b_i)'} \mid 1 \leq i \leq n\} \cup \{a' \rightarrow \lambda \mid a \in V\}.$$

The simulation task here is simple for two reasons: we took the simpler model of R systems, and using promoters besides inhibitors makes it possible to remove unneeded objects easily. We also note that the number of objects and rules can be decreased by not producing a' when a participates in the left side of any rule, and using $d_{\min\{j \mid a_j = b, 1 \leq j \leq n\}}$ instead of b' as promoter and inhibitor.

If $|V| = k$, then $|O| = n + 2k$ and $|R_1| = 2n + 2k$. Moreover, the optimization described in the previous paragraph decreases both $|O|$ and $|R_1|$ by the number of symbols appearing on the left side of some rule in R; in the rest of the paper, this number will be denoted by k'', and $k - k''$ will be denoted by k' (representing the number of symbols not appearing on the left side of some rule of S).

The multiplicities of symbols may grow. When the same symbol is produced simultaneously by multiple rules, a multiplicative effect happens. It is, however, fairly easy to reset the multiplicities of the objects in V to one, at the cost of one more step, $2k + 3$ additional symbols in O and $3k + 3$ additional rules, also using an additional object I_1 in the initial configuration:

$$\Pi_2 = (O, w_1 = w_0 I_1, R_1 = R_{1,1} \cup R_{1,2} \cup R_{1,3}) \text{ where}$$
$$O = V \cup \{a', a'', \overline{a} \mid a \in V\} \cup \{d_i \mid 1 \leq i \leq n\} \cup \{I_1, I_2, I_3\}$$
$$R_{1,1} = \{I_1 \to I_2\} \cup \{a \to a' \prod\nolimits_{a_i = a, 1 \leq i \leq n} d_i \mid a \in V\},$$
$$R_{1,2} = \{I_2 \to I_3 \prod\nolimits_{a \in V} \overline{a}\} \cup \{a' \to \lambda \mid a \in V\}$$
$$\cup \{d_i \to (c_i)''|_{\neg(b_i)'}, \ d_i \to \lambda|_{(b_i)'} \mid 1 \leq i \leq n\},$$
$$R_{1,3} = \{I_3 \to I_1\} \cup \{\overline{a} \to a|_{a''}, \ \overline{a} \to \lambda|_{\neg a''}, \ a'' \to \lambda \mid a \in V\}.$$

In the third step of the P system Π_2, exactly one copy of each symbol from V is generated which has been generated as a "reactant" in the second step.

3.3   Triples of Sets

Now the task becomes more complicated. Generating a set C_i instead of one symbol c_i is straightforward. Yet instead of verifying that a_i is present and b_i is absent, rule applicability now is defined as presence of *all* symbols from set A_i and absence of *all* symbols from set B_i. We recall that our task is to find a constant-time solution. Notice that the rule is not applicable if and only if some symbol from A_i is absent or some symbol from B_i is present.

Consider such an R system $S = (V, w_0, R)$ with the set of rules $R = \{(A_i, B_i, C_i) \mid 1 \leq i \leq n\}$. We construct a P system Π_3 simulating S where the simulation takes only 3 steps:

$$\Pi_3 = (O, w_1 = w_0 I_1, R_1 = R_{1,1} \cup R_{1,2} \cup R_{1,3}) \text{ where}$$
$$O = V \cup \{d_i \mid 1 \leq i \leq n\} \cup \{I_1, I_2, I_3\},$$
$$R_{1,1} = \{I_1 \to d_1 \cdots d_n I_2\},$$
$$R_{1,2} = \{I_2 \to I_3\} \cup \{d_i \to \lambda|_{\neg a}, \ d_i \to \lambda|_b \mid a \in A_i, \ b \in B_i, \ 1 \leq i \leq n\},$$
$$R_{1,3} = \{I_3 \to I_1\} \cup \{d_i \to \prod\nolimits_{c \in C_i} c|_{I_3} \mid 1 \leq i \leq n\} \cup \{a \to \lambda|_{I_3} \mid a \in V\}.$$

If $|V| = k$, then $|O| = n + k + 3$ and $|R_1| = n + k + \sum_{1 \leq i \leq k}(|A_i| + |B_i|) + 3$. Moreover, notice that, besides objects from V, no object ever appears in multiple copies. As for each object from V, its multiplicity represents the number of rules in S that has produced it in the last simulation step. Unlike the construction from the previous subsection, the multiplicative effect does not carry over to the next step of computation of S, since each object from V (except the instances in the starting configuration) is produced from some object d_i, produced in one copy, effectively resetting the multiplicities of the previous step. However, producing objects in V in a single copy requires additional overhead. Similarly to obtaining Π_2 from Π_1, we can obtain Π_4 from Π_3, at the price of one more step, $2k + 1$ additional symbols in O and $3k + 1$ additional rules. We skip the details.

3.4   Using only Promoters

It should not be any surprise that (in the maximally parallel mode) the effect of inhibitors can be obtained by non-cooperative rules with promoters only. Informally, to verify that some object b is absent, we first check if b is present by some rule $a \rightarrow a'|_b$, and it suffices to check in the next step whether a is unchanged. The reverse, i.e., replacing promoters with inhibitors, is even easier to see, since promoting a rule by b can be modeled by inhibiting a rule by some immediately-erased object b', the creation of which is inhibited by b. We still think it is interesting to consider the use of only promoters or only inhibitors, for two reasons. First, the reduction of promoters/inhibitors in the *general* case of P systems is too complicated, and second, we would like to explore how little overhead in terms of slowdown and descriptional complexity suffices to achieve our task.

First, we construct a P system for an R system $S = (V, w_0, R)$ with the set of rules $R = \{(a_i, b_i, c_i) \mid 1 \le i \le n\}$, i.e., with only triples of symbols (a_i, b_i, c_i) as rules in R.

$$\Pi_5 = (O, w_1 = w_0 I_1, R_1 = R_{1,1} \cup R_{1,2} \cup R_{1,3}) \text{ where}$$
$$O = V \cup \{a' \mid a \in V\} \cup \{d_i \mid 1 \le i \le n\} \cup \{I_1, I_2, I_3\},$$
$$R_{1,1} = \{I_1 \rightarrow I_2\} \cup \{a \rightarrow a' \prod_{a_i = a, 1 \le i \le n} d_i \mid a \in V\},$$
$$R_{1,2} = \{I_2 \rightarrow I_3\} \cup \{d_i \rightarrow \lambda|_{(b_i)'} \mid 1 \le i \le n\} \cup \{a' \rightarrow \lambda \mid a \in V\},$$
$$R_{1,3} = \{I_3 \rightarrow I_1\} \cup \{d_i \rightarrow c_i|_{I_3}, \mid 1 \le i \le n\}.$$

This construction is obtained from the first one with promoters and inhibitors, by implementing the group of rules with inhibitors (contrasted with existing rules with the same objects as promoters) in the next step, promoted by the "timer" I_3. We also note that, similarly to Π_1, the number of objects and rules can be decreased by not producing a' when a participates in the left side of any rule, and using $d_{\min\{j \mid a_j = b, 1 \le j \le n\}}$ instead of b' as promoter, thus for this purpose using only k' instead of k rules. Once again, this simulation has a multiplicative effect, and the multiplicities can be reset to one, at the price of one more step, $2k + 1$ additional symbols in O and $3k + 1$ additional rules. Let us call the obtained system Π_6. We omit the details, only mentioning that instead of rules $\bar{a} \rightarrow \lambda|_{\neg a''}$ as in Π_2, we can erase these symbols in the next step (i.e., in the first step of the next simulation cycle) by rules $\bar{a} \rightarrow \lambda|_{I_1}$.

Now consider the general case of simulating an R system $S = (V, w_0, R)$ with $R = \{(A_i, B_i, C_i) \mid 1 \leq i \leq n\}$. The simulating P system Π_7 using only atomic promoters is given below.

$$\Pi_7 = (O, w_1 = w_0 I_1 \prod_{a \in V} a', R_1 = R_{1,1} \cup R_{1,2} \cup R_{1,3}) \text{ where}$$
$$O = V \cup \{a' \mid a \in V\} \cup \{d_i \mid 1 \leq i \leq n\} \cup \{I_1, I_2, I_3\},$$
$$R_{1,1} = \{I_1 \rightarrow d_1 \cdots d_n I_2\} \cup \{a' \rightarrow \lambda|_a \mid a \in V\},$$
$$R_{1,2} = \{I_2 \rightarrow I_3\} \cup \{a \rightarrow \lambda|_{I_2}, \ a' \rightarrow \lambda|_{I_2} \mid a \in V\}$$
$$\cup \{d_i \rightarrow \lambda|_{a'}, \ d_i \rightarrow \lambda|_b \mid a \in A_i, \ b \in B_i, \ 1 \leq i \leq n\},$$
$$R_{1,3} = \{I_3 \rightarrow I_1 \prod_{a \in V} a'\} \cup \{d_i \rightarrow \prod_{c \in C_i} c|_{I_3} \mid 1 \leq i \leq n\}.$$

This construction is obtained from the second one with promoters and inhibitors, as follows. The role of objects a' is to survive for one step if and only if the corresponding object a is not present, to be used as a promoter instead of inhibitor a; the objects a' are recreated in the last step, for the next simulation cycle. Moreover, as now objects from V are no longer used as inhibitors, they can be removed one step earlier.

The system above needs only 3 steps to simulate one step of S, and if $|V| = k$, then $|O| = n + 2k + 3$ and $|R_1| = n + 3k + \sum_{1 \leq i \leq n}(|A_i| + |B_i|) + 3$. Of course, alternatively, the objects a' could be created from one additional initial object, at the price of an additional step and a few extra rules, but we currently focus on constructions that are efficient in time and descriptional complexity. We again comment that, although this construction has no multiplicative effect, the number of copies of a symbol in V having been produced in the end of the simulation equals the number of rules in S that have produced this symbol in the last simulation step. Producing exactly one copy needs one more step, $2k + 1$ additional symbols in O and $3k + 1$ additional rules. We call this system Π_8, but give no more details, since obtaining it from Π_7 is exactly like obtaining Π_6 from Π_5.

3.5 Using only Inhibitors

First, we construct a P system for an R system $S = (V, w_0, R)$ with the set of rules $R = \{(a_i, b_i, c_i) \mid 1 \leq i \leq n\}$, i.e., with only triples of symbols (a_i, b_i, c_i) as rules in R.

$$\Pi_9 = (O, w_1 = w_0 I_1, R_1 = R_{1,1} \cup R_{1,2} \cup R'_{1,1}) \text{ where}$$
$$O = V \cup \{a' \mid a \in V\} \cup \{d_i \mid 1 \leq i \leq n\} \cup \{I_1, I_2\},$$
$$R_{1,1} = \{I_1 \rightarrow I_2\} \cup \{a \rightarrow a' \prod_{a_i = a, 1 \leq i \leq n} d_i \mid a \in V\},$$
$$R_{1,2} = \{I_2 \rightarrow I_1\} \cup \{d_i \rightarrow c_i|_{\neg(b_i)'} \mid 1 \leq i \leq n\},$$
$$R'_{1,1} = \{d_i \rightarrow \lambda|_{\neg I_2} \mid 1 \leq i \leq n\} \cup \{a' \rightarrow \lambda|_{\neg I_2} \mid a \in V\}.$$

This construction is obtained from the one with promoters and inhibitors by implementing the group of rules with promoters (contrasted with existing rules with the same objects as inhibitors) in the next step, inhibited by the "timer" I_2. Moreover, removing objects a' is delayed for one step, to make sure that the rules inhibited by them in the second step are not applied in the third step. Notice also that the simulation of a computation step of S only takes two steps of computation in Π; the third step of computation cleaning objects d_i and a' overlaps with the first step of the simulation of the next step in S. However, this produces no interference, since the sub-alphabets $\{d_i \mid 1 \leq i \leq n\} \cup \{a' \mid a \in V\}$ and $\{I_1\} \cup V$ are disjoint. We also note that, similarly to Π_1, the number of objects and rules can be decreased by not producing a' when a participates in the left side of any rule, and using $d_{\min\{j|a_j=b,1\leq j\leq n\}}$ instead of b' as promoter.

The problem of a multiplicative effect can be solved in the usual way, resetting multiplicities to one: produce one copy of each candidate-object, and erase the objects where the multiplicity is zero. However, with inhibitors it takes longer: one additional step to erase objects $\bar{a}$ when the corresponding object a'' is absent, and one further step to rewrite $\bar{a}$ into a.

$$\Pi_{10} = (O, w_1 = w_0 I_1, R_1 = R_{1,1} \cup R_{1,2} \cup R_{1,3} \cup R_{1,4}) \text{ where}$$
$$O = V \cup \{a', a'', \bar{a} \mid a \in V\} \cup \{d_i \mid 1 \leq i \leq n\} \cup \{I_1, I_2, I_3, I_4\},$$
$$R_{1,1} = \{I_1 \rightarrow I_2\} \cup \{a \rightarrow a' \prod\nolimits_{a_i=a,1\leq i\leq n} d_i \mid a \in V\},$$
$$R_{1,2} = \{I_2 \rightarrow I_3 \prod\nolimits_{a\in V} \bar{a}\} \cup \{d_i \rightarrow (c_i)''|_{\neg(b_i)'} \mid 1 \leq i \leq n\},$$
$$R_{1,3} = \{I_3 \rightarrow I_4\} \cup \{d_i \rightarrow \lambda|_{\neg I_2} \mid 1 \leq i \leq n\}$$
$$\cup \{a \rightarrow \lambda|_{\neg I_2}, \ \bar{a} \rightarrow \lambda|_{\neg a''} \mid a \in V\},$$
$$R_{1,4} = \{I_4 \rightarrow I_1\} \cup \{\bar{a} \rightarrow a|_{\neg I_3}, \ a'' \rightarrow \lambda|_{\neg I_3} \mid a \in V\}.$$

Hence, the total additional price for resetting the multiplicities of elements of V to one using only atomic inhibitors is two more steps, $2k + 2$ additional objects, and $3k + 2$ additional rules.

Now consider the general case of simulating an R system $S = (V, w_0, R)$ with $R = \{(A_i, B_i, C_i) \mid 1 \leq i \leq n\}$. The simulating P system Π_{11} using only atomic inhibitors is given below.

$$\Pi_{11} = (O, w_1 = w_0 I_1 J \prod\nolimits_{b\in V} b', R_1 = R_{1,1} \cup R_{1,2} \cup R_{1,3}) \text{ where}$$
$$O = V \cup \{b', b'' \mid b \in V\} \cup \{d_i \mid 1 \leq i \leq n\} \cup \{I_1, I_2, I_3, J\},$$
$$R_{1,1} = \{I_1 \rightarrow d_1 \cdots d_n I_2 J, J \rightarrow \lambda\} \cup \{b' \rightarrow b''|_{\neg b} \mid b \in V\},$$
$$R_{1,2} = \{I_2 \rightarrow I_3, \ J \rightarrow \lambda\} \cup \{b' \rightarrow \lambda|_{\neg I_1} \mid b \in V\}$$
$$\cup \{d_i \rightarrow \lambda|_{\neg a}, \ d_i \rightarrow \lambda|_{\neg b''} \mid a \in A_i, \ b \in B_i, \ 1 \leq i \leq n\},$$
$$R_{1,3} = \{I_3 \rightarrow I_1 J \prod\nolimits_{b\in V} b'\} \cup \{d_i \rightarrow \prod\nolimits_{c\in C_i} c|_{\neg I_2} \mid 1 \leq i \leq n\}$$
$$\cup \{a \rightarrow \lambda|_{\neg J} \mid a \in V\} \cup \{b'' \rightarrow \lambda|_{\neg I_2} \mid b \in V\}.$$

This construction is obtained from the second one with promoters and inhibitors, as follows. The role of objects b' is to change into b'' if and only if the corresponding object b is not present, so b'' can be used as an inhibitor instead of promoter b; objects b' are recreated in the last step, for the next simulation cycle. Moreover, to make sure that the rules erasing d_i in the absence of a are applied in the second step, objects a can only be removed in the third step. This is why an additional object J is present in each of the first two steps of the simulation, inhibiting premature removal of objects a. The rule erasing J is written both in $R_{1,1}$ and $R_{1,2}$ only to highlight that it is applied both in the first and in the second step.

The system above needs only 3 steps to simulate one step of S, and if $|V| = k$, then $|O| = n + 3k + 4$ and $|R_1| = n + 4k + \sum_{1 \leq i \leq n}(|A_i| + |B_i|) + 4$. Of course, alternatively, the objects b' could be created from one additional initial object, at a price of an additional step and a few extra rules, but we currently focus on constructions that are efficient in time and descriptional complexity. Resetting to one the multiplicities of objects in V can be done exactly how Π_{10} was constructed from Π_9. Hence, the new system Π_{12}, compared to Π_{11}, will need two more steps, $2k + 2$ additional objects, and $3k + 2$ additional rules.

4 Using Antimatter

This section is devoted to a different control mechanism: matter/antimatter annihilation rules are used instead of promoters and/or inhibitors. We assume the annihilation rules to have weak priority over the remaining non-cooperative rules, which is the most common variant of the antimatter model in the area of P systems. First, we notice that erasing with a promoter, say, $d \rightarrow \lambda|_b$, in the case the promoting object b is erased without being used anywhere else, and when the number of copies of d is bounded, can be modeled by antimatter as follows:

- replace the promoting object b by the anti-object d^- of the promoted object, in sufficient copies to erase all possible copies of the promoted object d;
- add erasing rules for this anti-object d^- to remove the copies of the anti-objects which did not annihilate.

We construct the P system Π_{13} equivalent to Π_1 now using antimatter.

$$\Pi_{13} = (O, w_1 = w_0, R_1 = R_{1,1} \cup R_{1,2}) \text{ where}$$
$$O = V \cup \{d_i, d_i^- \mid 1 \leq i \leq n\},$$
$$R_{1,1} = \{a \rightarrow \prod_{b_i = a, 1 \leq i \leq n} d_i^- \prod_{a_i = a, 1 \leq i \leq n} d_i \mid a \in V\},$$
$$R_{1,2} = \{d_i d_i^- \rightarrow \lambda, \ d_i \rightarrow c_i, \ d_i^- \rightarrow \lambda \mid 1 \leq i \leq n\}.$$

In each rule of $R_{1,1}$, it is enough to produce a single copy of d_i^-, because at most one d_i may be generated by the system in the same step, since every rule uniquely determines its left side. The simulation only takes two steps, and uses $2n + k$ objects and $3n + k$ rules.

This construction again has multiplicative effect. Resetting multiplicities to one can be done by a two-step annihilation. Having got some number (possibly zero) of objects c'', we only want to know whether this number is positive. Then we produce one copy of $(c'')^-$ and rewrite it to c' if it does not immediately annihilate. One step later, we produce one copy of $(c')^-$, and rewrite it to c if it does not immediately annihilate. As a result, c will appear if and only if $(c')^-$ did not annihilate, i.e., c' did not appear one step before. But this happened if and only if $(c'')^-$ has been annihilated, i.e., there has been at least one copy of c'' two steps before. Performing this routine to the objects in V of Π_{13}, we obtain the following P system:

$$\Pi_{14} = (O, w_1 = w_0 I_1, R_1 = R_{1,1} \cup R_{1,2} \cup R_{1,3} \cup R_{1,4}) \text{ where}$$
$$O = V \cup \{a', a'', (a')^-, (a'')^- \mid a \in V\}$$
$$\cup \{d_i, d_i^- \mid 1 \le i \le n\} \cup \{I_1, I_2, I_3, I_4\},$$
$$R_{1,1} = \{I_1 \to I_2\} \cup \{a \to \prod_{b_i = a, 1 \le i \le n} d_i^- \prod_{a_i = a, 1 \le i \le n} d_i \mid a \in V\},$$
$$R_{1,2} = \{I_2 \to I_3 \prod_{a \in V}(a'')^-\} \cup \{d_i d_i^- \to \lambda, \ d_i \to (c_i)'', \ d_i^- \to \lambda \mid 1 \le i \le n\},$$
$$R_{1,3} = \{I_3 \to I_4 \prod_{a \in V}(a')^-\} \cup \{a''(a'')^- \to \lambda, \ (a'')^- \to a' \mid a \in V\},$$
$$R_{1,4} = \{I_4 \to I_1\} \cup \{a'(a')^- \to \lambda, \ (a')^- \to a \mid a \in V\}.$$

As one can see, resetting multiplicities with antimatter has the price of two more steps, $4k + 4$ additional objects, and $4k + 4$ additional rules.

Now consider the general case of simulating an R system $S = (V, w_0, R)$ with $R = \{(A_i, B_i, C_i) \mid 1 \le i \le n\}$. The simulating P system is given below.

$$\Pi_{15} = (O, w_1 = w_0 I_1, R_1 = R_{1,1} \cup R_{1,2} \cup R_{1,3}) \text{ where}$$
$$O = V \cup \{a', (a')^-, a'' \mid a \in V\} \cup \{d_i, d_i^- \mid 1 \le i \le n\} \cup \{I_1, I_2, I_3\},$$
$$R_{1,1} = \{I_1 \to I_2 d_1 \cdots d_n \prod_{a \in V} a'\} \cup \{a \to (a')^- a'' \mid a \in V\},$$
$$R_{1,2} = \{I_2 \to I_3\} \cup \{a'(a')^- \to \lambda, \ (a')^- \to \lambda \mid a \in V\}$$
$$\cup \{a' \to \prod_{a \in A_i} d_i^- \mid a \in A_i \text{ for some } i, \ 1 \le i \le n\}$$
$$\cup \{b'' \to \prod_{b \in B_i} d_i^- \mid b \in B_i \text{ for some } i, \ 1 \le i \le n\},$$
$$R_{1,3} = \{I_3 \to I_1\} \cup \{d_i d_i^- \to \lambda, \ d_i \to \prod_{c \in C_i} c, \ d_i^- \to \lambda \mid 1 \le i \le n\}.$$

Symbols from C_i are produced from d_i if and only if d_i has not been annihilated, i.e., neither a' nor b'' should produce d_i^- for any $a \in A_i$ and $b \in B_i$. Since a' is annihilated if and only if a is present, and b'' is not produced if and only if b is absent, the simulation of an application of rule i of the R system happens if and only if all symbols from the first set A_i are present and all symbols from the second set B_i are absent. The simulation takes three steps, using an alphabet of $2n + 4k + 3$ symbols and a set of $3n + 3k + k'' + \bar{k} + 3$ rules, where now $\bar{k}$ now denotes the number of symbols appearing in some inhibitor set of any rule.

This construction produces each symbol in a multiplicity equal to the number of rules of S that have produced it, not carrying the multiplicative effect to the simulation of the next evolution step in the R system. If needed, resetting multiplicities can also be done, which costs two more steps, $4k + 2$ additional objects, and $4k + 2$ additional rules. We call this system Π_{16}, but we do not provide more details since it can be obtained from Π_{15} exactly as Π_{14} is obtained from Π_{13}.

5   Non-standard P Systems

Some difficulty in the simulation of R systems by P systems arises from the differences in their standard derivation modes. We now would like to discuss how varying this may affect the problem.

First, if we consider P systems *with sets* instead of multisets, where the production of a symbol multiple times still yields only one single copy of this symbol, then *all* constructions in this paper still hold literally, i.e., no changes in the description of these P systems are needed. However, some things may become even simpler, as, for example, in this case resetting multiplicities to one is done by the model itself, and thus does not require additional time, symbol or rule complexity.

We note that, in a non-distributed case, P systems with sets of objects are no longer universal, since the number of possible configurations is bounded by two to the power of the cardinality of the alphabet. However, universality is not needed to simulate R systems by P systems (for example, non-universality has also been shown for the case of deterministic P systems with promoters and/or inhibitors).

Second, if we consider P systems which deterministically apply *all* individually applicable rules, even with overlapping left sides (i.e., competing for resources), then of course the existing solutions still literally hold, but in some cases there are much easier ways: we would have no need to explicitly produce multiple objects from one. For instance, the constructions given in this paper usually involve the production of rule labels d_i, either from the corresponding reactant a_i, or from some "timer" object I_j, and then we have different rules processing these label objects. In this "auto-replication" mode, these various processing rules could be applied directly to the corresponding original object a_i or I_j, the replication being done by the model itself. This would definitely simplify the simulation. Let us refer to this aspect as "*auto-replication*".

For example, the P system Π_1 then can be simplified to the following P system Π_1':

$$\Pi_1' = (O = V, w_1 = w_0, R_1 = \{a_i \to c_i|_{\neg b_i} \mid 1 \leq i \leq n\} \cup \{a \to \lambda \mid a \in V\}),$$

i.e., we need just one step, no additional objects and only k additional rules. The problem with resetting the multiplicities also becomes much simpler; instead of the P system Π_2 we then get the following P system Π_2':

$$\Pi_2' = (O, w_1 = w_0 I_1, R_1) \text{ where}$$
$$O = V \cup \{a' \mid a \in V\} \cup \{I_1, I_2\},$$
$$R_1 = \{I_1 \to I_2\} \cup \{a_i \to (c_i)'|_{\neg b_i} \mid 1 \le i \le n\} \cup \{a \to \lambda \mid a \in V\}$$
$$\cup \{I_2 \to I_1\} \cup \{I_2 \to c|_{c'}\} \cup \{c' \to \lambda \mid c \in V\},$$

Π_2' requires only one more step, $k + 2$ additional symbols, and $2k + 2$ additional rules (compared to the increase of complexity from Π_1 to Π_2 by one more step as well as $2k + 3$ additional symbols and additional $3k + 3$ rules).

Third, if we consider P systems where idle objects (i.e., those not consumed by applied rules) do not contribute to the next configuration, we call this aspect *"no persistence"*. Then many erasing rules (in particular, all erasing promoted or inhibited by some "timer" I_j) would no longer be needed, while occasionally some renaming rules should be added when an object has been designed to be used later than in the next step after its production. For instance, in case of no-persistence, all $n + k'$ erasing rules of Π_1 may be removed, leaving just $n + k$ rules. Similarly, all erasing rules of Π_2 may be removed; hence, the subtask of resetting the multiplicities to one in this case only needs $k + 3$ instead of $3k + 3$ additional rules.

However, testing for presence of some object b by "failing to apply a rule with inhibitor b and finding the reactant unchanged in the next step" would not work. The working solution is to use b as an inhibitor in a rule producing some object b', and to use b' as an inhibitor in the next step. Testing for absence by "failing to apply a rule with a promoter and finding the reactant unchanged in the next step" would no longer be possible, so such a model with promoters without persistence of idle objects seems to be considerably weaker.

We would also like to note that, in case of P systems with sets and auto-replication, the aspect of no-persistence can be simulated as follows: add rules $a \to \lambda$ for each $a \in V$; they will make sure that such objects are not carried over to the next step, in the same time not adding anything to the result (as for productive objects, erasing them is just another option, which in the auto-replication case neither grows nor shrinks the set of objects obtained from them). This simulation takes one step, k objects and $n + k$ rules.

Finally, if we consider P systems with all these features, i.e., with sets, auto-replication, and without object persistence, then a single object rule (a, b, c) of an R system becomes *identical* to the rule $a \to c|_{\neg b}$ in the corresponding P system, while a set rule (A, B, C) of an R system can be simulated by a rule $a \to \prod_{c \in C} c|_{\{\prod_{a \in A} a\}, \{\neg b \mid b \in B\}}$, for any $a \in A$, so the simulation is rather trivial, requiring only one step, k objects and n rules of type $(ncoo, inh_{1,1})$ and $(ncoo, pro_{1,*} + inh_{*,1})$, respectively.

6   Conclusions

We recall that although deterministic P systems with promoters and/or inhibitors are not universal and have subregular characterizations, their power is sufficient to simulate R systems.

All constructions presented in this paper (except those in the previous section) simulate R systems in their standard derivation mode by P systems in *their* standard derivation mode, with the slowdown by a constant factor, where the descriptional complexity of the simulating P system is linear with respect to the descriptional complexity of the simulated R system. The proportionality constants vary depending on whether R systems are defined as triples of symbols or as triples of sets of symbols, and on whether promoters, inhibitors or both are used in the simulating P system. All constructions are deterministic: while the multiset of rules to be applied to a given configuration may not be unique, the next configuration is unique. Indeed, in all these constructions, if two rules have the same left side, then either their applicability is mutually exclusive (one is being promoted and the other one is being inhibited by the same symbol), or also the right side is the same (and thus, if there are multiple choices which object would promote or inhibit the rule, such a choice would not influence the result).

Table 1. Comparative table of simulating R systems by P systems.

P	R	Mult	Features	Steps	$|O|$	$|R_1|$
Π_0	s	L	$(ncoo, pro_{1,1} + inh_{1,1})$	1	$n + k + 1$	$3n + k + 1$
Π_0	g	L	$(ncoo, pro_{1,*} + inh_{*,1})$	1	$n + k + 1$	$2n + k + m' + 1$
Π_1	s	M	$(ncoo, pro_{1,1}, inh_{1,1})$	2	$n + k + k'$	$2n + k + k'$
Π_2	s	1	$(ncoo, pro_{1,1}, inh_{1,1})$	3	$n + 3k + k' + 3$	$2n + 4k + k' + 3$
Π_3	g	L	$(ncoo, pro_{1,1}, inh_{1,1})$	3	$n + k + 3$	$n + k + m + 3$
Π_4	g	1	$(ncoo, pro_{1,1}, inh_{1,1})$	4	$n + 3k + 4$	$n + 4k + m + 4$
Π_5	s	M	$(ncoo, pro_{1,1})$	3	$n + k + k' + 3$	$2n + k + k' + 3$
Π_6	s	1	$(ncoo, pro_{1,1})$	4	$n + 3k + k' + 4$	$2n + 4k + k' + 4$
Π_7	g	L	$(ncoo, pro_{1,1})$	3	$n + 2k + 3$	$n + 3k + m + 3$
Π_8	g	1	$(ncoo, pro_{1,1})$	4	$n + 4k + 4$	$n + 6k + m + 4$
Π_9	s	M	$(ncoo, inh_{1,1})$	2	$n + k + k' + 2$	$2n + k + k' + 2$
Π_{10}	s	1	$(ncoo, inh_{1,1})$	4	$n + 3k + k' + 4$	$2n + 4k + k' + 4$
Π_{11}	g	L	$(ncoo, inh_{1,1})$	3	$n + 3k + 4$	$n + 4k + m + 4$
Π_{12}	g	1	$(ncoo, inh_{1,1})$	5	$n + 5k + 6$	$n + 7k + m + 6$
Π_{13}	s	M	$(ncoo, antim/pri)$	2	$2n + k$	$3n + k$
Π_{14}	s	1	$(ncoo, antim/pri)$	4	$2n + 5k + 4$	$3n + 5k + 4$
Π_{15}	g	L	$(ncoo, antim/pri)$	3	$2n + 4k + 3$	$3n + 3k + k'' + \bar{k} + 3$
Π_{16}	g	1	$(ncoo, antim/pri)$	5	$2n + 8k + 5$	$3n + 7k + k'' + \bar{k} + 5$

Seventeen constructions of simple P systems have been elaborated, see Table 1, P systems using specific control ingredients for simulating *simple* (rules with triples of symbols) and *general* (rules with triples of sets of symbols) R systems:

(0) P_0, using single higher-weighted promoters together with multiple atomic inhibitors for simulating a simple or a general R system;

(1) P_1, using promoters and inhibitors,
simulating a simple R system;

(2) P_2 using promoters and inhibitors and resetting multiplicities to one, simulating a simple R system;

(3) P_3, using promoters and inhibitors,
simulating a general R system;

(4) P_4, using promoters and inhibitors and resetting multiplicities to one, simulating a general R system;

(5) P_5, using promoters,
simulating a simple R system;

(6) P_6, using promoters and resetting multiplicities to one,
simulating a simple R system;

(7) P_7, using promoters,
simulating a general R system;

(8) P_8, using promoters and resetting multiplicities to one,
simulating a general R system;

(9) P_9, using inhibitors,
simulating a simple R system;

(10) P_{10}, using inhibitors and resetting multiplicities to one,
simulating a simple R system;

(11) P_{11}, using inhibitors,
simulating a general R system;

(12) P_{12}, using inhibitors and resetting multiplicities to one,
simulating a general R system;

(13) P_{13}, using antimatter,
simulating a simple R system;

(14) P_{14}, using antimatter and resetting multiplicities to one,
simulating a simple R system;

(15) P_{15}, using antimatter,
simulating a general R system;

(16) P_{16}, using antimatter and resetting multiplicities to one,
simulating a general R system.

Table 1 shows the alphabet size, the number of rules, and the number of steps of the simulating P system to simulate one step of the underlying R system:

- n is the number of rules in S;
- k is the number of symbols in S;
- k' is the number of symbols that do not appear in the left side of any rule of the simulated system,
- $k'' := k - k'$;
- $\bar{k}$ is the number of symbols that appear in the inhibitor set of any rule of the simulated system;
- $m := \sum_{1 \leq i \leq k}(|A_i| + |B_i|)$;
- $m' := \sum_{1 \leq i \leq k} |B_i|$.

Column R describes the type of the simulated system, where s stands for simple (rules with triples of symbols) and g stands for general (rules with triples of sets).

Column *mult* describes the multiplicities of symbols in the simulating P system, where M stands for multiplicative effect, L stands for last multiplicity, and 1 stands for multiplicities at most 1, i.e., 0 or 1.

Column *features* describes the kinds of rules used in the P system.

We note that in Π_6, Π_8 and Π_9 intermediate objects are removed one step later, i.e., in parallel with the first step of the simulation of the evolution step of the simulated R system, but not interfering with it.

Finally, in the previous section we discussed how (qualitatively and quantitatively) adopting some aspects of R systems (such as sets instead of multisets, auto-replication or no-persistence of objects) into the working model of P systems simplifies the simulation of R systems by such P systems.

References

1. Alhazov, A.: P systems without multiplicities of symbol-objects. Inf. Process. Lett. **100**(3), 124–129 (2006). http://dx.doi.org/10.1016/j.ipl.2005.01.017
2. Alhazov, A., Aman, B., Freund, R.: P systems with anti-matter. In: Gheorghe, M., Rozenberg, G., Salomaa, A., Sosík, P., Zandron, C. (eds.) CMC 2014. LNCS, vol. 8961, pp. 66–85. Springer, Heidelberg (2014). doi:10.1007/978-3-319-14370-5_5
3. Alhazov, A., Cojocaru, S., Colesnicov, A., Malahov, L., Petic, M.: A P system for annotation of romanian affixes. In: Alhazov, A., Cojocaru, S., Gheorghe, M., Rogozhin, Y., Rozenberg, G., Salomaa, A. (eds.) CMC 2013. LNCS, vol. 8340, pp. 80–87. Springer, Heidelberg (2014). doi:10.1007/978-3-642-54239-8_7
4. Alhazov, A., Freund, R.: Asynchronous and maximally parallel deterministic controlled non-cooperative P systems characterize *NFIN* and *coNFIN*. In: Csuhaj-Varjú, E., Gheorghe, M., Rozenberg, G., Salomaa, A., Vaszil, G. (eds.) CMC 2012. LNCS, vol. 7762, pp. 101–111. Springer, Heidelberg (2013). doi:10.1007/978-3-642-36751-9_8
5. Brijder, R., Ehrenfeucht, A., Main, M.G., Rozenberg, G.: A tour of reaction systems. Int. J. Found. Comput. Sci. **22**(7), 1499–1517 (2011)
6. Ehrenfeucht, A., Rozenberg, G.: Reaction systems. Fundamenta Informaticae **75**(1), 263–280 (2007)
7. Margenstern, M., Rogozhin, Y., Verlan, S.: Time-varying distributed H systems with parallel computations: the problem is solved. In: Chen, J., Reif, J. (eds.) DNA 2003. LNCS, vol. 2943, pp. 48–54. Springer, Heidelberg (2004). doi:10.1007/978-3-540-24628-2_6
8. Păun, G.: Computing with membranes. J. Comput. Syst. Sci. **61**, 108–143 (1998)
9. Păun, G.: DNA computing based on splicing: universality results. Theor. Comput. Sci. **231**(2), 275–296 (2000). https://dx.doi.org/10.1016/S0304-3975(99)00104-8
10. Păun, G., Pérez-Jiménez, M.J.: Towards bridging two cell-inspired models: P systems and R systems. Theor. Comput. Sci. **429**, 258–264 (2012). http://dx.doi.org/10.1016/j.tcs.2011.12.046
11. Păun, G., Rozenberg, G., Salomaa, A.: Computing by splicing. Theor. Comput. Sci. **168**(2), 321–336 (1996). https://dx.doi.org/10.1016/S0304-3975(96)00082-5

12. Păun, G., Rozenberg, G., Salomaa, A.: DNA Computing - New Computing Paradigms. Texts in Theoretical Computer Science. An EATCS Series. Springer, Heidelberg (1998). http://dx.doi.org/10.1007/978-3-662-03563-4
13. Păun, G., Rozenberg, G., Salomaa, A.: The Oxford Handbook of Membrane Computing. Oxford University Press Inc., New York (2010)
14. Sburlan, D.: Further results on P systems with promoters/inhibitors. Int. J. Found. Comput. Sci. **17**(1), 205–221 (2006)
15. The P Systems Website. http://ppage.psystems.eu, http://ppage.psystems.eu

Purely Catalytic P Systems over Integers and Their Generative Power

Artiom Alhazov[1], Omar Belingheri[2], Rudolf Freund[3]([✉]), Sergiu Ivanov[4], Antonio E. Porreca[2], and Claudio Zandron[2]

[1] Academy of Sciences of Moldova, Institute of Mathematics and Computer Science, Strada Academiei 5, 2028 Chişinău, Moldova
artiom@math.md

[2] Dipartimento di Informatica, Sistemistica e Comunicazione, Università Degli Studi di Milano-Bicocca, Viale Sarca 336/14, 20126 Milano, Italy
o.belingheri@campus.unimib.it, {porreca,zandron}@disco.unimib.it

[3] Faculty of Informatics, TU Wien, Favoritenstraße 9–11, 1040 Vienna, Austria
rudi@emcc.at

[4] Université Paris Est, Champs-sur-Marne, France
sergiu.ivanov@u-pec.fr

Abstract. We further investigate the computing power of the recently introduced P systems with $\mathbb{Z}$-multisets (also known as hybrid sets) as generative devices. These systems apply catalytic rules in the maximally parallel way, even consuming absent non-catalysts, thus effectively generating vectors of arbitrary (not just non-negative) integers. The rules may only be made inapplicable by dissolution rules. However, this releases the catalysts into the immediately outer region, where new rules might become applicable to them. We discuss the generative power of this model. Finally, we consider the variant with mobile catalysts.

1 Introduction

Membrane systems (cell-like, with symbol objects) have traditionally been viewed as collections of hierarchically arranged multiset processors, e.g., see [12]. In the list of open problems disseminated in 2015, see [11], Gheorghe Păun suggested to go beyond the traditional setting where symbol multiplicities in multisets are restricted to non-negative integers. In [6] generalized multisets are defined as taking multiplicities from arbitrary finitely generated, totally ordered commutative groups.

In [3], a different approach is taken: only catalytic rules are allowed, and the applicability of a rule only depends on the presence of the corresponding catalyst in the given region. Consuming an absent non-catalyst makes its multiplicity negative. While in [3] it was already established that such a model is not universal, we found it interesting to investigate its generative power more precisely.

Since the number of catalysts remains finite and does not change throughout the computation, this induces a finite set of "rule teams " which can be applied

© Springer International Publishing AG 2017
A. Leporati et al. (Eds.): CMC 2016, LNCS 10105, pp. 67–82, 2017.
DOI: 10.1007/978-3-319-54072-6_5

in parallel in one step. The virtual absence of applicability conditions and the finiteness of the "teams" hints at the possibility of seeing them as integer vectors; in this case the P system itself can be seen as evolving by sequentially adding such vectors (possibly having negative components) to the contents of its membranes. In [2], this general model is compared with vector addition systems (see [5,9] for standard definitions; adapted to allow negative vector components in [8]) and blind register machines, e.g., see [7].

Here we return to the particular model from [3], discussing the lower bound of its generative power and giving some results on the variants with target indications and with multiple membrane dissolutions.

2   Preliminaries

The reader is assumed to be familiar with the basic notions of formal languages and membrane computing; see [13] for a comprehensive introduction and the webpage [14] of P systems.

We only recall a few basic notations as they are used in this paper: $\mathbb{N}$ denotes the set of non-negative integers; $\mathbb{Z}$ denotes the set of integers. Multisets over the set of objects O can be seen as functions from O to $\mathbb{N}$; thus, the set of all multisets over O is $\mathbb{N}^O$ (the set of all functions from O to $\mathbb{N}$). In membrane computing, the set of all multisets over O is commonly denoted by $O^\circ = \mathbb{N}^O$, while the multisets themselves are represented by strings in O^*, keeping in mind that the order of symbols is not relevant.

2.1   Extending Multisets

To represent also negative multiplicities, multisets over a set of objects O have to be extended to $\mathbb{Z}$. A $\mathbb{Z}$-multiset, allowing integer multiplicities (called a *hybrid set* in [4]) then is from $\mathbb{Z}^O$; it can be represented by a string in $(O \cup O^-)^*$, where $O^- = \{a^- \mid a \in O\}$ is a set of symbols that represents objects in multiplicity "negative one". Note that, as opposed to P systems with matter/antimatter [1], symbol a^- here is not an actual object, but simply a convenient way to represent a deficit of a, and the actual multiplicity of a represented by a string w is $|w|_a - |w|_{a^-}$. We also do not distinguish between notations a^{-k} and $(a^-)^k$. The superscript $^-$ can be used as a morphism, producing a multiset with opposite multiplicities, e.g., $(a^k)^-$ represents the same $\mathbb{Z}$-multiset as a^{-k}. As the strings here are only used to represent $\mathbb{Z}$-multisets, we may write an equality sign between the strings representing the same $\mathbb{Z}$-multiset. For conciseness, let us use the notation $O^\bullet = (O \cup O^-)^*$. Finally, since it will be always clear from the context, we may call an element of $O^\bullet$ "multiset", omitting the word "representing". Assuming an order is fixed on O, for $u \in O^\bullet$, vector $(|u|_a - |u|_{a^-})_{a \in O}$ is denoted by $\psi_O(u)$; the subscript O may be omitted when it is clear from the context. This vector is called the *Parikh image* of u.

2.2 Linear Sets

The *linear* set generated by a set of vectors $A = \{\mathbf{a}_i \mid 1 \leq i \leq d\} \subset_{fin} \mathbb{Z}^n$ (here $A \subset_{fin} B$ indicates that A is a finite subset of B) and an offset $\mathbf{a}_0 \in \mathbb{Z}^n$ is defined as follows:

$$\langle A, \mathbf{a}_0 \rangle_{\mathbb{N}} = \left\{ \mathbf{a}_0 + \sum_{i=1}^{d} k_i \mathbf{a}_i \mid k_i \in \mathbb{N}, \ 1 \leq i \leq d \right\}.$$

If the offset $\mathbf{a}_0$ is the zero vector, we will call the corresponding linear set *homogeneous*; we also will use the short notation $\langle A \rangle_{\mathbb{N}} = \langle A, \mathbf{0} \rangle_{\mathbb{N}}$.

We use the notation $\mathbb{Z}^n LIN_{\mathbb{N}} = \{ \langle A, \mathbf{a}_0 \rangle_{\mathbb{N}} \mid A \subset_{fin} \mathbb{Z}^n, \ \mathbf{a}_0 \in \mathbb{Z} \}$, to refer to the class of all linear sets. Semilinear sets are defined as finite unions of linear sets. We use the notations $\mathbb{Z}^n SLIN_{\mathbb{N}}$ to refer to the classes of semilinear sets of n-dimensional vectors. In case no restriction is imposed on the dimension, n is replaced by $*$. We may omit n if $n = 1$. A finite union of linear sets which only differ in the starting vectors is called *uniform* semilinear:

$$\mathbb{Z}^n SLIN_{\mathbb{N}}^U = \left\{ \textstyle\bigcup_{\mathbf{b} \in B} \langle A, \mathbf{b} \rangle_{\mathbb{N}} \mid A \subset_{fin} \mathbb{Z}^n, \ B \subset_{fin} \mathbb{Z}^n \right\}$$

Let us denote such a set by $\langle A, B \rangle_{\mathbb{N}}$.

Note that a uniform semilinear set $\langle A, B \rangle_{\mathbb{N}}$ can be seen as a pairwise sum of the finite set B and the homogeneous linear set $\langle A \rangle_{\mathbb{N}}$:

$$\langle A, B \rangle_{\mathbb{N}} = \{ \mathbf{a} + \mathbf{b} \mid \mathbf{a} \in \langle A \rangle_{\mathbb{N}}, \mathbf{b} \in B \}.$$

This observation immediately yields the conclusion that the sum of two uniform semilinear sets $\langle A_1, B_1 \rangle_{\mathbb{N}}$ and $\langle A_2, B_2 \rangle_{\mathbb{N}}$ is uniform semilinear as well and can be computed in the following way:

$$\langle A_1, B_1 \rangle_{\mathbb{N}} + \langle A_2, B_2 \rangle_{\mathbb{N}} = \{ \mathbf{a} + \mathbf{b} \mid \mathbf{a} \in \langle A_1 \cup A_2 \rangle_{\mathbb{N}}, \mathbf{b} \in B_1 + B_2 \}.$$

3 Purely Catalytic P Systems over Integers

In purely catalytic P systems over integers the set of objects is a disjoint union of catalysts C and the regular objects O. The regular objects are allowed to have any integer multiplicity, while the catalysts are only allowed to appear in a non-negative number of copies.

Formally, a *(generating) purely catalytic P system over integers* Π is defined as a construct

$$\Pi = (O, C, \mu, w_1, \cdots, w_n, R_1, \cdots, R_n, i_0)$$

where

- O is a finite set of objects,
- $C \subset O$ is the set of catalysts,
- μ is a membrane structure of n hierarchically arranged membranes, labeled by 1 to n,

- R_i, $1 \leq i \leq n$, is the set of rules associated with membrane region i, and
- i_0 is the output membrane.

The rules can be of the two following types:

- *catalytic rules*: $cu \rightarrow cv$, where $c \in C$ and $u, v \in O^*$;
- *catalytic rules with dissolution*: $cu \rightarrow cv\delta$, where $c \in C$, $u, v \in O^*$, and $\delta \notin C \cup O$ is the symbol indicating membrane dissolution.

The rules applied in parallel cannot involve more catalysts than available in the system; the multiplicities of regular objects, on the other hand, do not influence the applicability of rules. An application of a rule $cu \rightarrow cv$ in a region containing cw, $c \in C$, $u, v \in O^*$, $w \in O^\bullet$, produces $cw(cu)^- cv = cwv(u^-)$, or, in terms of vectors, ignoring the catalyst, the vector $\psi(w) + \psi(v) - \psi(u)$ represents the contents of that region after the rule has been applied. An application of a rule $cu \rightarrow cv\delta$ produces the same effect, and then dissolves the enclosing membrane, moving the contents of the dissolved membrane into the parent membrane.

Purely catalytic P systems over integers evolve under the maximally parallel semantics, so each catalyst induces the application of exactly one rule (non-deterministically chosen), unless the given region has no rules associated with this catalyst. A computation is called successful if no rule is applicable any more, i.e., if the system *halts*.

By $\mathbb{Z}^d O_{\mathbb{Z}} P_m(pcat_k, \delta)$ we denote the family of sets of d-dimensional vectors of integers generated by purely catalytic P systems over integers with dissolution, at most m membranes and at most k catalysts. If any of parameters d, m, k is unbounded, it is replaced by $*$ in this notation.

We also use notations for extended features (listed in parentheses in the notation of the sets of $\mathbb{Z}$-vectors generated by the corresponding families of P systems). Target indications, denoted by tar, allow the non-catalysts to be sent to a different membrane. In the right side of the rules, sending object a is written by (a, tar), where $tar \in \{out\} \cup \{in_j \mid 1 \leq j \leq m\}$; j here is the label of an immediately inner membrane. In this paper, we write $tar_{\mathbb{Z}}$ in the notation of a set of $\mathbb{Z}$-vectors generated by a family of P systems; this generalization reflects the possibility to assign targets even to negative multiplicities of objects.

Another feature is *mobile catalysts*, e.g., see [10], i.e., targets may also be associated to the catalysts, and thus the catalysts move across the membrane structure; we denote this feature by $mpcat_k$ since the systems we consider are purely catalytic. We use the plus sign between the features of catalytic mobility and dissolution when it is allowed for the *same* rule to move a catalyst and to dissolve the membrane currently containing it.

4   Results

Before elaborating our results and giving characterizations of various families of linear sets by purely catalytic P systems, we discuss some general observations which allow us to simplify these systems.

4.1 Observations and Simplifications

First, we would like to explicitly allow rules of the form $c \to cx$, $(c \in C, x \in O^{\bullet})$, i.e., the multiset of regular objects in the left side being empty. This does not change the model, since any $\mathbb{Z}$-multiset x can be written as $u(v^{-})$, $u, v \in O^{*}$, and, fixing some $a \in O$, $c \to cx$ is equivalent to $cau \to av$. Moreover, any rule $cu \to cv$ is equivalent to $c \to cu(v^{-})$, so it suffices to only consider rules of types $c \to cx$ and $c \to cx\delta$ $(c \in C, x \in O^{\bullet})$.

Second, we claim that it is enough to start with a single catalyst in every region. To show that, we will consider that membrane i of the P system contains the catalysts $c_{i,k}$, $1 \le k \le n_i$, in the *initial* configuration. Now we will define the sets $X_{i,k,j}$ of right-hand sides of catalytic rules of membrane j involving the catalysts initially located in membrane i:

$$X_{i,k,j} = \{x \in O^{\bullet} \cup O^{\bullet}\delta \mid (c_{i,k} \to c_{i,k}x) \in R_j\},$$

where R_j is the set of rules associated with membrane j. To simplify subsequent explanations, we will adopt the following convention: If, for a given i and j, there exists such a k that $X_{i,k,j} \neq \emptyset$, then we will replace all empty $X_{i,k',j}$ by $\{\lambda\}$.

We now remark that the catalysts $c_{i,k}$ initially present in membrane i will always stay together, because dissolution cannot separate them. We will replace each such group ("band") by a new catalyst having the combined effect of the group. More formally, we will replace all the catalysts $c_{i,k}$ initially present in membrane i by one new catalyst c_i, and the rules associated with membrane j by the following set:

$$R'_j = \{c_i \to c_i x_1 \cdots x_{n_i} \mid x_k \in X_{i,k,j}, 1 \le k \le n_i, 1 \le i \le m\}, \ 1 \le j \le m,$$

where m is the number of membranes of the membrane system. Note that R'_j contains rules for every catalyst c_i representing the original "band" from membrane i which may have an effect in region j.

The argument in the previous paragraph shows that we can replace multiple catalysts in a region by a single one. On the other hand, having no catalyst in some region is equivalent to having one catalyst with no associated rules. Therefore, without restricting the generality, in the following we assume that in the initial configuration of an arbitrary purely catalytic P system over integers, each membrane region i, $1 \le i \le m$, contains precisely one catalyst, and we can call it c_i.

Third, notice that the symbols may only travel from the inner membranes to the outer ones, so if the output region i_0 is not the skin, only the contents of the membrane substructure inside i_0 (including i_0) is relevant for the result. The only way in which a membrane i not contained within i_0 could influence the evolution of the system is by preventing it from halting. If the computations inside the substructure of membrane i halt after i_0, but in a finite number of steps, then this only influences the moment when we are allowed to retrieve the result, but not the result itself. If the computations inside the substructure of membrane i never halt, then the result of the system is always empty. If both halting in a finite number of steps or never halting are an option, then it is sufficient to only consider the halting computations, and, as we have just shown, in this case what happened inside the substructure of membrane i does not have any influence on the result of the whole system.

According to this reasoning, the membranes not contained within the output membrane i_0 may influence the power of the system only trivially (by reducing its result to the empty set). We will therefore assume that the output region is always the skin.

Fourth, every elementary membrane having no rules associated to the catalysts available there may be removed from the system without affecting the result (unless it is the output membrane, in which case a singleton is generated, which is a degenerate case), so in the following we assume that every elementary membrane has some applicable rules. Clearly, the P system will not reach the halting until all these membranes are dissolved.

Consider this reasoning starting from the elementary membranes, by induction. Take any non-elementary membrane i which becomes elementary during a computation. Assume i is not dissolved (i.e., it has no rules associated to any of the catalysts that were placed within the membrane substructure inside i, including i), but it is not the output membrane. Then all the computations in the membrane substructure inside i, including i, do not contribute to the result, and can be removed from the system without affecting the result.

As a summary of the fourth observation, without restricting the generality (except, possibly the degenerate cases generating the empty set or some singleton), we may assume that any purely catalytic P system over integers has applicable rules associated to all elementary membranes, and all membranes except the skin must be dissolved at some moment during the computation.

Finally, for every region except the skin, a catalyst c_i without associated rules is equivalent to a catalyst with a rule $c_i \rightarrow c_i$. Hence, without restricting the generality, we may assume that each catalyst is *never* idle before it reaches the skin membrane. Clearly, (excluding the degenerate case generating the empty set), the skin should have no rules associated to any catalyst of the system.

We would like to note that even without pruning the membrane structure by removing membrane substructures not contributing to the result, the membrane structure obtained at halting (if at all reachable) is unique.

We recall that in [2], the following generalized approach is taken – there is a finite number of reachable membrane structures. These could be used as states of a sequential P system, which may be obtained, separately for each membrane structure, by combining the behavior of all catalysts in all regions of the P system. Indeed, having fixed a reachable membrane structure, we know which membranes have been dissolved, and thus the resulting location of each catalyst. Then, for each catalyst, associated rules in its current location are considered and combined, similarly to the second observation above, but globally. Having obtained a sequential system, the catalyst is no longer needed. Then, in [2] it was shown that such a generalization is nothing else but a sequential blind vector addition system with states, and it was claimed that it characterizes precisely the family of all semilinear vectors of integers.

Indeed, in this way any purely catalytic P system over integers can be substituted by a sequential blind vector addition system with states, so the upper bound of the family of all semilinear sets of vectors of integers, or, equivalently, the family of all integer vector sets, generated by blind register machines, holds. However, the reverse is not necessarily true, i.e., it does not follow that for any sequential blind vector addition system with states there would exist an equivalent purely catalytic P system over integers.

In the present paper we investigate the particularities of how dissolution affects the computation, and the lower bounds.

4.2 Generative Power

Since, by definition, the output region cannot be dissolved and any other applicable rule can never be stopped, single-membrane purely catalytic P systems over integers are degenerate (we will not mention these degenerate cases any more when considering multiple membranes):

Theorem 1. $\mathbb{Z}^d O_\mathbb{Z} P_1(pcat_*, \delta) = \{\emptyset\} \cup \{\{\mathbf{a}\} \mid \mathbf{a} \in \mathbb{Z}^d\}$.

With two membranes, a characterization is still straightforward:

Theorem 2. $\mathbb{Z}^d O_\mathbb{Z} P_2(pcat_*, \delta) = \mathbb{Z}^d SLIN_\mathbb{N}^U$.

Proof. Let A be the finite set of vectors corresponding to the non-dissolving rules in the elementary membranes, and let B be the finite set of sums of two vectors: the one corresponding to the initial configuration and vectors corresponding to the dissolving rules in the elementary membrane; the skin should have no rules. If the catalyst in the elementary membrane is c_2, then the correspondence mentioned above is $c_2 \rightarrow c_2 x \leftrightarrow \psi(x)$, and similarly with dissolution. An arbitrary computation of a P system consists of an arbitrary number of applications of non-dissolving rules and one application of a dissolving rule. Hence, the resulting vector sums up from the "initial" vector, one arbitrary "dissolving" vector, and an arbitrary linear combination of "non-dissolving" vectors.   □

It is worth noting that, by a similar reasoning, for a P system with multiple membranes, if the chronological order of dissolving the membranes is fixed, the result is still $\mathbb{Z}^d SLIN_\mathbb{N}^U$. Indeed, each combination of rules (one for each catalyst) yields one vector, so all such possible combinations of non-dissolving rules yield a finite set of vectors, and multiple non-dissolving steps yield a linear set generated by these vectors. Thus, over the whole computation the result sums up from the initial configuration, a finite number of dissolution vectors, and a finite number of linear sets corresponding to the membrane structures reached during that computation. Since the total number of chronological orders of dissolving membranes is bounded, we infer the following known result:

Theorem 3. $\mathbb{Z}^d O_\mathbb{Z} P_*(pcat_*, \delta) \subseteq \mathbb{Z}^d SLIN_\mathbb{N}$.

P systems with more than two membranes

Even with three membranes, in case two of them are elementary, the power of such purely catalytic P systems over integers is still $\mathbb{Z}^d SLIN_{\mathbb{N}}^U$, but for a different reason: each elementary membrane contributes with its uniform semilinear set, and a sum of two uniform semilinear sets is still uniform semilinear.

Let us now examine a P system with three nested membranes – as we will see, the minimal number to obtain a set which is not in $\mathbb{Z}^d SLIN_{\mathbb{N}}^U$. Let the vector obtained by joining the initial contents of all membranes be $\mathbf{a_0}$. In the elementary membrane 3, there are two sets of integers associated with the catalyst c_3: the set of non-dissolving vectors is denoted by $A_{3,3}$, the set of dissolving vectors by $B_{3,3}$. In the middle membrane 2, associated with the catalyst c_2, we have the sets of non-dissolving and dissolving vectors $A_{2,2}$ and $B_{2,2}$. When c_3 arrives in membrane 2, other rules may become applicable there with this catalyst, and we denote the corresponding sets of integers associated with catalyst c_3 in membrane 2 by $A_{3,2}$ and $B_{3,2}$. As we may assume the P system to be reduced according to the observations above, we collect the result of halting computations in the skin membrane and therefore, no rules are assigned to any catalyst there. Let us now see what the resulting vector set may be built from, besides $\mathbf{a_0}$.

In each non-dissolving computation step, in the inner two membranes, an element of $A_{3,3}$ is added to the elementary membrane 3 and an element of $A_{2,2}$ is added to the middle membrane 2; throughout every successful computation, nothing is added any more in the skin membrane, although finally all objects will arrive to the skin to constitute the result of a halting computation. Hence, during that non-dissolving phase of a computation, we get an arbitrary element from $\langle A_{3,3} + A_{2,2} \rangle_{\mathbb{N}}$. Then there are three possibilities:

1. Both membranes 2 and 3 are dissolved at the same moment, hence, by such halting computations in total we get

$$\mathbf{a_0} + \langle A_{3,3} + A_{2,2} \rangle_{\mathbb{N}} + (B_{2,2} + B_{3,3}).$$

2. If membrane 2 is dissolved first, then the system continues by only applying the rules in membrane 3 (no rules are applicable in the skin membrane), and eventually dissolving membrane 3, we have obtained an element from $(B_{2,2} + A_{3,3}) + \langle A_{3,3} \rangle_{\mathbb{N}} + B_{3,3}$ during this phase of the computation, hence, by such halting computations in total we get

$$\mathbf{a_0} + \langle A_{3,3} + A_{2,2} \rangle_{\mathbb{N}} + ((B_{2,2} + A_{3,3}) + \langle A_{3,3} \rangle_{\mathbb{N}} + B_{3,3}).$$

As the zero-vector is an element of $\langle A_{3,3} \rangle_{\mathbb{N}}$, we observe that this expression can be combined with the previous one, thus in sum yielding

$$\mathbf{a_0} + \langle A_{3,3} + A_{2,2} \rangle_{\mathbb{N}} + B_{3,3} + B_{2,2} + \langle A_{3,3} \rangle_{\mathbb{N}}.$$

3. If membrane 3 is dissolved first, then both catalysts are active in membrane 2; eventually dissolving it, this phase of the computation yields an element from

$$B_{3,3} + \langle A_{2,2} + A_{3,2} \rangle_{\mathbb{N}} + ((A_{3,2} + B_{2,2}) \cup (A_{2,2} + B_{3,2}) \cup (B_{3,2} + B_{2,2})).$$

The three expressions $(A_{3,2} + B_{2,2})$, $(A_{2,2} + B_{3,2})$, $(B_{3,2} + B_{2,2})$ describe the three possibilities for dissolving membrane 2. Hence, by such halting computations in total we get

$$\mathbf{a_0} + \langle A_{3,3} + A_{2,2} \rangle_{\mathbb{N}} + B_{3,3} +$$
$$\langle A_{2,2} + A_{3,2} \rangle_{\mathbb{N}} + ((A_{3,2} + B_{2,2}) \cup (A_{2,2} + B_{3,2}) \cup (B_{3,2} + B_{2,2})) .$$

Therefore, the total set of integer vectors generated by such a purely catalytic P system over integers with three nested membranes is

$$\mathbf{a_0} + B_{3,3} + \langle A_{3,3} + A_{2,2} \rangle_{\mathbb{N}} + \Big((B_{2,2} + \langle A_{3,3} \rangle_{\mathbb{N}}) \cup$$
$$\big(\langle A_{2,2} + A_{3,2} \rangle_{\mathbb{N}} + ((A_{3,2} + B_{2,2}) \cup (A_{2,2} + B_{3,2}) \cup (B_{3,2} + B_{2,2})) \big) \Big),$$

An immediate reduction of this formula is to omit $\mathbf{a_0}$ as it can be included in $B_{3,3}$, hence, from now on we omit $\mathbf{a_0}$. Let us denote the resulting expression by

$$M (B_{3,3}, B_{2,2}, B_{3,2}, A_{3,3}, A_{2,2}, A_{3,2}) .$$

We also note that the power of the nested case subsumes the power of the case with two elementary membranes, as in that case we only get some uniform semilinear set, which formally can also be described by

$$M (B, \emptyset, \emptyset, A, \emptyset, \emptyset) ,$$

although, using our notation, the correct formula would be

$$(\langle A_{2,2} \rangle_{\mathbb{N}} + B_{2,2}) + (\langle A_{3,3} \rangle_{\mathbb{N}} + B_{3,3}) .$$

Therefore the power of all purely catalytic P systems over integers with three membranes can be described as follows:

$$\mathbb{Z}^d O_{\mathbb{Z}} P_3 (pcat_*, \delta) = \{ M (B_{3,3}, B_{2,2}, B_{3,2}, A_{3,3}, A_{2,2}, A_{3,2}) \mid$$
$$B_{3,3}, B_{2,2}, B_{3,2}, A_{3,3}, A_{2,2}, A_{3,2} \subset_{fin} \mathbb{Z}^d \},$$

where $M (B_{3,3}, B_{2,2}, B_{3,2}, A_{3,3}, A_{2,2}, A_{3,2})$ is the expression defined above.

Unfortunately, it is not obvious what more could be simplified in this expression, hence, to achieve our goal of showing how to get a non-uniform semilinear set, we have to consider some particular cases.

The expression $M (B_{3,3}, B_{2,2}, B_{3,2}, A_{3,3}, A_{2,2}, A_{3,2})$ contains the three bounded B-terms $B_{3,3}$, $B_{2,2}$, $B_{3,2}$, but the three independent finite sets of vectors $A_{3,3}$, $A_{2,2}$, $A_{3,2}$ appear as the three unbounded terms $\langle A_{3,3} + A_{2,2} \rangle_{\mathbb{N}}$, $\langle A_{2,2} + A_{3,2} \rangle_{\mathbb{N}}$, $\langle A_{3,3} \rangle_{\mathbb{N}}$ which are not independent any more. It is, however, possible to separate them in some particular cases.

Let us choose $A_{3,3}$ to be a singleton, i.e., $A_{3,3} := \{\mathbf{e}\}$ for some vector $\mathbf{e}$, and $A_{2,2} = -A_{3,3} := \{-\mathbf{e}\}$, as well as, for some non-empty set of vectors C, $A_{3,2} := C - A_{2,2}$. Hence, the first unbounded term $\langle A_{3,3} + A_{2,2} \rangle_{\mathbb{N}}$ does not contribute any more, as $\langle A_{3,3} + A_{2,2}\rangle_{\mathbb{N}} = \langle \mathbf{0}\rangle_{\mathbb{N}} = \mathbf{0}$, where $\mathbf{0}$ denotes the zero-vector. Moreover, we get $\langle A_{2,2} + A_{3,2}\rangle_{\mathbb{N}} = \langle C\rangle_{\mathbb{N}}$ and $\langle A_{3,3}\rangle_{\mathbb{N}} = \langle \{\mathbf{e}\}\rangle_{\mathbb{N}}$.

If we choose $B_{3,3} = B_{2,2} = B_{3,2} = \{\mathbf{0}\}$, the expression for M simplifies to

$$\langle \{\mathbf{e}\}\rangle_{\mathbb{N}} \cup \Big(\langle C\rangle_{\mathbb{N}} + \big((C - \{-\mathbf{e}\}) \cup \{-\mathbf{e}\}\big)\Big)$$

or to $\langle \{\mathbf{e}\}\rangle_{\mathbb{N}} \cup \Big(\langle C\rangle_{\mathbb{N}} + \big((C + \{\mathbf{e}\}) \cup \{-\mathbf{e}\}\big)\Big)$, respectively, which can be seen as the union of a homogenous linear set and a uniform semilinear set. As e and C can be chosen independently from each other, we conclude

$$\mathbb{Z}^d O_{\mathbb{Z}} P_n(pcat, \delta) \supsetneq \mathbb{Z}^d SLIN_{\mathbb{N}}^{U}, \quad \text{for all } n \geq 3.$$

Alternatively, to avoid dealing with the union of three cases when membrane 2 is divided last, we may choose $B_{2,2} = A_{2,2}$ and $B_{3,2} = A_{3,2}$; then the last parenthesis in the general expression of set M simply reduces to $A_{2,2} + A_{3,2}$. Let us define $C := A_{2,2} + A_{3,2}$ and, moreover, choose $B_{3,3} := \{\mathbf{0}\}$, $A_{3,3} := \{\mathbf{e}\}$, and $A_{2,2} := \{-\mathbf{e}\}$, then we get the reduced expression

$$(\{-\mathbf{e}\} + \langle \{\mathbf{e}\}\rangle_{\mathbb{N}}) \cup \big(\langle C\rangle_{\mathbb{N}} + (C)\big),$$

Since $\mathbf{0} \in \langle \{\mathbf{e}\}\rangle_{\mathbb{N}} - \{\mathbf{e}\}$ and $(\langle C\rangle_{\mathbb{N}} + C) \cup \{\mathbf{0}\} = \langle C\rangle_{\mathbb{N}}$ as well as $\{-\mathbf{e}\} + \langle \{\mathbf{e}\}\rangle_{\mathbb{N}} = -\{\mathbf{e}\} \cup \langle \{\mathbf{e}\}\rangle_{\mathbb{N}}$, in this case we can rewrite M to

$$-\{\mathbf{e}\} \cup \langle \{\mathbf{e}\}\rangle_{\mathbb{N}} \cup \langle C\rangle_{\mathbb{N}},$$

which is the "clean union" of two arbitrary homogeneous linear sets, such that the first one has only one generator, only "contaminated" by the union with the opposite vector of that singleton generator.

Another interesting variant is to choose $B_{3,2} = \emptyset$, i.e., catalyst c_3 has no associated dissolution rules in membrane region 2. Then the general expression of set M is immediately simplified to

$$B_{3,3} + B_{2,2} + \langle A_{3,3} + A_{2,2}\rangle_{\mathbb{N}} + \Big(\langle A_{3,3}\rangle_{\mathbb{N}} \cup \big(\langle A_{2,2} + A_{3,2}\rangle_{\mathbb{N}} + A_{3,2}\big)\Big).$$

Choosing $A_{3,3} := \{\mathbf{e}\}$, $A_{2,2} := \{-\mathbf{e}\}$, $A_{3,2} := C + \{\mathbf{e}\}$, and $B_{3,3} + B_{2,2} := \{-\mathbf{e}\}$, the expression for the set M becomes

$$\{-\mathbf{e}\} + \Big(\langle \{\mathbf{e}\}\rangle_{\mathbb{N}} \cup \big(\langle C\rangle_{\mathbb{N}} + C + \{\mathbf{e}\}\big)\Big),$$

which can be reduced to $\{-\mathbf{e}\} \cup \langle \{\mathbf{e}\}\rangle_{\mathbb{N}} \cup \langle C\rangle_{\mathbb{N}}$, i.e., we again have obtained an "almost clean union" as already deduced above. Finally, we notice that we can equivalently write our last set of integers as

$$\langle \{\mathbf{e}\}, -\mathbf{e}\rangle_{\mathbb{N}} \cup \langle C\rangle_{\mathbb{N}}.$$

We can extend the approach we used for deriving M to construct precise characterizations of the vector languages generated by purely catalytic P systems over integers with an arbitrary membrane structure of more than three membranes.

For every membrane i, except the skin membrane, of such a P system Π, according to the previous observations and simplifications, we may assume exactly one catalyst to be found there at the beginning; moreover, as all the inner membranes in the skin should be able to contribute to a result, we also may assume that no catalyst arriving in such a membrane will ever be able to be idle there, i.e., at least the rule $c_j \to c_j$ can assumed to be assigned to c_j in membrane i.

For every catalyst c_i and every membrane j, $2 \le i, j \le n$, we define the following sets of vectors:

- $A_{i,j}$ contains the vectors corresponding to the right-hand sides of *non-dissolving* rules associated with the catalyst c_i in membrane j;
- $B_{i,j}$ contains the vectors corresponding to the right-hand sides of *dissolving* rules associated with the catalysts c_i in membrane j.

In fact, we only need these sets $A_{i,j}$ and $B_{i,j}$ if membrane i is located somewhere within membrane j in the membrane structure μ of the P system.

For a fixed order of dissolution of membranes, the set of vectors generated by Π then can be written as a linear combination of various specific sets $A_{i,j}$ and $B_{i,j}$ plus the initial vector $\mathbf{a_0}$. The final vector language generated by Π can be characterized as a union of such linear combinations. Actually writing down such a characterization is a matter of technicality, but we refrain from doing it to avoid boring the reader with very tedious details.

4.3 Communication

We would like to remark that adding target indications to the regular objects should not increase the power of purely catalytic P systems over integers. Indeed, looking at a purely catalytic P system over integers, it is easily decidable which membranes will eventually be dissolved. Hence, the only question is whether the contents of a region specified by target, after possible dissolutions, will be in the output. There is no need to examine the future of a moved regular object, since the resources in purely catalytic P systems over integers are unbounded, and we can view this copy of a moved object as staying in that region until the end of the computation.

However, if also the catalysts are allowed to have target indications associated, it does make a difference. We claim the following characterizations.

Theorem 4. *For all $k \ge 1$,*

$$\mathbb{Z}^d O_\mathbb{Z} P_*(mpcat_k, tar_\mathbb{Z}) = \mathbb{Z}^d SLIN_\mathbb{N},$$
$$\mathbb{Z}^d O_\mathbb{Z} P_*(mpcat_k + \delta) = \mathbb{Z}^d SLIN_\mathbb{N}, \quad and$$
$$\mathbb{Z}^d O_\mathbb{Z} P_*(mpcat_*, \delta) = \mathbb{Z}^d SLIN_\mathbb{N}.$$

Proof. The upper bound in either case is easy to see because the number of possible arrangements of catalysts across the given membrane structure (and any possible structures obtained from it by membrane dissolutions) is bounded. Hence, purely catalytic P systems over integers with mobile catalysts are still not more powerful than blind vector-addition systems with states, which characterize $\mathbb{Z}^* SLIN_{\mathbb{N}}$, see [2].

We now proceed to the $\supseteq$ inclusions and consider an arbitrary semilinear set $\bigcup_{1 \leq i \leq m} \langle A_i, \mathbf{b}_i \rangle_{\mathbb{N}}$, where for each i, $1 \leq i \leq m$, $A_i \cup \{\mathbf{b}_i\} \subset_{fin} \mathbb{Z}^d$.

We first construct the following purely catalytic P system over integers Π_1 showing the first inclusion $\mathbb{Z}^d O_{\mathbb{Z}} P_*(mpcat_1, tar_{\mathbb{Z}}) \supseteq \mathbb{Z}^d SLIN_{\mathbb{N}}$.

$$\Pi_1 = (O, C = \{c\}, \mu, w_1, \cdots, w_{2m+1}, R_1, \cdots, R_{2m+1}, i_0 = 1) \text{ where}$$
$$O = \{a_i \mid 1 \leq i \leq d\} \cup \{c\},$$
$$\mu = [\,[\,[\ ]_{m+2}\,]_2 \cdots [\,[\ ]_{2m+1}\,]_{m+1}\,]_1,$$
$$w_1 = c,$$
$$w_{i+1} = \lambda, \ 1 \leq i \leq 2m,$$
$$R_1 = \{c \rightarrow (c, in_{i+1})v_i \mid 1 \leq i \leq m, \ \psi(v_i) = \mathbf{b}_i\},$$
$$R_{i+1} = \{c \rightarrow c(v, out) \mid \psi(v) \in A_i\} \cup \{c \rightarrow (c, in_{m+i+1})\}, \ 1 \leq i \leq m,$$
$$R_{m+i+1} = \emptyset, \ 1 \leq i \leq m.$$

The work of Π_1 consists of a non-deterministic choice of the i-th linear set to be generated, by moving the single catalyst c from the skin membrane into membrane $i + 1$, at the same time producing $\mathbf{b}_i$ in the skin membrane. After having sent an arbitrary combination of vectors from A_i to the skin membrane, the catalyst enters membrane $m + i + 1$, getting disabled there, and the system halts.

For showing the second inclusion $\mathbb{Z}^d O_{\mathbb{Z}} P_*(mpcat_1 + \delta) \supseteq \mathbb{Z}^d SLIN_{\mathbb{N}}$, where the catalyst may move, but at the same time may dissolve its surrounding membrane, we construct the purely catalytic P system over integers Π_2:

$$\Pi_2 = (O, C = \{c\}, \mu, w_1, \cdots, w_{m+2}, R_1, \cdots, R_{m+2}, i_0 = 1) \text{ where}$$
$$O = \{a_i \mid 1 \leq i \leq d\} \cup \{c\},$$
$$\mu = [\,[\,[\ ]_3 \cdots [\ ]_{m+2}\,]_2\,]_1,$$
$$w_1 = \lambda,$$
$$w_2 = c,$$
$$w_{i+2} = \lambda, \ 1 \leq i \leq m,$$
$$R_1 = \emptyset,$$
$$R_2 = \{c \rightarrow (c, in_{i+2})v_i \delta \mid 1 \leq i \leq m, \ \psi(v_i) = \mathbf{b}_i\},$$
$$R_{i+2} = \{c \rightarrow cv \mid \psi(v) \in A_i\} \cup \{c \rightarrow c\delta\}, \ 1 \leq i \leq m.$$

In Π_2, the single catalyst c from the second membrane is sent into membrane $i+2$, at the same time dissolving membrane 2, thus also producing $\mathbf{b}_i$ in the skin membrane. Now a linear combination of vectors from A_i is generated directly in membrane $i + 1$, and is released into the skin upon the dissolution of membrane $i + 1$. As the skin membrane contains no rules, the system must halt.

If moving the catalyst and dissolving the surrounding membrane are not allowed to be carried out within one single rule, a more complicated construction is needed, involving two catalysts, with the second catalyst being needed in multiple copies depending on m. For proving the inclusion

$$\mathbb{Z}^d O_{\mathbb{Z}} P_*(mpcat_*, \delta) \supseteq \mathbb{Z}^d SLIN_{\mathbb{N}},$$

we now construct the following purely catalytic P system over integers Π_3:

$$\Pi_3 = (O, C = \{c, c'\}, \mu, w_1, \cdots, w_{3m+1}, R_1, \cdots, R_{3m+1}, i_0 = 1) \text{ where}$$
$$O = \{a_i \mid 1 \leq i \leq d\} \cup \{c, c'\},$$
$$\mu = [\,[\,[\,[\ ]_{2m+2}\,]_{m+2}\,]_2 \cdots [\,[\,[\ ]_{3m+1}\,]_{2m+1}\,]_{m+1}\,]_1,$$
$$w_1 = c,$$
$$w_{i+1} = \lambda, \ 1 \leq i \leq 2m,$$
$$w_{2m+1+i} = c', \ 1 \leq i \leq m,$$
$$R_1 = \{c \to (c, in_{i+1})v_i \mid 1 \leq i \leq m, \ \psi(v_i) = \mathbf{b}_i\},$$
$$R_{i+1} = \{c \to cv \mid \psi(v) \in A_i\}$$
$$\qquad \cup \{c \to (c, in_{m+i+1}), \ c' \to c'\delta\}, \ 1 \leq i \leq m,$$
$$R_{m+i+1} = \{c \to (c, in_{2m+i+1}), \ c' \to (c', out)\}, \ 1 \leq i \leq m,$$
$$R_{2m+i+1} = \{c \to c\delta\}, \ 1 \leq i \leq m.$$

With each linear set i, $1 \leq i \leq n$, three nested membranes are associated ($i + 1$, $m + i + 1$, and $2m + i + 1$). At the beginning, catalyst c is sent from the skin membrane into membrane $i + 1$, at the same time producing $\mathbf{b}_i$ in the skin membrane. After having produced an arbitrary combination of vectors from A_i in membrane $i+1$, the catalyst enters membrane $m+i+1$; observe that membrane $i + 1$ is not dissolved yet. Then, c enters the elementary membrane $2m + i + 1$ and dissolves it, releasing catalyst c' into the surrounding membrane $m + i + 1$. Clearly, c cannot reenter membrane $2m + i + 1$, which no longer exists, so it has no applicable associated rules. Catalyst c', however, is sent out to membrane $i+1$, and now can dissolve it, which releases all generated regular objects to the skin and halts the computation.

In sum, we have shown that using mobile catalysts we get characterizations for the semilinear sets over integers, i.e., for $\mathbb{Z}^d SLIN_{\mathbb{N}}$, with also using dissolution (together with moving catalysts or as a separate operation) or with using targets for integer values (not only for a positive number of objects).   □

5   Multiple Dissolution

In this section we focus on extensions of usual dissolution which allow dissolving multiple nested membranes in one step by adding multiple instances of the dissolution symbol δ. Thus, if the multiset δ^n is introduced into a membrane h

at depth d, membrane h and $n-1$ of its parent membranes are dissolved and the contents of h is transferred into its n-th parent membrane h_p. One may now consider two different semantics for the contents of the $n-1$ dissolved parent membranes of h:

- *forgetting semantics* (δ^*) — the contents of the intermediate dissolved membranes is discarded, and
- *conservative semantics* (δ'^*) — the contents of the intermediate dissolved membranes is merged with that of h and moved into the n-th parent membrane h_p.

Multiple dissolutions allow characterizing semilinear sets relatively easily, even if only one catalyst is available:

Lemma 1. *For all $k \geq 1$,*

$$\mathbb{Z}^d O_{\mathbb{Z}} P_*(pcat_k, \delta^*) \cap \mathbb{Z}^d O_{\mathbb{Z}} P_*(pcat_k, \delta'^*) \supseteq \mathbb{Z}^d SLIN_{\mathbb{N}}.$$

Proof. To prove the inclusion $\mathbb{Z}^d O_{\mathbb{Z}} P_*(pcat_k, \delta^*) \supseteq \mathbb{Z}^d SLIN_{\mathbb{N}}$, consider an arbitrary semilinear set $L = \bigcup_{1 \leq i \leq m} \langle A_i, b_i \rangle_{\mathbb{N}}$, with $A_i \cup \{b_i\} \subset_{fin} \mathbb{Z}^d$. We now construct the following purely catalytic P system over integers generating this semilinear set:

$$\Pi_4 = (O, C = \{c\}, \mu, w_1, \cdots, w_{m+2}, R_1, \cdots, R_{m+2}, i_0 = 1), \text{ where}$$
$$O = \{a_i \mid 1 \leq i \leq d\} \cup \{c\},$$
$$\mu = [\,[\cdots[\,]_{m+2}\cdots]_2\,]_1,$$
$$w_k = \lambda, 1 \leq k < m+2,$$
$$w_{m+2} = c,$$
$$R_1 = \emptyset,$$
$$R_{k+1} = \{c \to cv \mid \psi(v) \in A_k\} \cup \{c \to cw\delta^k \mid \psi(w) = b_k\}, 1 \leq k \leq m,$$
$$R_{m+2} = \{c \to \delta^{m-k+1} \mid 1 \leq k \leq m\}.$$

Π_4 contains a linear membrane structure: the skin membrane has no rules, the innermost membrane contains some dissolution rules, while the other membranes contain rules representing the generators of one of the linear sets forming L.

Initially, the only catalyst c is located in the innermost membrane. In the first step, c non-deterministically dissolves 1 to m membranes, thereby choosing one of the linear sets of L. Then, by the rules of R_{k+1}, $1 \leq k \leq m$, c adds some generators from A_k to the initially empty membrane. At a certain moment, c decides to stop the generation and uses the rule $c \to cw\delta^k$ to add the offset b_k and to dissolve the remaining membranes, thus putting the generated result into the skin.

Remark now that in Π_4 almost all membranes stay empty during the whole evolution. Specifically, whenever multiple membranes are dissolved, all the parent membranes are empty. This means that choosing a different semantics for multiple dissolution, i.e., having in mind the primed delta, also allows for covering all semilinear sets; hence, we immediately also infer

$$\mathbb{Z}^d O_{\mathbb{Z}} P_*(pcat_1, \delta'^*) \supseteq \mathbb{Z}^d SLIN_{\mathbb{N}}.$$

This observation completes the proof.   □

Finally, note that the discussion from Subsect. 4.2 establishing the upper bound at semilinear sets of vectors can be adapted for both semantics of multiple dissolutions. Alternatively, to establish this upper bound, one could show that any evolution of a purely catalytic P system over integers can be simulated by a blind register machine, see [2]. In both cases, we may infer the following characterization result:

Theorem 5. *For all $k \geq 1$,*

$$\mathbb{Z}^d O_{\mathbb{Z}} P_*(pcat_k, \delta^*) = \mathbb{Z}^d O_{\mathbb{Z}} P_*(pcat_k, \delta'^*) = \mathbb{Z}^d SLIN_{\mathbb{N}}.$$

Multiple membrane dissolutions in a row are also considered in [2]. In that work, however, one rule may influence multiple membranes (or even all of them) at a time, and is inapplicable if one of the membranes it affects has already been dissolved. This is an additional means of global synchronisation which allows for a simpler the proof in [2].

6   Conclusions

We have reproved that the power of purely catalytic P systems over integers is contained in the family of all semilinear sets of vectors of integers. We then have shown that with one membrane purely catalytic P systems over integers give degenerate results, and with two membranes they exactly characterize the family of all uniform semilinear sets of vectors of integers. With more membranes, this equality becomes a strict inclusion, and specific unions of linear sets with different base vectors have been obtained. More specifically, for any vector $\mathbf{e} \in \mathbb{Z}^d$ and any finite set $C \subseteq \mathbb{Z}^d$, purely catalytic P systems over integers can generate

$$\langle \{\mathbf{e}\}, -\mathbf{e} \rangle_{\mathbb{N}} \cup \langle C \rangle_{\mathbb{N}}.$$

The most interesting open question remaining is whether $\mathbb{Z}^* O_{\mathbb{Z}} P_*(pcat_*, \delta)$ is closed under union. While in almost all cases in membrane computing closure under union is trivial, e.g., by making a non-deterministic choice in the first step of the computation, the current situation is rather surprising.

Finally, we have considered the variants with mobile catalysts, and showed a few combinations of features leading to characterizations of semilinear sets of $\mathbb{Z}$-vectors.

References

1. Alhazov, A., Aman, B., Freund, R., Păun, G.: Matter and anti-matter in membrane systems. In: Jürgensen, H., Karhumäki, J., Okhotin, A. (eds.) DCFS 2014. LNCS, vol. 8614, pp. 65–76. Springer, Heidelberg (2014). doi:10.1007/978-3-319-09704-6_7
2. Alhazov, A., Belingheri, O., Freund, R., Ivanov, S., Porreca, A.E., Zandron, C.: Semilinear sets, register machines, and integer vector addition (P) systems. In: Leporati, A., Zandron, C. (eds.) Proceedings of the Seventeenth International Conference on Membrane Computing (CMC17), 25–29 July 2016, Milan, Italy, pp. 39–56. Università degli Studi di Milano-Bicocca (2016)
3. Belingheri, O., Porreca, A.E., Zandron, C.: P systems with hybrid sets. In: Gheorghe, M., Konur, S. (eds.) Proceedings of the Workshop on Membrane Computing WMC 2016, Manchester (UK), 11–15 July 2016. School of Electrical Engineering and Computer Science, University of Bradford, Bradford, BD7 1DP, UK. Technical Report UB-20160819-1, pp. 34–41. University of Bradford (2016)
4. Carette, J., Sexton, A.P., Sorge, V., Watt, S.M.: Symbolic domain decomposition. In: Autexier, S., Calmet, J., Delahaye, D., Ion, P.D.F., Rideau, L., Rioboo, R., Sexton, A.P. (eds.) CICM 2010. LNCS (LNAI), vol. 6167, pp. 172–188. Springer, Heidelberg (2010). doi:10.1007/978-3-642-14128-7_16
5. Freund, R., Ibarra, O., Păun, G., Yen, H.C.: Matrix languages, register machines, vector addition systems. In: Naranjo, M.A.G., Riscos-Núñez, A., Romero-Campero, F.J., Sburlan, D. (eds.) Third Brainstorming Week on Membrane Computing, pp. 155–167. Fénix Editora, Sevilla, España (2005)
6. Freund, R., Ivanov, S., Verlan, S.: P systems with generalized multisets over totally ordered abelian groups. In: Rozenberg, G., Salomaa, A., Sempere, J.M., Zandron, C. (eds.) CMC 2015. LNCS, vol. 9504, pp. 117–136. Springer, Heidelberg (2015). doi:10.1007/978-3-319-28475-0_9
7. Greibach, S.A.: Remarks on blind and partially blind one-way multicounter machines. Theoret. Comput. Sci. 7(3), 311–324 (1978)
8. Haase, C., Halfon, S.: Integer vector addition systems with states. In: Ouaknine, J., Potapov, I., Worrell, J. (eds.) RP 2014. LNCS, vol. 8762, pp. 112–124. Springer, Heidelberg (2014). doi:10.1007/978-3-319-11439-2_9
9. Hopcroft, J., Pansiot, J.J.: On the reachability problem for 5-dimensional vector addition systems. Theoret. Comput. Sci. 8(2), 135–159 (1979)
10. Krishna, S.N., Păun, A.: Results on catalytic and evolution-communication P systems. New Gener. Comput. 22(4), 377–394 (2004)
11. Păun, G.: Some quick research topics. http://www.gcn.us.es/files/OpenProblems_bwmc15.pdf
12. Păun, G.: Computing with membranes. J. Comput. Syst. Sci. 61, 108–143 (1998)
13. Păun, G., Rozenberg, G., Salomaa, A.: The Oxford Handbook of Membrane Computing. Oxford University Press Inc., New York (2010)
14. The P Systems Website: http://ppage.psystems.eu

P Systems Working in Maximal Variants of the Set Derivation Mode

Artiom Alhazov[1], Rudolf Freund[2(✉)], and Sergey Verlan[3]

[1] Institute of Mathematics and Computer Science Academy of Sciences of Moldova,
Academiei 5, 2028 Chişinău, Moldova
artiom@math.md

[2] Faculty of Informatics, TU Wien, Favoritenstraße 9–11, 1040 Wien, Austria
rudi@emcc.at

[3] LACL, Université Paris Est – Créteil Val de Marne,
61, av. Général de Gaulle, 94010 Créteil, France
verlan@u-pec.fr

Abstract. In P systems working in the set derivation mode, even in the maximally parallel derivation mode, rules are only applied in at most one copy in each derivation step. We also consider the set mode in the cases of taking those sets of rules with the maximal number of applicable rules or with affecting the maximal number of objects. For many variants of P systems, the computational completeness proofs even literally still hold true for these new set derivation modes. On the other hand, we obtain new results for P systems using target selection for the rules to be chosen together with these set derivation modes.

1 Introduction

Membrane systems with symbol objects are a theoretical framework of parallel distributed multiset processing. Usually, multisets of rules are applied in parallel to the objects in the underlying configuration; for example, in the maximally parallel derivation mode (abbreviated max), a non-extendable multiset of rules is applied to the current configuration. In this paper we now consider variants of these derivation modes, where each rule is only used in at most one copy, i.e., we consider sets of rules to be applied in parallel, for example, in the *set-maximally parallel derivation mode* (abbreviated $smax$) we apply non-extendable *sets* of rules, and in two other set derivation modes we apply sets of rules which contain a maximal number of applicable rules (abbreviated $smax_{rules}$) and sets of rules which affect a maximal number of objects (abbreviated $smax_{objects}$).

Taking sets of rules instead of multisets is a quite natural restriction which has already appeared implicitly in [9] as the variant of the min_1-derivation mode where each rule forms its own partition. Other motivations arise when we consider firing a maximal set of transitions in Petri Nets [5,10] or optimizing an implementation of FPGA simulators [19]. A natural question arises concerning the power of set-based modes in contrast to multiset-based ones. In an explicit way, the set derivation mode first was investigated in [13] where the derivation

© Springer International Publishing AG 2017
A. Leporati et al. (Eds.): CMC 2016, LNCS 10105, pp. 83–102, 2017.
DOI: 10.1007/978-3-319-54072-6_6

mode *smax* was called *flat maximally parallel derivation mode*. Yet we here keep the notation of the *set-maximally parallel derivation mode* as we have already used it at the Conference on Membrane Computing 2015. In [13] it was already shown that in some cases the computational completeness results established for the *max*-mode also hold for the flat maximally parallel derivation mode, i.e., for the *smax*-mode.

In this paper we continue this line of research and we show that for several well-known variants of P systems the proofs for computational completeness for *max* can be taken over even literally for *smax* as well as for the derivation modes max_{rules}, $max_{objects}$ and $smax_{rules}$, $smax_{objects}$, where multisets or sets of rules with the maximal number of rules and multisets or sets of rules affecting the maximal number of objects, respectively, are taken into account. For P systems using target selection for the rules to be chosen these set derivation modes yield even stronger new results. Full proofs of some of the results mentioned in this paper and a series of additional results can be found in [4].

2   Definitions

We assume the reader to be familiar with the underlying notions and concepts from formal language theory, e.g., see [7,15].

2.1   Prerequisites

The set of non-negative integers is denoted by $\mathbb{N}$. Given an alphabet V, a finite non-empty set of abstract symbols, the free monoid generated by V under the operation of concatenation is denoted by V^*. The elements of V^* are called strings, the empty string is denoted by λ, and $V^* \setminus \{\lambda\}$ is denoted by V^+. For an arbitrary alphabet $V = \{a_1, \ldots, a_n\}$, the number of occurrences of a symbol a_i in a string x is denoted by $|x|_{a_i}$, while the length of a string x is denoted by $|x| = \sum_{a_i \in V} |x|_{a_i}$. With respect to a specific order on the elements $a_1, \ldots, a_n$ of the alphabet V, the n-tuple $(|x|_{a_1}, \ldots, |x|_{a_n})$ is called the Parikh vector of $|x|$.

A finite multiset over an alphabet $V = \{a_1, \ldots, a_n\}$ is a mapping $f : V \to \mathbb{N}$ and can be represented by $\left\langle a_1^{f(a_1)}, \ldots, a_n^{f(a_n)} \right\rangle$ or by any string x for which $(|x|_{a_1}, \ldots, |x|_{a_n}) = (f(a_1), \ldots, f(a_n))$. The set of all multisets over V is denoted by V° or by $Ps(V^*)$.

The families of recursively enumerable string languages is denoted by RE. For any family of languages X, $Ps(X)$ denotes the set of Parikh sets of the languages in X; if we do not distinguish between different symbols and only consider sets of numbers, we write $N(X)$.

2.2   Register Machines

A *register machine* is a tuple $M = (d, B, l_0, l_h, R)$, where d is the number of registers, B is a set of labels, $l_0 \in B$ is the initial label, $l_h \in B$ is the final label, and R is the set of instructions bijectively labeled by elements of B. The instructions of M can be of the following forms:

- $p : (ADD\,(r)\,, q, s)$, with $p \in B \smallsetminus \{l_h\}$, $q, s \in B$, $1 \le r \le d$.
  Increases the value of register r by one, followed by a non-deterministic jump to instruction p or s. This instruction is usually called *increment*.
- $p : (SUB\,(r)\,, q, s)$, with $p \in B \smallsetminus \{l_h\}$, $q, s \in B$, $1 \le r \le d$.
  If the value of register r is zero, then the register machine jumps to instruction s; otherwise, the value of register r is decreased by one, followed by a jump to instruction q. The two cases of this instruction are usually called *zero-test* and *decrement*, respectively.
- $l_h : HALT$. Stops the computation of the register machine.

A *configuration* of a register machine is described by the contents (i.e., by the number stored in the register) of each register and by the current label, which indicates the next instruction to be executed. Computations start by executing the instruction l_0 of R, and terminate with reaching the HALT-instruction l_h.

As is well known (e.g., see [12]), register machines constitute a computationally complete model for generating or accepting sets of (vectors of) non-negative numbers, and thus they are often used as a reference model to be simulated in the area of membrane computing.

For accepting recursively enumerable sets of numbers, deterministic register machines with (at most) three registers are sufficient. In a deterministic register machine, the ADD-instructions are of the form $p : (ADD\,(r)\,, q)$, with $p \in B \smallsetminus \{l_h\}$, $q \in B$, $1 \le r \le d$.

In the succeeding proofs, for a register machine $M = (d, B, l_0, l_h, R)$ we will denote the sets of deterministic ADD-instructions, of non-deterministic ADD-instructions, and of SUB-instructions in R by $ADD^1(R)$, $ADD^2(R)$, and $SUB(R)$, respectively. Moreover, by B_{ADD} we denote the set of labels for ADD-instructions, and by B_{SUB} we denote the set of labels for SUB-instructions of M in R.

Finally, without loss of generality, for a register machine $M = (d, B, l_0, l_h, R)$ with d registers and $m \le d$ decrementable registers, we will assume that the following conditions hold: the output registers are $m + 1, \cdots, d$, and they are never decremented; moreover, the decrementable registers $1, \cdots, m$ are empty in any reachable halting configuration.

3   Variants of P Systems

In this section we recall the well-known definitions of several variants of P systems as well as some variants of derivation modes and also introduce the variants of set derivation modes considered in the following.

For all the notions and results not referred to otherwise we refer the reader to the Handbook of Membrane Computing [14] as well as to the webpage [18] of P systems.

A (cell-like) P system is a construct

$$\Pi = (O, C, \mu, w_1, \ldots, w_m, R_1, \ldots, R_m, f_O, f_I) \quad \text{where}$$

- O is the alphabet of objects,
- $C \subset O$ is the set of catalysts,
- μ is the membrane structure (with m membranes, labeled by 1 to m),
- $w_1, \ldots, w_m$ are multisets of objects present in the m regions of μ at the beginning of a computation,
- $R_1, \ldots, R_m$ are finite sets of rules, associated with the regions of μ,
- f_O is the label of the membrane region from which the outputs are taken (in the generative case),
- f_I is the label of the membrane region where the inputs are put at the beginning of a computation (in the accepting case).

$f_O = 0/f_I = 0$ indicates that the output/input is taken from the environment. If f_O and f_I indicate the same label, we only write f for both labels.

If a rule $u \to v$ has at least two objects in u, then it is called *cooperative*, otherwise it is called *non-cooperative*. *Catalytic rules* are of the form $ca \to cv$, where $c \in C$ is a special object called *catalyst* which never evolves and never passes through a membrane, it just assists object a to evolve to the multiset v.

In *catalytic P systems* we use non-cooperative as well as catalytic rules. In a *purely catalytic P system* we only allow catalytic rules.

We call a P system *simple* if it contains only one membrane (the skin membrane), which also serves as input and output membrane. Only specifying the relevant parts, we then may write $\Pi = (O, C, w_1, R_1)$ where

- O is the alphabet of objects,
- $C \subset O$ is the set of catalysts,
- w_1 is the finite multiset of objects over O present in the skin membrane at the beginning of a computation,
- R_1 is a finite set of rules.

We omit the set C if the P system contains no catalysts.

3.1   Derivation Modes

The definitions and the corresponding notions used in this subsection follow the definitions and notions elaborated in [9]. Given a P system Π, the set of multisets of rules applicable to a configuration C is denoted by $Appl(\Pi, C)$; this set also equals the set $Appl(\Pi, C, asyn)$ of multisets of rules applicable in the *asynchronous derivation mode* (abbreviated *asyn*). The set $Appl(\Pi, C, sequ)$ denotes the set of multisets of rules applicable in the *sequential derivation mode* (abbreviated *sequ*), where in each derivation step exactly one rule is applied.

In the *maximally parallel derivation mode* (abbreviated by *max*), in any computation step of Π we choose a multiset of rules from $\mathcal{R}$ (which is defined as the union of the sets $R_1, \ldots, R_m$; in this context, rules in different rule sets R_i and R_j with $i \neq j$ are always considered to be different rules) in such a way that no further rule can be added to it so that the obtained multiset would still be applicable to the existing objects in the regions $1, \ldots, m$:

$$Appl(\Pi, C, max) = \{R \in Appl(\Pi, C) \mid \text{there is no } R' \in Appl(\Pi, C)$$
$$\text{such that } R' \supset R\}$$

The basic set derivation mode is defined as the derivation mode where in each derivation step at most one copy of each rule may be applied in parallel with the other rules; this variant of a basic derivation mode corresponds to the asynchronous mode with the restriction that only those multisets of rules are applicable which contain at most one copy of each rule, i.e., we consider *sets* of rules:

$$Appl(\Pi, C, set) = \{R \in Appl(\Pi, C, asyn) \mid |R|_r \leq 1 \text{ for each } r \in \mathcal{R}\}$$

In the *set-maximally parallel derivation mode* (this derivation mode is abbreviated by *smax* for short), in any computation step of Π we choose a non-extendable multiset R of rules from $Appl(\Pi, C, set)$:

$$Appl(\Pi, C, smax) = \{R \in Appl(\Pi, C, set) \mid \text{there is no } R' \in Appl(\Pi, C, set)$$
$$\text{such that } R' \supset R\}$$

The *smax*-derivation mode corresponds to the min_1-mode with the discrete partitioning of rules (each rule forms its own partition), see [9].

As already introduced for multisets of rules in [6], we now consider the variant where the maximal number of rules is chosen. In the derivation mode $max_{rules}max$ only a maximal multiset of rules is allowed to be applied. But it can also be seen as the variant of the basic mode *max* where we just take a multiset of applicable rules with the maximal number of rules in it, hence, we will also call it the max_{rules} derivation mode. Formally we have:

$$Appl(\Pi, C, max_{rules}) = \{R \in Appl(\Pi, C, asyn) \mid$$
$$\text{there is no } R' \in Appl(\Pi, C, asyn)$$
$$\text{such that } |R'| > |R|\}$$

The derivation mode $max_{rules}smax$ is a special variant where only a maximal set of rules is allowed to be applied. But it can also seen as the variant of the basic set mode where we just take a set of applicable rules with the maximal number of rules in it, hence, we will also call it the $smax_{rules}$ derivation mode. Formally we have:

$$Appl(\Pi, C, smax_{rules}) = \{R \in Appl(\Pi, C, set) \mid$$
$$\text{there is no } R' \in Appl(\Pi, C, set)$$
$$\text{such that } |R'| > |R|\}$$

We also consider the derivation modes $max_{objects}max$ and $max_{objects}smax$ where from the multisets of rules in $Appl(\Pi, C, max)$ and from the sets of rules in $Appl(\Pi, C, smax)$, respectively, only those are taken which affect the maximal number of objects. As with affecting the maximal number of objects, such multisets and such sets of rules are non-extendable anyway, we will also use the notations $max_{objects}$ and $smax_{objects}$.

As usual, with all these variants of derivation modes as defined above, we consider halting computations. We may generate or accept or even compute functions or relations. The inputs/outputs may be multisets or strings, defined in the well-known way.

For any derivation mode γ,

$$\gamma \in \{sequ, asyn, max, smax\} \cup$$
$$\{max_{rules}, smax_{rules}, max_{objects}, smax_{objects}\},$$

the families of number sets $(Y = N)$ and Parikh sets $(Y = Ps)$ $Y_{\gamma,\delta}(\Pi)$, generated $(\delta = gen)$ or accepted $(\delta = acc)$ by P systems with at most m membranes and rules of type X, are denoted by $Y_{\gamma,\delta}OP_m(X)$.

4   Computational Completeness Proofs also Working for Set Derivation Modes

In this section we list several variants of P systems where the computational completeness proofs also work for the set derivation modes even being taken literally from the literature.

4.1   P Systems with Cooperative Rules

We first consider *simple P systems with cooperative rules* having only one membrane (the skin membrane), which also serves as input and output membrane, and cooperative rules of the form $u \to v$. Only specifying the relevant parts, we may write $\Pi = (O, w_1, R_1)$ where

- O is the alphabet of objects,
- w_1 is the finite multiset of objects over O present in the skin membrane at the beginning of a computation,
- R_1 is a finite set of cooperative rules.

For a rule $u \to v \in R_1$, $|uv|$ is called its *size*.

Theorem 1. *For any register machine $M = (d, B, l_0, l_h, R)$, with $m \leq d$ being the number of decrementable registers, we can construct a simple P system $\Pi = (O, w_1 = l_0, R_1)$ with cooperative rules of size at most 3 working in any of the derivation modes γ,*

$$\gamma \in \{max, max_{rules}, max_{objects}, smax, smax_{rules}, smax_{objects}\},$$

and simulating the computations of M such that

$$|R_1| \leq 1 \times |ADD^1(R)| + 2 \times |ADD^2(R)| + 5 \times |SUB(R)|.$$

Proof. Let $M = (m, B, l_0, l_h, R)$ be an arbitrary register machine. We now construct a simple P system with cooperative rules of size at most 3 simulating M. The number in register r is represented by the corresponding number of symbol objects o_r.

A deterministic ADD-instruction $p : (ADD(r), q)$ is simulated by the rule $p \to o_r q$.

An ADD-instruction $p : (ADD(r), q, s)$ is simulated by the two rules $p \to o_r q$ and $p \to o_r s$.

A SUB-instruction $p : (SUB(r), q, s)$ is simulated by the following rules:

1. $p \to p'p''$;
2. $p' \to \tilde{p}$, $p''o_r \to \bar{p}$
   (executed in parallel if register r is not empty);
3. $\tilde{p}p'' \to s$ (if register r has been empty),
   $\tilde{p}\bar{p} \to q$ (if register r has not been empty).

In the case of a deterministic register machine, the simulation by the P system is deterministic, too.

We observe that the construction works for every maximal derivation mode, even if only sets of rules are taken into account. □

4.2 Catalytic and Purely Catalytic P Systems

We now investigate proofs elaborated for catalytic and purely catalytic P systems working in the *max*-mode for the derivation modes $smax$, max_{rules}, $smax_{rules}$, $max_{objects}$, and $smax_{objects}$.

Based on the proof construction elaborated in [2] we state the following result:

Theorem 2. *For any register machine $M = (d, B, l_0, l_h, R)$, with $m \leq d$ being the number of decrementable registers, we can construct a simple catalytic P system $\Pi = (O, C, w_1, R_1)$ working in any of the derivation modes γ,*

$$\gamma \in \{max, smax, max_{rules}, smax_{rules}, max_{objects}, smax_{objects}\},$$

and simulating the computations of M such that

$$|R_1| \leq 1 \times |ADD^1(R)| + 2 \times |ADD^2(R)| + 5 \times |SUB(R)| + 5 \times m + 1.$$

Proof. We first check the construction for simulating a register machine $M = (d, B, l_0, l_h, R)$ by a catalytic P system Π, with $m \leq d$ being the number of decrementable registers, elaborated in [2] for the *max*-mode, and argue why it works for the derivation mode $smax$ and the other maximal (set) derivation modes, too.

For all d registers, n_i copies of the symbol o_i are used to represent the value n_i in register i, $1 \leq i \leq d$. For each of the m decrementable registers, we take a catalyst c_i and two specific symbols d_i, e_i, $1 \leq i \leq m$, for simulating SUB-instructions on these registers. For every $p \in B$, we use p, and also its variants $\bar{p}, \hat{p}, \tilde{p}$ for $p \in B_{SUB}$, where B_{SUB} denotes the set of labels of SUB-instructions.

For $r < m$, $r \oplus_m 1$ simply is $r + 1$, whereas for $r = m$ we define $m \oplus_m 1 = 1$; w_0 stands for additional input present at the beginning.

Usually, every catalyst c_i, $i \in \{1, \ldots, m\}$, is kept busy with the symbol d_i using the rule $c_i d_i \to c_i$, as otherwise the symbols d_i would have to be trapped by the rule $d_i \to \#$, and the trap rule $\# \to \#$ then enforces an infinite non-halting computation. We use the following shortcuts:

$$D_m = \prod_{i \in \{1, \ldots, m\}} d_i,$$
$$D_{m,r} = \prod_{i \in \{1, \ldots, m\} \setminus \{r\}} d_i,$$
$$D'_{m,r} = \prod_{i \in \{1, \ldots, m\} \setminus \{r, r \oplus_m 1\}} d_i.$$

Only during the simulation of SUB-instructions on register r the corresponding catalyst c_r is left free for decrementing or for zero-checking in the second step of the simulation, and in the decrement case both c_r and its "coupled" catalyst $c_{r \oplus_m 1}$ are needed to be free for specific actions in the third step of the simulation.

$$\Pi = (O, C, w_1 = c_1 \ldots c_m d_1 \ldots d_m p_1 w_0, R_1),$$
$$O = C \cup D \cup E \cup \Sigma \cup \{\#\} \cup B \cup \{\bar{p}, \hat{p}, \tilde{p} \mid l \in B_{SUB}\},$$
$$C = \{c_i \mid 1 \le i \le m\},$$
$$D = \{d_i \mid 1 \le i \le m\},$$
$$E = \{e_i \mid 1 \le i \le m\},$$
$$\Sigma = \{o_i \mid 1 \le i \le d\},$$
$$R_1 = \{p \to o_r q D_m, p \to o_r s D_m \mid p : (ADD(r), q, s) \in R\}$$
$$\cup \{p \to \hat{p} e_r D_{m,r}, p \to \bar{p} D_{m,r}, \hat{p} \to \tilde{p} D'_{m,r},$$
$$\tilde{p} \to q D_m, \bar{p} \to s D_m \mid p : (SUB(r), q, s) \in R\}$$
$$\cup \{c_r o_r \to c_r d_r, c_r d_r \to c_r, c_{r \oplus_m 1} e_r \to c_{r \oplus_m 1} \mid 1 \le r \le m\},$$
$$\cup \{d_r \to \#, c_r e_r \to c_r \# \mid 1 \le r \le m\}$$
$$\cup \{\# \to \#\}.$$

The HALT-instruction labeled l_h is simply simulated by not introducing the corresponding state symbol l_h, i.e., replacing it by λ, in all rules defined in R_1.

Each ADD-instruction $p : (ADD(r), q, s)$, for $r \in \{1, \ldots, d\}$, can easily be simulated by the rules $p \to o_r q D_m$ and $p \to o_r s D_m$; in parallel, the rules $c_i d_i \to c_i$, $1 \le i \le m$, have to be carried out, as otherwise the symbols d_i would have to be trapped by the rules $d_i \to \#$.

Each SUB-instruction $p : (SUB(r), q, s)$, is simulated as shown in the table listed below (the rules in brackets [and] are those to be carried out in case of a wrong choice):

Simulation of the SUB-instruction $p : (SUB(r), q, s)$ if

register r is not empty	register r is empty
$p \to \hat{p} e_r D_{m,r}$	$p \to \bar{p} D_{m,r}$
$c_r o_r \to c_r d_r$ $[c_r e_r \to c_r \#]$	c_r should stay idle
$\hat{p} \to \tilde{p} D'_{m,r}$	$\bar{p} \to s D_m$
$c_r d_r \to c_r$ $[d_r \to \#]$	$[d_r \to \#]$
$\tilde{p} \to q D_m$	
$c_{r \oplus_m 1} e_r \to c_{r \oplus_m 1}$	

In the first step of the simulation of each instruction (ADD-instruction or SUB-instruction) due to the introduction of D_m in the previous step (we also start with that in the initial configuration) every catalyst c_r is kept busy by the corresponding symbol d_r, $1 \leq r \leq m$.

We finally observe that the catalytic P system constructed above not only works correctly with the maximally parallel derivation mode max, but also for the derivation modes max_{rules} and $max_{objects}$ as well as for the set derivation modes $smax$, $smax_{rules}$, and $smax_{objects}$. Each maximality condition guarantees that the rules are applied in a correct way in every step.

The only difference is that in the set derivation modes smax-mode, smax_{rules}, and smax_{objects} only one trap rule $\# \rightarrow \#$ will be carried out! ☐

For the purely catalytic case, one additional catalyst c_{m+1} is needed to be used with all the non-cooperative rules. Unfortunately, in this case a slightly more complicated simulation of SUB-instructions is needed, a result established in [17], where for catalytic P systems

$$|R_1| \leq 2 \times |ADD^1(R)| + 3 \times |ADD^2(R)| + 6 \times |SUB(R)| + 5 \times m + 1,$$

and for purely catalytic P systems

$$|R_1| \leq 2 \times |ADD^1(R)| + 3 \times |ADD^2(R)| + 6 \times |SUB(R)| + 6 \times m + 1$$

is shown. We observe that again the construction works for every maximal derivation mode, even if only sets of rules are taken into account.

4.3 Computational Completeness of (Purely) Catalytic P Systems with Additional Control Mechanisms

In this subsection we mention results for (purely) catalytic P systems with additional control mechanisms, in that way reaching computational completeness with only one (two) catalyst(s).

P Systems with Label Selection

For all the variants of P systems of type X, we may consider labeling all the rules in the sets $R_1, \ldots, R_m$ in a one-to-one manner by labels from a set H and taking a set W containing subsets of H. In any transition step of a *P system with label selection* Π we first select a set of labels $U \in W$ and then, in the given derivation mode, we apply a non-empty multiset R of rules such that all the labels of these rules from R are in U.

The families of sets $Y_{\gamma,\delta}(\Pi)$, $Y \in \{N, Ps\}$, $\delta \in \{gen, acc\}$, and

$$\gamma \in \{sequ, asyn, max, smax, max_{rules}, smax_{rules}, max_{objects}, smax_{objects}\},$$

computed by P systems with label selection with at most m membranes and rules of type X are denoted by $Y_{\gamma,\delta}OP_m(X, ls)$.

Theorem 3. $Y_{\gamma,\delta}OP_1\left(cat_1,ls\right) = Y_{\gamma,\delta}OP_1\left(pcat_2,ls\right) = YRE$ *for any* $Y \in \{N, Ps\}$, $\delta \in \{gen, acc\}$, *and any (set) derivation mode* γ,

$$\gamma \in \{max, smax, max_{rules}, smax_{rules}, max_{objects}, smax_{objects}\}.$$

The proof given in [8] for the maximally parallel mode max can be taken over for the other maximal (set) derivation modes word by word; the only difference again is that in set derivation modes, in non-successful computations where more than one trap symbol $\#$ has been generated, the trap rule $\# \to \#$ is only applied once.

Controlled P Systems and Time-Varying P Systems

Another method to control the application of the labeled rules is to use control languages (see [3,11]). In a *controlled P system* Π, in addition we use a set H of labels for the rules in Π, and a string language L over 2^H (each subset of H represents an element of the alphabet for L) from a family FL. Every successful computation in Π has to follow a control word $U_1 \ldots U_n \in L$: in transition step i, only rules with labels in U_i are allowed to be applied (in the underlying derivation mode, for example, max or $smax$), and after the n-th transition, the computation halts; we may relax this end condition, i.e., we may stop after the i-th transition for any $i \leq n$, and then we speak of *weakly controlled P systems*. If $L = (U_1 \ldots U_p)^*$, Π is called a *(weakly) time-varying P system*: in the computation step $pn + i$, $n \geq 0$, rules from the set U_i have to be applied; p is called the *period*.

The family of sets $Y_{\gamma,\delta}\left(\Pi\right)$, $Y \in \{N, Ps\}$, computed by (weakly) controlled P systems and (weakly) time-varying P systems with period p, with at most m membranes and rules of type X as well as control languages in FL is denoted by $Y_{\gamma,\delta}OP_m\left(X, C\left(FL\right)\right)$ $\left(Y_{\gamma,\delta}OP_m\left(X, wC\left(FL\right)\right)\right)$ and $Y_{\gamma,\delta}OP_m\left(X, TV_p\right)$ $\left(Y_{\gamma,\delta}OP_m\left(X, wTV_p\right)\right)$, respectively, for $\delta \in \{gen, acc\}$ and

$$\gamma \in \{sequ, asyn, max, smax\} \cup$$
$$\{max_{rules}, smax_{rules}, max_{objects}, smax_{objects}\}.$$

Theorem 4. $Y_{\gamma,\delta}OP_1\left(cat_1, \alpha TV_6\right) = Y_{\gamma,\delta}OP_1\left(pcat_2, \alpha TV_6\right) = YRE$, *for any* $\alpha \in \{\lambda, w\}$, $Y \in \{N, Ps\}$, $\delta \in \{gen, acc\}$, *and*

$$\gamma \in \{max, smax, max_{rules}, smax_{rules}, max_{objects}, smax_{objects}\}.$$

The proof given in [8] for the maximally parallel mode max again can be taken over for the other maximal (set) derivation modes word by word, e.g., see [4].

5   P Systems with Toxic Objects

In many variants of (catalytic) P systems, for proving computational completeness it is common to introduce a trap symbol $\#$ for the case that the derivation goes the wrong way as well as the rule $\# \to \#$ (or $c\# \to c\#$ with a catalyst c)

guaranteeing that the derivation will never halt. Yet most of these rules can be avoided if we specify a specific subset of *toxic* objects O_{tox}.

The P system with toxic objects is only allowed to continue a computation from a configuration C by using an applicable multiset of rules covering all copies of objects from O_{tox} occurring in C; moreover, if there exists no multiset of applicable rules covering all toxic objects, the whole computation having yielded the configuration C is abandoned, i.e., no results can be obtained from this computation.

For any variant of P systems, we add the set of *toxic* objects O_{tox} and in the specification of the families of sets of (vectors of) numbers generated by P systems with toxic objects using rules of type X we add the subscript tox to O, thus obtaining the families $Y_{\gamma,\delta}O_{tox}P_m(X)$, for any $m \geq 1$, $Y \in \{N, Ps\}$, $\delta \in \{gen, acc\}$, and

$$\gamma \in \{max, smax, max_{rules}, smax_{rules}, max_{objects}, smax_{objects}\}.$$

The following theorem stated in [1] only for the *max*-mode obviously holds for the other maximal (set) derivation modes, too.

Theorem 5. $PsRE = Ps_{\gamma,gen}O_{tox}P_1([p]cat_2)$ *for every*

$$\gamma \in \{max, smax, max_{rules}, smax_{rules}, max_{objects}, smax_{objects}\}.$$

In general, we can formulate the following "metatheorem":

Metatheorem: *Whenever a proof has been established for the derivation mode max and literally also holds true for the derivation mode smax, then the omitting of trap rules by using the concept of toxic objects works for both derivation modes in the same way.*

In the following sections, we now turn our attention to models of P systems where the derivation mode *smax* yields different, in fact, stronger results than the derivation mode *max*.

6   Atomic Promoters and Inhibitors

As shown in [16], P systems with non-cooperative rules and atomic inhibitors are not computationally complete when the maximally parallel derivation mode is used. P systems with non-cooperative rules and atomic promoters can at least generate $PsET0L$. On the other hand, already in [13], the computational completeness of P systems with applying maximal sets of non-cooperative rules and atomic promoters has been shown. In the following we recall our new proof from [4] for the simulation of a register machine where the overall number of promoters only depends on the number of decrementable registers of the register machine. Moreover, we also recall the proof of a new rather surprising result, establishing computational completeness of P systems with applying maximal sets of non-cooperative rules and atomic inhibitors, where the number of inhibitors again only depends on the number of decrementable registers of the simulated register machine. Finally, in both cases, if the register machine is deterministic, then the P system is deterministic, too.

6.1 Atomic Promoters

We now recall our new proof from [4] for the computational completeness of P systems with non-cooperative rules and atomic promoters when using any of the set derivation modes $smax, smax_{rules}, smax_{objects}$. The overall number of promoters only is $5m$ where m is the number of decrementable registers of the simulated register machine.

Theorem 6. *For any register machine $M = (d, B, l_0, l_h, R)$, with $m \leq d$ being the number of decrementable registers, we can construct a simple P system with atomic inhibitors $\Pi = (O, w_1 = l_0, R_1)$ working in any of the set derivation modes $smax, smax_{rules}, smax_{objects}$ and simulating the computations of M such that*

$$|R_1| \leq 1 \times |ADD^1(R)| + 2 \times |ADD^2(R)| + 5 \times |SUB(R)| + 7 \times m.$$

The number of atomic inhibitors is $5m$. Finally, if the register machine is deterministic, then the P system is deterministic, too.

Proof. The numbers of objects o_r represent the contents of the registers r, $1 \leq r \leq d$; moreover, we denote $B_{SUB} = \{p \mid p : (SUB(r), q, s) \in R\}$.

$$O = \{o_r \mid 1 \leq r \leq d\} \cup \{o'_r, c_r, c'_r, c''_r, c'''_r \mid 1 \leq r \leq m\}$$
$$\cup\, (B \setminus \{l_h\}) \cup \{p', p'', p''' \mid p \in B_{SUB}\}$$

The symbols from $\{o'_r, c_r, c'_r, c''_r, c'''_r \mid 1 \leq r \leq m\}$ are used as promoters.

An ADD-instruction $p : (ADD(r), q, s)$ is simulated by the two rules $p \to qo_r$ and $p \to so_r$.

A SUB-instruction $p : (SUB(r), q, s)$ is simulated in four steps as follows:

1. $p \to p'c_r$;
2. $p' \to p''c'_r$, $o_r \to o'_r \mid_{c_r}$, $c_r \to \lambda$;
3. $p'' \to p'''c''_r$, $c'_r \to c''_r \mid_{o'_r}$, $o'_r \to \lambda$;
4. $p''' \to q \mid_{c'_r}$, $p''' \to s \mid_{c'_r}$, $c'_r \to \lambda \mid_{c'''_r}$, $c''_r \to \lambda$, $c'''_r \to \lambda$.

As final rule we could use $l_h \to \lambda$, yet we can omit this rule and replace every appearance of l_h in all rules as described above by λ. □

6.2 Atomic Inhibitors

We now show that even P systems with non-cooperative rules and atomic promoters using one of the derivation modes $smax, smax_{rules}, smax_{objects}$ can simulate any register machine needing only $2m+1$ inhibitors where m is the number of decrementable registers of the simulated register machine.

Theorem 7. *For any register machine $M = (d, B, l_0, l_h, R)$, with $m \leq d$ being the number of decrementable registers, we can construct a P system with atomic* *inhibitors $\Pi = (O, w_1 = l_0, R_1)$ working in any of the set derivation modes smax, $smax_{rules}$, $smax_{objects}$ and simulating the computations of M such that*

$$|R_1| \leq 1 \times |ADD^1(R)| + 2 \times |ADD^2(R)| + 5 \times |SUB(R)| + 3 \times m + 1.$$

The number of atomic inhibitors is $2m + 1$. Finally, if the register machine is deterministic, then the P system is deterministic, too.

Proof. The numbers of objects o_r represent the contents of the registers r, $1 \leq r \leq d$. The symbols d_r prevent the register symbols o_r, $1 \leq r \leq m$, from evolving.

$$O = \{o_r \mid 1 \leq r \leq d\} \cup \{o'_r \mid 1 \leq r \leq m\} \cup \{d_r \mid 0 \leq r \leq m\}$$
$$\cup (B \setminus \{l_h\}) \cup \{p', p'', \tilde{p} \mid p \in B_{SUB}\}$$

We denote $D = \prod_{i=1}^m d_i$ and $D_r = \prod_{i=1, i \neq r}^m d_i$.

An ADD-instruction $p : (ADD(r), q, s)$ is simulated by the two rules $p \to qo_r D$ and $p \to so_r D$.

A SUB-instruction $p : (SUB(r), q, s)$ is simulated in four steps as follows:

1. $p \to p' D_r$;
2. $p' \to p'' D d_0$; in parallel, the following rules are used:
   $o_r \to o'_r \mid_{\neg d_r}$; $d_k \to \lambda$, $1 \leq k \leq m$;
3. $p'' \to \tilde{p} D \mid_{\neg o'_r}$; $o'_r \to \lambda$, $d_0 \to \lambda$;
   again, in parallel the rules $d_k \to \lambda$, $1 \leq k \leq m$, are used;
4. $p'' \to qD \mid_{\neg d_0}$, $\tilde{p} \to sD$.

As final rule we could use $l_h \to \lambda$, yet we can omit this rule and replace every appearance of l_h in all rules as described above by λ. □

7 P Systems with Target Selection

In P systems with target selection, all objects on the right-hand side of a rule must have the same target, and in each derivation step, for each region a (multi)set of rules – non-empty if possible – having the same target is chosen. In [4] it was shown that for P systems with target selection in the derivation mode *smax* **no** catalyst is needed any more, and with $smax_{rules}$, we even obtain a deterministic simulation of deterministic register machines.

Theorem 8. *For any register machine $M = (d, B, l_0, l_h, R)$, with $m \leq d$ being the number of decrementable registers, we can construct a P system with non-cooperative rules working in the set derivation mode smax and simulating the computations of M.*

Proof. As usual, we take an arbitrary register machine M with d registers satisfying the following conditions: the output registers are $m + 1, \cdots, d$, and they are never decremented; moreover, registers $1, \cdots, m$ are empty in any reachable halting configuration.

We now construct the following P system Π simulating M. The value of each register r is represented by the multiplicity of objects o_r in the skin.

The correct behavior of the objects associated with the simulated instruction of M is the following:

In the decrement case, we have in_{r+2}, *out*, in_2, idle, *out*, in_2, *here*, *out*, *here* (9 steps in total), whereas in the zero-test case, we have the same as before, except that the fourth and the fifth steps are *out* and *here* instead of idle and *out*, respectively.

In case of an increment instruction, we get *here*, *here*, *here*, *here*, in_2, *here*, *out*, *here* (8 steps in total). We remark that the first four steps are carried out in the skin, while the last four steps repeat the cases of zero-test and decrement.

For every decrementable register r, there is a rule sending o_r into region $r+2$. However, this rule may only be applied safely in the first step of the simulation of the SUB-instruction, as otherwise some other object will also enter the same region as $\#$ (either one of e, e', e'', $\hat{e}$, $\hat{e}'$, which in the following we will refer to as the *guards*, or an object associated to the label of the simulated instruction, which in the following we will call a *program symbol*) forcing an unproductive computation, see the rules in brackets in the tables below.

The "correct" target selection for the inner regions normally coincides with that of the program symbol (described above) and no rule is applied there if the program symbol is not there, with the following exceptions. In the first step of simulating an instruction, object e exits membrane 2, as it is the only rule applicable there in this step. In the last step of simulating an instruction, object $\bar{e}$ is rewritten into e in membrane 2, as it is the only rule applicable there in this step. In the fourth step of the decrement case, the program symbol is idle while object d is erased. The "correct" target selection for the skin coincides with that of the program symbol, and is *here* if the program symbol is missing in the skin.

Most trapping rules, given in brackets in the tables and listed in rule groups $R_{i,j,\#}$ below, are only needed to force the "correct" target selection. The exception are some rules in steps 4 and 5 of the simulation of SUB-instructions, needed for verifying that the decrement and the zero-test have been performed correctly (the guess is made at step 3 by the program symbol, and is reflected in its subscript). Indeed, the zero-test being chosen while d is present (signifying that the register has been decremented), causes a target conflict, and either p_0 or d in any case will be rewritten into $\#$. On the other hand, if the decrement is chosen while d is absent (signifying that the register has been zero), then p_- will appear in the skin in step 4 instead of step 5, causing a target conflict, and either p'_- or e'' in any case will be rewritten into $\#$.

$$\Pi = (O, \mu, w_1, \cdots, w_{m+2}, R_1, \cdots, R_{m+2}) \text{ where}$$

$$O = \{o_r \mid 1 \leq r \leq d\} \cup \{\bar{p}, p, p' \mid p \in B\} \cup \{p'', \hat{p}, \tilde{p} \mid p \in B_{ADD}\}$$
$$\cup \{p', p_-, p'_-, p_0, p'_0, p''_0 \mid p \in B_{SUB}\} \cup \{\bar{e}, e, e', e'', \hat{e}, \hat{e}', d, \#\},$$

$$\mu = [\,[\,]_2 \cdots [\,]_{m+2}]_1,$$

$$w_1 = l_0, \ w_2 = e, \ w_{r+2} = \lambda, \ 1 \leq r \leq m,$$

$$R_1 = \bigcup_{i=1}^{m+2} (R_{1,i,s} \cup R_{1,i,\#}),$$

$$R_i = R_{i,1,s} \cup R_{i,1,\#} \cup R_{i,i,s} \cup R_{i,i,\#}, \ 2 \leq j \leq m+2,$$

$$R_{1,1,s} = \{e \to e', e' \to e'', e'' \to \hat{e}, \hat{e} \to \hat{e}', \hat{e}' \to \lambda\}$$
$$\cup \{p'_0 \to p''_0 \mid p \in B_{SUB}\} \cup \{\bar{p} \to p \mid p \in B\}$$
$$\cup \{p \to \tilde{p}o_r \mid p : (ADD(r), q, s) \in P\}$$
$$\cup \{\tilde{p} \to p', p' \to p'', p'' \to \hat{p} \mid p \in B_{ADD}\},$$

$$R_{1,2,s} = \{p' \to (p_-, in_2), p' \to (p_0, in_2), p'_- \to (p'_-, in_2), p''_0 \to (p''_0, in_2)$$
$$\mid p \in B_{SUB}\} \cup \{\hat{p} \to (\hat{p}, in_2) \mid p \in B_{ADD}\} \cup \{d \to (d, in_2)\}$$

$$R_{1,r+2,s} = \{o_r \to (o_r, in_{r+2})\} \cup \{p \to (p, in_{r+2})$$
$$\mid p : (SUB(r), q, s) \in P\}, \ 1 \leq r \leq m,$$

$$R_{1,1,\#} = \{p' \to \#, p''_0 \to \#, p'_- \to \# \mid p \in B_{SUB}\}$$
$$\cup \{\hat{p} \to \# \mid p \in B_{ADD}\} \cup \{\# \to \#\},$$

$$R_{1,2,\#} = \{p'_0 \to (\#, in_2), e'' \to (\#, in_2) \mid p \in B_{SUB}\}$$
$$\cup \{\bar{p} \to (\#, in_2) \mid p \in B\},$$

$$R_{1,r+2,\#} = \{x \to (\#, in_{r+2}) \mid x \in \{e, e', e'', \hat{e}, \hat{e}'\}$$
$$\cup \{p_0, p''_0, p'_- \mid p \in B_{SUB}\} \cup \{\bar{p} \mid p \in B\}\}$$
$$\cup \{p \to (\#, in_{r+2}) \mid p : (SUB(i), q, s) \in P, \ i \neq r\}$$
$$\cup \{p' \to (\#, in_{r+2}) \mid p \in B_{SUB}\}, \ 1 \leq r \leq m,$$

$$R_{2,1,s} = \{e \to (e, out)\} \cup \{\bar{p} \to (\bar{p}, out) \mid p \in B\}$$
$$\cup \{p_0 \to (p'_0, out), p_- \to (p'_-, out) \mid p \in B_{SUB}\},$$

$$R_{2,2,s} = \{d \to \lambda, \bar{e} \to e\}$$
$$\cup \{p''_0 \to \bar{s}\bar{e}, p'_- \to \bar{q}\bar{e} \mid p : (SUB(r), q, s) \in P\}$$
$$\cup \{\hat{p} \to \bar{q}\bar{e}, \hat{p} \to \bar{s}\bar{e} \mid p : (ADD(r), q, s) \in P\},$$

$$R_{2,1,\#} = \{d \to (\#, out), \# \to (\#, out)\},$$

$$R_{2,2,\#} = \{p_0 \to \# \mid p \in B_{SUB}\} \cup \{\bar{p} \to \# \mid p \in B\},$$

$$R_{r+2,1,s} = \{p \to (p', out) \mid p \in B_{SUB}\} \cup \{o_r \to (d, out)\}, \ 1 \leq r \leq m,$$

$$R_{r+2,1,\#} = \{\# \to (\#, out)\}, \ R_{r+2,r+2,s} = R_{r+2,r+2,\#} = \emptyset, \ 1 \leq r \leq m.$$

Simulation of a SUB-instruction (p:(SUB(r),q,s))

$r+2$	1	2
- -	$o_r \to (o_r, in_{r+2})$ $p \to (p, in_{r+2})$ $[p \to (\#, in_{i+2}), i \neq r]$	$e \to (e, out)$
$p \to (p', out)$ $o_r \to (d, out)$	$e \to e'$ $[e \to (\#, in_{i+2})]$	-
-	$p' \to (p_-, in_2)$ $p' \to (p_0, in_2)$ $d \to (d, in_2)$ $[p' \to \#]$ $[p' \to (\#, in_{i+2})]$ $[e' \to (\#, in_{i+2})]$	-

$1,-$	$1,0$	$2,-$	$2,0$
$e' \to e''$		$d \to \lambda$ $[p_- \to (p'_-, out)]$	$p_0 \to (p'_0, out)$ $[d \to (\#, out)]$ $[p_0 \to \#]$
$e'' \to \hat{e}$ $[p'_- \to (p'_-, in_2)]$ $[p'_- \to \#]$ $[e'' \to (\#, in_t)]$ $[for\ t \geq 2]$	$p'_0 \to p''_0$ $e'' \to \hat{e}$ $[p'_0 \to (\#, in_t)]$ $[e'' \to (\#, in_t)]$ $[for\ t \geq 2]$	$p_- \to (p'_-, out)$	-
$p'_- \to (p'_-, in_2)$ $[p'_- \to \#]$ $[p'_- \to (\#, in_{i+2})]$	$p''_0 \to (p''_0, in_2)$ $[p''_0 \to \#]$ $[p''_0 \to (\#, in_{i+2})]$	-	
$\hat{e} \to \hat{e}'$ $[\hat{e} \to (\#, in_{i+2})]$		$p'_- \to \bar{q}\bar{e}$	$p''_0 \to \bar{s}\bar{e}$
$\hat{e}' \to \lambda$ $[\hat{e}' \to (\#, in_{i+2})]$		$\bar{q} \to (\bar{q}, out)$ $[\bar{q} \to \#]$	$\bar{s} \to (\bar{s}, out)$ $[\bar{s} \to \#]$
$\bar{q} \to q$ $[\bar{q} \to (\#, in_t)]$	$\bar{s} \to s$ $[\bar{s} \to (\#, in_t)]$	$\bar{e} \to e$	

Nearly half of the steps in the preceding constructions is needed for releasing the auxiliary symbol e in the first step of a simulation from membrane 2, yet in our construction, e and its derivatives are needed to control the correct target selection in the skin membrane, and especially to keep the register objects o_r from moving into membrane $r + 2$.

Auxiliary trap rules

$r+2$	1	2
$[\# \to (\#, out)]$	$[\# \to \#]$	$[\# \to (\#, out)]$

Simulation of an ADD-instruction $(p:(ADD(r),q,s))$

	1	2
1	$p \to \tilde{p}o_r$	$e \to (e, out)$
2	$\tilde{p} \to p'$	-
	$e \to e'$	
3	$p' \to p''$	-
	$e' \to e''$	
4	$p'' \to \hat{p}$	-
	$e'' \to \hat{e}$	
5	$\hat{p} \to (\hat{p}, in_2)$	-
	$[\hat{p} \to \#]$	
6	$\hat{e} \to \hat{e}'$	$\hat{p} \to \bar{x}\bar{e}, \ x \in \{q, s\}$
7	$\hat{e}' \to \lambda$	$\bar{x} \to (\bar{x}, out)$
		$[\bar{x} \to \#]$
8	$\bar{x} \to x$	$\bar{e} \to e$

Again we mention that any application of one of the rules given in brackets in the tables above leads to non-halting computations, not contributing to the result. □

We now show that taking the maximal sets of rules which are applicable, the simulation of SUB-instructions can even be carried out in a deterministic way.

Theorem 9. *For any register machine $M = (d, B, l_0, l_h, R)$, with $m \le d$ being the number of decrementable registers, we can construct a P system with non-cooperative rules*

$$\Pi = (O, \mu = [\ [\ ]_2 \dots [\ ]_{2m+1}\ ]_1, w_1, \lambda, \dots, \lambda, R_1 \dots R_{2m+1}, f = 1)$$

working in the derivation mode $smax_{rules}$ and simulating the computations of M such that

$$|R_1| \le 1 \times |ADD^1(R)| + 2 \times |ADD^2(R)| + 4 \times |SUB(R)| + 10 \times m + 3.$$

Proof. The contents of the registers r, $1 \le r \le d$, is represented by the numbers of objects o_r, and for the decrementable registers we also use a copy of the symbol o'_r for each copy of the object o_r. This second copy o'_r is needed during the simulation of SUB-instructions to allow for distinguishing between the decrement and the zero-test case. For each r, $1 \le r \le m$, the two objects o_r and o'_r can only be affected by the rules $o_r \to (\lambda, in_{r+1})$ and $o'_r \to (\lambda, in_{r+1})$ sending them into the membrane $r + 1$ corresponding to register r (and at the same time erasing them; in fact, we could also leave them in the membrane unaffected forever as a garbage). These are already two rules, so any other combination of rules with different targets has to contain at least three rules.

One of the main ideas of the proof construction is that in the skin membrane the label p of an ADD-instruction is represented by the three objects p and e, e', and the label p of any SUB-instruction is represented by the eight objects $p, e, e', e'', d_r, d'_r, \tilde{d}_r, \tilde{d}_r{}'$. Hence, for each $p \in (B \setminus \{l_h\})$ we define $R(p) = pee'$ for $p \in B_{ADD}$ and $R(p) = pee'e''d_r d'_r \tilde{d}_r \tilde{d}_r{}'$ for $p \in B_{SUB}$ as well as $R(l_h) = \lambda$; as initial multiset w_1 in the skin membrane, we take $R(l_0)$.

$$O = \{o_r \mid 1 \le r \le d\} \cup \{o'_r \mid 1 \le r \le m\} \cup (B \setminus \{l_h\})$$
$$\cup \left\{d_r, d'_r, \tilde{d}_r, \tilde{d}_r{}' \mid 1 \le r \le m\right\} \cup \{e, e', e''\}$$

An ADD-instruction $p : (ADD(r), q, s)$ is simulated by the rules $e \to \lambda$ and $e' \to \lambda$ as well as by the rules $p \to R(q)o_r$ and $p \to R(s)o_r$ for $m < r \le d$, and, in the case of the decrementable registers, for $1 \le r \le m$, by the rules $p \to R(q)o_r o'_r$ and $p \to R(s)o_r o'_r$. Any possible maximal combination of these rules yields a (multi)set of three rules and thus supersedes any combination of rules $o_r \to (\lambda, in_{r+1})$ and $o'_r \to (\lambda, in_{r+1})$, for some $1 \le r \le m$.

A SUB-instruction $p : (SUB(r), q, s)$ is simulated in two steps as follows:

1. In R_1, for the first step we take one of the following tuples of rules:
   $p \to (p, in_{r+1})$, $d_r \to (\lambda, in_{r+1})$, $d'_r \to (\lambda, in_{r+1})$, $\tilde{d}_r \to (\lambda, in_{r+1})$,
   $o_r \to (\lambda, in_{r+1})$, $o'_r \to (\lambda, in_{r+1})$;
   $p \to (p, in_{m+r+1})$, $d_r \to (\lambda, in_{m+r+1})$, $d'_r \to (\lambda, in_{m+r+1})$,
   $\tilde{d}_r \to (\lambda, in_{m+r+1})$, $\tilde{d}_r{}' \to (\lambda, in_{m+r+1})$;
   the application of the rules $o_r \to (\lambda, in_{r+1})$, $o'_r \to (\lambda, in_{r+1})$ in contrast to the application of the rule $\tilde{d}_r{}' \to (\lambda, in_{m+r+1})$ determines whether the first or the second tuple of rules has to be chosen. Here it becomes clear why we have to use the two register symbols o_r and o'_r, as we have to guarantee that the target $r + 1$ cannot be chosen if none of these symbols is present, as in this case then only four rules could be chosen in contrast to the five rules for the zero-test case. On the other hand, if some of these symbols o_r and o'_r are present, then six rules are applicable superseding the five rules which could be used for the zero-test case.

2. In the second step, the following three or four rules, again superseding any combination of rules $o_r \to (\lambda, in_{r+1})$ and $o'_r \to (\lambda, in_{r+1})$ for some $1 \le r \le m$, are used in the skin membrane:
   $e \to \lambda$, $e' \to \lambda$, $e'' \to \lambda$, and in the decrement case also the rule $\tilde{d}_r{}' \to \lambda$.
   In the second step, we either find the symbol p in membrane $r + 1$, if a symbol o_r together with its copy o'_r has been present for decrementing or in membrane $m + r + 1$, if no symbol o_r has been present (zero-test case).
   In the decrement case, the following rule is used in R_{r+1}: $p \to (R(q), out)$.
   In the zero-test case, the following rule is used in R_{m+r+1}: $p \to (R(s), out)$.

The simulation of the SUB-instructions works deterministically, hence, although the P system itself is not deterministic syntactically, it works in a deterministic way if the underlying register machine is deterministic. □

In contrast to the derivation mode $smax_{rules}$ where we take the maximal sets of rules which are applicable, in the $smax$-derivation mode we may have several non-extendable sets of rules which are applicable to the current configuration although being of different sizes, which has made that proof much more difficult than in the case of $smax_{rules}$.

8 Conclusion and Future Work

It is not very surprising that many of the computational completeness proofs elaborated in the literature for the derivation mode max also work for the set derivation mode $smax$ and usually even for the other (set) derivation modes max_{rules} and $smax_{rules}$ as well as for $max_{objects}$ and $smax_{objects}$, because many constructions just "break down" maximal parallelism to near sequentiality in order to work for the simulation of register machines. On the other hand, we also have shown that due to this fact some variants of P systems become even stronger with the modes $smax$ and $smax_{rules}$. A comprehensive overview of variants of P systems we have already investigated can be found in [4], many more variants wait for future research.

References

1. Alhazov, A., Freund, R.: P systems with toxic objects. In: Gheorghe, M., Rozenberg, G., Salomaa, A., Sosík, P., Zandron, C. (eds.) CMC 2014. LNCS, vol. 8961, pp. 99–125. Springer, Cham (2014). doi:10.1007/978-3-319-14370-5_7
2. Alhazov, A., Freund, R.: Small catalytic P systems. In: Dinneen, M.J. (ed.) Proceedings of the Workshop on Membrane Computing 2015 (WMC2015), (Satellite workshop of UCNC2015), CDMTCS Research Report Series, vol. CDMTCS-487, pp. 1–16. Centre for Discrete Mathematics and Theoretical Computer, Science Department of Computer Science, University of Auckland, Auckland, New Zealand (2015), August 2015
3. Alhazov, A., Freund, R., Heikenwälder, H., Oswald, M., Rogozhin, Y., Verlan, S.: Sequential P systems with regular control. In: Csuhaj-Varjú, E., Gheorghe, M., Rozenberg, G., Salomaa, A., Vaszil, G. (eds.) CMC 2012. LNCS, vol. 7762, pp. 112–127. Springer, Heidelberg (2013). doi:10.1007/978-3-642-36751-9_9
4. Alhazov, A., Freund, R., Verlan, S.: Computational completeness of P systems using maximal variants of the set derivation mode. In: Proceedings 14th Brainstorming Week on Membrane Computing, Sevilla, February 1–5, 2016 (2016)
5. Burkhard, H.: Ordered firing in Petri nets. Elektronische Informationsverarbeitung und Kybernetik **17**(2/3), 71–86 (1981)
6. Ciobanu, G., Marcus, S., Păun, G.: New strategies of using the rules of a P system in a maximal way. Power and Complexity. Rom. J. Inf. Sci. Technol. **12**(2), 21–37 (2009)
7. Dassow, J., Păun, G.: Regulated Rewriting in Formal Language Theory. EATCS Monographs in Theoretical Computer Science, vol. 18. Springer, Heidelberg (1989)
8. Freund, R., Păun, G.: How to obtain computational completeness in P systems with one catalyst. In: Neary, T., Cook, M. (eds.) Proceedings Machines, Computations and Universality 2013, MCU 2013, Zürich, Switzerland, September 9–11, 2013. EPTCS, vol. 128, pp. 47–61 (2013)

9. Freund, R., Verlan, S.: A formal framework for static (Tissue) P systems. In: Eleftherakis, G., Kefalas, P., Păun, G., Rozenberg, G., Salomaa, A. (eds.) WMC 2007. LNCS, vol. 4860, pp. 271–284. Springer, Heidelberg (2007). doi:10.1007/978-3-540-77312-2_17

10. Frisco, P., Govan, G.: P systems with active membranes operating under minimal parallelism. In: Gheorghe, M., Păun, G., Rozenberg, G., Salomaa, A., Verlan, S. (eds.) CMC 2011. LNCS, vol. 7184, pp. 165–181. Springer, Heidelberg (2012). doi:10.1007/978-3-642-28024-5_12

11. Krithivasan, K., Păun, Gh., Ramanujan, A.: On controlled P systems. In: Valencia-Cabrera, L., García-Quismondo, M., Macías-Ramos, L., Martínez-del-Amor, M., Păun, Gh., Riscos-Núñez, A. (eds.) Proceedings 11th Brainstorming Week on Membrane Computing, Sevilla, February 4–8, 2013, pp. 137–151. Fénix Editora, Sevilla (2013)

12. Minsky, M.L.: Computation: Finite and Infinite Machines. Prentice Hall, Englewood Cliffs (1967)

13. Pan, L., Păun, G., Song, B.: Flat maximal parallelism in P systems with promoters. Theoret. Comput. Sci. **623**, 83–91 (2016)

14. Păun, G., Rozenberg, G., Salomaa, A. (eds.): The Oxford Handbook of Membrane Computing. Oxford University Press, New York (2010)

15. Rozenberg, G., Salomaa, A. (eds.): Handbook of Formal Languages, vol. 1–3. Springer, Heidelberg (1997)

16. Sburlan, D.: Further results on P systems with promoters/inhibitors. Int. J. Found. Comput. Sci. **17**(1), 205–221 (2006)

17. Sosík, P., Langer, M.: Small (purely) catalytic P systems simulating register machines. Theoret. Comput. Sci. **623**, 65–74 (2015)

18. The P Systems Website: http://ppage.psystems.eu, http://ppage.psystems.eu

19. Verlan, S., Quiros, J.: Fast hardware implementations of P systems. In: Csuhaj-Varjú, E., Gheorghe, M., Rozenberg, G., Salomaa, A., Vaszil, G. (eds.) CMC 2012. LNCS, vol. 7762, pp. 404–423. Springer, Heidelberg (2013). doi:10.1007/978-3-642-36751-9_27

Computational Power of Protein Networks

Bogdan Aman$^{(\boxtimes)}$ and Gabriel Ciobanu

Romanian Academy, Institute of Computer Science,
Blvd. Carol I no. 8, 700505 Iaşi, Romania
`bogdan.aman@gmail.com`, `gabriel@info.uaic.ro`

Abstract. Cell biology provides useful ideas to computer scientists in order to construct models which can provide more efficient computations. In this paper we prove that an abstract model of protein-protein interaction derived from membrane computing has the same computational power as a Turing machine by using a rather small number of proteins having at most length two, where length is an abstract measure of complexity.

1 Introduction

Biological cells are complex systems composed of many components which are themselves components in a large system of organs. The processes inside a cell are integrated through a complex protein-protein network. It is widely known the importance of proteins as active agents and targets in cellular biology. Membrane proteins play critical roles in many biological and pathological processes, and constitute the majority of all drug targets. During the last years, several studies were devoted to protein-protein interaction networks and their role in new therapeutic methods for numerous diseases.

Membrane proteins are often arranged in large complexes and are important for many biological functions. For example, signals from the exterior of a cell are mediated to the inside of that cell by protein-protein interactions of the signalling molecules. Proteins might interact to form part of a protein complex, a protein may be transporting another protein, or a protein may interact briefly with another protein just to modify it. Such a (conformation) modification of proteins can itself change protein-protein interactions. Most of the reactions taking place in a cell are in fact controlled by proteins bound on cell membrane. These proteins can be of two types: peripheral proteins (placed on the internal or external side of a membrane), and integral proteins (have parts on both internal and external sides of a membrane). Freely floating molecules interact with the proteins bounded on membranes, and can be activated, manipulated, and pushed across the cell membranes. According to [1], proteins constitute about 50% of the mass of most animal cell membranes. The increasing complexity of protein-protein interactions has driven the selection of longer proteins by the addition of functional motifs. This increasing is an important evolutionary strategy for achieving complex systems. In order to cope with the increased complexity of

© Springer International Publishing AG 2017
A. Leporati et al. (Eds.): CMC 2016, LNCS 10105, pp. 103–118, 2017.
DOI: 10.1007/978-3-319-54072-6_7

protein-protein interactions that arise within complex systems, protein lengths are correlated with systems size [22].

The living cells provide useful ideas to theoretical computer scientists in order to define models which can provide more efficient computations, models which can be used by biologists. It is not about simply applying computer science to biology, but by a systemic approach of the biological phenomena in terms of computational inspiration in which the processing of information is essential [16]. "Life is computation. Every single cell reads information from a memory, rewrites it, receives data input (information about the state of its environment), processes the data and acts according to the results of all this computation. Globally, the zillions of cells populating the biosphere certainly perform more computation steps per unit of time than all man made computers put together" [15].

Membrane systems [20] represent such a class of computing devices inspired by living cells which are complex hierarchical membrane structures with a flow of materials and information which underlies their functioning, involving parallel application of rules, communication between membranes and membrane dissolution. The structure of the cell is represented by a set of hierarchically embedded regions, each delimited by a surrounding boundary (called membrane), and all contained inside a so called "skin membrane". A membrane without any other membrane inside is said to be elementary, while a membrane with other membranes inside is said to be non-elementary. Multisets of objects are distributed inside these regions, and they can be modified or communicated between adjacent compartments. Objects represent the formal counterpart of molecular species (ions, proteins, etc.) floating inside cellular compartments, and multisets of objects are described by means of strings over a given alphabet. Evolution rules represent the formal counterpart of chemical reactions, and are given in the form of rewriting rules which operate on the objects, as well as on the structure by membrane influx, membrane efflux and elementary division.

A *computation* in membrane systems starts from an initial structure and the system evolves by applying the rules in a nondeterministic and maximally parallel manner. The maximally parallel way of using the rules means that in each step we apply a maximal multiset of rules such that no further rule can be added to the multiset being applicable. A rule is applicable when all the objects that appear on its left-hand side are available in the region where the rule is placed (the objects are not used by other rules applied in the same step). Due to the competition for available objects, some rules are applied nondeterministically. A halting configuration is reached when no rule can be applied anymore; the result is then given by the number of objects (in a specified region or in the entire system as done in this paper).

There are various models of computation (e.g., Turing machines) providing different interpretations for the notion of algorithm. Turing computable functions are the formalized analogue of the intuitive notion of algorithm. By considering an abstract measure of complexity that we call length, we prove that protein interaction networks using proteins of small lengths and acting according to various biological inspired operations can simulate all computable functions.

2   Protein-Protein Interaction Systems

The study of many complex biological systems has reached a stage where much is known about the molecular components and their functional capacity and interactions. A real challenge is how to integrate this wealth of information to explain complex behaviours at various system levels [14]; cell polarity represents one such example. Functional analysis of the proteins involved have uncovered several subfunctions in the establishment and maintenance of cell polarity, including GTPase signalling, exocytic deposition of membrane components and cell wall materials, and endocytic recycling.

After presenting some technical notions, we define the protein-protein interaction systems. Their rules are applicable whenever there is a agreement between membranes expressed by appropriate proteins, or protein complexes represented by bonds between proteins, and co-proteins, or co-protein complexes, on their surfaces. Let $\mathbb{N}$ be the set of non-negative integers, and consider a finite alphabet V of proteins. A multiset over V is a mapping $u : V \rightarrow \mathbb{N}$. The empty multiset is represented by ε. We use the string representation of multisets that is widely used in the membrane protein systems; when a multiset is represented by a string u, it means that every permutation of this string is allowed as a representation of the multiset. An example of such a representation is $u = aabaca$, where $u(a) = 4$, $u(b) = 1$, $u(c) = 1$. Using such a representation, the operations over multisets are defined as operations over strings. Given two multisets u, v over V, for any $a \in V$, we have $(u \uplus v)(a) = u(a) + v(a)$ as the multiset union, and $(u \backslash v)(a) = max\{0, u(a) - v(a)\}$ as the multiset difference.

Consider an alphabet $V = \{a_i, \overline{a_i} \mid 1 \leq i \leq n\}$ in which if a denotes a protein, then $\overline{a}$ denotes the corresponding co-protein. We denote by V^* the set of all strings over V. V^* is a monoid with ε as its unit element (as strings are used to denote multisets), and $V^+ = V^* \backslash \{\varepsilon\}$. For a string $u \in V^*$, $|u|$ denotes the number of occurrences of symbols from V in the string u. By $V^\sim = \{a_1 \sim \ldots \sim a_n \mid a_1, \ldots, a_n \in V, n \geq 1\}$ we denote protein complexes, where proteins in protein complexes of length greater than two are bonded. We use $\overline{a_1 \sim \ldots \sim a_n}$ as a shorthand notation for $\overline{a_1} \sim \ldots \sim \overline{a_n}$.

Protein-protein interaction systems represent a rule-based formalism involving parallelism and mobility introduced in order to model more specific biological systems [6,7]. The biologically inspired rules taken from the immune system [18] and describing the mobility of membrane proteins inside the structure are: pinocytosis (engulfing zero external membranes), phagocytosis (engulfing just one external membrane), and exocytosis (expelling the content of a membrane outside the membrane where it is placed). Pinocytosis and phagocytosis represent different types of endocytosis. In these rules membranes agree on their movement by using complementary objects a and $\overline{a}$. Biologically speaking, the objects a and their corresponding co-objects $\overline{a}$ fit properly.

Definition 1. *A protein-protein interaction system with n membranes is a tuple*

$$\Pi = (V, \mu, u_1, \ldots, u_n, v_1, \ldots, v_n, R),$$

where

1. V is a finite (non-empty) alphabet of proteins;
2. μ is a membrane hierarchical structure (i.e., a rooted tree) with $n \geq 2$ membranes; the membranes are bijectively mapped to $\{1, \ldots, n\}$;
3. $u_1, \ldots, u_n$ are finite multisets of proteins (represented by strings over V) bounded to the n membranes at the beginning of the evolution;
4. $v_1, \ldots, v_n$ are finite multisets of proteins (represented by strings over V) placed inside the n membranes at the beginning of the evolution;
5. R is a finite set of rules of the following forms:
   - $[a]_b \rightarrow [\ ]_{a \sim b}$, for $a \in V$, $b \in V^\sim$ (bondin)
   - $[\ ]_b a \rightarrow [\ ]_{b \sim a}$, for $a \in V$, $b \in V^\sim$ (bondout)
   - $u[v]_{a\,\bar{a}} \rightarrow [[u']_c v']_d$, for $a, \bar{a} \in V^\sim, u, v, u', v' \in V^*, c, d \in (V^\sim)^*$ (pino)
   - $[[u]_a v]_{\bar{a}} \rightarrow u'[v']_{c\,d}$, for $a, \bar{a} \in V^\sim, u, v, u', v' \in V^*, c, d \in (V^\sim)^*$ (exo)
   - $[u]_a [v]_{\bar{a}} \rightarrow [[[u']_c]_d v']_b,$ (phago)
     $\qquad$ for $a, \bar{a} \in V^\sim, u, v, u', v' \in V^*, c, d, b \in (V^\sim)^*$

In rule (bondin), a bond is created between the protein labelled by a placed inside a membrane and the protein labelled by b placed on the membrane, while in rule (bondout), a bond is created between the protein labelled by a placed outside a membrane and the protein labelled by b placed on the membrane. The newly created protein complex has the length equal with the sum of lengths of a and b, and is able to interact with other protein complexes.

In rule (pino), a protein complex labelled by a together with a complementary protein complex labelled by $\bar{a}$ model the creation of an empty membrane within the membrane on which a and $\bar{a}$ proteins are attached. The connection between these proteins (a and $\bar{a}$) is activated by the presence of the multisets of proteins u and v. We should imagine that the original membrane protein receptor buckles towards the inside, and pinches off by breaking the connection between a and $\bar{a}$. The multiset of proteins u' inside the new created membrane is transferred from outside the initial membrane. The proteins a and $\bar{a}$, as well as the multisets u and v, can be modified during this step to the multisets c, d, u' and v', respectively. On the surface of the membrane appearing in the left hand side of the rule there are some proteins (others than $a\bar{a}$) which are ignored; these proteins are also not specified on the right hand side of the rule, being randomly distributed between the two resulting membranes. Graphically, this rule can be depicted as follows:

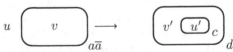

In rule (exo), a protein complex labelled by a together with a complementary protein complex labelled by $\bar{a}$ model the merging of a nested membrane with its surrounding membrane. The connection between these proteins (a and $\bar{a}$) is activated by the presence of the multisets of proteins u and v. We should imagine that the connection between a and $\bar{a}$ represent the point where the membranes connect each other. In this merging process (which is a smooth and continuous process), the membrane having the protein a on its surface gets expelled to the outside, and all proteins placed on the surface of the two membranes are united into a multiset on the membrane which initially contained $\bar{a}$. The proteins a and $\bar{a}$, as well as the multisets u and v, can be modified during this step to the multisets c, d, u' and v', respectively. If the membrane protein receptor having on its surface the protein a is non-elementary, then its content is released near the newly merged membrane after applying the rule. On the surface of the membranes appearing in the left hand side of the rule there are some proteins (others than a and $\bar{a}$) which are ignored; these proteins are also not specified on the right hand side of the rule, being moved by default on the resulting membrane. Graphically, this process can be depicted as follows:

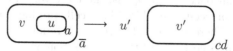

In rule (phago), a protein complex labelled by a together with its complementary protein complex labelled by $\bar{a}$ model a membrane (the one with $\bar{a}$ on its surface) "eating" an elementary membrane (the one with a on its surface). The connection between these proteins (a and $\bar{a}$) is activated by the presence of the multisets of proteins u and v. The membrane having $\bar{a}$ on its surface wraps around the membrane having a on its surface. An additional membrane is created around the eaten membrane; the proteins a and $\bar{a}$, as well as the multisets u and v, can be modified during this step to the multisets b, c, d, u' and v', respectively (the multiset c corresponds to a and remains on the eaten membrane, while the multisets b and d correspond to $\bar{a}$ and are placed on the new created membrane and the surrounding one). On the surface of the membranes appearing in the left hand side of the rule there are some proteins (others than a and $\bar{a}$) which are ignored, and these proteins are also not specified on the right hand side of the rule. The proteins appearing on the membrane having initially the protein a on surface remain unchanged, while the proteins appearing on the membrane having initially the protein $\bar{a}$ on surface are randomly distributed between the two resulting membranes (the ones with d and b). Graphically, this process can be depicted as follows:

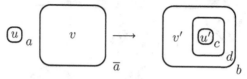

Starting from an initial configuration of the newly defined protein-protein interaction system (given by the initial membrane structure and multisets of proteins), the evolution takes place by applying the rules activated by protein-protein interactions. A rule is applicable when all the involved proteins and membranes appearing in its left hand side are available. In each step a membrane can be used in at most one rule (pino), (exo) or (phago). In this way the evolution is parallel at the level of membranes. A halting configuration is reached when no rule is applicable. The result of a halting evolution consists of all the vectors describing the multiplicity of proteins inside and on all the membranes (a non-halting evolution provides no output).

3   Protein-Protein Interactions of the Immune System

The immune system is described well in [18], a book which is revised every few years to keep the pace with the new discoveries in this field. The cells of the immune system work together with different proteins to seek out and destroy anything dangerous which enters our body. It takes some time for the immune cell to be activated, but once this happens, there are very few hostile organisms having a chance. Immune cells are white blood cells produced in huge quantities in the bone marrow. There are a wide variety of immune cells, each of them with its own utility and selectivity of the antigen. Some seek out and engulf the invaders, while other destroy the infected or mutated body cells. Another type of cells, namely the B cells, following the binding to the antigen, have the ability to release special proteins called antibodies which mark intruders in order to be destroyed by macrophages. The immune system has also the ability to produce antibodies able to remember enemies which it fought in the past. In this way, once the immune system recognizes an invader, it attacks more quickly and strongly against it. Based on certain previous articles [3,11], we illustrate here how the protein interaction networks work against infections. The description presented in [3] is based on the theoretical approach presented in [4,5,12].

Dendritic cells can engulf bacteria, viruses and other cells. Once a dendritic cells engulfs a bacterium, it dissolves this bacterium and places portions of bacterium proteins on its surface. These surface markers serve as an alarm to other immune cells, namely helper T cells, which then infer the form of the invader. This mechanism makes sensitive the T cells to recognize the antigens or other foreign agents which triggers a reaction from the immune system. Antigens are often found on the surface of bacterium and viruses.

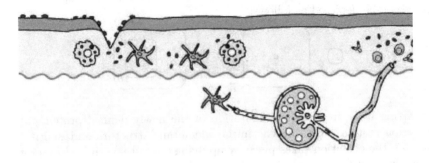

Fig. 1. Protection against infection [6]

In order to simulate the evolution presented in Fig. 1, we need first to encode all the component of the immune system into our model. This can be realized by associating a membrane to each component, and some objects to the signals, states and parts of molecules. For the steps done by the dendritic cells presented in Fig. 1, we use the following encodings:

- dendritic cell: $[eat]_{\overline{a_1}\,\overline{a_2}\,\overline{a_3}\,l}$
  An immature dendritic cell is willing to eat any bacterium it encounters, so we translate it into a membrane which has inside an object eat used to engulf the bacterium and some proteins bounded to the membrane $\overline{a_1}$, $\overline{a_2}$, $\overline{a_3}$ (these are used to recognize viruses) and l (used to enter the lymph node). Once the dendritic cell matures, the object eat is consumed.
- bacterium cell: $[antigen]_{a_1}$
  A bacterium cell contains antigen so we simply represent it as a membrane containing a single object $antigen$ which contains the information of the bacterium and a protein a_1.
- lymph node: $[\ ]_{\overline{l}}$
  The lymph node is the place where the mature dendritic cells migrate in order to start the immune response, so we translate it into a membrane that has bounded a protein $\overline{l}$.

Using the above encodings, we can describe the whole system as follows:

$$[eat]_{\overline{a_1}\,\overline{a_2}\,\overline{a_3}\,l}[\ ]_{\overline{l}}[antigen]_{a_1},$$

together with the following rules describing its evolution:

* $[eat]_{\overline{a_1}}[antigen]_{a_1} \rightarrow [eat[[antigen]_{a_1}]_{\overline{a_1}}]_{\overline{a_1}}$
  Once an immature dendritic cell becomes sibling to a bacterium, it "eats" the bacterium by performing a phagocytosis rule. Until this moment the bacterium has controlled its own movement; in this step of the evolution the movement becomes controlled by the dendritic cell which eats the bacterium.
* $[[antigen]_{a_1}]_{\overline{a_1}} \rightarrow antigen[\ ]_{a_1}$
  Once the bacterium has entered the dendritic cell, the content of the bacterium is released into the dendritic cell.
* $[[\ ]_{a_1}]_{\overline{a_1}} \rightarrow [\ ]_{a_1}$
  The remaining parts of the membrane used to engulf the bacterium is joined with the membrane of the dendritic cell by a exocytosis rule.
* $[antigen]_l[\ ]_{\overline{l}} \rightarrow [[[antigen]_{l'}]_{\overline{l'}\sim antigen}]_{\overline{l}}$
  Once the dendritic cell contains parts of antigen, it enters the lymph node in order to activate a special class of T cells, namely the helper T cells.
* $[antigen]_{l'} \rightarrow [\ ]_{l'\sim antigen}$
  Once the dendritic cell enters the lymph node it displays on its surface the antigen of the bacterium in order to be able to interact with T cells.
* $[[eat]_{l'\sim antigen}]_{\overline{l'\sim antigen}} \rightarrow [\ ]_{l'\sim antigen}$
  Once the dendritic cell enters the lymph node it matures and the capacity to engulf bacteria disappear, namely the eat object is consumed.

Using only these rules, we can simulate the way a bacterium is engulfed and its content is displayed by the eater cell. The proteins produced by helper T cells activate the B cells. Using the proteins produced by helper T cells, the B cell starts to divide and produce clones of itself. During this process, two new cell types are created: plasma cells which produce an antibody, and memory cells which are used to "remember" specific intruders.

This example motivates the introduction of the new class of membranes; more exactly, it motivates the new rules and the way they can be used in modelling some biological systems.

4   Computational Power of Interaction Networks

Formal languages and automata theory [21] are usually used to introduce abstract computing devices and investigating their computational power. Turing machines represent a classical model of computation. Actually, a Turing machine is a mathematical model that mechanically operates 0 and 1 symbols on an infinite tape according to a table of three simple operations: go left, go right, change symbol. Despite its simplicity, a Turing machine can simulate the logic of any computer algorithm. According to Church-Turing thesis, computable functions are exactly the functions that can be calculated using a Turing machine [23].

In this section we prove that protein-protein interaction networks can simulate all the computable functions by using a rather small number of components, small proteins (having at most length two, meaning actually two components) and operations inspired by membrane influx (pino, phago) and efflux (exo). The rules (pino) and (phago) are used to increase the number of membranes, while rule (exo) is used to decrease the number of membranes. Thus, we combine the rules (pino) and (phago) with (exo) just to balance the number of membranes. The result of a halting evolution consists of all the vectors describing the multiplicity of proteins inside and on all the membranes (a non-halting evolution provides no output).

In what follows, we study the computational power of the pair (pino, exo) of operations and prove its universality by using at most three membranes, while the lengths of the membrane proteins in both (pino) and (exo) operations are at most two. The number of three membranes represents the minimum number with respect to the movement rules provided in our approach. In order to prove this result, we construct a protein-protein interaction system with three nodes (membranes) able to simulate any function computed by a Turing machine (i.e., computable functions). This computational power supports the possibility of protein-protein interaction networks to describe algorithmically any normal and abnormal biological evolution.

The basic results used for proving the computational power are described in [17], where it was shown that any Turing machine can be simulated by a register machine with only two registers. The actions of such register machines can easily be simulated by matrix grammars with appearance checking [13]. We define the notions used in what follows. A *matrix grammar with appearance* *checking* is a construct $G = (N, T, S, M, F)$ where N, T are disjoint alphabets of non-terminals and terminals, $S \in N$ is the axiom, M is a finite set of matrices of the form $mat = (A_1 \rightarrow x_1, \ldots, A_n \rightarrow x_n)$, $A_i \in N$, $x_i \in (N \cup T)^*$, $1 \leq i \leq n$, of context-free rules, and F is a set of occurrences of rules in M. For $w, z \in (N \cup T)^*$, we write $w \Rightarrow_{mat} z$ whenever (i) there is a matrix in M whose rules can be applied in order to obtain z from w, or whenever (ii) the j-th rule r_j of a matrix in M is not applicable to w_j ($w \Rightarrow_{mat} w_j$ in j steps) and $r_j \in F$, in which case r_j can be skipped obtaining $w_{j+1} = w_j$. The language generated by G is $L(G) = \{x \in T^* \mid S \Rightarrow^*_{mat} x\}$, where by $\Rightarrow^*_{mat}$ we denote the reflexive and transitive closure of the binary relation $\Rightarrow_{mat}$. A *matrix grammar in the strong binary normal form* is a construct $G = (N, T, S, M, F)$, where $N = N_1 \cup N_2 \cup \{S, \#\}$ with these three sets mutually disjoint, two distinguished symbols $B^{(1)}, B^{(2)} \in N_2$, and the matrices in M are of one of the following forms:

(type-1) $(S \rightarrow XA)$ with $X \in N_1, A \in N_2$;

(type-2) $(X \rightarrow Y, A \rightarrow x)$ with $X, Y \in N_1$, $A \in N_2$, $x \in (N_2 \cup T)^*$, $|x| \leq 2$;

(type-3) $(X \rightarrow Y, B^{(j)} \rightarrow \#)$ with $X, Y \in N_1$ and
$B^{(j)} \rightarrow \# \in F$ for $j = 1, 2$;

(type-4) $(X \rightarrow \varepsilon, A \rightarrow x)$ with $X \in N_1, A \in N_2, x \in T^*, |x| \leq 2$

If we do not use the empty string ε, then the rules of type (4) can be considered of the form $(X \rightarrow a, A \rightarrow x)$, with $X \in N_1, a \in T, A \in N_2, x \in T^*$, $|x| \leq 2$.

Other notions and notations used here can be found in [21].

Theorem 1. *A protein-protein interaction system with three membranes, proteins of length two and using rules of types* (bondin), (bondout), (pino) *and* (exo) *has the same computational power as a Turing machine, i.e., are able to describe algorithmically any normal and abnormal biological evolution.*

Proof. We simulate a matrix grammar with appearance checking $G = (N, T, S, M, F)$ in the strong binary normal form. We construct a protein-protein interaction system Π with three membranes,

$$\Pi = (V, [\,[\,[\,]_2]_3]_1, \varepsilon, X, \overline{X}, \varepsilon, A, \overline{A}, R).$$

able to simulate a matrix grammar with appearance checking in the strong binary normal form. The symbols X, A correspond to the symbols of the initial type-1 matrix $(S \rightarrow XA)$ with $X \in N_1, A \in N_2$. Let there be n_1 matrices of type-2 and type-4 labelled $1, \ldots, n_1$ and n_2 matrices of type-3 labelled $n_1 + 1, \ldots, n_1 + n_2$.

The finite alphabet V of proteins is defined as follows:

$$V = \{\beta, \overline{\beta}, x, x', A, \overline{A}, Y, \overline{Y}, a\} \cup \{B^{(j)}, \alpha_j, \overline{\alpha_j}, \alpha'_j, \overline{\alpha'_j} \mid 1 \leq j \leq 2\}$$
$$\cup \{X, \overline{X}, X_l, \overline{X_l}, X'_l, \overline{X'_l}, X''_l, \overline{X''_l}, X_l^{(j)}, \overline{X_l^{(j)}} \mid$$
$$X \in N_1, 1 \leq l \leq n_1 + n_2, 1 \leq j \leq 2\}.$$

The set R of rules is constructed as follows:

(i) For each type-2 matrix $m_l : (X \rightarrow Y, A \rightarrow x)$ with $1 \leq l \leq n_1, X, Y \in N_1$, $A \in N_2, x \in (N_2 \cup T)^*$ and $|x| \leq 2$ we consider the rules:

1. $[A]_X \to [\ ]_{A \sim X}$
   $[\overline{A}]_{\overline{X}} \to [\ ]_{\overline{A} \sim \overline{X}}$
2. $[\ [\ ]_{A \sim X}]_{\overline{A} \sim \overline{X}} \to A[\overline{A}]_{X_l \overline{X_l}}$
3. $[\ ]_{X_l} A \to [\ ]_{X_l \sim A}$
   $[\overline{A}]_{\overline{X_l}} \to [\ ]_{\overline{A} \sim \overline{X_l}}$
4. $[\ ]_{\overline{A} \sim \overline{X_l} A \sim X_l} \to [\ [\ ]_{X_l}]_{\overline{X_l}}$, if $x = \varepsilon$
   $[\ ]_{\overline{A} \sim \overline{X_l} A \sim X_l} \to [\ [x]_{X_l}]_{\overline{X_l}}$, if $x \in T^*$
   $[\ ]_{\overline{A} \sim \overline{X_l} A \sim X_l} \to [\ [x']_{X_l}]_{\overline{X_l}}$, otherwise
   (If $m_l : (X \to Y, A \to \alpha_1 \alpha_2), \alpha_1 \in N_2, \alpha_2 \in T \cup \{\varepsilon\}$ then $x' = \alpha'_1 \alpha_2$,
   and if $m_l : (X \to Y, A \to \alpha_1 \alpha_2), \alpha_1, \alpha_2 \in N_2$ then $x' = \alpha'_1 \alpha'_2$)
5. $[\ [\ ]_{X_l}]_{\overline{X_l}} \to [\ ]_{X'_l \overline{X'_l}}$
6. $\alpha'_1 [\ ]_{X'_l \overline{X'_l}} \to [\ [\alpha'_1]_{X'_l} \overline{\alpha'_1}]_{\overline{X'_l}}$
7. $[\ ]_{X'_l} \alpha'_1 \to [\ ]_{X'_l \sim \alpha'_1}$
   $[\overline{\alpha'_1}]_{\overline{X'_l}} \to [\ ]_{\overline{\alpha'_1} \sim \overline{X'_l}}$
8. $[\ ]_{\overline{\alpha'_1} \sim \overline{X'_l} X'_l \sim \alpha'_1} \to [\ [\alpha_1]_{X'_l} \overline{\alpha_1}]_{\overline{X'_l}}$
9. $[\ [\ ]_{X'_l}]_{\overline{X'_l}} \to [\ ]_{X''_l \overline{X''_l}}$
10. $\alpha'_2 [\ ]_{X''_l \overline{X''_l}} \to [\ [\alpha'_2]_{X''_l} \overline{\alpha'_2}]_{\overline{X''_l}}$
11. $[\ ]_{X''_l} \alpha'_2 \to [\ ]_{X''_l \sim \alpha'_2}$
    $[\overline{\alpha'_2}]_{\overline{X''_l}} \to [\ ]_{\overline{\alpha'_2} \sim \overline{X''_l}}$
12. $[\ ]_{\overline{\alpha'_2} \sim \overline{X''_l} X''_l \sim \alpha'_2} \to [\ [\alpha_2]_{X'_l} \overline{\alpha_2}]_{\overline{X'_l}}$
13. $[\ ]_{X''_l \overline{X''_l}} \to [\ [\ ]_Y]_{\overline{Y}}$
14. $[\ ]_{X'_l \overline{X'_l}} \to [\ [\ ]_Y]_{\overline{Y}}$
15. $[\ [\ ]_x]_{\overline{X}} \to [\ ]_{\beta \overline{\beta}}$ (X does not correspond to a nonterminal matrix)
16. $[\ ]_{\beta \overline{\beta}} \to [\ [\ ]_\beta]_{\overline{\beta}}$
17. $[\ [\ ]_\beta]_{\overline{\beta}} \to [\ ]_{\beta \overline{\beta}}$

The simulation of a type-2 matrix can be done as follows:

- Whenever there exist proteins A, X, $\overline{A}$ and $\overline{X}$, by using two rules 1 applied in parallel, two protein complexes $A \sim X$ and $\overline{A} \sim \overline{X}$ are created. These protein complexes are able to interact, and by using rule 2, the proteins A and $\overline{A}$ break their bonds, while X and $\overline{X}$ are replaced by X_l and $\overline{X_l}$, marking the beginning of the simulation. Using two rules 3 in parallel, two new protein complexes $A \sim X_l$ and $\overline{A} \sim \overline{X_l}$ are created. This is followed by rule 4, where A and $\overline{A}$ break their bonds, and are replaced by either x (if $x \in T^*$) or x' (if $x \notin T^*$ and $x \neq \varepsilon$). Also by rule 4, the elements X_l and $\overline{X_l}$ are distributed between the two obtained membranes. Then, by applying rule 5, X_l and $\overline{X_l}$ are replaced by X'_l and $\overline{X'_l}$ to prevent replacing A's anymore. One of the following evolutions is possible:
  - * Whenever there exists a protein α'_1, rule 6 is applied to introduce the corresponding protein $\overline{\alpha'_1}$. Rules 7 and 8 use protein complexes, and replace the proteins α'_1 and $\overline{\alpha'_1}$ by the proteins α_1 and $\overline{\alpha_1}$. Rule 9 is used to reach a configuration in which one of the following rule can be applied:

· rule 10 if there exists the protein α_2', in order to introduce the corresponding protein $\overline{\alpha_2'}$; rules 11 and 12 use protein complexes, and replace the proteins α_2' and $\overline{\alpha_2'}$ by the proteins α_2 and $\overline{\alpha_2}$;

· if it does not exist a protein α_2', rule 13 is used to replace X_l'' and $\overline{X_l''}$ by Y and $\overline{Y}$, respectively.

* Whenever it does not exist proteins α_1' and α_2', then rule 14 is applied to replace X_l' and $\overline{X_l'}$ by Y and $\overline{Y}$, respectively.

Rules 13 and 14 end a successfully simulation of a type-2 matrix, and return to the initial membrane structure. The proteins $\overline{\alpha_1}$ and $\overline{\alpha_2}$ are introduced in order to be able to use the corresponding proteins $\overline{\alpha_1}$ and $\overline{\alpha_2}$ when simulating other matrices.

- If the symbol $A \in N_2$ is not present (i.e., we cannot apply rule 1), then rule 15 introduces two symbols β and $\overline{\beta}$ which lead to an infinite evolution (by using rules 16 and 17).

(ii) For each type-3 matrix $m_l' : (X \to Y, B^{(j)} \to \#)$, $X, Y \in N_1$ and $B^{(j)} \to \# \in F$, where $n_1 + 1 \leq l \leq n_1 + n_2$, $l \in lab_j$, $j = 1, 2$, we consider the rules:

18. $[\,[\,]x]_{\overline{X}} \to [\,]_{X_l^{(j)}\overline{X_l^{(j)}}}$

19. $[B^{(j)}]_{X_l^{(j)}\overline{X_l^{(j)}}} \to [\,[\,]_\beta B^{(j)}]_{\overline{\beta}}$

20. $[\,]_{X_l^{(j)}\overline{X_l^{(j)}}} \to [\,[\,]Y]_{\overline{Y}}$

Rule 18 starts the simulation of a type-3 matrix by replacing X and $\overline{X}$ with $X_l^{(j)}$ and $\overline{X_l^{(j)}}$, and thereby remembering the index l of the matrix and the index j of the possibly present symbol $B^{(j)}$. This is followed by rule 19 that checks if the symbol $B^{(j)} \in N_2$ is present. If this is the case, $X_l^{(j)}$ and $\overline{X_l^{(j)}}$ are replaced by β and $\overline{\beta}$ which lead to an infinite evolution (by using rules 16 and 17). Regardless the presence of $B^{(j)}$, rule 20 is applied replacing $X_l^{(j)}$ and $\overline{X^{(j)}}$ by Y and $\overline{Y}$, thus successfully simulating a type-3 matrix, and returning to the initial membrane structure.

(iii) For a terminal type-4 matrix $m_l : (X \to a, A \to x)$ with $1 \leq l \leq n_1$, $X \in N_1$, $a \in T$, $A \in N_2$, $x \in T^*$ and $|x| \leq 2$, we consider the rules

21. $[\,]_{X_l\overline{X_l}} \to [\,[a]]$

22. $[\,]_{X_l''\overline{X_l''}} \to [\,[a]]$

We do not involve the protein $\overline{a}$, because $a \in T$. By replacing rule 14 with rule 21, and rule 13 by rule 22 in the sequence 1–17, a terminal type-4 matrix is faithfully simulated. The result of the simulation consists of the vector describing the multiplicity of proteins inside and on all the membranes.

We also investigate the computational power of the pair (phago, exo) of operations and prove its universality by using at most four membranes, while the length of proteins of (phago) and (exo) operations are at most two. We consider initially a system of three membranes. Comparing with Theorem 1, the higher number (four) of membranes is triggered by the use of (phago) operation.

Theorem 2. *A protein-protein interaction system with four membranes, proteins of length two and using rules of types* (bondin), (phago) *and* (exo) *has* *the same computational power as a Turing machine, i.e., are able to describe algorithmically any normal and abnormal biological evolution.*

Proof. We simulate a matrix grammar with appearance checking $G = (N, T, S, M, F)$ in the strong binary normal form. We construct a protein-protein interaction system Π with three membranes,

$$\Pi = (V, [\,[\,]_2[\,]_3]_1, \varepsilon, X, \overline{X}, \varepsilon, A, \overline{A}, R)$$

able to simulate a matrix grammar with appearance checking in the strong binary normal form. The symbols X, A correspond to the symbols of the initial type-1 matrix $(S \rightarrow XA)$ with $X \in N_1, A \in N_2$. Let there be n_1 matrices of type-2 and type-4 labelled $1, \ldots, n_1$ and n_2 matrices of type-3 labelled $n_1 + 1, \ldots, n_1 + n_2$.

The finite alphabet V of proteins is defined as

$$V = \{\beta, \overline{\beta}, \gamma, \overline{\gamma}, x, x', Y, \overline{Y}, a\} \cup \{B^{(j)}, \alpha_j, \overline{\alpha_j}, \alpha'_j, \overline{\alpha'_j} \mid 1 \le j \le 2\}$$
$$\cup \{A, \overline{A}, A_l, \overline{A_l} \mid A \in N_2, 1 \le l \le n_1 + n_2\}$$
$$\cup \{X, \overline{X}, X_l, \overline{X_l}, X'_l, \overline{X'_l}, X''_l, \overline{X''_l}, X_l^{(j)}, \overline{X_l^{(j)}} \mid$$
$$X \in N_1, 1 \le l \le n_1 + n_2, 1 \le j \le 2\}.$$

The set R of rules is constructed as follows:

(i) For each type-2 matrix $m_l : (X \rightarrow Y, A \rightarrow x)$ with $1 \le i \le n_1$, $X, Y \in N_1$, $A \in N_2$, $x \in (N_2 \cup T)^*$ and $|x| \le 2$, we consider the rules:

1. $[A]_X \rightarrow [\,]_{A \sim X}$
   $[\overline{A}]_{\overline{X}} \rightarrow [\,]_{\overline{A} \sim \overline{X}}$
2. $[\,]_{A \sim X}[\,]_{\overline{A} \sim \overline{X}} \rightarrow [\,[\,[A_l]_{X_l}]x]_{\overline{X}}$
3. $[\,[\,]_x]_{\overline{X}} \rightarrow [A_l]_{\overline{X_l}}$
4. $[A_l]_{X_l} \rightarrow [\,]_{A_l \sim X_l}$
   $[\overline{A_l}]_{\overline{X_l}} \rightarrow [\,]_{\overline{A_l} \sim \overline{X_l}}$
5. $[\,]_{A_l \sim X_l}[\,]_{\overline{A_l} \sim \overline{X_l}} \rightarrow [\,[\,[\,]_{\overline{X'_l}}]x_l]_{\overline{X_l}}$, if $x = \varepsilon$
   $[\,]_{A_l \sim X_l}[\,]_{\overline{A_l} \sim \overline{X_l}} \rightarrow [\,[\,[x]_{\overline{X'_l}}]x_l]_{\overline{X_l}}$, if $x \in T^*$
   $[\,]_{A_l \sim X_l}[\,]_{\overline{A_l} \sim \overline{X_l}} \rightarrow [\,[\,[x']_{\overline{X'_l}}]x_l]_{\overline{X_l}}$, otherwise
   (If $m_l : (X \rightarrow Y, A \rightarrow \alpha_1 \alpha_2), \alpha_1 \in N_2, \alpha_2 \in T \cup \{\varepsilon\}$ then $x' = \alpha'_1 \alpha_2$, and if $m_l : (X \rightarrow Y, A \rightarrow \alpha_1 \alpha_2), \alpha_1, \alpha_2 \in N_2$ then $x' = \alpha'_1 \alpha'_2$)
6. $[\,[\,]_{x_l}]_{\overline{X_l}} \rightarrow [\,]_{\overline{X'_l}}$
7. $[\alpha'_1]_{X'_l}[\,]_{\overline{X'_l}} \rightarrow [\,[\,[\alpha'_1]_{X'_l}]x'_l \overline{\alpha'_1}]_{\overline{X'_l}}$
8. $[\,[\,]_{X'_l} \overline{\alpha'_1}]_{\overline{X'_l}} \rightarrow [\alpha'_1]_{\overline{X'_l}}$
9. $[\alpha'_1]_{X'_l} \rightarrow [\,]_{\alpha'_1 \sim X'_l}$
   $[\overline{\alpha'_1}]_{\overline{X'_l}} \rightarrow [\,]_{\overline{\alpha'_1} \sim \overline{X'_l}}$
10. $[\,]_{\alpha'_1 \sim X'_l}[\,]_{\overline{\alpha'_1} \sim \overline{X'_l}} \rightarrow [\,[\,[\alpha_1]_{X''_l}]x'_l \overline{\alpha_1}]_{\overline{X'_l}}$
11. $[\,[\,]_{X'_l} \overline{\alpha_1}]_{\overline{X'_l}} \rightarrow [\alpha_1]_{\overline{X''_l}}$
12. $[\alpha'_2]_{X''_l}[\,]_{\overline{X''_l}} \rightarrow [\,[\,[\alpha''_2]_{X''_l}]x''_l \overline{\alpha'_2}]_{\overline{X''_l}}$
13. $[\,[\,]_{X''_l} \overline{\alpha'_2}]_{\overline{X''_l}} \rightarrow [\alpha'_2]_{\overline{X''_l}}$
14. $[\alpha'_2]_{X''_l} \rightarrow [\,]_{\alpha'_2 \sim X''_l}$
    $[\overline{\alpha'_2}]_{\overline{X''_l}} \rightarrow [\,]_{\overline{\alpha'_2} \sim \overline{X''_l}}$

15. $[\ ]_{\alpha_2' \sim X_l''}[\ ]_{\overline{\alpha_2'} \sim \overline{X_l''}} \rightarrow [\ [\ [\alpha_2]_{X_l''}]_{X_l''}\overline{\alpha_2}]_{\overline{X_l''}}$

16. $[\ [\ ]_{X_l''}\overline{\alpha_2}]_{\overline{X_l''}} \rightarrow [\overline{\alpha_2}]_{\overline{X_l''}}$

17. $[\ ]_{X_l'}[\ ]_{\overline{X_l'}} \rightarrow [\ [\ [\ ]_Y]_{X_l'}]_{\overline{X_l'}}$

$[\ ]_{X_l''}[\ ]_{\overline{X_l''}} \rightarrow [\ [\ [\ ]_Y]_{X_l'}]_{\overline{X_l'}}$

18. $[\ [\ ]_{X_l'}]_{\overline{X_l'}} \rightarrow [\ ]_{\overline{Y}}$

19. $[\ ]_X[\ ]_{\overline{X}} \rightarrow [\ [\ [\ ]_\beta]_\beta]_{\overline{\beta}}$ (X does not correspond to a nonterminal matrix)

20. $[\ [\ ]_\beta]_{\overline{\beta}} \rightarrow [\ ]_{\overline{\beta}}$

21. $[\ ]_\beta[\ ]_{\overline{\beta}} \rightarrow [\ [\ [\ ]_\beta]_\beta]_{\overline{\beta}}$

The simulation of a type-2 matrix can be done as follows:

- Whenever there exist proteins A, X, $\overline{A}$ and $\overline{X}$, by using two rules 1 applied in parallel, two protein complexes $A \sim X$ and $\overline{A} \sim \overline{X}$ are created. These protein complexes are able to interact, and by using rule 2, the proteins A and $\overline{A}$ break their bonds and the proteins A_l, X_l, X and $\overline{X}$ are created, marking the beginning of the simulation. This is followed by rule 3, where X and $\overline{X}$ are replaced by $\overline{A_l}$, $\overline{X_l}$. Using two rules 4 in parallel, two new protein complexes $A \sim X_l$ and $\overline{A} \sim \overline{X_l}$ are created. This is followed by rule 5, where A and $\overline{A}$ break their bonds and are replaced by either x (if $x \in T^*$) or x' (if $x \notin T^*$ and $x \neq \varepsilon$). Also, by rule 5, the elements X_l and $\overline{X_l}$ are replaced by the proteins X_l', X_l and $\overline{X_l}$. Then, by applying rule 6, X_l and $\overline{X_l}$ are replaced by $\overline{X_l'}$ in order to prevent replacing A's anymore. Now one of the evolutions is possible:

  * Whenever there exists a protein α_1', rule 7 is applied to introduce the corresponding protein $\overline{\alpha_1'}$, and is followed by rule 8 that simplifies the membrane structure. Rules 9 and 10 use protein complexes, and replace the proteins α_1' and $\overline{\alpha_1'}$ by the proteins α_1 and $\overline{\alpha_1}$, respectively. Rule 11 is used to reach a configuration in which one of the following rule can be applied:

    · rule 12 if exists a protein α_2', in order to introduce the protein $\overline{\alpha_2'}$; it is followed by rule 13 that simplifies the membrane structure. Rules 14 and 15 use protein complexes, and replace the proteins α_2' and $\overline{\alpha_2'}$ by the proteins α_2 and $\overline{\alpha_2}$, respectively.

    · whenever it does not exist such a protein α_2', rules 17 and 18 are used to replace X_l'' and $\overline{X_l''}$ by Y and $\overline{Y}$, respectively.

  * Whenever it does not exist proteins α_1' and α_2', then rules 17 and 18 are applied to replace X_l' and $\overline{X_l'}$ by Y and $\overline{Y}$, respectively.

  Rules 17 and 18 end a successfully simulation of a type-2 matrix, and return to the initial membrane structure. The proteins $\overline{\alpha_1}$ and $\overline{\alpha_2}$ are introduced in order to be able to use the corresponding proteins $\overline{\alpha_1}$ and $\overline{\alpha_2}$ when simulating other matrices.

- Whenever the symbol $A \in N_2$ is not present (i.e., we cannot apply rule 1), then rule 19 is applied introduces two symbols β and $\overline{\beta}$ which lead to an infinite evolution (by using rules 20 and 21).

(ii) For each type-3 matrix $m'_l : (X \rightarrow Y, B^{(j)} \rightarrow \#)$, $X, Y \in N_1$ and $B^{(j)} \rightarrow \# \in F$, where $n_1 + 1 \leq i \leq n_1 + n_2$, $i \in lab_j$, $j = 1, 2$, we consider the rules:

22. $[\,]_X[\,]_{\overline{X}} \rightarrow [\,[\,[\,]_{X_l^{(j)}}]_X]_{\overline{X}}$

23. $[\,[\,]_X]_{\overline{X}} \rightarrow [\,]_{\overline{X_l^{(j)}}}$

24. $[B^{(j)}]_{X_l^{(j)}}[\,]_{\overline{X_l^{(j)}}} \rightarrow [\,[\,[B^{(j)}]_\beta]_\beta]_{\overline{\beta}}$

25. $[\,]_{X_l^{(j)}}[\,]_{\overline{X_l^{(j)}}} \rightarrow [\,[\,[\,]_Y]_\gamma]_{\overline{\gamma}}$

26. $[\,[\,]_\gamma]_{\overline{\gamma}} \rightarrow [\,]_{\overline{Y}}$

Rule 22 starts the simulation of a type-3 matrix by replacing X and $\overline{X}$ by $X_l^{(j)}$, X and $\overline{X}$, and thereby remembering the index l of the matrix and the index j of the possibly present symbol $B^{(j)}$. This is followed by rule 23 in which the proteins X and $\overline{X}$ are replaced by $X_l^{(j)}$. At this step we need to verify if the symbol $B^{(j)} \in N_2$ is present. If $B^{(j)}$ is present, rule 24 replaces $X_l^{(j)}$ and $\overline{X_l^{(j)}}$ with two proteins β placed on the inner membranes, while keeping the protein $\overline{\beta}$ on the outer membrane leads to an infinite evolution (by using rules 20 and 21). Regardless the presence of $B^{(j)}$, rule 25 is applied and $X_l^{(j)}$ and $\overline{X^{(j)}}$ are replaced by Y, γ and $\overline{\gamma}$ on the outer membrane. Rule 26 involves the creation of $\overline{Y}$, successfully simulating a type-3 matrix and returning to the initial membrane structure.

(iii) For a terminal type-4 matrix $m_l : (X \rightarrow a, A \rightarrow x)$ with $1 \leq i \leq n_1$, $X \in N_1$, $a \in T$, $A \in N_2$, $x \in T^*$ and $|x| \leq 2$, we consider the rules:

27. $[\,]_{X'_l}[\,]_{\overline{X'_l}} \rightarrow [\,[\,[\,]_a]_{X'_l}]_{\overline{X'_l}}$

    $[\,]_{X''_l}[\,]_{\overline{X''_l}} \rightarrow [\,[\,[\,]_a]_{X'_l}]_{\overline{X'_l}}$

28. $[\,[\,]_{X_l}]_{\overline{X_l}} \rightarrow [\,]$

We do not involve the protein $\overline{a}$, because $a \in T$. By replacing rules 17 and 18 with rules 27 and 28 in the sequence 1-21, a terminal type-4 matrix is faithfully simulated. The result of the simulation consists of the vector describing the multiplicity of proteins inside and on all the membranes.

5   Conclusion

In this work we proposed a computing system inspired by protein-protein interaction networks that uses a minimal number of membranes with respect to the cell movement operations that are initiated by proteins of different length. We proved that such protein-protein interaction networks can simulate all computable functions. We prove that protein-protein interaction networks have the same computational power as a Turing machine by using a rather small number of proteins having at most length two, where length is an abstract measure of complexity. Up to our knowledge, this is one of the first qualitative and quantitative approach in terms of an abstract measure of complexity (called length) studying the computational power of protein-protein interaction systems.

Inspired by the proteins of the living cell and by fact that membranes proteins are highly dynamic, several types of membrane proteins were previously investigated. In [9] there were defined several (biological inspired) transformations of membranes as (pino) (engulfing zero external membranes), (exo) (the process of expelling some material), (phago) (engulfing just one external membrane), (mate) (merging of membranes), (drip) (splitting off zero internal membranes), (bud) (splitting off one internal membrane). These operations were defined in terms of membrane computing, and used in defining classes of membrane systems where objects are placed on membranes [2]. Other approaches have considered proteins placed both on the membranes and in their compartments. In [19] the objects do not change their places (those bound on membranes remain there), while in [8,10] the objects can move from compartments to membranes and back.

References

1. Alberts, B., Johnson, A., Lewis, J., Raff, M., Roberts, K., Walter, P.: Molecular Biology of the Cell, 5th edn. Garland Science, Taylor & Francis Group, New York (2008)
2. Aman, B., Ciobanu, G.: Mutual mobile membranes with objects on surface. Nat. Comput. **10**, 777–793 (2011)
3. Aman, B., Ciobanu, G.: Describing the immune system using enhanced mobile membranes. Elect. Notes Theor. Comput. Sci. **194**(3), 5–18 (2008)
4. Aman, B., Ciobanu, G.: Turing completeness using three mobile membranes. In: Calude, C.S., Costa, J.F., Dershowitz, N., Freire, E., Rozenberg, G. (eds.) UC 2009. LNCS, vol. 5715, pp. 42–55. Springer, Heidelberg (2009). doi:10.1007/978-3-642-03745-0_12
5. Aman, B., Ciobanu, G.: Simple, enhanced and mutual mobile membranes. In: Priami, C., Back, R.-J., Petre, I. (eds.) Trans. on Comput. Syst. Biol. XI. LNCS, vol. 5750, pp. 26–44. Springer, Heidelberg (2009). doi:10.1007/978-3-642-04186-0_2
6. Aman, B., Ciobanu, G.: Mobility in Process Calculi and Natural Computing. Natural Computing Series. Springer, Heidelberg (2011)
7. Aman, B., Ciobanu, G.: Computational power of protein interaction networks. In: Mauri, G., Dennunzio, A., Manzoni, L., Porreca, A.E. (eds.) UCNC 2013. LNCS, vol. 7956, pp. 248–249. Springer, Heidelberg (2013). doi:10.1007/978-3-642-39074-6_25
8. Brijder, R., Cavaliere, M., Riscos-Núñez, A., Rozenberg, G., Sburlan, D.: Membrane systems with proteins embedded in membranes. Theor. Comput. Sci. **404**, 26–39 (2008)
9. Cardelli, L.: Brane calculi. Interactions of biological membranes. In: Danos, V., Schachter, V. (eds.) CMSB 2004. LNCS, vol. 3082, pp. 257–278. Springer, Heidelberg (2005). doi:10.1007/978-3-540-25974-9_24
10. Cavaliere, M., Sedwards, S.: Decision problems in membrane systems with peripheral proteins, transport and evolution. Theor. Comput. Sci. **404**, 40–51 (2008)
11. Ciobanu, G.: Modeling cell-mediated immunity by means of P systems. In: Ciobanu, G., Păun, G., Pérez-Jiménez, M.J. (eds.) Applications of Membrane Computing, pp. 159–180. Springer, Heidelberg (2006)
12. Ciobanu, G., Krishna, S.N.: Enhanced mobile membranes: computability results. Theory Comput. Syst. **48**, 715–729 (2011)
13. Freund, R., Ibarra, O.H., Păun, G., Yen, H.C.: Matrix languages, register machines, vector addition systems. In: Proceedings 3rd Brainstorming Week on Membrane Computing, pp. 155–168 (2005)

14. Gao, J.T., Guimera, R., Li, H., Pinto, I.M., Sales-Pardo, M., Wai, S., Rubinstein, B., Li, R.: Modular coherence of protein dynamics in yeast cell polarity system. Proc. Natl. Acad. Sci. **198**(18), 7647–7652 (2011)
15. Gramss, T., Bornholdt, S., Gross, M., Mitchel, M., Pellizzari, T. (eds.): Non-Standard Computation. Wiley-VCH, New York (1998)
16. Manca, V.: Infobiotics. Information in Biotic Systems. Springer, Heidelberg (2013)
17. Minsky, M.L.: Computation: Finite and Infinite Machines. Prentice-Hall, Upper Saddle River (1967)
18. Murphy, K., Weaver, C.: Janeway's Immunobiology, 9th edn. Garland Publishing, New York (2016)
19. Păun, A., Popa, B.: P systems with proteins on membranes. Fundamenta Informaticae **72**, 467–483 (2006)
20. Păun, G., Rozenberg, G., Salomaa, A. (eds.): The Oxford Handbook of Membrane Computing. Oxford University Press, Oxford (2010)
21. Salomaa, A.: Formal Languages. Academic Press, New York (1973)
22. Tan, T., Frenkel, D., Gupta, V., Deem, M.: Length, protein-protein interactions, and complexity. Phys. A **350**, 52–62 (2005)
23. Turing, A.M.: On computable numbers, with an application to the entscheidungsproblem. Proc. Lond. Math. Soc. **42**, 230–265 (1937)

Comparative Analysis of Statistical Model Checking Tools

Mehmet Emin Bakir[1(✉)], Marian Gheorghe[2], Savas Konur[2],
and Mike Stannett[1]

[1] Department of Computer Science, The University of Sheffield,
Regent Court, 211 Portobello, Sheffield S1 4DP, UK
{mebakir1,m.stannett}@sheffield.ac.uk
[2] School of Electrical Engineering and Computer Science,
University of Bradford, West Yorkshire, Bradford BD7 1DP, UK
{m.gheorghe,s.konur}@bradford.ac.uk

Abstract. Statistical model checking is a powerful and flexible approach for formal verification of computational models, e.g. P systems, which can have very large search spaces. Various statistical model checking tools have been developed, but choosing the most efficient and appropriate tool requires a significant degree of experience, not only because different tools have different modelling and property specification languages, but also because they may be designed to support only a certain subset of property types. Furthermore, their performance can vary depending on the property types and membrane systems being verified. In this paper, we evaluate the performance of various common statistical model checkers based on a pool of biological models. Our aim is to help users select the most suitable SMC tools from among the available options, by comparing their modelling and property specification languages, capabilities and performances.

Keywords: Membrane computing · P systems · Statistical model checking · Biological models · Performance benchmarking

1 Introduction

In order to understand the structure and functionality of biological systems, we need methods which can highlight the spatial and time-dependent evolution of systems. To this end, researchers have started to utilize the computational power of machine-executable models, including implementations of membrane system models, to get a better and deeper understanding of the spatial and temporal features of biological systems [21]. In particular, the executable nature of computational models enables scientists to conduct experiments, in silico, in a fast and cheap manner.

The vast majority of models used for describing biological systems are based on ordinary differential equations (ODEs) [9], but researchers have recently

© Springer International Publishing AG 2017
A. Leporati et al. (Eds.): CMC 2016, LNCS 10105, pp. 119–135, 2017.
DOI: 10.1007/978-3-319-54072-6_8

started to use *computational models* as an alternative to mathematical modelling. The basis of such models is *state machines*, which can be used to model numerous variables and relate different system states (configurations) to one another [21]. There have been various attempts to model biological systems from a computational point of view, including the use of Boolean networks [30], Petri nets [43], the π-calculus [38], interacting state machines [25], L-systems [36] and variants of P systems (membrane systems) [22,37]. A survey of computational models applied in biology can be found here [21]. These techniques are useful for investigating the qualitative features of the biological systems, as are their stochastic counterparts (e.g., stochastic Petri Nets [26], stochastic P systems [7,41]) or deterministic systems (so called, MP systems [10]) useful for investigating the quantitative features of computation models.

Having built a model, the goal is typically to *analyse* it, so as to determine the underlying system's properties. Various approaches have been devised for analysing computational models. One widely used method, for example, based on generating the execution traces of a model, is *simulation*. Although the simulation approach is widely applicable, the large number of potential execution paths in models of realistic systems means that we can often exercise only a fraction of the complete trace set using current techniques. Especially for non-deterministic and stochastic systems each state may have more than one possible successor, which means that different runs of the same basic model may produce different outcomes [5]. Consequently, some computational paths may never be exercised, and their conformance to requirements never assessed.

Model checking is another widely recognized approach for analysis and verification of models, which has been successfully applied both to computer systems and biological system models. This technique involves representing each (desired or actual) property as a temporal logic formula, which is then verified against a model. It formally demonstrates the correctness of a system by means of strategically investigating the whole of the model's state space, considering all paths and guaranteeing their correctness [4,15,28]. Model checking has advantages over conventional approaches like simulation and testing, because it checks all computational paths and if the specified property is not satisfied it provides useful feedback by generating a counter-example (i.e. execution path) that demonstrates how the failure can occur [28].

Initially, model checking was employed for analysing *transition systems* used for describing discrete systems. A transition system regards time as discrete, and describes a set of states and the possible transitions between them, where each state represents some instantaneous configuration of the system. More recently, model checking has been extended by adding probabilities to state transitions (*probabilistic model checking*); in practice, such systems include discrete-time Markov chains (DTMC), continuous-time Markov chains (CTMC), and Markov decision processes (MDP). Probabilistic models are useful for verifying quantitative features of systems.

Typically, the model checking process comprises the following steps [4,28]:

1. Describing the system model in a high-level modelling language, so as to provide an unambiguous representation of the input system.
2. Specifying the desired properties (using a property specification language) as a set of logical statements, e.g., temporal logic formulas.
3. Verifying whether each property is valid on the model. For non-probabilistic models the response is either 'yes' or 'no'. For probabilistic systems the response may instead be some estimate of the 'probability of correctness'.

"Exact" model checking considers whole state spaces while verifying a property, but if the model is relatively large, the verification process can be prohibitively resource intensive and time consuming which is known as 'state-space explosion' problem, so this approach can only be applied to a small number of biological models. Nonetheless, the intrinsic power of the approach has gained a good deal of attention from researchers, and model checking has been applied to various biological phenomena, including, for example, gene regulator networks (GRNs) and signal-transduction pathways [7,13] (see [20] for a recent survey of the use of model checking in systems biology).

To overcome the state-space explosion problem, the *statistical* model checking (SMC) approach does not analyse the entire state space, but instead generates a number of independent simulation traces and uses statistical (e.g., Monte Carlo) methods to generate an approximate measure of system correctness. This approach does not guarantee the absolute correctness of the system, but it allows much larger models be verified (within specified confidence limits) in a faster manner [12,35,47,49]. This approach allows verifying much larger models with significantly improved performance.

The number of tools using statistical model checking has been increasing steadily, as has their application to biological systems [14,51]. Although the variety of SMC tools gives a certain amount of flexibility and control to users, each model checker has its own specific pros and cons. One tool may support a large set of property operators but perform property verifications slowly, while another may be more efficient at analysing small models, and yet another may excel at handling larger models. In such cases, the user may need to cover all of their options by using more than one model checker, but unfortunately the different SMCs generally use different modelling and property specification languages. Formulating properties using even a single SMC modelling language can be a cumbersome, error-prone, and time wasting experience for non-experts in computational verification (including many biologists), and the difficulties multiply considerably when more than one SMC needs to be used.

In order to facilitate the modelling and analysis tasks, several software suites have been proposed, such as Infobiotics Workbench [8] (based on stochastic P systems [9]) and kPWorkbench framework (based on kernel P systems [17]) [17,32]. As part of the computational analysis, these tools employ more than one model checker. Currently, they allow only a manual selection of the tools, relying on the user expertise for the selection mechanism. These systems automatically translate the model and queries into the target model checker's specification language. While this simplifies the checking process considerably, one still has to know which target model checker best suits ones needs, and this requires a significant degree of experience. It is desirable, therefore, to introduce another processing layer, so as to reduce human intervention by *automatically* selecting the best model checker for any given combination of P system and property query.

As part of this wider project (Infobiotics Workbench) to provide machine assistance to users, by automatically identifying the best model checker, we evaluate the performance of various statistical model checkers against a pool of biological models. The results reported here can be used to help select the most suitable SMC tools from the available options, by comparing their modelling and property specification languages, capabilities and performances (see also [6]).

Paper structure. We begin in Sect. 2 by describing some of the most commonly used SMC tools, together with their modelling and property-specification languages. Section 3 compares the usability of these tools in terms of expressibility of their property specification languages. In Sect. 4 we benchmark the performance of these tools when verifying biological models, and describe the relevant experiment settings. We conclude in Sect. 5 with a summary of our findings, and highlight open problems that warrant further investigation.

2   A Brief Survey of Current Statistical Model Checkers

In this section, we review some of the most popular and well-maintained statistical model checking tools, together with their modelling and property specification languages.

2.1   Tools

PRISM. PRISM (Probabilistic and Symbolic Model Checker) is a widely-used, powerful probabilistic model checker tool [27,33]. It has been used for analysing a range of systems including biological systems, communication, multimedia and security protocols and many others [44]. It allows building and analysing several types of probabilistic systems including discrete-time Markov chains (DTMCs) and continuous-time Markov chains (CTMCs) with their 'reward' extension. PRISM can carry out both probabilistic model checking based on numerical techniques with exhaustive traversal of model, and statistical model checking with a discrete-event simulation engine [34,44]. The associated modelling language, the PRISM language (a high-level state-based language), is the probabilistic variant of Reactive Modules [1,33] (for a full description of PRISMs modelling language, see [44]), which subsumes several property specification languages, including PCTL, PCTL*, CSL, probabilistic LTL. However, statistical model checking can only be applied to a limited subset of properties; for example, it does not support steady-state and LTL-style path properties.

PRISM can be run via both a Graphical User Interface (GUI) or directly from the command line. Both options facilitate model checking process by allowing to modify a large set of parameters. The command line option is particularly useful when users need to run a large number of models. PRISM is open source software and is available for Windows, Linux and Mac OS X platforms.

PLASMA-Lab. PLASMA-Lab is a software platform for statistical model checking of stochastic systems. It provides a flexible plug-in mechanism which allows users to personalise their own simulator, and it also facilitates distributed simulations [11]. The tool has been applied to a range of problems, such as systems biology, rare events, motion planning and systems of systems [42].

The platform supports four modelling languages: Reactive Module Language (RML) implementation of the PRISM tool language, with two other variants of RML (see Table 1), and Biological Language [11,42]. In addition, it provides a few simulator plug-ins which enable external simulators to be integrated with PLASMA-Lab, e.g., MATLAB/Simulink. The associated property specification language is based on Bounded Linear Temporal Logic (B-LTL) which bounds the number of states by number of steps or time units.

PLASMA-Lab can be run from a GUI or command line with plug-in system, and while it is not open source it can be embedded within other software programs as a library. It has been developed using the Java programming language, which provides compatibility with different operating systems.

Ymer. Ymer is a statistical model checking tool for verifying continuous-time Markov chains (CTMCs) and generalized semi-Markov processes (GSMPs). The tool supports parallel generation of simulation traces, which makes Ymer a fast SMC tool [48].

Ymer uses the PRISM language grammar for its modelling and property specification language. It employs the CSL formalism for property specification [46].

Ymer can be invoked via a command line interface only. It has been developed using the C/C++ programming language, and the source code is open to the public.

MRMC. MRMC is a tool for numerical and statistical model checking of probabilistic systems. It supports DTMC, CTMC, and using the reward extension of DTMC and CTMC [29].

The tool does not employ a high-level modelling language, but instead requires a sparse matrix representation of probabilities or rates as input. Describing systems in transition matrix format is very hard, especially for large systems, and external tools should be used to automatically generate the required inputs. Both PRISM and Performance Evaluation Process Algebra (PEPA) have extensions which can generate inputs for the MRMC tool [50]. The matrix representation also requires that state labels with atomic propositions be provided in another structure. Properties can be expressed with PCTL and CSL, and with their reward extensions.

MRMC is a command line tool. It has been developed using the C programming language, and the source code is publicly available. Binary distributions for Windows, Linux and Mac OS X are also available [40].

MC2. The MC2 tool enables statistical model checking of simulation traces, and can perform model checking in parallel.

MC2 does not need a modelling language, instead it imports simulation traces generated by external tools for stochastic and deterministic models. The tool uses probabilistic LTL with numerical constraints (PLTLc) for its property specification language, which enables defining numerical constraints on free variables [16].

MC2 can be executed only through its command line interface. The tool was developed using the Java programming interfaces and is distributed as a `.jar` file, therefore the source code is not available to public. The tool is bundled with a Gillespie simulator, called *Gillespie2*. As will be explained in the following section, it is possible to use Gillespie2 to generate simulation traces for the MC2 tool.

2.2 Modelling Languages

As part of the model checking process the system needs to be described in the target SMC modelling language. If the SMC tool relies on external tools, as in the case of MRMC and MC2, users will also have to learn the usage and modelling language of these external tools as well. For example, if users want to use the MRMC tool, they also have to learn how to use PRISM and how to model in the PRISM language.

Table 1. Modelling languages and external dependency of SMC tools.

SMCs	Modelling language(s)	Needs an external tool?	External tool modelling language
PRISM	PRISM language	NO	N/A
PLASMA-Lab	RML of PRISM, Adaptive RML (extension of RML for adaptive systems), RML with importance sampling, Biological Language	NO	N/A
Ymer	PRISM language	NO	N/A
MRMC	Transition matrix	YES, e.g., PRISM	PRISM language
MC2	N/A	YES, e.g., Gillespie2	Systems Biology Markup Language (SBML)

Table 1 summarises the modelling languages associated with each SMC tool. The PLASMA and Ymer tools provide fair support for the PRISM language. MRMC expects a transition matrix input, but in practice, for large models, it is not possible to generate the transition matrix manually, so an external tool should be used for generating the matrix. MC2 also relies on external tools, because it does not employ a modelling language, instead it expects externally generated simulation traces. If users want to use the MC2 tool, they first have to learn a modelling language and usage of an appropriate simulation tool. For example, in order to use the Gillespie2 simulator as an external tool for MC2, the user should be able to describe their model using the Systems Biology Markup Language (SBML).

3   Usability

Model checking uses *temporal logics* as property specification languages. In order to query probabilistic features, probabilistic temporal logics should be used. Several probabilistic property specification languages exist, such as Probabilistic Linear Temporal Logic (PLTL) [4], probabilistic LTL with numerical constraints (PLTLc) [16] and Continuous Stochastic Logic (CSL) [2,3,34].

In order to ease the property specification process, frequently used properties, called *patterns*, have been identified by previous studies [18,24]. Patterns represent recurring properties (e.g., something is *always* the case, something is *possibly* the case), and are generally represented by natural language-like keywords. An increasing number of studies have been conducted to identify appropriate pattern systems for biological models [23,31,39]. Table 2 lists various popular patterns [24], giving a short description and explaining how they can be represented using existing temporal logic operators.

The SMCs investigated here employ different grammar syntaxes for property specification, which makes it harder to use other tools at the same time. Although Ymer uses the same grammar as PRISM, it excludes some operators, such as the Always (G) operator. In addition, different SMCs tools may support different sets of probabilistic temporal logics. In the following, we compare the expressibility of their specification languages, by checking if the properties can be defined using just one temporal logic operator, namely directly supported (DS), which will be easier for practitioners to express; or as a combination of multiple operators, indirectly supported (IS); or not supported at all, not supported (NS). Qualitative and quantitative operators, with five property patterns which are identified as widely used by [24], are listed in Table 3.

The PRISM, Ymer and MC2 tools directly support both Qualitative and Quantitative operators, but MRMC supports only the Qualitative operator. While PLASMA-Lab does not allow these operators to be expressed directly with B-LTL, the verification outputs contain information about the probability of the property, hence users can interpret the results. Existence, Until and Universality properties are directly supported by all SMCs, except that Ymer does not employ an operator for Universality patterns (it needs to be interpreted using the

Table 2. Property patterns

Patterns	Description	Temporal logic
Existence	ϕ_1 will eventually hold, within the $\bowtie p$ bounds	$P_{\bowtie p}[F\ \phi_1]$ or $P_{\bowtie p}[true\ \text{U}\ \phi_1]$
Until	ϕ_1 will hold continuously until ϕ_2 eventually holds, within the $\bowtie p$ bounds	$P_{\bowtie p}[\phi_1\ \text{U}\ \phi_2]$
Response	If ϕ_1 holds, then ϕ_2 must hold within the $\bowtie p$ bounds	$P_{\geq 1}[G\ (\phi_1 \rightarrow (P_{\bowtie p}[F\ \phi_2]))]$
Steady-State (Long-run)	In the long-run ϕ_1 must hold, within the $\bowtie p$ bounds	$S_{\bowtie p}[\phi_1]$ or $P_{\bowtie p}[FG\ (\phi_1)]$
Universality	ϕ_1 continuously holds, within the $\bowtie p$ bounds	$P_{\bowtie p}[G\ \phi_1]$ or $P_{\overline{\bowtie}(1-p)}[(F\ (\neg\phi_1)]$

Key. ϕ_1, and ϕ_2 are state formulas; $\bowtie$ is one of the relations in $\{<, >, \leq, \geq\}$; $p \in [0, 1]$ is a probability with rational bounds; and $\overline{\bowtie}$ is negation of inequality operators. $P_{\bowtie p}$ is the *qualitative* operator which enables users to query qualitative features, those whose result is either 'yes' or 'no'. In order to query *quantitative* properties, $P_{=?}$ (quantitative operator) can be used to returns a numeric value which is the probability that the specified property is true.

Table 3. Specifying various key patterns using different SMC tools.

SMCs	Qualitative operator	Quantitative operator ($P_{=?}$)	Existence	Until	Response	Steady-state	Universality
PRISM	DS	DS	DS	DS	**NS**	**NS**	DS
PLASMA-Lab	**NS**	**NS**	DS	DS	IS	IS	DS
Ymer	DS	DS	DS	DS	**NS**	**NS**	IS
MRMC	DS	**NS**	DS	DS	IS	DS	DS
MC2	DS	DS	DS	DS	IS	IS	DS

Key. DS = Directly Supported; IS = Indirectly Supported; NS = Not Supported.

Not (!) and Eventually (F) operators, i.e. it is indirectly supported). There is no single operator to represent the Response pattern directly, but it is indirectly supported by PLASMA-Lab, MRMC and MC2. The Steady-State pattern can be either represented by one operator, S, or two operators, F and G. Only the MRMC tool employs the S operator to allow Steady-State to be expressed directly, while PLASMA-Lab and MC2 allow it to be expressed indirectly.

4   Experimental Findings

The wide variety of SMC tools gives a certain flexibility and control to users, but practitioners need to know which of the tools is the most suitable for their particular models and queries. The expressive power of the associated modelling and specification languages is not the only criterion, because SMC performance may also depend on the nature of the models and property specifications. We have therefore conducted a series of experiments to determine the capabilities and performances of the most commonly used tools [6]. The experiments are conducted on an Intel i7-2600 CPU @ 3.40 GHz 8 cores, with 16 GB RAM running on Ubuntu 14.04.

We tested each of the five tools against a representative selection of 465 biological models (in SBML format) taken from the BioModels database [19] (as modified in [45] to fix the stochastic rate constants of all reactions to 1). The models tested ranged in size from 2 species and 1 reaction, to 2631 species and 2824 reactions. Figure 1 shows the distribution of models size, we take "size" to be the product of species count and reaction count. X-axis (log scale) indicates the model size and Y-axis represents the frequency of models with their sizes represented on the X-axis.

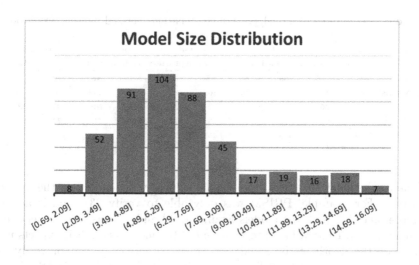

Fig. 1. The distribution of models size in the logarithmic scale.

Each tool/model pair was tested against five different property specification patterns [24], namely Existence, Until, Response, Steady-State and Universality. We have developed a tool for translating SBML models to SMC modelling languages, and translating property patterns to the corresponding SMC specification languages. For each SMC, the number of simulation traces was set to 500, and the depth of each trace was set to 5000.

The time required for each run is taken to be the combined time required for model parsing, simulation and verification. Each SMC/model/pattern combination was tested three times, and the figures reported here give the average total time required. When an SMC depends on external tools, we also added the external tool execution time into the total execution time. In particular, there-fore, the total times reported for verifying models with MRMC and MC2 tools are not their execution times only, but include the time consumed for generating transition matrices and simulation traces, respectively. We used the PRISM tool for generating transition matrices requested by MRMC, and the Gillespie2 for generating simulation traces utilised by MC2. When the external tool failed to generate the necessary input for its corresponding SMC, we have recorded the SMC as being incapable of verifying the model. In order to keep the experiment tractable, when an SMC required more than 1 h to complete the run, we halted the process and again recorded the model as unverifiable.

Table 4 shows the experiment results. The SMCs and the property patterns are represented in the first column and row, respectively. The *Verified* columns under each pattern show the number of models that could be verified by the corresponding SMC. The *Fastest* column shows the number of models for which the corresponding SMC was the fastest tool.

Table 4. The number of model/pattern combinations verified by each SMC tool.

	Existence		Until		Response		Steady-State		Universality	
	Verified	Fastest	Verified	Fastest	Verified	Fastest	Verified	Fastest	Verified	Fastest
PRISM	337	15	435	84	NS	NS	NS	NS	370	57
PLASMA-Lab	465	143	465	54	465	390	465	392	465	80
Ymer	439	304	439	324	NS	NS	NS	NS	439	325
MRMC	75	0	72	0	75	17	57	11	77	0
MC2	458	3	458	3	458	58	458	62	458	3

Key. NS = Not Supported.

The results show that SMC tool capabilities vary depending on the queried properties. For example, PRISM was only able to verify 337 models against Existence, and 435 and 370 models against Until and Universality, respectively. The main reason PRISM failed to verify *all* of the models is that it expects user to increase the depth of the simulation traces, otherwise it cannot verify the unbounded properties with a reliable approximation. In contrast, PLASMA-Lab was able to verify all of the models within 1 h. Ymer could verify 439 models for those patterns it supports, thus failing to complete 26 models in the time available. MRMC was able to verify relatively few models, because it relied on the PRISM model checker to construct the model and export the associated transition matrices. Especially for relatively large models PRISM crashed while generating these matrices (we believe this is related to its CU Decision Diagram (CUDD) library). MC2 was able to verify 458 models against all of the patterns tested, and only failed for 7 of them.

The second column of the patterns shows the number of models which were verified by the corresponding model checker tools. The distribution of models size across the fastest model checkers for different patterns are shown in the following set of violin plots (Figs. 2, 3, 4, 5 and 6). Each of the inner swarm points represents a model. X-axis represents the logarithmic scale of models size.

For the models in the white background region, we can uniquely identify the fastest SMC tool for their verification, whereas for the models in grey background region the fastest model checker is not clear.

Ymer was the fastest for most model/pattern pairs (where those patterns were supported). However, it is the fastest tool only for verification of relatively small size models. Ymer was the fastest for verifying 304 models against Existence pattern, the minimum model size verified by Ymer was 2, maximum 2128, mean 256.8 and median 137.5. It was the fastest tool for larger number of models, 324 (min = 2, max = 2128, mean = 312.9, median = 144), against Until pattern verification, and 325 models (min = 2, max = 2346, mean = 335, median = 144) against Universality pattern verification. PLASMA-Lab is the fastest tool for relatively large size models. It was the fastest tool for verifying 143 models (min = 380, max = 7429944, mean =464498.9, median = 11875) against Existence pattern, 54 models (min = 1224, max = 7429944, mean = 837193.5, median = 288162) against Until pattern, and 80 models (min = 575, max = 7429944, mean = 773247.5, median = 43143) against Universality pattern verification. It did particularly well against Response, 390 models (min = 12, max = 7429944, mean = 170734.5, median = 604.5) and Steady-State patterns, 392 models (min = 9, max = 7429944, mean = 169862.1, median = 600), where it was only competing with MRMC and MC2. PRISM is generally the fastest tool for medium to large size models. It was the fastest only for 15 models (min = 1023, max = 39770, mean = 5860.9, median = 2304) against Existence pattern verification, but it was able to verify larger number of models, 84 (min = 1665, max = 2928904, mean = 253327.3, median = 7395), against Until pattern verification and 57 models (min = 960, max = 1633632, mean = 92998.4, median = 3364) against Universality pattern verification. MC2 (with Gillespie2) is the fastest for relatively small size models. It could verify only 3 models (min = 722, max = 1892, mean = 1138, median = 800) against Existence, Until and Universality patterns, although it did better with 58 models (min = 2, max = 1892, mean = 103.2, median = 30) against Response pattern, and 62 models (min = 2, max = 1892, mean = 105.9, median = 36) against Steady-State patterns. Finally, MRMC (with PRISM dependency) was slower than other tools for Existence, Until and Universality patterns verification, but did better handling Response (fastest for 17 models: min = 6, max = 42, mean = 18.5, median = 20) and Steady-State (fastest for 11 models: min = 6, max = 42, mean = 22.3, median = 20).

As we stated previously, the background color of Figs. 2, 3, 4, 5 and 6 gives an indication of whether the fastest model checker can be identified for the models within a region of the graph, that is, for models in the white background region, the fastest SMC tool can be identified, but the models in grey background region it is less clear-cut. For verification of Existence pattern, we can uniquely identify the fastest SMC tool for both the 232 smallest models (size ranging from 2 to 380), and the 55 largest models (size = 39984 to 7429944), namely Ymer and PLASMA-Lab respectively, but for remaining 178 medium-sized models

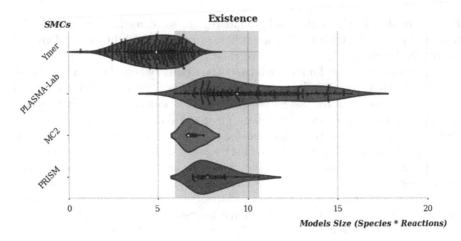

Fig. 2. The distribution of models size across fastest SMC tools for Existence pattern verification.

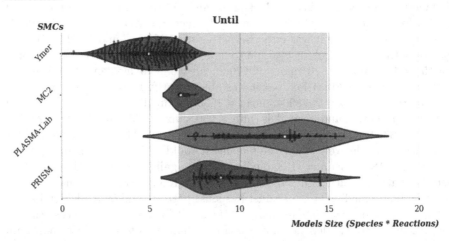

Fig. 3. The distribution of models size across fastest SMC tools for Until pattern verification.

(size = 380 to 39770), there is no obvious 'winner'. Similarly, for Until pattern verification, the smallest 283 models (size ranging from 2 to 714), and only for the 5 largest models (size = 3605380 to 7429944) we can identify the fastest SMC tool (Ymer and PLASMA-Lab respectively), but there are more than one candidates for remaining 177 medium-sized models (size = 722 to 2928904). Despite, we have only three SMC tools, namely PLASMA-Lab, MRMC and MC2, which support the verification of Response and Steady-State patterns, their performance on small and medium size models are close to each other, which makes harder to

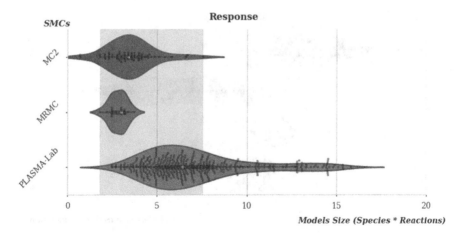

Fig. 4. The distribution of models size across fastest SMC tools for Response pattern verification.

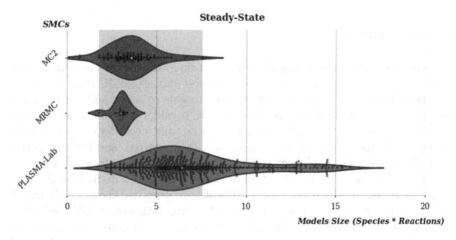

Fig. 5. The distribution of models size across fastest SMC tools for Steady-State pattern verification.

identify the fastest tool. Therefore, only for the smallest 4 models (size = 2 to 6) and for the largest 128 models (size = 1927 to 7429944) the fastest tool (MC2 and PLASMA-Lab respectively) can be identified. Lastly, for Universality pattern verification, the fastest SMC tool for both smallest 262 models (size = 2 to 572) and largest 17 models (size = 1823582 to 7429944), Ymer and PLASMA-Lab respectively, can be identified, for the remained 186 medium size models we cannot assign a unique model checker tool.

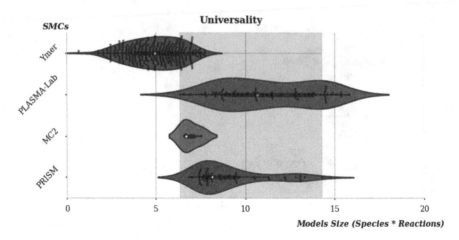

Fig. 6. The distribution of models size across fastest SMC tools for Universality pattern verification.

5   Conclusion

The experimental results clearly show that certain SMC tools are best for certain tasks, but there are also situations where the best choice of SMC is far less clear-cut, and it is not surprising that users may struggle to select and use the most suitable SMC tool for their needs. Users need to consider the modelling language of tools and the external tools they may rely on, and need detailed knowledge as to which property specification operators are supported, and how to specify them. Even then, the tool may still fail to complete the verification within a reasonable time, whereas another tool might be able to run it successfully.

These factors make it extremely difficult for users to know which model checker to choose, and point to a clear need for automation of the SMC-selection process. We are currently working to identify novel methods and algorithms to automate the selection of best SMC tool for a given computational model (more specifically for P system models) and property patterns. We aim to enable the integration of our methods within larger software platforms, e.g., IBW and kPWorkbench, and while this is undoubtedly a challenging task, we are encouraged by recent developments in related areas, e.g., the automatic selection of stochastic simulation algorithms [45].

References

1. Alur, R., Henzinger, T.A.: Reactive modules. Form. Methods Syst. Des. **15**(1), 7–48 (1999). http://dx.doi.org/10.1023/A:1008739929481
2. Aziz, A., Sanwal, K., Singhal, V., Brayton, R.: Model-checking continuous-time markov chains. ACM Trans. Comput. Logic **1**(1), 162–170 (2000). http://doi.acm.org/10.1145/343369.343402

3. Baier, C., Haverkort, B., Hermanns, H., Katoen, J.P.: Model-checking algorithms for continuous-time markov chains. IEEE Trans. Softw. Eng. **29**(6), 524–541 (2003)
4. Baier, C., Katoen, J.P.: Principles of Model Checking. The MIT Press, Cambridge (2008)
5. Bakir, M.E., Konur, S., Gheorghe, M., Niculescu, I., Ipate, F.: High performance simulations of kernel P systems. In: 2014 IEEE 16th International Conference on High Performance Computing and Communications (HPCC) (2014)
6. Bakir, M.E., Stannett, M.: Selection criteria for statistical model checking. In: Gheorghe, M., Konur, S. (eds.) Proceedings of the Workshop on Membrane Computing WMC 2016, Manchester (UK), 11–15 July 2016, pp. 55–57 (2016). http:// bradscholars.brad.ac.uk/handle/10454/8840, Available as: Technical Report UB-20160819-1, University of Bradford
7. Bernardini, F., Gheorghe, M., Romero-Campero, F.J., Walkinshaw, N.: A hybrid approach to modeling biological systems. In: Eleftherakis, G., Kefalas, P., Păun, G., Rozenberg, G., Salomaa, A. (eds.) WMC 2007. LNCS, vol. 4860, pp. 138–159. Springer, Heidelberg (2007). doi:10.1007/978-3-540-77312-2_9
8. Blakes, J., Twycross, J., Romero-Campero, F.J., Krasnogor, N.: The infobiotics workbench: An integrated in silico modelling platform for systems and synthetic biology. Bioinformatics **27**(23), 3323–3324 (2011)
9. Blakes, J., Twycross, J., Konur, S., Romero-Campero, F.J., Krasnogor, N., Gheorghe, M.: Infobiotics workbench: A P systems based tool for systems and synthetic biology. In: Frisco, P., Gheorghe, M., Pérez-Jiménez, M.J. (eds.) Applications of Membrane Computing in Systems and Synthetic Biology. Emergence, Complexity and Computation, vol. 7, pp. 1–41. Springer, Heidelberg (2014). doi:10. 1007/978-3-319-03191-0_1
10. Bollig-Fischer, A., Marchetti, L., Mitrea, C., Wu, J., Kruger, A., Manca, V., Drăghici, S.: Modeling time-dependent transcription effects of HER2 oncogene and discovery of a role for E2F2 in breast cancer cell-matrix adhesion. Bioinformatics **30**(21), 3036–3043 (2014)
11. Boyer, B., Corre, K., Legay, A., Sedwards, S.: PLASMA-lab: A flexible, distributable statistical model checking library. In: Joshi, K., Siegle, M., Stoelinga, M., D'Argenio, P.R. (eds.) QEST 2013. LNCS, vol. 8054, pp. 160–164. Springer, Heidelberg (2013). doi:10.1007/978-3-642-40196-1_12
12. Buchholz, P.: A new approach combining simulation and randomization for the analysis of large continuous time Markov chains. ACM Trans. Model Comput. Simul. **8**(2), 194–222 (1998). http://doi.acm.org/10.1145/280265.280274
13. Carrillo, M., Góngora, P.A., Rosenblueth, D.A.: An overview of existing modeling tools making use of model checking in the analysis of biochemical networks. Front. Plant Sci. **3**(155), 1–13 (2012)
14. Cavaliere, M., Mazza, T., Sedwards, S.: Statistical model checking of membrane systems with peripheral proteins: Quantifying the role of estrogen incellular mitosis and DNA damage. In: Frisco, P., Gheorghe, M., Pérez-Jiménez, M.J. (eds.) Applications of Membrane Computing inSystems and Synthetic Biology. Emergence, Complexity and Computation, vol. 7, pp. 43–63. Springer, Heidelberg (2014). doi:10.1007/978-3-319-03191-0_2
15. Clarke, E.M., Grumberg, O., Peled, D.: Model Checking. MIT Press, Cambridge (1999)
16. Donaldson, R., Gilbert, D.: A Monte Carlo model checker for Probabilistic LTL with numerical constraints. Technical report, University of Glasgow, Department of Computing Science (2008)

17. Dragomir, C., Ipate, F., Konur, S., Lefticaru, R., Mierla, L.: Model checking kernel P systems. In: Alhazov, A., Cojocaru, S., Gheorghe, M., Rogozhin, Y., Rozenberg, G., Salomaa, A. (eds.) CMC 2013. LNCS, vol. 8340, pp. 151–172. Springer, Heidelberg (2014). doi:10.1007/978-3-642-54239-8_12

18. Dwyer, M.B., Avrunin, G.S., Corbett, J.C.: Patterns in property specifications for finite-state verification. In: ICSE 1999, pp. 411–420. ACM, New York (1999)

19. The European Bioinformatics Institute. http://www.ebi.ac.uk/. Accessed 25 Sept 2016

20. Fisher, J., Piterman, N.: Model checking in biology. In: Kulkarni, V.V., Stan, G.-B., Raman, K. (eds.) A Systems Theoretic Approach to Systems and Synthetic Biology I Models and System Characterizations, pp. 255–279. Springer, Heidelberg (2014)

21. Fisher, J., Henzinger, T.A.: Executable cell biology. Nat. Biotech. **25**(11), 1239–1249 (2007)

22. Frisco, P., Gheorghe, M., Pérez-Jiménez, M.J. (eds.): Applications of Membrane Computing in Systems and Synthetic Biology. Emergence, Complexity and Computation, vol. 7. Springer, Heidelberg (2014)

23. Gheorghe, M., Konur, S., Ipate, F., Mierla, L., Bakir, M.E., Stannett, M.: An integrated model checking toolset for kernel P systems. In: Rozenberg, G., Salomaa, A., Sempere, J.M., Zandron, C. (eds.) CMC 2015. LNCS, vol. 9504, pp. 153–170. Springer, Cham (2015). doi:10.1007/978-3-319-28475-0_11

24. Grunske, L.: Specification patterns for probabilistic quality properties. In: ICSE 2008, pp. 31–40. ACM, New York (2008)

25. Harel, D.: Statecharts: a visual formalism for complex systems. Sci. Comput. Program. **8**(3), 231–274 (1987)

26. Heiner, M., Gilbert, D., Donaldson, R.: Petri nets for systems and synthetic biology. In: Bernardo, M., Degano, P., Zavattaro, G. (eds.) SFM 2008. LNCS, vol. 5016, pp. 215–264. Springer, Heidelberg (2008). doi:10.1007/978-3-540-68894-5_7

27. Hinton, A., Kwiatkowska, M., Norman, G., Parker, D.: PRISM: A tool for automatic verification of probabilistic systems. In: Hermanns, H., Palsberg, J. (eds.) TACAS 2006. LNCS, vol. 3920, pp. 441–444. Springer, Heidelberg (2006). doi:10.1007/11691372_29

28. Huth, M., Ryan, M.: Logic in Computer Science: Modelling and Reasoning about Systems, 2nd edn. Cambridge University Press, Cambridge (2004)

29. Katoen, J.P., Zapreev, I.S., Hahn, E.M., Hermanns, H., Jansen, D.N.: The ins and outs of the probabilistic model checker MRMC. In: Quantitative Evaluation of Systems (QEST), pp. 167–176. IEEE Computer Society (2009)

30. Kauffman, S.A.: Metabolic stability and epigenesis in randomly constructed genetic nets. J. Theoret. Biol. **22**, 437–467 (1969)

31. Konur, S., Gheorghe, M.: A property-driven methodology for formal analysis of synthetic biology systems. IEEE/ACM Trans. Comput. Biol. Bioinform. **12**(2), 360–371 (2015)

32. kPWorkbench. http://kpworkbench.org/. Accessed 25 Sept 2016

33. Kwiatkowska, M., Norman, G., Parker, D.: PRISM: Probabilistic symbolic model checker. In: Field, T., Harrison, P.G., Bradley, J., Harder, U. (eds.) TOOLS 2002. LNCS, vol. 2324, pp. 200–204. Springer, Heidelberg (2002). doi:10.1007/3-540-46029-2_13

34. Kwiatkowska, M., Norman, G., Parker, D.: Stochastic model checking. In: Bernardo, M., Hillston, J. (eds.) SFM 2007. LNCS, vol. 4486, pp. 220–270. Springer, Heidelberg (2007). doi:10.1007/978-3-540-72522-0_6

35. Legay, A., Delahaye, B., Bensalem, S.: Statistical model checking: An overview. In: Barringer, H., Falcone, Y., Finkbeiner, B., Havelund, K., Lee, I., Pace, G., Roşu, G., Sokolsky, O., Tillmann, N. (eds.) RV 2010. LNCS, vol. 6418, pp. 122–135. Springer, Heidelberg (2010). doi:10.1007/978-3-642-16612-9_11

36. Lindenmayer, A., Jürgensen, H.: Grammars of development: Discrete-state models for growth, differentiation, and gene expression in modular organisms. In: Rozenberg, G., Salomaa, A. (eds.) Lindenmayer Systems: Impacts on Theoretical Computer Science, Computer Graphics, and Developmental Biology, pp. 3–21. Springer, Heidelberg (1992). doi:10.1007/978-3-642-58117-5_1

37. Manca, V.: Infobiotics: Information in Biotic Systems. Emergence, Complexity and Computation, vol. 3. Springer, Heidelberg (2013)

38. Milner, R.: Communicating and Mobile Systems: The Pi-Calculus. Cambridge University Press, New York (1999)

39. Monteiro, P.T., Ropers, D., Mateescu, R., Freitas, A.T., de Jong, H.: Temporal logic patterns for querying dynamic models of cellular interaction networks. Bioinformatics 24(16), i227–i233 (2008). http://dx.doi.org/10.1093/bioinformatics/btn275

40. Markow Reward Model Checker (MRMC). http://www.mrmc-tool.org/. Accessed 18 Feb 2015

41. Pérez-Jiménez, M.J., Romero-Campero, F.J.: P systems, a new computational modelling tool for systems biology. In: Priami, C., Plotkin, G. (eds.) Transactions on Computational Systems Biology VI. LNCS, vol. 4220, pp. 176–197. Springer, Heidelberg (2006). doi:10.1007/11880646_8

42. Plasma-Lab. https://project.inria.fr/plasma-lab/. Accessed 18 Feb 2015

43. Reisig, W.: The basic concepts. In: Understanding Petri Nets: Modeling Techniques, Analysis Methods, Case Studies, pp. 13–24. Springer, Heidelberg (2013). http://dx.doi.org/10.1007/978-3-642-33278-4_2

44. Probabilistic and Symbolic Model Checker (PRISM). http://www.prismmodelchecker.org/. Accessed 08 Jan 2015

45. Sanassy, D., Widera, P., Krasnogor, N.: Meta-stochastic simulation of biochemical models for systems and synthetic biology. ACS Synth. Biol. 4(1), 39–47 (2015). pMID: 25152014. http://dx.doi.org/10.1021/sb5001406

46. Ymer website. http://www.tempastic.org/ymer/. Accessed 25 Aug 2015

47. Younes, H., Kwiatkowska, M., Norman, G., Parker, D.: Numerical vs. statistical probabilistic model checking. Int. J. Softw. Tools Technol. Transfer (STTT) 8(3), 216–228 (2006)

48. Younes, H.L.S.: Ymer: A statistical model checker. In: Etessami, K., Rajamani, S.K. (eds.) CAV 2005. LNCS, vol. 3576, pp. 429–433. Springer, Heidelberg (2005). doi:10.1007/11513988_43

49. Younes, H.L.S., Simmons, R.G.: Probabilistic verification of discrete event systems using acceptance sampling. In: Brinksma, E., Larsen, K.G. (eds.) CAV 2002. LNCS, vol. 2404, pp. 223–235. Springer, Heidelberg (2002). doi:10.1007/3-540-45657-0_17

50. Zapreev, I.S., Jansen, C.: Markov reward model checker manual. http://www.mrmc-tool.org/downloads/MRMC/Specs/MRMC_Manual.pdf

51. Zuliani, P.: Statistical model checking for biological applications. Int. J. Softw. Tools Technol. Transfer 17(4), 527–536 (2014). http://dx.doi.org/10.1007/s10009-014-0343-0

Chemical Term Reduction
with Active P Systems

Péter Battyányi and György Vaszil$^{(\boxtimes)}$

Department of Computer Science, Faculty of Informatics, University of Debrecen,
Kassai út 26, Debrecen 4028, Hungary
{battyanyi.peter,vaszil.gyorgy}@inf.unideb.hu

Abstract. We present an attempt to translate the terms of a variant of
the γ-calculus into membrane systems, such that the reduction sequences
in the calculus are simulated by the computation of the corresponding
membrane system. Finding such translations could help to reason about
properties of membrane computations and properties of the reduction
sequences of chemical calculi in terms of each other. By translating chemical computing formalisms to membrane systems, we might also obtain
a high-level programming language for P systems which could also serve
as an elegant and efficient way of presenting P system algorithms.

1 Introduction

In the following, we continue the investigations concerning the relationship of
the "chemical calculus" of Banâtre and Le Métayer [3,5] and membrane systems.
The chemical calculus is a formal representation of the Gamma programming
style introduced in [5,6]. The intention behind the Gamma formulation of programs was the purpose of freeing programs from "artificial" sequentiality, that
is, sequentiality which is not inherent in the particular problem being solved, but
only a consequence of the programming language and the underlying machine
model. In the chemical calculus a computation can be seen as the global evolution of a collection of data, represented as molecules, acting freely in a chemical
solution (cf. [4]).

P systems represent a related, but quite different model of computation where
the components evolve in different compartments in a distributed, synchronous
manner (see [10]). In [1,7] we have studied the possibilities of describing membrane system computations with chemical terms and their reduction sequences.
We managed to give a translation of the membrane system with dissolution
into the chemical calculus such that the two systems compute the same sets of
numbers.

In this paper we are attempting to present a translation in the reverse direction: given a chemical term we render a membrane system with active membranes
such that the computation sequences of each system can be bijectively mapped
to each other. To simplify matters, we restrict our attention to the untyped
chemical formalism of [4]. Moreover, we resort to another restriction by considering only γ-abstraction in which the conditional parts are the constant term

© Springer International Publishing AG 2017
A. Leporati et al. (Eds.): CMC 2016, LNCS 10105, pp. 136–150, 2017.
DOI: 10.1007/978-3-319-54072-6_9

true (see Sect. 2 for the definitions). On one hand we expect from the translation that the description of membrane systems using one of the chemical computing formalisms would enable us to reason about properties of membrane systems and their computations which can be connected to properties of the reduction sequences of chemical calculi and vice versa. For example, to the authors' knowledge, the properties of reduction sequences like existence of reduction strategies (e.g. call-by-value, call-by-name) are yet not studied very extensively neither for membrane systems nor for the chemical calculus. Should some of these properties seem to be obtainable more easily form one computational model than from the other, we could acquire the equivalent of the property in the other computational model almost "for free". The same is true for classifying objects in he computational models as ones obeying the property of strong normalization, weak normalization, or having only infinite computation sequences. On the other hand, by being able to translate chemical computing formalisms to membrane systems, we could obtain a high-level programming language for P systems which could also serve as an elegant and efficient way of presenting P system algorithms.

A preliminary study of turning certain simple chemical programs to P systems was initiated in [9]. Here we present an attempt to continue the investigations in this direction, that is, to describe chemical terms and their reduction sequences by membrane system computations.

The paper is organized as follows. First we present a version of the γ-calculus, which is still in experimental form, and which, according to our expectations, admits us to grasp the connection between the chemical metaphor and the membrane system computational model in a more adequate form. The emerging calculus is a parallel version of the γ-calculus, where the reduction rule is the original γ-rule with the exception that it can be applied in one reduction step to several redexes in the original term, provided there is no overlap between the chosen redexes. Next we review the type of membrane systems with active membranes that we are going to use (a version of the active P system model described in [2]). The third part of the paper is a translation of the chemical calculus into the membrane system such that the chemical terms compute exactly the same results as the corresponding membrane systems.

2   About the γ-Calculus

In this section we provide the basic notions of the γ-calculus following the presentation in [4]. However, unlike in [4], we use a generalized version of the chemical calculus: molecules are formed by arbitrary, finite multisets instead of pairs, and we allow several γ-redexes to be reduced simultaneously. The only stipulation is that these redexes cannot have terms in common, that is, they should be disjoint. To distinguish our calculus from that of [4], we call it γ_p-calculus meaning that we are talking about a parallel version of the γ-calculus. In what follows we define the terms and reduction rules of the γ_p-calculus. As an abuse of notation we may still talk about γ-terms, γ-redexes etc. when it causes no confusion.

The syntactical elements of *molecules, reaction conditions,* and *patterns,* denoted by M, C and P, respectively, are defined as follows.

$$A := true \mid false \mid x \mid \langle M \rangle \mid \gamma(P)[C].M$$
$$M := (A_1, \ldots, A_n)$$

where x is a variable standing for any molecule, *true* and *false* are two constants, $(A_1, \ldots, A_n)$ is a compound molecule, considered as a multiset formed by elements of the set A, $\langle M \rangle$ is called a *solution,* and $\gamma(P)[C].M$ is called a γ-abstraction with pattern P, reaction condition C, result M. Reaction conditions can be arbitrary elements of M. We call variables, constants, abstractions and solutions together as atomic terms or atoms. The solution $\langle M \rangle$ encapsulates the molecule M which is inside the solution, and thus, insulated from molecules outside the solution. The contents of solutions can only be changed by reactions which occur inside the solution.

The γ-*abstraction* encodes a rewriting rule: when the pattern P is respected and the condition C is met, a substituted variant of M is created as a result. A pattern is

$$AP := x \mid \langle P \rangle$$
$$P := (AP_1, \ldots, AP_n)$$

where x matches any molecule, P, and $\langle P \rangle$ matches an *inert solution,* that is, a solution where no reaction in the outermost level can occur. (The contained solutions can still be active, however.)

A (γ-)redex is a term of the form $(\gamma(P)[C].M, N)$. The reaction rule (γ-rule) (cf. [4]) is originally defined as

$$\gamma(P)[C].M, N \rightarrow_\gamma \phi M,$$

where $match(P, N) = \phi$ assigns values to variables in such a way that $\phi(C)$ reduces to *true*. The abbreviation $\gamma(P).M$ stands for the term $\gamma(P)[true].M$.

As an example, consider the γ-term $(\gamma(x, y)[x = y].x, \ 1, 2, 3, 1, 4)$ where (x, y) is a pattern, and $x = y$ is a reaction condition. In order for the condition to evaluate to *true*, the pattern needs to be matched so that $\phi(x) = \phi(y)$, and then the result is $(\gamma(x, y)[x = y].x, \ 1, 2, 3, 1, 4) \rightarrow (1, 2, 3, 4)$.

We use the reaction in a broader sense: unlike in [4], *match* compares multisets and not just molecules formed with the help of the pair forming operator. Moreover, every distinct constituent of a molecule can take part in a reaction separately. Prior to defining the reduction relation, we settle what we understand on matching between patterns and molecules.

Definition 1. *Let x denote a variable, P a pattern, and M a molecule. The operator match takes a pattern and a molecule as arguments and gives back a substitution as result.*

$$match(x, \mathcal{M}) = \{x \mapsto \mathcal{M}\}, \text{ where } \mathcal{M} \text{ is a finite,}$$
$$\text{nonempty multiset of } \gamma\text{-terms}$$
$$match((P_1, \ldots, P_n), (M_1, \ldots, M_m)) = match(P_1, (M_{i_{11}}, \ldots, M_{i_{1k_1}})) \oplus \ldots$$
$$\oplus \; match(P_n, (M_{i_{n1}}, \ldots, M_{i_{nk_n}}))$$
$$match(\langle P \rangle, \langle M \rangle) = match(P, M) \text{ provided } inert(M)$$
$$match(P, M) = \boldsymbol{fail} \text{ in every other case,}$$

where the operator $\oplus$ *denotes the composition of substitutions provided that the matchings* $match(P_j, (M_{i_{j1}}, \ldots, M_{i_{jk_j}}))$ $(1 \leq j \leq n)$ *agree on their common variables. Furthermore, at the second equation,*

$$\{M_{i_j1}, \ldots, M_{i_j k_j}\}, (1 \leq j \leq n) \tag{1}$$

are non-empty multisets forming a partition of the set $\{M_1, \ldots, M_m\}$.

Observe that unlike in [4], the *match* operator in can have several results depending on the choice of the index sets $\{i_{j1}, \ldots, i_{jk_j}\}$ $(1 \leq j \leq n)$ in (1).

Example 1. The example below illustrates some of the assignments performed by *match*.

$$match((x, y, \langle u, v \rangle), (1, 2, 3, \langle 4, 5 \rangle))$$

can have any of the following results:

$$\{x \longmapsto (1,2), y \longmapsto 3, u \longmapsto 4, v \longmapsto 5\}, \text{or} \{x \longmapsto 1, y \longmapsto (2,3), u \longmapsto 4, v \longmapsto 5\}, \text{or}$$
$$\{x \longmapsto 2, y \longmapsto (1,3), u \longmapsto 5, v \longmapsto 4\}.$$

We restate the definition of the γ-reduction, where *match* is understood as above. We denote our new reduction by γ_p.

Definition 2.

$$(\gamma(P)[C].M, N) \to_{\gamma_p} \phi M,$$

where $match(P, N) = \phi$, $\phi(C) \twoheadrightarrow_{\gamma_p} true$, *and if* $\to$ *denotes a reduction relation,* $\twoheadrightarrow$ *denotes the reflexive, transitive closure of* $\to$. *(We will also use* $\to^+$ *for the transitive closure of* $\to$.)

The left hand side of the reduction rule is the multiset formed by the abstraction and N, and the result is ϕM, which is a substituted instance of the multiset M. We implicitly assume that, when we have calculated the result ϕM of a reduction, then the elements of the multiset ϕM become elements of the multiset to which the abstraction and the arguments of the redex belonged. The elements of N are called the arguments for the abstraction $\gamma(P)[C].M$. We remark that, if $(\gamma(P)[C].M, N)$ is a redex of S, it is not necessarily a multiset of S.

As usual, we assume that the γ_p is compatible with the term forming rules, that is, a solution reduces to a solution when their contents are in relation with respect to γ_p-reduction. The same is true for arbitrary multisets: the difference is that, unlike the γ-reduction, we allow γ_p-calculus to perform several reductions in parallel, with the stipulation that these reductions cannot overlap. When an abstraction takes part in a redex, reduction cannot take place inside that abstraction. The same is true for the arguments. Some of the terms can remain intact in a multiset during a γ_p-reduction step.

Example 2. We present some examples of a γ_p-reduction relation below.

$$(\gamma\langle x\rangle.(x,y), \langle \gamma x.x, 1, 3\rangle, \langle 4, 5\rangle) \rightarrow (4, 5, \langle \gamma x.x, 1, 3\rangle), \text{ or}$$
$$(\gamma\langle x\rangle.(x,y), \langle \gamma x.x, 1, 3\rangle, \langle 4, 5\rangle) \rightarrow (\gamma x.x, 1, 3, \langle 4, 5\rangle), \text{ or}$$
$$(\gamma\langle x\rangle.(x,y), \langle \gamma x.x, 1, 3\rangle, \langle 4, 5\rangle) \rightarrow (4, 5, \langle 1, 3\rangle), \text{ but}$$
$$(\gamma\langle x\rangle.(x,y), \langle \gamma x.x, 1, 3\rangle, \langle 4, 5\rangle) \nrightarrow (1, 3, 4, 5).$$

Remark 1. We assert a simple statement to illustrate how γ_p relates to the original γ-reduction. As expected, the γ_p-reduction relation is somewhere between a γ-reduction step and the reflexive and transitive closure of $\rightarrow_\gamma$.

If $\rightarrow_{\gamma_p}$ is defined as above, then

$$\rightarrow_\gamma \subsetneq \rightarrow_{\gamma_p} \subsetneq \twoheadrightarrow_\gamma = \twoheadrightarrow_{\gamma_p}.$$

Remark 2. In the following, we also use an additional simplification by assuming that the abstractions are of the form $\gamma(P).M$ with *true* as conditional element C. This assumption does not reduce the computational power of the γ-calculus (cf. [3]).

3   How to Associate P Systems to γ-Terms

Let M be a γ-calculus term. We define the P-system associated with M as

$$\Pi = (O, \mu, w_1, \ldots, w_n, H, R_1, \ldots, R_n, \rho_1, \ldots, \rho_n)$$

where

- O is an alphabet of objects, $O = Atom$, where $Atom$ is a set of atomic objects.
- μ is a membrane structure of n membranes,
- $w_i \in \mathcal{M}(O)$, $1 \leq i \leq n$, are the initial contents of the n regions,
- Let $H = Var \cup \{\sigma, \rho, \rho_1, \rho_2\}$, where Var is the set of variables occurring in M and $Atom$ is the set of atomic objects in M different from variables. Then H is the set of labels. For the sake of simplicity we assume that we only have variables, as in the untyped γ-calculus.
- R_i, $1 \leq i \leq n$, are the sets of evolution rules associated with the regions.
- We also use promoters and inhibitors assigned to rules. Moreover, besides the usual parities we introduce new values ? and ?? for unknown parities.

Intuitively, solutions are coded by the label σ and patterns are abstractions are coded as pairs, the first elements of which are the patterns labeled by ρ_1 and the second ones are the bodies of the abstractions with labels ρ_2. The variables occurring in patterns also appear as labels. Labels in the pattern part of an abstraction get an additional subscript p. Moreover, pattern variables occurring also in the body of the pattern also receive the subscript p. The membrane implicitly containing the whole structure is the skin membrane. For example, the term $\gamma\langle x, y\rangle.(x, y, z)$ corresponds to a system

$$[[[\,]_{x_p}, [\,]_{y_p}]_{\sigma_p}]_{\rho_1}, [[\,]_{x_p}, [\,]_{y_p}, [\,]_z]_{\rho_2}]_\rho.$$

Notation 1. *We use the following types of rules (cf. [2])*

1. $s, [u_1]_{\alpha_1}^{a_1}, \ldots, [u_k]_{\alpha_k}^{a_k} \rightarrow [v_{i_1}]_{\alpha_{i_1}}^{b_{i_1}}, \ldots, [v_{i_l}]_{\alpha_{i_l}}^{b_{i_l}}, t$
   where $s, u_1, \ldots, u_k, v_{i_1}, \ldots, v_{i_l}, t \in O^*, 1 \le i_1 < i_2 < \ldots < i_l \le k$ *(filtering)*
2. $s, [u_1]_{\alpha_1}^{a_1}, \ldots, [u_k]_{\alpha_k}^{a_k} \rightarrow t, [v_1]_{\alpha_1}^{b_1}, [w_1]_{\alpha_1}^{c_1}, \ldots, [v_k]_{\alpha_k}^{b_k}, [w_k]_{\alpha_k}^{c_k}$
   where $s, u_i, v_i, w_i, 1 \le i \le k, t \in O^*$ *(membrane division)*
3. $u, [\,]_\alpha^a, [\,]_{\beta_1}^{b_1}, \ldots, [\,]_{\beta_k}^{b_k} \rightarrow [v, [\,]_{\beta_1}^{c_1}, \ldots, [\,]_{\beta_k}^{c_k}]_\alpha^d, w$
   where $u, v, w \in O^*$ *(subordination)*

We assume that filtering has the highest priorities among all the rules. Observe that membrane dissolution acts as a special case of filtering.

Remark 3. We note that the rules above are generalization of those applied in [2]. In our system we allow arbitrary number of membranes on the left- and righthand side of the rules, moreover, we assume that any membrane has an infinite stock of these rules. This unusual assumption can, however, be eliminated if we take the rules in [2] and keep executing all prescribed operations until every intended element or membrane is processed. Thus, our rules can be seen as a "shorthand" notation for those in [2] that simplifies the presentation of the systems.

An other approach to limit the number of rules of our systems would be through upper bounds on the size of the reduction sequences of the γ-calculus. At present, since, according to our knowledge, upper bounds for the sizes and lengths of reductions for normalizable γ-terms are not known, in contrast to the λ-calculus (cf. [8,11]), we are not able to give an upper bound for the number of rules used in a membrane in order to keep a more parallel-like rule execution.

We simulate one γ_p-reduction step by several computational steps of the membrane system. We use promoters in addition, to make the presentation as accessible as possible. We assume that promoters are elements of the set $Prom = \{\Phi_i, \Theta_i, \Psi_i, \Delta_i \mid i \ge 1\}$.

The following group of rules finds the abstractions which are candidates for taking part of reductions together with their arguments, and then initiates the reductions by rendering the arguments to abstractions by subordination. We have to make sure that no reduction takes place in a term chosen as an argument of a redex. The elements in $Prom$ indicate the separate phases of the computation.

Proposition 1. *The following rules initiate a γ_p-reduction-step by choosing abstractions and arguments in the skin membrane and then letting the process continue in the contained solutions.*

$$
\begin{aligned}
r_{\varPhi 1} \quad & []^0_\rho, []^0_{\alpha_1}, \ldots, []^0_{\alpha_k} \rightarrow [\Theta_1, []^0_{\alpha_1}, \ldots, []^0_{\alpha_k}]^0_\rho, ?redex, \\
r_{\varPhi 2} \quad & []^0_\sigma \rightarrow [\varPhi_1]^0_\sigma, ?solution, \\
r_{\varPhi 3} \quad & []^0_\alpha \rightarrow []^0_\alpha, \\
r_{\varPhi 4} \quad & \varPhi_1 \rightarrow \varPhi_3, \\
& promoter: \quad \varPhi_1.
\end{aligned}
$$

The last line assigns the promoter for all the rules above it. In the sequel, we resort to such notation.

Explanation.

1. $r_{\varPhi 1}$: an instance of subordination rule, abstractions receive arguments by this rule. An element $?redex$ serves for keeping track of the successful reductions.
2. $r_{\varPhi 2}$: reduction propagates to some of the solutions
3. $r_{\varPhi 3}$: some of the terms remain unchanged ☐

Proposition 2. *The following rules initiate the matching process of a γ_p-reduction step.*

$$
\begin{aligned}
r_{\Theta 1} \quad & []^0_{\rho_1} \rightarrow, \quad (\text{ dissolution of } []^0_{\rho_1}) \\
r_{\Theta 2} \quad & []^0_{x_p}, []^0_{\alpha_1}, \ldots, []^0_{\alpha_k} \rightarrow [[]^0_{\alpha_1}, \ldots, []^0_{\alpha_k},]^+_{x_p}, \\
r_{\Theta 3} \quad & \Theta_1, []^0_{\sigma_p}, [inert]^0_\sigma \rightarrow \Theta_2, []^\triangle_{\sigma_p}, [inert]^\triangle_\sigma, \\
r_{\Theta 4} \quad & []^0_{\sigma_p}, [non\text{-}inert]^0_\sigma \rightarrow \#, \\
r_{\Theta 5} \quad & \Theta_1, []^0_\sigma \rightarrow []^1_\sigma, [\varPsi_1]^?_\sigma, \Theta_{in}, \\[6pt]
r_{\Theta 6} \quad & []^0_\alpha, \Theta_2 \rightarrow \#, \ (\alpha \neq \rho_2), \\
r_{\Theta 7} \quad & \Theta_2, []^\triangle_{\sigma_p} \rightarrow \Theta_3, []^\triangle_{\sigma_p}, \\
r_{\Theta 8} \quad & \Theta_2 \rightarrow \Theta_4, \\
r_{\Theta 9} \quad & \Theta_3, []^\triangle_{\sigma_p}, [inert]^\triangle_\sigma \rightarrow \Theta_1, \quad (\text{dissolution of membranes with } \triangle),
\end{aligned}
$$

where Θ_1 is the promoter of the first rule. Moreover, the first rule in the second block has priority higher than that of the second rule, the third one has the lowest priority. Moreover, $r_{\Theta 3} > r_{\Theta 5}$ and $r_{\Theta 4} > r_{\Theta 5}$.

Explanation.

1. $r_{\Theta 1}$: first we dissolve the membrane $[]^0_{\rho_1}$ so that the matching process can begin
2. $r_{\Theta 2}$: the pattern variables match to arbitrary multisets
3. $r_{\Theta 3}$: inert solutions match with pattern solutions- their processing is postponed by one step. Furthermore, only one membrane containing *inert* is treated at a time
4. $r_{\Theta 4}$: when a solution is non-inert, the reduction step fails

5. $r_{\Theta 5}$: when we have no information whether a solution is inert, a sequence of computational steps checks inertness. By introducing Θ_{in}, we achieve that only one solution is checked for inertness at a time.
6. $r_{\Theta 6}$: we make sure that no elements has been left out from the multisets matched to pattern variables and the solutions matched to solution patterns
7. $r_{\Theta 7}$: membranes of inert solutions disappear by virtue of $r_{\Theta 9}$ and $r_{\Theta 7}$ leads to $r_{\Theta 9}$
8. $r_{\Theta 8}$: the matching process will continue with the examination whether the obtained match itself is well defined
9. $r_{\Theta 9}$: an inert solution is dissolved and we are led back to the matching   □

By maximal parallelism, any solution which is not known to be inert will be checked for inertness, which is triggered by the promoter Ψ_1. We continue with the reduction step assuming we have a means already to test for inertness (we will return to this later on).

The promoter Θ_4 initiates a test required for the correctness of the matching process by the rule $\Theta_4 \to \Theta_4, init\_match$. Namely, we have to check whether any two membranes labeled with the same pattern variable contain membranes corresponding to equal γ-terms. We give a recursive algorithm which decides whether to every two occurrences of the same variable are assigned the same multiset of membranes. In addition, the algorithm simplifies the result of the matching by clearing the unnecessary repetitions. First we give an informal description of the algorithm.

Description.

- input: a multiset of membranes with labels in Var_p and polarity +
- output: a simplified assignment together with the element $matchsuccesful$ in the outermost membrane labeled ρ, or the element $matchfails$

1. Find two membranes with the same label in Var_p. We create auxiliary copies of them, let they have polarities * and ? and ** and ??, respectively. If there are no such membranes, the algorithm terminates with $matchsuccessful$. In each step of the algorithm the actual membranes will have copies * and ? and ** and ??.
2. Let us take the longest sequence of membranes with polarity * such that each element contains the next one in the sequence. Let Actual 1 be the copy of the endpoint membrane with polarity ?. Similarly, let Actual 2 be the copy with polarity ?? of the farthest membrane in the sequence of membranes denoted by **.
3. In Actual 1 we choose a membrane labeled by a variable. Delete that membrane and find in Actual 2 a membrane with the same label. Repeat the process with roles of Actual 1 and 2 interchanged as long as possible. If there are no membranes labeled by a variable in Actual 1 neither in Actual 2, go to Point 5. Otherwise continue with Point 4.

4. Delete Actual 1, take the original copy of Actual 1 labeled by $*$ and make a copy of it with polarity $?$. Delete Actual 2 and restore the original copy of Actual 2 and give it polarity $-$. If Actual 2 was the first element of the membrane sequence with polarity $??$, terminate with $match fails$. Otherwise, in Actual 2 choose a solution with polarity 0 and give it polarity $??$. If no such solution exists, indicate it with $match fails$. Otherwise, jump to Point 3.
5. Assume we are in Actual 1. If Actual 1 is empty, then go to Point 6. Otherwise choose a solution in Actual 1, make two copies of it, one with polarity $*$ and the other with $?$. Go to Actual 2, if Actual 2 is empty, go to Point 6. Otherwise, choose a solution, make two copies of it, one with polarity $**$ and the other with $??$. Jump to Point 3.
6. Either of the collections is non empty: terminate with $?match fails$. Otherwise delete Actual 1 and Actual 2. If the actual membranes were the outermost membranes with polarities $?$ and $??$, delete membrane with polarity $**$ and restore polarity $*$ to $+$. Jump to Point 1.   □

Now we present the algorithm corresponding to the equality check. We group the rules in blocks following the points in the hint above. Through the algorithm we use auxiliary elements to ensure control.

Algorithm.

r_{eq1}
$$\{init\_match, []^{+}_{x_p}, []^{+}_{x_p} \rightarrow []^{*?}_{x_p}, []^{**??}_{x_p} > init\_match \rightarrow matchsuccessful\},$$

r_{eq2} $\quad []^{*?}_{\beta} \rightarrow []^{*}_{\beta}, [compare\_vars]^{?}_{\beta},$
r_{eq3} $\quad []^{**??}_{\beta} \rightarrow []^{**}_{\beta}, [compare\_vars]^{??}_{\beta},$

r_{eq4} $\quad \{[compare\_vars, []^{0}_{y}]^{?}_{\beta} \rightarrow y\_found_1, []^{?}_{\beta},$
r_{eq5} $\quad [compare\_vars, []^{0}_{y}]^{??}_{\beta} \rightarrow y\_found_2, []^{??}_{\beta} >$
r_{eq6} $\quad compare\_vars \rightarrow compare\_solutions\},$
r_{eq7} $\quad y\_found_1, []^{??}_{\beta} \rightarrow [y\_find_2]^{??}_{\beta},$
r_{eq8} $\quad y\_found_2, []^{?}_{\beta} \rightarrow [y\_find_1]^{?}_{\beta},$
r_{eq9} $\quad \{[y\_find_1, []^{0}_{y}]^{?}_{\beta} \rightarrow [compare\_vars]^{?}_{\beta} >$
r_{eq10} $\quad [y\_find_1]^{?}_{\beta}, []^{??}_{\beta} \rightarrow [findnew]^{?}_{\beta}, [findnew]^{??}_{\beta}\},$
r_{eq11} $\quad \{[y\_find_2, []^{0}_{y}]^{??}_{\beta} \rightarrow [compare\_vars]^{??}_{\beta} >$
r_{eq12} $\quad []^{?}_{\beta}, [y\_find_2]^{??}_{\beta} \rightarrow [findnew]^{?}_{\beta}, [findnew]^{??}_{\beta}\},$
$$where \ \beta \in Var_p \cup \{\sigma\}$$

r_{eq13} $\quad [findnew]^{?}_{\beta} \rightarrow [findnew]^{\natural}_{\beta}, newcopy_1,$
r_{eq14} $\quad [findnew]^{??}_{\beta} \rightarrow [findnew]^{\natural}_{\beta}, newcopy_2,$
r_{eq15} $\quad newcopy_2, []^{**}_{\alpha} \rightarrow newargument, []^{-}_{\alpha}, \ (\alpha \notin Var_p),$
r_{eq16} $\quad newcopy_1, []^{*}_{\alpha} \rightarrow []^{*}_{\alpha}, [compare\_vars]^{?}_{\alpha},$
r_{eq17} $\quad \{newargument, []^{0}_{\alpha} \rightarrow []^{**}_{\alpha}, [compare\_vars]^{??}_{\alpha} >$
$\quad\quad newargument \rightarrow ?match fails\},$
r_{eq18} $\quad newcopy_2, []^{**}_{x_p} \rightarrow match fails,$

r_{eq19} $\quad \{ [compare\_solutions, []_{\sigma}^{0}]_{\beta}^{?} \to [[]_{\sigma}^{*}, [compare\_vars]_{\sigma}^{?}]_{\beta}^{?} >$

r_{eq20} $\quad\quad [compare\_solutions]_{\beta}^{?} \to empty_1, []_{\beta}^{\natural} \},$

$$\beta \in Var_p \cup \{\sigma\},$$

r_{eq21} $\quad \{ [compare\_solutions, []_{\sigma}^{0}]_{\beta}^{??} \to [, []_{\sigma}^{**}, [compare\_vars]_{\sigma}^{??}]_{\beta}^{??} >$

r_{eq22} $\quad\quad [compare\_solutions]_{\beta}^{??} \to empty_2, []_{\beta}^{\natural} \},$

$$\beta \in Var_p \cup \{\sigma\}$$

r_{eq23} $\quad\quad\quad \{ empty_1, empty_2 \to both\_empty >$

r_{eq24} $\quad\quad\quad\quad empty_1 \to matchfails,$

r_{eq25} $\quad\quad\quad\quad empty_2 \to matchfails \},$

r_{eq26} $\quad\quad both\_empty, []_{\sigma}^{*}, []_{\sigma}^{**} \to newsolutions$

r_{eq27} $\quad \{ [newsolutions, []_{\sigma}^{0}]_{\sigma}^{*} \to [[]_{\sigma}^{*?}]_{\sigma}^{*} >$

r_{eq28} $\quad\quad [newsolutions]_{\sigma}^{*} \to empty_1, \},$

r_{eq29} $\quad \{ [newsolutions, []_{\sigma}^{0}]_{\sigma}^{**} \to [[]_{\sigma}^{**??}]_{\sigma}^{**},$

r_{eq30} $\quad [newsolutions, []_{\sigma}^{-}]_{\sigma}^{**} \to [[]_{\sigma}^{**??}]_{\sigma}^{**} >$

r_{eq31} $\quad\quad [newsolutions]_{\sigma}^{**} \to empty_2, \},$

r_{eq32} $\quad\quad both\_empty, []_{x_p}^{*}, []_{x_p}^{**} \to iterate,$

r_{eq33} $\quad\quad\quad iterate, []_{x_p}^{+} \to init\_match, []_{x_p}^{\natural}.$ $\quad\quad\quad\square$

Explanation.

1. r_{eq1}: the matching process is initiated. When no two membranes with the same pattern variable as label exist, then the algorithm successfully terminates.

2. r_{eq4} and r_{eq5} find variables in $[]^{?}$ and $[]^{??}$.

3. y_found_i, y_find_i look for and delete the membranes with equal variable inside $[]^{?}$ and $[]^{??}$

4. r_{eq9}-r_{eq12}: when a variable is found in the other membrane of the comparison, too, the process starts all over again. Otherwise, we try for new submembranes.

5. r_{eq13}-r_{eq18}: the search for possible submembranes to compare begins. If there are no more new arguments in membrane $[]^{**}$ or we are back to the original membrane $[]_{x_p}^{**}$, then the comparison fails, and, by this, the matching also fails

6. r_{eq19}-r_{eq22}: if the membranes with variable labels are consumed at a certain level, then the contents of the solutions of that level are compared

7. r_{eq19}-r_{eq22}: depending on whether there exist new solutions to be compared in both membranes at the same level, we continue the process. If one of the submembranes at the same level contain less solution than the other, a message *matchfails* is evoked. $\quad\quad\quad\square$

Here *matchfails* acts as follows. Whenever *matchfails* is on the left side, the rule has highest priority of all the rules. The element *matchfails* penetrates every membrane until it reaches Θ_4. In that case the rule

$$\Theta_4, matchfails \to \#$$

applies. When $matchsuccessful$ is created, it also elevates to the level of Θ_4 and we have

$$\Theta_4, matchsuccessful \rightarrow \Theta_5.$$

The final stage in the reduction step is performing the substitutions themselves.

Proposition 3. *The rules below perform the substitution itself.*
Let $[w_1]^+_{x_{1p}}, \ldots, [w_j]^+_{x_{kp}}$ *be all the immediate submembranes of the membrane* $[]^+_\rho$ *with labels in* Var_p *and polarities* $+$.

$$r_{sub1} \quad \{ []^0_{\rho_2} \rightarrow,$$
$$r_{sub2} \quad \Theta_5, []^0_{\alpha_1}, \ldots, []^0_{\alpha_j} \rightarrow [\Theta_5]^?_{\alpha_1}, \ldots, [\Theta_5]^?_{\alpha_j}, \Theta_6,$$
$$remainder,$$
$$where \alpha_i \neq \rho_1 \text{ and } \alpha_i \notin Var_p \cup Var,$$
$$r_{sub3} \quad []^0_{y_{1p}}, \ldots, []^0_{y_{jp}} \rightarrow []^?_{y_{1p}}, \ldots, []^?_{y_{jp}}, ?var_{y_{1p}}, \ldots, ?var_{y_{jp}},$$
$$r_{sub4} \quad promoter: \quad \Theta_5, \}$$

$$r_{sub5} \quad \{ remainder, []^0_\alpha \rightarrow \# \quad > \quad (where \alpha \neq \rho_1, \alpha \notin Var),$$
$$r_{sub6} \quad remainder, []^?_\alpha \rightarrow []^?_\alpha \},$$

$$r_{sub7} \quad [?var_{y_{1p}}, \ldots, ?var_{y_{jp}}]^?_\alpha \rightarrow [s^j]^0_\alpha, ?var_{y_{1p}}, \ldots, ?var_{y_{jp}},$$
$$r_{sub8} \quad []^+_{x_{1p}}, \ldots, []^+_{x_{kp}}, ?var_{yp} \rightarrow ?sub_{yp}, []^+_{x_{1p}}, []^+_{x_{1p}}, \ldots, []^+_{x_{kp}}, []^+_{x_{kp}},$$
$$r_{sub9} \quad [s]^0_\alpha \rightarrow []^{++}_\alpha,$$
$$r_{sub10} \quad []^{++}_\alpha, []^+_{x_{1p}}, \ldots, []^+_{x_{kp}} \rightarrow [[]^+_{x_{1p}} \ldots, []^+_{x_{kp}}]^0_\alpha,$$
$$where \alpha \neq \rho_1 and \alpha \notin Var_p \cup Var,$$
$$r_{sub11} \quad []^?_{x_{jp}}, []^+_{x_{1p}}, \ldots, []^+_{x_{kp}} \rightarrow [sync_j, []^+_{x_{1p}}, \ldots, []^+_{x_{kp}}]^{??}_{x_{jp}}, \quad x_{jp} \in Var_p,$$
$$r_{sub12} \quad sync_j, []^+_{x_{1p}}, \ldots, []^+_{x_{jp}}, \ldots, []^+_{x_{kp}} \rightarrow sync'_j, []^\natural_{x_{1p}}, \ldots, []^\natural_{x_{kp}},$$
$$([]^+_{x_{jp}} \text{ is deleted}),$$
$$r_{sub13} \quad [sync'_j]^0_{x_{jp}} \rightarrow !sub_{x_{jp}} \ ([]^{??}_{x_{jp}} \text{ is deleted}).$$

Explanation. The rules r_{sub1}-r_{sub7} perform some preliminary steps before the actual substitution. They find the variables in the outermost submembrane $[] \rho_2$ and inform the membrane system about the maximal number of variables that must be substituted for. The counter elements s store that number.

Rules r_{sub8}-r_{sub13} perform the actual substitutions. Rule r_{sub8} produces the necessary copies of terms to be written in, while rule r_{sub9} and r_{sub10} pushes the terms to be substituted toward their correct places enabling as many as k terms to move inside a membrane. All membranes $[]^+_{x_{1p}}, \ldots, []^+_{x_{kp}}$ move together according to rules r_{sub10} and r_{sub11}. When a substitution is done, an element $!sub_{yp}$ is released.

The elements $?sub_{yp}, !sub_{yp}$ perform a synchronization, when both appear in the membrane containing Θ_6 they vanish. The inhibitor of creating an element $!redex$ and deleting the outside membrane with label ρ is any one of $?sub_{yp}$. In a similar way, $?redex$ is an inhibitor for sending out an element $!solution$ from any solution: when the same number of $!redex$ elements have appeared in the skin membrane as that of ?*redex* elements, and likewise for the pair of elements ?*solution* and !*solution*, then the promoter Φ_1 appears again and the reduction process is iterated. We assume that, in preparation to the simulation of the next γ_p-reduction step, we restore polarities of membranes to 0, except for those with polarity $\natural$, and remove all auxiliary elements from membranes with polarity 0. $\square$

Prior to the inertness check, we have to make some preparations. Inertness check starts with a solution with polarity ? and a promoter element Ψ_1 contained in the solution. We would like to search exhaustively for redexes formed by immediate submembranes of $[]_\sigma^?$ by giving all possible combinations of abstractions (functional parts) and their arguments. We first enumerate the immediate submembranes and designate the abstractions and possible combinations of arguments for them. We assume that an initial counter element, a_0, is already present in $[]_\sigma^?$.

Proposition 4. *We determine the number of immediate submembranes of $[]_\sigma^?$ by the following rules. Moreover, we also provide a unique numbering to the immediate submembranes which is expressed by the elements b.*

$$
\begin{aligned}
r_{in1} \quad & \{ []_\alpha^0, a_0 \rightarrow & []_\alpha^+, a_0, a \\
r_{in2} \quad & []_\alpha^+ \rightarrow & [b]_\alpha^+, \\
r_{in3} \quad & \Psi_1 \rightarrow & \Psi_2, \\
& promoter : & \Psi_1 \},
\end{aligned}
$$

where the third rule has priority lower than the first one.

Explanation.

1. r_{in1}: when a new immediate submembrane is met, a copy of a is added to $[]_\sigma^?$.
2. r_{in2}: at the same time, each immediate submembrane receives an element b.
3. r_{in3}: the process ends with the replacement of Ψ. Observe that every immediate submembrane will receive a unique number of b-s, which is between 1 and the number of a-s in the end. $\square$

Let us denote by s the number of immediate submembranes in $[]_\sigma^?$. The number of b-s in each immediate submembrane of $[]_\sigma^?$ is unique. In a way similar to the generation of a-s we can count and enumerate the abstractions in $[]_\sigma^?$. Let the number of e-s give the number of abstractions which are immediate submembranes of $[]_\sigma^?$, and let the f-s inside the abstractions denote their number in that enumeration.

Proposition 5. *We enumerate the abstractions in $[]_\sigma^?$: the e-s give the number of abstractions while the number of f-s provide a unique identifier to each abstraction.*

$$
\begin{aligned}
r_{in4} \quad & \{ []_\rho^+, e_0 \rightarrow & []_\rho^-, e_0, e, \\
r_{in5} \quad & []_\rho^- \rightarrow & [f]_\rho^-, \\
r_{in6} \quad & []_\sigma^? \rightarrow & [\ominus]_\sigma^?, \\
r_{in7} \quad & \Psi_2 \rightarrow & \Psi_3, \\
& promoter : & \Psi_2 \},
\end{aligned}
$$

where $r_{in4} > r_{in6}, r_{in7}$ and the inhibitor of r_{in6} is e.

Explanation. Rules r_{in4} and r_{in5} give the number of abstractions and enumerate the abstractions in $[]_\sigma^?$ simultaneously. Rule r_{in6} acts in the case when no abstraction is present. Then we immediately know that $[]_\sigma^?$ is inert, which is expressed by the element $\ominus$.   □

Let the number of abstractions present as immediate submembranes in $[]_\sigma^?$ be t.

Proposition 6. *The following rules produce t copies of $[]_\sigma^?$, where each copy contains a designated abstraction.*

$$
\begin{aligned}
r_{in8} \quad & [\Psi_3, e, e]_\sigma^? \rightarrow [\Psi_4, e, e]_\sigma^?, [\Psi_3, e]_\sigma^?, \\
r_{in9} \quad & [\Psi_3, e]_\sigma^? \rightarrow [\Psi_4, e]_\sigma^?, \\
r_{in10} \quad & e^i, [f^i]_\rho^- \rightarrow [?f]_\rho^{++}, ?e, \\
r_{in11} \quad & \{?e, e \rightarrow \# \; > \\
r_{in12} \quad & \quad ?e \rightarrow \}, \\
r_{in13} \quad & \{?f, f \rightarrow \#, \\
r_{in14} \quad & \quad ?f \rightarrow \}, \\
r_{in15} \quad & \Psi_4 \rightarrow \Psi_5,
\end{aligned}
$$

where the promoter of the third rule is Ψ_4 and the second rule has lower priority than the first.

Explanation. After executing Rule r_{in10}, the computation can be continued only if the number of e-s in the underlying copy of $[]_\sigma^?$ was exactly the same as the number of f-s in the abstraction with which a filtering rule was applied. Rules r_{in11}-r_{in14} achieve this fact. The abstraction obtains an individual polarity by Rule r_{in10}.

As the next step, we form all combination of arguments for all designated copies of abstractions.

Proposition 7. *The following rules produce all possible sets of arguments for the abstractions.*

$$
\begin{aligned}
r_{in16} \quad & []_\alpha^d, \Psi_5 \rightarrow []_\alpha^d, \Delta_1, \quad where \; d \neq ++ \\
r_{in17} \quad & [\Psi_5]_\sigma^? \rightarrow [\ominus]_\sigma^?, \\
r_{in18} \quad & [a, \Delta_1]_\sigma^? \rightarrow [c, \bar{a}, \overline{\Delta}]_\sigma^?, [c, \bar{\bar{a}}, \overline{\Delta}]_\sigma^?, \\
r_{in19} \quad & [b^i]_\alpha^d, c^i, \bar{a} \rightarrow [?b]_\alpha^{--}, ?c, \bar{c}^i, \\
r_{in20} \quad & \{?b, b \rightarrow \# \; > \\
r_{in21} \quad & \quad ?b \rightarrow \}, \\
r_{in22} \quad & \{?c, c \rightarrow \# \; > \\
r_{in23} \quad & \quad ?c \rightarrow , \\
r_{in24} \quad & \quad \bar{c} \rightarrow c\}, \\
r_{in25} \quad & \overline{\Delta}, \bar{a} \rightarrow \Delta_1, \\
r_{in26} \quad & \overline{\Delta}, \bar{\bar{a}} \rightarrow \Delta_1, \\
r_{in27} \quad & \Delta_1, []_\rho^{++}, []_{\alpha_1}^{--}, \ldots, []_{\alpha_j}^{--} \rightarrow [\Delta_2, []_{\alpha_1}^0, \ldots, []_{\alpha_j}^0]_\rho^{++}, \\
r_{in28} \quad & []_\alpha^{--} \rightarrow \#,
\end{aligned}
$$

where $r_{in16} > r_{in17}$ And the rules $r_{in20} - r_{in24}$ have priorities higher than those of rules r_{in25} and r_{in26}. Rule r_{in27} has lower priority than all the rules above it and $r_{in27} > r_{in28}$.

Explanation.

1. Rules r_{in16}-r_{in17} commence the process by either introducing a new control element Δ_1, or, when there are no arguments at all, an element $\ominus$ indicates that fact.
2. Rules r_{in18}-r_{in26} prepare the arguments by providing a term that will serve as an argument with polarity $--$. The trick is the same as by Proposition 6, we ensure that each time precisely the next argument in the enumeration with b-s follows. We choose or reject that membrane as an argument depending on $\bar{a}$ or $\bar{\bar{a}}$ is present in the actual copy of $[]^0_\alpha$.
3. Rule r_{in27} commences the reduction process itself.   □

From this point on, the inertness check is the same as the reduction process initiated by Rule $r_{\Phi 1}$. The difference is: in this case special elements, $\ominus$, take the role of $\#$. When during the reduction *matchfails* is encountered, it acts as before, only at the upper level instead of producing $\#$ it produces an element $\ominus$. Then

$$r_{fin1} \quad [\,\ominus\,]^?_\sigma \to []^\natural_\sigma,$$
$$r_{fin2} \quad []^?_\sigma \to []^?_\sigma,$$
$$r_{fin3} \quad \Theta_{in} \to [non\_inert]^0_\sigma, \Theta_1,$$

where $r_{fin2} > r_{fin3}$ and, moreover, the rules with labels *fin* have lower priorities than all the rules with labels *in*. The promoter for all the rules is Θ_{in}.

The element *matchsuccessful* acts as before with the exception that it allows $\oplus$ appear as an element of a membrane $[]^?_\sigma$. Then $\oplus$ obeys the rule

$$[\,\oplus\,]^?_\sigma \quad \to []^\natural_\sigma, \oplus,$$
$$\Theta_{in}, \oplus, []^!_\sigma \to [inert]^0_\sigma, \Theta_1.$$

By this the membrane system can return to the reduction process initiated by Θ_1, and, eventually, after eliminating all possible solutions where being inert is not known, the redex can be computed.

4   Conclusion

We have shown how chemical term reduction can be simulated as membrane system computation. Our approach is rather tedious, which is due to the chosen representation of γ-terms in the labeled membrane structure of the corresponding P system. We believe that with a different, and probably more appropriate representation could very much simplify the simulation, and not only that, but also would be able to take advantage of the parallel and nondeterministic rule execution of the membrane system model. One step in this direction we have already performed in the present paper by defining a parallel version of the γ reduction rule $\rightarrow_{\gamma_p}$ which could be a basis for finding a much more natural correspondence between the computations of membrane systems and the reduction sequences of the calculus. We intend to pursue this research direction in a forthcoming paper.

References

1. Aman, B., Battyányi, P., Ciobanu, G., Vaszil, G.: Simulating P systems with membrane dissolution in a chemical calculus. Nat. Comput. **15**, 521–532 (2016)
2. Atanasiu, A., Martin-Vide, C.: Recursive calculus with membranes. Fundam. Informaticae **49**(1–3), 45–59 (2002)
3. Banâtre, J.P., Fradet, P., Radenac, Y.: Principles of chemical programming. Electron. Notes Theor. Comput. Sci. **124**(1), 133–147 (2005)
4. Banâtre, J.P., Fradet, P., Radenac, Y.: Generalized multisets for chemical programming. Math. Struct. Comput. Sci. **16**, 557–580 (2006)
5. Banâtre, J.P., Le Métayer, D.: A new computational model and its discipline of programming. Technical report RR0566, INRIA (1986)
6. Banâtre, J.P., Le Métayer, D.: Programming by multiset transformation. Commun. ACM **36**, 98–111 (1986)
7. Battyányi, P., Vaszil, G.: Describing membrane computations with a chemical calculus. Fundam. Informaticae **134**, 39–50 (2014)
8. Battyányi, P.: Normalization properties of symmetric logical calculi. Ph.D. thesis, University of Chambéry (2007)
9. Fésüs, M., Vaszil, G.: Chemical programming, membrane systems. In: Proceedings of the 14th International Conference on Membrane Computing, Institute of Mathematics and Computer Science, Academy of Moldova, Chişinău, pp. 313–316 (2013)
10. Păun, G.: Computing with membranes. J. Comput. Syst. Sci. **61**(1), 108–143 (2000)
11. Xi, H.: Upper bounds for standardisation and an application. J. Symbolic Logic **64**(1), 291–303 (1999)

P Colonies with Evolving Environment

Lucie Ciencialová, Luděk Cienciala, and Petr Sosík[✉]

Research Institute of the IT4Innovations Centre of Excellence,
Faculty of Philosophy and Science, Silesian University, Opava, Czech Republic
{lucie.ciencialova,ludek.cienciala,petr.sosik}@fpf.slu.cz

Abstract. We study two variants of P colonies with dynamic environment changing due to an underlying 0L scheme: P colonies with two objects inside each agent that can only consume objects, and P colonies with one object inside each agent which uses rewriting and communication rules. We show that the first kind of P colonies with one consumer agent can generate all sets of natural numbers computed by partially blind register machines. The second kind of P colonies with two agents with rewriting/communication rules is computationally complete. Finally, we demonstrate that P colonies with one such agent with checking programs can simulate catalytic P systems with one catalyst, and consequently, another relation to partially blind register machines is established.

Keywords: P colony · Catalytic p system · 0L scheme · Computational completeness · Partially blind register machine

1 Introduction

P colony was introduced in [10] as a very simple variant of membrane systems inspired by so-called *colonies* of formal grammars. See [14] for more information about membrane systems and [11] for details on colonies in the context of grammar systems theory.

There are three basic entities in the P colony model: objects, agents and the environment. A P colony is composed of agents, each containing a collection of objects embedded in a membrane. The objects can be placed in the environment, too. Agents are equipped with programs composed of rules that allow interactions of objects. The number of objects inside each agent is set by definition and it is usually very low – 1, 2 or 3. The environment of a P colony serves as a communication channel for agents: an agent is able to affect the behaviour of another agent by sending objects via the environment, implementing thus a blackboard architecture. There is also a special type of *environmental objects* denoted by e which are present in the environment in an unlimited number of copies.

A specific variant of P colony called *eco-P colony* with two object inside each agent, where the environment can change independently of the agents, was introduced in [1]. Evolution of the environment is controlled by a 0L scheme

© Springer International Publishing AG 2017
A. Leporati et al. (Eds.): CMC 2016, LNCS 10105, pp. 151–164, 2017.
DOI: 10.1007/978-3-319-54072-6_10

applying context-free rules in parallel to all possible objects in the environment which are unused by the agents in the current step of computation.

The activity of agents is based on rules that can be rewriting, communication or checking; these three types were introduced in [10]. Furthermore, other three types of generating, consuming and transporting rules were introduced in [5].

Rewriting rule $a \rightarrow b$ allows an agent to rewrite (evolve) one object a placed inside the agent to object b.

Communication rule $c \leftrightarrow d$ exchanges one object c placed inside the agent for object d from the environment.

Checking rule r_1/r_2, where each of r_1, r_2 is a rewriting or a communication rule, sets a priority between these two rules. The agent tries to apply the first rule and if it cannot be performed, the agent executes the second rule.

Furthermore, other three types of generating, consuming and transporting rules were introduced in [5].

Generating rule $a \rightarrow bc$ creates two objects b, c from one object a.

Consuming rule $ab \rightarrow c$ rewrites two objects a, b to one object c.

Transporting rule of the form $(a\ in)$ or $(a\ out)$ is used to transport one object from the environment into the agent, or from the agent to the environment, respectively. The rule is always associated with a consuming/generating rule to keep a constant number of objects inside the agent.

The rules are combined into programs in such a way that all objects inside the agent are affected by execution of the rules in every step. Consequently, the number of rules in the program is the same as the number of objects inside the agent.

The programs that contain consuming rules are called consuming programs and the programs with generating rules are called generating programs. The agent that only contains consuming (resp. generating) programs is called consumer (resp. sender).

P colonies with senders and consumers without evolving environment were studied in [5] and the authors proved their computational completeness (in the Turing sense), as well as the computational completeness of P colonies with senders and consumers with 0L scheme for the environment. Many papers were devoted to P colonies with rewriting and communication rules without evolving environment, e.g., [4,6,12], and there are two book chapters in [3,14] describing this topic.

In this paper we focus on P colonies with evolving environment. The paper is structured as follows: The second section is devoted to definitions and notations used in the paper. The third section contains results obtained during studies of P colonies with consumers only. In the fourth section we study P colonies with one object inside the agent and rewriting/communication rules. The fifth section studies the relation of P colonies with evolving environment and catalytic P systems. The paper concludes with a summary of presented results and possibilities of future work.

2   Definitions

Throughout the paper we assume the reader to be familiar with basic of formal automata and language theory. We introduce notation used in the paper.

We use $\mathbb{N} \cdot \mathsf{RE}$ to denote the family of recursively enumerable sets of natural numbers and $\mathbb{N}$ to denote the set of natural numbers.

Σ is a notation for the alphabet. Let Σ^* be set of all words over alphabet Σ (including the empty word ε). For the length of the word $w \in \Sigma^*$ we use the notation $|w|$ and the number of occurrences of symbol $a \in \Sigma$ in w is denoted by $|w|_a$.

A *multiset* of objects M is a pair $M = (V, f)$, where V is an arbitrary (not necessarily finite) set of objects and f is a mapping $f : V \to N$; f assigns to each object in V its multiplicity in M. The cardinality of M, denoted by $card(M)$, is defined by $card(M) = \sum_{a \in V} f(a)$.

Any multiset of objects M with the set of objects $V = \{a_i, \dots ?a_n\}$ can be represented as a string w over alphabet V with $|w|_{a_i} = f(a_i)$; $1 \leq i \leq n$. Obviously, all words obtained from w by permuting the letters can also represent M, and ε represents the empty multiset. Because of string representation we can denote the set of all multisets over the set of objects V by V^*.

The mechanism of evolution of the environment is based on a *0L scheme*. It is a pair (Σ, P), where Σ is the alphabet of 0L scheme and P is the set of context-free rules fulfilling the condition $\forall a \in \Sigma \; \exists \alpha \in \Sigma^*$ such that $(a \to \alpha) \in P$. For $w_1, w_2 \in \Sigma^*$ we write $w_1 \Rightarrow w_2$ if $w_1 = a_1 a_1 \dots a_n, w_2 = \alpha_2 \alpha_2 \dots \alpha_n$, for $a_i \to \alpha_i \in P, 1 \leq i \leq n$

A *register machine* [13] is a construct $M = (m, H, l_0, l_h, P)$ where:

- m is the number of registers, H is a set of instruction labels,
- l_0 is the initial/start label, l_h is the final label,
- P is the finite set of instructions injectively labelled with the elements from the given set H.

The instructions of the register machine are of the following forms:

$l_1 :$ $(ADD(r), l_2, l_3)$ Add 1 to the contents of the register r and non-deterministically choose one of the instructions (labelled with) l_2 or l_3 to proceed with.

$l_1 :$ $(SUB(r), l_2, l_3)$ If the register r is not empty, then subtract 1 from its contents and go to instruction l_2, otherwise proceed to instruction l_3.

$l_h :$ *HALT* Stop the machine. The final label l_h is only assigned to this instruction.

Without loss of generality, one can assume that in each *ADD*-instruction $l_1 : (ADD(r), l_2, l_3)$ and in each conditional *SUB*-instruction $l_1 : (SUB(r), l_2, l_3)$ the labels l_1, l_2, l_3 are mutually distinct. The register machine M computes a set $N(M)$ of numbers in the following way: we start with all registers empty (hence storing the number zero) with the instruction with label l_0 and we proceed to apply the instructions as indicated by the labels (and made possible by the contents of registers). If we reach the halt instruction, then the number stored at that time in the register 1 is said to be computed by M and hence it is introduced in $N(M)$. Because of non-determinism of the machine, $N(M)$ can be an infinite set. The family of sets of numbers computed by register machines is denoted by $\mathbb{N} \cdot RM$.

Theorem 1 ([13]). $\mathbb{N} \cdot RM = \mathbb{N} \cdot \mathsf{RE}$.

Moreover, we call a register machine *partially blind* if we interpret the subtract instructions in the following way: $l_1 : (SUB(r); l_2; l_3)$ - if register r is not empty, then subtract one from its contents and non-deterministically choose to continue with one of the instructions l_2 or l_3; if register r is empty when attempting to decrement register r, then the program ends without yielding a result.

When the register machine reaches the final state, the result obtained in the first register is only taken into account if the remaining registers are empty. The family of sets of non-negative integers generated by partially blind register machines is denoted by $\mathbb{N} \cdot RM_{pb}$. The partially blind register machine accepts a proper subset of $\mathbb{N} \cdot \mathsf{RE}$:

Theorem 2 ([7]). $\mathbb{N} \cdot RM_{pb} = \mathbb{N} MAT$, where $\mathbb{N} MAT$ is the Parikh image of the class of languages generated by matrix grammars without appearance checking.

2.1 Catalytic P Systems

Definition 1. *An* extended catalytic P system *of degree $m \geq 1$ is a construct*

$$\Pi = (O, C, \mu, w_1, \ldots, w_m, R_1, \ldots, R_m, i_0) \ where$$

1. O *is the alphabet of objects;*
2. $C \subseteq O$ *is the alphabet of catalysts;*
3. μ *is a membrane structure of degree m with membranes labelled in a one-to-one manner with the natural numbers $1, 2, \ldots, m$;*
4. $w_1, \ldots, w_m \in O^*$ *are the multisets of objects initially present in the m regions of μ;*
5. R_i, $1 \leq i \leq m$, *are finite sets of evolution rules over O associated with the regions $1, 2, \ldots, m$ of μ; these evolution rules are of the forms $ca \to cv$ or $a \to v$, where c is a catalyst, a is an object from $O \setminus C$, and v is a string from $((O \setminus C) \times \{here, out, in\})^*$;*
6. $i_0 \in \{0, 1, \ldots, m\}$ *indicates the output region of Π.*

The membrane structure and the multisets in Π constitute a *configuration* of the P system; the *initial configuration* is given by the initial multisets $w_1, \ldots, w_m$. A transition between configurations is governed by the application of the evolution rules, which is done in the maximally parallel way, i.e., only applicable multisets of rules which cannot be extended by further rules have to be applied to the objects in all membrane regions.

The application of a rule $u \to v$ in a region containing a multiset M results in subtracting from M the multiset identified by u, and then in adding the multiset identified by v. The objects can eventually be transported through membranes due to the targets *in* and *out*. We refer to [14] for further details and examples.

The P system continues with applying multisets of rules in the maximally parallel way until there remain no applicable rules in any region of Π. Then the system halts. We consider the number of objects from $O \setminus C$ contained in the output region i_0 at the moment when the system halts as the *result* of the underlying computation of Π. The system is called *extended* since the catalytic objects in C are not counted to the result of a computation. The set of results of all computations possible in Π is called the set of natural numbers *generated by Π* and it is denoted by $N(\Pi)$.

The problem how to count the catalysts in the case of generating catalytic P systems can be avoided if using external output, i.e., the output is sent to the environment, indicated by $i_0 = 0$. Denote by $NOP_m(cat_k)$ the class of sets of natural numbers generated by catalytic P systems with external output, with at most m membranes and at most k catalysts.

2.2   Generalized P Colonies

Definition 2. *A P colony with capacity $c \geq 1$ is the structure*

$$\Pi = (\Sigma, e, f, v_E, D_E, B_1, \dots, B_n), \text{ where}$$

- *Σ is the alphabet of the colony, its elements are called objects,*
- *e is the basic (environmental) object of the colony, $e \in \Sigma$,*
- *f is final object of the colony, $f \in \Sigma$,*
- *v_E is the initial content of the environment, $v_E \in (\Sigma - \{e\})^*$,*
- *D_E is 0L scheme (Σ, P_E), where P_E is the set of context free rules,*
- *B_i, $1 \leq i \leq n$, are the agents, every agent is the structure $B_i = (o_i, P_i)$, where o_i is the multiset over Σ, it defines the initial state (content) of the agent B_i and $|o_i| = c$ and $P_i = \{p_{i,1}, \dots, p_{i,k_i}\}$ is the finite set of programs of three types:*
  - *(1) generating program with generating rules $a \to bc$ and transporting rules $(d \text{ out})$ - the number of generating rules is the same as the number of transporting rules.*
  - *(2) consuming program with consuming rules $ab \to c$ and transporting rules $(d \text{ in})$ - the number of consuming rules is the same as the number of transporting rules.*
  - *(3) rewriting/communication program can contain three types of rules:*
    - ⋄ *$a \to b$, called a rewriting rule,*
    - ⋄ *$c \leftrightarrow d$, called a communication rule,*
    - ⋄ *r_1/r_2, called a checking rule; each of r_1, r_2 is a rewriting or a communication rule.*

Every agent has only one type of programs. The agent with generating programs is called *sender* and the agent with consuming programs is called *consumer*. The capacity of a P colony with senders and consumers must be an even number.

The *initial configuration* of a P colony is the $(n + 1)$-tuple $(o_1, \ldots, o_n, v_E)$, with the interpretation of the symbols $o_1, \ldots, o_n, v_E$ as in Definition 2. In general, the *configuration* of the P colony Π is defined as $(n + 1)$-tuple $(w_1, \ldots, w_n, w_E)$, where w_i represents the multiset of objects inside the i-th agent, $|w_i| = c$, $1 \leq i \leq n$, and $w_E \in (\Sigma - \{e\})^*$ is the multiset of objects different from e placed in the environment.

At each step of the (parallel) computation every agent tries to find one of its programs to apply. If the number of applicable programs is higher than one, the agent non-deterministically chooses one. At each step of a computation, the set of active agents executing a program must be maximal, i.e., no further agent can be added to it.

By applying programs, the P colony passes from one configuration to another configuration. Objects in the environment unaffected by any program in the given step are rewritten by the 0L scheme D_E. A sequence of configurations starting from the initial configuration is called a *computation*. A configuration is *halting* if the P colony has no applicable program. Each halting computation has associated a *result* – the number of copies of the final object placed in the environment in a halting configuration.

$$N(\Pi) = \{|w_E|_f \mid (o_1, \ldots, o_n, v_E) \Rightarrow^* (w_1, \ldots, w_n, w_E)\},$$

where $(o_1, \ldots, o_n, v_E)$ is the initial configuration, $(w_1, \ldots, w_n, w_E)$ is the final configuration, and $\Rightarrow^*$ denotes reflexive and transitive closure of $\Rightarrow$.

Let us denote $NEPCOL(i, j, k, u, v, w)$ the family of the sets computing by P colonies with at most $j \geq 1$ agents with $i \geq 1$ objects inside the agent and with at most $k \geq 1$ programs associated with each agent such that:

$\quad u = check$ if the P colony uses rewriting/communication rules with checking rules

$\quad u = no\text{-}check$ if the P colony uses rewriting/communication rules without checking rules

$\quad u = s/c/sc$ if the P colony contains only sender/only consumer/both sender and consumer agents

$\quad v = pas$ if the rules of 0L scheme are of type $a \rightarrow a$ only,

$\quad v = act$ if the set of rules of 0L scheme disposes of at least one rule of another type than $a \rightarrow a$,

$\quad w = ini$ if the environment or agents contain initially objects different from e, otherwise w is omitted,

If a numerical parameter is unbounded, we denote it by $*$.

In [5] the authors deal with P colonies with senders and consumers with "passive" environment and they show that

$$NEPCOL(2, 3, *, sc, pas) = \mathbb{N} \cdot \text{RE}.$$

In [1] there are results of P colonies with active environment:

$$NEPCOL(2, 2, *, c, act, ini) = \mathbb{N} \cdot \text{RE}$$

$$NEPCOL(2, 2, *, sc, pas, ini) \supseteq \mathbb{N} \cdot RM_{pb}.$$

Other results are shown for P colonies with "passive" environment and rewriting/communication rules and with only one object inside the agent in [2]

$$NEPCOL(1, 4, *, check, pas) = \mathbb{N} \cdot \text{RE}$$

and in [5]

$$NEPCOL(1, 6, *, no\text{-}check, pas) = \mathbb{N} \cdot \text{RE}.$$

3   P Colonies with Consumer Agents

In this section we study computational power of P colonies with two objects inside the agent - consumer and with active environment. We extend the previous results reported in [1].

Theorem 3. $\mathbb{N} \cdot RM_{pb} \subseteq NEPCOL(2, 1, *, c, act, ini)$.

Proof. Consider register machine $M = (m, H, l_0, l_h, P)$. All labels from the set H are objects in the P colony. The content of register r is represented by the number of copies of objects a_r placed in the environment. We construct the P colony $\Pi = (\Sigma, e, a_1, l_0 d, D_E, B_1)$ with:

- $\Sigma = \{l_i, l'_i, l''_i, \overline{l}_i, \underline{l}_i, L_i \mid l_i \in H\} \cup \{a_i \mid 1 \leq i \leq m\} \cup \{e, d, f\}$,
- $B_1 = (de, P_1)$.

At the beginning of computation there is object l_0 and auxiliary object d in the environment. Object l_0 corresponds to the initial label of M.

An instruction $l_i = (ADD(r), l_j, l_k)$ is simulated by the environment and the agent by using the following rules and programs:

ENV :	B_1 :
$A : l_i \rightarrow a_r l_j d;$	$1 : \langle de \rightarrow e; d\ in \rangle;$
$B : l_i \rightarrow a_r l_k d;$	

The computation is done in such a way that 0L scheme works in the environment, it executes adding one to the content of register r (generate one copy of object a_r – the rule labelled A or B) and generating of the objects l_j or l_k, label of instruction which will be executed in the next steps of computation of register machine M. Agent B_1 consumes object d from the environment. Notice that there is at most one copy of d in the environment.

An instruction $l_i : (SUB(r), l_j, l_k)$ is simulated by following rules and programs:

ENV :

$C : l_i \rightarrow \overline{l_i} l'_i;$	
$D : l'_i \rightarrow l''_i;$	
$E : l''_i \rightarrow l_j l_k;$	
$F : l_j \rightarrow \overline{l_j} d;$	
$G : \overline{l_k} \rightarrow l_k d;$	

B_1 :

$2 : \langle de \rightarrow e; \overline{l_i}\ in \rangle;$
$3 : \langle \overline{l_i} e \rightarrow L_j; a_r\ in \rangle;$
$4 : \langle \overline{l_i} e \rightarrow f; e\ in \rangle;$
$5 : \langle L_j a_r \rightarrow e; l_j\ in \rangle;$
$6 : \langle L_j a_r \rightarrow e; \overline{l_k}\ in \rangle;$
$7 : \langle l_j e \rightarrow e; d\ in \rangle;$
$8 : \langle \overline{l_k} e \rightarrow e; d\ in \rangle;$
$9 : \langle \overline{f} e \rightarrow f; e\ in \rangle;$

If there is the object l_i (the label of *SUB*-instruction) in the environment, the 0L scheme generates (using the rule labelled C) the object $\overline{l_i}$. This is the message for the agent B_1 to try to consume one copy of object a_r from the environment (try to subtract one from the content of register r.).

If the agent is successful (using the program labelled 3), then in the next step the agent consumes $\overline{l_j}$ or $\overline{l_k}$ and the computation will follow in simulation of instruction labelled l_k or l_j.

If the agent does not consume object a_r – there is no a_r in the environment or the agent non-deterministically chooses program 4 instead of the applicable program 3 – the agent generates object f and the computation will never end because the program 9 will be applicable.

For the halting instruction we add the rule $l_h \rightarrow l_h$ to the 0L scheme, as well as "passive" 0L rules for other objects which are not changed by other environmental rules (for example $e \rightarrow e$, $a_r \rightarrow a_r, \dots$). Whenever the simulated register machine executes the HALT instruction, neither object d nor object $l_i \in H \setminus \{l_h\}$ will appear in the environment any more and the computation will halt.

P colony Π starts its computation with object l_0 in the environment and the simulation of the instruction labelled l_0. By the rules and programs it places and deletes from the environment the objects a_r and halts its computation only after object l_h appears in the environment. The result of a computation is the number of copies of object a_1 placed in the environment at the end of the computation. No other halting computation can be executed in the constructed P colony.

4   P Colonies with Rewriting/Communication Rules

In this section we deal with P colonies with active environment and with one object inside agents. We prove that such a P colony with two agents can generate every recursively enumerable set of natural numbers.

Theorem 4. *NEPCOL*$(1, 2, *, no\text{-}check, act, ini) = \mathbb{N} \cdot \text{RE}$.

Proof. Let us consider register machine $M = (m, H, l_0, l_h, P)$. For all labels in the set H we construct corresponding objects in the P colony Π. Again, the content of register i is represented by the number of copies of objects a_i placed in the environment.

We construct the P colony $\Pi = (\Sigma, e, a_1, l_0 d, D_E, B_1)$ with:

- $\Sigma = \{l_i, l_i', l_i'', \overline{l_i}, \overline{\overline{l_i}}, \underline{l_i}, l_i^1, l_i^2, l_i^3, l_i^4, M_i, M_i^1, M_i^2, M_i^3, M_i^4, N_i, N_i^1, N_i^2, N_i^3, N_i^4 \mid l_i$
  $\in H\} \cup \{a_i \mid 1 \le i \le m\} \cup \{e, d, f, g\}$,
- $B_1 = (e, P_1)$
- $B_2 = (e, P_2)$.

The object l_0 corresponds to the label of the first instruction executed by the register machine.

The instruction $l_i : (ADD(r), l_j, l_k)$ will be simulated by the environment and the agent B_1 by using following rules and programs:

ENV :	B_1 :
$A : l_i \rightarrow a_r l_j'$;	$1 : \langle e \leftrightarrow d \rangle$;
$B : l_i \rightarrow a_r l_k'$;	$2 : \langle d \rightarrow e \rangle$;
$C : l_j' \rightarrow l_j d$;	
$D : l_k' \rightarrow l_k d$;	

The simulation of the ADD-instruction starts by rewriting the object l_i to object a_r (adds one to the content of register r) by executing rule A or B and object l_j (rule C) or object l_k (rule D).

The instruction $l_i : (SUB(r), l_j, l_k)$ is simulated by using the following rules and programs:

ENV :	B_1 :	B_2 :
$E : l_i \rightarrow l_i^1 \overline{l_i}$;	$3 : \langle e \leftrightarrow g \rangle$;	$7 : \langle e \leftrightarrow \overline{l_i} \rangle$;
$F : l_i^1 \rightarrow l_i^2 d$;	$4 : \langle g \rightarrow f \rangle$;	$8 : \langle \overline{l_i} \rightarrow \overline{\overline{l_i}} \rangle$;
$G : l_i^2 \rightarrow l_i^3$;	$5 : \langle f \leftrightarrow \overline{\overline{l_i}} \rangle$;	$9 : \langle \overline{\overline{l_i}} \leftrightarrow a_r \rangle$;
$H : l_i^3 \rightarrow l_i^4 d$;	$6 : \langle \overline{\overline{l_i}} \rightarrow e \rangle$;	$10 : \langle a_r \rightarrow g \rangle$;
$I : l_i^4 \rightarrow M_i N_i$;		$11 : \langle g \leftrightarrow N_i \rangle$;
$J : M_i \rightarrow M_i^1$;		$12 : \langle N_i \rightarrow e \rangle$;
$K : M_i^1 \rightarrow M_i^2$;		$13 : \langle \overline{\overline{l_i}} \leftrightarrow M_i \rangle$;
$L : M_i^2 \rightarrow M_i^3$;		$14 : \langle M_i \rightarrow e \rangle$;
$M : M_i^3 \rightarrow M_i^4$;		
$N : M_i^4 \rightarrow l_j d$;		
$O : N_i \rightarrow N_i^1 g$;		
$P : N_i^1 \rightarrow N_i^2$;		
$Q : N_i^2 \rightarrow N_i^3$;		
$R : N_i^3 \rightarrow N_i^4$;		
$S : N_i^4 \rightarrow l_k d$;		

The simulation starts with rule E generating objects $l_i^1 \overline{l_i}$. Object l_i^1 keeps the environmental rules busy for 6 steps until actions of agents are completed. Object $\overline{l_i}$ causes the agent B_2 to generate object $\overline{\overline{l_i}}$ and, in turn, to consume object a_r.

Table 1 shows the example of the simulation of the SUB-instruction when the register to be decremented stores a value greater than zero. Symbol w in

Table 1. The simulation of the SUB-instruction when register r is not empty

Step	w_E	w_1	w_2	Applicable rules and programs		
0	$l_i da_r w$	e	e	E	1	–
1	$l_i^1 \overline{l}_i a_r w$	d	e	F	2	7
2	$l_i^2 da_r w$	e	$\overline{l}_i$	G	1	8
3	$l_i^3 a_r w$	d	$\overline{\overline{l}}_i$	H	2	9
4	$l_i^4 d\overline{\overline{l}}_i w$	e	a_r	I	1	10
5	$M_i N_i \overline{\overline{l}}_i \mathrm{w}$	d	g	J	2	11
6	$M_i^1 g\overline{\overline{l}}_i w$	e	N_i	K	3	12
7	$M_i^2 L_k \overline{l}_i w$	g	e	L	4	–
8	$M_i^3 \overline{l}_i w$	f	e	M	5	–
9	$M_i^4 f w$	$\overline{\overline{l}}_i$	e	N	6	–
10	$l_j df w$	e	e	$?$	1	–

the environment (column w_E) denotes an arbitrary multiset containing objects in $\{a_i \mid 1 \le i \le m\}$. Symbol ? in the last row means that the applicable rule depends on the next simulated instruction labelled l_j.

Table 2 shows the example of the simulation of the SUB-instruction when register to be decremented stores zero. Symbol w in the environment (column w_E) denotes an arbitrary multiset containing objects in $\{a_i \mid 1 \le i \le m, i \ne r\}$. Symbol ? in the last row means that the applicable rule depends on the next simulated instruction labelled l_k.

Table 2. The simulation of the SUB-instruction when register r is empty

Step	w_E	w_1	w_2	Applicable rules and programs		
0	$l_i d\, \mathrm{w}$	e	e	E	1	–
1	$l_i^1 \overline{l}_i w$	d	e	F	2	7
2	$l_i^2 dw$	e	$\overline{l}_i$	G	1	8
3	$l_i^3 w$	d	$\overline{\overline{l}}_i$	H	2	–
4	$l_i^4 dw$	e	$\overline{\overline{l}}_i$	I	1	–
5	$M_i N_i w$	d	$\overline{\overline{l}}_i$	O	2	13
6	$N_i^1 g\overline{\overline{l}}_i w$	e	M_i	P	3	14
7	$N_i^2 \overline{l}_i w$	g	e	Q	4	–
8	$N_i^3 \overline{l}_i w$	f	e	R	5	–
9	$N_i^4 f w$	$\overline{\overline{l}}_i$	e	S	6	–
10	$l_k df w$	e	e	$?$	1	–

For instruction $l_h : HALT$ we add the rule $T : l_h \rightarrow l_h$. The environment does not produce object d any more. The computation halts as no agent can execute a program. The result is the number of objects a_1 placed in the environment and it corresponds to the result of a successful computation in the register machine.

5   P Colonies Versus Catalytic P Systems

In this section we study the relation of P colonies with communication rules, and catalytic P systems in the generating mode. We show that any catalytic P system with one catalyst can be simulated by a P colony with checking rules and with one agent. As a consequence, a relation of these P colonies and partially blind register machines is established.

Theorem 5. *For an arbitrary extended catalytic P system Π with one catalyst there exists a P colony Π' with checking rules and one agent containing one object such that $N(\Pi) = N(\Pi')$.*

Proof. Note first that in the generating case, due to the existence of flattening procedures described, e.g., in [8], one can assume without loss of generality that the catalytic P system $\Pi = (O, C, [], w, R, i_0)$ has a single membrane and that its output is collected in the environment, i.e., $i_0 = 0$.

We construct the P colony $\Pi' = (\Sigma, e, f, w \setminus C, D_E, B_1)$ as follows: each step of Π is simulated by two steps of Π'.

1. In the first step the P colony checks whether the P system can apply at least one rule (if not, the P colony halts in the next step). Then both catalytic and non-catalytic rules are randomly applied in the environment, rewriting all objects to their primed versions.
2. In the second step the agent checks whether at most one catalytic rule was applied (if not, a trap symbol is produced). Simultaneously the environment signals whether there had been unused objects in the previous step to which catalytic rules could have been applied. If yes, and simultaneously if no catalytic rules was chosen, the agent produces the trap symbol in the next step (which is the first step of a new cycle). All primed objects are rewritten back to their original versions.

Formally, let

$$O_c = \{a \in (O \setminus C) \mid \exists u : (ca \rightarrow cu) \in R \text{ and } \not\exists v : (a \rightarrow v) \in R\}$$

be the set of objects to which only catalytic rules can be applied. Let the alphabet of the P colony be constructed as

$$\Sigma = O \cup \{a' \mid a \in (O \setminus C)\} \cup \{a'' \mid a \in O_c\} \cup \{c, f, k, n, s, t\}$$

such that the newly added symbols do not appear in O. Define further a mapping $\varphi : (O \setminus C) \times \{here, out\} \longrightarrow \Sigma$ as follows:

$$\varphi(a, dest) = \begin{cases} f & \text{if } dest = out, \\ a' & \text{otherwise.} \end{cases}$$

Let the agent of the P colony adopt the form $B_1 = (n, P_1)$. We construct the rules of the environment and the agent as specified in the following table:

Step	Programs of the agent	Rules of the environment
1	$\langle n \leftrightarrow s/n \rightarrow k \rangle$ $\langle c \rightarrow k \rangle$	$\{a \rightarrow \varphi(u)n \mid (a \rightarrow u) \in R\} \cup$ $\{a \rightarrow \varphi(u)c \mid (ca \rightarrow cu) \in R\} \cup$ $\{a \rightarrow a''n \mid a \in O_c\} \cup \{s \rightarrow \varepsilon\}$
2	$\langle k \leftrightarrow c/k \leftrightarrow n \rangle$	$\{a' \rightarrow a \mid a \in O\} \cup$ $\{a'' \rightarrow as \mid a \in O_c\} \cup$ $\{c \rightarrow t, \ n \rightarrow \varepsilon\}$

In addition, the agent contains programs $\langle k \leftrightarrow t \rangle$, $\langle t \rightarrow t \rangle$, $\langle s \rightarrow s \rangle$, and the environment contains rules $a \rightarrow a$ for each object $a \in \Sigma$ not affected by any of the rules described above.

In the first simulation step the agent contains object n and there is no s in the environment, hence $n \rightarrow k$ is the only applicable rule. Simultaneously the environment simulates the application of rules of the P system to all objects to which any rule can be applied. If more than one rule is applicable to an object, one is randomly chosen. Each application of a catalytic rule produces also one object c and a non-catalytic rule produces n.

When the simulated P system sends an object to the output region 0 by applying a rule with target *out*, the P colony produces instead the final object f, hence the number of final objects equals the number of objects in the output region of the simulated P system.

In the second step the agent checks whether any rule of the P system was applicable, i.e., whether there is at least one c or n in the environment. If not, the agent can run no program and the colony halts. Simultaneously, if there were more than one object c in the environment, indicating that more than one catalytic rule has been applied, then at least one object c is rewritten by the environment to t. Object t is the trap object – whenever it appears, the colony never halts and produces no output (note the programs $\langle k \leftrightarrow t \rangle$ and $\langle t \rightarrow t \rangle$ of the agent).

Finally, rules of the form $a'' \rightarrow as$ in the environment produce the object s. If there is n in the agent and s in the environment in the next step, this means that no catalytic rule was applied even if there were unused objects to which such a rule was applicable, i.e., the maximal parallelism condition of the P system was broken. In this situation the rule $n \leftrightarrow s$ is selected, and s enters the agent where it acts as another trap symbol.

The whole cycle repeats again and again for each simulated step of the P system Π. As explained above, any incorrect simulation results in the appearance of the trap symbol s or t which forces the P colony to run forever and produce no result. Hence only correct simulation results can be produced, and the P colony halts if and only if so does the simulated P system. We can conclude that $N(\Pi) = N(\Pi')$.

Corollary 1. $\mathbb{N} \cdot RM_{pb} \subseteq NEPCOL(1, 1, *, check, act, ini)$.

Proof. The paper [9] demonstrates that $\mathbb{N} \cdot RM_{pb} \subseteq NOP_1(cat_1)$. Then the statement follows by Theorem 5.

6 Conclusions

In this paper we presented the results obtained during the study of P colonies with evolving environment. We have shown that P colonies with one consumer agent can generate all sets of natural numbers computable by partially blind register machines. If we place two agents with one object inside each of them and with no-checking rewriting/communication programs into the evolving environment, the obtained P colony is computationally complete in the Turing sense.

Finally, we have demonstrated that when checking programs are allowed, then a P colony with one agent is sufficient to simulate a catalytic P system with one catalyst. Consequently, these colonies can generate all sets of natural numbers computable by partially blind register machines. We conjecture that this simulation principle is extensible to the case of more catalysts/more agents.

It remains an *open problem* whether any of the presented results can be further strengthened by using a P colony with weaker parameters, or whether the class $\mathbb{N} \cdot RM_{pb}$, forming a lower bound of generative power of the two mentioned types of P colonies, is also their upper bound.

Acknowledgements. This work was supported by The Ministry of Education, Youth and Sports from the National Programme of Sustainability (NPU II) project IT4Innovations excellence in science - LQ1602, and by the Silesian University in Opava under the Student Funding Scheme, project SGS/13/2016.

References

1. Cienciala, L., Ciencialová, L.: Eco-P colonies. In: Pre-Proceedings of the 10th Workshop on Membrane Computing, pp. 201–209. Romania, Curtea de Arges (2009)
2. Cienciala, L., Ciencialová, L., Kelemenová, A.: On the number of agents in P colonies. In: Eleftherakis, G., Kefalas, P., Păun, G., Rozenberg, G., Salomaa, A. (eds.) WMC 2007. LNCS, vol. 4860, pp. 193–208. Springer, Heidelberg (2007). doi:10.1007/978-3-540-77312-2_12
3. Cienciala, L., Ciencialová, L.: P colonies and their extensions. In: Kelemen, J., Kelemenová, A. (eds.) Computation, Cooperation, and Life. LNCS, vol. 6610, pp. 158–169. Springer, Heidelberg (2011). doi:10.1007/978-3-642-20000-7_13
4. Ciencialová, L., Cienciala, L., Csuhaj-Varjú, E., Kelemenová, A., Vaszil, G.: On very simple P colonies. In: Proceeding of The Seventh Brainstorming Week on Membrane Computing, vol. 1, pp. 97–108 (2009)
5. Ciencialová, L., Kelemenová, A., Csuhaj-Varjú, E., Vaszil, G.: Variants of P colonies with very simple cell structure. Int. J. Comput. Commun. Control **3**(IV), 224–233 (2009)

6. Freund, R., Oswald, M.: P colonies working in the maximally parallel and in the sequential mode. In: Proceedings - Seventh International Symposium on Symbolic and Numeric Algorithms for Scientific Computing, SYNASC 2005, pp. 419–426, September 2005

7. Freund, R., Ibarra, O.H., Păun, Gh., Yen, H.C.: Matrix languages, register machines, vector addition systems. In: Proceeding of the Third Brainstorming Week on Membrane Computing, vol. 1, pp. 155–167. E.T.S. de Ingeniería Informática, Universidad de Sevilla (2005)

8. Freund, R., Leporati, A., Mauri, G., Porreca, A.E., Verlan, S., Zandron, C.: Flattening in (Tissue) P systems. In: Alhazov, A., Cojocaru, S., Gheorghe, M., Rogozhin, Y., Rozenberg, G., Salomaa, A. (eds.) CMC 2013. LNCS, vol. 8340, pp. 173–188. Springer, Heidelberg (2014). doi:10.1007/978-3-642-54239-8_13

9. Freund, R., Sosík, P.: On the power of catalytic p systems with one catalyst. In: Rozenberg, G., Salomaa, A., Sempere, J.M., Zandron, C. (eds.) CMC 2015. LNCS, vol. 9504, pp. 137–152. Springer, Cham (2015). doi:10.1007/978-3-319-28475-0_10

10. Kelemen, J., Kelemenová, A., Păun, Gh: Preview of P colonies: a biochemically inspired computing model. In: Ninth International Conference on the Simulation and Synthesis of Living Systems (Alife IX), Workshop and Tutorial Proceedings, pp. 82–86. Mass, Boston (2004)

11. Kelemen, J., Kelemenová, A.: A grammar-theoretic treatment of multiagent systems. Cybern. Syst. **23**(6), 621–633 (1992)

12. Kelemen, J., Kelemenová, A.: On P colonies, a biochemically inspired model of computation. In: Proceedings of the 6th International Symposium of Hungarian Researchers on Computational Intelligence, pp. 40–56 (2005)

13. Minsky, M.L.: Computation: Finite and Infinite Machines. Prentice-Hall, Inc., Upper Saddle River (1967)

14. Păun, G., Rozenberg, G., Salomaa, A.: The Oxford Handbook of Membrane Computing. Oxford University Press, Inc., New York (2010)

Continuation Passing Semantics
for Membrane Systems

Gabriel Ciobanu[1]($\boxtimes$) and Eneia Nicolae Todoran[2]

[1] Romanian Academy, Institute of Computer Science, Iaşi, Romania
gabriel@info.uaic.ro
[2] Department of Computer Science, Technical University, Cluj-Napoca, Romania
eneia.todoran@cs.utcluj.ro

Abstract. Membrane systems are described by a language in which multisets of objects are encapsulated in hierarchical structures of compartments. The language provides primitives for parallel communication of objects across membranes and a primitive for membrane creation. The behaviour of each membrane is specified by means of multiset rewriting rules. We provide a compositional semantics for membrane systems by using the continuation passing style and metric spaces.

1 Introduction

Membrane systems are presented in [12], and several of their applications in [5]. In this paper we investigate membrane systems by using continuation passing style in the tradition of programming language semantics. By using metric spaces, we provide a denotational semantics for a simple concurrent language in which computations are specified by means of multiset rewriting rules distributed into membrane-delimited compartments. The language provides a primitive for membrane creation, but we ignore other operations that can be used for expressing the dynamics of systems with active membranes, such as membrane division or membrane dissolution [12]. However, we are confident that most of the membrane computing concepts that are investigated in the literature can receive a denotational semantics by using the techniques that we employ in this paper.

The essential tools in this semantic investigation are the classic continuation-passing style in which the control is passed explicitly in the form of a continuation [2], as well as the continuations for concurrency [9,14]; both are used to describe in a compositional manner the behaviour of dynamic hierarchical systems. An important feature of this semantic approach is *compositionality*: the meaning of a compound construction is determined solely on the basis of the meanings of its components.

The aim of this paper is to offer a semantic investigation in the area of membrane computing by using methods and tools from the tradition of programming language semantics, viz., denotational semantics and continuations. We use a language $\mathcal{L}_{MC}$ in which the syntactic constructions are *statements* and *programs*. When referring to the behaviour of an $\mathcal{L}_{MC}$ program we use the term

© Springer International Publishing AG 2017
A. Leporati et al. (Eds.): CMC 2016, LNCS 10105, pp. 165–176, 2017.
DOI: 10.1007/978-3-319-54072-6_11

execution. An $\mathcal{L}_{MC}$ program comprises a list of membrane declarations, which is similar to a list of class declarations in an object-oriented language. The list of membrane declarations is followed by an $\mathcal{L}_{MC}$ statement which is executed in the skin membrane.

1.1   Semantic Investigation of Membrane Systems

We present a semantic investigation in the area of membrane computing employing the discipline of *denotational semantics*, a formal method consecrated in the tradition of programming language semantics. In the denotational approach semantic definitions are *compositional*: the semantics of a compound language construction is determined solely on the basis of the semantics of its components. The foundations of denotational semantics are given by the mathematical theory of domains. In the definition of a denotational semantics, one can use classic domains [11] or complete metric spaces [4]. In this paper we employ the mathematical methodology of metric semantics. The main mathematical tool in the metric approach to semantics is Banach's theorem, which states that contracting functions on complete metric spaces have *unique* fixed points. In Sect. 2 we recall some basic notions from metric semantics; for further details the reader may consult the monograph [4].

A denotational semantics can describe rigorously the behaviour of computer programs. In this paper we investigate the possibility of using denotational semantics to describe the behaviour of membrane systems. For this purpose we define a formal language $\mathcal{L}_{MC}$ in which multisets of objects are encapsulated in hierarchical structures of compartments delimited by membranes. $\mathcal{L}_{MC}$ provides primitives for parallel communication of objects across membranes and a primitive for membrane creation. The behaviour of each membrane is specified by means of multiset rewriting rules. We define a denotational (compositional) semantics for $\mathcal{L}_{MC}$. We employ a fixed point construction to describe the semantics of multiset rewriting computations. The denotational semantics is designed with metric spaces and continuations. The final yield of the denotational semantics is an element of a metric powerdomain [13] which is used to describe nondeterministic behaviour in $\mathcal{L}_{MC}$. An element of the powerdomain is a collection of sequences of observables representing dynamic membrane structures.

1.2   Contribution

In previous papers we have defined the operational semantics for membrane systems [3,6], and proved certain semantic properties. In [7,8] we have applied continuation semantics for concurrency [14] in providing denotational semantics for a simple multiset rewriting concurrent language. In [10] we have investigated the semantics of a language where computations are distributed to membrane-delimited regions, but without any feature for transmembrane communication.

The languages described in [7,10] are all subsumed by the language $\mathcal{L}_{MC}$ investigated in this paper. The language $\mathcal{L}_{MC}$ combines various advanced control concepts, including maximal parallelism, nondeterministic behaviour and the sequencing of phases within each computation step. In order to achieve a compositional approach of the complex control structures incorporated in $\mathcal{L}_{MC}$, we employ a domain of continuations combined with a powerdomain construction. This is the first paper presenting a denotational semantics for the combination of features embodied in $\mathcal{L}_{MC}$.

2   Mathematical Preliminaries

Mathematical preliminaries are those presented in [10]. The notation $(x \in)X$ introduces the set X with typical element x ranging over X. $\mathcal{P}(X)$ denotes the set of all subsets (the powerset) of X. $\mathcal{P}_\pi(X)$ denotes the set of all subsets of X with property π. A *multiset* is a generalization of a set; intuitively, a multiset is a collection in which an element may occur more than once. One can represent the concept of a multiset of elements of type X by using functions from $X \to \mathbb{N}$, or partial functions from $X \to \mathbb{N}^+$, where $\mathbb{N}^+ = \mathbb{N} \setminus \{0\}$. Let $(x \in)X$ be a countable set. We use the notation $[X] \overset{not.}{=} \bigcup_{A \in \mathcal{P}_{finite}(X)} \{m \mid m \in (A \to \mathbb{N}^+)\}$, where $\mathcal{P}_{finite}(X)$ is the set of all *finite* subsets of X. Since X is countable, $\mathcal{P}_{finite}(X)$ is also countable. $[X]$ is the set of all finite multisets of elements of type X.

It is also possible to represent a multiset $m \in [X]$ by enumerating its elements between parentheses '[' and ']'. For example, [] is the empty multiset, i.e. the function with empty graph. As another example, $[x_1, x_2, x_2]$ is the multiset with one occurrence of x_1 and two occurrence of x_2, i.e. the function $m : \{x_1, x_2\} \to \mathbb{N}^+$, $m(x_1) = 1$, $m(x_2) = 2$. Note that the elements of a multiset are *not* ordered. For example, $m = [x_1, x_2, x_2] = [x_2, x_1, x_2] = [x_2, x_2, x_1]$. There are several operations defined on multisets $m_1, m_2 \in [X]$, defined as in [10].

2.1   Metric Spaces

The denotational semantics given in this paper is built within the mathematical framework of *1-bounded complete metric spaces*. We work with the following notions which we assume known: *metric* and *ultrametric* space, *isometry* (distance preserving bijection between metric spaces, denoted by '$\cong$'), *complete* metric space, and *compact* set. For details the reader may consult [4]. We recall that if (M_1, d_1), (M_2, d_2) are metric spaces, a function $f: M_1 \to M_2$ is a *contraction* if $\exists c \in \mathbb{R}$, $0 \le c < 1$, $\forall x, y \in M_1 : d_2(f(x), f(y)) \le c \cdot d_1(x, y)$. In metric semantics it is customary to attach a contracting factor $c = \frac{1}{2}$ to each computation step. When $c = 1$ the function f is called *nonexpansive*. In what follows we denote the set of all nonexpansive functions from M_1 to M_2 by $M_1 \overset{1}{\to} M_2$. The following theorem is at the core of metric semantics.

Theorem 1 (Banach). *Let (M, d) be a non-empty complete metric space. Each contraction $f : M \to M$ has a* unique *fixed point.*

If $(x, y \in)M$ is any non-empty set, one can define the *discrete metric* on M $(d : M \times M \to [0, 1])$ as follows: $d(x, y) = 0$ if $x = y$, and $d(x, y) = 1$ otherwise. (M, d) is a complete ultrametric space.

Definition 1. *Let* $(M, d_M), (M_1, d_{M_1}), (M_2, d_{M_2})$ *be (ultra) metric spaces. On* $(x \in)M$, $(f \in)M_1 \rightarrow M_2$ *(the function space)*, $(x_1, x_2) \in M_1 \times M_2$ *(the Cartesian product)*, $u, v \in M_1 + M_2$ *(the disjoint union of M_1 and M_2, which can be defined by:* $M_1 + M_2 = (\{1\} \times M_1) \cup (\{2\} \times M_2))$, *and* $U, V, W \in \mathcal{P}(M)$ *(the powerset of M, i.e. the set of all subsets of M) one can define the following metrics:*

(a) $d_{\frac{1}{2} \cdot M} : M \times M \rightarrow [0, 1]$, $\quad d_{\frac{1}{2} \cdot M}(x, x') = \frac{1}{2} \cdot d_M(x, x')$,

(b) $d_{M_1 \rightarrow M_2} : (M_1 \rightarrow M_2) \times (M_1 \rightarrow M_2) \rightarrow [0, 1]$,
$\quad d_{M_1 \rightarrow M_2}(f, f') = \sup_{x_1 \in M_1} d_{M_2}(f(x_1), f'(x_1))$,

(c) $d_{M_1 \times M_2} : (M_1 \times M_2) \times (M_1 \times M_2) \rightarrow [0, 1]$,
$\quad d_{M_1 \times M_2}((x_1, x_2), (x_1', x_2')) = max\{d_{M_1}(x_1, x_1'), d_{M_2}(x_2, x_2')\}$,

(d) $d_{M_1 + M_2} : (M_1 + M_2) \times (M_1 + M_2) \rightarrow [0, 1]$,
$\quad d_{M_1 + M_2}(u, v) = $ if $(u, v \in M_1)$ then $d_{M_1}(u, v)$
$\qquad\qquad\qquad\qquad$ else if $(u, v \in M_2)$ then $d_{M_2}(u, v)$ else 1,

(e) $d_H : \mathcal{P}(M) \times \mathcal{P}(M) \rightarrow [0, 1]$,
$\quad d_H(U, V) = max\{\sup_{x \in U} d(x, V), \sup_{x' \in V} d(x', U)\}$,
$\quad$ *where* $d(x, W) = \inf_{x' \in W} d_M(x, x')$ *and by convention* $\sup \emptyset = 0, \inf \emptyset = 1$ *(d_H is the Hausdorff metric).*

We use the abbreviation $\mathcal{P}_{nco}(\cdot)$ to denote the powerset of *non-empty and compact* subsets of '$\cdot$'. We often suppress the metrics in domain definitions, and write, e.g., $\frac{1}{2} \cdot M$ instead of $(M, d_{\frac{1}{2} \cdot M})$.

Remark 1. Let $(M, d_M), (M_1, d_{M_1})(M_2, d_{M_2}), d_{\frac{1}{2} \cdot M}, d_{M_1 \rightarrow M_2}, d_{M_1 \times M_2}, d_{M_1 + M_2}$ and d_H be as in Definition 1. In case d_M, d_{M_1}, d_{M_2} are ultrametrics, so are $d_{\frac{1}{2} \cdot M}, d_{M_1 \rightarrow M_2}, d_{M_1 \times M_2}, d_{M_1 + M_2}$ and d_H. Moreover, if $(M, d_M), (M_1, d_{M_1}),$ (M_2, d_{M_2}) are complete, then $\frac{1}{2} \cdot M, M_1 \rightarrow M_2, M_1 \overset{1}{\rightarrow} M_2, M_1 \times M_2, M_1 + M_2,$ and $\mathcal{P}_{nco}(M)$ (with the metrics defined above) are also complete metric spaces [4].

3   Syntax and Semantics of $\mathcal{L}_{MC}$

We assume that O is a countable set. Let $(w \in)W = [O]$ be the set of all finite multisets of O objects, and $(M \in)Mname$ be a set of *membrane names*.

Syntax of $\mathcal{L}_{MC}$ is given by

(a) (Statements) $x(\in X) ::= o \mid in(o) \mid out(o) \mid new(M, y) \mid x \| x$
$\quad$ where $y(\in Y) ::= o \mid y \| y$

(b) (Rules) $r(\in R) ::= r_\epsilon \mid w \Rightarrow x; r$

(c) (Membrane declarations)
$\quad d(\in MD) ::= $ membrane $M \{r\}$
$\quad D(\in MDs) ::= d \mid d; D$

(d) (Programs) $\rho(\in \mathcal{L}_{MC}) ::= D; x$.

An $\mathcal{L}_{MC}$ statement may be either an object o, a communication statement $\mathsf{in}(o)$ or $\mathsf{out}(o)$, a membrane creation statement of the form $\mathsf{new}(M, y)$, where M is a membrane name and y is a statement of the type Y, or a parallel composition of two $\mathcal{L}_{MC}$ statements of the form $x_1 \parallel x_2$. Note that a statement $y \in Y$ may be either an object, or a parallel composition of two or more objects, but y cannot contain communication or membrane creation primitives. Obviously, $Y \subseteq X$.

A statement $\mathsf{out}(o)$ indicates that the object o must leave the membrane where it is currently located, and becomes an element of the surrounding region. A statement $\mathsf{in}(o)$ indicates that the object o must enter one of the child membranes, nondeterministically chosen.

The execution of a membrane created by a statement $\mathsf{new}(M, y)$ will always begin by a multiset rewriting step. In the first step after its creation, a membrane cannot perform any communication or membrane creation operations. However, by using the rewriting rules specified in the definition of M, the newly created membrane (instance) can next immediately create new inner membranes and communication objects and it can proceed as any other membrane.

An $\mathcal{L}_{MC}$ program $D; x$ consists of a list $D \in MDs$ of membrane declarations and a statement $x \in X$. A membrane declaration introduces a type of membranes, which can be instantiated. In $\mathcal{L}_{MC}$ we speak of *membrane types*, and *membrane instances*. Each membrane instance has a (unique) label. The execution of the program $D; x$ starts with the creation of an instance of the first membrane type in the declarations list D, which becomes a *skin* membrane; the skin membrane starts the execution of the program by executing statement x.

A membrane declaration **membrane** $M \{r\}$ indicates the name $M \in Mname$ of the membrane (type) and a (possibly empty) list of rules $r \in R$, which specify the behaviour of objects inside any instance of a membrane of the type M. A rule $w \Rightarrow x$ is composed of two elements: a multiset $w \in W$ and a statement $x \in X$. An $\mathcal{L}_{MC}$ statement is a concurrent composition of objects, which behave as a multiset. In this interpretation $w \Rightarrow x$ is a multiset rewriting rule, specifying that w is rewritten as x. Intuitively, a rule $w \Rightarrow x$ is like a 'procedure' definition, with 'name' w and 'body' x. The objects $o_1, \cdots, o_n$ in the multiset $w = [o_1 \cdots o_n]$ are 'fragments' of the procedure name. Only when all the 'fragments' of such a 'procedure name' are prepared for interaction a rewriting rule is applied, and so replaces the 'name of the procedure' with its 'body'. The 'body' (the right hand side) of a rule is a statement. Further explanations concerning the syntactic constructions for specifying membranes and rules in $\mathcal{L}_{MC}$ are provided in [10].

If we consider the analogy with object-oriented programming, we can state clearly that in $\mathcal{L}_{MC}$ an object $o \in O$ is *not* an instance of a membrane. In $\mathcal{L}_{MC}$, an object is just an elementary statement, a symbol taken from the alphabet O. The reader may wonder why we use the semantic notion of a *multiset* in the syntax definition of $\mathcal{L}_{MC}$. According to the syntax, we can use rules of the form $j \Rightarrow x$, where $j ::= o \mid j \& j$ is the set of 'method names'. We use multisets as 'method names' because the order in which fragments occur in such a 'method name' is irrelevant.

Semantics of $\mathcal{L}_{MC}$ is given by using a denotational approach. Denotational semantics (known also as mathematical semantics) is an important step in formalizing the meanings of languages/systems. The most important principle in denotational semantics is *compositionality*: the meaning of a compound construction is determined solely on the basis of the meanings of its components. In general, denotational semantics assigns to every construction of a language a certain formal *meaning*, which is an element from a suitably chosen mathematical model. Following [4], we choose to use the mathematical framework of *complete metric spaces* for our semantic description. In this approach, one can prove the semantic properties by making use of Banach's theorem which states that contracting functions on complete metric spaces have *unique* fixed points.

We introduce the metric domains to express the behaviour of $\mathcal{L}_{MC}$ programs, and then give a continuation-based denotational semantics for $\mathcal{L}_{MC}$. The final yield of the denotational semantics is an element of a linear time domain [4].

We assume given a (countably) infinite set $(l \in)L$ of *membrane labels*. Let also $(\varsigma \in)\mathcal{P}_{finite}(L)$ be the set of all finite subsets of L. We also assume given a function $\nu : \mathcal{P}_{finite}(L) \to L$, such that $\nu(\varsigma) \notin \varsigma$, for any $\varsigma \in \mathcal{P}_{finite}(L)$. We obtain a possible example of such a set L and function ν by putting $L = \mathbb{N}$, and $\nu(\varsigma) = 1 + max\{n \mid n \in \varsigma\}$, with the convention that $\nu(\emptyset) = 0$.

Following [3], we define the set $(\mu \in)Mb$ of *membranes* inductively:

- If $M \in Mname$ is a membrane name, $l \in L$ is a label and $w \in W = [O]$ is a multiset of O objects then $\langle M, l \mid w; \rangle \in Mb$; $\langle M, l \mid w; \rangle$ is called a (*simple* or) *elementary membrane*;
- If $M \in Mname$ is a membrane name, $l \in L$ is a label, $w \in W$ is a multiset of O objects, and $\mu_1, \ldots, \mu_n \in Mb$ then $\langle M, l \mid w; \mu_1, \ldots, \mu_n \rangle \in Mb$; $\langle M, l \mid w; \mu_1, \ldots, \mu_n \rangle$ is called a *composite membrane*.

We provide a continuation-based denotational semantics for $\mathcal{L}_{MC}$ in which we use the linear time domain $(p \in)\mathbf{P} = \mathcal{P}_{nco}(\mathbf{Q})$, where $(q \in)\mathbf{Q} \cong \{\epsilon\} + (Mb \times \frac{1}{2} \cdot \mathbf{Q})$. In this domain equation, the set Mb is endowed with the discrete metric (i.e. an ultrametric). The composed metric spaces are built up using the composite metrics of Definition 1. According to [4], the above domain equation has a *unique* solution (up to isomorphism). The solution is a complete ultrametric space.

An element of the domain $\mathbf{P}$ is a non-empty and compact collection of $\mathbf{Q}$ sequences. $\mathbf{Q}$ is a domain of finite and infinite sequences over Mb; ϵ is the empty sequence. Instead of $(\mu_1, (\mu_2, \ldots (\mu_n, \epsilon) \ldots))$ and $(\mu_1, (\mu_2, \ldots))$, we write $\mu_1\mu_2\ldots\mu_n$ and $\mu_1\mu_2\ldots$, respectively. In particular, instead of (μ, ϵ) (a sequence of length 1) we write just μ. Nondeterministic behaviour in $\mathcal{L}_{MC}$ is defined by using the operator $+ : (\mathbf{P} \times \mathbf{P}) \to \mathbf{P}$ defined by $p_1 + p_2 = \{q \mid q \in p_1 \cup p_2, q \neq \epsilon\}$ $\cup \{\epsilon \mid \epsilon \in p_1 \cap p_2\}$. It is easy to see that $+$ is well-defined, non-expansive, associative and commutative [4]. Also, we use the following notations: $\mu \cdot q = (\mu, q)$ and $\mu \cdot p = \{\mu \cdot q \mid q \in p\}$, for any $\mu \in Mb, q \in \mathbf{Q}, p \in \mathbf{P}$. Based on the results presented in [4], we have $d(\mu \cdot p_1, \mu \cdot p_2) = \frac{1}{2} \cdot d(p_1, p_2)$.

Let $(\alpha \in)A = Mb \to \mathcal{P}_{finite}(Mb)$. We define a set $(\theta, \vartheta \in)\Theta$ of *actions*:

- $\theta_0 \in \Theta$ (θ_0 is a distinct element of Θ);
- If $\alpha \in A$ then $\alpha \in \Theta$, for any $\alpha \in A$;
- If $\alpha \in A$ and $\theta \in \Theta$, then $(\cdot, \alpha, \theta) \in \Theta$; we use a triple $(\cdot, \alpha, \theta)$ to represent a sequential composition between α and θ, but write $\alpha \cdot \theta$ instead of $(\cdot, \alpha, \theta)$;
- If $\theta_1, \theta_2 \in \Theta$, then $(\parallel, \theta_1, \theta_2) \in \Theta$; instead of $(\parallel, \theta_1, \theta_2)$, we use $\theta_1 \parallel \theta_2$ for parallel composition between θ_1 and θ_2.

We define a valuation $\mathcal{T}[\![\cdot]\!] : \Theta \to A$ by

$$\begin{aligned}
\mathcal{T}[\![\theta_0]\!] &= \lambda\mu.\{\mu\}, \\
\mathcal{T}[\![\alpha]\!] &= \mathcal{T}[\![\alpha \cdot \theta_0]\!] = \alpha, \\
\mathcal{T}[\![\alpha \cdot \theta]\!] &= \lambda\mu.\bigcup\{\mathcal{T}[\![\theta]\!](\mu') \mid \mu' \in \alpha(\mu)\} \quad \text{if } \theta \neq \theta_0, \\
\mathcal{T}[\![\theta \parallel \theta_0]\!] &= \mathcal{T}[\![\theta_0 \parallel \theta]\!] = \mathcal{T}[\![\theta]\!], \\
\mathcal{T}[\![\theta_1 \parallel \theta_2]\!] &= \mathcal{T}[\![\theta_1]\!] \,\hat{\parallel}\, \mathcal{T}[\![\theta_2]\!],
\end{aligned}$$

where the operator $\hat{\parallel} : (A \times A) \to A$ is given by

$$\alpha_1 \,\hat{\parallel}\, \alpha_2 = \lambda\mu.(\{\mu_2 \mid \mu_1 \in \alpha_1(\mu), \mu_2 \in \alpha_2(\mu_1)\} \cup \{\mu_1 \mid \mu_2 \in \alpha_2(\mu), \mu_1 \in \alpha_1(\mu_2)\}).$$

Clearly, $\hat{\parallel}$ is well-defined, i.e. $\theta_1 \,\hat{\parallel}\, \theta_2 \in A$ for any $\theta_1, \theta_2 \in A$. Well-definedness of $\mathcal{T}[\![\theta]\!]$ follows by an easy induction on the structure of θ.

In the following definitions, Θ is just a set endowed with the discrete metric. We define the domain $\mathbf{D}$ of *computations*, and the domain $\mathbf{K}$ of *continuations* by $(\varphi \in)\mathbf{D} = \mathbf{K} \xrightarrow{1} F$ and $(\kappa \in)\mathbf{K} = (\Theta \times \Theta) \to F$, where $F = \mathcal{P}_{finite}(L) \to Mb \to \mathbf{P}$. In the domain definitions, the sets Θ, $\mathcal{P}_{finite}(L)$ and Mb are endowed with discrete metrics, and $\mathbf{D}$ is a domain of *nonexpansive* functions [4].

Definition 2. (*Semantics of parallel composition*)

(a) We define $\parallel: (\mathbf{D} \times \mathbf{D}) \xrightarrow{1} \mathbf{D}$ by

$$\varphi_1 \parallel \varphi_2 = \lambda\kappa.\varphi_1(\lambda(\theta_1, \vartheta_1).\varphi_2(\lambda(\theta_2, \vartheta_2).\kappa(\theta_1 \,\hat{\parallel}\, \theta_2, \vartheta_1 \,\hat{\parallel}\, \vartheta_2)));$$

(b) For any $n \in \mathbb{N}$ we define $\parallel^n (\cdot) : \mathbf{D}^n \to \mathbf{D}$ ($\mathbf{D}^n = \mathbf{D} \times \cdots \times \mathbf{D}$ n times, $n \geq 1$) by $\parallel^1 (\varphi) = \varphi$, and $\parallel^{n+1} (\varphi_1, \ldots, \varphi_{n+1}) = \varphi_1 \parallel (\parallel^n (\varphi_2, \ldots, \varphi_{n+1}))$. For readability, we write $\varphi_1 \parallel \cdots \parallel \varphi_n$ instead of $\parallel^n (\varphi_1, \ldots, \varphi_n)$.

Proposition 1. *The operator for parallel composition $\parallel$ is well-defined and non-expansive in both arguments.*

The above property is not difficult to prove. Other properties, e.g., the associativity or the commutativity of $\parallel$, are more difficult to establish. A formal proof of the fact that $\parallel$ is associative employs the technique introduced in [9].

In order to define the semantics of $\mathcal{L}_{MC}$ statements we need some auxiliary operators on membranes. Given a membrane μ, $add(o, l', \mu)$ adds the object o to the multiset stored in the membrane region indicated by label l'.

$new_M(M_{new}, l_{new}, l', \mu)$ creates a new membrane region with label l_{new} of the type M_{new} as an inner membrane (a child) of the membrane region with label l'. The operator $out(o, l', \mu)$ sends the object o from its membrane (instance) to the surrounding region. The operator $in(o, l', \mu)$ sends the object o from its membrane into a child membrane, nondeterministically chosen. The operator in is used to specify the fact that an object enters into a child membrane which is nondeterministically selected. If there is no child membrane, in is inoperative.

The operators are defined by induction on the structure of the membrane hierarchy, considering the fact that membranes (regions) are labelled in a one-to-one manner with labels from the given set L. All definitions are recursive. We only provide the definitions for some representative (non-recursive) cases, leaving the other cases to the reader. $\uplus$ is the multiset sum operation [1].

$add : (O \times L \times Mb) \to Mb,$
$$add(o, l', \langle M, l \mid w; \rangle) = \begin{cases} \langle M, l \mid [o] \uplus w; \rangle & \text{if } l' = l \\ \langle M, l \mid w; \rangle & \text{if } l' \neq l \end{cases}$$

$new_M : (Mname \times L \times L \times Mb) \to Mb,$
$$new_M(M_{new}, l_{new}, l', \langle M, l \mid w; \rangle) = \begin{cases} \langle M, l \mid w; \langle M_{new}, l_{new} \mid [ ]; \rangle \rangle & \text{if } l' = l \\ \langle M, l \mid w; \rangle & \text{if } l' \neq l \end{cases}$$

$in : (O \times L \times Mb) \to \mathcal{P}_{finite}(Mb),$
$in(o, l, \langle M, l \mid w; \rangle) = \{\langle M, l \mid [o] \uplus w; \rangle\},$
$in(o, l, \langle M, l \mid w; \mu_1, \ldots, \langle M_i, l_i \mid w_i; \mu_{i1}, \ldots, \mu_{in_i} \rangle, \ldots, \mu_n \rangle) =$
$\quad \{\langle M, l \mid w; \mu_1, \ldots, \langle M_i, l_i \mid [o] \uplus w_i; \mu_{i1}, \ldots, \mu_{in_i} \rangle, \ldots, \mu_n \rangle \mid 1 \leq i \leq n\},$

$out : (O \times L \times Mb) \to Mb,$
$out(o, l', \langle M, l \mid w; \mu_1, \ldots, \mu_n \rangle) = \langle M, l \mid [o] \uplus w; \mu_1, \ldots, \mu_n \rangle,$
$\quad \text{if } l' \in \{label(\mu_1), \ldots, label(\mu_n)\} .$

Definition 3. *Denotational semantics* $\llbracket \cdot \rrbracket : X \to L \to \mathbf{D}$ *of* $\mathcal{L}_{MC}$ *statements is defined by*

$$\llbracket o \rrbracket(l) = \lambda\kappa . \kappa(\lambda\mu . \{ add(o, l, \mu) \}, \theta_0),$$
$$\llbracket \mathsf{in}(o) \rrbracket(l) = \lambda\kappa . \kappa(\lambda\mu . in(o, l, \mu), \theta_0),$$
$$\llbracket \mathsf{out}(o) \rrbracket(l) = \lambda\kappa . \kappa(\lambda\mu . \{ out(o, l, \mu) \}, \theta_0),$$
$$\llbracket \mathsf{new}(M, y) \rrbracket(l) = \lambda\kappa . \lambda\varsigma . \text{ let } l' = \nu(\varsigma); \varsigma' = \{l'\} \cup \varsigma \text{ in}$$
$$\llbracket y \rrbracket(l')(\lambda(\theta, \vartheta) . \kappa(\theta_0, (\lambda\mu . \{ new_M(M, l', l, \mu) \}) \cdot (\theta \parallel \vartheta)))(\varsigma'),$$
$$\llbracket x_1 \parallel x_2 \rrbracket(l) = (\llbracket x_1 \rrbracket(l)) \parallel (\llbracket x_2 \rrbracket(l)).$$

Proposition 2. *The denotational mapping* $\llbracket \cdot \rrbracket$ *is well-defined.*
In particular, $\llbracket x \rrbracket(l)$ *is non-expansive for any* $x \in X$, $l \in L$.

The denotational mapping $\llbracket x \rrbracket(l)$ takes as parameters a statement $x \in X$ and a label $l \in L$. The parameter l is the membrane label where the statement x is executed. Each continuation takes as parameter a pair of actions (θ, ϑ). The action θ represents the behaviour of object and communication actions. The action ϑ represents the behaviour of membrane creation actions. Within each computation step the two actions θ and ϑ are executed in this sequence by the initial continuation κ_0: first the action θ, then the action ϑ. However, note that only one observable is produced by each computation step.

All equations are straightforward, except the equation handling membrane creation. In the equation defining the semantics of $\mathsf{new}(M, y)$, a new label l' is created. Next, the body y of the statement $\mathsf{new}(M, y)$ is executed. The membrane creation action $\lambda\mu . \{ new_M(M, l', l, \mu)\})$ is executed before $\theta \parallel \vartheta$. Thus, the actions produced by $[\![y]\!]$ are executed in the newly created membrane with label l' only *after* the new membrane is created.

The mapping $appRules(r, w')$ computes a (finite) set of pairs, each pair consisting of a multiset of rules applicable to w' and an irreducible submultiset of w'. $\subseteq$ and $\backslash$ are operations for submultiset testing and multiset difference [1].

$$appRules : (R \times W) \rightarrow \mathcal{P}_{finite}(R \times W),$$
$$appRules(r, w) = \text{ if } aux(r, w) = \emptyset \text{ then } \{(r_\epsilon, w)\} \text{ else}$$
$$\{(\overline{w} \Rightarrow \overline{x} \square r', w'') \mid ((\overline{w}, \overline{x}), w') \in aux(r, w), (r', w'') \in appRules(r, w')\},$$
$$\text{where } aux : (R \times W) \rightarrow \mathcal{P}_{finite}((W \times X) \times W),$$
$$aux(r_\epsilon, w) = \emptyset,$$
$$aux(w' \Rightarrow x' \square r, w) =$$
$$\text{if } (w' \subseteq w) \text{ then } \{((w', x'), w \backslash w')\} \cup aux(r, w) \text{ else } aux(r, w).$$

We define a scheduler mapping $sched : (Mb \times MDs) \rightarrow \mathcal{P}_{finite}(\mathbf{D} \times Mb)$ by induction on the structure of the membrane. The function $sched(\mu, D)$ takes as arguments a membrane μ and a list of membrane declarations D, and yields a finite set of pairs, each pair consisting of a computation and a corresponding membrane. It uses $appRules$ to compute the applicable rules for each membrane region. We use $sched$ in a fixed point construction required to define the semantics of parallel rewriting of multisets in a compositional manner.

$$sched(\langle M, l \mid w; \rangle, D) =$$
$$\{(([\![x_1]\!](l) \parallel \cdots \parallel [\![x_n]\!](l) \parallel [\![o_1]\!](l) \parallel \cdots \parallel [\![o_m]\!](l), \langle M, l \mid [\,]; \rangle)$$
$$\mid (r', w') \in appRules(rules(D, M), w),$$
$$r' = w_1 \Rightarrow x_1; \ldots; w_n \Rightarrow x_n; r_\epsilon, w' = [o_1, \ldots, o_m]\},$$
$$sched(\langle M, l \mid w; \mu_1, \ldots, \mu_k \rangle, D) =$$
$$\{(([\![x_1]\!](l) \parallel \cdots \parallel [\![x_n]\!](l) \parallel [\![o_1]\!](l) \parallel \cdots \parallel [\![o_m]\!](l) \parallel$$
$$\varphi_1 \parallel \cdots \parallel \varphi_k, \langle M, l \mid [\,]; \mu'_1, \ldots, \mu'_k \rangle)$$
$$\mid (r', w') \in appRules(rules(D, M), w),$$
$$r' = w_1 \Rightarrow x_1; \ldots; w_n \Rightarrow x_n; r_\epsilon, w' = [o_1, \ldots, o_m],$$
$$(\varphi_1, \mu'_1) \in sched(\mu_1, D), \ldots, (\varphi_k, \mu'_k) \in sched(\mu_k, D)\}.$$

Given a list of membrane declarations, we also define a mapping $haltMb : (Mb \times MDs) \rightarrow Bool$ which decides whether the membrane system has reached a halting configuration. $haltMb$ is defined with the aid of an auxiliary mapping $haltM : (Mname \times MDs \times W) \rightarrow Bool$, based on the mapping $appRules$.

$$haltMb(\langle M, l \mid w; \rangle, D) = haltM(M, D, w),$$
$$haltMb(\langle M, l \mid w; \mu_1, \ldots, \mu_n \rangle, D) =$$
$$haltM(M, D, w) \wedge haltMb(\mu_1, D) \wedge \cdots \wedge haltMb(\mu_n, D),$$
$$haltM(M, D, w) = (appRules(rules(D, M), w) = \{(r_\epsilon, w)\}).$$

We define a mapping $\Psi : MDs \to \mathbf{K} \to \mathbf{K}$ by

$$\Psi(D)(k)(\theta, \vartheta)(\varsigma)(\mu) =$$
$$+\{\mu_2 \cdot (\text{ if } (haltMb(\mu, D)) \text{ then } \{\epsilon\} \text{ else } \varphi(\kappa)(\varsigma)(\mu_2'))$$
$$| \mu_1 \in \mathcal{T}[\![\theta]\!](\mu), \mu_2 \in \mathcal{T}[\![\vartheta]\!](\mu_1), (\varphi, \mu_2') \in sched(\mu_2, D)\}.$$

For any $D \in MDs$, we define the *initial continuation* $\kappa_0 \in \mathbf{K}$ by $\kappa_0 = fix(\Psi(D))$. This definition is justified by Proposition 3 which states that $\Psi(D)$ is $\frac{1}{2}$ contractive for any $D \in MDs$. According to Banach's Theorem, $\Psi(D)$ has a *unique* fixed point for any $D \in MDs$.

Proposition 3. $\Psi(D) \in \mathbf{K} \xrightarrow{\frac{1}{2}} \mathbf{K}$ *for any* $D \in MDs$, *i.e.*

$$d(\Psi(D)(\kappa_1)(\theta, \vartheta)(\varsigma)(\mu), \Psi(D)(\kappa_2)(\theta, \vartheta)(\varsigma)(\mu)) \leq \frac{1}{2} \cdot d(\kappa_1, \kappa_2)$$

for any $D \in MDs$, $\kappa_1, \kappa_2 \in \mathbf{K}$, $(\theta, \vartheta) \in \Theta \times \Theta$, $\varsigma \in \mathcal{P}_{finite}(A)$ *and* $\mu \in Mb$.

Proof. If $haltMb(\mu, D) = true$, then

$$d(\Psi(D)(\kappa_1)(\theta, \vartheta)(\varsigma)(\mu), \Psi(D)(\kappa_2)(\theta, \vartheta)(\varsigma)(\mu)) = 0 \leq \frac{1}{2} \cdot d(\kappa_1, \kappa_2).$$

Otherwise, if $haltMb(\mu, D) = false$, we have

$$d(\Psi(D)(\kappa_1)(\theta, \vartheta)(\varsigma)(\mu), \Psi(D)(\kappa_2)(\theta, \vartheta)(\varsigma)(\mu)) \qquad [\text{+ is nonexpansive}]$$
$$\leq \frac{1}{2} \cdot max\{d(\varphi(\kappa_1)(\varsigma)(\mu_2'), \varphi(\kappa_2)(\varsigma)(\mu_2'))$$
$$| \mu_1 \in \mathcal{T}[\![\theta]\!](\mu), \mu_2 \in \mathcal{T}[\![\vartheta]\!](\mu_1), (\varphi, \mu_2') \in sched(\mu_2, D)\}$$
$$\qquad\qquad [\text{since } \varphi \in \mathbf{D}, \varphi \text{ is nonexpansive}]$$
$$\leq \frac{1}{2} \cdot d(\kappa_1, \kappa_2).$$

Definition 4. *Semantics of* $\mathcal{L}_{MC}$ *programs is defined by* $\mathcal{D}[\![\cdot]\!] : \mathcal{L}_{MC} \to \mathbf{P}$,
$$\mathcal{D}[\![D; x]\!] = [\![x]\!](l_0)(\kappa_0)(\varsigma_0)(\mu_0),$$
where $D = $ membrane $M_0 \{r_0\}$; $\cdots$; membrane $M_m \{r_m\}$, $\kappa_0 = fix(\Psi(D))$, $l_0 = \nu(\emptyset)$, $\varsigma_0 = \{l_0\}$ *and* $\mu_0 = \langle M_0, l_0 \mid [\,]; \rangle$.

The function $\mathcal{D}[\![\rho]\!]$ defines the semantics of an $\mathcal{L}_{MC}$ program $\rho = D; x$, where $D \in MDs$ and $x \in X$. The execution of an $\mathcal{L}_{MC}$ program begins with the creation of the skin which is an instance of the first membrane type in the declaration list D. The label of the skin is $\nu(\emptyset)$; the statement x is executed in the skin membrane. In the spirit of denotational semantics, the initial continuation $\kappa_0 \in \mathbf{K}$ is defined as a fixed point of the higher-order mapping Ψ.

Example 1. We consider the $\mathcal{L}_{MC}$ program $\rho = D; x$, where D is:

```
membrane M_0 {
    [o_1, o_4] ⇒ o_2 || o_4;
    [o_2] ⇒ in(o_5) || new(M_1, o_1 || o_5);
    [o_2] ⇒ o_4;
    [o_5] ⇒ in(o_4);
    [o_3] ⇒ in(o_5)
};
```

```
membrane M₁ {
    [o₁] ⇒ o₂ ∥ out(o₃);
    [o₂] ⇒ o₃
};
```

and $x = o_1 \parallel o_4$. Let $\mu_1, \mu_2, \mu_3, \mu_4, \mu_5, \mu_6 \in Mb$

$$\mu_1 = \langle M_0, l_0 \mid [o_1, o_4]; \rangle$$
$$\mu_2 = \langle M_0, l_0 \mid [o_2, o_4]; \rangle$$
$$\mu_3 = \langle M_0, l_0 \mid [o_4, o_4]; \rangle$$
$$\mu_4 = \langle M_0, l_0 \mid [o_4, o_5]; \langle M_1, l_1 \mid [o_1, o_5]; \rangle \rangle$$
$$\mu_5 = \langle M_0, l_0 \mid [o_3, o_4]; \langle M_1, l_1 \mid [o_2, o_4, o_5]; \rangle \rangle$$
$$\mu_6 = \langle M_0, l_0 \mid [o_4]; \langle M_1, l_1 \mid [o_3, o_4, o_5, o_5]; \rangle \rangle$$

One can check that $\mathcal{D}[\![\rho]\!] = \{\mu_1\mu_2\mu_3, \mu_1\mu_2\mu_4\mu_5\mu_6\}$.

The denotational specification presented in this paper was developed following a prototyping approach; we used the functional language Haskell as a prototyping tool (and metalanguage) for this denotational semantics. A couple of $\mathcal{L}_{MC}$ programs (including the $\mathcal{L}_{MC}$ example discussed above) are provided, and can be tested by using the semantic interpreter available at

http://users.utcluj.ro/~eneia/CMC17-semMC.hs.

The semantic interpreter is a complete Haskell implementation of the denotational semantics presented in this paper.

4 Conclusion

In this paper we introduce a language $\mathcal{L}_{MC}$ in which computations are specified by means of multiset rewriting rules applied in a maximal parallel way into membrane-delimited compartments. In $\mathcal{L}_{MC}$ there is a notion of membrane declaration, and membranes are grouped into classes based on their rewriting rules. There exist primitives for parallel communication of objects between adjacent membranes, and a primitive for membrane creation (instantiation).

We present a denotational semantics designed with complete metric spaces for $\mathcal{L}_{MC}$. For illustration, we presented a small $\mathcal{L}_{MC}$ example program; other examples are available on our Haskell implementation webpage.

References

1. Alexandru, A., Ciobanu, G.: Mathematics of multisets in the Fraenkel-Mostowski framework. Bull. Math. Soc. Sci. Math. Roumanie **58**(106), 3–18 (2015). Tome
2. Appel, A.W.: Compiling with Continuations. Cambridge University Press, New York (2007)
3. Andrei, O., Ciobanu, G., Lucanu, D.: A rewriting logic framework for operational semantics of membrane systems. Theor. Comput. Sci. **373**, 163–181 (2007)
4. de Bakker, J.W., de Vink, E.P.: Control Flow Semantics. MIT Press, Cambridge (1996)

5. Ciobanu, G., Păun, G., Pérez-Jiménez, M.J.: Applications of Membrane Computing. Natural Computing Series. Springer, Heidelberg (2006)
6. Ciobanu, G.: Semantics of P systems. In: Handbook of Membrane Computing, pp. 413–436. Oxford University Press (2009)
7. Ciobanu, G., Todoran, E.N.: Metric denotational semantics for parallel rewriting of multisets. In: Proceedings 13th Symposium on Symbolic and Numeric Algorithms for Scientific Computing (SYNASC), pp. 276–283. IEEE Computer Press (2011)
8. Ciobanu, G., Todoran, E.N.: Relating two metric semantics for parallel rewriting of multisets. In: Proceedings 14th Symposium on Symbolic and Numeric Algorithms for Scientific Computing (SYNASC), pp. 273–280. IEEE Computer Press (2012)
9. Ciobanu, G., Todoran, E.N.: Continuation semantics for asynchronous concurrency. Fundamenta Informaticae **131**(3–4), 373–388 (2014)
10. Ciobanu, G., Todoran, E.N.: Continuation semantics for dynamic hierarchical systems. In: Proceedings of 17th Symposium on Symbolic and Numeric Algorithms for Scientific Computing (SYNASC), pp. 281–288. IEEE Computer Press (2015)
11. Gierz, G., Hofmann, K.H., Keimel, K., Lawson, J.D., Mislove, M., Scott, D.S.: Continuous Lattices and Domains. Cambridge University Press, Cambridge (2003)
12. Păun, G.: Membrane Computing. An Introduction. Springer, Heidelberg (2002)
13. Plotkin, G.: A powerdomain construction. SIAM J. Comput. **5**(3), 452–487 (1976)
14. Todoran, E.N.: Metric semantics for synchronous and asynchronous communication: a continuation-based approach. Electronic Notes in Theoretical Computer Science **28**, 101–127 (2000)

Minimal Multiset Grammars for Recurrent Dynamics

Alessandro Farinelli, Giuditta Franco$^{(\boxtimes)}$, and Romeo Rizzi

Dipartimento di Informatica, Università di Verona, Verona, Italy
giuditta.franco@univr.it

Abstract. A biochemical network modeled by a multiset grammar may be investigated from a dynamical viewpoint by a linear recurrence system. This interesting connection between computation by a multiset grammar and a (network) recurrent dynamics poses a minimization problem, which turns out to be NP-hard.

Keywords: Metabolic computing · Multiset grammar · NP-hardness · Optimization

1 Introduction

Metabolic networks (usually having many more interactions/edges than substances/nodes) may be modeled by a set of (usually thousands) rewriting rules (see, for example [21]), where reactants are replaced by their products in each step of computation. Namely, multiset grammars represent a computational model for substances transformation (i.e., a metabolic dynamics), where rewriting rules process in parallel mutisets of objects/substances (i.e., symbols of a given alphabet), according to an application strategy. The structure of such a grammar may be pictured by a direct network over the substances (see Fig. 1), labeled by natural numbers (where labels equal to one are omitted).

The intent to employ multiset processing as a framework to study real biological systems is vivid in literature, along with variants of P systems enriched with other features, often inspired by biology [10], and having a specific rule application strategy different from the traditional nondeterministic maximal parallelism [20]. A very applicative trend of membrane computing provides us with models for metabolism called MP systems [15,16], which are monomembrane multiset grammars, with rules regulated by (real) state functions computed by regression from observed data [6,10,15]. Other approaches in membrane computing to model biological systems include state probability functions, assigned to rules to guide their application at each step [5]. All biological models based on membrane systems (even those employing the strategy of non-deterministic maximal parallelism [8]) exhibit a computation strategy where the multiset of rules which is applied at each step depends on the current state of the system. This is indeed very intuitive, as any rule to be applied requires the presence of sufficient matter in the system. For example, $aab \to c$ needs $2n$ copies of object

© Springer International Publishing AG 2017
A. Leporati et al. (Eds.): CMC 2016, LNCS 10105, pp. 177–189, 2017.
DOI: 10.1007/978-3-319-54072-6_12

a and n copies of b in order to be applied n times. In fact, the system state (or current multiset) is usually seen as the vector of object quantities, i.e., a natural vector.

Although motivated by an applicative interest towards computation of multiset grammars meant as dynamics of metabolic networks, in this paper we work at an abstract level, where a multiset grammar transforms multisets with possibly negative multiplicities (states are integer vectors), and focus (as an initial setting) on minimal grammars keeping given dynamical/computational properties (indipendently on where the states of the dynamics are located in the vector space). This setting has been recently investigated in membrane computing, in terms of computational power and complexity [2,3].

In this work, we search for the smallest cohorts of rewriting rules, from a given grammar, required to exhibit one given dynamics (for all variables involved in the system). We formalize such a search as a quadratically constrained optimization problem, so finding a standard way to "efficiently" (as possible) compute a *minimal* grammar (i.e., having a minimal set of rules) which guarantees a given systemic dynamical pattern (e.g., periodic, oscillating, increasing, decreasing ...). In other words, we reduce the problem to that of finding solutions of minimal support to integer linear problem in canonical form ($Ax = b$, of which a solution $\bar{x}$ is given).

The problem arises by an interest both in discrete modeling of metabolic dynamics and in integer multiset grammar computation. It has been however already investigated in this form [1], under different assumptions and in different contexts [18,22]. Namely, this work has been ispired by problems opened up in [9], in the context of metabolic computing, where also rule covering properties have been discussed.

Similarly to our approach of minimization, in recent literature of synthetic biology, synthetic genomes are generated by suitable assemblying of a minimal set of genes necessary to keep the cell working, or performing a given specific function. For instance, the genome of *Mycoplasma mycoides* was replaced with a synthetic genome in 2010 [12], while more complex organisms (of yeast species) have been synthetically generated more recently [4,13]. In these cases, original genomic sequences are "edited", namely by specific deletion of "dispensable" DNA sequences and by replacement of particular regions by others performing the same task. Deletion of the "non-essential genes" allows the genome size to be reduced: a feature designed to determine the smallest cohorts of genes required to perform a given function (or necessary for survival under a particular growth condition).

A description and a formalization of our problem is proposed in the fist two sections, along with a simple example, while its complexity is analyzed in the third section, followed by some conclusions.

2   Grammar Computation as a Recurrent Dynamics

Deterministic evolution of an abstract container of objects, having integer multiplicities, may be naturally modeled by a grammar where a multiset of rules is applied at each step to transform integer vectors (states). Hence, an application strategy is established for the number of times that each rule is applied. On multisets with integer multiplicities, namely, rules have no conflict to be applied (just as in some traditional P models, where an environment was assumed to provide our system with unlimited resourses [20]). Our interest is focused on the dynamics of the system, that is, on the string of states.

Let us consider a one-membrane P system with integer multiplicities, having numerical vectors emerging as a sequence of states computed by transitions, where rules are applied a natural number of times. This is the most intuitive strategy, although to model biological phenomena rational numbers are often necessary to meet different scales of times (or velocity) for different rules [7].

Example 1. As a toy example, we are given a grammar with five reactions (we call in the order r_1, r_2, r_3, r_4, r_5):

$$\mathcal{G} = \begin{cases} ab \rightarrow aa \\ bcc \rightarrow a \\ abc \rightarrow bb \\ c \rightarrow ab \\ ab \rightarrow c \end{cases}.$$

they may be all applied in one transition, *each of them once*, to modify an arbitrary (initial) state (α, β, γ), which is an integer vector. The transition is computed by means of the stoichiometric matrix:

$$\mathcal{M} = \begin{pmatrix} 1 & 1 & -1 & 1 & -1 \\ -1 & -1 & 1 & 1 & -1 \\ 0 & -2 & -1 & -1 & 1 \end{pmatrix}$$

according to the equation $\mathcal{M} \times (1,1,1,1,1) + (\alpha, \beta, \gamma) = (\alpha + 1, \beta - 1, \gamma - 3)$, where $\times$ denotes the ordinary matrix product.

In general, given a multiset grammar over the alphabet $X = \{x_1, x_2, \ldots, x_n\}$, with rules $R = \{r_1, r_2, \ldots, r_m\}$, with $m \geq n$, if k_i represents the number of times each rule r_i is applied (in one transition step), for $i = 1, \ldots, m$, then the following recurrent dynamics describes the grammar computation:

$$X[i+1] = \sum_{i=1}^{m} k_i v_i + X[i] = \mathcal{M} \times U + X[i]$$

where $X[i] \in \mathbb{Z}^n$ is the current state of the system, i the computational step, $U = (k_1, k_2, \ldots, k_m) \in \mathbb{N}^m$, and $v_1, v_2, \ldots, v_m$ the m columns of the stochiometric matrix $\mathcal{M}$, reporting the substance variation by application of $r_1, r_2, \ldots, r_m$.

This is an MP system with natural fluxes, where the dynamics is formalized by a recurrence equation, which updates the current state $X[i]$ by adding the vector $\mathcal{M} \times U$, given by the specific linear combination $\sum_{i=1}^{m} k_i v_i$ of the m vectors of Z^n corresponding to the rules. Our goal here is to minimize the number of rules in the system, by keeping unaltered such a state variation at each step (i.e., the dynamics). To be able to reduce the number of rules (i.e., vectors v_i, $i = 1, \ldots, m$) of course we need to change the given U into a different vector U^* with a smaller number of positive components, and the question is:

which is the minimum number p of rules, $p \leq m$, such that: $k_{j_1} v_{j_1} + k_{j_2} v_{j_2} + \ldots, k_{j_p} v_{j_p} = k_1 v_1 + k_2 v_2 \cdots + k_m v_m$ and $j_i \in \{1, 2, \ldots, m\}$ for $i \in \{1, 2, \ldots, p\}$?

In the toy system above, we have a given state variation $b = \mathcal{M} \times U$ of $(1, -1, -3)$, with $U = (1, 1, 1)$ and $\mathcal{M} = \begin{pmatrix} 1 & 1 & -1 & 1 & -1 \\ -1 & -1 & 1 & 1 & -1 \\ 0 & -2 & -1 & -1 & 1 \end{pmatrix}$, and by basic algebra one realizes that $4v_1 + 3v_3 = v_1 + v_2 + v_3 + v_4 + v_5$. The minimal set of rules to get the dynamics in that step is $\{r_1, r_3\}$ (see Fig. 1). In fact, the cardinality of such a set cannot be further reduced, as no column of $\mathcal{M}$ is a multiple of $(1, -1, -3)$. This solution p for one step of computation needs to be extended with those for the other steps, as one wants to minimize the grammar generating the whole dynamics.

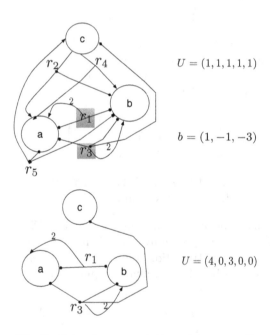

$$U = (1, 1, 1, 1, 1)$$

$$b = (1, -1, -3)$$

$$U = (4, 0, 3, 0, 0)$$

Fig. 1. Network representation of grammar $\mathcal{G}$.

The above question recalls a problem of flux balance analysis [5, 21], where the equation system $\mathcal{M} \times U = b$ is studied as the homogeneous system obtained by adding $-b$ as a further column of $\mathcal{M}$ and 1 as a further component of U. Network freedom degrees are here given by the dimension of the matrix rank and the solution is found in the flux cone computed by positive linear combinations of the matrix columns.

In our case, instead, the minimum number p has no relation with $rank_{\mathcal{M}}$. Consider the following counterexamples: $\mathcal{M} \times U = b$, with either $\mathcal{M} = \begin{pmatrix} 1 & 2 \\ 1 & 0 \end{pmatrix}$, $U = (0, 3)$ and $b = (6, 0)$, or $\mathcal{M} = \begin{pmatrix} 1 & 2 \\ -1 & -2 \end{pmatrix}$, $U = (1, 1)$ and $b = (3, -3)$.

If the vector U is constant, the dynamics of X is linear, that is, each variable increases or decreases monotonically. Let us thus assume that U is not constant at each step, but we have its value for each of r steps of given dynamics: $U_1, U_2, \ldots, U_r$, with corresponding values $\mathcal{M} \times U_i = b_i$. In this case, all solutions of minimal support for the r systems $\mathcal{M} \times U_i = b_i$ have to be compared, and the ones having a maximal common support, meaning that share more zeros on same components, have to be chosen. A more elegant formulation (see next section) requires to find a *further constrained* minimal support for the linear problem having as matrix a $(r \times n) \times (r \times m)$-dimensional block matrix, with blocks equal to $\mathcal{M}$ along the diagonal, and the remaining blocks equal to the null matrix, variable equals to $(U_1, U_2, \ldots, U_r)$ and product vector given by $(b_1, b_2, \ldots, b_r)$. The constraint on the solution U^* requires to maximize the number of components which are all zero when equivalent *modulo n*.

In order to compute any function as a dynamics, we need a vector U which depends on the state, as it is usually the case for multiset grammars in both traditional P systems (where the number of times to apply rules depends on the current multiset) and MP systems, where U is given by state functions computed by data-driven regression [17]. It has been shown [15,19] how efficiently complex functions may be computed by such a (universal) discrete model of computation.

Next section reports in mathematical terms the problem introduced so far.

3   A Minimization Problem

For every natural n, let $[n] := \{1, \ldots, n\}$ denote the set of the first n natural numbers. Let $A \in \mathbf{Z}^{[m] \times [n]}$ be an integral $m \cdot n$ matrix with $n > m$, and $b \in \mathbf{Z}^{[n]}$ be an integral vector of dimension n. The *support* of a vector $x \in \mathbf{N}^{[n]}$ is the set $S(x) := \{i \in [n] : x_i > 0\}$. Among the integral solutions to an integer linear programming problem in canonical form $\{Ax = b, x \geq 0, x \text{ integral}\}$ we are interested in those for which $|S(x)|$ is minimum.

We may consider $|S(x)|$ as the *cost* of solution x, and define the problem as:

INPUT: an integral $m \cdot n$-matrix $A \in \mathbf{Z}^{[m] \times [n]}$, an integral n-vector $b \in \mathbf{Z}^{[n]}$, and an m-vector $\bar{x} \in \mathbf{N}^{[m]}$ such that $A \times \bar{x} = b$.
OUTPUT: a minimum cost vector $x \in \mathbf{N}^{[n]}$ which is also a solution to $\{Ax = b, x \geq 0, x \text{ integral}\}$.

3.1   Formulation as a Quadratic Problem

A clear formalization of the problem is in terms of quadratically constrained optimization:

$$\begin{cases} min \sum_i^m y_i \\ \\ y_i \in \{0,1\} \quad z_i \in \mathbb{Z} \quad z_i \geq 0 \\ \sum_i^m z_i y_i v_i = b \end{cases}$$

where v_i are the columns of given matrix A.

Intuitively this is a version of the knapsack problem [1], where a minimum number of objects is taken, even in quantity, for the knapsack where the whole volume has to be filled in.

As informally introduced in the previous section, the problem above presented for one step of dynamics computation makes sense and is complete when proposed for the entire given dynamics, with r steps.

In conclusion, we are interested in the following problem:

$$\begin{cases} min \sum_{i=1}^m y_i \\ \\ \sum_i^m z_i y_i v_i = b \\ y_i \in \{0,1\} \quad z_i \in \mathbb{Z} \quad z_i \geq 0 \end{cases}$$

where v_i are the columns of the A-block-diagonal-matrix of dimesion $(r \times n) \times (r \times m)$, which may be computed by the Kronecker product $\mathcal{M} \otimes \mathcal{I}_{r \times r}$ of the stoichiometrix matrix by the identity matrix, and $b = (b_1, b_2, \ldots, b_r)$ of dimension $r \times n$, with single components computed by $b_i = A \times \overline{u_i}$ for given m-dimensional u_i, $i = 1, \ldots, r$.

Since we are seeking to eliminate rules from the grammar (i.e., to minimize it) by keeping the whole dynamics as an invariant, we need to add this further constraint on the solution x:

$$\begin{cases} max \sum_{k=1}^m y_k \\ \\ \sum_i^m z_i y_i v_i = b \\ y_k \in \{0,1\} \quad z_i = 0 \quad i \equiv k \cdot y_k \mod m \end{cases}$$

Notice that the dimension of this problem for real applications is quite high. As an example, the real metabolic network analyzed in [21] involves 1,445 metabolites and 2,589 reactions. If observed along 100 steps, it would provide us with a quadratic system, having matrix of dimensions $14,450 \times 25,890$.

The assumption to work on integer vectors (as states) did not simplify the complexity: indeed, the constraint of having a dynamics with natural vectors would just bound the values of integer variables z in the system above.

4   Computational Complexity

In this section, we prove that the problem presented above is NP-hard in the weak sense even when matrix A contains one single row. This negative result is sharp, as shown in Subsect. 4.3 where the existence of pseudo-polynomial algorithms and other positive results is discussed for the special case in which the number of rows of A is bounded by any fixed constant. The proof is organized into stages so that a richer and modular variety of negative results is actually obtained, or can easily be foreseen from the treatment in this section.

Short Reminder on Weak NP-hardness and Pseudo-Polynomial Algorithms (see [11]). We assume some knowledge about the standard notion of NP-hardness: (1) when a problem is NP-hard then, unless $P = NP$, no algorithm solves it in time polynomial in the length of a reasonable encoding of the input; (2) to prove that a target problem is NP-hard, we reduce to it, by means of a polynomial transformation, another problem A already known to be NP-hard.

A positional system for the representation of numbers (like our base 10 system, and, in general, as soon as the base b is at least 2) allows to compactly represent (and manipulate), in just n digits, all naturals from 0 to $b^n - 1$, that is, we represent numbers whose *magnitude* (i.e., their face value) is exponential in the encoding lenght n. This tremendous power might well be the reason behind the computational complexity of certain problems comprising numbers in their inputs. Indeed, whereas no algorithm with running time bounded by a polynomial in the encoding length of the instance is known for SUBSETSUM (see more below for the definition of this problem), and no such algorithm can actually exist unless $P = NP$, since SUBSETSUM was shown to be *NP-hard (in the weak/standard sense)*, still a practical algorithm of complexity $O(nB)$ is known. Such an algorithm is called *pseudo-polynomial* since its running time is bounded by a polynomial in two key parameters of the instance: its encoding length but also the magnitude of the biggest number occurring into it. The standard notion of (weak) NP-completeness does not rule out the possibility of pseudo-polynomial algorithms. A problem is called *strongly NP-hard* if it remains NP-hard even when restricted to those instances where all numbers in the input are bounded by some polynomial in the length of the input. No pseudo-polynomial algorithm can exist for a strongly NP-hard problem (unless $P = NP$).

SUBSETSUM is a problem appearing in the list of NP-complete problems compiled in [11]. It was proven to be NP-complete in the weak sense by Richard Karp in its celebrated 1972 paper [14]. Let $I = (w_1, \ldots, w_n; B) \in \mathbf{N}^{n+1}$ be an instance of SUBSETSUM. The problem asks to find out whether there exists an index set $J \subseteq [n]$ such that $B = \sum_{j \in J} w_j$. As such, SUBSETSUM is a decision problem. Given our purposes, we are naturally interested into the following optimization version of SUBSETSUM.

INPUT: an instance $I = (w_1, \ldots, w_n; B) \in \mathbf{N}^{n+1}$ of SUBSETSUM and a first solution to it, i.e., an index set $\overline{J} \subseteq [n]$ such that $B = \sum_{j \in \overline{J}} w_j$.
OUTPUT: a solution $J \subseteq [n]$ to the equation $B = \sum_{j \in J} w_j$, with $|J|$ as small as possible.

This optimization version of SUBSETSUM admits the following ILP formulation.

$$\begin{cases} \min \sum_{j \in [n]} x_j \\ \sum_{j \in [n]} w_j x_j = B, \\ x_j \in \{0, 1\} \text{ for every } j \in [n]. \end{cases}$$

In Subsect. 4.1, our optimization version of SUBSETSUM is shown to be NP-hard. This result, combined with the above ILP formultation, shows the NP-hardness of finding a minimum support 0/1-solution to a single equation all of whose parameters are natural numbers, even in the case at least one 0/1-solution is guaranteed to exist (and actually one such 0/1-solution has been possibly provided).

Our main interest is however in minimizing the support for solution vectors whose components are over the naturals (not restricted to be 0/1). To cover for this case, the proof will comprise a subsequent and more technical stage. Recall that SUBSETSUM is known to be NP-complete even in its version with multiplicities, a fact that is generally phrased by saying that even checking the feasibility of the unbounded knapsack problem (UKP) is NP-complete. Let $I = (w_1, \ldots, w_n; B) \in \mathbf{N}^{n+1}$ be an instance of UKP. The UKP problem asks to find out whether there exists a vector of multiplicities $x \in \mathbf{N}^n$ such that $B = \sum_{j \in [n]} w_j x_j$. Again, we will consider the following optimization version of UKP.

INPUT: an instance $I = (w_1, \ldots, w_n; B) \in \mathbf{N}^{n+1}$ of UKP and a first solution to it, i.e., a vector $\bar{x} \in \mathbf{N}^n$ such that $B = \sum_{j \in [n]} w_j \bar{x}_j$.
OUTPUT: a solution $x \in \mathbf{N}^n$ to the equation $B = \sum_{j \in [n]} w_j x_j$, with the support of x as small as possible.

In Subsect. 4.2, our optimization version of UKP is shown to be NP-hard, building on top of the result obtained in the previous stage. As above, this negative result directly implies the NP-hardness of finding a minimum support solution vector, now over the naturals, to a single equation all of whose parameters are natural numbers, even in the case at least one 0/1-solution is guaranteed to exist (and actually one such 0/1-solution has been possibly provided).

4.1   Weak NP-hardness: The SUBSETSUM Case (Zero-one Solutions)

In this subsection, SUBSETSUM in our non-standard optimization form is shown to be weakly NP-hard by reducing the generic instance $I = (w_1, \ldots, w_n; B)$ from the SUBSETSUM problem in its classical decision form.

Given I, we have to find an index set $J \subseteq [n]$ such that $\sum_{j \in J} w_j = B$. Notice first that, for every possible solution J to I (we possibly have no solutions), the fact that $|J| \leq n - 2$ can be enforced. Indeed, this can be easily achieved by simply adding two extra objects, both of weight $B + 1$ (and thus of no use) to the list of n objects.

Let $\Sigma := \sum_{j \in [n]} w_j$. Consider now the instance $I' = (w_1, \ldots, w_n, w_{n+1} := \Sigma - B; B' := \Sigma) \in \mathbf{N}^{n+1}$, plus $\overline{J'} = [n]$, of SUBSETSUM in our non-standard optimization form. Notice that the new instance I' has the following three properties.

1. the index set $\overline{J'} = [n]$ is a solution for I' with $|\overline{J'}| = n$.
2. If J is a solution for I, i.e., $B = \sum_{j \in J} w_j$, then $\Sigma = (\Sigma - B) + B = w_{n+1} + \sum_{j \in J} w_j$. Therefore, $J' := J \cup \{n + 1\}$ is a solution for I' with $|J'| = |J| + 1 \leq n - 1$.
3. If J' is a solution for I' with $|J'| \leq n-1$, then, since $\sum_{j \in J'} w_j = \Sigma$, it must be the case that $w_{n+1} \in J'$ and $\sum_{j \in J' \setminus \{n+1\}} w_j = \Sigma - (\Sigma - B) = B$. Therefore, $J := J' \setminus \{n + 1\}$ is a solution for the original instance I of SUBSETSUM in its classical decision form.

Therefore, the above reduction shows that given an instance I' of SUBSETSUM in its non-standard optimization form, it is NP-hard (in the weak sense) to compute a solution whose size of the support is minimum, even in case we have been given in input a proof of the fact that I' is feasible in the form of a first feasible solution $\overline{J'}$.

4.2 Weak NP-hardness: The UKP Case (Solutions over the Naturals)

We build on the result in the previous subsection as follows. We propose a reduction from SUBSETSUM to UKP, in which every item w_j of the SUBSETSUM instance gets represented by three items $w_{j,1}, w_{j,2}, w_{j,3}$ of the UKP instance in such a way that: for every solution λ of the UKP instance, and for every $j \in [n]$, either $\lambda_{j,1} = 1$ and $\lambda_{j,2} = \lambda_{j,3} = 0$ or $\lambda_{j,1} = 0$ and $\lambda_{j,2} = \lambda_{j,3} = 1$, with the first option simulating the picking up of item w_j in the original instance of SUBSETSUM and the second option simulating that item w_j is not used.

Now, to implement this ideal plan, assume all numbers $w_1, \ldots, w_n, B$ comprising the original instance are represented in binary, with say t bits, and, for $q = 1, \ldots, t$, let $w_1[q], \ldots, w_n[q], B[q]$ denote the q-th bits of these numbers (less significant bit for $q = 1$). Then, the set of numbers $\{w_{j,1}, w_{j,2}, w_{j,3} : j = 1, \ldots n\} \cup \{B'\}$ comprising the new instance are specified by their binary encodings in $4n + t$ bits which are defined as follows.

low/parity zone:

(1) $w_{j,1}[2q - 1] = w_{j,2}[2q - 1] = w_{j,3}[2q - 1] = w_{j,1}[2q] = w_{j,2}[2q] = w_{j,3}[2q] = 0$ for every $j \in [n]$ and every $q \in [n]$, $q \neq j$;
(2) $w_{j,1}[2j - 1] = w_{j,1}[2j] = B'[2j - 1] = B'[2j] = 1$ for every $j \in [n]$;
(3) $w_{j,2}[2j - 1] = w_{j,3}[2j] = 1$ for every $j \in [n]$;
(4) $w_{j,3}[2j - 1] = w_{j,2}[2j] = 0$ for every $j \in [n]$;

middle zone:

(5) $B'[q + 2n] = B[q]$ for every $q \in [t]$;
(6) $w_{j,1}[q + 2n] = w_j[q]$ for every $j \in [n]$ and every $q \in [t]$;
(7) $w_{j,3}[q + 2n] = w_{j,2}[q + 2n] = 0$ for every $j \in [n]$ and every $q \in [t]$;

high/heavy zone:

(8) $w_{j,1}[2q + 2n + t - 1] = w_{j,2}[2q + 2n + t - 1] = w_{j,3}[2q + 2n + t - 1] = w_{j,1}[2q + 2n + t] = w_{j,2}[2q + 2n + t] = w_{j,3}[2q + 2n + t] = 0$ for every $j \in [n]$ and every $q \in [n]$, $q \neq j$;
(9) $w_{j,1}[2j + 2n + t - 1] = B'[2j + 2n + t - 1] = 0$ for every $j \in [n]$;
(10) $w_{j,1}[2j + 2n + t] = B'[2j + 2n + t] = 1$ for every $j \in [n]$;
(11) $w_{j,2}[2j + 2n + t - 1] = w_{j,3}[2j + 2n + t - 1] = 1$ for every $j \in [n]$;
(12) $w_{j,3}[2j + 2n + t] = w_{j,2}[2j + 2n + t] = 0$ for every $j \in [n]$.

Just to get the key idea, explore what these values imply on the first item $j = 1$, where the situation is as follows:

1. the binary encoding of B' ends in 11 (i.e., $B' \equiv_4 3$).
2. the binary encoding of all items ends in 00 (i.e., all divisible by 4) except for the binary encoding of

$w_{j,1}$ which ends in 11.
$w_{j,2}$ which ends in 01.
$w_{j,3}$ which ends in 10.

3. $w_{j,1}$ is so big that we can take at most one copy of this item.
4. $w_{j,2}$ and $w_{j,3}$ are two roughly equal numbers such that $w_{j,1} + w_j = w_{j,2} + w_{j,3}$.

Notice that for none of them a feasible solution can pick up more then two copies. If a feasible solution takes $w_{j,1}$, then it picks up no copies of them. Otherwise, if it avoids $w_{j,1}$, then it must pick up at least one $w_{j,3}$ copy (to make for an odd sum) and picking up precisely two would set us with the wrong parity; therefore, in this case, it would necessarily pick precisely one copy of both $w_{j,2}$ and $w_{j,3}$. Since $w_{j,2} + w_{j,3} = w_{j,1} + w_j$, this faithfully simulates having picked up item w_j in the original instance. And leaves a clean situation after the choice of what to do with these three items, so that inductive thinking can be applied.

Notice that, after having performed the above check for $j = 1$, one can work out a sound proof of the "hard lemma" for the correctness of the reduction by working recursively on j, emplying the very same arguments above, which each time force a binary choice. As for the "easy lemma", that can be proven by observing that the definitions of the numbers comprising the target instance, as given in (1–12), comply with our ideal plan that the picking up of $w_{j,1}$ ($\lambda_{j,1} = 1, \lambda_{j,2} = \lambda_{j,3} = 0$) simulates taking w_j ($\lambda_j = 1$) whereas the simultaneous picking up of $w_{j,2}$ and $w_{j,3}$ ($\lambda_{j,1} = 0, \lambda_{j,2} = \lambda_{j,3} = 1$) simulates not taking w_j ($\lambda_j = 0$).

4.3 Pseudo-Polynomial Solutions When the Number of Equality Constraints is Bounded

In this section we give a pseudo-polynomial algorithm for the case of one single equality constraint. We remark that this positive result holds even for natural multiplicities and can be easily extended to the case where the number of equality constraints is bounded by any fixed constant. Moreover, it proves that the weak NP-hardness result for the case of one single row is essentially tight and makes clear that the relation between this special case of our problem and the SUBSETSUM (or the UKP) problem is a very close one, to the point that it can also be exploited on the positive, allowing to translate a great whealt of positive results (approximations, FPTASes, approaches to exact algorithms) from a well studied problem like SUBSETSUM (or UKP) to our problem in the case matrix A has one single row. Most of these positive results retain their validity under the weaker assumption that A has at most k rows, for some constant k (with k small, for the theoretical result to retain any practical validity).

We exemplify all this by adapting the classical dynamic programming pseudo-polynomial algorithm for SUBSETSUM (or UKP) to our problem (both in the case a 0/1-vector x is seeked for and in the case a vector $x \in \mathbf{N}^n$ is seeked for).

Assume the equation is $\sum_{i \in [n]} a_i x_i = B$.

The family of problems is the following:

for every $j \in [n]$, and for every natural $b \in [B]$, denote by $cost[j, b]$ (or by $cost_{0/1}[j, b]$) the minimum cost of a non-negative integral (or binary, resp.) solution to $\sum_{i \in [j]} a_i x_i = b$.

The recurrence is

$$cost[j, b] = \min\{cost[j-1, b], 1 + cost[j-1, b'] \text{ with } b' = b - ha_j \text{ for some } h \in [\lceil b/a_j \rceil]\}$$

In the 0/1-case the recurrence is

$$cost_{0/1}[j, b] = \min\{cost_{0/1}[j-1, b], 1 + cost_{0/1}[j-1, b-a_j]\}$$

where, in both case, the inizialization is $cost_{0/1}[0, b] := cost[0, b] := \infty$ for every $b \in [B]$.

In the 0/1-case the time complexity of this dynamic programming is $O(nB)$. In the case of general (non-negative) integer multipliers, note that the possible values of h that have to be considered in the recurrence are at most $b \leq B$, thus a dynamic programming computation of all the $cost[j, b]$ values based on the above recurrence will take $O(nB^2)$ time. Though more expensive, this anyhow delivers a pseudo-polynomial algorithm.

5   Conclusion

Given a multiset grammar and one of its computations in a certain number of steps, this is seen as a discrete dynamics over integer vectors. Here we pose the problem of finding a minimal number of rules (of the grammar) generating the same dynamics. This problem corresponds to find solutions with minimal support to an integer linear system, which turns out to be NP-hard.

A related apparently simplified problem could be that one to (initially) select a set of rules involving all the variables as own reactants, as this is a necessary condition to effect the whole dynamics, and starting from such a "covering set" to build up a minimal set of rules reproducing the given dynamics.

References

1. Bradley, S.P., Hax, A.C., Magnanti, T.L.: Applied Mathematical Programming. Addison-Wesley, Boston (1977)
2. Alhazov, A., Aman, B., Freund, R., Păun, G.: Matter and anti-matter in membrane systems. In: Jürgensen, H., Karhumäki, J., Okhotin, A. (eds.) DCFS 2014. LNCS, vol. 8614, pp. 65–76. Springer, Heidelberg (2014). doi:10.1007/978-3-319-09704-6_7
3. Alhazov, A., Belingheri, O., Freund, R., Ivanov, S., et al.: Semilinear sets, machines, and integer vector addition (P) systems. In: Leporati, A., Zandron, C. (eds.) Preproceedings of the 17th International Conference on Membrane Computing, CMC 17, Milano, pp. 39–55 (2016)
4. Annaluru, N., Muller, H., Mitchell, L.A., Ramalingam, S., et al.: Total synthesis of a functional designer eukaryotic chromosome. Science **344**(6186), 816 (2014)
5. Besozzi, D., Cazzaniga, P., Pescini, D., Mauri, G.: Modelling metapopulations with stochastic membrane systems. BioSystems **91**(3), 499–514 (2008)
6. Castellini, A., Franco, G., Pagliarini, R.: Data analysis pipeline from laboratory to MP models. Nat. Comput. **10**, 55–76 (2011)
7. Cazzaniga, P., Damiani, C., Besozzi, D., Colombo, R., et al.: Computational strategies for a system-level understanding of metabolism. Metabolites **4**(4), 1034–1087 (2014)
8. Franco, G., Jonoska, N., Osborn, B., Plaas, A.: Knee joint injury and repair modeled by membrane systems. BioSystems **91**, 473–488 (2008)
9. Franco, G., Manca, V., Pagliarini, R.: Regulation and covering problems in MP systems. In: Păun, G., Pérez-Jiménez, M.J., Riscos-Núñez, A., Rozenberg, G., Salomaa, A. (eds.) WMC 2009. LNCS, vol. 5957, pp. 242–251. Springer, Heidelberg (2010). doi:10.1007/978-3-642-11467-0_18
10. Frisco, P., Gheorghe, M., Péréz-Jiménez, M.J. (eds.): Applications of Membrane Computing in Systems and Synthetic Biology. Springer, Heidelberg (2014)
11. Garey, M.R., Johnson, D.S.: Computers and Intractability: A Guide to the Theory of NP-Completeness. W. H. Freeman & Co., NY (1979)
12. Gibson, D.G., Glass, J.I., Lartigue, C., Noskov, V.N., et al.: Creation of a bacterial cell controlled by a chemically synthesized genome. Science **329**(5987), 52–56 (2010)
13. Gibson, D.G., Venter, J.C.: Synthetic biology: construction of a yeast chromosome. Nature **509**, 168–169 (2014)
14. Karp, R.M.: Reducibility among combinatorial problems. In: Miller, R.E., et al. (eds.) Complexity of Computer Computations. Plenum Press, NY (1972)
15. Manca, V.: Infobiotics. Springer, Heidelberg (2013)
16. Manca, V., Castellini, A., Franco, G., Pagliarini, R.: Metabolic P systems: a discrete model for biological dynamics. Chin. J. Electron. **22**, 717–723 (2013)

17. Manca, V., Marchetti, L.: Recurrent solutions to dynamics inverse problems: a validation of MP regression. J. of Appl. Comput. Math. **3**, 1–8 (2014)
18. Mangasarian, O.L.: Minimum-support solutions of polyhedral concave programs. Optimization **45**(1–4), 149–162 (1999)
19. Mante, V., Sussillo, D., Shenoy, K.V., Newsome, W.T.: Context-dependent computation by recurrent dynamics in prefrontal cortex. Nature **503**(7474), 78–84 (2013)
20. Păun, G.: Membrane Computing - An Introduction. Springer, Heidelberg (2002)
21. Pagliarini, R., Sangiovanni, M., Peron, A., Di Bernardo, D.: Combining flux balance analysis and model checking for metabolic network validation and analysis. Nat. Comput. **14**(3), 341–354 (2015)
22. Szalkai, I., Dósa, G., Tuza, Z., Szalkai, B.: On minimal solutions of systems of linear equations with applications. Miskolc Math. Notes **13**(2), 529–541 (2012)

Solution to Motif Finding Problem in Membranes

Katrina B. Gapuz, Ephraim D. Mendoza, Richelle Ann B. Juayong,
Nestine Hope S. Hernandez$^{(\boxtimes)}$, Francis George C. Cabarle,
and Henry N. Adorna

Algorithms and Complexity Lab, Department of Computer Science,
University of the Philippines Diliman, Diliman, 1101 Quezon City, Philippines
{kbgapuz,rbjuayong,fccabarle,hnadorna}@up.edu.ph,
mendoza.eph@gmail.com, nshernandez@dcs.upd.edu.ph

Abstract. The study of genes is an important field of biology. A way to understand genetic composition is through finding regularly occurring nucleotide sequences, or motifs, in a DNA sequence. However, finding these motifs is difficult and is shown to be NP-complete. In this paper, we use a variant of P systems called Evolution-Communication P systems with Energy using string objects to solve the Motif Finding Problem in $O(lt)$-time where l is the length of the motif and t is the number of DNA sequences given.

Keywords: Membrane computing · Evolution-communication P systems with energy · Motif finding

1 Introduction

Genes are very important in the field of biology. They not only contain information about the traits of an organism, but also instructions on carrying out biological functions e.g. production of antibodies to counteract antigens. Identifying what gene affects a specific function can be very helpful to scientists. For example, in [6], various fruit fly immunity genes contain a specific string of nucleotides that occur regularly in the genome. These strings are called *NF-kB binding sites*, an example of *regulatory motifs*. It is said that these motifs are involved in the production of proteins that would destroy the pathogen that infected the fruit fly. Motifs of small non-coding RNAs called miRNAs, are also critical in understanding the pathogenesis of diseases (analysis relating to associations between miRNA and diseases can be found in [13,14]).

The problem of finding a pattern within a given set of strings (or DNA sequences) is better known as the Motif Finding Problem (in short, MFP) [6]. Finding regularly occurring nucleotide sequences, or motifs, can be challenging since the pattern describing these motifs is not known at the onset. Motifs may also vary across genomic regions due to mutations. As a consequence, solving MFP entails finding a set of substrings that are the most similar, given a set of

© Springer International Publishing AG 2017
A. Leporati et al. (Eds.): CMC 2016, LNCS 10105, pp. 190–208, 2017.
DOI: 10.1007/978-3-319-54072-6_13

sequences from a genome. With the exponential number of possible combination of substrings, a brute force algorithm (in [6]) solves MFP in $O(ln^t)$-time where l is the length of the motif, n is the number of nucleotides in a DNA sequence, and t is the number of DNA sequences given. In [13], a comprehensive discussion of techniques to identify disease-related miRNAs using biological interaction information is given.

In this paper, we use the maximally parallel nature of P systems [9] to address MFP. This paper is a continuation of the effort in [5] where we introduced a P system variant for solving a restricted version of MFP (referred as MFP'). To the best of our knowledge, solving MFP in the context of membrane computing have not yet been explored in literature earlier than our work. In our previous study, we used a modified variant of Evolution-Communication P systems with energy [1] that manipulates strings as objects. We call this system Evolution-Communication P systems with energy using string objects or ECPe-str. In this system, we introduced nature-inspired string operations in our P system solution. These string operations are inspired from the processes in the Central Dogma of Biology: transcription and translation [7]. Using this system, we have achieved a solution to MFP' in P systems that runs in $O(lt)$-time where l is the length of the motif and t is the number of DNA sequences. For this study, we use the same P system variant, ECPe-str. However, this time, we use it for the unrestricted Motif Finding Problem. We have achieved a solution to MFP in a P system that also runs in $O(lt)$-time where l is the length of the motif and t is the number of DNA sequences.

The outline of this paper is as follows: Sect. 2 provides a description of MFP. Section 3 includes a discussion on ECPe-str, the model used to solve MFP. The main contribution of this paper can be found in Sect. 4. Here, we utilize new and previous results to form an ECPe-str solution to MFP. We conclude our work in Sect. 5.

2   Motif Finding Problem

Readers are assumed to be familiar with common string operations and notations used in formal language theory [12]. Before we proceed with the discussion of our problem of interest, we will first define some terms.

Definition 1 (l-mer). *An l-mer of a string s is an l-length substring s' of s.*

We now introduce the following notations given n-length string(s) and l-mers where $n \geq l$:

- Given an n-length string s and a length l, let $LMERS(s, l)$ be the set of all l-mers of s. Note that the cardinality of $LMERS(s, l)$ is at most $n - l + 1$.
- Given a set S of n-length strings and a length l, let $LMERS_{set}(S, l) = \{LMERS(s, l) \mid s \in S\}$.

In Motif Finding Problem (MFP), a set Seq of DNA sequences and a length l are given. The main goal is to find a combination of l-mers (one for each string in Seq) such that the chosen l-mers are 'most similar'. The next definitions are used to formalize the concept of similarity:

Definition 2 (Alignment Matrix). *Given a set $L = \{s_1, s_2, ..., s_t\}$ of l-mers and each string $s_i = s_{i1}s_{i2} \ldots s_{il}$, the alignment matrix of L is a $t \times l$ matrix $M = [m_{ij}]_{t \times l}$ where $m_{ij} = s_{ij}, 1 \leq i \leq t, 1 \leq j \leq l$.*

Definition 3 (Profile Matrix). *Given a set $L = \{s_1, s_2, ..., s_t\}$ of l-mers and its corresponding alignment matrix $M = [m_{ij}]_{t \times l}$, the profile matrix of M is a $4 \times l$ matrix $[p_{ij}]_{4 \times l}$ such that $p_{1j} = A_j$, $p_{2j} = C_j$, $p_{3j} = T_j$, $p_{4j} = G_j$. The value X_j represents the count of X's in the jth column of M, the base $X \in \{A, C, T, G\}$.*

As can be observed, the alignment matrix is formed when the strings in a given set of DNA sequences are stacked such that each string occupies a row. The profile matrix given an alignment matrix is used to count the number of occurrence of each base per column. Figure 1 illustrates an example of an alignment matrix and a profile matrix for a set $L = \{ATTGACT, CAATGTC, AACTGCT, GAATCTC\}$. The top four rows in Fig. 1 corresponds to the alignment matrix while the profile matrix is in the bottom four rows. The value 2 in the first column and first row of the profile matrix is obtained by counting the number of A's in the first column of the alignment matrix. The values 1, 0 and 1 in the succeeding rows of the profile matrix corresponds to the count of C, T and G, respectively, in the first column of the alignment matrix. The other columns of the profile matrix are filled up in a similar manner.

$$
\begin{array}{llllllll}
A & T & T & G & A & C & T \\
C & A & A & T & G & T & C \\
A & A & C & T & G & C & T \\
G & A & A & T & C & T & C \\
\underline{A}\ 2 & 3 & 2 & 0 & 1 & 0 & 0 \\
\underline{C}\ 1 & 0 & 1 & 0 & 1 & 2 & 2 \\
\underline{T}\ 0 & 1 & 1 & 3 & 0 & 2 & 2 \\
\underline{G}\ 1 & 0 & 0 & 1 & 2 & 0 & 0
\end{array}
$$

Fig. 1. An example alignment matrix (top four rows) and profile matrix (bottom four rows). The underlined letters (not part of the profile matrix) indicate the letters to consider per row in the profile matrix.

Definition 4 (Consensus Score). *Given a set L of l-mers, the $t \times l$ alignment matrix M for L, and the $4 \times l$ profile matrix P for M,*

$$
Score(L) = \sum_{j=1}^{l} max\{p_{ij} \mid 1 \leq i \leq 4\}. \tag{1}
$$

The consensus score can be used to define the degree of similarity among a set of l-mers. As can be observed, higher score implies greater similarity. The score ranges from $lt/4$ to lt. The highest possible score implies that the pattern is highly conserved, i.e. only one base per column in the profile matrix has a nonzero value. The minimum score implies that on each column of the profile matrix, all bases have the same number of occurrences. We go back to the profile matrix in Fig. 1 to compute for the score of a set $L = \{ATTGACT, CAATGTC, AACTGCT, GAATCTC\}$. By summing the maximum value per column of the profile matrix, we have $Score(L) = 2 + 3 + 2 + 3 + 2 + 2 + 2 = 16$.

We now give a formal definition of the Motif Finding Problem (MFP). At this point, it is apparent that MFP is an optimization problem where the aim is to find a set L of l-mers that maximizes $Score(L)$. We recall from [2] that a combinatorial optimization problem can be defined as a 4-tuple (I, f, m, g) where I is a set of instances, f is a function with input $x \in I$ and $f(x)$ is the set of all feasible solutions for instance x. The function m takes as input an instance x and a feasible solution $y \in f(x)$. The value $m(x, y)$ is a real number that indicates the score of solution y for instance x. Finally, g is a function that takes x as input and outputs either the minimum or maximum of function m. As a shorthand, the 4th element of the tuple can be one of min or max. The notation max implies $g(x) = max\{m(x, y') \mid y' \in f(x)\}$.

Definition 5 (Motif Finding Problem). *The Motif Finding Problem (MFP) is a combinatorial optimization problem represented by the quadruple (I, f, m, g), where:*

- $I = \{(Seq, l) \mid Seq$ *is a set of n-length strings,* $l < n\}$,
- $f(x) = S_1 \times S_2 \times \ldots \times S_t$ *where each* $S_i \in LMERS_{set}(x)$ *and* $x = (Seq, l) \in I$,
- $m(x, y) = Score(y)$, *given* $x = (Seq, l) \in I$, $y \in f(x)$,
- $g = max$.

Notice that given an instance x, the set $f(x)$ can have a cardinality at most $(n - l + 1)^t$, where t is the number of strings in an instance of the problem.

3 A P System for MFP

The P system we used to solve MFP is an extension of a model defined in [1] called the Evolution-Communication P system with energy (ECPe system). An ECPe system computes by evolving objects through evolution rules and communicating objects through symport and antiport rules (similar to Evolution-Communication P system (ECP system) introduced in [3]). The main difference that distinguishes ECPe from ECP system is the requirement imposed during communication. This is where the special object e, called *energy*, plays an important role. During evolution, it is possible to produce some copies of e through rules of the form $a \rightarrow ve^i$ (a is an object, v is a multiset, $i \geq 0$). In such rule, i copies of e are produced. The object e's are eventually consumed as a requirement during communication. Symport rules of the form (ae^i, in) or (ae^i, out)

requires that i copies of e be consumed in order to transfer a. Similarly, antiport rule of the form $(ae^i, in; be^j, out)$ require that j copies from a region h and i copies outside region h be used to swap objects a and b across membrane h.

We extended ECPe systems to handle string objects so that there is a direct encoding of the input strings in the system used. Handling string objects have also been explored in several P system papers (e.g. in [8]). In such case, regions contain several strings instead of having several atomic objects. While there are no order on the strings present in a region, there is an arrangement on the symbols comprising a single string. We shall thus refer to a group of strings in a region as a *multiset of strings*. A string is treated as a single entity as it passes through membranes. Also, each string is processed by one rule only. Maximal parallelism is manifested when all strings with an appliable rule are processed simultaneously. If several rules are applicable to a string, then we take only one rule and only one possibility to apply it.

We handle string objects using the idea of some rules found in [8]. One type of rule is called the *rewriting rule*. Given strings u and v, where $|u| > 0$, a rewriting rule is of the form $u \rightarrow v$. When this rule is applied to a string $s = xuy$, s becomes xvy in the next step. When there are several occurrences of u in a string s, all occurrences of u are replaced with v.

Another type of rule is called the *replication rule*. Given strings $u, v_1, v_2, ..., v_n$, where $|u| > 0$ and $n \geq 2$, a replication rule is of the form $u \rightarrow v_1 || v_2 || ... || v_n$. When this rule is applied to a string $s = xuy$, s is consumed producing n strings $xv_1y, xv_2y, ..., xv_ny$. As in a rewriting rule, when several occurrences of u exists in a string s, all occurrences of u are replaced. Note that in such case, n strings are still produced; in one resulting string, all u is replaced with v_1, in another string, all u is replaced with v_2, etc.

Apart from general features, the system we used to handle MFP employs additional features. First, we shall introduce a type of rule called a *projection rule* inspired by DNA-based biological processes in cells. We also include some modification to the evolution rules so that several strings can be consumed to produce a string. Finally, we employ the use of priority on rules.

Introducing Projection Rules. We model the phenomena transcription and translation in Central Dogma of Biology through the use of what we call *projection rules*. These rules are of the form $Project(\kappa, \kappa', \kappa'')$, where κ is a start symbol, κ' is a stop symbol, and κ'' is a new symbol. When a rule of this form is applied to a string $x = x_1 \kappa u \kappa' x_2$, x becomes $x_1 \kappa' u \kappa' x_2$ and produces a string $\kappa'' u \kappa''$. When there is more than one occurrence of the start and stop symbols in the strings present in the region, we only consider the leftmost occurrence of the start and stop symbol.

Upon application of projection rule x, a copy of the substring u is produced. This is abstracted from the way a portion of the DNA sequence is copied during transcription. The symbols κ and κ' works in a similar manner as how start and stop codons work during translation. At the end of the application of projection rule, the produced copy is identified using the new symbol κ'' which replaces the start and stop symbols in the original string x.

Modification on Evolution Rules. In the P system that we will use for solving MFP, we include an evolution rule of the form $u_1, u_2, \ldots, u_n \rightarrow v$, where $u_1, u_2, \ldots, u_n$ and v are strings, $|u_i| > 0$ and $n \geq 2$. We call this *multi-string cooperative rule*. When a rule of this form is applied on a region h, the strings $u_1, u_2, \ldots, u_n$ found in region h are all consumed to produce a string v.

Priority on Rules. Given a priority relation, a rule with a higher priority is executed first. A rule with a lower priority can be executed if and only if a rule with higher priority is not applicable to the objects present in the region. This gives a way to control the flow of computation by lessening the degree of nondeterminism in P system. In [10], the notation $\rho = r_i > r_j, \ldots, r_k > r_l$ is introduced, where r_i, r_j, r_k and r_l are rules and the symbol $>$ denotes the priority relation over the rules. The rule on the left of $>$ symbol has higher priority than the rule on the right.

We now provide the P system we used for MFP. This was initially introduced in [5]. The system mainly manipulates strings, however, one special symbol e functions as an atomic object. Some copies of this special object e can be produced during evolution and consumed during communication, however, it cannot be a part of any other string.

Definition 6. *Evolution-Communication P Systems with Energy Using String Objects (ECPe-str) is a construct of the form*

$$\Pi = (\bar{O}, e, \mu, w_1, \ldots, w_m, R_1, R_1', \rho_1, \ldots, R_m, R_m', \rho_m, i_o),$$

- m is the number of membranes;
- $\bar{O}$ is the tuple (O, S, Z, N);
  - O is the alphabet of string objects;
  - S is the set of start symbols, $S \subset O$;
  - Z is the set of stop symbols, $Z \subset O$;
  - N is the set of new symbols, $N \subset O$;
  The sets S, Z and N are disjoint;
- e is a special object for energy and $e \notin O$. The value e cannot be a part of any string and is treated as a separate object in the region;
- μ is the membrane structure of the system;
- $w_1, \ldots, w_m$ are multiset of strings over O^* where w_i denotes the multiset of strings present in the region i;
- $R_1, \ldots, R_m$ are sets of evolution rules, with each R_k associated with a region k. An evolution rule can be:
  - A rewriting rule of the form $u \rightarrow v, e^i$, where $u \in O^+$, $v \in O^*$ and $i \geq 0$. This rule is applicable to a string s containing u. When this rule is applied to a string s, every occurrence of u in string s is replaced by v and i copies of e are produced in the region.

- A replication rule of the form $u \rightarrow v_1||v_2|| \ldots ||v_n, e^i$, where $u, v_j \in O^+$ for $1 \leq j \leq n$, $n \geq 2$ and $i \geq 0$. This rule is applicable to a string s containing u. When this rule is applied to string s, the string s is consumed and n strings $y_1, y_2, \ldots, y_n$ and i copies of e are produced in the region. Each string y_j is obtained by replacing all occurrences of u in s by the string v_j. It is also possible that $v_1 = \ldots = v_n$. In such case, suppose all $v_i = v$ $(1 \leq i \leq n)$, we use the form $u \rightarrow v||^{(n)}v$ as a shorthand notation.
- A multi-string cooperative rule of the form $u_1, u_2, \ldots, u_n \rightarrow v, e^i$, where $u_1, u_2, \ldots, u_n \in O^+$, $v \in O^*$, $n \geq 2$, and $i \geq 0$. Upon application of this rule, the strings $u_1, u_2, \ldots, u_n$ found in region k are all consumed to produce a string v and i copies of e in the region.
- A projection rule of the form $Project(\kappa, \kappa', \kappa''), e^i$, where $\kappa \in S$, $\kappa' \in Z$, $\kappa'' \in N$, and $i \geq 0$. When this rule is applied to a string $x = x_1\kappa u\kappa'x_2$, (where $u, x_1, x_2 \in O^*$), in the next step, x is replaced with $x_1\kappa u\kappa'x_2$. In addition, a string $\kappa''u\kappa''$ and i copies of e appear in the region. When two or more occurrences of κ and κ' a in x, only the leftmost κ and κ' are considered.

For the above rules, when $i = 0$ (meaning no e is produced), we omit the notation e^i for simplicity.

- $R_1', \ldots, R_m'$ are sets of communication rules; each R_k' is associated with a membrane k in μ. A communication rule can be:
  - A symport rule of the form (a, e^i, in) or (a, e^i, out), where $a \in O^+$ and $i \geq 1$. During the application of this rule, i copies of e are consumed to transport string with substring a inside (denoted by in) or outside (denoted by out) membrane k.
  - An antiport rule is of the form $(a, e^i, in; b, e^j, out)$ where $a, b \in O^+$ and $i, j \geq 1$. Applying this rule, there should be a string with substring a in the region immediately outside membrane k. Also, a string with substring b should exist inside the region bounded by membrane k. The string with substring a and the string with substring b are then swapped, consuming i and j copies of object e in their respective regions.
- $\rho_1, \ldots, \rho_m$ are partial order relations over evolution rules, each ρ_i $(1 \leq i \leq m)$ is associated with the evolution rules of region i.
- $i_o \in \{0, 1, \ldots, m\}$ is the output membrane. If $i_o = 0$, this means that the output of the computation of this system will go to the environment.

The rules in ECPe-str are applied in a nondeterministic and maximally parallel manner. If there are two or more rules applicable to a string, the system will nondeterministically choose only one rule to be applied to the said string. Also, all strings with an applicable rule are processed simultaneously. Strong priority (as defined in [10]) is employed in ECPe-str system, i.e. when a rule r_1 has priority over rule r_2 and rule r_1 is applicable, r_2 cannot be applied regardless if there are objects that were not affected by r_1.

An Example. We adapt an example from [5] to demonstrate how the system works. The system checks if two strings s and s' with distinct symbols are anagrams of each other. Each input string is encoded in the system such that a symbol α and a symbol β are placed before and after every element of the string, respectively. In effect, an input string $s = s_1 s_2 \ldots s_n$ has the encoding $enc(s) = \alpha s_1 \beta \alpha s_2 \beta \ldots \alpha s_n \beta$ where n is the length of string s. The system used to determine if s and s' are anagrams has the form:

$$\Pi = (\bar{O}, e, \mu, w_1, R_1, R_1', \rho_1, i_o),$$

where: $\bar{O} = (O, S, Z, N)$; $O = \{A, B, C, \ldots, Z, \theta, \$\}$; $S = \{\alpha\}$; $Z = \{\beta\}$; $N = \{\gamma\}$; $\mu = [_1]_1$; $w_1 = \{enc(s), enc(s')\}$; $R_1 = \{r_1 : Project(\alpha, \beta, \gamma), r_2 : \gamma \to \lambda, r_3 : A, A \to \theta, e, r_4 : B, B \to \theta, e, \ldots, r_{28} : Z, Z \to \theta, e, r_{29} : A \to \$, r_{30} : B \to \$, \ldots, r_{54} : Z \to \$, r_{55} : \$ \to \$\}$; $R_1' = \{r_1' : (\theta, e, out)\}$; $\rho_1 = \{r_1, r_3, r_4, \ldots, r_{28} > r_{29}, r_{30}, \ldots, r_{54}\}$; $i_o = 0$;

We say the strings are anagrams of each other if the system halts. If the system does not halt, regardless of the objects in the environment, then the two strings are not anagrams of each other. The system computes as follows:

Given input strings s and s', the initial configuration of the system has the encoding $enc(s)$ and $enc(s')$ in region 1. In the next time step, the system applies projection rule r_1 on $enc(s)$ and $enc(s')$. This produces two 3-length strings; one containing the first symbol of s and the other containing the first symbol of s'. The produced strings start and end with the symbol γ. After applying rule r_1 in $enc(s)$ and $enc(s')$, the first occurrence of the start symbol α in each string evolves to the stop symbol β. As a result, the symbol next to the occurrence of the first α in these strings will become the target of application of projection rule r_1 in the next time step. In the second time step, aside from the application of rule r_1, rule r_2 will also be used to erase the γ symbols in the strings produced from the previous step. Application of rule r_1 and use of rule r_2 in the next step continues until all α in the encodings have been replaced by β.

After every application of rule r_2, it is possible that in the next time step, one or two letter will occur twice in region 1. This indicates that the letter occurs in both input strings. When this happens, the next time step will also include the use of at most two rules from r_3 to r_{28}. As a result, each application will consume the involved letter in order to produce a string θ as well as a copy of the special object e. This e is used to communicate the string θ to the environment via the symport rule r_1'.

When all letters in the input strings were processed this way, then the system will halt. This shows that all letter of input s is also present in input s' and vice versa. Since the strings are assumed to have distinct symbols, s and s' are anagrams. On the other hand, if the input strings are not an anagram of each other, the system will reach a configuration where no rules from r_1 to r_{28} are applicable yet there are still some distinct letters floating in region 1. This letters will eventually evolve to a trap symbol $\$$ through any rule from r_{29} to r_{54}. This trap symbol will evolve continuously through the rule r_{55}. This prevents the system from halting.

Shown below is the step-by-step computation for two input strings $s = ARMY$ and $s' = MARY$. String s has the encoding $enc(s) = \alpha A \beta \alpha R \beta \alpha M \beta \alpha Y \beta$ and string s' will have the encoding $enc(s') = \alpha M \beta \alpha A \beta \alpha R \beta \alpha Y \beta$. For each config-uration below, we use paired square brackets to represent a membrane, and the strings contained in a membrane are separated by commas.

$t = 0$: $[_1 \; \alpha A \beta \alpha R \beta \alpha M \beta \alpha Y \beta, \; \alpha M \beta \alpha A \beta \alpha R \beta \alpha Y \beta \;]_1$

$t = 1$: $[_1 \; \beta A \beta \alpha R \beta \alpha M \beta \alpha Y \beta, \; \beta M \beta \alpha A \beta \alpha R \beta \alpha Y \beta, \; \gamma A \gamma, \; \gamma M \gamma \;]_1$

$t = 2$: $[_1 \; \beta A \beta \beta R \beta \alpha M \beta \alpha Y \beta, \; \beta M \beta \beta A \beta \alpha R \beta \alpha Y \beta, \; A, \; M, \; \gamma R \gamma, \; \gamma A \gamma \;]_1$

$t = 3$: $[_1 \; \beta A \beta \beta R \beta \beta M \beta \alpha Y \beta, \; \beta M \beta \beta A \beta \beta R \beta \alpha Y \beta, \; A, \; M, \; R, \; A, \; \gamma M \gamma, \; \gamma R \gamma \;]_1$

$t = 4$: $[_1 \; \beta A \beta \beta R \beta \beta M \beta \beta Y \beta, \; \beta M \beta \beta A \beta \beta R \beta \beta Y \beta, \; M, \; R, \; M, \; R, \; \gamma Y \gamma,$
$\qquad \gamma Y \gamma, \; \theta, \; e \;]_1$

$t = 5$: $[_1 \; \beta A \beta \beta R \beta \beta M \beta \beta Y \beta, \; \beta M \beta \beta A \beta \beta R \beta \beta Y \beta, \; Y, \; Y, \; \theta, \; \theta, \; e, e \;]_1 \; \theta$

$t = 6$: $[_1 \; \beta A \beta \beta R \beta \beta M \beta \beta Y \beta, \; \beta M \beta \beta A \beta \beta R \beta \beta Y \beta, \; \theta, \; e \;]_1 \; \theta, \; \theta, \; \theta$

$t = 7$: $[_1 \; \beta A \beta \beta R \beta \beta M \beta \beta Y \beta, \; \beta M \beta \beta A \beta \beta R \beta \beta Y \beta \;]_1 \; \theta, \; \theta, \; \theta, \; \theta$

4   A Solution to Motif Finding Problem Using ECPe-str

In this section, we present a modification of a solution presented in our previous work [5]. We take note of the parameters in building the system for our solution: n is the length of the DNA sequences, t is the number of DNA sequences, and l is the length of the motif. Furthermore, to simplify the solution in the next subsections, we denote some expressions as: $p = n - l + 1$, and $q = p^t = (n - l + 1)^t$.

Throughout the whole section, we shall use the definition and notations for MFP in Definition 5. That is, we represent MFP as (I, f, m, g), such that for each instance $x \in I$, $x = (Seq, l)$ where $Seq = \{D_1, D_2, \ldots, D_t\}$ and $D_i = d_{i1} d_{i2} \ldots d_{in}$ for $1 \leq i \leq t$. Also, we let $y \in f(x)$ as a possible solution, where from Definition 5, $f(x) = S_1 \times \ldots S_t$, each $S_i \in LMERS_{set}(x)$.

For this solution, we refer to each nucleotide in each DNA sequence (D_i) as d_{ij}. For example, given $Seq = \{ACCTG, GGACT, TGATG\}$, d_{11} represents A, since it is the nucleotide that is in the first position in the first DNA sequence. The symbol d_{25} represents T, since it is in the fifth position of the second sequence. We use this notation in constructing our P system.

4.1   Previous Work: On Alignment Matrices and Computing Score

We first recall the approach presented in [5]. In previous work, only a restricted version of the problem (referred in the paper as MFP') was addressed. The task of solving MFP' was divided into three main parts: generation of alignment matrices, computation of score, and the search for a maximum score. The last part can be represented as finding the largest number in a given set of numbers. It was assumed that the largest number is unique (no two numbers have the largest value). Each part of solving MFP' was formulated as a problem, and an ECPe-str solution was provided for each of this problem. These solutions were then incorporated as subsystems of an ECPe-str system that solves MFP'.

For our solution to MFP, we shall employ two of the subsystems given in [5] (with some slight modification). Specifically, we use the subsystems for generating alignment matrices and computation of score. The main difference between the solution in [5] and in this paper is the subsystem for determining the largest score. In our previous work, it was assumed that the largest number among a set of scores must be unique. The subsystem developed can only find the largest score, if the largest is unique. In this work, such restriction is already removed. As a consequence, we have improved our previous work such that our solution is applicable to any instance of MFP. The first part of the Motif Finding Problem is the generation of alignment matrices.

Definition 7 *Generation of Alignment Matrices Problem (GAM). Given an instance* $x = (Seq, l)$ *where* $Seq = \{D_1, D_2, \ldots, D_t\}$, $|D_i| = n$, *and a length* $l < n$, *generate a set* $ALG = \{M \mid M$ *is an alignment matrix for* $y \in f(x)\}$.

Note that $|ALG|$ is at most q. For every D_i, there are at most p l-mers. Given t DNA sequences, we generate q possible combinations of l-mers.

Lemma 1 [5]. *The GAM problem can be solved using ECPe-str in* $O(t)$-*time where* t *is the number of DNA sequences.*

To illustrate the constructed ECPe-str for Lemma 1, we provide an example construction for a given set of DNA sequences. We shall name the subsystem, Π_1. Given a set of DNA sequences $Seq = \{ACTG, ATTG, CTGG\}$ with $l = 3, n = 4$ and $t = 3$, we obtain the following system:

$$\Pi_1 = (\bar{O}, e, \mu, w_1, R_1, R'_1, \rho_1, 1),$$

where $\bar{O} = (O, S, Z, N)$; $O = \{A, C, T, G, \beta_1, \ldots, \beta_4, 1, 2\}$; $S = \{\alpha_{11}, \ldots, \alpha_{33}\}$; $Z = \{\alpha'_{11}, \ldots, \alpha'_{33}\}$; $N = \emptyset$; $\mu = [_1]_1$; $R'_1 = \rho_1 = \emptyset$; $w_1 = \beta_1$. The rules of R_1 are as given below:

$$
\begin{aligned}
R_1 = \{ r_1 : \beta_1 &\rightarrow \alpha_{11}A\alpha'_{11}\alpha_{12}C\alpha'_{12}\alpha_{13}T\alpha'_{13}\beta_2 1 \parallel \alpha_{11}C\alpha'_{11}\alpha_{12}T\alpha'_{12}\alpha_{13}G\alpha'_{13}\beta_2 2, \\
\beta_2 &\rightarrow \alpha_{21}A\alpha'_{21}\alpha_{22}T\alpha'_{22}\alpha_{23}T\alpha'_{23}\beta_3 1 \parallel \alpha_{21}T\alpha'_{21}\alpha_{22}T\alpha'_{22}\alpha_{23}G\alpha'_{23}\beta_3 2, \\
\beta_3 &\rightarrow \alpha_{31}C\alpha'_{31}\alpha_{32}T\alpha'_{32}\alpha_{33}G\alpha'_{33}\beta_4 1 \parallel \alpha_{31}T\alpha'_{31}\alpha_{32}G\alpha'_{32}\alpha_{33}G\alpha'_{33}\beta_4 2 \}
\end{aligned}
$$

[1]We now proceed with a description of the computation:

At $t = 0$, region 1 only contains β_1. Applying a rule r_1 to β_1 produces two strings $\alpha_{11}A\alpha'_{11}\alpha_{12}C\alpha'_{12}\alpha_{13}T\alpha'_{13}\beta_2 1$ and $\alpha_{11}C\alpha'_{11}\alpha_{12}T\alpha'_{12}\alpha_{13}G\alpha'_{13}\beta_2 2$. These strings represent l-mers ACT and CTG respectively. These l-mers correspond to the possible first rows of all alignment matrices from Seq. At $t = 2$, β_2 evolves the same way as β_1 using a rule r_1. These strings represent all possible first and second rows of all alignment matrices from Seq. This process continues until the strings contain β_4. At the last time step, the strings given below are present in region 1. These strings represent all alignment matrices, as follows:

---

[1] In [5], the formal definition of Π_1 has an initial membrane structure containing two membranes, i.e. $\mu = [_1[_2]_2]_1$. However, it is apparent that even when removing membrane 2 and relocating the initial content of membrane 2, i.e. β_1, and the rules of region 2 in the skin region, the algorithm still works almost the same. The only difference is the resources used.

$$\alpha_{11}Aa'_{11}\alpha_{12}Ca'_{12}\alpha_{13}Ta'_{13}\alpha_{21}Aa'_{21}\alpha_{22}Ta'_{22}\alpha_{23}Ta'_{23}\alpha_{31}Ca'_{31}\alpha_{32}Ta'_{32}\alpha_{33}Ga'_{33}\beta_4 111$$
$$\alpha_{11}Aa'_{11}\alpha_{12}Ca'_{12}\alpha_{13}Ta'_{13}\alpha_{21}Aa'_{21}\alpha_{22}Ta'_{22}\alpha_{23}Ta'_{23}\alpha_{31}Ta'_{31}\alpha_{32}Ga'_{32}\alpha_{33}Ga'_{33}\beta_4 211$$
$$\alpha_{11}Aa'_{11}\alpha_{12}Ca'_{12}\alpha_{13}Ta'_{13}\alpha_{21}Ta'_{21}\alpha_{22}Ta'_{22}\alpha_{23}Ga'_{23}\alpha_{31}Ca'_{31}\alpha_{32}Ta'_{32}\alpha_{33}Ga'_{33}\beta_4 121$$
$$\alpha_{11}Aa'_{11}\alpha_{12}Ca'_{12}\alpha_{13}Ta'_{13}\alpha_{21}Ta'_{21}\alpha_{22}Ta'_{22}\alpha_{23}Ga'_{23}\alpha_{31}Ta'_{31}\alpha_{32}Ga'_{32}\alpha_{33}Ga'_{33}\beta_4 221$$
$$\alpha_{11}Ca'_{11}\alpha_{12}Ta'_{12}\alpha_{13}Ga'_{13}\alpha_{21}Aa'_{21}\alpha_{22}Ta'_{22}\alpha_{23}Ta'_{23}\alpha_{31}Ca'_{31}\alpha_{32}Ta'_{32}\alpha_{33}Ga'_{33}\beta_4 112$$
$$\alpha_{11}Ca'_{11}\alpha_{12}Ta'_{12}\alpha_{13}Ga'_{13}\alpha_{21}Aa'_{21}\alpha_{22}Ta'_{22}\alpha_{23}Ta'_{23}\alpha_{31}Ta'_{31}\alpha_{32}Ga'_{32}\alpha_{33}Ga'_{33}\beta_4 212$$
$$\alpha_{11}Ca'_{11}\alpha_{12}Ta'_{12}\alpha_{13}Ga'_{13}\alpha_{21}Ta'_{21}\alpha_{22}Ta'_{22}\alpha_{23}Ga'_{23}\alpha_{31}Ca'_{31}\alpha_{32}Ta'_{32}\alpha_{33}Ga'_{33}\beta_4 122$$
$$\alpha_{11}Ca'_{11}\alpha_{12}Ta'_{12}\alpha_{13}Ga'_{13}\alpha_{21}Ta'_{21}\alpha_{22}Ta'_{22}\alpha_{23}Ga'_{23}\alpha_{31}Ta'_{31}\alpha_{32}Ga'_{32}\alpha_{33}Ga'_{33}\beta_4 222$$

At this point, there are no more rules left to apply. This, in effect, halts the computation of the system. In the halting configuration, each string represents one possible alignment matrix. Specifically, a string having a suffix of ijk represents the alignment matrix involving the following l-mers: (a) l-mer of the *first* input string starting at the kth position, (b) l-mer of the *second* input string starting at the jth position, (c) l-mer of the *third* string input starting at the ith position. We now proceed with the problem of computing score given an alignment matrix.

Definition 8 *Computation of Score Problem (CoS). Given an instance $x = (Seq, l)$, $y \in f(x)$, an alignment matrix $M = [m_{uv}]_{t \times l}$ for y, and a profile matrix $P = [p_{ij}]_{4 \times l}$ for y, compute for the consensus score of y i.e. $Score(y)$.*

Lemma 2 [5]. *The CoS problem can be solved using ECPe-str in a constant amount of time.*

To illustrate the constructed ECPe-str for Lemma 2, we provide an example construction. We shall name the subsystem, Π_2. For our illustration, we consider the same set $Seq = \{ACTG, ATTG, CTGG\}$ (in example for Lemma 1), with $l = 3, n = 4$ and $t = 3$. We choose an alignment matrix M with starting positions 111. The alignment matrix M is

$$ACT$$
$$ATT$$
$$CTG.$$

We construct the following system:

$$\Pi_2 = (\bar{O}, e, \mu, w_s, w_1, w_2, w_3, R_s, R'_s, \rho_s, R_1, R'_1, \rho_1, R_2, R'_2, \rho_2, R_3, R'_3, \rho_3, s),$$

where $\bar{O} = (O, S, Z, N)$; $O = \{A, C, T, G, a_s\}$; $S = \emptyset$; $Z = \emptyset$; $N = \emptyset$; $\mu = [_s[_1]_1[_2]_2[_3]_3]_s$; $w_1 = \{A, A, C\}$; $w_2 = \{C, T, T\}$; $w_3 = \{T, T, G\}$; $w_s = R_s = R'_s = \rho_s = \emptyset$. The following rules are for each R_i ($1 \le i \le 3$):

$$R_i = \{\; r_1 : A, C, T, G \to a_s, e,\; r_2 : A, C, T \to a_s, e,$$
$$r_3 : A, C, G \to a_s, e,\; r_4 : C, T, G \to a_s, e,$$
$$r_5 : A, T, G \to a_s, e, r_6 : A, C \to a_s, e,$$
$$r_7 : A, T \to a_s, e, r_8 : A, G \to a_s, e, r_9 : C, T \to a_s, e,$$
$$r_{10} : C, G \to a_s, e, r_{11} : T, G \to a_s, e, r_{12} : A \to a_s, e,$$
$$r_{13} : C \to a_s, e, r_{14} : T \to a_s, e, r_{15} : G \to a_s, e\};$$

Also, for $1 \leq i \leq 3, R'_i = \{r'_1 : (a_s, e, out)\}$ and $\rho_i = \{r_1 > r_2, \ldots, r_5 > r_6, \ldots, r_{11} > r_{12}, \ldots, r_{15}\}$; The step-by-step computation for the example is given below:

$$t = 0: [_s \ [_1 \ A, \ A, \ C \ ]_1 \ [_2 \ C, \ T, \ T \ ]_2 \ [_3 \ T, \ T, \ G \ ]_3 \ ]_s$$
$$t = 1: [_s \ [_1 \ A, \ a_s, \ e \ ]_1 \ [_2 \ a_s, \ e, \ T \ ]_2 \ [_3 \ T, \ a_s, \ e \ ]_3 \ ]_s$$
$$t = 2: [_s \ [_1 \ a_s, \ e \ ]_1 \ [_2 \ a_s, \ e \ ]_2 \ [_3 \ a_s, \ e \ ]_3 \ a_s, \ a_s, \ a_s \ ]_s$$
$$t = 3: [_s \ [_1 \ ]_1 \ [_2 \ ]_2 \ [_3 \ ]_3 \ a_s, \ a_s, \ a_s, \ a_s, \ a_s, \ a_s \ ]_s$$

Computation proceeds as follows: At the initial configuration, nucleotides are grouped according to their columns in M. Each column is represented by one membrane. For column 1, it corresponds to membrane 1. Column 2 corresponds to membrane 2. Lastly, column 3 corresponds to membrane 3. For $t = 1$, rule $r_6 :$ $A, C \rightarrow a_s, e$ is applied in region 1 since there are no other possible combinations available. While in region 2, rule $r_9 : C, T \rightarrow a_s, e$ is applied and lastly, in region 3, rule $r_{11} : T, G \rightarrow a_s, e$ is applied. At $t = 2$, the a_s strings produced in region $1, 2$ and 3 from $t = 1$ are transported to region s. Rule $r_{12} : A \rightarrow a_s, e$ is used in region 1 and rule $r_{14} : T \rightarrow a_s, e$ is used in regions 2 and 3. For the last time step, all a_s strings inside the column membranes are transported to region s. Here we see 6 copies of a_s strings in membrane s. This is interpreted as the score computed for the given alignment matrix M, which is 6.

4.2   Search for Maximum Score

Our main contribution in this paper is a solution for finding the maximum score. Recall that this is the last part in solving MFP. To search for the maximum score, we first define a problem for finding the maximum integer.

Definition 9 *Search for the Maximum Integer Problem (SM). Given v positive integers $\eta_1, \eta_2, \ldots, \eta_v$, find the maximum integer. The output to the problem is the maximum integer η_i such that $\forall j \neq i, \eta_i \geq \eta_j$.*

Lemma 3 *The SM problem can be solved using ECPe-str in time linear with respect to the value of the maximum input number.*

Proof We now provide a formal definition for the subsystem that will be used in solving the search for the maximum integer problem. The subsystem is of the form:

$$\Pi_3 = (\bar{O}, e, \mu, w_s, w_1, \ldots, w_v, R_s, R'_s, \rho_s, R_1, R'_1, \rho_1, \ldots, R_v, R'_v, \rho_v, 0),$$

where $\bar{O} = (O, S, Z, N); O = \{a_i, z_i, z'_i, z''_i, \chi_i, c_i, b_i, b'_i \mid 1 \leq i \leq v\} \cup \{\bigstar, \$\}; S = \emptyset; Z = \emptyset; N = \emptyset; \mu = [_s[_1]_1 \ldots [_v]_v]_s; w_s = \{c_i \mid 1 \leq i \leq v\} \cup D = \{\$, \ldots, \$\}$ and $|D| = v$; For $1 \leq i \leq v, w_i = \{z_i, \chi_i, \$\} \cup G$ where $|G| = \eta_i$ and $G = \{a_i, \ldots, a_i\}$. The next set of rules are for R_s:

$$R_s = \{ \ r_1 : \$ \rightarrow e, r_2 : a_i z_i \rightarrow a_i z'_i \ || \ c_i, e, r_3 : a_i z'_i \rightarrow a_i z''_i, r_4 : b_i \rightarrow b'_i \ || \ a_i z_i,$$
$$r_5 : b'_1, \ldots, b'_v \rightarrow \bigstar, r_6 : \bigstar, a_i z'_i \rightarrow \bigstar a_i z''_i \mid 1 \leq i \leq v\};$$

The set $R'_s = \{r'_1 : (\bigstar a_i z''_i, e, out)\}$; also, $\rho_s = \{r_6 > r_3\}$. The next set of rules are for each R_i ($1 \leq i \leq v$,):

$$R_i = \{ r_7 : \$ \to e, r_8 : c_i \to z_i, e, r_9 : a_i, z_i \to a_i z_i, r_{10} : \chi_i, z_i \to b_i\};$$

For $1 \leq i \leq v$, the set $R'_i = \{r'_2 : (a_i z_i, e, out; c_i, e, in), r'_3 : (b_i, e, out)\}$; and lastly, $\rho_i = \{r_9 > r_{10}\}$.

The solution for finding the maximum integer is based on the vertical search found in [4], but we changed a few rules to separate the evolution from communication rules, and incorporate energy objects. We also included some modification to handle the case wherein the maximum integer is not unique.[2] System Π_3 consists of an outer membrane (labeled s), and v inner membranes (labeled i, where $1 \leq i \leq v$). Membrane i corresponds to η_i. In the initial configuration, the integer η_i is represented by the multiplicity of string a_i in region i.

During the first part of the solution, there are v copies of $\$$ strings in region s, one for each η_i, and also one $\$$ string inside each inner membrane. These $\$$ strings evolve to produce one copy of e each using rules r_1 and r_7. At the same time, z_i strings are concatenated to the a_i strings in each inner membrane using rules of the form r_9. Then, using rules of the form r'_2, exactly one $a_i z_i$ string is transported outside of each inner membrane and one c_i string is transported inside membrane i at the same time step. After this, rules of the form r_2 is applied to all $a_i z_i$ strings, each producing an $a_i z'_i$ string, a c_i string, and an e object. Simultaneously, rules of the form r_8 is applied in each region i, causing the evolution of the c_i strings to z_i strings, and producing an e object each. In the next time step, $a_i z'_i$ strings evolve to $a_i z''_i$ strings using rules of the form r_3. Concurrently, the z_i strings produced in the previous time step are again concatenated to a_i strings in region i. This enables us to apply rule r'_2 again. For each inner membrane, we repeat the whole process until there are no more a_i strings left in the region.

Once there are no more a_i strings inside region i, a rule of the form r_9 is no longer applicable. This allows a rule of the form r_{10} to be applied, consuming the z_i and χ_i strings in the region to produce a b_i string. A rule of the form r'_3 is then applied, communicating the b_i string outside of membrane i. This signals that membrane i is already empty. Once the b_i string is transported to membrane s, a rule of the form r_4 will be applied, producing a b'_i and an $a_i z_i$ string. In the next time step, a rule of the form r_2 would be applied to the $a_i z_i$ string. The $a_i z'_i$ string produced this way would evolve using a rule r_3 in the next time step. Note that not all inner membranes would be emptied out at the same time since the multiplicity of each a_i string in each membrane are different from each other. Thus, the b_i strings in each membrane would not be transported to the skin membrane at the same time.

---

[2] This is an entirely new subsystem compared to the subsystem Π_3 in [5]. In [5], we were only able to solve for the restricted version of MFP because it can only find the motif if it has a unique maximum score. Otherwise, the system will just output an indication that the maximum score is not unique and therefore, won't solve the problem.

Once all b_i strings from each inner membrane are transported to region s and have evolved to b_i', rule r_5 can then be applied, producing a $\bigstar$ string. Prioritizing rule r_6 over rule r_3, we consume the $\bigstar$ string and an $a_i z_i'$ string to produce a string of the form $\bigstar a_i z_i''$, instead of evolving $a_i z_i'$ to $a_i z_i''$. In the case that there are multiple strings of the form $a_i z_i'$, the system will nondeterministically choose to apply a rule of the form r_6.

Observe that the strings $a_i z_i'$ are produced from b_i strings that are the latest to evolve to b_i'. This means that strings of the form $a_i z_i'$ that can be consumed in rule r_6 denote the maximum integer, since the membranes with the maximum integer are the last to transport their b_i string. At the end of the process, a string of the form $\bigstar a_i z_i''$ is transported outside of membrane s using the rule r_1'. The system halts after this.

From Definition 9, the SM problem requires that the maximum integer is output. Using system Π_3, this occurs when the system halts with a $\bigstar a_i z_i''$ string in the environment. The a_i substring in the $\bigstar a_i z_i''$ string represents the maximum integer, η_i. Note that in the case where two or more η_i have values equal to the maximum, only one of those would be outputted by this subsystem.

The steps needed for the solution depends on the value of the maximum integer, M. One step is needed for starting the system through the evolution of \$ and the application of rule r_9. Afterwards, there are $3M + 1$ steps needed to empty all inner membranes. Then, one step each is taken to apply rules of the form r_4, r_5, and r_6. One last step is taken for transporting the string of the form $\bigstar a_i z_i''$ to the environment. The total steps needed is $3M + 6$.   □

An Example for Finding the Maximum Score. Given $v = 3$ and positive integers $1, 2, 2$, we construct the following subsystem to find the maximum value:

$$\Pi_3 = (\bar{O}, e, \mu, w_s, w_1, w_2, w_3, R_s, R_s', \rho_s, R_1, R_1', \rho_1, R_2, R_2', \rho_2, R_3, R_3', \rho_3, 0),$$

where $\bar{O} = (O, \emptyset, \emptyset, \emptyset)$; $O = \{a_i, z_i, z_i', z_i'', \chi_i, c_i, b_i, b_i' \mid 1 \le i \le 3\} \cup \{\bigstar, \$\}$; membrane structure $\mu = [_s[_1]_1[_2]_2[_3]_3]_s$; $w_s = \{c_1, c_2, c_3, \$, \$, \$\}$; $w_1 = \{z_1, \chi_1, \$, a_1\}$; $w_2 = \{z_2, \chi_2, \$, a_2, a_2\}$; $w_3 = \{z_3, \chi_3, \$, a_3, a_3\}$. For the set R_s:

$$R_s = \{ \; r_1 : \$ \to e, \qquad\qquad r_4 : b_1 \to b_1' \; || \; a_1 z_1,$$
$$r_2 : a_1 z_1 \to a_1 z_1' \; || \; c_1, e, \qquad b_2 \to b_2' \; || \; a_2 z_2,$$
$$r_9 : a_i, z_i \to a_i z_i, \qquad\qquad b_3 \to b_3' \; || \; a_3 z_3,$$
$$a_3 z_3 \to a_3 z_3' \; || \; c_3, e, \quad r_5 : b_1', b_2', b_3' \to \bigstar,$$
$$r_3 : a_1 z_1' \to a_1 z_1'', \qquad r_6 : \bigstar, a_1 z_1' \to \bigstar a_1 z_1'',$$
$$a_2 z_2' \to a_2 z_2'', \qquad\qquad \bigstar, a_2 z_2' \to \bigstar a_2 z_2'',$$
$$a_3 z_3' \to a_3 z_3'', \qquad\qquad \bigstar, a_3 z_3' \to \bigstar a_3 z_3'' \; \};$$

The set $R_s' = \{r_1' : (\bigstar a_i z_i'', e, out) \mid 1 \le i \le v\}$ and $\rho_s = \{r_6 > r_3\}$. For each set R_i $(1 \le i \le v)$: $R_i = \{r_7 : \$ \to e, r_8 : c_i \to z_i, e, r_9 : a_i, z_i \to a_i z_i, r_{10} : \chi_i, z_i \to b_i\}$; The set $R_i' = \{r_2' : (a_i z_i, e, out; c_i, e, in), r_3' : (b_i, e, out)\}$ and $\rho_i = \{r_9 > r_{10}\}$.

An example step-by-step computation for the example is given below:

$t = 0$: $[_s$ $[_1$ \$, a_1, z_1, χ_1 $]_1$ $[_2$ \$, a_2, a_2, z_2, χ_2 $]_2$ $[_3$ \$, a_3, a_3, z_3, χ_3 $]_3$
$\quad$ \$, \$, \$, c_1, c_2, c_3 $]_s$

$t = 1$: $[_s$ $[_1$ $e, a_1 z_1, \chi_1$ $]_1$ $[_2$ $e, a_2, a_2 z_2, \chi_2$ $]_2$ $[_3$ $e, a_3, a_3 z_3, \chi_3$ $]_3$
$\quad$ e, e, e, c_1, c_2, c_3 $]_s$

$t = 2$: $[_s$ $[_1$ c_1, χ_1 $]_1$ $[_2$ a_2, c_2, χ_2 $]_2$ $[_3$ a_3, c_3, χ_3 $]_3$ $a_1 z_1, a_2 z_2, a_3 z_3$ $]_s$

$t = 3$: $[_s$ $[_1$ e, z_1, χ_1 $]_1$ $[_2$ e, a_2, z_2, χ_2 $]_2$ $[_3$ e, a_3, z_3, χ_3 $]_3$
$\quad$ $a_1 z_1', a_2 z_2', a_3 z_3', c_1, c_2, c_3, e, e, e$ $]_s$

$t = 4$: $[_s$ $[_1$ e, b_1 $]_1$ $[_2$ $e, a_2 z_2, \chi_2$ $]_2$ $[_3$ $e, a_3 z_3, \chi_3$ $]_3$
$\quad$ $a_1 z_1'', a_2 z_2'', a_3 z_3'', c_1, c_2, c_3, e, e, e$ $]_s$

$t = 5$: $[_s$ $[_1$ $]_1$ $[_2$ c_2, χ_2 $]_2$ $[_3$ c_3, χ_3 $]_3$
$\quad$ $a_1 z_1'', a_2 z_2'', a_3 z_3'', c_1, b_1, a_2 z_2, a_3 z_3, e$ $]_s$

$t = 6$: $[_s$ $[_1$ $]_1$ $[_2$ e, z_2, χ_2 $]_2$ $[_3$ e, z_3, χ_3 $]_3$ c_1, c_2, c_3, e, e, e
$\quad$ $a_1 z_1'', a_2 z_2'', a_3 z_3'', b_1', a_1 z_1, a_2 z_2'', a_2 z_2', a_3 z_3'', a_3 z_3'$ $]_s$

$t = 7$: $[_s$ $[_1$ $]_1$ $[_2$ e, b_2 $]_2$ $[_3$ e, b_3 $]_3$ $b_1', c_1, c_1, c_2, c_3, e, e, e, e$
$\quad$ $a_1 z_1', a_1 z_1'', a_2 z_2'', a_2 z_2'', a_3 z_3'', a_3 z_3''$ $]_s$

$t = 8$: $[_s$ $[_1$ $]_1$ $[_2$ $]_2$ $[_3$ $]_3$ $b_1', b_2, b_3, c_1, c_1, c_2, c_3, e, e, e, e$
$\quad$ $a_1 z_1'', a_1 z_1'', a_2 z_2'', a_2 z_2'', a_3 z_3'', a_3 z_3''$ $]_s$

$t = 9$: $[_s$ $[_1$ $]_1$ $[_2$ $]_2$ $[_3$ $]_3$ $b_1', b_2', b_3', c_1, c_1, c_2, c_3, e, e, e, e$
$\quad$ $a_1 z_1'', a_1 z_1'', a_2 z_2, a_2 z_2'', a_2 z_2'', a_3 z_3, a_3 z_3'', a_3 z_3''$ $]_s$

$t = 10$: $[_s$ $[_1$ $]_1$ $[_2$ $]_2$ $[_3$ $]_3$ $c_1, c_1, c_2, c_2, c_3, c_3, \bigstar, e, e, e, e, e, e$
$\quad$ $a_1 z_1'', a_1 z_1'', a_2 z_2', a_2 z_2'', a_2 z_2'', a_3 z_3', a_3 z_3'', a_3 z_3''$ $]_s$

$t = 11$: $[_s$ $[_1$ $]_1$ $[_2$ $]_2$ $[_3$ $]_3$ $c_1, c_1, c_2, c_2, c_3, c_3, e, e, e, e, e, e$
$\quad$ $a_1 z_1'', a_1 z_1'', a_2 z_2', a_2 z_2'', a_2 z_2'', \bigstar a_3 z_3'', a_3 z_3'', a_3 z_3''$ $]_s$

$t = 12$: $[_s$ $[_1$ $]_1$ $[_2$ $]_2$ $[_3$ $]_3$ $c_1, c_1, c_2, c_2, c_3, c_3, e, e, e, e, e$
$\quad$ $a_1 z_1'', a_1 z_1'', a_2 z_2'', a_2 z_2'', a_2 z_2'', a_3 z_3'', a_3 z_3''$ $]_s$ $\bigstar a_3 z_3''$

Note that At time $t = 11$, it also possible that a string $\bigstar a_2 z_2''$ is produced instead of the string $\bigstar a_3 z_3''$. The string $\bigstar a_3 z_3''$ implies that the number represented by the string a_3 possesses (one of the) the largest value.

4.3 Integrating All Subsystems to Solve MFP

We now provide a theorem for solving the Motif Finding Problem using the subsystems discussed.

Theorem 1 *The Motif Finding Problem can be solved using ECPe-str in $O(lt)$-time where l is the length of the motif and t is the number of DNA sequences.*

Proof We construct the system for solving MFP using the systems defined in the previous lemmas as subsystems of our solution. We now have the system:

$$\Pi_{MFP} = (\bar{O}, e, \mu, w_u, w_1, \ldots, w_i, w_{11}, \ldots, w_{id}, R_u, R_u', \rho_u, R_1, R_1', \rho_1,$$
$$\ldots, R_i, R_i', \rho_i, R_{11}, R_{11}', \rho_{11}, \ldots, R_{id}, R_{id}', \rho_{id}),$$

where $\bar{O} = (O, S, Z, N)$; $O = \{A, C, T, G, \beta_1, \ldots, \beta_{t+1}, 1, \ldots, p, a_i, z_i, z_i', z_i'',$
$\chi_i, c_i,\ b_i, b_i' \mid 1 \leq i \leq q\} \cup \{\star, \$\}$; $S = \{\alpha_{11}, \ldots, \alpha_{tl}\}$; $Z = \{\alpha_{11}', \ldots, \alpha_{tl}'\}$;
$N = \{\gamma_{11}, \ldots, \gamma_{tl}\}$; $\mu = [_u[_1[_{11}]_{11} \cdots [_{1d}]_{1d}]_1 \cdots [_i[_{i1}]_{i1} \cdots [_{id}]_{id}]_i]_u$ where $1 \leq i \leq$
q and $1 \leq d \leq l$; $w_u = \{\beta_1\} \cup \{c_i \mid 1 \leq i \leq q\} \cup D = \{\$, \ldots, \$\}$ where $|D| = q$;
For $1 \leq i \leq q$ and $1 \leq d \leq l$, $w_i = \{z_i, \chi_i, \$\}$; $w_{id} = \emptyset$. The set of rules and
priority relations are as follows. For $1 \leq i \leq q$ and $1 \leq d \leq l$:

$$R_u = \{\ r_1 : \beta_k \to L_{k1}\beta_{k+1}1 \| \ldots \| L_{kp}\beta_{k+1}p \mid 1 \leq k \leq t\} \text{ where}$$
$$L_{kj} = \alpha_{11}d_{kj}\alpha_{11}' \ldots \alpha_{kl}d_{k(j+l-1)}\alpha_{kl}' \text{ for all } 1 \leq k \leq t, 1 \leq j \leq p$$
$$\cup\ \{r_2 : \$ \to e,\ r_3 : a_i z_i \to a_i z_i' \| c_i, e,$$
$$r_4 : a_i z_i' \to a_i z_i'',\ r_5 : b_i \to b_i' \| a_i z_i,$$
$$r_6 : b_1', \ldots, b_q' \to \star, r_7 : \star, a_i z_i' \to \star a_i z_i'' \mid 1 \leq i \leq q\}$$
$$\cup\ \{r_8 : \beta_{t+1} \to \lambda\};$$
$$R_i = \{\ r_9 : \$ \to e,\ r_{10} : c_i \to z_i, e,$$
$$r_{11} : a_i, z_i \to a_i z_i,\ r_{12} : \chi_i, z_i \to b_i\}$$
$$\cup\ \{r_{13} : Project(\alpha_{cd}, \alpha_{cd}', \gamma_{cd}), e \mid 1 \leq c \leq t, 1 \leq d \leq l\};$$
$$R_{id} = \{\ r_{14} : A, C, T, G \to a_i, e,\ r_{15} : A, C, T \to a_i, e,$$
$$r_{16} : A, C, G \to a_i, e,\ r_{17} : C, T, G \to a_i, e,$$
$$r_{18} : A, T, G \to a_i, e, r_{19} : A, C \to a_i, e,$$
$$r_{20} : A, T \to a_i, e, r_{21} : A, G \to a_i, e, r_{22} : C, T \to a_i, e,$$
$$r_{23} : C, G \to a_i, e, r_{24} : T, G \to a_i, e, r_{25} : A \to a_i, e,$$
$$r_{26} : C \to a_i, e, r_{27} : T \to a_i, e, r_{28} : G \to a_i, e\}$$
$$\cup\ \{r_{29} : \gamma_{cd} \to \lambda \mid 1 \leq c \leq t\};$$
$$R_u' = \{r_1' : (\star a_i z_i'', e, out) \mid 1 \leq i \leq q\};$$
$$R_i' = \{r_2' : (a_i z_i, e, out; c_i, e, in), r_3' : (b_i, e, out)\} \cup \{r_4' : (map(i), e, in)\};$$
$$R_{id}' = \{r_5' : (a_i, e, out)\} \cup \{r_6' : (\gamma_{cd}, e, in) \mid 1 \leq c \leq t, 1 \leq d \leq l\};$$
$$\rho_u = \{r_7 > r_4\};$$
$$\rho_i = \{r_{11} > r_{12}\};$$
$$\rho_{id} = \{r_{14} > r_{15}, \ldots, r_{18} > r_{19}, \ldots, r_{24} > r_{25}, \ldots, r_{28}\};$$

Membrane 1 in Π_1 (used in Lemma 1) coincides with membrane s of Π_3 (used
in Lemma 3). For Π_{MFP}, we label this membrane as membrane u. In the same
region bounded by membrane u, we have q number of Π_2 subsystems and we
label these as membrane i for $1 \leq i \leq q$. We call each membrane i as *score
membranes*. Lastly, inside each score membrane i are the column membranes
and we label these as membrane id for $1 \leq d \leq l$.

Recall that the system Π_2 (used in Lemma 2 solves the score of only one
alignment matrix. Since there are q possible alignment matrices, we assign each
alignment matrix to a membrane i. To do this, we define a one-to-one mapping
function $map(i)$:

$1 \mapsto 11\ldots11$	$p+1 \mapsto 11\ldots21$		$q-p+1 \mapsto pp\ldots p1$	
$2 \mapsto 11\ldots12$	$p+2 \mapsto 11\ldots22$		$q-p+2 \mapsto pp\ldots p2$	
$\vdots$	$\vdots$	$\cdots$	$\vdots$	
$p \mapsto 11\ldots1p$	$2p \mapsto 11\ldots2p$		$q \mapsto pp\ldots pp$	

The system works as follows: subsystem Π_1 will work in the same way as discussed in Sect. 4.1. Once Π_1 halts, all strings representing an alignment matrix is now found in membrane u. These strings contain substring s_i. Observe that s_i is similar to the values of $map(i)$ discussed above. We utilize this similarity to transport each alignment matrix (represented by a string) to their assigned score membranes. To do this, we use communication rules of the form $r'_4 : (map(i), e, in)$ associated to each score membrane i. The energy objects needed for this rule will come from evolving β_{t+1} present in each string representing an alignment matrix to λ using rule r_8.

After transporting all these strings, we project each nucleotide using projection rules of the form $r_{13} : Project(\alpha_{cd}, \alpha'_{cd}, \gamma_{cd}), e$, for $1 \leq c \leq t$ and $1 \leq d \leq l$ defined in each score membrane i. We use the e objects produced by this rule to transport each nucleotide to their respective column membranes. We do this through communication rules of the form $r'_6 : (\gamma_{cd}, e, in)$ associated to each column membrane id.

Once all nucleotides are in their respective column membranes, we use an evolution rule $r_{29} : \gamma_{cd} \to \lambda$ associated to each region bounded by each column membrane id. Notice that each score membrane i resembles the initial configuration of Π_2. For the system to proceed with the process discussed in Sect. 4.1, we change some rules in Π_2. Instead of evolving combinations of nucleotides to string a_s, we now evolve it to a_i since the score membranes are now labeled as i where $1 \leq i \leq q$. Once the system is done with the process in Sect. 4.1, the score of the alignment matrix assigned to each membrane i is now represented by the multiplicity of string a_i found in membrane i.

Lastly, the system now executes the process discussed in Sect. 4.2. Note that the variable v in Π_3 is now equal to q since we are now searching for the maximum value among q positive integers. These q positive integers are the scores of our alignment matrices. As seen in Sect. 4.2, the $\bigstar a_i z''_i$ string corresponding to the integer with the maximum value will be found in the environment once Π_3 halts. Thus, once Π_3 halts, the $\bigstar a_i z''_i$ string that is found in the environment will be pertaining to an alignment matrix with the maximum score.

Getting the i from $\bigstar a_i z''_i$ string that is now in the environment of out Π_{MFP}, we use our $map(i)$ function to know the corresponding alignment matrix of i. Reading the value of $map(i)$ from right to left, we now have the starting positions of the l-mers that produces the maximum consensus score.

The total time steps needed for the whole solution to MFP using the system above is $3lt + l + t + 14$: t time steps are needed for Π_1, the transition from Π_1 to Π_2 takes $l + 3$ time steps, 5 time steps are needed for Π_2 and $3lt + 6$ time steps are needed for Π_3. □

5   Final Remarks

In this paper, we have presented a solution to MFP using ECPe-str. Through this system, MFP is solved with the maximum runtime equal to $3lt + l + t + 14$ where l is the length of the motif and t is the number of DNA sequences. It can

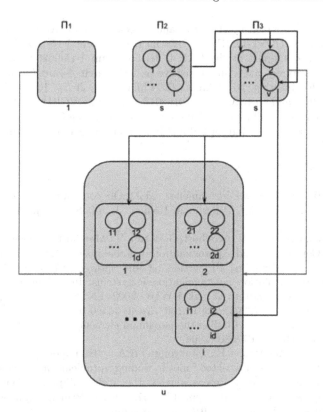

Fig. 2. Schematic diagram illustrating the membrane structure of Π_{MFP} from the membrane structures of Π_1, Π_2 and Π_3.

be observed that our initial solution can still be further improved by looking into several factors. First, the set of rules and membranes used are exponential and very powerful rules are employed in our solution. Thus, our improvement may be in the direction of minimizing the resources used, and exploring solutions where some of the additional features in the current system are not included. We may also look into how the current solution can be improved if we capitalize the use of energy objects. Finally, the solution presented is non-uniform [11]. It remains an open problem to explore a uniform solution for MFP (Fig. 2).

Future studies may look into another way to solve MFP faster using a branch and bound algorithm, discussed in [6]. In this paper, we computed for the score of all possible alignment matrices and then compare all of them to find the maximum. Through the branch and bound method in [6], one can devise a solution that would enable the system to sort through "bad" solutions and reduce the number of alignment matrices compared.

Acknowledgements. R. Juayong would like to thank the DOST-ERDT Scholarship Program and the DOST-PCIEERD for the HRIDD HRDP grant I-15-0715-2.

N. Hernandez is supported by the Vea Family Technology for All Centennial professorial chair and the DOST-PCIEERD HRIDD HRDP grant I-15-1006-19. F. Cabarle is grateful for the support of the HRIDD HRDP grant I-15-0626-06 of the DOST PCIEERD, Philippines, a Faculty Incentive and Research Award (2015–2016) from the College of Engineering, UP Diliman, the PhDIA Project No. 161606 from the UP Diliman, OVCRD, and an RLC grant 20162017 also from OVCRD. H. Adorna is supported by the following, all from UP Diliman: Semirara Mining Corp. professorial chair, the Gawad Tsanselor Award grant 2015–2016 and an OVCRD RLC grant 2014–2015.

References

1. Adorna, H., Păun, G., Pérez-Jiménez, M.J.: On communication complexity in evolution-communication P systems. Roman. J. Inf. Sci. Technol. **13**, 113–130 (2010)
2. Ausiello, G., Crescenzi, P., Gambosi, G., Kann, V., Marchetti-Spaccamela, A., Protasi, M.: Complexity and Approximation: Combinatorial Optimization Problems and Their Approximability Properties, 1st edn. Springer, Heidelberg (1999)
3. Cavaliere, M.: Evolution–communication P systems. In: PĂun, G., Rozenberg, G., Salomaa, A., Zandron, C. (eds.) WMC 2002. LNCS, vol. 2597, pp. 134–145. Springer, Heidelberg (2003). doi:10.1007/3-540-36490-0_10
4. Fontana, F., Franco, G.: Finding the maximum element using P systems. J. Univ. Comput. Sci. **10**(5), 567–580 (2004)
5. Gapuz, K., Mendoza, E., Juayong, R.A., Hernandez, N.H., Adorna, H.: Solution to a restricted motif finding problem in membranes. In: Sioson, A., et al. (eds.) Proceedings of the 16th Philippine Computing Science Congress (PCSC 2016), pp. 136–147. Puerto Princesa, Palawan (2016). https://sites.google.com/site/2016pcsc/proceedings
6. Jones, N., Pevzner, P.: An Introduction to Bioinformatics Algorithms. Massachusetts Institute of Technology Press, Cambridge (2004)
7. Leavitt, S.A.: Deciphering the Genetic Code. https://history.nih.gov/exhibits/nirenberg/glossary.htm. Accessed 20 Feb 2016
8. Naranayan, K.S.: Language of P systems; computability and complexity. Master's thesis, Indian Institute of Technology Madras (2001)
9. Păun, G.: Membrane Computing. Springer, Heidelberg (2002)
10. Păun, G.: Introduction to Membrane Computing. In: Ciobanu, G., Păun, G., Pérez-Jiménez, M.J. (eds.) Applications of Membrane Computing. Natural Computing Series, pp. 1–42. Springer, Heidelberg (2006). http://dx.doi.org/10.1007/3-540-29937-8_1
11. Pérez–Jiménez, M.J.: A computational complexity theory in membrane computing. In: Păun, G., Pérez-Jiménez, M.J., Riscos-Núñez, A., Rozenberg, G., Salomaa, A. (eds.) WMC 2009. LNCS, vol. 5957, pp. 125–148. Springer, Heidelberg (2010). doi:10.1007/978-3-642-11467-0_10
12. Sipser, M.: Introduction to the Theory of Computation, 2nd edn. Thomson Course Technology, San Francisco (2006)
13. Zeng, X., Zhang, X., Zou, Q.: Integrative approaches for predicting microRNA function and prioritizing disease-related microRNA using biological interaction networks. Brief. Bioinform. **17**(2), 193–203 (2016)
14. Zou, Q., Li, J., Song, L., Zeng, X., Wang, G.: Similarity computation strategies in the microRNA-disease network: a survey. Brief. Funct. Genomics **15**(1), 55–64 (2016)

Remarks on the Computational Power of Some Restricted Variants of P Systems with Active Membranes

Zsolt Gazdag$^{(\boxtimes)}$ and Gábor Kolonits

Department of Algorithms and Their Applications,
Faculty of Informatics,
Eötvös Loránd University, Budapest, Hungary
{gazdagzs,kolomax}@inf.elte.hu

Abstract. In this paper we consider three restricted variants of P systems with active membranes: (1) P systems using send-out communication rules only, (2) P systems using elementary membrane division and dissolution rules only, and (3) polarizationless P systems using dissolution and unit evolution rules only. We show that every problem in **P** can be solved with uniform families of any of these variants using reasonably weak uniformity conditions. This, using known results on the upper bound of the computational power of variants (1) and (3) yields new characterizations of the class **P**. In the case of variant (2) we provide a further characterization of **P** by giving a semantic restriction on the computations of P systems of this variant.

Keywords: Membrane computing · P systems with active membranes · Computational complexity

1 Introduction

P systems with active membranes were introduced in [20]. These P systems have the possibility of dividing elementary (or even non-elementary) membranes. It was soon discovered that this feature (combined with maximal parallelism) makes this variant a rather powerful computational device, and efficient solutions of problems that are complete in **NP** [10, 20, 25, 31] (or even in **PSPACE** [1, 29]) were given. In order to establish the connection between classical complexity classes and P system families, recognizer P systems were introduced in [24]. Since then recognizer P systems are considered as the natural framework to study the computational power of various classes of P system families. Among the many research lines in Membrane Computing, one is to find efficient solutions of computationally hard problems by various types of recognizer P systems with active membranes (see e.g. [2–4, 17, 18, 23]).

It is not too surprising that membrane division is necessary in these systems to solve computationally hard problems efficiently [31]. However, in [21] Păun conjectured that polarization is also necessary. More precisely, Păun's conjecture

© Springer International Publishing AG 2017
A. Leporati et al. (Eds.): CMC 2016, LNCS 10105, pp. 209–232, 2017.
DOI: 10.1007/978-3-319-54072-6_14

(which is also known as the *P conjecture* in the literature) sounds as follows: polarizationless P systems with active membranes working in polynomial time can solve only problems in **P** if non-elementary membrane division rules are not allowed. Although the P conjecture has not been proven yet, there are some partial results. In [8] it was shown that without dissolution rules these systems can solve exactly the problems in **P**. The conjecture was also confirmed in the following cases: when dissolution rules are allowed, but the P systems can employ only restricted, so-called symmetric, division rules [12], and when the initial membrane structure is a linearly nested sequence of membranes, and the system can employ only dissolution and elementary membrane division rules [30].

It was observed in [13] that the **P** lower bound in the characterization of **P** in [8] comes from the polynomial uniformity of the examined P systems. In fact, according to [11] the used uniformity condition dominates the computational power of uniform families of polarizationless P systems with no dissolution rules. This initiated a sequence of papers where P systems with active membranes under reasonably tight uniformity conditions were examined [15,16]. Moreover, several solutions of problems in **P** with restricted classes of P systems under tight uniformity conditions were given [5,9,14,15].

In this paper we continue the work in this research line. First we show that uniform families of P systems with active membranes using send-out communication rules only can solve every problem in **P**. Then we show a similar result when the applicable rules are elementary membrane division and dissolution rules. The proofs are given by solving a restricted, but still **P**-complete variant of the well know HORNSAT problem, the satisfiability problem of Horn formulas.

Finally, we show that uniform families of polarizationless P systems with active membranes using dissolution and unit rules can simulate polynomial time Turing machines efficiently (a unit rule is such an evolution rule which introduces exactly one object during its application). This result is stronger than the one appearing in [6] since there communication and not restricted evolution rules were used too. In [15] a solution of a **P**-complete problem was given using dissolution and restricted evolution rules only, however the presented family of P systems was semi-uniform.

Using the **P** upper bound given in [31], our first and third results give new characterizations of **P** in terms of Membrane Computing techniques. In our second result we use P systems where the initial membrane structure is a linearly nested sequence of membranes, and during the computation the number of membranes on the deepest level is at most two. It can be seen that the set of those problems that can be solved by those P systems with active membranes which have this semantic restriction during their computations are in **P**. This yields another characterization of the complexity class **P**.

2   Preliminaries

Here we recall the necessary notions used later. Nevertheless, we assume that the reader is familiar with the basic concepts of formal language theory, propositional logic, and Membrane Computing techniques (for a comprehensive guide to these topics see e.g. [7,22,27], respectively). $\mathbb{N}$ denotes the set of natural numbers. For $n, m \in \mathbb{N}$, $n < m$, $[n, m]$ denotes the set $\{n, n+1, \ldots, m\}$. If $n = 1$, then $[n, m]$ is denoted by $[m]$.

Propositional Formulas and the HORNSAT *Problem.* A *propositional variable* is a variable whose value can be either *true* or *false*. If it is not confusing, we will often call propositional variables simply *variables*. We fix an infinite set $Var = \{v_1, v_2, v_3, \ldots\}$ of variables. For a number $n \in \mathbb{N}$, Var_n is the set $\{v_1, \ldots, v_n\}$. An *interpretation* of the variables in Var_n is a function $\mathcal{I} : Var_n \rightarrow \{true, \ false\}$.

The propositional variables and their *negations* are called *literals*. l is a *positive* (resp. *negative*) literal, if $l = x$ (resp. $l = \neg x$), for some $x \in Var$, where the operator $\neg$ denotes the *negation*. A *clause* $\mathcal{C}$ is a *disjunction* of finitely many pairwise different literals satisfying that there is no $x \in Var$ such that both x and $\neg x$ occur in $\mathcal{C}$. A clause $\mathcal{C}$ is a *positive unit clause* if it contains exactly one positive literal and no negative literals. A formula in *conjunctive normal form* (CNF) is a conjunction of finitely many clauses. For example, the following is a formula in CNF: $x \wedge y \wedge (\neg x \vee \neg y)$, where $x, y \in Var$ and the operators $\wedge$ and $\vee$ denote the *conjunction* and *disjunction*, respectively. Due to the commutativity of these operators, a formula in CNF can be considered as a finite set of clauses, where the clauses are finite sets of literals. Let φ be a formula in CNF. φ is *satisfiable*, if there is an interpretation under which φ evaluates to *true*. Moreover, φ is a *Horn formula* if every clause in φ contains at most one positive literal.

The HORNSAT problem sounds as follows: *given a Horn formula φ, decide if φ is satisfiable.* It is known that HORNSAT is **P**-complete (see e.g. [19]). Let HORN3SAT be that restriction of HORNSAT where every clause of the input formula can contain at most three literals. Moreover, let HORN3SATNORM be that restriction of HORN3SAT where the input formula is in the following normal form: every clause of the formula is either a positive unit clause or it contains exactly two negative literals and at most one positive literal. For example, $x \wedge (\neg x \vee y) \wedge (\neg y \vee \neg z \vee u)$ $(x, y, z, u \in Var)$ is an instance of HORN3SAT, but not of HORN3SATNORM, since $(\neg x \vee y)$ neither is a positive unite clause nor contains exactly two negative literals. However, $x \wedge (\neg x \vee \neg y) \wedge (\neg y \vee \neg z \vee u)$ is an instance of HORN3SATNORM.

Next we show that HORN3SATNORM is **P**-complete. The proof resembles the standard **NP**-completeness proof of the 3SAT problem (the 3SAT problem is the satisfiability problem of those formulas in CNF which can have only clauses with three literals, see e.g. [28]).

Proposition 1. HORN3SATNORM *is **P**-complete.*

Proof. Since this problem is a restriction of HORNSAT, it is in **P**. Thus, it is enough to show that HORNSAT can be reduced using logarithmic space to HORN3SATNORM. First we show that HORNSAT reduces to HORN3SAT. Let φ be a Horn formula over the variables in Var_n $(n \in \mathbb{N})$. We construct an instance φ' of HORN3SAT such that φ' is satisfiable if and only if φ is satisfiable. Let $\mathcal{C}$ be a clause in φ. If $\mathcal{C}$ has at most three literals, then let $\mathcal{C}$ be a clause of φ'. Otherwise, assume that $\mathcal{C} = x_1 \vee \neg x_2 \vee \cdots \vee \neg x_k$ for some $k \in [4, n]$ and $x_i \in Var_n$ ($i \in [k]$). It can be easily seen that $\mathcal{C}$ is satisfiable if and only if $(x_1 \vee \neg x_2 \vee \neg y) \wedge (y \vee \neg x_3 \vee \cdots \vee \neg x_k)$ is satisfiable, where y is a new variable, not included in Var_n. In this way we can construct the formula $(x_1 \vee \neg x_2 \vee \neg y_1) \wedge (y_1 \vee \neg x_3 \vee \neg y_2) \wedge \cdots \wedge (y_{k-3} \vee \neg x_{k-1} \vee \neg x_k)$, which is satisfiable (over $Var_n \cup \{y_1, \ldots, y_{k-3}\}$) if and only if $\mathcal{C}$ is satisfiable (over Var_n). To a clause with no positive literals one can give a very similar construction. Then we add these new clauses to φ'. Clearly, φ' is satisfiable if and only if φ is satisfiable, and the mapping $\varphi \mapsto \varphi'$ can be carried out by a deterministic Turing machine using logarithmic space in the size of φ.

Next we show that HORN3SAT reduces to HORN3SATNORM. To this end let φ be an instance of HORN3SAT with variables in Var_n. We construct an instance φ' of HORN3SATNORM such that φ' is satisfiable if and only if φ is satisfiable. For every clause $\mathcal{C}$ of φ, if $\mathcal{C}$ corresponds to the restrictions made on the instances of HORN3SATNORM, then let $\mathcal{C}$ be a clause of φ'. Otherwise we replace $\mathcal{C}$ with the set $\mathcal{C}'$ of clauses defined as follows:

- if $\mathcal{C} = \neg x$, then let $\mathcal{C}' = \{\neg x \vee \neg y, y\}$,
- if $\mathcal{C} = x_1 \vee \neg x_2$, then let $\mathcal{C}' = \{x_1 \vee \neg x_2 \vee \neg y, y\}$, and
- if $\mathcal{C} = \neg x_1 \vee \neg x_2 \vee \neg x_3$, then let $\mathcal{C}' = \{\neg x_1 \vee \neg x_2 \vee y, \neg y \vee \neg x_3\}$,

where $x, x_1, x_2, x_3 \in Var_n$ and y is always a new variable not used yet during the construction. Clearly the clauses in $\mathcal{C}'$ have the desired forms, and φ' is satisfiable if and only if φ is satisfiable. Moreover, the described construction can be carried out by a logarithmic space Turing machine. Thus, since logarithmic space reductions are closed under composition, we have that HORNSAT can be efficiently reduced to HORN3SATNORM, which finishes the proof of the statement.

Turing Machines. In this paper we will use that variant of Turing machines which appears, e.g., in [28]. A *(deterministic) Turing machine* is a 7-tuple $M = (Q, \Sigma, \Gamma, \delta, q_0, q_a, q_r)$ where

- Q is the finite set of *states*,
- Σ is the *input alphabet*,
- Γ is the tape alphabet including Σ and a distinguished symbol $\sqcup \notin \Sigma$, called the *blank symbol*,
- $\delta : (Q - \{q_a, q_r\}) \times \Gamma \to Q \times \Gamma \times \{-1, 1\}$ is the *transition function*; the ith component of $\delta(q, X)$ ($i \in [1, 3], q \in Q - \{q_a, q_r\}, X \in \Gamma$) is denoted by $\mathrm{proj}_i(\delta(q, X))$,
- q_0, q_a, and q_r are the *initial*, *accepting*, and *rejecting states*, respectively.

M works on a single infinite tape that is closed on the left-hand side. During the computation of M, the tape contains only finitely many non-blank symbols, and it is blank elsewhere. Let $w \in \Sigma^*$. The *initial configuration* of M on w is that where w is placed at the beginning of the tape, the head points to the first letter of w, and the current state of M is q_0. A computation step performed by M is described as follows. If M is in state p and the head of M reads the symbol X, then M changes its state to q and writes X' onto X if and only if $\delta(p, X) = (q, X', d)$, for some $d \in \{-1, 1\}$. Moreover, if $d = 1$ (resp. $d = -1$), then M moves its head one position to the right (resp. to the left) (by definition, M can never move the head off the left-hand end of the tape even if the head points to the first cell and $d = -1$). We say that M *accepts* (resp. *rejects*) w, if M can reach q_a (resp. q_r) starting from the initial configuration on w. We note here that M can stop only in these states. The *language accepted by M* is the set $L(M)$ consisting of those words in Σ^* that are accepted by M.

P Systems with Active Membranes. In this paper we consider several restricted variants of P systems with active membranes. In general, a *P system* with active membranes [20] is a construct of the form $\Pi = (\Gamma, H, \mu, w_1, \ldots, w_m, R)$, where m is the initial *degree* of the system, Γ is the alphabet of *objects*, H is a finite set of *labels* of the membranes; μ is a *membrane structure* consisting of m membranes and labelled with elements of H; $w_1, \ldots, w_m \subseteq \Gamma^*$ are the *initial multisets of objects* placed in the m regions of μ; and R is a finite set of *rules* defined as follows:

(a) $[a \rightarrow v]_h^e$, for $e \in \{+, -, 0\}$, $h \in H, a \in \Gamma, v \in \Gamma^*$
    (object *evolution* rules, associated with membranes and depending on the label and the charge of the membranes, but not directly involving the membranes);

(b) $a[\ ]_h^{e_1} \rightarrow [b]_h^{e_2}$, for $e_1, e_2 \in \{+, -, 0\}$, $h \in H$, $a, b \in \Gamma$
    (*send-in communication* rules; an object is sent into a membrane, maybe modified during this process; also the polarization of the membrane can be modified, but not its label);

(c) $[a]_h^{e_1} \rightarrow [\ ]_h^{e_2} b$, for $e_1, e_2 \in \{+, -, 0\}$, $h \in H$, $a, b \in \Gamma$
    (*send-out communication* rules; an object is sent out of the membrane, maybe modified during this process; also the polarization of the membrane can be modified, but not its label);

(d) $[a]_h^e \rightarrow b$, for $e \in \{+, -, 0\}$, $h \in H$, $a, b \in \Gamma$
    (*membrane dissolving* rules; in reaction with an object, a membrane can be dissolved, while the object specified in the rule can be modified);

(e) $[a]_h^{e_1} \rightarrow [b]_h^{e_2} [c]_h^{e_3}$, for $e_1, e_2, e_3 \in \{+, -, 0\}$, $h \in H$, $a, b, c \in \Gamma$
    (*division* rules for elementary membranes; in reaction with an object, the membrane is divided into two membranes with possibly different polarizations; the object a specified in the rule is replaced in the two new membranes by (possibly new) objects b and c respectively, and the remaining objects are duplicated).

As it is usual in membrane computing, P systems with active membranes work in a *maximally parallel* manner: at each step the system first nondeterministically assigns appropriate rules to the objects of the system such that the assigned multiset S of rules satisfies the following properties: (i) at most one rule from S is assigned to any object of the system, (ii) a membrane can be the subject of at most one rule in S, and (iii) S is maximal among the multisets of rules satisfying (i) and (ii).

We call an evolution rule $[a \rightarrow v]_h^e$ with $|v| = 1$ a *unit rule*. A *layer* is a non-branching membrane structure, that is a layer has the form $[\ldots [\ ]_{h_1} \ldots]_{h_n}$ $(n \geq 1, h_1, \ldots, h_n \in H)$. For two layers $\mu_1 = [\ldots [\ ]_{h_1} \ldots]_{h_j}$ and $\mu_2 = [\ldots [\ ]_{g_1} \ldots]_{g_k}$ $(j, k \geq 1, h_1, \ldots, h_j, g_1, \ldots, g_k \in H)$, the *composition* $\mu_1[\mu_2]$ of μ_1 and μ_2 is the layer $[\ldots [[\ldots [\ ]_{g_1} \ldots]_{g_k}]_{h_1} \ldots]_{h_j}$. For improving the readability of the paper, we will often call a composition of finitely many layers a *block*.

Recognizer P Systems. A *recognizer P system* [24,26] is a P system Π with a designated *input* membrane and having the following properties. The alphabet Γ of objects has two designated elements *yes* and *no*. Every computation of Π halts and sends to the environment the same object which is either *yes* or *no*, and these objects are sent out in the last step of the computation (if the examined P system model does not have send-out communication rules, then the output of the system appears in the skin membrane). The *input* of Π is a multiset over Γ, which is added to the input membrane of the system in the initial configuration.

Uniform Families of P Systems. A family $\mathbf{\Pi} = \{\Pi(n)\}_{n \in \mathbb{N}}$ of recognizer P systems *decides a problem* L if, for every instance x of L with length n, starting $\Pi(n)$ with an appropriate encoding of x in its input membrane the following holds: $\Pi(n)$ sends into the environment *yes* if and only if $x \in L$.

We will use uniform families of recognizer P systems to solve problems in $\mathbf{P}$. Clearly, we should use such a uniformity condition that is reasonably weak to work with in class $\mathbf{P}$. According to the widely believed fact that Turing machines using logarithmic space are strictly weaker than Turing machines working in polynomial time, we will use logarithmic space uniform families of P systems. We denote by $\mathbf{L}$ the family of functions that can be computed by Turing machines using logarithmic amount of space.

Assume that a family $\mathbf{\Pi} = \{\Pi(n)\}_{n \in \mathbb{N}}$ of recognizer P systems decides a problem L. $\mathbf{\Pi}$ is called $(\mathbf{L}, \mathbf{L})$-*uniform* if and only if (i) there are functions $f, cod \in \mathbf{L}$ such that, for every $n \in \mathbb{N}$, $\Pi(n) = f(1^n)$ (i.e., the P system $\Pi(n)$ can be constructed by a logarithmic space Turing machine from the unary representation of n); (ii) for every instance x of L with size n, $cod(x)$ is a multiset encoding x over the alphabet of objects in $\Pi(n)$.

For a type $\mathcal{F}$ of recognizer P systems, we denote by $(\mathbf{L}, \mathbf{L}) - \mathbf{PMC}_{\mathcal{F}}$ the class of those problems that can be decided by $(\mathbf{L}, \mathbf{L})$-uniform families of P systems of type $\mathcal{F}$ working in polynomial time. $\mathcal{AM}_{+out}$ (resp. $\mathcal{AM}_{+e,+d}$) denotes the family of P systems with active membranes having send-out communication (resp. division and dissolution) rules only. Similarly, $\mathcal{AM}_{+u,+d}^0$ denotes the family of polarizationless P systems having unit rules and dissolution rules only.

3   Results

Here we show that recognizer P systems of type $\mathcal{AM}_{+out}$, $\mathcal{AM}_{+e,+d}$, or $\mathcal{AM}_{+u,+d}^0$ and working in polynomial time are capable to solve every problem in **P**. First we consider two solutions of HORN3SATNORM, then we give an efficient simulation of Turing machines.

3.1   The Solution of HORN3SATNORM

By definition, if φ is an instance of HORN3SATNORM, then every clause of φ is either a positive unit clause or it has exactly two negative literals. In the rest of this section by a clause we mean a clause having this property. Using the well known equivalences of propositional logic, a clause having exactly two negative literals $\neg x$ and $\neg y$ can be written in the form $x \wedge y \rightarrow \downarrow$ or $x \wedge y \rightarrow z$, where z is a variable, $\rightarrow$ denotes the operation of *implication* and $\downarrow$ denotes a formula with constant *false* truth value. We will often use these expressions to denote the corresponding clauses of the input formula (in fact, we will often call these expressions clauses, although strictly speaking they are not clauses). Moreover, for the sake of simplicity, we will not indicate the operator $\wedge$ in the left-hand side of these expressions. Notice that the order of the variables on the left-hand side is irrelevant, since, as we have mentioned above, clauses can be considered as sets of literals.

   Let φ be an instance of HORN3SATNORM with variables in Var_n $(n \geq 1)$. Clearly, if φ is *true* in an interpretation $\mathcal{I}$, then $\mathcal{I}(x) = true$ must hold for every positive unite clause $\{x\}$ in φ. Assume now that $\mathcal{C} = xy \rightarrow z$ $(x, y \in Var_n,$ $z \in Var_n \cup \{\downarrow\})$ is a clause of φ. We observe that if $\mathcal{I}(x) = \mathcal{I}(y) = true$, then $\mathcal{C}$ is *true* in $\mathcal{I}$ if and only if z is *true* too. That is, if $z = \downarrow$, then x, y, z cannot be all *true* in $\mathcal{I}$. We will use these observations in the following algorithm H3SN, which decides if φ is satisfiable or not. Let $\mathcal{N}(n)$ denote the set of those clauses over variables in Var_n which contain exactly two negative literals, and let $m = |\mathcal{N}(n)|$. In the rest of this section we assume a fixed enumeration $c_1, \ldots, c_m$ of clauses in $\mathcal{N}(n)$.

Algorithm. H3SN

1. **input:** A formula φ in CNF with variables in Var_n $(n \geq 1)$
2. $X := \{x \in Var_n \mid x \in \varphi\}$ // x is a positive unit clause of φ
3. **For** $i = 1 \ldots n$ **do**
4.   **For** $j = 1 \ldots m$ **do**
5.   **If** $c_j = xy \rightarrow u \in \varphi$ **and** $x, y \in X$ **then** $X := X \cup \{u\}$
6. **If** $\downarrow$ is in X **then return** *no*
7. **else return** *yes*

To demonstrate the work of H3SN consider the following example (see also the solution of HORNSAT in [19]). Let $\varphi = x \wedge y \wedge (xy \rightarrow z) \wedge (xz \rightarrow \downarrow)$, where $x, y, z \in Var_n$. Then, initially, $X = \{x, y\}$. Since $x, y \in X$ and $xy \rightarrow z \in \varphi$, X becomes $\{x, y, z\}$. Then, since $x, z \in X$ and $xz \rightarrow \downarrow \in \varphi$, X becomes $\{x, y, z, \downarrow\}$. After this the value of X remains the same until H3SN halts. Thus, since $\downarrow \in X$, H3SN outputs *no*. This is correct as φ is unsatisfiable.

   In this section we give two families of P systems with rather restricted sets of applicable rules to solve the HORN3SATNORM problem in polynomial time. Both solutions are based on Algorithm H3SN. In these solutions the P systems cannot employ evolution and send-in communication rules. In addition, in the first solution dissolution and membrane division rules, while in the second solution send-out communication rules are also not allowed.

In both solutions the constructed P system, roughly, works as follows. Let φ be an instance of HORN3SATNORM with variables in Var_n ($n \geq 1$). The initial membrane structure consists of n blocks, and the innermost membrane contains $cod(\varphi)$ (that is, the encoding of φ). The ith block, counted from the innermost membrane, will be used to implement the ith round of the main loop in Algorithm H3SN.

For an arbitrary clause $\mathcal{C}$ with variables in Var_n, $cod(\varphi)$ contains an object $O_{\mathcal{C}}^{\exists}$ or $O_{\mathcal{C}}^{\#}$ (but not both) according to whether $\mathcal{C}$ occurs in φ or not. Moreover, for every clause $xy \to u \in \mathcal{N}(n)$, the ith block has a layer l whose membranes are indexed by this clause. The objects in the inner membrane of l go through l (either by send-out communication or by dissolution rules, according to the used model), and during this the system performs the following task. It first checks whether all the objects $O_{xy \to u}^{\exists}$, $O_x^{\exists}$, $O_y^{\exists}$, and $O_u^{\#}$ are present in the innermost membrane of l. If yes, then the system rewrites $O_u^{\#}$ to $O_u^{\exists}$. In this way the system can determine which variables of φ must be *true* in order to make φ *true* in an interpretation. After performing the above task in all layers of the nth block, the skin contains either $O_{\downarrow}^{\exists}$ or $O_{\downarrow}^{\#}$. If $O_{\downarrow}^{\exists}$ occurs in the skin, then φ cannot be satisfied and the system introduces an object *no*, otherwise it introduces an object *yes*. Notice that while H3SN computes the set of those variables that must be *true* in order make φ *true* in an interpretation, the above described computation considers these variables as they were positive unit clauses of the formula. However, this behaviour is correct, since if we know that a variable x should be *true* in any interpretation that makes φ *true*, then $\varphi \wedge x$ is satisfiable if and only if φ is satisfiable.

Formally, we encode an instance φ of HORN3SATNORM with variables in Var_n as follows. First, let

$$\Sigma(n) = \{O^e \mid O \in V(n) \cup C(n), e \in \{\exists, \#\}\},$$

where $V(n) = \{V_u \mid u \in Var_n \cup \{\downarrow\}\}$ and $C(n) = \{C_{\mathcal{C}} \mid \mathcal{C} \in \mathcal{N}(n)\}$. Then the encoding of φ is $cod(\varphi) = \{O_{\mathcal{C}}^{\exists} \in \Sigma(n) \mid \mathcal{C} \in \varphi\} \cup \{O_{\mathcal{C}}^{\#} \in \Sigma(n) \mid \mathcal{C} \notin \varphi\} \cup \{V_{\downarrow}^{\#}\}$. That is, for an object $O_{\mathcal{C}}^e$ ($\mathcal{C} \in Var_n \cup \mathcal{N}(n), e \in \{\exists, \#\}$), if $O = C$, then this object corresponds to a clause having exactly two negative literals, while if $O = V$, then it corresponds to a positive unit clause. Consider, for example, $\varphi = x \wedge (\neg x \vee \neg y)$, where $x, y \in Var_2$. Then $cod(\varphi) = \{V_x^{\exists}, V_y^{\#}, V_{\downarrow}^{\#}, C_{xy \to \downarrow}^{\exists}\}$. We note here that there is no need to distinguish in the notation between positive unite clauses and clauses having exactly two negative literals. Nevertheless, we decided to do so to improve the readability of the constructions. Since the size of φ is clearly polynomial in n, it can be seen that cod is a function in **L**.

A Solution Using Send-Out Communication Rules Only.

Here we solve HORN3SATNORM with a family $\mathbf{\Pi_1} = \{\Pi_1(n)\}_{n \in \mathbb{N}}$ of recognizer P systems

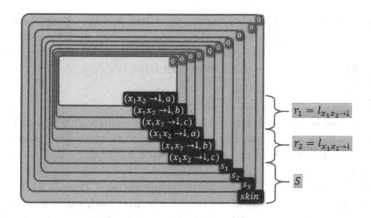

Fig. 1. The initial membrane structure of $\Pi_1(2)$

of type $\mathcal{AM}_{+out}$, where $\Pi_1(n) = (\Gamma(n), H(n), \mu(n), W(n), R(n))$ is defined as follows:

- $\Gamma(n) = \Sigma(n) \cup \{V_x^{\exists+} \mid x \in Var_n \cup \{\downarrow\}\} \cup \{yes, no\}$.
- $H(n) = \{(\mathcal{C}, \alpha) \mid \mathcal{C} \in \mathcal{N}(n), \alpha \in \{a, b, c\}\} \cup \{s_k \mid k \in [m+n]\} \cup \{skin\}$.
- $\mu(n) = S[r_n[r_{n-1}[\ldots r_2[r_1]\ldots]]]$, where $S = [[[\ ]_{s_1} \ldots]_{s_{m+n}}]_{skin}$ and, for every $i \in [n]$, r_i is a block defined as follows. $r_i = l_{c_m}[\ldots l_{c_2}[l_{c_1}]\ldots]$, where, for every $j \in [m]$, the layer l_{c_j} has the form $[[[\ ]_{(c_j,a)}]_{(c_j,b)}]_{(c_j,c)}$ (the initial structure of $\Pi_1(2)$ can be seen in Fig. 1; notice that in this case the only clause in $\mathcal{N}(2)$ is $x_1 x_2 \to \downarrow$).
- The input membrane is the innermost membrane in the initial membrane structure.
- $W(n)$ is the sequence of empty initial multisets.
- $R(n)$ consists of the following subsets of rules, where $xy \to u$ is a clause in $\mathcal{N}(n)$:
  (1) $[C_{xy \to u}^{\exists}]_{(xy \to u, a)}^{0} \to [\ ]_{(xy \to u, a)}^{+} C_{xy \to u}^{\exists}$,
  $[C_{xy \to u}^{\exists}]_{(xy \to u, \beta)}^{0} \to [\ ]_{(xy \to u, \beta)}^{0} C_{xy \to u}^{\exists}$,
  $[C_{xy \to u}^{\nexists}]_{(xy \to u, \alpha)}^{0} \to [\ ]_{(xy \to u, \alpha)}^{-} C_{xy \to u}^{\nexists}$ $(\alpha \in \{a, b, c\}, \beta \in \{b, c\})$.
  These rules are used to initialize the layers in the following sense: an object representing a clause in φ sets the charge of the first membrane in the corresponding layer to positive, and keeps the neutral charges of the second and third membranes in that layer, while an object representing a clause not in φ sets the charges of all membranes in the corresponding layer to negative.
  (2) $[\mathcal{O}]_{(xy \to u, \alpha)}^{-} \to [\ ]_{(xy \to u, \alpha)}^{-} \mathcal{O}$ $(\mathcal{O} \in \Sigma(n))$.
  Every membrane with negative charge lets all of the objects in $\Sigma(n)$ pass through itself.
  (3) $[V_x^{\exists}]_{(xy \to u, a)}^{+} \to [\ ]_{(xy \to u, a)}^{-} V_x^{\exists+}$,
  $[V_x^{\exists+}]_{(xy \to u, b)}^{0} \to [\ ]_{(xy \to u, b)}^{+} V_x^{\exists}$.

If a membrane with label $(xy \to u, a)$ has positive charge (notice that in this case φ must contain the clause $xy \to u$) and $V_x^{\exists}$ exists in this membrane, then these rules are used to store this information in the positive charge of the membrane with label $(xy \to u, b)$.

(4) $[V_y^{\exists}]_{(xy \to u,b)}^+ \to [\,]_{(xy \to u,b)}^- V_y^{\exists +}$,

$[V_y^{\exists +}]_{(xy \to u,c)}^0 \to [\,]_{(xy \to u,c)}^+ V_y^{\exists}$.

If the membrane with label $(xy \to u, b)$ has positive charge and $V_y^{\exists}$ exists in this membrane, then these rules are used to store this information in the positive charge of the membrane with label $(xy \to u, c)$.

(5) $[V_u^{\not\exists}]_{(xy \to u,c)}^+ \to [\,]_{(xy \to u,c)}^- V_u^{\exists}$.

The positive charge of the membrane with label $(xy \to u, c)$ indicates that $xy \to u$ is a clause of the system and that both variables x and y has to be *true* in an interpretation in order to make φ *true*. Thus, with this rule the system rewrites $V_u^{\not\exists}$ to $V_u^{\exists}$ indicating that u must be also *true* to make φ *true*.

(6) $[V_u^{\exists}]_{(xy \to u,\alpha)}^p \to [\,]_{(xy \to u,\alpha)}^- V_u^{\exists}$ $(p \in \{+, 0\}, \alpha \in \{a, b, c\})$.

If the system already knows that u must be *true* to make φ *true*, then the charges of the corresponding membranes are set to negative by these rules.

(7) $[V_x^{\not\exists}]_{(xy \to u,\alpha)}^p \to [\,]_{(xy \to u,\alpha)}^- V_x^{\not\exists}$,

$[V_y^{\not\exists}]_{(xy \to u,\alpha)}^p \to [\,]_{(xy \to u,\alpha)}^- V_y^{\not\exists}$ $(p \in \{+, 0\}, \alpha \in \{a, b, c\})$.

If any of the variables on the left-hand side of a clause $xy \to u$ is not considered to be *true* yet, then the charges of membranes of the corresponding layer are set to negative by these rules; in this way $V_u^{\exists}$ cannot be introduced in this layer by the rule in (5).

(8) $[V_{\downarrow}^e]_{s_k}^0 \to [\,]_{s_k}^0 V_{\downarrow}^e$, $[V_{\downarrow}^{\exists}]_{skin}^0 \to [\,]_{skin}^0 no$, $[V_{\downarrow}^{\not\exists}]_{skin}^0 \to [\,]_{skin}^0 yes$

$(k \in [m + n], e \in \{\exists, \not\exists\})$.

The first rule is used to move object $V_{\downarrow}^{\exists}$ or $V_{\downarrow}^{\not\exists}$ towards the skin membrane. When they arrive at the skin, the system sends to the environment the correct answer.

Correctness, Running Time, and $(\mathbf{L}, \mathbf{L})$-*uniformity.* First we observe that during the computation of $\Pi_1(n)$ the following holds.

1. If all the membranes in a layer l have negative charge, then l does not contribute to the computation, i.e. all objects pass through the membranes of l without any change.
2. For every $\mathcal{C} \in \mathcal{N}(n)$, either $C_{\mathcal{C}}^{\exists}$ or $C_{\mathcal{C}}^{\not\exists}$ (but not both) occurs in the system (the same object during the whole computation).
3. For every $x \in Var_n \cup \{\downarrow\}$, exactly one of $V_x^{\exists}$, $V_x^{\exists +}$ or $V_x^{\not\exists}$ occurs in the system (not counting the last configuration, where $V_{\downarrow}^{\exists}$ (resp. $V_{\downarrow}^{\not\exists}$) is already rewritten to no (resp. yes)). Indeed, the rules that can change an object of this form before the last step are rules in (3)–(5). Rules in (3) (resp. in (4)) change $V_x^{\exists}$ to $V_x^{\exists +}$ (resp. $V_y^{\exists}$ to $V_y^{\exists +}$) and $V_x^{\exists +}$ to $V_x^{\exists}$ (resp. $V_y^{\exists +}$ to $V_y^{\exists}$). Rules in (5) remove $V_u^{\not\exists}$ and introduce $V_u^{\exists}$. Thus the observation remains true after applying these rules.

4. If an object $V_x^{\exists}$ occurs in the systems, then $V_x^{\not\exists}$ will not be introduced during the computation.

Now consider a layer $l_{xy \to u}$ for some $xy \to u \in \mathcal{N}(n)$. For every object in $\Gamma \setminus \{yes, no\}$ passing through this layer the following holds.

5. $C_{xy \to u}^{\exists}$, $C_{xy \to u}^{\not\exists}$, $V_x^{\not\exists}$, $V_y^{\not\exists}$, and $V_u^{\exists}$ are unchanged (but they may change the polarizations of the membranes in the layer).
6. $V_x^{\exists}$ and $V_y^{\exists}$ can evolve only when the corresponding membrane's charge is positive (first rules in (3) and (4)). However, if they evolve, then the second rules in (3) and (4) will be applied in the next step.
7. $V_u^{\not\exists}$ can evolve to $V_u^{\exists}$ only when the corresponding membrane's charge is positive (rules in (5)).
8. Any other objects are unchanged (and they do not change any of the polarizations in the layer). Moreover, they can only pass through membranes with negative polarization in this layer.

Using these observations and also the comments given after the rules, the computation in the layer $l_{xy \to u}$ can be described as follows. At the beginning of the computation every membrane in $l_{xy \to u}$ has neutral charge. Now, according to the objects that occur in the system at the beginning of the computation in this layer we can distinguish the following two cases.

1. All of the objects $C_{xy \to u}^{\exists}$, $V_x^{\exists}$, $V_y^{\exists}$, and $V_u^{\not\exists}$ occur in the system. It can be seen that these objects can pass through the membranes of $l_{xy \to u}$ only in the above order (i.e., $C_{xy \to u}^{\exists}$ is the first one that leaves the layer, and $V_u^{\not\exists}$ is the last one). Thus, the last such step of a computation involving all the above objects must be the application of the rule in (5). That is, in this case the system rewrites $V_u^{\not\exists}$ to $V_u^{\exists}$.
2. Any of the objects $C_{xy \to u}^{\not\exists}$, $V_x^{\not\exists}$, $V_y^{\not\exists}$, or $V_u^{\exists}$ occurs in the system. Then by observations 2 and 3 above, the system cannot contain all of the objects $C_{xy \to u}^{\exists}$, $V_x^{\exists}$, $V_y^{\exists}$, and $V_u^{\not\exists}$. Thus, although a computation described in the previous case may start here as well, it cannot be completed. On the other hand, using any of the objects $C_{xy \to u}^{\not\exists}$, $V_x^{\not\exists}$, $V_y^{\not\exists}$, or $V_u^{\exists}$, the system can set the charge of every membrane in $l_{xy \to u}$ to negative. In this way the system can ignore this layer (see observation 1 above) and continue the computation in the next layer. (Notice that in this case the computation is not deterministic but confluent, i.e., all the possible computations in the layer yield the same result. For an example of such a computation see Fig. 2.)

As one can see from the above discussion, the objects passing through layer $l_{xy \to u}$ simulate step 5 of Algorithm H3SN. Thus, sending objects through a block corresponds to performing steps 4–5 of this algorithm. Since steps 4–5 are performed n times by the algorithm, the work of the P system in the n blocks corresponds to the work of the algorithm. Thus, $V_{\downarrow}^{\exists}$ or $V_{\downarrow}^{\not\exists}$ eventually appears in membrane s_1. In the next $m + n$ steps this object gets to the skin by rules in (8). There the system computes yes or no accordingly, which is then sent to the

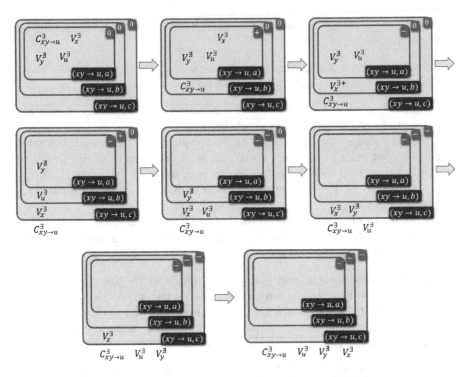

Fig. 2. One of the possible computations in a layer $l_{xy \to u}$ of $\Pi_1(n)$ when it contains $C^{\exists}_{xy \to u}$, $V^{\exists}_x$, $V^{\nexists}_y$, and $V^{\exists}_u$.

environment. It can be seen that during this computation all the other objects occurring in the system arrive to membrane s_1, and the computation halts.

This justifies the correctness of $\Pi_1(n)$. Since $\Pi_1(n)$ has polynomial number of objects in the initial configuration and no evolution rules are performed during its work, sending all the objects through a block takes polynomial steps. Thus the running time of $\Pi_1(n)$ is also polynomial.

It can be seen that all the ingredients of $\Pi_1(n)$ can be enumerated by a logarithmic space Turing machine. Thus, using Proposition 1, we get the following result.

Theorem 1. $\mathbf{P} \subseteq (\mathbf{L}, \mathbf{L}) - \mathbf{PMC}_{\mathcal{AM}_{+out}}$.

A Solution Using Elementary Membrane Division and Dissolution Rules Only. In this subsection we solve HORN3SATNORM with a family $\mathbf{\Pi_2} = \{\Pi_2(n)\}_{n \in \mathbb{N}}$ of recognizer P systems of type $\mathcal{AM}_{+e,+d}$. The solution is similar to the one given in the previous subsection, however, there is a substantial difference: here the presence of the necessary objects to simulate step 5 of Algorithm H3SN are checked by the application of membrane division rules. Consequently, those objects that do not take part in the simulation are duplicated several times. In particular, at certain points of the computation the P system has multiple copies of objects of the form $V_x^{\#}$. However, the correctness of the computation requires that at the beginning of the work in a layer there is at most one copy of these objects. Therefore we will apply special layers that will remove those objects that could cause the system to give incorrect results. The following is the formal definition of $\Pi_2(n) = (\Gamma(n), H(n), \mu(n), W(n), R(n))$:

- $\Gamma(n) = \Sigma(n) \cup \{w, \overline{w}_1, \overline{w}_2, \#, \$\} \cup \{yes, no\}$.
- $H(n) = \{skin, s\} \cup \{(\mathcal{C}, \alpha) \mid \mathcal{C} \in \mathcal{N}(n), \alpha \in \{a, b, c, d\}\} \cup \{d_O \mid O \in V(n) \cup C(n) \cup \{w\}\}$.
- $\mu(n)$ is defined as follows (see also Fig. 3). Let $\mathcal{C} = xy \rightarrow u$ be a clause in $\mathcal{N}(n)$ and $l_{\mathcal{C}}$ be the layer $D_{\mathcal{C}}[M_{\mathcal{C}}]$, where $D_{\mathcal{C}}$ and $M_{\mathcal{C}}$ are defined as follows:

$$M_{\mathcal{C}} = [[[[[[\ ]_{(\mathcal{C},a)}]_{(\mathcal{C},b)}]_{d_w}]_{(\mathcal{C},c)}]_{d_w}]_{(\mathcal{C},d)}$$

and $D_{\mathcal{C}}$ is a layer which, for every $O \in V(n) \cup C(n)$, contains the membrane $[\ ]_{d_O}$ once if $O = V_u$, and fifteen times, otherwise. Intuitively, $M_{\mathcal{C}}$ is that part

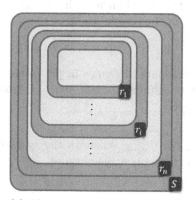

(a) The structure of the regions in $\Pi_2(n)$

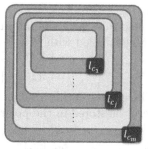

(b) The structure of the layers in a region r_i

(c) The structure of a layer l_{c_j}

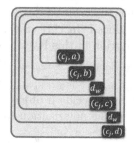

(d) The membranes in a layer M_{c_j}

Fig. 3. The initial membrane structure of $\Pi_2(n)$

of the layer which is responsible to simulate step 5 in Algorithm H3SN, and layer D_C is used (together with membranes with label d_w in M_C) to remove those objects that are produced by the used division rules, but should be removed in order to keep the behaviour of the system correct.

To finish the construction, let $\mu(n) = S[r_n[r_{n-1}[\ldots r_2[r_1]\ldots]]]$, where $S = [[\ ]_s]_{skin}$ and, for every $i \in [n]$, r_i is the block $l_{c_m}[\ldots l_{c_2}[l_{c_1}]\ldots]$.

- The input membrane is the innermost membrane in the initial membrane structure.
- $W(n)$ is a sequence of empty initial multisets.
- $R(n)$ consists of the following subsets of rules, where $xy \to u$ is a clause in $\mathcal{N}(n)$:

(1) $[V_u^{\not\exists}]^0_{(xy \to u,a)} \to [w]^-_{(xy \to u,a)}[\#]^-_{(xy \to u,a)}$,

$[V_u^\exists]^0_{(xy \to u,a)} \to [\overline{w}_1]^-_{(xy \to u,a)}[\#]^-_{(xy \to u,a)}$.

These rules are used to decide if $V_u^{\not\exists}$ or $V_u^\exists$ is present in a membrane with label $(xy \to u,a)$. If $V_u^{\not\exists}$ is present, then the system introduces w which indicates that the system should work further to decide if $V_u^\exists$ should be introduced or not. Object $\overline{w}_1$ indicates that $V_u^\exists$ is present in the system and thus it should not be introduced later. $\#$ indicates that the membrane containing it is not used effectively in the computation.

(2) $[w]^-_{(xy \to u,a)} \to w, [\overline{w}_1]^-_{(xy \to u,a)} \to \overline{w}_1$,

$[\#]^-_{(xy \to u,a)} \to \$$.

These rules pass the information computed by rules in (1) to the membrane labelled with $(xy \to u,b)$. $\$$ is a dummy object not used later.

(3) $[C^\exists_{xy \to u}]^0_{(xy \to u,b)} \to [C^\exists_{xy \to u}]^+_{(xy \to u,b)}[C^\exists_{xy \to u}]^+_{(xy \to u,b)}$,

$[C^{\not\exists}_{xy \to u}]^0_{(xy \to u,b)} \to [C^{\not\exists}_{xy \to u}]^-_{(xy \to u,b)}[C^{\not\exists}_{xy \to u}]^-_{(xy \to u,b)}$.

These rules decide if object $C^\exists_{xy \to u}$ or $C^{\not\exists}_{xy \to u}$ exists in the system. The result is stored in the polarizations of the new membranes.

(4) $[w]^+_{(xy \to u,b)} \to w, [w]^-_{(xy \to u,b)} \to \overline{w}_2$,

$[\overline{w}_1]^+_{(xy \to u,b)} \to \overline{w}_1, [\overline{w}_1]^-_{(xy \to u,b)} \to \overline{w}_1$.

These rules introduce objects that will control the computation according to the information computed by the previous subsets of rules. For example, if w and $C^{\not\exists}_{xy \to u}$ is present in the inner membrane, then $\overline{w}_2$ is introduced. In this case $V_u^\exists$ will not be introduced at the end of the computation in this layer (see rules in (8)).

(5) $[V_y^\exists]^0_{(xy \to u,c)} \to [V_y^\exists]^+_{(xy \to u,c)}[V_y^\exists]^+_{(xy \to u,c)}$,

$[V_y^{\not\exists}]^0_{(xy \to u,c)} \to [V_y^{\not\exists}]^-_{(xy \to u,c)}[V_y^{\not\exists}]^-_{(xy \to u,c)}$.

These rules decide if object $V_y^\exists$ or $V_y^{\not\exists}$ exists in the system. The result is stored in the polarizations of the new membranes.

(6) $[w]^+_{(xy \to u,c)} \to w, [w]^-_{(xy \to u,c)} \to \overline{w}_2$,

$[\overline{w}_1]^+_{(xy \to u,c)} \to \overline{w}_1, [\overline{w}_1]^-_{(xy \to u,c)} \to \overline{w}_1$,

$[\overline{w}_2]^+_{(xy \to u,c)} \to \overline{w}_2, [\overline{w}_2]^-_{(xy \to u,c)} \to \overline{w}_2$.

These rules introduce objects that will control the computation according to the information computed by the previous subset of rules.

(7) $[V_x^{\exists}]^0_{(xy \to u,d)} \to [V_x^{\exists}]^+_{(xy \to u,d)} [V_x^{\exists}]^+_{(xy \to u,d)}$,

$[V_x^{\nexists}]^0_{(xy \to u,d)} \to [V_x^{\nexists}]^-_{(xy \to u,d)} [V_x^{\nexists}]^-_{(xy \to u,d)}$.

These rules decide if object $V_x^{\exists}$ or $V_x^{\nexists}$ exists in the system. The result is stored in the polarizations of the new membranes.

(8) $[w]^+_{(xy \to u,d)} \to V_u^{\exists}, [w]^-_{(xy \to u,d)} \to V_u^{\nexists}$,

$[\overline{w}_1]^+_{(xy \to u,d)} \to V_u^{\exists}, [\overline{w}_1]^-_{(xy \to u,d)} \to V_u^{\exists}$

$[\overline{w}_2]^+_{(xy \to u,d)} \to V_u^{\nexists}, [\overline{w}_2]^-_{(xy \to u,d)} \to V_u^{\exists}$.

These rules are used to handle the different cases of possible computations in a layer. For example, w indicates that at the beginning of the computation in a layer the system contained objects $V_u^{\nexists}$, $C_{xy \to u}^{\exists}$, and $V_y^{\exists}$.

(9) $[O^e]^0_{d_O} \to \$, [w]^0_{d_w} \to \$, [\overline{w}_i]^0_{d_w} \to \$$

$(O \in V(n) \cup C(n), e \in \{\exists, \nexists\}, i \in [2])$.

These rules are used to remove certain objects from the system.

(10) $[V_{\downarrow}^{\nexists}]^0_s \to [no]^-_s [\$]^-_s, [V_{\downarrow}^{\exists}]^0_s \to [yes]^-_s [\$]^-_s, [\kappa]^-_s \to \kappa \quad (\kappa \in \{yes, no\})$.

These rules are used to introduce the computed answer in the skin membrane.

Correctness, Running Time, and $(\mathbf{L}, \mathbf{L})$-*uniformity.* First we observe that during the computation of $\Pi_2(n)$ the following holds.

1. The membrane structure has the form $[\dots [M]_{h_1} \dots]_{h_k}$ $(h_1, \dots, h_k \in H(n))$, where M is either a membrane or it is of the form $[\ ]_{g_1} [\ ]_{g_2}$ $(g_1, g_2 \in H(n))$, and
2. Objects occur only in the innermost membranes.

The correctness of the system follows from the following lemma.

Lemma 1. *Let* $C = xy \to u$ *be a clause in* $\mathcal{N}(n)$ *and consider the layer* $l_C = D_C[M_C]$. *Assume that, for every* $O \in C(n) \cup V(n)$, *either one copy of* $O^{\exists}$ *or one copy of* $O^{\nexists}$ *occurs in* l_C. *Let* $\mathcal{O}$ *be an object in* l_C. *Then the following holds:*

1. *If* $\mathcal{O} \in \Sigma(n) - \{V_u^{\nexists}\}$, *then after dissolving all the membranes in* l_C, $\Pi_2(n)$ *contains exactly one copy of* $\mathcal{O}$.
2. *If* $\mathcal{O} = V_u^{\nexists}$ *and* l_C *contains all of the objects* $C_C^{\exists}$, $V_x^{\exists}$, *and* $V_y^{\exists}$, *then after dissolving all the membranes in* l_C, $\Pi_2(n)$ *contains no* $V_u^{\nexists}$ *and exactly one copy of* $V_u^{\exists}$.
3. *If* $\mathcal{O} = V_u^{\nexists}$ *and* l_C *contains* $C_C^{\nexists}$, $V_x^{\nexists}$, *or* $V_y^{\nexists}$, *then after the work in* l_C $\Pi_2(n)$ *contains exactly one copy of* $V_u^{\nexists}$.

Proof. By assumption, l_C contains exactly one copy of $\mathcal{O}$. Then Statement 1 can be seen by distinguishing the following two sub-cases:

Case 1. $\mathcal{O} \neq V_u^{\exists}$. Then during the work in M_C, O is duplicated by the corresponding rules in (1), (3), (5), and (7), and the other rules are not applied to $\mathcal{O}$ in M_C. This yields sixteen copies of $\mathcal{O}$ in D_C. Out of these copies fifteen ones are removed during the computation in D_C.

Case 2. $\mathcal{O} = V_u^{\exists}$. Then the second rule in (1) removes first $V_u^{\exists}$ and introduces one copy of $\overline{w}_1$. After this, the membrane with label $(\mathcal{C}, a)$ is dissolved using rules in (2). In the next two steps, $\overline{w}_1$ is duplicated first due the division of membrane $(\mathcal{C}, b)$ by rules in (3), then the yielded membranes are dissolved by rules in (4). Thus, at this point of the computation two copies of $\overline{w}_1$ are in membrane d_w. However, in the next step one copy is removed due to the corresponding rule in (9). After this, membrane $(\mathcal{C}, c)$ is divided (rules in (5)) and the new membranes are dissolved (rules in (6)). At this point, two copies of $\overline{w}_1$ are in membrane d_w, and one copy is removed by the corresponding rule in (9). Finally, $\overline{w}_1$ is duplicated by rules in (7), and then the two copies of $\overline{w}_1$ introduce two copies of $V_u^{\exists}$. During the dissolution of membranes in $D_{\mathcal{C}}$ one copy of $V_u^{\exists}$ is removed which proves the statement.

Statement 2 can be seen as follows. The computation starts with removing the object $V_u^{\nexists}$ and introducing one w (first rule in (1)). Then the new membranes with label $(\mathcal{C}, a)$ are dissolved by the corresponding rules in (2). In membrane $(\mathcal{C}, b)$ the first rule of (3) is applied and thus w is duplicated. At this point membranes with label $(\mathcal{C}, b)$ have positive charges, thus only the first rule in (4) can be applied. After this the corresponding rule in (9) removes one copy of w. During the next step the first rule in (5) is applied, and then only the first rule in (6) can be used. Again, one copy of w is removed by the corresponding rule in (9). Then the first rule in (7) divides membrane $(\mathcal{C}, d)$, w is again duplicated, and by the first rule in (8) each w introduces one copy of $V_u^{\exists}$. During the work in $D_{\mathcal{C}}$, one copy of $V_u^{\exists}$ is removed.

The system has several different computations in the case of Statement 3. We discuss here only one of them, the remaining ones can be treated similarly. Assume for example that $l_{\mathcal{C}}$ contains $C_{\mathcal{C}}^{\exists}$ and $V_y^{\nexists}$. Then the computation goes in the same way as in the case of Statement 2 until the application of the corresponding dissolution rules in (4). But then the second rule in (5) is applied, and thus, in the next step, only the second rule in (6) can be applied. Therefore here two copies of $\overline{w}_2$ are introduced. Then the computation continues similarly as in Case 2 in the proof of Statement 1. However here, when rules from (8) are applied the system has two copies of $\overline{w}_2$, and thus two copies of $V_u^{\nexists}$ are introduced by the fifth and sixth rules in (8). One of these copies is eliminated during the work in $D_{\mathcal{C}}$. □

By definition, the initial configuration of $\Pi_2(n)$ satisfies the conditions of Lemma 1. Then, by the iterated application of this lemma, we get that the computation in a layer $l_{\mathcal{C}}$ in a block r_k ($k \in [n]$) corresponds to the step 5 of Algorithm H3SN when $i = k$ and $c_j = \mathcal{C}$. Therefore, the whole computation of $\Pi_2(n)$ corresponds to the complete work of this algorithm. This justifies the correctness of $\Pi_2(n)$.

Since $\Pi_2(n)$ has polynomial number of membranes in layer $l_{\mathcal{C}}$, and in $l_{\mathcal{C}}$ the number of the applied division rules is constant, we have that dissolving all the membranes in $l_{\mathcal{C}}$ takes polynomial time. As in the initial configuration there are n blocks and each block has polynomial number of layers, it follows that the running time of $\Pi_2(n)$ is also polynomial.

Finally, it can be seen that all the ingredients of $\Pi_2(n)$ can be enumerated by a logarithmic space Turing machine. This, using Proposition 1 yields the following theorem.

Theorem 2. $\mathbf{P} \subseteq (\mathbf{L}, \mathbf{L}) - \mathbf{PMC}_{\mathcal{AM}_{+e,+d}}.$

3.2 Simulating Turing Machines

Here we show that, for every polynomial time Turing machine M, an $(\mathbf{L}, \mathbf{L})$-uniform family Π_3 of polarizationless recognizer P systems can be constructed such that the members of Π_3 can simulate the work of M efficiently using only dissolution and unit rules.

Let $M = (Q, \Sigma, \Gamma, \delta, q_0, q_a, q_r)$ be an $f(n)$-time Turing machine, for some polynomial $f(n)$. Notice that M can use at most $f(n)$ cells of its tape during its computations. Let $k = |Q|$ and $m = |\Gamma|$. Assume that $Q = \{s_1, \ldots, s_k\}$, where $s_1 = q_0, s_{k-1} = q_a$ and $s_k = q_r$. Likewise, assume that $\Gamma = \{X_1, \ldots, X_m\}$, where $X_m = \sqcup$. The idea of the simulation is the following. The initial membrane structure μ is a composition of $f(n)+1$ blocks (see Fig. 4). The input membrane is the innermost membrane. During the simulation of the tth step of M, the objects in the innermost membrane will dissolve all the membranes in the tth block as follows. Assume that after $t - 1$ steps M is in state s_i ($i \in [k - 2]$), the position of the head is p, and the head scans X_j. Then the innermost membrane of the tth block contains an object O that represents s_i and p, and another object O' representing X_j on the pth position of the tape. The blocks are composed of $k \cdot m \cdot f(n)$ membranes (that is, in every block, for every state–tape symbol–position triple there is a corresponding membrane). During the simulation of the tth step of M, O dissolves all the membranes that correspond to a state $s_{i'}$ with $i' < i$ or a position $p' < p$. Meanwhile O' evolves using a counter and at the appropriate time step it starts to dissolve all the membranes corresponding to

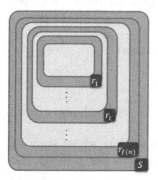

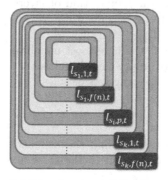

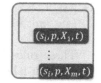

(a) The structure of the regions in $\Pi_3(n)$ (b) The structure of the layers in a region r_i (c) The membranes in a layer $l_{s_i,p,t}$

Fig. 4. The initial membrane structure of $\Pi_3(n)$

s_i, p, and tape symbol $X_{j'}$ with $j' < j$. After this the simulation of one step of M is performed using the value $\delta(s_i, X_j)$. Then the remaining membranes in the tth block are dissolved, and the system continues with the simulation of the next step of M.

Construction of the P System. The uniform family of P systems that will perform the above described simulation is defined as follows. Let $w = a_1 \ldots a_n$ be an input of M ($a_1, \ldots, a_n \in \Sigma$) and $N = f(n) \cdot k \cdot m$. Let $cod(w)$ be a multiset over the alphabet

$$\Sigma(n) = \{(X_j, p, t)^{(c)}, (s_i, p, t)^{(c')} \mid$$
$$j \in [m], i \in [k], p \in [f(n)], t \in [0, f(n)], c \in [0, N], c' \in [0, N + m]\}$$

defined as follows: $cod(w) = \{(a_1, 1, 0)^{(0)}, \ldots, (a_n, n, 0)^{(0)}\} \cup \{(\sqcup, n + 1, 0)^{(0)}, \ldots, (\sqcup, f(n), 0)^{(0)}\} \cup (s_1, 1, 0)^{(0)}$. Intuitively, an object $(X_j, p, t)^{(c)}$ in $\Sigma(n)$ represents the fact that after t steps M has X_j on the pth position of its tape. We call these objects *position objects*. Similarly, an object $(s_i, p, t)^{(c')}$ represents the fact that after t steps M is in state s_i and the head points to the pth position of the tape. We call these objects *state objects*. The indexes c, c' are counters used for technical reasons. It can be seen that $cod \in \mathbf{L}$.

Let $\mathbf{\Pi_3} = \{\Pi_3(n)\}_{n \in \mathbb{N}}$ be a uniform family of P systems, where $\Pi_3(n) = (\Gamma(n), H(n), \mu(n), W(n), R(n))$ is defined as follows:

- $\Gamma(n) = \Sigma(n) \cup \{yes, no\}$.
- $H(n) = \{(s_i, p, X_j, t) \mid i \in [k], p, t \in [f(n)], j \in [m]\}$.
  Intuitively, a label (s_i, p, X_j, t) corresponds to the following configuration of M after t steps on w: the current state is s_i, the position of the head is p, and the scanned symbol is X_j. We will often call s_i, p, and t the *state*, *position*, and *time* labels of the corresponding membrane, respectively.
- $\mu(n)$ is a composition $S[r_{f(n)}[\ldots [r_1]]]$ of blocks, where $S = [\ ]_{skin}$, and a block r_t ($t \in [f(n)]$) is a composition of layers defined as follows. For every $i \in [k]$ and $p \in [f(n)]$, let $l_{s_i, p, t} = [\ldots [\ ]_{(s_i, p, X_1, t)} \cdots]_{(s_i, p, X_m, t)}$, and let $r_t = l_{s_k, f(n), t}[\cdots [l_{s_k, 1, t}[\cdots [l_{s_1, f(n), t}[\cdots [l_{s_1, 1, t} \cdots]] \cdots]] \cdots]$ (see also Fig. 4).
- The input membrane is the innermost membrane in $\mu(n)$.
- $W(n)$ is a sequence of empty initial multisets.
- $R(n)$ consists of the following sets of rules:
  (1) $[(s_i, p, t)^{(0)}]_{(s_{i'}, p', X_j, t+1)} \rightarrow (s_i, p, t)^{(0)}$
  ($j \in [m]$, $i \in [k - 2]$, $i' \in [k]$, $p, p' \in [f(n)]$, $t \in [0, f(n) - 1]$, and $i' < i$ or $p' < p$).
  These rules are used to find the first such membrane whose state and position labels correspond to the state and position stored in the state object.
  (2) $[(X_j, p, t)^{(c)} \rightarrow (X_j, p, t)^{(c+1)}]_{(s_i, p', X_{j'}, t+1)}$
  ($j, j' \in [m]$, $i \in [k]$, $p, p' \in [f(n)]$, $t \in [0, f(n) - 1]$, $c \in [0, N - 1]$).
  These rules are used to increment the counter c in the position objects. When this counter equals to N, the system can start to use rules in (3).

(3) $[(X_j, p, t)^{(N)}]_{(s_i, p, X_l, t+1)} \to (X_j, p, t)^{(N)}$,

$[(X_j, p, t)^{(N)} \to (X_{j'}, p, t+1)^{(0)}]_{(s_i, p, X_j, t+1)}$,

$[(X_j, p', t)^{(N)} \to (X_j, p', t+1)^{(0)}]_{(s_i, p, X_l, t+1)}$

$(j, l \in [m], l < j, i \in [k-2], p, p' \in [f(n)], p \neq p', t \in [0, f(n) - 1]$, and $X_{j'} = \mathrm{proj}_2(\delta(s_i, X_j)))$.

If the position stored in an object $(X_j, p, t)^{(N)}$ corresponds to the position label of the current membrane, then this object starts to dissolve the membranes until a membrane whose label stores X_j is found. When this membrane is found, $(X_j, p, t)^{(N)}$ evolves according to the value of $\delta(s_i, X_j)$, its counter is reset, and its component t is incremented. Those position objects that store a different position than the position label of the current membrane evolve immediately such that their counter is reset and their component t is incremented. Notice that after performing the computations by these rules, the position objects have no impact on the computation in block r_{t+1}.

(4) $[(s_i, p, t)^{(c)} \to (s_i, p, t)^{(c+1)}]_{(s_i, p, X_l, t+1)}$,

$[(s_i, p, t)^{(N+m)} \to (s_{i'}, p', t+1)^{(0)}]_{(s_i, p, X_l, t+1)}$

$(i \in [k-2], i' \in [k], p \in [f(n)], t \in [0, f(n) - 1], c \in [N+m-1], l \in [m],$

$s_{i'} = \mathrm{proj}_1(\delta(s_i, X_l)), p' = \max\{p + \mathrm{proj}_3(\delta(s_i, X_l)), 1\})$.

The counter of the state object is incremented using the first rule. Until this counter reaches $N + m$, the appropriate position object can find the corresponding membrane using rules in (3). Then the state object evolves according to the value of the transition function of M. Moreover, its counter is reset and its component t is incremented.

(5) $[(s_i, p, t+1)^{(0)}]_{(s_{i'}, p', X_j, t+1)} \to (s_i, p, t+1)^{(0)}$

$(i \in [k-2], i' \in [k], p, p' \in [f(n)], j \in [m], t \in [0, f(n) - 1])$.

After simulating a step of M using rules in (1)–(4), the remaining membranes in block r_{t+1} are dissolved by these rules.

(6) $[(s_{k-1}, p, t)^{(0)} \to yes]_h$, $[(s_k, p, t)^{(0)} \to no]_h$,

$[yes]_{h'} \to yes$, and $[no]_{h'} \to no$

$(p, t \in [f(n)], h \in H(n), h' \in H(n) - \{skin\})$.

These rules are used to produce the answer of $\Pi_3(n)$ according to which halting state is reached by M on the input.

Correctness, Running Time, and (**L, L**)*-uniformity.* Let $w = a_1 \ldots a_n$ be an input of M $(a_1, \ldots, a_n \in \Sigma)$. We show that $\Pi_3(n)$ produces *yes* started with $cod(w)$ in its input membrane if and only if $w \in L(M)$. The work of $\Pi_3(n)$ can be described as follows. Initially, the object $(s_1, 1, 0)^{(0)}$ (representing that M starts its work in its initial state and the head is positioned to the first letter of the input) is in the innermost membrane of block r_1. Now assume that $\Pi_3(n)$ has already simulated t steps of M, that is, the innermost membrane of $\Pi_3(n)$ is the most deeply nested membrane of block r_{t+1}, and this membrane contains an object $(s_i, p, t)^{(0)}$, for some $i \in [k]$ and $p \in [f(n)]$ (see Fig. 5). If $i \in [k-1, k]$, i.e., M has reached one of its halting states, then $\Pi_3(n)$, using rules in (6) computes the answer of the system accordingly. Otherwise, rules from (1) are applied until

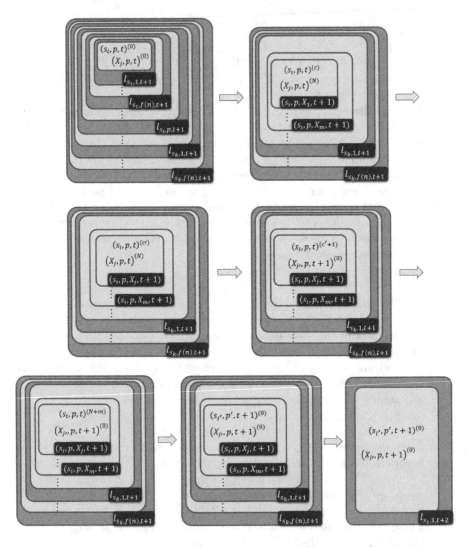

Fig. 5. Simulating the $(t + 1)$th step of a TM by $\Pi_3(n)$ (c and c' are appropriate counters in $[N + m]$)

a membrane with label $(s_i, p, X_1, t + 1)$ is reached. Meanwhile, the counter c in position objects is incremented using rules in (2). By the time this counter becomes N, the corresponding membrane is reached by the rules in (1). Now those position objects that store different positions than p evolve by the third rule in (3) to such objects that will be used next time only in the next block r_{t+2} (i.e., in the simulation of the next step of M).

Concerning the position object storing p, assume that this object is $(X_j, p, t)^{(N)}$. Then $(X_j, p, t)^{(N)}$ is used to find that membrane in layer $l_{s_i, p, t+1}$ whose label contains X_j. When this membrane is found, $(X_j, p, t)^{(N)}$ evolves according to the transition function of M. Moreover, its counter is reset and its time component is incremented. Thus this object is not used any more in this block.

Meanwhile, rules in (4) are used to increment the counter c of $(s_i, p, t)^{(c)}$. By the time this counter becomes $N + m$, the position object $(X_j, p, t)^{(N)}$ has reached the membrane it searched for. Now the second rule in (4) is used to produce object $(s_{i'}, p', t + 1)^{(0)}$ where $s_{i'}$ and p' are calculated according to the transition function of M. Finally, $(s_{i'}, p', t+1)^{(0)}$ is used to dissolve the remaining membranes of r_{t+1}. If this is done, the system is ready to simulate the next step of M. With this we have seen that $\Pi_3(n)$ simulates correctly the computation of M on w^1.

It can be seen that dissolving a block in the membrane structure takes $O(N)$ steps and $N = O(f(n))$. Moreover, $\Pi_3(n)$ has $f(n)$ blocks. Thus the running time of the system is $O(f^2(n))$, that is, polynomial in n. The $(\mathbf{L}, \mathbf{L})$-uniformity of Π_3 follows from the observation that the size of $\Pi_3(n)$ is also polynomial in n. Thus we have the following result.

Theorem 3. $\mathbf{P} \subseteq (\mathbf{L}, \mathbf{L}) - \mathbf{PMC}_{\mathcal{AM}^0_{+u, +d}}$.

As we have observed on page 16, our solution of HORN3SATNORM by P systems of type $\mathcal{AM}_{+e, +d}$ is such that the number of membranes occurring on the same level in the membrane structure is at most two during the whole computation of the system. Let k be a fixed positive integer. We say that a P system Π is k-bounded, if the number of membranes occurring on the same level in the membrane structure is at most k in every configuration of each computation of Π. For a type $\mathcal{F}$ of P systems, denote $(\mathbf{L}, \mathbf{L}) - \mathbf{PMC}_{\mathcal{F}_{\leq k}}$ the set of those problems that can be decided in polynomial time by such $(\mathbf{L}, \mathbf{L})$-uniform families of P systems of type $\mathcal{F}$ which have k-bounded members only. Denote $\mathcal{AM}_{-e}$ those P systems with active membranes that do not employ membrane division rules. It was shown in [31] that $\mathbf{PMC}_{\mathcal{AM}_{-e}} \subseteq \mathbf{P}$. It can be seen by the generalization of the proof of this result that $(\mathbf{L}, \mathbf{L}) - \mathbf{PMC}_{\mathcal{AM}_{\leq 2}} \subseteq \mathbf{P}$ also holds. Using these and the results obtained in the paper we can give the following new characterizations of $\mathbf{P}$.

Corollary 1. $\mathbf{P} = (\mathbf{L}, \mathbf{L}) - \mathbf{PMC}_{\mathcal{AM}_{+out}} = (\mathbf{L}, \mathbf{L}) - \mathbf{PMC}_{\mathcal{AM}_{+e, +d, \leq 2}} = (\mathbf{L}, \mathbf{L}) - \mathbf{PMC}_{\mathcal{AM}^0_{+u, +d}}$.

---

[1] As we have seen, the main idea in the proof is to use dissolution and object evolution rules to pass information from the state objects to the position objects, and vice versa. According to a clever idea appearing in one of the referee reports on a previous version of this paper, this cooperation could be implemented using only a constant number of cells per blocks in the initial membrane structure.

4   Conclusions

In this paper we have shown that uniform families of the following restricted variants of P systems with active membranes can solve all problems in **P**: (1) P systems where only send-out communication rules are used, (2) P systems where only elementary membrane division and dissolution rules are used, and (3) polarizationless P systems where only dissolution and unit rules are used. Using the obtained results concerning variants (1) and (3), and known results about the upper bound on the power of these variants we could give new characterizations of **P** in terms of Membrane Computing techniques.

It remained an open question if the variant (2) could solve problems outside of **P**. It is known that this is not possible if the polarizations of the membranes are not used and the initial membrane structure is a linearly nested sequence of membranes [30]. It fact, giving a solution of a **P**-complete problem with variant (2) when polarizations are not allowed seems to be a challenging task. Nevertheless, we could give another characterization of **P** using variant (2) where we made a simple semantic restriction on the computations of this variant.

References

1. Alhazov, A., Martín-Vide, C., Pan, L.: Solving a PSPACE-complete problem by P systems with restricted active membranes. Fundamenta Informaticae **58**, 67–77 (2003)
2. Alhazov, A., Pan, L., Păun, G.: Trading polarizations for labels in P systems with active membranes. Acta Inf. **41**(2–3), 111–144 (2004)
3. Gazdag, Z.: Solving SAT by P systems with active membranes in linear time in the number of variables. In: Alhazov, A., Cojocaru, S., Gheorghe, M., Rogozhin, Y., Rozenberg, G., Salomaa, A. (eds.) CMC 2013. LNCS, vol. 8340, pp. 189–205. Springer, Heidelberg (2014). doi:10.1007/978-3-642-54239-8_14
4. Gazdag, Z., Kolonits, G.: A new approach for solving SAT by P systems with active membranes. In: Csuhaj-Varjú, E., Gheorghe, M., Rozenberg, G., Salomaa, A., Vaszil, G. (eds.) CMC 2012. LNCS, vol. 7762, pp. 195–207. Springer, Heidelberg (2013). doi:10.1007/978-3-642-36751-9_14
5. Gazdag, Z., Gutiérrez-Naranjo, M.A.: Solving the ST-connectivity problem with pure membrane computing techniques. In: Gheorghe, M., Rozenberg, G., Salomaa, A., Sosík, P., Zandron, C. (eds.) CMC 2014. LNCS, vol. 8961, pp. 215–228. Springer, Heidelberg (2014). doi:10.1007/978-3-319-14370-5_13
6. Gazdag, Z., Kolonits, G., Gutiérrez-Naranjo, M.A.: Simulating turing machines with polarizationless P systems with active membranes. In: Gheorghe, M., Rozenberg, G., Salomaa, A., Sosík, P., Zandron, C. (eds.) CMC 2014. LNCS, vol. 8961, pp. 229–240. Springer, Heidelberg (2014). doi:10.1007/978-3-319-14370-5_14
7. Gensler, H.J.: Introduction to Logic. Routledge, London (2002)
8. Gutiérrez–Naranjo, M.A., Pérez–Jiménez, M.J., Riscos–Núñez, A., Romero–Campero, F.J.: On the power of dissolution in P systems with active membranes. In: Freund, R., Păun, G., Rozenberg, G., Salomaa, A. (eds.) WMC 2005. LNCS, vol. 3850, pp. 224–240. Springer, Heidelberg (2006). doi:10.1007/11603047_16

9. Kolonits, G.: A solution of Horn-SAT with P systems using antimatter. In: Rozenberg, G., Salomaa, A., Sempere, J.M., Zandron, C. (eds.) CMC 2015. LNCS, vol. 9504, pp. 236–250. Springer, Heidelberg (2015). doi:10.1007/978-3-319-28475-0_16

10. Krishna, S.N., Rama, R.: A variant of P systems with active membranes: solving NP-complete problems. Rom. J. Inf. Sci. Technol. **2**(4), 357–367 (1999)

11. Murphy, N.: Uniformity conditions for membrane systems: uncovering complexity below P. Ph.D. thesis, National University of Ireland, Maynooth (2010)

12. Murphy, N., Woods, D.: Active membrane systems without charges and using only symmetric elementary division characterise P. In: Eleftherakis, G., Kefalas, P., Păun, G., Rozenberg, G., Salomaa, A. (eds.) WMC 2007. LNCS, vol. 4860, pp. 367–384. Springer, Heidelberg (2007). doi:10.1007/978-3-540-77312-2_23

13. Murphy, N., Woods, D.: A characterisation of NL using membrane systems without charges and dissolution. In: Calude, C.S., Costa, J.F., Freund, R., Oswald, M., Rozenberg, G. (eds.) UC 2008. LNCS, vol. 5204, pp. 164–176. Springer, Heidelberg (2008). doi:10.1007/978-3-540-85194-3_14

14. Murphy, N., Woods, D.: On acceptance conditions for membrane systems: characterisations of **L** and **NL**. In: Neary, T., Woods, D., Seda, T., Murphy, N. (eds.) Proceedings International Workshop on the Complexity of Simple Programs. Electronic Proceedings in Theoretical Computer Science, Cork, Ireland, vol. 1, pp. 172–184. Open Publishing Association (2009)

15. Murphy, N., Woods, D.: The computational power of membrane systems under tight uniformity conditions. Nat. Comput. **10**(1), 613–632 (2011)

16. Murphy, N., Woods, D.: Uniformity is weaker than semi-uniformity for some membrane systems. Fundam. Inf. **134**(1–2), 129–152 (2014)

17. Pan, L., Alhazov, A., Ishdorj, T.-O.: Further remarks on P systems with active membranes, separation, merging, and release rules. Soft Comput. **9**(9), 686–690 (2004)

18. Pan, L., Ishdorj, T.-O.: P systems with active membranes and separation rules. J. Univ. Comput. Sci. **10**(5), 630–649 (2004)

19. Papadimitriou, C.H.: Computational Complexity. Addison-Wesley Publishing Company, Inc., Boston (1994)

20. Păun, G.: P systems with active membranes: attacking NP-complete problems. J. Autom. Lang. Comb. **6**(1), 75–90 (2001)

21. Păun, G.: Further twenty six open problems in membrane computing. In: Third Brainstorming Week on Membrane Computing, Fénix Editora, Sevilla, pp. 249–262 (2005)

22. Păun, G., Rozenberg, G., Salomaa, A. (eds.): The Oxford Handbook of Membrane Computing. Oxford University Press, Oxford (2010)

23. Pérez-Jiménez, M.J., Romero-Campero, F.J.: Trading polarization for bi-stable catalysts in P systems with active membranes. In: Mauri, G., Păun, G., Pérez-Jiménez, M.J., Rozenberg, G., Salomaa, A. (eds.) WMC 2004. LNCS, vol. 3365, pp. 373–388. Springer, Heidelberg (2005). doi:10.1007/978-3-540-31837-8_24

24. Pérez-Jiménez, M.J., Romero-Jiménez, Á., Sancho-Caparrini, F.: A polynomial complexity class in P systems using membrane division. In: Csuhaj-Varjú, E., Kintala, C., Wotschke, D., Vaszil, G. (eds.) Proceeding of the 5th Workshop on Descriptional Complexity of Formal Systems, DCFS 2003, pp. 284–294 (2003)

25. Pérez-Jiménez, M.J., Romero-Jiménez, Á., Sancho-Caparrini, F.: Complexity classes in models of cellular computing with membranes. Nat. Comput. **2**(3), 265–285 (2003)

26. Pérez-Jiménez, M.J., Romero-Jiménez, Á., Sancho-Caparrini, F.: A polynomial complexity class in P systems using membrane division. J. Autom. Lang. Comb. **11**(4), 423–434 (2006)
27. Salomaa, A.: Formal Languages. Academic Press, New York (1973)
28. Sipser, M.: Introduction to the Theory of Computation, 3rd edn. Cengage Learning, Boston (2012)
29. Sosík, P.: The computational power of cell division in P systems. Nat. Comput. **2**(3), 287–298 (2003)
30. Woods, D., Murphy, N., Pérez-Jiménez, M.J., Riscos-Núñez, A.: Membrane dissolution and division in P. In: Calude, C.S., Costa, J.F., Dershowitz, N., Freire, E., Rozenberg, G. (eds.) UC 2009. LNCS, vol. 5715, pp. 262–276. Springer, Heidelberg (2009). doi:10.1007/978-3-642-03745-0_28
31. Zandron, C., Ferretti, C., Mauri, G.: Solving NP-complete problems using P systems with active membranes. In: Antoniou, I., Calude, C.S., Dinneen, M.J. (eds.) Unconventional Models of Computation, UMC'2K. DISCMATH, pp. 289–301. Springer, London (2001)

Kernel P Systems Modelling, Testing and Verification - Sorting Case Study

Marian Gheorghe[1]([✉]), Rodica Ceterchi[2], Florentin Ipate[2,3], and Savas Konur[1]

[1] School of Electrical Engineering and Computer Science,
University of Bradford, Bradford BD7 1DP, UK
{m.gheorghe,s.konur}@bradford.ac.uk
[2] Department of Computer Science, University of Bucharest,
Str. Academiei nr. 14, 010014 Bucharest, Romania
rceterchi@gmail.com
[3] Department of Computer Science, University of Piteşti,
Str Targul din Vale, nr 1, 110040 Argeş, Romania
florentin.ipate@ifsoft.ro

Abstract. A kernel P system (kP system, for short) integrates in a coherent and elegant manner many of the P system features most successfully used for modelling various applications and, consequently, it provides a framework for analyzing these models. In this paper, we illustrate the modelling capacity of kernel P systems by providing a number of kP system models for sorting algorithms. Furthermore, the problem of testing systems modelled as kP systems is also discussed and a test generation method based on automata is proposed. We also demonstrate how formal verification can be used to validate that the given models work as desired.

1 Introduction

Membrane systems were introduced in [27] as a new natural computing paradigm inspired by the structure and distribution of the compartments of living cells, as well as by the main bio-chemical interactions occurring within compartments and at the inter-cellular level. They were later also called *P systems*. An account of the basic fundamental results can be found in [28] and a comprehensive description of the main research developments in this area is provided in [29]. The key challenges of the membrane systems area and a discussion on some future research directions, are available in a more recent survey paper [20].

In recent years, significant progress has been made in using P systems to model and simulate systems and problems from various areas. However, in order to facilitate the modelling, in many cases various features have been added in an ad-hoc manner to these classes of P systems. This has led to a multitude of P systems variants, without a coherent integrating view. There have been investigations aiming to produce unifying approaches for several variants of P systems [13,14], looking mainly at the computational aspects, syntax and semantics. The concept of *kernel P systems (kP systems)* [17,18] integrates in a coherent and

© Springer International Publishing AG 2017
A. Leporati et al. (Eds.): CMC 2016, LNCS 10105, pp. 233–250, 2017.
DOI: 10.1007/978-3-319-54072-6_15

elegant manner many of the P system features most successfully used for modelling various applications and provides a generic framework for specifying and analyzing these models. Furthermore, the expressive power of these systems has been illustrated by a number of representative case studies [18,19]. The kP system model is supported by a modelling language, called kP-Lingua, capable of mapping a kP system specification into a machine readable representation. Furthermore, kP systems are supported by a software framework, kPWORKBENCH [21], which integrates a set of related simulation and verification tools and techniques.

Another complementary method to simulation and verification is testing, a major activity in the lifecycle of software systems. In practice, software products are almost always validated through testing. Testing has been discussed for cell-like P systems and various strategies, such as rule coverage based and automata based techniques have been proposed [16,24]. Until now, however, testing has not been discussed in the context of kP systems.

In this paper we further illustrate the modelling capacity of kP systems by providing a number of kP system models for sorting algorithms. Furthermore, the problem of testing and formally verifying systems modelled as kP systems is also discussed.

The key contributions of the paper are: (a) illustrate the modelling capability of kP systems by implementing a number of sorting methods - the method presented in Sect. 3.1 is an extension of the approach introduced in [17,18] which includes a stopping condition, whereas the other sorting methods are new; (b) integrate the kP systems with a test generation method based on automata; and (c) formally verifying the sorting problems using the kPWORKBENCH environment.

2   kP Systems - Main Concepts and Definitions

We consider that standard P system concepts such as strings, multisets, rewriting rules, and computation are well-known and refer to [28] for their formal notations and precise definitions. The kP system concepts and definitions introduced below are from [17,18]; some are slightly changed and this will be mentioned.

Definition 1. T *is a* set of compartment types, $T = \{t_1, \ldots, t_s\}$, *where* $t_i = (R_i, \sigma_i)$, $1 \leq i \leq s$, *consists of a set of rules,* R_i, *and an execution strategy,* σ_i, *defined over* $Lab(R_i)$, *the labels of the rules of* R_i.

Remark 1. The compartments that appear in the definition of the kP systems will be instantiated from these compartment types. The types of rules and the execution strategies will be discussed later.

Definition 2. *A* kernel P (kP) system *of degree* n *is a tuple*

$$k\Pi = (A, \mu, C_1, \ldots, C_n, i_0),$$

where A *is a finite set of elements called* objects; μ *defines the* initial membrane structure, *which is a graph,* (V, E), *where* V *are vertices indicating components, and E edges;* $C_i = (t_i, w_i)$, $1 \leq i \leq n$, *is a* compartment *of the system consisting of a compartment type* t_i *from* T *and an* initial multiset, w_i *over* A; i_o *is the* output compartment *where the result is obtained.*

2.1   kP System Rules

Each rule r may have a **guard** g and its generic form is r $\{g\}$. The guards are constructed using multisets over A, as operands, and relational and Boolean operators. Let us first introduce some notations.

For a multiset w over A and an element $a \in A$, we denote by $|w|_a$ the number of objects a occurring in w. Let us denote $Rel = \{<, \leq, =, \neq, \geq, >\}$, the set of relational operators, $\gamma \in Rel$, a relational operator, and a^n a multiset. We first introduce an *abstract relational expression*.

Definition 3. *If* g *is an* abstract relational expression γa^n *and* w *a multiset, then* g *applied to* w *denotes the* relational expression $|w|_a \gamma n$; g *is true with respect to the multiset* w, *if* $|w|_a \gamma n$ *is true.*

One can consider the Boolean operators $\neg$ (negation), $\wedge$ (conjunction) and $\vee$ (disjunction). An *abstract Boolean expression* is either an abstract relational operator or if g and h are abstract Boolean expressions then $\neg g$, $g \wedge h$ and $g \vee h$ are abstract Boolean expressions. The concept of a guard is a generalisation of the promotor and inhibitor concepts utilised by some variants of P systems.

Definition 4. *If* g *is an* abstract Boolean expression *containing* g_i, $1 \leq i \leq n$, *abstract relational expressions and* w *a multiset, then* g *applied to* w, *denoted* gw, *means the* Boolean expression *obtained from* g *by applying* g_i, $1 \leq i \leq n$, *to* w. *The guard* g *is true with respect to the multiset* w, *if the Boolean expression* gw *is true.*

Example 1. If g is the guard $\geq a^5 \wedge \geq b^3 \vee \neg > c$ and w a multiset, then gw is true if it has at least 5 a's and 3 b's or no more than one c.

If r $\{g\}$ denotes a rule then its guard, g, is defined by an abstract Boolean expression. A rule may or may not have a guard. A rule r $\{g\}$ is applicable to a multiset w when the left-hand side of r is contained into w and gw is true.

Definition 5. *A rule from a compartment* $C_{l_i} = (t_{l_i}, w_{l_i})$ *will have one of the following types:*

- *(a)* **rewriting and communication** *rule:* $x \rightarrow y$ $\{g\}$,
   where $x \in A^+$ *and* y *has the form* $y = (a_1, t_1) \ldots (a_h, t_h)$, $h \geq 0$, $a_j \in A$ *and* t_j *indicates a compartment type from* T – *see Definition 2* – *with instance compartments linked to the current compartment;* t_j *might also indicate the type of the current compartment,* t_{l_i}, *(in this case it is not present on the right hand side of the rule); if a link does not exist (i.e., there is no link between the two compartments in* E) *then the rule is not applied; if a target,* t_j, *refers to a compartment type that has more than one instance connected to* C_{l_i}, *then one of them will be non-deterministically chosen;*

- *(b)* **structure changing rules***; the following types of rules are considered:*
  - *(b1)* **membrane division** *rule:* $[x]_{t_{l_i}} \rightarrow [y_1]_{t_{i_1}} \cdots [y_p]_{t_{i_p}} \{g\}$,
    where $x \in A^+$ *and* $y_j \in A^*$, $1 \leq j \leq p$; *the compartment* C_{l_i} *will be replaced by* p *compartments; the* j-*th compartment, instantiated from the compartment type* t_{i_j} *contains the same objects as* C_{l_i}, *but* x, *which will be replaced by* y_j; *all the links of* C_{l_i} *are inherited by each of the newly created compartments;*
  - *(b2)* **membrane dissolution** *rule:* $[]_{t_{l_i}} \rightarrow \lambda \{g\}$;
    the compartment C_{l_i} *will be destroyed together with its links;*
  - *(b3)* **link creation** *rule:* $[x]_{t_{l_i}}; []_{t_{l_j}} \rightarrow [y]_{t_{l_i}} - []_{t_{l_j}} \{g\}$;
    the current compartment is linked to a compartment of type t_{l_j} *and* x *is transformed into* y; *if more than one instance of the compartment type* t_{l_j} *not yet linked to* t_{l_i} *exist then one of them will be non-deterministically picked up;* g *is a guard that refers to the compartment instantiated from the compartment type* t_{l_1};
  - *(b4)* **link destruction** *rule:* $[x]_{t_{l_i}} - []_{t_{l_j}} \rightarrow [y]_{t_{l_i}}; []_{t_{l_j}} \{g\}$;
    is the opposite of link creation and means that the compartments are disconnected.

The membrane division is defined slightly differently here compared to [17, 18], where each y_j, $1 \leq j \leq p$, is composed of objects with target compartments.

2.2 kP System Execution Strategies

In kP systems the way in which rules are executed is defined for each compartment type t from T – see Definition 1 and Remark 1. As in Definition 1, $Lab(R)$ is the set of labels of the rules R.

Definition 6. *For a compartment type* $t = (R, \sigma)$ *from* T *and* $r \in Lab(R)$, $r_1, \ldots, r_s \in Lab(R)$, *the execution strategy,* σ, *is defined by the following*

- $\sigma = \lambda$, *means no rule from the current compartment will be executed;*
- $\sigma = \{r\}$ – *the rule* r *is executed once;*
- $\sigma = \{r_1, \ldots, r_s\}$ – *one of the rules labelled* $r_1, \ldots, r_s$ *will be chosen non-deterministically and executed; if none is applicable then none is executed; this is called* alternative *or* choice;
- $\sigma = \{r_1, \ldots, r_s\}^*$ – *the rules are applied an arbitrary number of times (*arbitrary parallelism*);*
- $\sigma = \{r_1, \ldots, r_s\}^\top$ – *the rules are executed according to* maximal parallelism *strategy;*
- $\sigma = \sigma_1 \& \ldots \& \sigma_s$, *means executing sequentially* $\sigma_1, \ldots, \sigma_s$, *where* σ_i, $1 \leq i \leq s$, *describes any of the above cases, namely* λ, *one rule, a choice, arbitrary parallelism or maximal parallelism; if one of* σ_i *fails to be executed then the rest is no longer executed;*
- *for any of the above* σ *strategy only one single structure changing rule is allowed.*

Arbitrary parallelism and maximal parallelism for rewriting and communication rules, as well as for structure changing rules (cell division, dissolution), are discussed in [29].

Remark 2. In certain cases the operator & will be ignored and the sequential execution will be denoted as $\sigma = \sigma_1 \ldots \sigma_s$.

3 Sorting with kP Systems

Sorting is a central topic in Computer Science (see [25]). A variety of approaches to sorting have been investigated, for different algorithms, and with different P system models. A first approach was [3], in which a BeadSort algorithm was implemented with tissue P systems. Another approach was [6], in which algorithms inspired from sorting networks were implemented using P systems with communication. Other papers ([1, 30]) use different types of P systems, and refine the sorting problem to sorting by ranking. A first overview of sorting algorithms implemented with P systems was [2]. A dynamic sorting algorithm was proposed in [7]. The bitonic sort was implemented with P systems [8], spiking neural P systems were used for sorting [10], other network algorithms were implemented using P systems [9]. Another overview of sorting algorithms implemented with P systems is provided by [11]. First implementations of sorting with kP systems were proposed in [17, 18].

The problem can be stated as follows: suppose we want to sort $x_1, \cdots, x_n, n \geq 1$, in ascending order, where x_i, $1 \leq i \leq n$, are positive integer values. Each such number, x_i, $1 \leq i \leq n$, will be represented as a multiset $a_i^{x_i}$, $1 \leq i \leq n$, where a_i is an object from a given set. In the next sections we will present two sorting algorithms using different representations of the sequence of positive integer numbers. More precisely, we start with an algorithm already studied in several other papers, [2, 6] for various types of P systems. Here we implement it using kP systems, by representing each element x_i by a^{x_i}, $1 \leq i \leq n$. The multisets a^{x_i}, $1 \leq i \leq n$, are stored in separate compartments, C_i, $1 \leq i \leq n$ (Sect. 3.1). In Sect. 3.2 these positive integer numbers are represented by $a_i^{x_i}$, $1 \leq i \leq n$, and stored in one compartment C_1; an additional one, C_2, is used for implementation purposes. In Sect. 3.3 is used again the representation $a_i^{x_i}$, $1 \leq i \leq n$, but a more complex structure of compartments is provided in order to maximise the parallel behaviour of the system implementing the sorting algorithm. The algorithm used in Sects. 3.1 and 3.2 makes comparisons of adjacent compartments by employing a two stage process. In the first stage all pairs "odd-even" are compared (C_{2i-1} with C_{2i}, $i \geq 1$) and in the second stage all pairs "even-odd" are involved (C_{2i} with C_{2i+1}, $i \geq 1$).

3.1 Sorting Using kP Systems with an Element per Compartment

The approach presented below follows [17, 18], but stopping conditions have been also considered and the sequence of numbers is obtained in ascending order.

Let us consider a kP system, $k\Pi_1$, having n compartments $C_i = (t_i, w_{i,0})$, where $t_i = (R_i, \sigma_i)$, $1 \leq i \leq n$, and a set of objects $A = \{a, b, c, p, p'\}$. In each compartment, C_i, the initial multiset, $w_{i,0}$, $1 \leq i \leq n$, includes the representation of the positive integer number x_i, i.e., a^{x_i}, the multiset $c^{2(n-1)}$ and the object p for all odd index values, when n is an even number, and for all odd index values, but the last, when n is odd. The objects p stored initially in compartments indexed by odd values indicate that one starts with stage one, whereby "odd-even" compartment pairs are compared first. The multiset $c^{2(n-1)}$ will be used in a counting process, in each of the compartments, that will help stopping the algorithm when the sorting is complete.

Let us consider for $n = 6$ the sequence 3, 6, 9, 5, 7, 8. Then the initial multisets are: $w_{1,0} = a^3 c^{10} p$; $w_{2,0} = a^6 c^{10}$; $w_{3,0} = a^9 c^{10} p$; $w_{4,0} = a^5 c^{10}$; $w_{5,0} = a^7 c^{10} p$; $w_{6,0} = a^8 c^{10}$. As n is even, p appears in all compartments indexed by odd values, i.e., C_1, C_3, and C_5.

In each compartment C_i, t_i contains the following set of rules, denoted R_i, $1 \leq i \leq n$,

$r_{1,i} : a \rightarrow (b, i+1) \{\geq p\}$, $i < n$;
$r_{2,i} : p \rightarrow p'$;
$r_{3,i} : p' \rightarrow (p, i+1)$, for i odd and $i < n$;
$r'_{3,i} : p' \rightarrow (p, i-1)$, for i even and $i > 1$;
$r_{4,i} : ab \rightarrow a(a, i-1)$, $i > 1$;
$r_{5,i} : b \rightarrow a$, $i > 1$;
$r : c \rightarrow \lambda$.

The rule r is used for implementing the counting process mentioned above. By using the two stage process of comparing "odd-even" pairs of compartments and then "even-odd" ones, one needs at most $n-1$ stages to complete the sorting. As will be explained below, each stage will involve two steps and consequently after $2(n-1)$ steps one expects to stop the sorting process.

In each compartment C_i, the execution strategy is defined according to $\sigma_i = \{r\}\{r_{1,i}, r_{2,i}, r_{3,i}, r_{4,i}\}^\top \{r_{5,i}\}^\top$, if i is odd; for even values of i, $r_{3,i}$ is replaced by $r'_{3,i}$. The execution strategy, σ_i, tells us that a sequence of three sets of rules are executed in each step. The first one indicates that one single rule is applied and then two sets of rules are used, each of them applied in a maximal parallel manner.

We assume that any two compartments, C_i, C_{i+1}, $1 \leq i < n$, are connected.

In the first step, of the "odd-even" stage, in every compartment one c is removed by applying $r : c \rightarrow \lambda$; then the only applicable rules are $r_{1,i}, r_{2,i}$ in all compartments indexed by an odd value. Given the presence of p in these compartments, rules $r_{1,i}$ move all objects a from each compartment with an odd index value, i, $i < n$, to the compartment C_{i+1} by transforming them into bs and rules $r_{2,i}$ transforming p into p'. In the next step, another c is removed from every compartment and rules $r_{3,i}, r_{4,i}, r_{5,i}$ are then applied. The rules $r_{3,i}$ are applied in compartments with an odd index value and $r_{4,i}$ are applied in compartments with an even index value, this means p' is moved as p from each C_i, i an odd value and $i < n$, to compartment C_{i+1} and every ab, in each C_j,

j an even value and $j > 1$, is transformed into an a kept in the compartment and another a moved to C_{j-1}. At the end of the step, in each compartment C_j, j an even value and $j > 1$, and in accordance with the execution strategy, the remaining b objects, if any, are transformed into as. These two steps implement comparators between two adjacent compartments, in this case "odd-even" pairs. If a^{x_i} from C_i and $a^{x_{i+1}}$ from C_{i+1}, $i < n$, are such that $x_i > x_{i+1}$ then the multiset a^{x_i} is moved to C_{i+1} and $a^{x_{i+1}}$ to C_i. In the next step, the first of the second stage, ps appear in even compartments and the comparators are now acting between pairs of compartments C_i, C_{i+1}, where i is even and $i < n$.

Given that the algorithm must stop in maximum $2(n - 1)$ steps, one can notice that in step $2(n - 1)$ the counter, c, disappears, i.e., becomes λ, and the first rule from the execution strategy, r, is no longer applicable and then the next sets of rules are not executed either. Hence, the process stops with the multisets codifying the positive integer values in ascending order.

The table below presents the first four steps of the sorting process.

Compartments - Step	C_1	C_2	C_3	C_4	C_5	C_6
0	$a^3 c^{10} p$	$a^6 c^{10}$	$a^9 c^{10} p$	$a^5 c^{10}$	$a^7 c^{10} p$	$a^8 c^{10}$
1	$c^9 p'$	$a^6 b^3 c^9$	$c^9 p'$	$a^5 b^9 c^9$	$c^9 p'$	$a^8 b^7 c^9$
2	$a^3 c^8$	$a^6 c^8 p$	$a^5 c^8$	$a^9 c^8 p$	$a^7 c^8$	$a^8 c^8 p$
3	$a^3 c^7$	$c^7 p'$	$a^5 b^6 c^7$	$c^7 p'$	$a^7 b^9 c^7$	$a^8 c^7 p'$
4	$a^3 c^6 p$	$a^5 c^6$	$a^6 c^6 p$	$a^7 c^6$	$a^9 c^6 p$	$a^8 c^6$

Now, one can state the result of the algorithm presented above and the number of steps involved.

Proposition 1. *The above algorithm sorts in ascending order a sequence of n, $n \geq 1$, positive integer numbers in $2(n - 1)$ steps.*

3.2 Sorting Using kP Systems with Two Compartments

In this section we use a representation of the positive integer numbers $x_1, \cdots, x_n$ as multisets $a_1^{x_1}, \cdots, a_n^{x_n}$, where $a_1, \cdots, a_n$ are from a given set of distinct objects. We consider a kP system, $k\Pi_2$, with two compartments $C_j = (t_j, w_{j,0})$, $1 \leq j \leq 2$, which are linked and $A = \{a_1, \ldots, a_n, c\}$. The initial multisets are $w_{1,0} = a_1^{x_1} \cdots a_n^{x_n} c^{n-1}$ and $w_{2,0} = c^{n-1}$.

Finally, the kP system $k\Pi_2$ will lead to a multiset $a_1^{x_{i_1}} \cdots a_n^{x_{i_n}}$ in compartment C_1, such that $x_{i_1} \leq \cdots \leq x_{i_n}$.

In compartment C_1 the rules are

$R_{1,1} = \{a_i a_{i+1} \rightarrow (a_i, 2)(a_{i+1}, 2) \mid 1 \leq i < n \wedge i \text{ is odd}\}$;
$R_{2,1} = \{a_i \rightarrow (a_{i+1}, 2) \mid 1 \leq i < n \wedge i \text{ is odd}\}$;
$R_{3,1} = \{a_i \rightarrow (a_i, 2) \mid 1 \leq i \leq n\}$.

We also consider the rule $r : c \to \lambda$, like in the previous section.

Compartment C_2 has the rules

$R_{1,2} = \{a_i a_{i+1} \to (a_i, 1)(a_{i+1}, 1) \mid 1 \leq i < n \wedge i \text{ is even}\};$
$R_{2,2} = \{a_i \to (a_{i+1}, 1) \mid 1 \leq i < n \wedge i \text{ is even}\};$
$R_{3,2} = \{a_i \to (a_i, 1) \mid 1 \leq i \leq n\};$

and the rule r defined above.

The execution strategies of these compartments are the following: $\sigma_j = \{r\} Lab(R_{1,j})^\top Lab(R_{2,j})^\top Lab(R_{3,j})^\top$, $j = 1, 2$.

In compartment C_1 one implements "odd-even" comparison steps and in C_2 "even-odd" steps. The process starts with compartment C_1. The execution strategy in each compartment starts by decrementing the counter (using r), then the comparators are implemented by executing first $R_{1,j}$ and then $R_{2,j}$, $j = 1, 2$, both in maximally parallel manner. After that all the pairs a_i, a_{i+1} are sent to the other compartment and when $a_i^{x_i}$ and $a_{i+1}^{x_{i+1}}$ are such that $x_i > x_{i+1}$ then a_i is transformed into a_{i+1} and sent to the other compartment, i.e., a_i and a_{i+1} are swapped and sent to the other compartment. In the last part, are moved to the other compartment all the objects a_i, $1 \leq i \leq n$, that remained there after comparisons. This is the case when a pair a_i and a_{i+1} has its objects with their multiplicities, x_i and x_{i+1}, respectively, in the right order, i.e., $x_i \leq x_{i+1}$.

Clearly after at most $n - 1$ steps the objects $a_1, \cdots, a_n$ have their multiplicities in the ascending order and the sorting process stops at step $n - 1$ as r is no longer applicable and the execution strategy is not applicable any more.

Proposition 2. *The above algorithm sorts in ascending order a sequence of $n, n \geq 1$, positive integer numbers in $n - 1$ steps.*

One can produce a similar implementation whereby the comparison of two neighbours is made more directly and with simpler rules, but with more complex guards.

In this case we extend the definition of a guard, by allowing θa^n to be of the form $\theta a^{f(z)}$, where $f(z)$ is a function over the multisets of objects returning a positive integer value. For the current multiset z, one can define, for instance, $f_b(z) = |z|_b$, Then a rule $a \to b\{> a^{f_b(\cdot)}\}$ is applicable to z if the guard is true, i.e., $|z|_a > |z|_b$.

The *extended definition of the guard* allows us to implement a comparator with simpler rules than in the previous case. We have the pair of integers x_1, x_2 represented as $a_1{}^{x_1}, a_2{}^{x_2}$. Consider the pair of guarded rewriting rules

$$a_1 \to a_2\{> a_1{}^{f_{a_2}(\cdot)}\} \quad \text{and} \quad a_2 \to a_1\{< a_2{}^{f_{a_1}(\cdot)}\}$$

where $f_{a_2}(w) = |w|_{a_2}$ and $f_{a_1}(w) = |w|_{a_1}$. Then both guards codify the condition $x_1 > x_2$.

If $x_1 \leq x_2$ the rules are not applicable, while if $x_1 > x_2$, then the x_1 copies of a_1 are rewritten as a_2, and x_2 copies of a_2 are rewritten as a_1, interchanging the values and achieving eventually $x_1 \leq x_2$.

A kP system, $k\Pi_3$, is defined now for sorting the sequence of $n, n \geq 1$, positive integer numbers. It consists of two compartments C_1 and C_2 which are linked. They have the same initial multisets like $k\Pi_2$. The sets of rules associated with these compartments are

- R_1 consisting of the following subsets of rules (R_1 is responsible for "odd-even" stages):
  - $\{c \rightarrow \lambda\}$;
  - $R_{1,1} = \{a_i \rightarrow (a_{i+1}, 2)\{> a_i^{f_{a_{i+1}}(\cdot)}\} \mid i = 1, 3 \cdots \wedge i \leq n\}$;
  - $R_{2,1} = \{a_{i+1} \rightarrow (a_i, 2)\{< a_{i+1}^{f_{a_i}(\cdot)}\} \mid i = 1, 3 \cdots \wedge i \leq n\}$;
  - $R_{3,1} = \{a_i \rightarrow (a_i, 2) \mid i = 1, \cdots, n\}$.

The function f_{a_i} is defined $f_{a_i}(z) = |z|_{a_i}$, $1 \leq i \leq n$, for any multiset z.

Similarly, one defines R_2 in compartment C_2, which is used to implement the "even-odd" stage. The execution strategy is given by $\sigma_j = \{r\}Lab(R_{1,j} \cup R_{2,j})^\top Lab(R_{3,j})^\top, j = 1, 2$.

Proposition 3. *The above algorithm sorts in ascending order a sequence of $n, n \geq 1$, positive integer numbers in $n - 1$ steps.*

Remark 3.

1. The kP system $k\Pi_3$ has simpler rules (non-cooperative) than $k\Pi_2$ (cooperative rules), but the guards of the rules in $k\Pi_2$ are simpler than those belonging to $k\Pi_3$.
2. The number of rules applied in each step to interchange $a_i^{x_i}$ and $a_{i+1}^{x_{i+1}}$ is $max\{x_i, x_{i+1}\}$ for $k\Pi_2$ and $x_i + x_{i+1}$ for $k\Pi_3$. Hence, $k\Pi_2$ uses less rules than $k\Pi_3$ in each one of the $n - 1$ steps.

3.3 A kP System for Sorting in Constant Time

We present two sorting methods exploiting more the massive parallelism of the P systems in general and of the kP systems in particular. In both cases we consider the integers to be sorted $x_1, \cdots x_n$ distinct. In the first case one uses $n^2 + 2n$ compartments with specific initial multisets and a special arrangement of links amongst them. In the second case the n^2 compartments are replaced by n compartments with simpler initial multisets.

For the first sorting method we consider $n^2 + 2n$ compartments:

- $C_{i,j}$, $1 \leq i, j \leq n$, where each $C_{i,j}$ will be responsible for a comparison;
- C_i, $1 \leq i \leq 2n$, where each C_i, $1 \leq i \leq n$, will collect the results of comparing x_i to the rest; and C_i, $n + 1 \leq i \leq 2n$, will collect the sorted result.

The connections between compartments are given by the set of edges

$$E = \cup_{i=1}^n E_i$$

where

$$E_i = \{(C_i, C_{i,j}) \mid 1 \leq j \leq n\} \cup \{(C_i, C_k) \mid n+1 \leq k \leq 2n\}, 1 \leq i \leq n.$$

Each $C_{i,j}$, $1 \leq i, j \leq n$, will contain the initial multiset $w_{i,j,0} = a_i{}^{x_i} a_j{}^{x_j} a$ and the rules

$$r'_{i,j} : a_i \rightarrow a_j F\{> a_i{}^{f_j(\cdot)}\}; \ r''_{i,j} : a_j \rightarrow a_i\{< a_j{}^{f_i(\cdot)}\}; \ r'''_{i,j} : a \rightarrow a';$$
$$r_{i,j} : a' \rightarrow (F, i)\{\geq F\},$$

where $f_i(z) = |z|_{a_i}$ and $f_j(z) = |z|_{a_j}$.

The execution strategy is $\sigma_{i,j} = \{r'_{i,j}, r''_{i,j}, r'''_{i,j}, r_{i,j}\}^\top$.

Note that the rules $r'_{i,j}, r''_{i,j}$ implement a comparator between x_i and x_j, similar to the one of the previous section. The modified comparator produces also a symbol F (False) when $x_i > x_j$, signifying that $x_i \leq x_j$ is false. If the rewriting rules $r'_{i,j}, r''_{i,j}$ and $r'''_{i,j}$ have acted, then a single F will be sent to compartment C_i (by using the rule $r_{i,j}$).

In compartment $C_i, 1 \leq i \leq n$, we have the initial multiset $w_{i,0} = a_i{}^{x_i} a$ and the rules

$$r'_i : a \rightarrow a'; \ r''_i : a' \rightarrow a'';$$
$$r_{i,0} : a_i \rightarrow (a, n+1)\{< F \wedge = a''\}; \ r_{i,k} : a_i \rightarrow (a, n+k+1)\{= F^k \wedge = a''\},$$
$$1 \leq k \leq n-1.$$

The execution strategy is $\sigma_i = \{r'_i, r''_i, r_{i,0}, \cdots, r_{i,n-1}\}^\top$.

Compartments $C_i, n+1 \leq i \leq 2n$, are initially empty and contain no rules.

The functioning of the system is as follows. Initially, in compartments $C_{i,j}$, $1 \leq i, j \leq n$, the rules $r'_{i,j}$, $r''_{i,j}$, and $r'''_{i,j}$ act. If $x_i > x_j$ the values will be interchanged and some Fs will be produced (rules $r'_{i,j}$, $r''_{i,j}$ are used), signifying that $x_i \leq x_j$ is false. Also $r'''_{i,j}$ is used to transform a in a'. If at least one F is produced in $C_{i,j}$, then a single F will be sent to C_i, using rule $r_{i,j}$. In parallel, in each compartment $C_i, 1 \leq i \leq n$, in the first two steps the rules r'_i and r''_i are applied.

After these two steps, no rules are applicable in $C_{i,j}$, $1 \leq i, j \leq n$, and in $C_i, 1 \leq i \leq n$, the rules $r_{i,k}$, $0 \leq k \leq n-1$, might be applicable, depending on the number of Fs collected. The number of Fs tells us how many comparisons $x_i \leq x_j$, $1 \leq j \leq n$, are false. If we have k such Fs in C_i, it means that x_i is greater than exactly k other values, which means that in the sorted order it must be the $(k+1)$-th component. This is accomplished by sending a^{x_i} in C_{n+k+1}. The maximum number of Fs in C_i is $n-1$ because $C_{i,i}$ will never produce an F. If there are no Fs in C_i, this means that x_i is the minimum, and a^{x_i} will be sent to C_{n+1}. Compartments $C_{n+i}, 1 \leq i \leq n$, collect the result of sorting. Each such C_{n+i} will contain at the end of the computation the string $a^{x_{k_i}}$, x_{k_i} being the i-th value in the sorted order. The computation has three steps, the first two ones in which $C_{i,j}$, $1 \leq i, j \leq n$, work, and a third one in which $C_i, 1 \leq i \leq n$, work.

Proposition 4. *The above kP system sorts n integers in 3 steps.*

Remark 4. This algorithm makes extensive use of the n^2 additional compartments, $C_{i,j}$, $1 \le i, j \le n$, their contents, $a_i^{x_i}$ and $a_j^{x_j}$, and links with the first n components, C_i, $1 \le i \le n$. This solution, although computationally efficient, requires an initial, quite complex, setting, i.e., some precomputed resources of size $O(n^2)$. This can be simplified as shown by the next sorting method.

In the second sorting method we consider $2n$ compartments C_i, $1 \le i \le 2n$, as above and replace the n^2 compartments, $C_{i,j}$, $1 \le i, j \le n$, by a much simpler set of n compartments from which $C_{i,j}$, $1 \le i, j \le n$, compartments are obtained by using membrane division rules. Let us say that the new set of compartments are C_k, $2n + 1 \le k \le 3n$, and each C_k is connected to a C_i, $1 \le i \le n$, such that $k - 2n = i$. Each compartment C_k, $2n + 1 \le k \le 3n$, contains the initial multiset $w_{k,0} = s$, where s is a new object. Membrane division rules can be used to transform each C_k, $2n + 1 \le k \le 3n$, in one step, into n compartments $C_{i,j}$, $1 \le j \le n$ and $k - 2n = i$, $1 \le i \le n$. We could use the rules

$$[s]_k \rightarrow [a_1{}^{x_1} a_i{}^{x_i} a]_{i,1} \cdots [a_j{}^{x_j} a_i{}^{x_i} a]_{i,j} \cdots [a_n{}^{x_n} a_i{}^{x_i} a]_{i,n}$$

$2n + 1 \le k \le 3n, k - 2n = i$.

Hence one additional step will be added to the algorithm. The rules of C_i will be modified to account for this additional step. We can now formulate the following result.

Proposition 5. *The above kP system sorts n integers in 4 steps.*

Remark 5. This algorithm requires $3n$ compartments, the first $2n$ have similar structure to the first $2n$ compartments presented in the first sorting method, hence the entire initial settings is much simpler.

4   Simulating and Verifying kP Systems

In Sect. 3, we have illustrated that kP systems provide a coherent and expressive language that allows us to model various systems that were originally implemented by different P system variants. In addition to the modelling aspect, there has been a significant progress on analysing kP systems using various simulation and verification methodologies. The methods and tools developed in this respect have been integrated into a software platform, called kPWORKBENCH, to support the modelling and analysis of kP systems.

The ability of simulating kernel P systems is an important feature of this tool. Currently, there are two different simulation approaches, kPWORKBENCH SIMULATOR and FLAME (Flexible Large-Scale Agent Modelling Environment). Both simulators receive as input a kP system model written in kP–Lingua and output a trace of the execution, which is mainly used for checking the evolution of a system and for extracting various results out of the simulation. The simulators provide traces of execution for a kP system model, and an interface displaying the current configuration (the content of each compartment) at each step. It

Table 1. List of properties derived from the property language and their representations in different formats.

Prop.	Pattern	(i) Informal query, (ii) Formal query using patterns
1	Existence	(i) *The numbers will be eventually sorted, i.e. the multisets representing the numbers will be in ascending order in the compartments*
		(ii) **eventually** $(c_1.a <= c_2.a$ & $c_2.a <= c_3.a$ & $c_3.a <= c_4.a$ && $c_4.a <= c_5.a$ & $c_5.a <= c_6.a)$
2	Universality	(i) *Counters in different compartments are always sync'ed*
		(ii) **always** $(c_1.c = c_2.c$ & $c_2.c = c_3.c$ & $c_3.c = c_4.c$ & $c_4.c = c_5.c$ & $c_5.c = c_6.c)$
3	Steady-state	(i) *In the steady-state, the numbers are sorted*
		(ii) **steady-state** $(c_1.a <= c_2.a$ & $c_2.a <= c_3.a$ & $c_3.a <= c_4.a$ && $c_4.a <= c_5.a$ & $c_5.a <= c_6.a)$
4	Existence	(i) *The algorithm will eventually stop*
		(ii) **eventually** $(c_i.c = 0)$
5	Response	(i) *An unsorted state of two adjacent compartments will always be followed by a sorted one*
		(ii) $(c_i.a > c_{i+1}.a)$ **followed-by** $(c_i.a <= c_{i+1}.a)$

is useful for checking the temporal evolution of a kP system and for inferring various information from the simulation results.

Another important analysis method that kPWORKBENCH features is formal verification, requiring an exhaustive analysis of system models against some queries to be verified. The automatic verification of kP systems brings in some challenges as they feature a dynamic structure by preserving the structure changing rules such as membrane division, dissolution and link creation/destruction. kPWORKBENCH employs different verification strategies to alleviate these issues. The framework supports both *Linear Temporal Logic (LTL)* and *Computation Tree Logic (CTL)* properties by making use of the SPIN [22] and NUSMV [15] model checkers.

In order to facilitate the formal specification, kPWORKBENCH features a property language, called *kP-Queries*, comprising a list of natural language statements representing formal property patterns, from which the formal syntax of the SPIN and NUSMV formulas are automatically generated. The property language editor interacts with the kP-Lingua model in question and allows users to directly access the native elements in the model, which results in less verbose and shorter state expressions, and hence more comprehensible formulas. *kP-Queries* also features a grammar for the most common property patterns. These features and the natural language like syntax of the language make the property construction much easier.

Some of the commonly used patterns are "existence", "absence", "universality", "recurrence", "steady-state", "until", "next", "response" and "precedence". The details can be found in [21].

We now illustrate the usage of the query patters on the sorting algorithm given in Sect. 3.1. The other algorithms can be considered in a similar manner. In order to verify that the algorithm works as desired, we have constructed a set of properties specified in kP-Queries, listed in Table 1. The applied pattern types are given in the second column of the table. For each property we provide the following information; (i) informal description of each kP-Query, and (ii) the formal kP-Query using the patterns. The queries given in Table 1 capture that the algorithm given in Sect. 3.1 works as desired.

We note that both the kP–Lingua model and the queries are automatically converted into the languages required by the corresponding model checkers. So, the verification process in kPWORKBENCH is carried out in an automatic manner.

5   Testing kP Systems Using Automata Based Techniques

In this section we outline how the kP systems obtained in the previous sections can be tested using automata based testing methods. The approach presented here follows the blueprint presented in [16,24] for cell-like P systems. We illustrate our approach on $k\Pi_1$, the application of our approach on the other kP system modelling sorting algorithms is similar.

Naturally, in order to apply an automata based testing method to a kP model, a finite automata needs to be obtained first. In general, the computation of a kP system cannot be fully modelled by a finite automaton and so an *approximate* automaton will be sought. The problem will be addressed in two steps.

- Firstly, the computation tree of a P system will be represented as a deterministic finite automaton. In order to guarantee the finiteness of this process, an upper bound k on the length of any computation will be set and only computations of maximum k transitions will be considered at a time.
- Secondly, a *minimal* model, that preserves the required behaviour, will be defined on the basis of the aforementioned derivation tree.

Let $M_k = (A_k, Q_k, q_{0,k}, F_k, h_k)$ be the finite automaton representation of the computation tree, where A_k is the finite input alphabet, Q_k is the finite set of states, $q_{0,k} \in Q_k$ is the initial state, $F_k \subseteq Q_k$ is the set of final states, and $h_k : Q_k \times A_k \longrightarrow Q_k$ is the next-state function. A_k is composed of the tuples of multisets that label the transition of the computation tree. The states of T_k correspond to the nodes of the tree. For testing purposes we will consider all the states as final. It is implicitly assumed that a non-final "sink" state q_{sink} that receives all "rejected" transitions, also exists.

Consider $k\Pi_1$, the kP system in Sect. 3.1, $n = 6$ and the sequence to be sorted 3, 6, 9, 5, 7, 8. Then the initial multisets are: $w_{1,0} = a^3 c^{10} p; w_{2,0} = a^6 c^{10}; w_{3,0} = a^9 c^{10} p; w_{4,0} = a^5 c^{10}; w_{5,0} = a^7 c^{10} p; w_{6,0} = a^8 c^{10}$. As $k\Pi_1$ is a deterministic kP system, there is no ramification in the computation tree. For $k = 3$, this is represented below.

Compartments - Step	C_1	C_2	C_3	C_4	C_5	C_6
0	$rr_{1,1}^3 r_{2,1}$	r	$rr_{1,3}^9 r_{2,3}$	r	$rr_{1,5}^7 r_{2,5}$	r
1		$rr_{3,1}$	$rr_{4,2}^3$	$rr_{3,3}$	$rr_{4,4}^5 r_{5,4}^4$	$rr_{3,5}$	$rr_{4,6}^7$
2		r	$rr_{1,2}^6 r_{2,2}$	r	$rr_{1,4}^9 r_{2,4}$	r	$rr_{2,6}$
3		r	$rr_{3,2}'$	$rr_{1,3}^5 r_{5,3}$	$rr_{3,4}'$	$rr_{1,5}^7 r_{5,5}^2$	$rr_{3,6}'$

Let us denote

$$\alpha_1 = (rr_{1,1}^3 r_{2,1}, r, rr_{1,3}^9 r_{2,3}, r, rr_{1,5}^7 r_{2,5}, r),$$
$$\alpha_2 = (rr_{3,1}, rr_{4,2}^3, rr_{3,3}, rr_{4,4}^5 r_{5,4}^4, rr_{3,5}, rr_{4,6}^7),$$
$$\alpha_3 = (r, rr_{1,2}^6 r_{2,2}, r, rr_{1,4}^9 r_{2,4}, r, rr_{2,6}),$$
$$\alpha_4 = (r, rr_{3,2}', rr_{1,3}^5 r_{5,3}, rr_{3,4}', rr_{1,5}^7 r_{5,5}^2, rr_{3,6}').$$

Then, for $k = 3$, $M_k = (A_k, Q_k, q_{0,k}, F_k, h_k)$, where $A_k = \{\alpha_1, \alpha_2, \alpha_3, \alpha_4\}$, $Q_k = \{q_{0,k}, q_{1,k}, q_{2,k}, q_{3,k}, q_{4,k}\}$, $F_k = Q_k$, and h_k, the next-state function, is defined by: $h_k(q_{i-1,k}, \alpha_i) = q_{i,k}$, $1 \le i \le 4$.

As M_k is a deterministic finite automaton over A_k, one can find the minimal deterministic finite automaton that accepts *exactly* the language defined by M_k. However, as only sequences of at most k transitions are considered, it is irrelevant how the constructed automaton will behave for longer sequences. Consequently, a deterministic finite cover automaton of the language defined by M_k will be sufficient.

A *deterministic finite cover automaton* (*DFCA*) of a finite language U is a deterministic finite automaton that accepts all sequences in U and possibly other sequences that are longer than any sequence in U [4,5]. A *minimal DFCA* of U is a DFCA of U having the least possible states. A minimal DFCA may not be unique (up to a renaming of its states). The great advantage of using a minimal DFCA instead of the minimal deterministic automaton that accepts precisely the language U is that the size (number of states) of the minimal DFCA may be much less than that of the minimal deterministic automaton that accepts U. Several algorithms for constructing a minimal DFCA (starting from the deterministic automaton that accepts the language U) exist, the best known algorithm [26] requires $O(n \log n)$ time, where n denotes the number of states of the original automaton. For details about the construction of a minimal DFCA we refer the reader to [24,26].

A minimal DFCA of the language defined by M_k, $k = 3$, is the following: $M = (A, Q, q_0, F, h)$, where $A = A_k$, $Q = \{q_0, q_1, q_2, q_3\}$, $F = Q$ and h defined by: $h(q_{i-1}, \alpha_i) = q_i$, $1 \le i \le 3$ and $h(q_3, \alpha_4) = q_0$.

Now, suppose we have a finite state model (automaton) of the system we want to test. In *conformance testing* one constructs a finite set of input sequences, called *test suite*, such that the implementation passes all tests in the test suite if and only if it behaves identically as the specification on any input sequence. Naturally, the implementation under test can also be modelled by an unknown deterministic finite automaton, say M'. This is not known, but one can make assumptions about it (e.g. that may have a number of incorrect transitions, missing or extra states). One of the least restrictive assumptions refers to its size (number of states). The W-*method* [12] assumes that the difference between the number of states of the implementation model and that of the specification has to be at most β, a non-negative integer estimated by the tester. The W-method involves the selection of two sets of input sequences, a state cover S and a characterization set W [12].

In our case, we have constructed a DFCA model of the system and we are only interested in the behavior of the system for sequences of length up to an upper bound k. Then, the set suite will only contain sequences of up to length k and its successful application to the implementation under test will establish that the implementation will behave identically to the specification for any sequence of length less then or equal to k. This situation is called conformance testing for bounded sequences. Recently, it was shown that the underlying idea of the W-method can also be applied in the case of bounded sequences, provided that the sets S and W used in the construction of the test suite satisfy some further requirements; these are called a proper state cover and strong characterization set, respectively [23]. In what follows we informally define these two concepts and illustrate them on our working example. For formal definitions we refer the reader to [23] or [24].

A *proper state cover* of a deterministic finite automaton $M = (A, Q, q_0, F, h)$ is a set of sequences $S \subseteq A^*$ such that for every state $q \in Q$, S contains a sequence of *minimum length* that reaches q. Consider M the DFCA in our example. Then λ is the sequence of minimum length that reaches q_0, σ_1 is a sequence of minimum length that reaches q_1, $\alpha_1\alpha_2$ is a sequence of minimum length that reaches q_2, $\alpha_1\alpha_2\alpha_3$ is a sequence of minimum length that reaches q_3. Furthermore, we can use any input symbol in $A \setminus \{\alpha_1\}$ to reach the (implicit) "sink" state, for example α_2. Thus, $S = \{\lambda, \alpha_1, \alpha_1\alpha_2, \alpha_1\alpha_2\alpha_3, \alpha_2\}$ is a proper state cover of M.

A *strong characterization set* of a minimal deterministic finite automaton $M = (A, Q, q_0, F, h)$ is a set of sequences $W \subseteq A^*$ such that for every two distinct states $q_1, q_2 \in Q$, W contains a sequence of minimum length that distinguishes between q_1 and q_2. Consider again our running example. λ distinguishes between the (non-final) "sink" state and all the other (final) states. A transition labelled α_1 is defined from q_0, but not from q_1, q_2 or q_3, so α_1 is a sequence of minimum length that distinguishes q_0 from q_1, q_2 and q_3. Similarly, α_2 is a sequence of minimum length that distinguishes q_1 from q_2 and q_3 and α_3 is a sequence of minimum length that distinguishes between q_2 and q_3. Thus $W = \{\lambda, \alpha_1, \alpha_2, \alpha_3\}$ is a strong characterization set of M,

Once we have established the sets S and W and the maximum number β of extra states that the implementation under test may have, a test suite is constructed by extracting all sequences of length up to k from the set

$$S(A^0 \cup A^1 \cup \cdots \cup A^\beta)W,$$

where A^i denotes the set of input sequences of length $i \geq 0$.

Note that some test sequences may be accepted by the DFCA model - these are called *positive tests* - but some others may not be accepted (they end up in the (non-final) "sink" state) - these are called *negative tests*.

6   Conclusions

In this paper, we have illustrated the modelling power of kernel P systems by providing a number of kP system models for sorting algorithms. These prove that the kP systems approach provides a coherent and expressive language that allows us to model various systems that were originally implemented by different P system variants. We have also discussed the problem of testing systems modelled as kernel P systems and proposed a test generation method based on automata. Namely, we have outlined how the kP systems can be tested using automata based testing methods. Furthermore, we have demonstrated how formal verification can be used to validate that the given models work as desired.

In our future work we aim to show how other problems can be solved, tested and verified by using kP systems and also to prove how existing classes of P systems can be expressed with this formalism.

Acknowledgements. The authors are indebted to the anonymous reviewers for carefully reading and providing comments allowing us to improve the content and presentation of the paper. MG and SK acknowledge the support provided for synthetic biology research by EPSRC ROADBLOCK (project number: EP/I031812/1). The work of FI and MG was supported by a grant of the Romanian National Authority for Scientific Research, CNCS-UEFISCDI (project number: PN-II-ID-PCE-2011-3-0688).

References

1. Alhazov, A., Sburlan, D.: Static sorting algorithms for P systems. In: Alhazov, A., et al. (eds.) Pre-Proceedings of 4th Workshop on Membrane Computing, GRLMC report 28/03, Tarragona, pp. 17–40 (2003)
2. Alhazov, A., Sburlan, D.: Static Sorting P Systems. In: [16], pp. 215–252 (2006)
3. Arulanandham, J.J.: Implementing bead-sort with P systems. In: Calude, C.S., Dinneen, M.J., Peper, F. (eds.) UMC 2002. LNCS, vol. 2509, pp. 115–125. Springer, Heidelberg (2002). doi:10.1007/3-540-45833-6_10
4. Câmpeanu, C., Sântean, N., Yu, S.: Minimal cover-automata for finite languages. In: Champarnaud, J.-M., Ziadi, D., Maurel, D. (eds.) WIA 1998. LNCS, vol. 1660, pp. 43–56. Springer, Heidelberg (1999). doi:10.1007/3-540-48057-9_4
5. Câmpeanu, C., Santean, N., Yu, S.: Minimal cover-automata for finite languages. Theor. Comput. Sci. **267**(1–2), 3–16 (2001)
6. Ceterchi, R., Martín-Vide, C.: P systems with communication for static sorting. In: Cavaliere, M., et al. (eds.) Pre-proceedings of 1st Brainstorming Week on Membrane Computing, Technical report no 26, pp. 101–117. Rovira i Virgili University, Tarragona (2003)
7. Ceterchi, R., Martín-Vide, C.: Dynamic P Systems. In: Păun, G., Rozenberg, G., Salomaa, A., Zandron, C. (eds.) WMC 2002. LNCS, vol. 2597, pp. 146–186. Springer, Heidelberg (2003). doi:10.1007/3-540-36490-0_11
8. Ceterchi, R., Pérez-Jiménez, M.J., Tomescu, A.I.: Simulating the bitonic sort using P systems. In: Eleftherakis, G., Kefalas, P., Păun, G., Rozenberg, G., Salomaa, A. (eds.) WMC 2007. LNCS, vol. 4860, pp. 172–192. Springer, Heidelberg (2007). doi:10.1007/978-3-540-77312-2_11

9. Ceterchi, R., Pérez-Jiménez, M.J., Tomescu, A.I.: Sorting Omega Networks Simulated with P Systems: Optimal Data Layouts. In: Diaz-Pernil, D., et al. (eds.) Proceedings of 6th Brainstorming Week on Membrane Computing, RGNC report 01/08, Fénix Editora, pp. 79–92 (2008)

10. Ceterchi, R., Tomescu, A.I.: Implementing sorting networks with spiking neural P systems. Fundamenta Informaticae **87**(1), 35–48 (2008)

11. Ceterchi, R., Sburlan, D.: Membrane Computing and Computer Science, Chap. 22 of [30], pp. 553–583 (2010)

12. Chow, T.S.: Testing Software design modeled by finite-state machines. IEEE Trans. Softw. Eng. **4**(3), 178–187 (1978)

13. Freund, R., Pérez-Hurtado, I., Riscos-Núñez, A., Verlan, S.: A formalization of membrane systems with dynamically evolving structures. Int. J. Comput. Math. **90**(4), 801–815 (2013)

14. Freund, R., Verlan, S.: A formal framework for static (tissue) P systems. In: Eleftherakis, G., Kefalas, P., Păun, G., Rozenberg, G., Salomaa, A. (eds.) WMC 2007. LNCS, vol. 4860, pp. 271–284. Springer, Heidelberg (2007). doi:10.1007/978-3-540-77312-2_17

15. Cimatti, A., Clarke, E., Giunchiglia, E., Giunchiglia, F., Pistore, M., Roveri, M., Sebastiani, R., Tacchella, A.: NuSMV 2 version 2: an opensource tool for symbolic model checking. In: Brinksma, E., Larsen, K.G. (eds.) CAV 2002. LNCS, vol. 2404, pp. 359–364. Springer, Heidelberg (2002). doi:10.1007/3-540-45657-0_29

16. Gheorghe, M., Ipate, F.: On testing P systems. In: Corne, D.W., Frisco, P., Păun, G., Rozenberg, G., Salomaa, A. (eds.) WMC 2008. LNCS, vol. 5391, pp. 204–216. Springer, Heidelberg (2009). doi:10.1007/978-3-540-95885-7_15

17. Gheorghe, M., Ipate, F., Dragomir, C.: Kernel P systems. In: Martínez-del-Amor, M.A., et al. (eds.) Proceedings of 10th Brainstorming Week on Membrane Computing, pp. 153–170. Fénix Editora, Universidad de Sevilla (2012)

18. Gheorghe, M., Ipate, F., Dragomir, C., Mierlă, L., Valencia-Cabrera, L., García-Quismondo, M., Pérez-Jiménez, M.J.: Kernel P systems - version 1. In: Valencia-Cabrera, L., et al. (eds.) Proceedings of 11th Brainstorming Week on Membrane Computing, pp. 97–124. Fénix Editora, Universidad de Sevilla (2013)

19. Gheorghe, M., Ipate, F., Lefticaru, R., Pérez-Jiménez, M.J., Ţurcanu, A., Valencia-Cabrera, L., García-Quismondo, M., Mierlă, L.: 3-COL problem modelling using simple kernel P systems. Int. J. Comput. Math. **90**(4), 816–830 (2013)

20. Gheorghe, M., Păun, Gh, Pérez-Jiménez, M.J., Rozenberg, G.: Research frontiers of membrane computing: open problems and research topics. Int. J. Found. Comput. Sci. **24**, 547–624 (2013)

21. Gheorghe, M., Konur, S., Ipate, F., Mierla, L., Bakir, M.E., Stannett, M.: An integrated model checking toolset for kernel P systems. In: Rozenberg, G., Salomaa, A., Sempere, J.M., Zandron, C. (eds.) CMC 2015. LNCS, vol. 9504, pp. 153–170. Springer, Cham (2015). doi:10.1007/978-3-319-28475-0_11

22. Holzmann, G.J.: The model checker SPIN. IEEE Trans. Softw. Eng. **23**(5), 275–295 (1997)

23. Ipate, F.: Bounded sequence testing from deterministic finite state machines. Theor. Comput. Sci. **411**(16–18), 1770–1784 (2010)

24. Ipate, F., Gheorghe, M.: Finite state based testing of P systems. Nat. Comput. **8**(4), 833–846 (2009)

25. Knuth, D.E.: The Art of Computer Programming. Sorting and Searching, vol. 3, 2nd edn. Addison Wesley Longman Publishing Co., Inc., Redwood City (1998). ISBN: 0-201-89685-0

26. Körner, H.: On minimizing cover automata for finite languages in $O(n \log n)$ time. In: Champarnaud, J.-M., Maurel, D. (eds.) CIAA 2002. LNCS, vol. 2608, pp. 117–127. Springer, Heidelberg (2003). doi:10.1007/3-540-44977-9_11

27. Păun, Gh: Computing with membranes. J. Comput. Syst. Sci. **61**(1), 108–143 (2000)

28. Păun, Gh: Membrane Computing - An Introduction. Springer, Heidelberg (2002)

29. Păun, Gh, Rozenberg, G., Salomaa, A. (eds.): The Oxford Handbook of Membrane Computing. Oxford University Press, New York (2010)

30. Sburlan, D.: A static sorting algorithm for P systems with mobile catalysts. Analele Ştiinţifice Universitatea Ovidius Constanţa **11**(1), 195–205 (2003)

Walking Membranes: Grid-Exploring P Systems with Artificial Evolution for Multi-purpose Topological Optimisation of Cascaded Processes

Thomas Hinze[1,2(✉)], Lea Louise Weber[2], and Uwe Hatnik[3]

[1] Department of Bioinformatics, Friedrich Schiller University Jena,
Ernst-Abbe-Platz 2, 07743 Jena, Germany
thomas.hinze@uni-jena.de
[2] Institute of Computer Science, Brandenburg University
of Technology, Postfach 10 13 44, 03013 Cottbus, Germany
weberlea@b-tu.de
[3] Design Automation Division EAS, Fraunhofer Institute for Integrated Circuits IIS,
Zeunerstraße 38, 01069 Dresden, Germany
uwe.hatnik@eas.iis.fraunhofer.de

Abstract. The capability of *self-organisation* belongs to the most fascinating features of many living organisms. It results in formation and continuous adjustment of dedicated *spatial structures* which in turn can sustain a high fitness and efficient use of resources even if environmental conditions or internal factors tend to vary. Spatial structures in this context might for instance incorporate *topological arrangements* of cellular compartments and filaments towards fast and effective signal transduction. Due to its discrete nature, the P systems approach represents an ideal candidate in order to capture emergence and evolution of topologies composed of membranes passable by molecular particles. We introduce *grid-exploring P systems* in which generalised membranes form the grid elements keeping the grid structure variable. Particles initially placed at different positions of the grid's boundary individually run through the grid visiting a sequence of designated membranes in which they become successively processed. Using artificial evolution, the arrangement of membranes within the grid becomes optimised for shortening the total time duration necessary for complete passage and processing of all particles. Interestingly, the corresponding framework comprises numerous practical applications beyond modelling of biological self-organisation. When replacing membranes by queue-based treads, tools, or processing units and particles by customers, workpieces, or raw products, we obtain a multi-purpose optimisation strategy along with a simulation framework. Three case studies from cell signalling, retail industry, and manufacturing demonstrate various benefits from the concept.

1 Introduction and Background

Living organisms appear almost perfectly adapted to environmental conditions. A plethora of elaborated survival strategies in concert with highly *optimised*

© Springer International Publishing AG 2017
A. Leporati et al. (Eds.): CMC 2016, LNCS 10105, pp. 251–271, 2017.
DOI: 10.1007/978-3-319-54072-6_16

form and function enables maintenance of individuals (*autopoiesis*) as well as long-term persistence of entire biological species or colonies. Impressive examples range from nanoscaled intracellular pathway mechanisms [9,14] via shapes of tissues or seeds [17] up to complex behavioural patterns of ant colonies, construction of insects' nests, or positioning of foxholes within a bumpy landscape [3,4,18]. All these phenomena have in common that spatial structures and arrangements follow the best possible way to fulfil a useful function in helping the organism to cope with realities.

Sometimes, a more or less static formation of a structure is sufficient. Let us consider for instance the common sunflower (*Helianthus annuus*). Its florets in the head are arranged in a way to assure a maximum exploitation of light energy since the individual florets have small offsets to each other. This in turn gives two advantages: Firstly, the shadow induced by a floret cannot significantly cover another floret. Secondly, the total number of florets within the sunflower's head reaches its maximum by close packaging [20]. To this end, the florets form centered spiral structures (Fermat's spirals) whose rotation angle resembles the golden ratio expressed by Fibonacci numbers, see Fig. 1 left part.

The scenario becomes more complicated when considering temporally *dynamic control* of spatial structures in an adaptively continuous manner instead of a one-time static formation. Resulting systems turn out to be highly robust against perturbations and damages [8]. An illustrative example in this context can be seen in the wide cardiovascular network of human blood vessels [21]. The existence and reliability of this circulatory system is essential for supply of each single cell with nutrients, metabolites, hormones, and other messengers. The underlying topology of the cardiovascular network obviously follows its function taking into account a minimum need of material resources and mechanical energy [23]. Mostly, this becomes evident by the placement of branches and junctions successively dividing arteries and capillaries towards more and more fine-grained spatial structures sketched in Fig. 1 right part. Interestingly, the cardiovascular network topology re-organises during the whole life time [15].

Both aforementioned biological examples – arrangement of florets in sunflower heads as well as the cardiovascular network topology of human blood vessels – demonstrate the capability of *self-organisation*. There are much more examples in many facets of biology and medicine. In all cases, spatial structures exhibit a certain flexibility which has been permanently utilised to find out the best possible topology to achieve adaptively under present constraints. Modifications affecting the topology have been initiated endogenously which means without any external control. Inspired by its potential in nature, we are going to develop an abstract descriptive framework for exploration of self-organisation *in-silico* on a two-dimensional grid along with a corresponding software for system's configuration and behavioural simulation. The P systems approach in general provides an ideal candidate to formalise this framework since it can directly cope with dynamical structures due to its employment of algebraic elements and flexible hierarchically nested compositions from that.

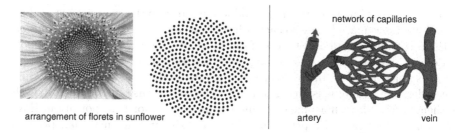

Fig. 1. Biological examples of spatial structures emerged from self-organising formation and maintenance. **Left:** Close two-dimensional packaging of florets in a sunflower head forming Fermat's spirals [20]. **Right:** Schematic representation of a cardiovascular network structure composed of blood vessels by self-organisation.

What stands out after study of diverse systems equipped with self-organisation is that in a majority of cases the optimised topology has been passed by *particles*. Typically, the particles carry a dedicated *meaning* for the underlying system such as providing information, energy supply, or messages. For instance, hormones as particles within the blood stream should fast and safely reach their specific destination cells coupled to the blood vessels. Photons assumed as particles should intensively and homogeneously penetrate the sunflower florets instead of getting lost aside. In other words, the entirety of particles passing through the topology defines the *fitness* of the topology on its own. During passage, a particle is allowed to consult a predetermined sequence of destinations within the topology in terms of a signalling cascade. Here, each destination acts as a processing unit for particles which in turn successively proceed and finally leave the system or get consumed. In the end, the whole amount of time necessary to completely process a given initial setting of particles measures the quality of the underlying topology under study. Slight *modifications* of the topology can lead to a better, worse, or unchanged quality. Those producing a better quality are retained. Modifications of the topology characterise an adaptive self-organisation able to manage varying settings of particles over time.

2   Identification of Interdisciplinary Application Scenarios

Potential applications of self-organising topologies are not restricted to modelling of pure biological phenomena. Particularly, the fourth industrial revolution (*"Industry 4.0"*) comes along with an increased need of so-called self-X properties [13]. Formerly large-volume fabrication of uniform products has been more and more transformed into assembly of highly individualised products. To this end, instead of mass-products, a huge variety of customised goods emerges. In order to successfully manage the underlying production processes, a continuous self-configuration, self-optimisation, and self-organisation of involved machines, processing units, and manufacturing facilities becomes essential. So, the placement and arrangement of moveable machines within a factory building could re-organise according to the current production order. In this way, groups or clusters of machines placed close to each other enable a cascaded form of production with short transportation distances of raw products. Here, a self-organised topology of machines aims at fastest passage and successive processing of raw products towards final products. In this scenario, the raw products act as particles while the underlying two-dimensional grid is composed of regions ("membranes"), each of them covered by a machine or forming a paved area for transportation. Having in mind that several types of machines can exist and raw materials prior to raw products may enter the grid at different entries, a non-trivial optimisation problem occurs in which the best possible topology needs to be found. Whenever there is a change of the production order, the optimisation problem arises again. Coping with dynamical structures within a formal framework turns out to be a final clue which opens a new field of applications for the P systems approach.

Another non-biological example of a self-organising two-dimensional grid of membranes passed by particles comes from retail industry when considering a typical supermarket. Nowadays, the arrangement of products at the two-dimensional ground follows a sophisticated scheme resulting from modern sales psychology. Customers should stay for a long time in the supermarket discovering more and more attractive products alongside their route from the entry to the cashpoints. In contrast, let us imagine an alternative form called *"Supermarket 2.0"* reflecting the habit of educated customers: They know in advance what products they are looking for. In addition, they permanently suffer from lack of time. This type of customers is interested in finding all desired products as fast as possible walking across the supermarket at the shortest possible path. Scanners in concert with contact-free automatic payment could further accelerate the shopping. While passing a supermarket's exit, the customer confirms the price to pay simply by pressing a button and having the debit card in the pocket. This concept has been already under test study [6,25]. It avoids the queue in front of conventional cashpoints. In this context, an optimal placement of products adapted to the preferences of educated customers defines an appealing scenario for a self-organisation framework in which customers represent the particles.

Motivated by these and many further application scenarios, we introduce grid-exploring P systems for topological optimisation of cascaded processes. Here, self-organisation towards fastest passage and processing of particles is carried out using artificial evolution which in turn cares for variation of grid elements. Since grid elements constitute membranes able to be entered and left by particles, the metaphor of *walking membranes* depicts the central idea traced throughout this paper. Principles of self-organisation have been addressed in the field of membrane computing from time to time. Tissue P systems [16] reflect the idea of a membrane grid. By grid-exploring P systems, we extend the notion of tissue P systems by dedicated transmembranous instructions (sequences of processing units) to be executed by each particle. Modelling of swarm-based multi-agent systems succeeded using population P systems [27]. In [2], self-assembly by consecutive membrane division in population P systems was modelled. Self-adaptive and reconfigurable distributed computing systems were introduced in [1]. Here, self-organisation is employed to minimise failures in network partitioning. Each node in the network stands for a uniform type of processor. When looking at self-modifiable sequences of instructions able to compose functional chemical units (modules) on the fly, we refer the reader to [12]. In [10], evaluation, accumulation, and categorised counting of particles initially positioned at a planar two-dimensional surface was considered for image analysis using blotting P systems. Some approaches in membrane computing are directed at modelling of dynamical structures in various facets. For instance, variable molecular structures expressed by modifiable character strings became apparent in [11] while active membranes flank the notion of P systems almost from its beginning [19].

In the following section, we familiarise the reader with the general concept of grid-exploring P systems which also sheds light on the assumptions made towards an abstract, flexible, and nevertheless widely practicable framework. After that, Sect. 5 is dedicated to define the underlying formalisms and algorithms comprising the framework of grid-exploring P systems and their behaviour over time. Our model comes along with three case studies revealing the overall capability of explorative two-dimensional grid optimisation in different application scenarios. First, we address biological cell signalling by taking into consideration several pathways (Sect. 6.1). Placement of receptors in conjunction with downstream signalling cascade destinations can induce a broad spectrum of latencies prior to cell response depending on the type (urgency) of stimulus signal. Beyond biology, Sect. 6.2 is focused on a production scenario in manufacturing. Here, an optimised placement of processing units for cascaded production of several goods is exemplified by a cabinet maker's workshop. The advantage of specific islands of machine tools over conventional production lines becomes visible. In Sect. 6.3, we develop an experimental idea of a possible alternative supermarket in the future whose arrangement of products follows the needs of educated customers in hurry. Even if a bit visionary, this example could sketch a new prototype of supermarket dominated by groups of frequently chosen product combinations. Final remarks discuss the concept of grid-exploring P systems regarding its extensibility for further work.

3   General Concept

Basic prerequisite for the topological optimisation is a configurable initial $n \times m$ grid composed of *membranes* as grid elements. In this context, a membrane represents a square-shaped region or area able to be entered, passed, and left by particles. In addition, membranes can also process or consume particles during passage. According to its functional purpose, we assume different predefined types of membranes:

- A **paved area** allows particle transportation. The corresponding membrane can be passed by particles in all directions without any processing or modification. Each paved area comes with two individual parameters: Its *capacity* defines the maximum number of particles permitted to stay inside the membrane at the same time. In case of exhausted capacity, no further particles can enter. Another parameter is the *duration of passage*, expressed by a natural number > 0. Its value marks the minimum number of time steps each particle must reside inside the membrane. Afterwards, it can leave the membrane by entering an adjacent membrane if possible. In its entirety, paved areas make accessible the grid for particles. When placed adjacent to each other, sequenced paved areas develop pathes throughout the grid to be trodden by particles. Paved areas placed at the outer boundary of the grid act as combined entries and exits. Each grid must have at least one entry/exit.

- A **blocked area** is a permanently empty membrane forbidden to become entered by particles. Using blocked areas, fixed zones can be excluded from any topological consideration and variation. This enables incorporation of specific immutable features of the underlying landscape or ground.
- A **processing unit** specifies a membrane able to affect particles which are permitted to enter from all adjacent paved areas. Since processing of particles can happen in a varied manner, we distinguish different types of processing units. The number of processing unit types can be arbitrarily chosen but at least one is mandatory. For simplicity, we assign a capitalised letter starting from A for each processing unit type. The grid example shown in Fig. 2 utilises three types denoted by A, B, and C. Addressed by its name, each processing unit type comprises two attributes for its behavioural specification. The *processing duration*, a natural number > 0, indicates the number of time steps necessary

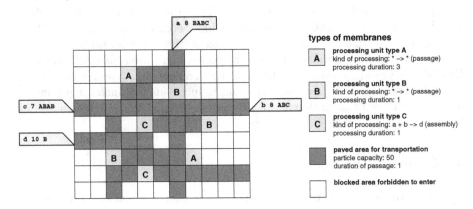

Fig. 2. Example of a predefined 9×11 grid with 7 entries/exits and 7 processing units marked by capitalised letters. From each processing unit, any processing unit of different type can be reached via paved areas. Initially, particles are placed in front of entries. There are four categories of particles called a, b, c, and d. Each particle is obliged to consult the corresponding sequence of processing units. By doing so, it can either be consumed within a processing unit (like in unit C which assembles $a + b \rightarrow d$ by consumption of particles a and b) or finally runs to the nearest entry/exit after completion of processing.

to carry out the processing. Furthermore, the *kind of processing* is given. Here, either the mode *passage* or *assembly* are available.

- **Passage**, marked by $* \to *$, leaves intact each entering particle which migrates to an adjacent membrane after processing as soon as possible. At the same time, at most one particle is allowed to be present in the processing unit.
- **Assembly** emulates a *composition, incorporation,* or *unification* of two particles which results in a particle again. Let particles a, b, and c be present within the grid, assembly can be of the form $a + b \to c$ (composition) but also $a + b \to a$ (incorporation) or $a + a \to b$ (unification). In the assembly mode, exactly two particles of the processed form are permitted to reside simultaneously within the processing unit. Along with assembly, these two particles are consumed releasing the corresponding product particle to leave the membrane as soon as possible.

Several instances of processing units of each type might be placed at the initial grid. Each processing unit must be reachable via at least one paved area. Adjacent positioning of processing units is forbidden in order to imply a transportation phase between subsequent processing steps.

Figure 2 illustrates an example of an initial grid configuration complemented by the placement of particles before passing the grid. For system's setup, we distinguish an arbitrarily chosen but final number of *particle categories*, for simplicity named by lower-case letters beginning from a. Each particle category comprises the total number of individual particles together with a uniform final sequence of processing unit identifiers to be passed. All particles from the same category are collectively placed in front of an arbitrary entry/exit of the grid. In the example shown in Fig. 2, there are four categories of particles (a, b, c, and d). Within this example setting, a total amount of 8 particles from category a are situated on top of the only entry/exit at the upper bound of the grid. Each particle from a must migrate to the nearest processing unit from type B, then A, B again, and finally C. Since C consumes particles of category a, their passage is finished there. Otherwise, particles after all steps of processing run to the next entry/exit to leave the grid.

Having the initial grid with its membranes and placement of particles at hand, a behavioural simulation traces the passage of the particles through the grid over time until all particles from all categories left the grid or got consumed. The corresponding total number of times steps taken from a global clock marks the *fitness* of the grid under study. The fitness measure reflects the suitability of the grid for processing all particles in the desired manner. In the example given in Fig. 2, we obtain a fitness of 98 time steps. Please note that a particle must wait inside a membrane if the subsequent membrane on its route cannot be entered since it is fully occupied. In this way, the passage could get delayed. By variation of the topological arrangement of processing units within the accessible part of the grid, the corresponding fitness values might deviate from each other. The faster a grid can process all particles, the higher its fitness. It may happen that a grid cannot completely process all particles due to two reasons: In case of a deadlock (circular path of membranes whose capacities are exhausted) or in case of persisting particles unable to become assembled due to lack of their counterparts, the overall duration of passage (execution time) is set to ∞ which implies worst possible fitness. Out of the initial grid, a variety ("population") of grids is generated using *artificial evolution*. To this end, we introduce two operators called *recombination* and *shift* able to modify the grid topology:

- **Recombination** randomly selects two processing units out of the whole grid. Both processing units get exchanged with each other. In case that either processing units are from the same type, the recombination has no effect, and the original grid is reproduced.
- **Shift** randomly picks one processing unit which swaps its place with one of the adjacent paved areas which in turn have been also identified by random in equipartition.

The initialisation phase of the artificial evolution creates a population of grids. Here, a number of copies ("individuals") from the initial grid is produced. Each of them undergoes either a recombination or a shift in which the occurrence of both operators is kept in parity. All grids emerged in this way are checked for validity. Invalid grids become removed from the population and replaced by additional ones until the desired population size is reached. A typical population size in our case studies comprises 50 grids. An individual fitness evaluation reveals the qualities of all grids in the population. The ascending order of fitness values identifies at its end a number of worst grids (20% of the population size) to be eliminated from the population. From the surviving grids, an appropriate number of copies is made and each of them tackled once by an evolutionary operator in order to fill up the population. So, the new generation of the grid population consists of a mixture of parents and offsprings in which the original initial grid always persists independently of its fitness in order to ensure a revitalisation of the population if necessary. We run the evolution loop until there is no improval of the best fitness over 100 generations. An optimisation result of the initial grid exemplified in Fig. 2 is shown in Fig. 3.

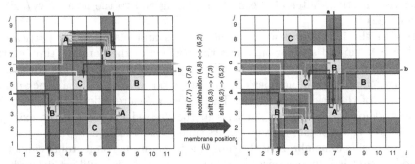

Fig. 3. Four evolutionary cycles can improve the fitness from 98 time steps (initial grid, left part) to 75 time steps (final grid, right part). Placement of particles and parameter setting of processing units and paved areas remain unchanged. The underlying artificial evolution carries out a self-organising optimisation of the grid topology in order to diminish the overall time of passage for all particles from the initial placement.

4   Reflecting Related Paradigms and Heuristic Concepts

The intended topological grid optimisation turns out to be a hard computational task. A complete enumeration of all potential grid layouts representing all combinations for placement of processing units implies a finite but huge search space. Its size exponentially grows with the number of grid areas. From a technical point of view, grids with approximately 30 or more areas elude an optimisation conducted by complete enumeration due to the infeasible need of computation time. In this context, employment of suitable *heuristics* appears to be the method of choice in order to obtain practicable results close to the global optimum within reasonable time. All heuristics have in common the incorporation of random in order to select elements from the search space whose quality as a solution candidate is evaluated. Based on this outcome, further search could prefer similar (related) elements in case of a high quality or distant elements otherwise. A large variety of heuristics at hand differs in the specific manner on how these steps are organised. Interestingly, the *no-free-lunch theorem* states that over many combinatorial optimisation problems and problem instances, different heuristics produce final solutions with similar quality and with similar performance in average. There is no "better" or "worse" heuristics in general [5]. Among the variety, artificial evolution comes with several beneficial properties. Most notably, effective evolutionary operators able to explore the search space intuitively result from the compositional nature of the grid. While *recombination* (see previous section) emphasises a rough exploration of the search space due to its strong influence on the grid topology, the *shift* operator in contrast carries out a fine tuning. This interplay of operators along with efficient fitness evaluation and well-tried experiences in setting and parameterisation of evolutionary programming schemes makes artificial evolution our favourite tool. Moreover, its intention comprising a population of individuals composed of algebraic elements comes close to the notion of membrane systems. Other formalisms like for instance cellular automata [24] or Petri nets [22] require additional effort in order to manage a population of grids. Furthermore, the practicability of fitness evaluation necessitates extensions of the formalisms as well. Alternative heuristics beyond artificial evolution are worth to be discussed [7]. Although inspired by different approaches, some of them lead to analogical implementations. *Reinforcement learning* gives an example for that. Here, a modification of the grid topology is also obtained by move or exchange of processing units. Modifications inducing a better solution become successively rewarded. *Simulated annealing* also follows the idea of stepwise grid modification taking into account that in the beginning of the optimisation process more tremendous topological changes are allowed than in a later phase which is controlled by a temperature function which in turn seems hard to parameterise for our purpose. *Swarm-based* methods and *hill climbing* exhibit a widely gradual approximation towards the optimum ideally for fitness landscapes with a low number of local optima. However, a topological grid optimisation needs to cope with numerous local optima widely distributed within the search space. In consequence, we decided on implementation of an evolutionary programming approach based on a membrane system.

5 Grid-Exploring P Systems: Definitions and Formalisms

5.1 Algebraic and String-Operational Prerequisites

Let A and B be arbitrary sets, $\emptyset$ the empty set, $\mathbb{N}$ the set of natural numbers including zero. The term $|A|$ denotes the number of elements in A (cardinality). The Cartesian product of A and B is written by $A \times B$. A multiset over A is a mapping $F : A \longrightarrow \mathbb{N}$. A multiset can also be specified by unordered enumeration of multiple elements like for instance $\{a, a, b, a, b\}$ instead of $\{(a, 3), (b, 2)\}$. The support $\mathrm{supp}(F) \subseteq A$ of F is defined by $\mathrm{supp}(F) = \{a \in A \mid F(a) > 0\}$. A multiset F over A is said to be empty iff $\forall a \in A : F(a) = 0$. The cardinality $|F|$ of F over A is $|F| = \sum\limits_{a \in A} F(a)$. Let A be a set, $a \in A$, and $F : A \longrightarrow \mathbb{N}$ a multiset. We define the removal $F \setminus \{a\} \Leftrightarrow F(a) := F(a) - 1$ and the incorporation $F \cup \{a\} \Leftrightarrow F(a) := F(a) + 1$, respectively.

Let Σ be an alphabet, ε the empty word, and $w \in \Sigma^*$ a word over Σ. The symbol $x \in \Sigma$ is called *prefix*(w) iff $w = xy$ and $y \in \Sigma^*$. The symbol $z \in \Sigma$ is called *suffix*(w) iff $w = yz$ and $y \in \Sigma^*$. Let $u, v \in \Sigma^*$ words over the same alphabet. Concatenation $u \oplus v := uv$ appends v to u. For removal of the leftmost symbol x from a word w, we define $w \ominus x := y$ with $w = xy$.

5.2 Definition of System Components

A grid exploring P system $\Pi_\square$ is a construct

$$\Pi_\square = (m, n, \Sigma_F, \Sigma_P, G_{\mathrm{mbrns}}, G_{\mathrm{capac}}, G_{\mathrm{durat}}, F, P)$$

with its components

$m \in \mathbb{N} \setminus \{0\}$ .... number of grid columns

$n \in \mathbb{N} \setminus \{0\}$ .... number of grid rows

Σ_F .... alphabet of processing unit types

Σ_P .... alphabet of particle categories

$G_{\mathrm{mbrns}} : \{1, \ldots, m\} \times \{1, \ldots, n\} \longrightarrow \Sigma_F \cup \{\#\} \cup \{\bot\}$
  grid of membranes, denoted by a matrix and represented by a function whose arguments identify column and row. Assigned function values provide the type of membrane at the corresponding grid position. Available types are processing units ($\in \Sigma_F$), paved areas ($\#$), and blocked areas ($\bot$).

$G_{\mathrm{capac}} : \{1, \ldots, m\} \times \{1, \ldots, n\} \longrightarrow \mathbb{N}$
  capacities of grid elements which define the maximum number of particles allowed to be present at the same grid membrane simultaneously. Blocked areas are assumed to have a capacity of 0. All other membranes should constitute individual capacities > 0.

$G_{\text{durat}} : \{1, \ldots, m\} \times \{1, \ldots, n\} \longrightarrow \mathbb{N} \setminus \{0\}$

> durations necessary for particle passage or processing individually assigned to each membrane within the grid. Each duration is expressed by a number of time steps.

$F : \Sigma_F \longrightarrow \{\star\} \cup \Sigma_P^3$. mode (kind of processing) for each processing unit type

$P : \{((i,j), p, f) \mid i \in \{1, \ldots, m\} \wedge j \in \{1, \ldots, n\} \wedge p \in \Sigma_p \wedge f \in \Sigma_F^*\} \longrightarrow \mathbb{N}$

> finite multiset of particles. Each particle comes with individual attributes such as its position (i,j) at the grid, its category p, and a finite sequence (word) f of processing unit types to be consecutively passed through.

5.3 Auxiliary Data to be Obtained Prior to System's Evolution

Undirected Graph (V, E) of Routes Through the Grid of Membranes

$V = \left\{ (a,b) \mid G_{\text{mbrns}}(a,b) \in \Sigma_F \cup \{\#\} \right\}$ and $E \subseteq V \times V$ with

$E = \{ \left((a,b), (c,d) \right), \left((c,d), (a,b) \right) \mid G_{\text{mbrns}}(a,b) \in \Sigma_F \cup \{\#\} \wedge$

$\quad G_{\text{mbrns}}(c,d) \in \Sigma_F \cup \{\#\} \wedge (((|a - c| = 1) \wedge (b = d)) \vee ((|b - d| = 1) \wedge (a = c))) \}$

The graph (V, E) identifies the adjacence structure of grid membranes. Each accessible membrane of the underlying grid results in a node while adjacent membranes get bidirectionally connected by edges.

Shortest Routes Through Graph (V, E)

Using the *Floyd-Warshall* algorithm [26], the shortest path from each node to each other node along with its length is calculated by filling two matrices.

matrix of shortest routes $H_{\text{route}} : V \times V \longrightarrow V^*$

matrix of shortest distances $H_{\text{dist}} : V \times V \longrightarrow \mathbb{N} \cup \{\infty\}$

```
for (i, j) ∈ V × V:
    H_route(i, j) := ε
    H_dist(i, j) := { 1  iff (i, j) ∈ E
                    { ∞ otherwise
for (k, l) ∈ V:
    for ((o, p), (q, r)) ∈ E:
        dist := H_dist((o, p), (k, l)) + H_dist((k, l), (q, r))
        if (dist < H_dist((o, p), (q, r))):
            H_dist((o, p), (q, r)) := dist
            H_route((o, p), (q, r)) := H_route((o, p), (k, l)) ⊕ (k, l) ⊕ H_route((k, l), (q, r))
```

Check for Validity of the Grid of Membranes

Since the grid must be passable by the particles in the desired sequence of processing units, a validity check of the grid prior to its fitness evaluation and optimisation is required. Invalid grids cannot be handled. We formulate the validity check by a number of constraints which have to be met in conjunction:

- at least one entry/exit is available in the grid
- no processing unit is placed at the outer grid boundaries
- there are no adjacent processing units
- each processing unit type is reachable from each other processing unit
- each route from an any processing unit to another one takes course exclusively via paved areas
- from any processing unit at least one entry/exit is reachable
- from each entry/exit each processing unit type is reachable

Auxiliary Function Estimating Next Membrane Towards Nearest Exit
After a particle has passed all processing units, it runs to the nearest exit. To do so, we provide an auxiliary function which detects for all accessible grid membranes (for all nodes in V) the next membrane to be entered in order to reach the nearest exit. We implement $\texttt{succ\_to\_exit} : V \longrightarrow V$ called by $\texttt{succ\_to\_exit}(i, j)$ in pseudocode.

```
min := ∞
x := ε
if (i = 1 ∨ i = m ∨ j = 1 ∨ j = n):
    succ_to_exit(i, j) := (i, j)
else
    for a ∈ {1, ..., m}:
        if (H_dist((i, j), (a, 1)) < min):
            min := H_dist((i, j), (a, 1))
            x := H_route((i, j), (a, 1))
        if (H_dist((i, j), (a, n)) < min):
            min := H_dist((i, j), (a, n))
            x := H_route((i, j), (a, n))
```

```
for b ∈ {1, ..., n}:
    if (H_dist((i, j), (1, b)) < min):
        min := H_dist((i, j), (1, b))
        x := H_route((i, j), (1, b))
    if (H_dist((i, j), (m, b)) < min):
    if (H_dist((i, j), (m, b)) < min):
        min := H_dist((i, j), (m, b))
        min := H_dist((i, j), (m, b))
        x := H_route((i, j), (m, b))
if (x = ε):
    succ_to_exit(i, j) := (i, j)
else
    succ_to_exit(i, j) := prefix(x)
```

Function Estimating Next Membrane Towards Next Processing Unit
Analogously, we make available an auxiliary function $\texttt{succ\_to\_proc\_unit} : V \times \Sigma_F \longrightarrow V$ which detects for all accessible grid membranes (for all nodes in V) the next membrane to be entered in order to reach the nearest processing unit from type $f \in F$. The function is called by $\texttt{succ\_to\_proc\_unit}((i, j), f)$.

```
min := ∞; x := ε
if (G_mbrns(i, j) = f): succ_to_proc_unit((i, j), f) := (i, j)
else
    for a ∈ {1, ..., m}:
        for b ∈ {1, ..., n}:
            if ((G_mbrns(a, b) = f) ∧ (H_dist((i, j), (a, b)) < min)):
                min := H_dist((i, j), (a, b))
                x := H_route((i, j), (a, b))
    if (x = ε): succ_to_proc_unit((i, j), f) := (i, j)
    else
        succ_to_proc_unit((i, j), f) := prefix(x)
```

5.4   Passing the Particles Throughout the Grid for Estimation of Total Overall Execution Time

The fitness of a grid together with its initial placement of particles is expressed by the overall execution time which means the number of time steps necessary to process all particles and run them outwards the grid. The formal description of the fitness evaluation is based on a global clock counting the number of time steps on the one hand and the successive progression of the P system's *configuration* on the other. Let $Q = \{((i,j),p,f) \mid i \in \{1,\dots,m\} \wedge j \in \{1,\dots,n\} \wedge p \in \Sigma_p \wedge f \in \Sigma_F^*\} \longrightarrow \mathbb{N}$ be an arbitrary multiset of particles located within the membrane at grid position (i,j). We capture a configuration of $\Pi_\square$ at time t by a triple $(Q_{\mathrm{processing}}, Q_{\mathrm{migratable}}, t)$ in which $t \in \mathbb{N} \cup \{\infty\}$ marks a point in time. $Q_{\mathrm{processing}} : V \longrightarrow (\mathrm{supp}(Q) \times \mathbb{N} \longrightarrow \mathbb{N})$ assigns to each grid position (i,j) a multiset of particles present in this membrane and being processed. Along with insertion of a particle into $Q_{\mathrm{processing}}$, a time stamp is assigned. This is necessary in order to decide when the processing is over. In addition, $Q_{\mathrm{migratable}} : V \longrightarrow Q$ contains for each grid position all particles locally processed and ready to migrate to the adjacent membrane as soon as possible. The fitness function $\mathtt{fitness} : (\Pi_\square) \mapsto t$ determines the number of time steps to pass all particles up to the finally empty grid. To this end, the global clock starts with 0, the initial configuration is set up, and afterwards a loop becomes iterated in which the configuration is updated and the number of elapsed time steps increased by 1.

$t := 0$
$\mathtt{for}\ a \in \{1,\dots,m\}:$
　　$\mathtt{for}\ b \in \{1,\dots,n\}:$
　　　　$Q_{\mathrm{processing}}(a,b) := \emptyset$
　　　　$Q_{\mathrm{migratable}}(a,b) := \emptyset$
　　　　$\mathtt{for}\ ((i,j),p,f) \in P:$
　　　　　　$\mathtt{if}\ ((a = i) \wedge (b = j)):$
　　　　　　　　$Q_{\mathrm{processing}}(a,b) := Q_{\mathrm{processing}}(a,b) \cup \{(((i,j),p,f),t)\}$

$\mathtt{while}\ \left(\sum\limits_{b=1}^{n}\sum\limits_{a=1}^{m}(|Q_{\mathrm{processing}}(a,b)| + |Q_{\mathrm{migratable}}(a,b)|) > 0\right):$
$t := t + 1$
$\mathtt{for}\ a \in \{1,\dots,m\}:$
　　$\mathtt{for}\ b \in \{1,\dots,n\}:$
　　　　$\mathtt{for}\ (((i,j),p,f),\tau) \in Q_{\mathrm{processing}}(a,b):$
　　　　　　$\mathtt{if}\ ((a = i) \wedge (b = j)):$
　　　　　　　　$\mathtt{if}\ (t \geq \tau + G_{\mathrm{durat}}(a,b)):$
　　　　　　　　　　$Q_{\mathrm{processing}}(a,b) := Q_{\mathrm{processing}}(a,b) \setminus \{(((i,j),p,f),\tau)\}$
　　　　　　　　　　$Q_{\mathrm{migratable}}(a,b) := Q_{\mathrm{migratable}}(a,b) \cup \{((i,j),p,f)\}$
　　　　　　　　$\mathtt{for}\ ((i,j),p,f) \in Q_{\mathrm{migratable}}(a,b):$
　　　　　　　　　　$\mathtt{if}\ (G_{\mathrm{mbrns}}(a,b) = \#):$
　　　　　　　　　　　　$\mathtt{if}\ (f = \varepsilon):$
　　　　　　　　　　　　　　$\mathtt{if}\ ((i = 1) \vee (i = m) \vee (j = 1) \vee (j = n)):$

$$Q_{\mathrm{migratable}}(a,b) := Q_{\mathrm{migratable}}(a,b) \setminus \{((i,j),p.f)\}$$

elseif $(|Q_{\mathrm{processing}}(\texttt{succ\_to\_exit}(i,j))| +$
$Q_{\mathrm{migratable}}(\texttt{succ\_to\_exit}(i,j))| < G_{\mathrm{capac}}(\texttt{succ\_to\_exit}(i,j)))$:
$$Q_{\mathrm{migratable}}(a,b) := Q_{\mathrm{migratable}}(a,b) \setminus \{((i,j),p,f)\}$$
$$Q_{\mathrm{processing}}(\texttt{succ\_to\_exit}(i,j)):=Q_{\mathrm{processing}}(\texttt{succ\_to\_exit}(i,j))$$
$$\cup \{((\texttt{succ\_to\_exit}(i,j),p,f),t)\}$$

if $(G_{\mathrm{mbrns}}(a,b) \in \Sigma_F \wedge F(G_{\mathrm{mbrns}}(a,b)) = \star)$:
  if $(f = \varepsilon)$:
    if $(|Q_{\mathrm{processing}}(\texttt{succ\_to\_exit}(i,j))| +$
    $Q_{\mathrm{migratable}}(\texttt{succ\_to\_exit}(i,j))| < G_{\mathrm{capac}}(\texttt{succ\_to\_exit}(i,j)))$:
    $$Q_{\mathrm{migratable}}(a,b) := Q_{\mathrm{migratable}}(a,b) \setminus \{((i,j),p,f)\}$$
    $$Q_{\mathrm{processing}}(\texttt{succ\_to\_exit}(i,j)):=Q_{\mathrm{processing}}(\texttt{succ\_to\_exit}(i,j))$$
    $$\cup \{((\texttt{succ\_to\_exit}(i,j),p,f),t)\}$$

    elseif $(|Q_{\mathrm{processing}}(\texttt{succ\_to\_proc\_unit}((i,j),\mathit{prefix}(f))| +$
    $Q_{\mathrm{migratable}}(\texttt{succ\_to\_proc\_unit}((i,j),\mathit{prefix}(f))| <$
    $G_{\mathrm{capac}}(\texttt{succ\_to\_proc\_unit}((i,j),\mathit{prefix}(f))))$:
    $$Q_{\mathrm{migratable}}(a,b) := Q_{\mathrm{migratable}}(a,b) \setminus \{((i,j),p,f)\}$$
    $$Q_{\mathrm{processing}}(\texttt{succ\_to\_proc\_unit}((i,j),\mathit{prefix}(f))) :=$$
    $$Q_{\mathrm{processing}}(\texttt{succ\_to\_proc\_unit}((i,j),\mathit{prefix}(f))) \cup$$
    $$\{((\texttt{succ\_to\_proc\_unit}((i,j),\mathit{prefix}(f)),p,f \ominus \mathit{prefix}(f)),t)\}$$

if $(G_{\mathrm{mbrns}}(a,b) \in \Sigma_F \wedge F(G_{\mathrm{mbrns}}(a,b)) \neq \star)$:
  if $(p = \mathit{prefix}(F(G_{\mathrm{mbrns}}(a,b))))$:
    $q := F(G_{\mathrm{mbrns}}(a,b)) \ominus \mathit{prefix}(F(G_{\mathrm{mbrns}}(a,b))) \ominus$
    $$\mathit{suffix}(F(G_{\mathrm{mbrns}}(a,b)))$$

    $\mathit{partner} := \mathit{false}$
    if $(((i,j+1),q,G_{\mathrm{mbrns}}(a,b+1)) \in Q_{\mathrm{migratable}}(a,b+1))$:
    $\mathit{partner} := \mathit{true}$
    $$Q_{\mathrm{migratable}}(a,b+1)) := Q_{\mathrm{migratable}}(a,b+1)) \setminus$$
    $$\{((i,j+1),q,G_{\mathrm{mbrns}}(a,b+1))\}$$
    elseif $(((i,j-1),q,G_{\mathrm{mbrns}}(a,b-1)) \in Q_{\mathrm{migratable}}(a,b-1))$:
    $\mathit{partner} := \mathit{true}$
    $$Q_{\mathrm{migratable}}(a,b-1)) := Q_{\mathrm{migratable}}(a,b-1)) \setminus$$
    $$\{((i,j-1),q,G_{\mathrm{mbrns}}(a,b-1))\}$$
    elseif $(((i+1,j),q,G_{\mathrm{mbrns}}(a+1,b)) \in Q_{\mathrm{migratable}}(a+1,b))$:
    $\mathit{partner} := \mathit{true}$
    $$Q_{\mathrm{migratable}}(a+1,b)) := Q_{\mathrm{migratable}}(a+1,b)) \setminus$$
    $$\{((i+1,j),q,G_{\mathrm{mbrns}}(a+1,b))\}$$
    elseif $(((i-1,j),q,G_{\mathrm{mbrns}}(a-1,b)) \in Q_{\mathrm{migratable}}(a-1,b))$:
    $\mathit{partner} := \mathit{true}$
    $$Q_{\mathrm{migratable}}(a-1,b)) := Q_{\mathrm{migratable}}(a-1,b)) \setminus$$
    $$\{((i-1,j),q,G_{\mathrm{mbrns}}(a-1,b))\}$$
    if $(\mathit{partner} = \mathit{true})$:
      if $(f = \varepsilon)$:
        if $(|Q_{\mathrm{processing}}(\texttt{succ\_to\_exit}(i,j))| +$
        $|Q_{\mathrm{migratable}}(\texttt{succ\_to\_exit}(i,j))| < G_{\mathrm{capac}}(\texttt{succ\_to\_exit}(i,j)))$:

$$Q_{\text{migratable}}(a, b) := Q_{\text{migratable}}(a, b) \setminus \{((\underline{i, j}), p, f)\}$$
$$Q_{\text{processing}}(\texttt{succ\_to\_exit}(\underline{i, j})) :=$$
$$Q_{\text{processing}}(\texttt{succ\_to\_exit}(\underline{i, j})) \cup$$
$$\{((\texttt{succ\_to\_exit}(\underline{i, j}), \mathit{suffix}(F(G_{\text{mbrns}}(a, b))), f \ominus \mathit{prefix}(f)), t)\}$$
$$\texttt{elseif} \ (|Q_{\text{processing}}(\texttt{succ\_to\_proc\_unit}((\underline{i, j}), \mathit{prefix}(f)))| +$$
$$|Q_{\text{migratable}}(\texttt{succ\_to\_proc\_unit}((\underline{i, j}), \mathit{prefix}(f)))| <$$
$$G_{\text{capac}}(\texttt{succ\_to\_proc\_unit}((\underline{i, j}), \mathit{prefix}(f)))):$$
$$Q_{\text{migratable}}(a, b) := Q_{\text{migratable}}(a, b) \setminus \{((\underline{i, j}), p, f)\}$$
$$Q_{\text{processing}}(\texttt{succ\_to\_proc\_unit}((\underline{i, j}), \mathit{prefix}(f))) :=$$
$$Q_{\text{processing}}(\texttt{succ\_to\_proc\_unit}((\underline{i, j}), \mathit{prefix}(f))) \cup$$
$$\{((\texttt{succ\_to\_proc\_unit}((\underline{i, j}), \mathit{prefix}(f)), \mathit{suffix}(F(G_{\text{mbrns}}(a, b))), f \ominus \mathit{prefix}(f)), t)\}$$
$$\texttt{fitness}(\Pi_{\square}) := t$$

We are aware of unlikely but potentially possible situations in which the number of time steps will infinitely grow without termination. This can happen due to two reasons: A circular path of membranes whose capacity is exhausted might cause a deadlock. Moreover, in case of utilisation of processing units assembling two particles into a resulting product, some particles could stuck in a membrane but their counterpart is permanently absent. These particles are unable to get completely processed. We can cope with both situations by inspection of $Q_{\text{processing}}$ and $Q_{\text{migratable}}$ over time. If there is no modification of both matrices over a long period of time steps, the fitness evaluation terminates by return of ∞.

5.5 Artificial Evolution

For the artificial evolution, we induce a list (population) of grid exploring P systems ($\Pi_{\square}^i$) in which the index i identifies the individuals. After the initialisation, the evolution loop drives the generations, see pseudocode:

```
g := 0;  i := 1;  φ₀ := fitness(Π⁰_□)
while(i < population_size) :
    Π^i_□ := duplicate(Π⁰_□)
    mutate(Π^i_□)
    if (validity_check(m, n, G_mbrns, H_dist, H_route)_i) :
        i := i + 1
while(g < max_number_of_generations) :
    φ_i := fitness(Π^i_□)  ∀i ∈ {1,..., population_size}
    sort_by_fitness()
    k := ⌊0.8 · population_size⌋
    remove(Π^j_□)  ∀j ∈ {k,..., population_size}
    j := 1
    while (j < population_size) :
        Π^j_□ := duplicate(Π^{random([0..k-1])}_□)
        mutate(Π^j_□)
        if (validity_check(m, n, G_mbrns, H_dist, H_route)_i) :
            j := j + 1
    g := g + 1
```

For duplication of an individual, we prepare the function `duplicate`. `mutate` randomly decides whether a recombination or a shift occurs and carries out the corresponding mutation. `remove` eliminates an individual from the list. `sort_by_fitness` permutates the list of individuals in ascending fitness order (Figs. 4, 5 and 6).

6   Case Studies

6.1   Cell Signalling Cascades

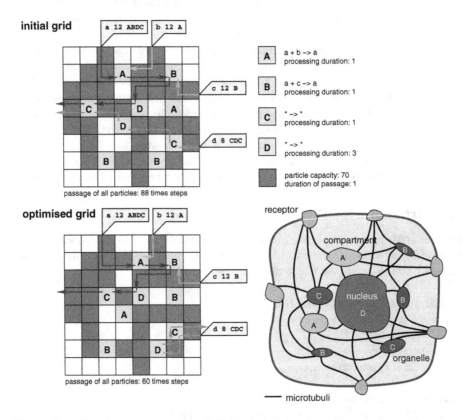

Fig. 4. Signalling in an eucaryotic cell. Signalling molecules a, b, c, and d reach receptors at the outer cell membrane. From there, they enter the cell (for instance by endocytosis) passing through a signalling cascade. Transported via microtubuli of the cytoskeleton, they become successively processed within compartments and organelles embedded into the cytosol. The initial grid predefines an abstracted cell structure which exhibits a fitness of 88 time steps to process all signalling molecules in the desired manner. Within A and B, complex formations are carried out incorporating b and c into a. D represents the nucleus for gene expression. The resulting cell response leaves the cell via C. There are two signalling pathways. One of them is initiated by a, the second one by d. Evolutionary structural optimisation improves the fitness to 60 time steps.

6.2   Manufacturing in a Cabinet Maker's Workshop

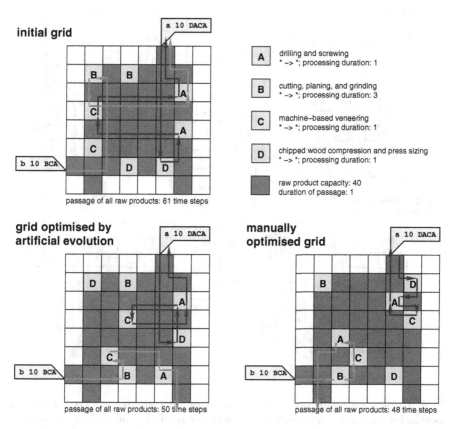

Fig. 5. Cascaded processing of raw products in a cabinet maker's workshop. Raw products called **a** and **b** have been delivered at different entries/exits of a factory work floor depicted as grid. Processing units available in multiple copies allow for completion of a specific work step. We distinguish four types of machines: A (drilling, screwing), B (cutting, planing, grinding), C (veneering), and D (press sizing). Raw products **a** require the processing sequence DACA while those called **b** need to pass BCA. The initial grid arranges all processing units at the outer walls. By evolutionary optimisation, we observe a self-organisation of so-called *production islands*, clusters of processing units corresponding to the individual workflows for both product lines. This diminishs the overall execution time from 61 to 50 time steps. A manual optimisation reveals a best possible result of 48 time steps. From a variety of independently conducted optimisation studies starting from the same initial grid, we obtained numerous topological arrangements. Interestingly, they achieved similar fitness values ranging from 50 to 52 which confirms the observation that artificial evolution typically ends up with results close to but away from the global optimum.

6.3   Alternative Supermarket

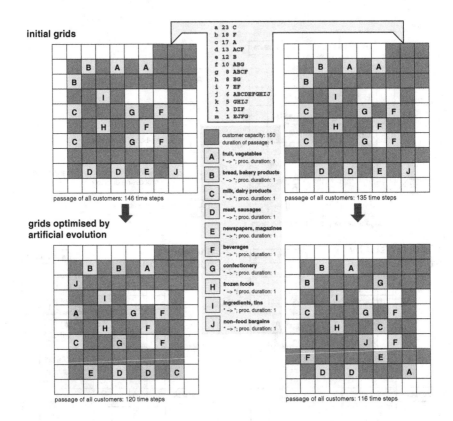

Fig. 6. Upper left grid: Initial placement of product groups in a typical German supermarket with *one central entry/exit*, customer routes in anticlockwise orientation and strictly separated classes of goods. In the example study, 131 customers reflecting frequently observed selections of product combinations visit the supermarket which requires 146 time steps in total. **Lower left grid:** After artificial evolution, a re-arrangement of product placement reveals clusters of complementary products like bread/breakfast cereals (**B**) with bargains (**J**) or frozen products (**H**) with confectionery (**G**). Some products like fruit/vegetables (**A**) are offered at different places. For the sample customers, the overall duration has been decreased to 120 time steps. **Upper right grid:** The same initial placement of product groups and the same setting of customers like in the upper left grid is considered but now the supermarket possess *two additional exits*. This action on its own without further optimisation succeeds by a corresponding fitness of 135 time steps. **Lower right grid:** The fitness can further improve by artificial evolution finally resulting in 116 time steps. To this end, the original ample straight-forward paths have been replaced by more or less local round tours preventing customers from crossing most parts of the supermarket. Especially products in demand near the new exits can effectively accelerate the shopping process for many customers in hurry. By leaving the supermarket earlier with all desired products, they less intensively hamper exhaustive shoppers which in turn can also finalise faster.

7 Discussion and Conclusions

The concept of topological grid optimisation by self-organising dynamical structures using grid-exploring P systems opens one more field of broad applications of membrane-based computing inspired by *bionics*. Interestingly, formalisation of modifiable spatial structures mainly exploits algebraic elements along with their nested composition. Dynamics on that is typically driven by algorithmic denotations in an imperatively or rule-controlled manner rather than prone to explicite formulas or closed analytical terms. We believe that the inherent complexity of structural dynamics suggests an incorporation of algorithmical components into corresponding P systems. In this paper, we exemplified this idea by means of artificial evolution which includes an algorithm for fitness evaluation. Its parameterisation follows common and empirically reliable assumptions. A population size of 50 grids seems to be large enough to create a sufficient variety in which 80% survive for the next generation. No improvement of the best fitness for 100 generations implies termination of the artificial evolution. This turns out to be enough to enable an effective *fine tuning* that can lead to grid structures with improved quality. Dedicated formation of *processing islands* is an example for this. We obtained the best experimental results by utilisation of both evolutionary operators (recombination, shift) in parity and by permanent survival of the initial grid within the population. Unequivocally, the success of artificial evolution also depends on predefinition of a suitable initial grid with a balanced degree of freedom. A free version of the software implemented in JavaScript is available at http://www-user.tu-cottbus.de/~weberlea/gridtool/ and from the authors upon request. This version supports processing units in passage mode as well as incorporation in assembly mode. Further work is aimed at making the fitness evaluation "smarter". Instead of simply running each particle to the *nearest* destination of the desired type, the underlying algorithm could interpret temporary delays, particle jam, or overcharged processing units which ends up with flexible generation of alternative bypass routes individually for each particle.

References

1. Bagchi, S.: Self-adaptive and reconfigurable distributed computing systems. Appl. Soft Comput. **12**, 3023–3033 (2012)
2. Bernardini, F., Gheorghe, M., Krasnogor, N., Giavitto, J.-L.: On self-assembly in population P systems. In: Calude, C.S., Dinneen, M.J., Păun, G., Pérez-Jímenez, M.J., Rozenberg, G. (eds.) UC 2005. LNCS, vol. 3699, pp. 46–57. Springer, Heidelberg (2005). doi:10.1007/11560319_6
3. Buhl, J., Deneubourg, J.L., Grimal, A., Theraulaz, G.: Self-organized digging activity in ant colonies. Behav. Ecol. Sociobiol. **58**, 9–17 (2005)
4. Camazine, S., Deneubourg, J.L., Franks, N.R., Sneyd, J., Theraulaz, G., Bonabeau, E.: Self-organization in Biological Systems. Princeton University Press, Princeton (2003)
5. Du, K.L., Swamy, M.N.S.: Search and Optimization by Metaheuristics: Techniques and Algorithms Inspired by Nature. Springer, Berlin (2016)

6. Fangwei, Z., Huang, J., Meagher, M.: The introduction and design of a new form of supermarket: smart market. In: Information Engineering and Electronic Commerce (IEEC 2009), pp. 608–611. IEEE Press (2009)
7. Gendreau, M., Potvin, J.Y. (eds.): Handbook of Metaheuristics. Springer, Berlin (2010)
8. Gheorghe, M., Păun, G.: Computing by self-assembly: DNA molecules, polyominoes, cells. Syst. Self-Assemb.: Multidiscipl. Snapshots Stud. Multidiscipl. **5**, 49–78 (2008). Elsevier
9. Hancock, J.T.: Cell Signalling. Oxford University Press, Oxford (2010)
10. Hinze, T., Grützmann, K., Höckner, B., Sauer, P., Hayat, S.: Categorised counting mediated by blotting membrane systems for particle-based data mining and numerical algorithms. In: Gheorghe, M., Rozenberg, G., Salomaa, A., Sosík, P., Zandron, C. (eds.) CMC 2014. LNCS, vol. 8961, pp. 241–257. Springer, Heidelberg (2014). doi:10.1007/978-3-319-14370-5_15
11. Hinze, T., Behre, J., Bodenstein, C., Escuela, G., Grünert, G., Hofstedt, P., Sauer, P., Hayat, S., Dittrich, P.: Membrane systems and tools combining dynamical structures with reaction kinetics for applications in chronobiology. In: Frisco, P., Gheorghe, M., Perez-Jimenez, M.J. (eds.) Applications of Membrane Computing in Systems and Synthetic Biology. Emergence, Complexity, and Computation, vol. 7, pp. 133–173. Springer, Heidelberg (2014)
12. Hinze, T., Kirkici, K., Sauer, P., Sauer, P., Behre, J.: Membrane computing meets temperature: a thermoreceptor model as molecular slide rule with evolutionary potential. In: Rozenberg, G., Salomaa, A., Sempere, J.M., Zandron, C. (eds.) CMC 2015. LNCS, vol. 9504, pp. 215–235. Springer, Heidelberg (2015). doi:10.1007/978-3-319-28475-0_15
13. Ivanov, D., Dolgui, A., Sokolov, B., Werner, F., Ivanova, M.: A dynamic model and an algorithm for short-term supply chain scheduling in the smart factory industry 4.0. Int. J. Prod. Res. **54**(2), 386–402 (2016)
14. Kholodenko, B.N.: Cell-signalling dynamics in time and space. Nat. Rev. Mol. Cell Biol. **7**, 165–176 (2006)
15. Kurz, H., Sandau, K., Wilting, J., Christ, B., Growth, B.V.: Mathematical analysis and computer simulation, fractality, and optimality. In: Little, C.D., et al. (eds.) Vascular Morphogenesis. Birkhäuser, Boston (1998)
16. Martin-Vide, C., Păun, G., Pazos, J., Rodriguez-Paton, A.: Tissue P systems. Theoret. Comput. Sci. **296**, 295–326 (2003)
17. Meyers, M.A., Chen, P.Y., Lin, A.Y.M., Seki, Y.: Biological materials: structure and mechanical properties. Prog. Mater. Sci. **53**, 1–206 (2007). Elsevier
18. Miller, P.: The Smart Swarm. Avery Publishing Group, New York (2010)
19. Păun, G.: Membrane Computing: An Introduction. Springer, Berlin (2002)
20. Prusinkiewicz, P., Lindenmayer, A.: The Algorithmic Beauty of Plants. Springer, New York (1990)
21. Reichold, J., Stampanoni, M., Keller, A.L., Buck, A., Jenny, P., Weber, B.: Vascular graph model to simulate the cerebral blood flow in realistic vascular networks. J. Cereb. Blood Flow Metab. **29**, 1429–1443 (2009)
22. Reisig, W.: Petri nets and algebraic specifications. Theoret. Comput. Sci. **80**(1), 1–34 (1991)
23. Rivron, N.C., Rouwkema, J., Truckenmüller, R., Karperien, M., de Boer, J., van Blitterswijk, A.: Tissue assembly and organization: developmental mechanisms in microfabricated tissues. Biomaterials **30**, 4851–4858 (2009)
24. Rozenberg, G., Bäck, T., Kok, J.N. (eds.): Handbook of Natural Computing. Springer, Berlin (2012)

25. Ruan, F., Chen, D.: Based on RFID and NFC technology retail chain supermarket mobile checkout mode research. In: The International Conference on Artificial Intelligence and Software Engineering (ICAISE). Atlantis Press (2013)
26. Sedgewick, R., Wayne, K.: Algorithms, 4th edn. Addison-Wesley, Boston (2011)
27. Stamatopoulou, I., Kefalas, P., Gheorghe, M.: $OPERAS_{CC}$: an instance of a formal framework for MAS modeling based on population P systems. In: Eleftherakis, G., Kefalas, P., Păun, G., Rozenberg, G., Salomaa, A. (eds.) WMC 2007. LNCS, vol. 4860, pp. 438–452. Springer, Heidelberg (2007). doi:10.1007/978-3-540-77312-2_27

Array-Rewriting P Systems with Basic Puzzle Grammar Rules and Permitting Features

Pradeep Isawasan[1], Ravie Chandren Muniyandi[2], Ibrahim Venkat[3], and K.G. Subramanian[4(✉)]

[1] Department of Computing, School of Engineering, Computing and Built Environment, KDU Penang University College, 10400 George Town, Penang, Malaysia
pradeep.isawasan@gmail.com
[2] School of Computer Science, Faculty of Information Science and Technology, Universiti Kebangsaan Malaysia, 43600 Bangi, Malaysia
[3] School of Computer Sciences, Universiti Sains Malaysia, 11800 Gelugor, Penang, Malaysia
[4] Department of Mathematics, Madras Christian College, Tambaram, Chennai 600059, India
kgsmani1948@gmail.com

Abstract. Motivated by the problem of tiling the plane, puzzle grammars were introduced as a mechanism for generating languages of picture arrays in the two-dimensional plane. On the other hand BPG array P system with array objects and basic puzzle grammar (BPG) rules was introduced as a variant of array generating P systems that were developed with a view to link the two areas of membrane computing and picture array grammars. Here we incorporate the feature of permitting symbols in the rules of the BPG array P system, thus introducing permitting array P system with BPG rules ($pAP(BPG)$). We show that the permitting feature gives more generative power to the BPG array P system with one or two membranes. We also show that a $pAP(BPG)$ with only two membranes under t–communication mode, can generate picture arrays of square frames.

1 Introduction

Syntactic methods of picture array generation are well-known [15, 16, 24, 31] for their structure-handling ability in the field of pattern recognition and image analysis. Among various kinds of picture array generating models [10], puzzle grammars [12] and a subclass called basic puzzle grammars introduced by Subramanian et al. [28] are array generating two-dimensional grammars motivated by the problem of tiling the plane. These grammars have been subsequently investigated for their different properties and applications [11, 19, 25–27, 29].

The area of membrane computing, initiated by Păun [13] introducing a new computability model known as P system, has proved to be a suitable frame work for a variety of application problems [14, 32]. The problem of handling picture

© Springer International Publishing AG 2017
A. Leporati et al. (Eds.): CMC 2016, LNCS 10105, pp. 272–285, 2017.
DOI: 10.1007/978-3-319-54072-6_17

array languages using P systems has been of great interest and investigation [20]. Ceterchi et al. [1] introduced array-rewriting P system, linking the two areas of membrane computing and picture grammars. Several variants of array P system have been proposed (see, for example, [2,3,8,22,23]). Using a well-known technique of regulating rewriting [7], permitting array P system was introduced in [22], associating permitting symbols with rules in the regions of an array P system [1] so that an array is rewritten by a rule only when the permitting symbols of the used rule are present in the array rewritten. On the other hand in [21,25], an array P system that uses BPG type of rules in its regions was considered. We denote this kind of array P system with m membranes as $AP_m(BPG)$.

Here we consider the array P system with BPG type of rules associating permitting symbols with the rules. Denoting the resulting array P system with m membranes as $pAP_m(BPG)$, we examine the generative power. In particular we show that the language family generated by $AP_i(BPG)$ is properly included in $pAP_i(BPG)$, for $i \in \{1,2\}$. We also show that when t–communication [21], is used, geometric figures such as a hollow square frame with "corner supports" is generated by $pAP_2(BPG)$. Thus in this approach, there is a reduction in the number of membranes in generating the picture arrays of square frames when compared to the BPG array P system model.

2 Preliminaries

We refer to [10] for notions related to picture array grammars and languages and to [13] for concepts pertaining to P systems. For notions of formal grammars and languages we refer to [17,18]. We recall here needed notions and results.

A word or string w over a finite alphabet Σ is a sequence of symbols from Σ. The set of all words over Σ, including the empty word λ with no symbols, is denoted by Σ^*. A picture array or simply an array over Σ in the two-dimensional plane is composed of a finite number of labelled pixels or unit squares, with the labels belonging to the alphabet Σ. The unit squares in the plane not labelled with symbols of Σ, are assumed to have the blank symbol $\# \notin \Sigma$. An array can be pictorially represented indicating the nonblank pixels. The set of all arrays over Σ will be denoted by Σ^{**}.

A formal representation of a picture array is to list the coordinates of the unit squares of the array and the corresponding labels of the unit squares. For example, for the picture array in Fig. 1 describing the picture token P, the coordinates of the unit squares of the array can be specified as follows, taking the origin $(0,0)$ at the lowermost unit square of the left vertical line of $a's$.

$$\{((0,0),a),\ ((0,1),a),\ ((0,2),a),\ ((0,3),a),\ ((0,4),a),\ ((0,5),a),((0,6),a),$$

$$((-1,6),a),\ ((-2,6),a),\ ((1,6),a),\ ((2,6),a),\ ((3,6),a),\ ((4,6),a),$$

$$((4,5),a),\ ((4,4),a),\ ((4,3),a),\ ((3,3),a),\ ((2,3),a),\ ((1,3),a)\}$$

We now recall the notion of a basic puzzle grammar [28].

$$\begin{array}{ccccccc}
a & a & a & a & a & a & a \\
 & & a & & & & a \\
 & & a & & & & a \\
 & & a & a & a & a & a \\
 & & a & & & & \\
 & & a & & & & \\
 & & a & & & &
\end{array}$$

Fig. 1. An array describing picture token P

Definition 1. *A basic puzzle grammar* (BPG) *is a 4-tuple* $G = (N, T, R, S)$ *where* N *and* T *are finite sets of symbols;* $N \cap T = \emptyset$*; Elements of* N *are called non-terminals and elements of* T*, terminals;* $S \in N$ *is the start symbol or the axiom;* R *consists of rules of the following forms:*

$$A \rightarrow \boxed{a}B,\ A \rightarrow a\boxed{B},\ A \rightarrow B\boxed{a},\ A \rightarrow \boxed{B}a,\ A \rightarrow \boxed{B},\ A \rightarrow \boxed{a},$$

$$A \rightarrow \begin{array}{c}\boxed{a}\\ B\end{array},\ A \rightarrow \begin{array}{c}a\\ \boxed{B}\end{array},\ A \rightarrow \begin{array}{c}B\\ \boxed{a}\end{array},\ A \rightarrow \begin{array}{c}\boxed{B}\\ a\end{array}$$

where $A, B \in N$ *and* $a \in T$*. We may omit the box in the rule with a single* a *on the right side.*

Derivations begin with S *written in a unit square in the two-dimensional plane. All the other squares contain the blank symbol* $\#$*, not in* $N \cup T$*. In a derivation step, denoted* $\Rightarrow$*, a non-terminal* A *in a unit square is replaced by the right-hand member of a rule whose left-hand side is* A*. In this replacement, the symbol enclosed by a box in the right-hand side of the rule used, occupies the square of the replaced symbol and the other symbol (not enclosed in a box) in the right side of the rule, occupies the square to the right or the left or above or below the square of the replaced symbol depending on the type of rule used. Note that the replacement of the square to be filled in by the symbol not enclosed in a box, is possible only if it contains a blank symbol.*

The basic puzzle language (BPL) *generated by the* BPG G*, is the set* $L(G)$ *of picture arrays over* T*, derivable in one or more steps from the start symbol. We denote the family of* BPL *by* $L(BPL)$*.*

Remark 1. (*i*) As an illustration of the application of the rules of a BPG, we exhibit the result of application of one of the BPG rules. For example, if $p_1 = \begin{array}{ccc}\# & A & \#\\ a & a & a\end{array}$ is an array which is rewritten by a rule $A \rightarrow a\boxed{C}$, then the resulting array is $p_2 = \begin{array}{ccc}a & C & \#\\ a & a & a\end{array}$. If the rule is $A \rightarrow \boxed{a}C$, then the resulting array is $p_3 = \begin{array}{ccc}\# & a & C\\ a & a & a\end{array}$.

(*ii*) Extending the Chomsky string grammars, array grammars were introduced and extensively investigated for theoretical properties as well as possible applications [10,15]. These array grammars generate picture languages consisting of picture arrays in the two-dimensional plane. A regular array grammar (RAG) [30,31] consists of array productions of the following forms:

$$A\# \rightarrow aB\,,\; \#A \rightarrow Ba\,,\quad \begin{matrix} A & a & \# & B \\ \rightarrow & , & \rightarrow & \\ \# & B & A & a \end{matrix}\,,\; A \rightarrow a$$

These rules can be written in the form of BPG rules and are respectively given by

$$A \rightarrow \boxed{a}B, A \rightarrow B\boxed{a}, A \rightarrow \dfrac{\boxed{a}}{B}, A \rightarrow \dfrac{B}{\boxed{a}}, A \rightarrow \boxed{a}.$$

We denote by $L(RAL)$ the family of the regular array languages (RAL) generated by $RAGs$. It is known [28] that $L(RAL) \subset L(BPL)$.

With a view to handle picture array languages by P systems, Ceterchi et al. [1] introduced array-rewriting P system with objects as arrays and array-rewriting rules as evolution rules in the regions of the system. When the rules are regular array rewriting rules, the language family of the system with m membranes is denoted as $AP_m(REGA)$. A variant of the array P system was considered in [21,25], by having the rules in the membranes as basic puzzle grammar (BPG) rules. We recall this system here.

Definition 2. [25] *An array P System of degree $m(\geq 1)$ with BPG type of rules is a construct*

$$\Pi = (V, T, \#, \mu, F_1, \cdots, F_m, R_1, \cdots, R_m, i_0)$$

where V is the total alphabet, $T \subseteq V$ is the terminal alphabet, $\#$ is the blank symbol, μ is a membrane structure with m membranes labeled in a one-to-one way with $1, \cdots, m$; $F_1, \cdots, F_m$ are finite sets of arrays over V initially associated with the m regions of μ; $R_1, \cdots, R_m$ are finite sets of BPG kind of rules over $V \cup T$ associated with the m regions of μ; the rules have attached targets, here, out, in (in general, here is omitted); finally, i_o is the label of an elementary membrane of μ (the output membrane).

A computation in this array P system is defined similar to a string rewriting P system [13]. Each array in every region of the system that can be rewritten by a rule associated with that region, should be rewritten. In other words one rule is applied with the rewriting being sequential at the level of arrays. The resulting array is placed in the region indicated by the target associated with the rule used; "here" means that the array remains in the same region, "out" means that the array exits the current membrane - thus, if the rewriting was done in the skin membrane, then it can exit the system; arrays leaving the system are "lost" in the environment, and "in" means that the array is immediately sent to one of the directly lower membranes, non-deterministically chosen if several exist (if no internal membrane exists, then a rule with the target indication in cannot be used). A computation is successful only if it stops reaching a configuration where no rule can be applied to the existing arrays. The result of a halting computation *consists of the arrays composed only of symbols from T placed in the membrane with label i_o in the halting configuration.*

The set of all such arrays computed (or generated) by a system Π is denoted by $AL(\Pi)$. The family of all array languages $AL(\Pi)$ generated by systems Π as above, with at most m membranes, is denoted by $AP_m(BPG)$. Note that the regular array rewriting (REGA) rules are also BPG rules and so when REGA rules only are used in the regions, we call the family as $AP_m(REGA)$. In [25], the families $AP_m(BPG)$ and $AP_m(REGA)$ are denoted as $EAP_m(BPG)$ and $EAP_m(REGA)$ respectively, with the letter E indicating that the array P system involves nonterminals.

We give an example.

Example 1. Consider the picture array language L_1 consisting of picture arrays (one of these is shown in Fig. 2) with two equal "arms" of $a's$ and "single protrusions" of $e's$ to the left of the vertical arm of $a's$ and below the horizontal arm of $a's$. This picture language is generated by the following array P system Π_1 with basic puzzle grammar rules.

$$\Pi_1 = \left(\{A, B, C, D, X, Y, Z, a, e\}, \{a, e\}, [_1 [_2 \ ]_2]_1, \begin{smallmatrix} & A & \\ e & a & B \\ & e & \end{smallmatrix}, \emptyset, R_1, R_2, 2 \right)$$

The rule sets are given by

$$R_1 = \{r_1 : A \to \frac{C}{\boxed{a}}, (in), \ r_2 : C \to e\boxed{X}, \ r_3 : X \to \frac{A}{\boxed{a}}, (in)\}$$

$$R_2 = \{r_4 : B \to \boxed{a}Y, (out), \ r_5 : Y \to \frac{\boxed{Z}}{e}, \ r_6 : Z \to \boxed{a}B, (out),$$

$$r_7 : Z \to \boxed{a}D, \ r_8 : A \to a, \ r_9 : D \to a\}$$

A computation starts with the initial array $p = \begin{smallmatrix} & A & \\ e & a & B \\ & e & \end{smallmatrix}$ in region 1. Note that there is no initial array in region 2. An application of the rule r_1 to p yields the array $\begin{smallmatrix} & C & \\ & a & \\ e & a & B \\ & e & \end{smallmatrix}$ which is sent to region 2 where an application of the rule r_4 yields

$$\begin{matrix} & & a & & \\ & e & a & & \\ & & a & & \\ e & a & a & a & a \\ & e & & e & \end{matrix}$$

Fig. 2. *L*–like Picture array with equal "arms" of $a's$ and "protrusions" of $e's$

the array
$$\begin{array}{l} C \\ a \\ e\ a\ a\ Y \\ e \end{array}$$
which is sent back to region 1. Here application of the rule

r_2 followed by r_3 yields the array
$$\begin{array}{l} A \\ e\ a \\ a \\ e\ a\ a\ Y \\ e \end{array}$$
which again is sent to region 2 where

the application of the rules r_5 followed by r_6 yields the array
$$\begin{array}{l} A \\ e\ a \\ a \\ e\ a\ a\ a\ B \\ e\ \ \ e \end{array}$$
which

again is sent to region 1. The process can repeat. On the other hand in region 2, if the rule r_5 is followed by r_7, then the rules r_8 and r_9 can be applied yielding a picture array as in Fig. 2, which remains in region 2 and is collected in the language generated. Thus Π_1 generates the picture language L_1.

3   Array Rewriting P Systems with BPG Rules and Permitting Symbols

Several mechanisms regulating rewriting in string grammars [6,7] as well as array grammars [9], are known. Associating symbols with a rule that permit the application of the rule when the symbols are present is one such technique which has been studied by researchers [6,7]. In [22], a permitting array P system with regular array rewriting rules having associated permitting symbols, is considered. We now introduce here a permitting P system with BPG kind of rules.

If q is a subarray of p then $p \setminus q$ denotes the array formed by the labelled squares of p that are not labelled squares of q. The set of all symbols in the labelled squares of the array p is denoted by $l(p)$. A permitting BPG rule is of the form (r, per), where r is the BPG rule and per is a subset of the set of nonterminals of the BPG. If $per = \emptyset$, then it is not mentioned in the rule. The application of permitting BPG rule (r, per) to an array p can be done only when all the symbols in per are present in $l(p) \setminus \{A\}$ where the left side of rule r has label A. For example, given the permitting BPG rules $(r_1, per1)$, $(r_2, per2)$ where r_1 is the rule $A \rightarrow a\boxed{C}$ with the set of permitting symbols $per1 = \{B\}$ and r_2 is the rule $B \rightarrow \boxed{a}D$ with the set of permitting symbols $per2 = \{C\}$.

The rule r_1 can be applied to the array $p = \begin{array}{l} A \\ a \\ e\ a\ B \\ e \end{array}$ as the permitting symbol B

is present while rule r_2 cannot be applied to p as the permitting symbol C is not present. Application of rule r_1 to p yields the array $q = \begin{matrix} a\,C \\ a \\ e\,a\,B \\ e \end{matrix}$. Now the rule r_2

can be applied to the array q to yield the array $\begin{matrix} a\,C \\ a \\ e\,a\,a\,D \\ e \end{matrix}$.

Definition 3. *A permitting array P system of degree $m \geq 1$ with BPG type rules, $(pAP_m(BPG)$, is a construct*

$$\Pi = (V, T, \#, \mu, F_1, \ldots, F_m, R_1, \ldots, R_m, i_o),$$

where the components $V, T, \#, \mu, F_1, \ldots, F_m, i_o$ are as in the array P system with BPG type rules given in Definition 2. The rules in the sets $R_1, \ldots, R_m$ are permitting BPG rules of the form (r, per) where r is a BPG rule and per $\subseteq V - T$ with $V - T$ being the set of nonterminals.

A computation in $pAP_m(BPG)$ takes place as in the array P system in Definition 2 except that a permitting BPG rule of the form (r, per) is applied in rewriting an array in any region. In fact, in deriving an array from a given array, the symbols of per regulate the application of the rule r as described earlier. The halting configuration gives rise to a successful computation. The picture arrays over the terminal alphabet T collected in the output membrane i_0 in the halting configuration, constitute the picture language generated by Π.

*   We denote by $pAP_m(BPG)$, the family of all array languages generated by permitting array P systems with BPG type rules and at the most m membranes.*

We illustrate with an example.

Example 2. Consider the picture language $L_\perp$ consisting of picture arrays p, which is similar to the "perpendicular" symbol ($\perp$). The picture array p has a horizontal line of $a's$ having the symbol c in the middle with single "protrusions" of $e's$ below the horizontal line on alternate squares and a vertical line of $a's$ above the unit square labelled c. One member of $L_\perp$ is shown in Fig. 3.

$$\begin{matrix} & & & & a & & & & \\ & & & & a & & & & \\ & & & & a & & & & \\ & & & & a & & & & \\ a & a & a & a & c & a & a & a & a \\ & e & & e & & e & & e & \end{matrix}$$

Fig. 3. An Array in $L_\perp$

A permitting array P system Π_2 of degree 2 with BPG type rules generating $L_\perp$ is given by

$$\Pi_2 = \left(\{A, B, C, D, X, Y, Z, a, c, e\}, \{a, c, e\}, [_1[_2 \ ]_2]_1, \left\{\begin{array}{c} C \\ A \ c \ B \end{array}\right\}, \emptyset, R_1, R_2, 2\right)$$

The rule sets are given by

$$R_1 = \left\{r_1 : \left(A \to \boxed{D}_e, \{B, C\}\right), r_2 : \left(B \to \boxed{E}_e, \{C, D\}\right)\right\}$$

$$\cup \left\{r_3 : \left(C \to \dfrac{F}{\boxed{a}}, \{D, E\}\right), r_4 : (D \to A\boxed{a}, \{E, F\}), r_5 : (E \to \boxed{a}B, \{A, F\})\right\}$$

$$\cup \left\{r_6 : \left(F \to \boxed{C}, \{A, B\}\right), r_7 : \left(F \to \boxed{Z}, \{A, B\}\right) (in)\right\}$$

$$R_2 = \{r_8 : Z \to a, \ r_9 : A \to a, \ r_{10} : B \to a\}$$

A computation starts with the initial array $p = \begin{array}{c} C \\ A \ c \ B \end{array}$ in region 1. Note that there is no initial array in region 2. The rule r_1 can be applied to p as the permitting symbols B, C are present, yielding the array $\begin{array}{c} C \\ D \ c \ B \\ e \end{array}$. Now the rule r_2 is applicable as the symbols C, D are present, yielding the array $\begin{array}{c} C \\ D \ c \ E \\ e \ \ \ e \end{array}$. Likewise, if the sequence of applicable rules r_3, r_4, r_5, r_6 is applied now, the resulting array is $\begin{array}{c} C \\ a \\ A \ a \ c \ a \ B \\ e \ \ \ e \end{array}$. The process can then repeat. On the other hand, if the rule r_7 is applied instead of r_6 yielding a picture array $\begin{array}{c} Z \\ a \\ A \ a \ c \ a \ B \\ e \ \ \ e \end{array}$, then the array is sent to region 2 where the application of the rules generates a picture array which remains in region 2 and is collected in the language generated. Thus Π_1 generates the picture language L_1. One member of L_1 is shown in Fig. 3.

We now examine the generative power of the permitting array P system with BPG rules. By definition it follows that for $m \geq 1$, $pAP_m(BPG) \subseteq pAP_{m+1}(BPG)$

Theorem 1. (i) $pAP_1(REG) - AP_2(REG) \neq \emptyset$
(ii) $pAP_1(REG) \subset pAP_1(BPG)$

Proof. In order to prove statement (i), consider the picture array language L_t consisting of T shaped arrays, one member of which is shown in Fig. 4, over the symbol a with the symbol c in the "junction" and having all three "arms" equal in length. In otherwords, the number of $a's$ to the left and right of c in the horizontal line and the number of $a's$ below c in the vertical line, are equal. A permitting array P system with two membranes and regular array rules is given in the proof of Theorem 5 in [22] to generate L_t (with a small change of the symbol a replacing symbol c, in the picture arrays of L_t). A slight modification in the construction of this permitting array P system as given in [22], enables us to generate L_t by a permitting P system Π_3 with one membrane and regular array rules, given by

$$\Pi_3 = (\{A, B, C, D, E, F, Z, a, c\}, \{a, c\}, [_1 \ ]_1, \left\{ \begin{matrix} A\, c\, B \\ C \end{matrix} \right\}, R_1, 1) \text{ where}$$

$$R_1 = \{(r_1 : \# \ A \to D \ a, \{B, C\}), (r_2 : B \ \# \to a \ E, \{D, C\}),$$
$$(r_3 : \begin{matrix} C \\ \# \end{matrix} \to \begin{matrix} a \\ F \end{matrix}, \{D, E\}), (r_4 : D \to A, \{E, F\}),$$
$$(r_5 : E \to B, \{A, F\}), (r_6 : F \to C, \{A, B\}),$$
$$(r_7 : F \to Z, \{A, B\}), (r_8 : A \to a, \{B, Z\}),$$
$$(r_9 : B \to a, \{Z\}), (r_{10} : Z \to a)\}.$$

$$a\ a\ a\ a\ c\ a\ a\ a\ a$$
$$a$$
$$a$$
$$a$$
$$a$$

Fig. 4. T–shaped array with equal arms

In a computation starting with the initial array, the sequence of rules r_1 to r_6 extend the three arms (to the left and right of the symbol c and the vertical line below c) by one a each and the process can be repeated. If insted of r_6 the rule r_7 is applied, then the rules r_8, r_9, r_{10} are to be applied generating a picture array in L_t. This language L_t cannot be generated by an array P system with two membranes and regular array rules, since regular array rules can maintain equal length at the most in only two arms, by sending back and forth the generated array in the two membranes. This proves statement (i).

The inclusion in statement (ii) is clear since every regular array rule is also a BPG rule. The proper inclusion in (ii) can be seen by noticing that the picture language L_l consisting of L–like picture arrays (one of these is shown in Fig. (2) with equal "arms" made of $a's$ and "single protrusions" of $e's$ on alternate squares to the left of the vertical line of $a's$ and below the horizontal line if $a's$, is generated by the permitting array P

system with one membrane and basic puzzle grammar rules given by $\Pi_4 =$

$$\left(\{A,B,C,D,E,F,X,a,e\}, [_1]_1, \left\{\begin{array}{c} A \\ e\ a\ B \\ e \end{array}\right\}, R_1, 1\right).$$

The rule set is given by

$$R_1 = \left\{r_1 : \left(A \to \dfrac{C}{\boxed{a}}, \{B\}\right), r_2 : \left(C \to e\boxed{D}, \{B\}\right)\right\}$$

$$\cup \left\{r_3 : (B \to \boxed{a}E, \{D\}), r_4 : \left(E \to \dfrac{\boxed{F}}{e}, \{D\}\right), r_5 : \left(D \to \dfrac{A}{\boxed{a}}, \{F\}\right)\right\}$$

$$\cup \left\{r_6 : (F \to \boxed{a}B, \{A\}), r_7 : \left(D \to \dfrac{X}{\boxed{a}}, \{F\}\right)\right\}$$

$$\cup \{r_8 : B \to a, \{X\}, r_9 : X \to a\}$$

The idea of a computation is that the rules r_1 to r_6 extend the vertical and horizontal arms simultaneouslybut when r_7 is applied, it should be followed by r_8 and r_9 generating picture arrays in the picture language L_l. Again regular array rules cannot handle the "protrusions" of $e's$ in the picture arrays of L_l even using permitting symbols, although equal growth between the horizontal and vertical directions can be maintained. This proves statement (ii).

Theorem 2. (i) $AP_1(BPG) \subset pAP_1(BPG)$
(ii) $AP_2(BPG) \subset pAP_2(BPG)$

Proof. The inclusions in both the statements follow from definition. In order to prove proper inclusion in statement (i), consider the picture array language L_l in the proof of proper inclusion of statement (ii) in Theorem 1. A permitting array P system with one membrane and BPG rules is shown in Theorem 1 to generate this language. But without the permitting symbols, this language cannot be generated in one membrane with BPG rules as the vertical and horizontal arms of the picture arrays in L_l can be "grown" freely and there is no way to regulate their growth. Hence $L_l \notin AP_1(BPG)$.

Proper inclusion in statement (ii) can be seen by considering the picture language L_{perp} in Example 2. The language L_{perp} cannot be generated by an array P system with two membranes and BPG rules (and without permitting symbols), since these rules can handle equal length at the most only in two arms of the picture arrays of L_{perp} by sending back and forth the generated array in the two membranes. Hence $L_{perp} \notin AP_2(BPG)$.

4 Array P Systems with *BPG* Rules and t-Communication

In several studies on grammar models for language description, a maximal mode or terminal mode (t-mode) of derivation has been considered. A t-communication mode has been introduced [4] in string rewriting P systems with a view to link string grammar systems [5] and string-objects P systems. As a natural extension of the study, Subramanian et al. [21] extended this t-mode of communication to array P systems.

We mention here only certain essential features of a t-communicating array P system of type tin considered in [21]. A t-communicating array P system [21] of degree $m \geq 1$ and of type tin, the components are defined in an array P system [21] but the system does not have rules with target indication in. In fact, the t-mode derivation performed enforces the in target command. This means that an array-rewriting rule can be without any target indication and the array to which this type of rule is applied, is retained in the same region so long as the array can be rewritten further. But if no further rule can be applied to the array in that region, then it is sent to the immediately direct inner region if one such region exists. On the other hand, if an array-rewriting rule with target indication out is applied to an array, then the resulting array is sent to its immediately direct upper region.

Generation of picture arrays corresponding to geometric figures like rectangles and squares over $\{a\}$ has been studied in the area of picture grammars [30]. In [21] array P systems with array objects and basic puzzle grammar rules in the regions of the system are considered incorporating the t–communication feature. Here we consider this t–communication in a permitting array P system with BPG rules. Let S_{hf} be the set of all "hollow square frames" represented as digitized picture arrays over the symbol $\{a\}$, a member of which is shown in Fig. 5. We construct a permitting tin type array P system Π_f with two membranes and having t–communication in order to generate S_{hf}. We note that a t-communicating array P system with five membranes and regular array rules is constructed to generate these picture arrays. Thus the use of permitting feature and BPG rules provide an advantage, although not unexpected, in reducing the number of membranes from five to two. The P system Π_f is given by

$$\Pi_4 = \left(\{A,B,C,D,E,F,X,Y,Z,K,P,Q,a\}, [_1 [_2]_2]_1, \left\{ \begin{array}{c} a \\ a\ a\ B \\ A \end{array} \right\}, \emptyset, R_1, R_2, 2 \right).$$

The rule sets are given by

$$R_1 = \left\{ r_1 : \left(A \to \boxed{\begin{array}{c} a \\ C \end{array}}, \{B\} \right), r_2 : (B \to \boxed{a}D, \{C\}), r_3 : \left(C \to \boxed{\begin{array}{c} a \\ X \end{array}}, \{D\} \right) \right\}$$

$$\cup \left\{ r_4 : \left(D \to a\boxed{Y}, \{X\} \right), r_5 : \left(C \to \boxed{A}, \{D\} \right), r_6 : \left(D \to \boxed{B}, \{A\} \right) \right\}$$

$$\cup \left\{ r_7 : \left(X \to \boxed{\begin{array}{c} E \\ a \end{array}}, \{Y\} \right), r_8 : \left(Y \to \boxed{F}a, \{E\} \right), r_9 : (E \to \boxed{a}I, \{F\}) \right\}$$

$$
\begin{array}{cccccccc}
a & & & & & & a \\
a & a & a & a & a & a & a & a \\
a & & & & & & a \\
a & & & & & & a \\
a & & & & & & a \\
a & & & & & & a \\
a & a & a & a & x & a & a & a \\
a & & & & & & a \\
\end{array}
$$

Fig. 5. A square frame of $a's$

$$\cup \left\{ r_{10} : \left(F \rightarrow \boxed{\frac{\text{a}}{J}}, \{I\} \right), r_{11} : \left(I \rightarrow \boxed{E}, \{J\} \right), \right\}$$

$$\cup \left\{ r_{12} : \left(J \rightarrow \boxed{F}, \{E\} \right), r_{13} : \left(I \rightarrow \boxed{\text{a}}Z, \{F\} \right) \right\}$$

$$R_2 = \left\{ r_{14} : (F \rightarrow a, \emptyset), r_{15} : (E \rightarrow \boxed{\text{a}}K, \{F\}), r_{16} : \left(K \rightarrow \boxed{P}a, \{F\} \right) \right\}$$

$$\cup \left\{ r_{17} : \left(P \rightarrow \boxed{\frac{\text{Q}}{a}}, \{F\} \right), r_{18} : (Q \rightarrow \boxed{\text{a}}, \{F\}) \right\}$$

The idea in the computation is that the upper and left "arms" are grown equally until the left arm begins to turn right and the upper arm, to turn down. The lower and right arms are then grown together until they meet at which point the rule $I \rightarrow \boxed{\text{a}}Z$ cannot be applied and no more rule is applicable in region. The array at this point enters region 2 due to tin type of the system. Note that the single "protrusions" at the corners are taken care of by the BPG rules. In region 2, the computation reaches a halting configuration and the square-frame generated is collected in the language.

5   Conclusion

Here we have considered array P system with BPG rules and with permitting symbols associated with the rules. It remains to investigate whether $pAP_1(BPG)$ is properly included in $pAP_2(BPG)$ and in more general terms whether $pAP_m(BPG)$ is properly included in $pAP_{m+1}(BPG)$. It also remains to examine whether the number of membranes in the constructions of the P systems can further be reduced.

Acknowledgements. The fourth author K.G. Subramanian is grateful to UGC, India, for the award of Emeritus Fellowship (No. F.6-6/2016-17/EMERITUS-2015-17-GEN-5933 / (SA-II)) to him to execute his work in the Department of Mathematics, Madras Christian College.

References

1. Ceterchi, R., Mutyam, M., Paun, G., Subramanian, K.G.: Array- rewriting P systems. Nat. Comput. **2**, 229–249 (2003)
2. Ceterchi, R., Gramatovici, R., Jonoska, N.: Tiling rectangular pictures with P systems. In: Martín-Vide, C., Mauri, G., Păun, G., Rozenberg, G., Salomaa, A. (eds.) WMC 2003. LNCS, vol. 2933, pp. 88–103. Springer, Heidelberg (2004). doi:10.1007/978-3-540-24619-0_7
3. Ceterchi, R., Gramatovici, R., Jonoska, N., Subramanian, K.G.: Tissue-like P systems with active membranes for picture generation. Fundam. Inform. **56**, 311–328 (2003)
4. Csuhaj-Varjú, E., Păun, G., Vaszil, G.: Grammar systems versus membrane computing: the case of CD grammar systems. Fundam. Inform. **76**(3), 271–292 (2007)
5. Csuhaj-Varjú, E., Dassow, J., Kelemen, J., Păun, Gh.: Grammar Systems: A Grammatical Approach to Distribution and Cooperation. Gordon and Breach Science Publishers. Topics in Computer Mathematics 5, Yverdon (1994)
6. Dassow, J.: Grammars with regulated rewriting. In: Martin-Vide, C., et al. (eds.) Formal Languages and Applications. Studies in Fuzziness and Soft Computing, vol. 148. Springer, Berlin (2004)
7. Dassow, J., Păun, G.: Regulated Rewriting in Formal Language Theory. Springer, Berlin (1989)
8. Fernau, H., Freund, R., Schmid, M.L., Subramanian, K.G., Wiederhold, P.: Contextual array grammars and array P systems. Ann. Math. Artif. Intell. **75**(1–2), 5–26 (2015)
9. Freund, R.: Control mechanisms on #–context-free array grammars. In: Păun, G. (ed.) Mathematical Aspects of Natural and Formal Languages, pp. 97–137. World Scientific Publishing, Singapore (1994)
10. Giammarresi, D., Restivo, A.: Two-dimensional languages. In: Rozenberg, G., Salomaa, A. (eds.) Handbook of Formal Languages, vol. 3, pp. 215–267. Springer, Berlin (1997)
11. Laroche, P., Nivat, M., Saoudi, A.: Context-sensitivity of puzzle grammars. Int. J. Pattern Recogn. Artif. Intell. **8**(2), 525–542 (1994)
12. Nivat, M., Saoudi, A., Subramanian, K.G., Siromoney, R., Dare, V.R.: Puzzle grammars and context-free array grammars. Int. J. Pattern Recogn. Artif. Intell. **5**, 663–676 (1991)
13. Păun, G.: Membrane Computing: An Introduction. Springer, Berlin (2000)
14. Păun, G., Rozenberg, G., Salomaa, A. (eds.): The Oxford Handbook of Membrane Computing. Oxford University Press Inc., New York (2010)
15. Rosenfeld, A.: Picture Languages. Academic Press, Cambridge (1979)
16. Rosenfeld, A., Siromoney, R.: Picture languages - a survey. Lang. Des. **1**, 229–245 (1993)
17. Rozenberg, G., Salomaa, A. (eds.): Handbook of Formal Languages, vol. 1–3. Springer, Berlin (1997)
18. Salomaa, A.: Formal Languages. Academic Press, London (1973)
19. Siromoney, R., Huq, A., Chandrasekaran, M., Subramanian, K.G.: Stochastic puzzle grammars. Int. J. Patt. Recogn. Artif. Intell. **06**, 257–273 (1992)
20. Subramanian, K.G.: P systems and picture languages. In: Durand-Lose, J., Margenstern, M. (eds.) MCU 2007. LNCS, vol. 4664, pp. 99–109. Springer, Heidelberg (2007). doi:10.1007/978-3-540-74593-8_9

21. Subramanian, K.G., Ali, R.M., Nagar, A.K., Margenstern, M.: Array P systems and t-communication. Fundam. Inform. **91**, 145–159 (2009)
22. Subramanian, K.G., Isawasan, P., Venkat, I., Pan, L., Nagar, A.K.: Array P systems with permitting features. J. Comput. Sci. **5**(2), 243–250 (2014)
23. Subramanian, K.G., Pan, L., Lee, S.K., Nagar, A.K.: A P system model with pure context-free rules for picture array generation. Math. Comput. Model. **52**(11–12), 1901–1909 (2010)
24. Subramanian, K.G., Rangarajan, K., Mukund, M. (eds.): Formal Models, Languages and Applications. Series in Machine Perception and Artificial Intelligence, vol. 66. World Scientific Publishing, Singapore (2006)
25. Subramanian, K.G., Saravanan, R., Geethalakshmi, M., Chandra, P.H., Margenstern, M.: P systems with array objects and array rewriting rules. Prog. Nat. Sci. **17**, 479–485 (2007)
26. Subramanian, K.G., Saravanan, R., Chandra, P.H.: Cooperating basic puzzle grammar systems. In: Reulke, R., Eckardt, U., Flach, B., Knauer, U., Polthier, K. (eds.) IWCIA 2006. LNCS, vol. 4040, pp. 354–360. Springer, Heidelberg (2006). doi:10.1007/11774938_28
27. Subramanian, K.G., Siromoney, R., Dare, V.R., Saoudi, A.: Basic puzzle grammars and isosceles right triangles. Int. J. Pattern Recogn. Artif. Intell. **6**(5), 799–816 (1992)
28. Subramanian, K.G., Siromoney, R., Dare, V.R., Saoudi, A.: Basic puzzle languages. Int. J. Pattern Recogn. Artif. Intell. **9**, 763–775 (1995)
29. Subramanian, K.G., Thomas, D.G., Chandra, P.H., Hoeberechts, M.: Basic puzzle grammars and generation of polygons. J. Automata Lang. Comb. **6**(4), 555–568 (2001)
30. Yamamoto, Y., Morita, K., Sugata, K.: Context-sensitivity of two-dimensional array grammars. In: Wang, P.S.P. (ed.) Array grammars, Patterns and recognizers, pp. 17–41. World Scientific, Singapore (1989)
31. Wang, P.S.P.: Array Grammars, Patterns and Recognizers. World Scientific, Singapore (1989)
32. Zhang, G., Pan, L.: A survey of membrane computing as a new branch of natural computing. Chin. J. Comput. **33**(2), 208–214 (2010)

Agent-Based Simulation of Kernel P Systems with Division Rules Using FLAME

Raluca Lefticaru[1,2]([⊠]), Luis F. Macías-Ramos[3], Ionuţ Mihai Niculescu[4], and Laurenţiu Mierlă[2,4]

[1] CENTRIC, Sheffield Hallam University, 153 Arundel Street, Sheffield S1 2NU, UK
[2] Department of Computer Science, University of Bucharest,
Str. Academiei nr. 14, 010014 Bucharest, Romania
raluca.lefticaru@fmi.unibuc.ro
[3] Research Group on Natural Computing,
Department Computer Science and Artificial Intelligence,
University of Seville, Avda. Reina Mercedes S/N, 41012 Sevilla, Spain
lfmaciasr@us.es
[4] Department of Mathematics and Computer Science,
University of Pitesti, Str. Targu din Vale 1, 110040 Pitesti, Romania
ionutmihainiculescu@gmail.com, laurentiu.mierla@gmail.com

Abstract. Kernel P systems (or *kP systems*) bring together relevant features from several P systems flavours into a unified *kernel* model which allows solving complex problems using a straightforward *code programming approach*. kPWorkbench is a software suite enabling specification, parsing and simulation of kP systems models defined in the kernel P–Lingua (or kP-Lingua) programming language. It has been shown that any computation of a kP system involving only rewriting and communication rules can be simulated by a family of Communicating Stream X-Machines (or *CSXM*), which are the core of FLAME *agent based simulation environment*. Following this, kPWorkbench enables translating kP-Lingua specifications into FLAME models, which can be simulated in a sequential or parallel (MPI based) way by using the FLAME framework. Moreover, FLAME GPU framework enables efficient simulation of CSXM on CUDA enabled GPGPU devices. In this paper we present an extension of kPWorkbench framework to generate FLAME models from kP–Lingua specifications including structural rules; and consider translation of FLAME specifications into FLAME GPU models. Also, we conduct a performance evaluation regarding simulation of equivalent kP systems and CSXM models in kPWorkbench and FLAME respectively.

Keywords: Membrane computing · Kernel P systems · Communicating stream X-machines · Agent-based simulation

1 Introduction

Membrane computing is, to date, the youngest Natural Computing discipline. It was introduced in 1998 by *Gheorghe Păun*, as a paradigm which addresses

© Springer International Publishing AG 2017
A. Leporati et al. (Eds.): CMC 2016, LNCS 10105, pp. 286–306, 2017.
DOI: 10.1007/978-3-319-54072-6_18

models taking inspiration form the structure and functioning of cells present in living beings, considering such cells as living entities themselves able to process and generate information.

Computing devices of membrane computing are called membrane systems or P systems [22]. Basic ingredients of a P system are (i) *a membrane structure*, consisting in a set of *regions* delimited by *membranes*; and (ii) *multisets of objects* placed within the regions. Objects may be transformed according to some *evolution rules*, which are applied in a non-deterministic maximally parallel way (emulating how chemical reactions take place among compounds). To emulate *cell membrane permeability*, *evolution rules* can transform existing objects within a region and, additionally, *transfer* them among *adjacent* regions – objects pass through the membrane separating the regions.

Basically, there are three ways to categorize membrane systems: *cell-like* P systems, *tissue-like* P systems and *neural-like* P systems. In cell-like P systems, membranes are arranged in a hierarchical way, inspired by the inner structure of the biological cells. In tissue-like P systems, cells are set in nodes of a directed graph, inspired from the cell inter-communication in tissues. Similarly, in neural-like P systems, cells are arranged in nodes of a directed graph, taking inspiration from the way in which neurons exchange information by the transmission of electrical impulses (spikes) along axons. Neither tissue-like nor neural-like consider the possibility of cells containing inner compartments, that is, in such variants cells are elemental compartments.

Kernel P systems (or *kP systems*) [6] are a novel variant of membrane systems aiming to bring together relevant features from several P systems flavours into a unified *kernel* model which allows solving complex problems using a straight-forward *code programming approach*. In particular, a kP system model is defined by placing *compartment type instances* in the nodes of a *dynamic graph*. Each type represents a kind of *elemental compartment* which is associated with a sequence of *rule blocks*. Following this, each rule block is defined by both a *set of guarded evolution rules* and an *execution strategy*. A guarded rule associated to a compartment type is an extension of a classic evolution rule where a new syntactical element, the *guard*, is added. A guard is a logical condition over the multiplicity of objects belonging to the multiset associated to any instance of the corresponding type. Evolution rules may be either *rewriting and communication* rules or *structure changing rules* (cell division, cell dissolution, link creation or link destruction rules). A given compartment instance executes its rule blocks sequentially, with applicable rules to be executed for each block according to the its own execution strategy.

P–Lingua framework [27], possibly the most widely known simulation software for membrane computing, provides support for a reduced version of kP systems, known as *simple kernel P systems*. As a separate effort from that of P–Lingua, a brand new software project, known as kPWorkbench [7,28], was created aiming to provide full support for kP systems as well as advanced model checking features. kPWorkbench allows the specification of kP systems in the kernel P–Lingua (or kP-Lingua) programming language, which share some similarities with the original P–Lingua one. kPWorkbench framework features a native simulator, allowing the simulation of kP system models written in kP–Lingua. On the other hand, kPWorkbench's model checking environment permits the formal verification of kernel P system models.

Regarding parallel simulation of kP systems, in [20] it was shown that any computation of a kP system involving only rewriting and communication evolution rules can be simulated by a family of *Communicating Stream X-Machines* (or *CSXM*), which are extended forms of state machines, having memory and processing functions. CSXM can be efficiently simulated in a parallel way by means of two template-based software frameworks called FLAME (*Flexible Large-Scale Agent Modelling Environment*) [29] and FLAME GPU [30]. FLAME allows MPI [31] based efficient simulation of CSXM models written in the FLAME agent-based specification language, while FLAME GPU allows *CUDA (Compute Unified Device Architecture)* [12,19,21,32] based efficient simulation of CSXM models written in the FLAME GPU specification language, an extension/variant of the FLAME one. Both FLAME and FLAME GPU have been used in several experiments, which were performed on *High Performance Computing (HPC)* platforms due to the scale of the associated models and, subsequently, resource-intensive simulation tasks. Some examples include modelling oxygen-responsive transcription factors in *Escherichia coli* [1] or the complex cellular tissue simulation [24].

Following this, in [8] kPWorkbench was extended to provide automated translation from kP systems models written in kP–Lingua into CSXM models written in FLAME specification language. This translation addressed kP systems involving only rewriting and communication evolution rules, with the transformation of systems involving structural rules left as an open issue. Moreover, no support for automated translation to FLAME GPU was provided either.

In this work, we take a step forward regarding the aforementioned results tackling new challenges. Firstly, we address an extension of the kPWorkbench framework to generate FLAME models from kP–Lingua specifications including structural rules such as division and dissolution rules. Secondly, we address the translation of FLAME specifications into FLAME GPU models. Finally, we conduct a performance study regarding the simulation of equivalent kP systems and CSXM models in kPWorkbench and FLAME (serial and parallel mode) respectively. This is conducted following the trail of [2,13]. In particular, [13] presented the first approach of implementing the pulse generator model in FLAME GPU [13], conducting a performance comparison with FLAME. Remarkably, the FLAME GPU model used was manually translated, since there was no public available tool to automate the conversion.

This paper is structured as follows. Section 2 outlines previous related work. Section 3 introduces the theoretical background. Section 4 presents our modelling approach in FLAME, while Sect. 5 presents the possible ways of extending it to FLAME GPU. A case study illustrating the cited approach is discussed in Sect. 6. Finally, conclusions and further work are drawn in Sect. 7.

2   Related Work

In this section, we briefly outline the state-of-the art of parallel simulation of P systems on High Performance Computing (HPC) platforms.

Both P–Lingua and kPWorkbench, as a vast majority of software tools for membrane computing, implement the simulation algorithms in a *sequential* way. This effectively neglects the inherent parallelism of P systems, and leads to non-efficient simulations from the computational complexity point of view. Fortunately, an increasing variety of simulators specially intended to run on *massively-parallel platforms* have been developed along the years. Such HPC platforms include *Field Programmable Gate Array circuits (FPGAs)* [23], *microcontrollers* [9], *computer clusters* [3,4,26] and *General–Purpose Graphic Processing Unit (GPGPU)* devices.

In particular, GPGPU hardware comprises a very affordable technology, providing in a *single* device *hundreds* of *massively parallel processors* supporting several *thousand* of concurrent *threads*. To date, many general purpose applications have been successfully migrated to GPGPU platforms, showing good *speed-ups* compared to their corresponding sequential versions. Two are the main programming models enabling software development oriented to GPG-PUs. On the one hand, *CUDA (Compute Unified Device Architecture)* programming model, [12,19,21,32] and on the other hand, *Open Computing Language (OpenCL)* framework [18,25,33].

An updated exhaustive list of parallel simulators for P systems regarding the aforementioned approaches can be consulted in [14], with the reader also encouraged to check [5,15], from where an encyclopaedic knowledge can be obtained. Finally, a couple of surveys summarising the topic can be consulted in [16,17].

With respect to parallel simulation of kernel P systems, to the best knowledge of the authors, there are only a few related software applications due to the novelty of the model. On the one hand, a parallel implementation on GPGPU architectures using CUDA is reported in [11]. On the other hand, regarding the simulation of kP systems with agents, FLAME and FLAME GPU simulation platforms are detailed in [2,13,20], as we discussed above.

3   Background

This section gives the basic definitions and major results regarding kernel P systems and communicating stream X-machines, largely following those in [6,20]. For this, we will assume that the reader is familiar with usual notations from formal languages, membrane computing and finite automata domains and refer to [6,10,20] for further technical details and examples.

We first begin recalling the formal definition of kernel P systems (or kP systems).

Definition 1. *A kP system of degree n is a tuple $k\Pi = (A, \mu, C_1, \ldots, C_n, i_0)$, where*

- A is a finite set of elements called objects;
- μ defines the membrane structure, which is a graph, (V, E), where V are vertices representing components (compartments), and E edges, i.e., links between components;
- $C_i = (t_i, w_{i,0})$, $1 \le i \le n$, is a compartment of the system consisting of a compartment type, t_i, from a set T and an initial multiset, $w_{i,0}$ over A; the type $t_i = (R_i, \rho_i)$ consists of a set of evolution rules, R_i, and an execution strategy, ρ_i;
- i_0 is the output compartment where the result is obtained.

A kernel P system can have several compartment instances of the same type: while they share the same set of rules and execution strategies, they may have different multiset of objects at different computation steps and different neighbours according to the graph relation specified by (V, E). Within the kernel P systems framework, the following kinds of evolution rules have been considered so far:

- *rewriting and communication* rule: $x \longrightarrow y\{g\}$, where $x \in A^+$ and y represents a multiset of objects over A^* with potential different compartment type targets (each symbol from the right side can be sent to a different compartment, specified by its type; if more compartments of the same type are linked to the current compartment, then one is randomly chosen).
  Compared to cell-like P systems, the targets in kP systems are the type of compartments to which the objects will be sent, not particular instances. Also, for kP systems, complex guards can be represented, using multisets over A with relational and Boolean operators.
  For example, rule $r : ab \longrightarrow bc\{\ge a^3 \wedge < b^2\}$ can be applied if and only if the current multiset includes the left hand side of r, i.e., ab and the guard holds: the current multiset has at least 3 a's and less then 2 b's.
- *structure changing* rules: membrane division, membrane dissolution, link creation and link destruction rules, which all may also incorporate complex guards and that are covered in detail in [6].

As we stated above, besides of a set of evolution rules, each compartment type in a kP system has an associated execution strategy. Execution strategies offer a lot of flexibility to the kP system designer, as the rules corresponding to a compartment can be grouped in several blocks, every block having one of the following strategies:

- *sequential*: if the current rule is applicable, then it is executed, advancing towards the next rule/block of rules; otherwise, the execution terminates;
- *choice*: a non-deterministic choice within a set of rules, one and only one applicable rule will be executed if such a rule exists, otherwise the whole block is simply skipped;
- *arbitrary*: the rules from the block can be executed zero or more times by nondeterministically choosing any of the applicable rules;
- *maximal parallel*: the classic execution mode used in membrane computing.

On the other hand, a stream X-machine is an extended form of finite state machine in which the transitions are labelled by (partial) functions (called *processing functions*) instead of simple symbols. Remarkably, the machine has a memory M, that can be imagined as the domain of the variables of the system to be modelled. The input received by the machine is processed in order: depending on the current state of the machine and the input symbol to be processed, one of the processing functions will read the current input symbol, discard it from the input sequence and produce an output symbol while (possibly) changing the value of the memory and taking the machine to a different state. Finally, if several processing functions can compute the same input, then one of them is randomly chosen (non-determinism). Formal definition of stream X-machines follows:

Definition 2. *A Stream X-Machine (SXM for short) is a tuple* $Z = (\Sigma, \Gamma, Q, M, \Phi, F, I, T, m_0)$, *where:*

- Σ *and* Γ *are finite sets called the input alphabet and output alphabet respectively;*
- Q *is the finite set of states;*
- M *is a (possibly) infinite set called memory;*
- Φ *is the type of* Z, *a finite set of function symbols. A basic processing function* $\phi : M \times \Sigma \longrightarrow \Gamma \times M$ *is associated with each function symbol* ϕ.
- F *is the (partial) next state function,* $F : Q \longrightarrow 2^Q$ *As for finite automata,* F *is usually described by a state-transition diagram.*
- I *and* T *are the sets of initial and terminal states respectively,* $I \subseteq Q$, $T \subseteq Q$;
- m_0 *is the initial memory value, where* $m_0 \in M$;
- *all the above sets, i.e.,* $\Sigma, \Gamma, Q, M, \Phi, F, I, T$, *are non-empty.*

Several theoretical frameworks have been developed addressing communicating stream X-machines, that is, concurrent systems where different stream X-machines work in parallel exchanging data via communication channels. In what follows, we recall the one from [10], which is the closest to the the implementation of FLAME, according to [20].

Definition 3. *A Communicating Stream X-Machine System (CSXMS for short) with n components is a tuple* $S_n = ((Z_i)_{1 \leq i \leq n}, E)$, *where:*

- $Z_i = (\Sigma_i, \Gamma_i, Q_i, M_i, \Phi_i, F_i, I_i, T_i, m_{i,0})$ *is the SXM with number* i, $1 \leq i \leq n$.
- $E = (e_{ij})_{1 \leq i,j \leq n}$ *is a matrix of order* $n \times n$ *with* $e_{ij} \in \{0,1\}$ *for* $1 \leq i,j \leq n$, $i \neq j$ *and* $e_{ii} = 0$ *for* $1 \leq i \leq n$.

The CSXMS works as follows:

- Each individual Communicating SXM (CSXM for short) is a SXM plus an infinite input queue (FIFO structure); the CSXM consumes inputs from its queue.
- An input symbol received from the external environment (also a FIFO structure) will move to the input queue of one CSXM, if it is contained in its input alphabet. If more than one CSXM satisfies such condition, then the symbol will enter the input queue of one of these in a non-deterministic fashion.

- Each pair of CSXMs, say Z_i and Z_j, have two unidirectional communication channels. The communication channel from Z_i to Z_j is enabled if $e_{ij} = 1$ and disabled otherwise
- There exists the possibility for an output symbol produced by a CSXM, say Z_i, to pass to the input queue of another CSXM, say Z_j, providing that the communication channel between them is enabled, and if the symbol is included in the input alphabet of Z_j. If several CSXMs satisfy these conditions one of them is non-deterministic chosen, whereas if none exists the symbol goes to the output environment (also a FIFO structure).

One important result proving the possibility of simulating kP systems with CSXMs is given in the following theorem from [20].

Theorem 1. *For any kP system, kΠ, of degree n and using only rewriting and communication rules, there is a communicating stream X-machine system, S_{n+1}, with $n + 1$ components such that for any multiset w computed by kΠ there is a complete sequence of transitions in S_{n+1} leading to s(w).*

In this theorem, w is the final configuration of the kP system, $w = (w_1, \ldots, w_n)$, where each w_i represents the final multiset occurring in compartment i. On the other hand, $s(w)$ corresponds to any of the strings obtained by concatenating the symbols occurring in w. Remarkably, the Proof of this Theorem, as shown in [20], suggests the manner in which a FLAME model for a given kP system can be constructed. We will briefly examine this in the next section.

4   Modelling Kernel P Systems with Structure Changing Rules in FLAME

In this section, we describe how kernel P systems incorporating structure changing rules can be mapped into FLAME specification language. We start recalling the way in which Communicating Stream X-Machines Systems are defined in that language.

FLAME framework provides an environment for defining communicating agents, specified in an XML format, which contains information regarding their memory variables, name of processing functions, message structures that can be exchanged for communication, etc. FLAME uses an implementation of CSXMs in which: (a) the associated automaton of each CSXM has no loops (this ensures that the execution will end after a finite number of processing functions calls); (b) the CSXMs receive no inputs from the environment – inputs are usually those produced in the previous computation step or the ones defined in the initial configuration file; and (c) the processing function scripts are written in C files.

The input Communicating Stream X-Machines System is defined in XMML format (X-Machine Mark-up Language), which is translated by FLAME into simulation program source code, either in its serial or parallel (MPI) version.

Next, this program can be compiled together with the agent processing functions script files (written in C) by any C/C++ compiler, giving place to simulation executable code can be run, in the case of the parallel version, on High Performance Computing (HPC) platforms.

To take advantage of the aforementioned efficient simulation capability of FLAME, in [8] kPWorkbench was extended to provide automated translation from kP systems models written in kP–Lingua into CSXM models written in FLAME specification language. This translation addressed kP systems involving only rewriting and communication evolution rules, with the transformation of systems involving structural rules left as an open issue. In what follows, we outline the main ideas in which such transformation process relies on (additional details can be found in [8,13,20]):

- Each compartment type in the kP system is associated an agent type in FLAME, while each compartment type instance is associated an agent of the corresponding agent type.
- Multisets of objects from each compartment type instance are stored in the corresponding agent memory using, in general, dynamic arrays of complex data types.
- Execution strategies (sequential, choice, arbitrary, maximal parallel) of the compartment types are encapsulated in C functions.
- Communication between compartments is materialized by using FLAME's agents message passing mechanism. In particular, communication among linked compartments is ensured by means of message filtering, while the non-deterministic choice among one of the possible target compartments is ensured by means of non-deterministic message processing.
- Finally, the graph structure of the kP system, which maps the links among compartments, can be stored in a distributed way among each agent memory as a dynamic array containing the identifiers of the agents representing the compartments sharing an active link with the compartment represented by the current agent.

Next, we address how kP systems incorporating structural rules (membrane division, membrane dissolution, link creation, link destruction) can be translated into FLAME. Let us notice that previous experiments regarding kP systems to FLAME translation, such as the ones references above, did not considered kP systems having structural rules. We start describing the process for membrane dissolution, link creation and link destruction, which is quite straightforward compared to that of membrane division:

- Membrane dissolution can be implemented by either (1) extending the agent memory with a flag-type data value storing whether the corresponding compartment is active or has been dissolved; or (2) removing the corresponding FLAME agent, when the membrane dissolution takes place. The first approach should be used when keeping trace of kP system evolution is required and, subsequently, agent deletion is not aimed. In both approaches, each time that

a dissolution takes place, all the agents having connections to the "dissolved" agent have to be notified via messages, in order to update their connection arrays.
- Link creation and link destruction rules can be implemented by adding or removing elements in the connection arrays accordingly.

In what follows we address transformation of kP systems involving division rules. Translation of such rules is the most challenging to implement and, consequently, we devote a specific part of this paper to its study.

4.1 Implementing kP Systems Division Rules in FLAME

Let us recall that, in general, P systems operate by applying rewriting rules defined over multisets of objects associated to the different membranes, in a synchronized non-deterministic maximally parallel way. P systems show a double level of parallelism: the first level comprises parallel application of rules within individual membranes, while the second level comprises all the membranes working simultaneously, that is, in parallel. These features make P systems powerful computing devices. In particular, the double levels of parallelism allow a space-time trade-off enabling *the generation of an exponential workspace in polynomial time*. This is usually accomplished by applying iteratively membrane creation rules, such as division rules.

As such, P systems are suitable to tackle relevant real-life problems, usually involving **NP**-complete problems. Moreover, P systems are excellent tools to investigate on the computational complexity boundaries, in particular tackling the **P versus NP** problem. In this way, by studying how the ingredients relative to their syntax and semantics affect to their ability to solve **NP**–complete problems in a feasible way, computational properties, sharper frontiers between efficiency and non-efficiency can be discovered.

In order to take advantage of the full power of P systems, it is required to simulate them on HPC platforms, which can suitably manage the demanding resource requirements of their inherent double parallelism. In the particular case of kernel P systems, this involves efficiently simulating division rules on massively parallel devices. This can be accomplished by transforming the corresponding kP systems models into FLAME specification language.

Regarding this, FLAME inherently favours the possibility of simulating membrane division, since it supports adding new agents during the simulation execution in such a way that all the newly created agents are introduced at the beginning of the next iteration. Nevertheless, several tasks have to be performed to properly simulate membrane division of a given compartment:

- The newly created agent memory has to be initialized with the data corresponding to the multiset of the underlying newly created compartment.
- The connection arrays of both the newly created agent and each agent representing a compartment linked to the original dividing one have to be updated. As such, it is required to implement a mechanism for the newly created agents to be associated unique identifiers.

– This is accomplished by creating in the system a single instance of a new agent type, called the *instance manager*. This agent will receive and process requests of new identifiers from agents representing dividing compartments via message passing. The instance manager will then provide – again via message passing – a new identifier that will be used by the "dividing" agent to initialize the newly created agents and to send a connection array update signal to all its linked agents.

Figure 1 shows the visual representation of a FLAME model incorporating different kind of translated evolution rules. In particular, this state machine visualisation is automatically drawn by the FLAME editor, based on the kPWorkbench generated model of a kP system solving SubSetSum. States are represented with ellipses, processing functions with rectangles, and messages exchanged between agents with green parallelograms.

Comparing the Main and Output compartments in Fig. 1, one can check that the Main compartment has additional states and transitions corresponding to the application of division rules, preliminaries for the creation of new membranes, request identifiers or receive identifiers messages.

It is worth pointing out that a FLAME agent structure will vary depending on the execution strategies and blocks from its corresponding kP system compartment. For example, comparing the kP–Lingua specification from Fig. 2 and its corresponding FLAME model in Fig. 1, one can easily identify that each *choice* block has a corresponding processing function and next state in the CSXM. Similarly, the execution order with respect to several strategies is reflected in the agent structure. In addition, ramifications may appear for the cases when a structural rule is chosen to be applied.

Following the process outlined above, the existing kP–Lingua to FLAME kPWorkbench translator module has been extended to support translation of division and dissolution rules with the corresponding algorithm included as an Appendix at the end of this paper. The new module has been successfully used to generate FLAME models for instances of SubSetSum. Such instances have then been used in the experiments detailed in Sect. 6.

5   Adapting the Modelling Approach to FLAME GPU

In this section we briefly discuss some design constraints when translating FLAME models to FLAME GPU and recommended workarounds.

Although FLAME GPU framework is an extension of FLAME, models designed for FLAME are not supported by FLAME GPU. Apart from small differences that could be easily tackled, e.g. using a slightly different XML schema, with different namespace or tag names, there are also important differences in the data types which can be used by each environment.

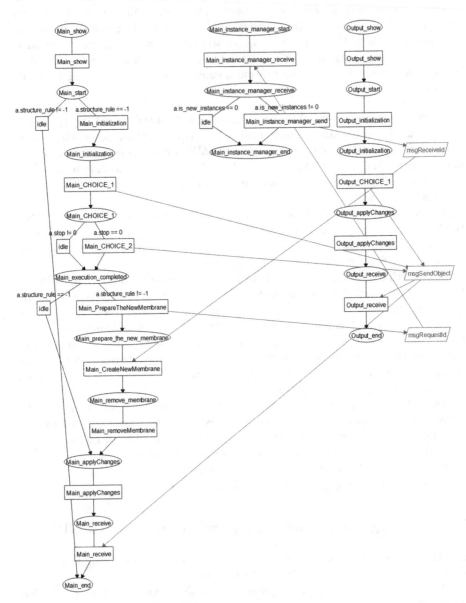

Fig. 1. Graph of the states, functions and messages between agents, corresponding to the FLAME model for Subset Sum problem, having two agent types for the compartments types Main and Output, plus an additional main instance manager agent in charge of the Main compartment division process (for allocation of new identifiers) (Color figure online)

In order to address these issues, some design guidelines have to be taken into account, as noted in [13], where authors manually translated a model of a pulse generator from FLAME to FLAME GPU, in order to have it implemented in both frameworks and compare their performance with kPWorkbench.

Firstly, memory in FLAME GPU is pre-allocated due to CUDA programming model constraints. As such, agents memory neither support dynamic arrays nor fixed arrays with complex types. The recommender workaround is the serialization of dynamic arrays (with/without composed objects) which appear in the FLAME models into static arrays of basic types, recommended to have fixed length equal to a power of 2.

Secondly, although in FLAME it is possible to add several new agents in one step, which is useful for example when a membrane is divided into 3 new compartments, in FLAME GPU only one agent is possible to be added per function. Consequently, the recommended workaround implies creating additional functions in the X-machine structure, to add the remaining membranes to be created.

Finally, contrary to FLAME, in FLAME GPU each agent can only create a single message, which clash with communication rules semantics, where multiple compartments may receive different objects. The recommended workaround is to expand the memory space for each message, allowing it to contain data for multiple targets.

6   Case Study: Subset Sum Problem

As previous work on modelling kP systems with FLAME [2,20] and FLAME GPU [13] addressed models with communication and rewriting rules, in this section we will illustrate the case of a kP–Lingua model consisting in a kP system family solving SubSetSum, which involves division rules as well as other kernel P systems specific features, such as presence of guards plus sequential and choice execution strategies.

The SubSetSum problem can be roughly described as: "Given the set $S_n = \{a_1, a_2, \ldots, a_n\}$, is there a subset of S_n, having the sum of elements equal to x?" Regarding to our model, in order to ensure that the computation will continue until all the possible membrane divisions have been applied, we have considered $S_n = \{1, 2, \ldots, n\}$ and the expected sum $x = n(n + 1)/2$, which will return the *yes* answer in this case. The kP-Lingua specification considered for $n = 4$ is given in Fig. 2, however corresponding files have been generated for each $n \in \{2, 3, \ldots, 20\}$, more details and a complete folder containing all the files and scripts needed to run the experiments are provided for download on the kPWorkbench website[5].

---

[5] http://kpworkbench.org/index.php/case-studies.

The model shown in Fig. 2 is a slightly adapted version from that of [8], and was chosen because of its programming-like structure (sequential blocks) and its simplicity regarding beforehand computation of the number of expected execution steps $(n+1)$ and number of membranes in the last configuration ($2^n +$ 1). Two compartment types are used, named *Main* and *Output*, respectively. The *Main* compartment type contains two choice blocks to (1) generate the *positive answer* when required; and (2) generate the subsets to be checked by applying division rules. The *Output* compartment type take care of (1) controlling the execution by means of a *counter* object; and (2) generating the *negative answer* when required.

Simplicity of the model eased the experimentation process, since the goal was to conduct non-deterministic experiments but assuring that the computation would end after the same number of steps, with a maximum number of membranes created by division, but different execution traces each time.

```
type Main {
choice {
= 10x: a -> {yes} (Output) .
> 10x: a -> halt .
}
choice {
!r1: a -> [a, r1][x, a, r1] .
!r2: a -> [a, r2][2x, a, r2] .
!r3: a -> [a, r3][3x, a, r3] .
!r4: a -> [a, r4][4x, a, r4] .
}
}
type Output {
choice {
start -> step .
<5step : step -> 2step .
<yes & =5step: step -> 2step, no, halt .
}
}
main {a} (Main) - output {start} (Output) .
```

Fig. 2. kP–Lingua specification for SubSetSum ($n = 4$)

In order to assess the performance of the different modelling approaches and implementations for kPWorkbench and FLAME, we conducted several experiments involving different instances of the presented kP system solution to SubSetSum, and their translated FLAME counterparts, respectively. With respect to FLAME, besides the serial simulation of the models, which was addressed in previous works like [2,13,20], also the parallel MPI based simulation provided by FLAME was considered. Since FLAME does not support MPI

Table 1. Average time for solving Subset sum problem for different n values

n	Compart	Flame	kPWorkbench	Flame NP 2	Flame NP 3	Flame NP 4
2	4	0.00	0.09	0.00	0.00	0.18
3	8	0.00	0.09	0.00	0.00	0.22
4	16	0.00	0.09	0.00	0.00	0.18
5	32	0.00	0.10	0.00	0.00	0.23
6	64	0.01	0.11	0.19	0.19	0.21
7	128	0.02	0.14	0.21	0.25	0.28
8	256	0.05	0.15	0.18	0.27	0.43
9	512	0.10	0.24	0.27	0.43	0.51
10	1024	0.15	0.36	0.47	0.67	0.85
11	2048	0.26	0.65	0.82	1.10	1.74
12	4096	0.53	1.29	1.52	2.19	3.42
13	8192	1.04	2.78	3.03	4.74	6.33
14	16384	2.33	6.73	6.47	9.59	14.91
15	32768	5.30	17.69	15.03	22.73	30.10
16	65536	13.41	52.56	35.56	53.58	70.36
17	131072	36.17	202.01	89.81	138.66	187.16
18	262144	106.16	832.31	250.45	387.24	507.62
19	524288	352.28	3388.19	793.75	1211.27	1609.34
20	1048576	1088.26	13605.23	3575.90	5787.97	7885.79

simulation in Windows environments, the Sevilla HPC Server [34] `mulhacen` was configured with FLAME and Open MPI [35] to conduct the experiments.

Comparisons were realised between average execution times for: kPWorkbench, FLAME in serial mode and FLAME in parallel version, run with different number of processors, $NP \in \{2, 3, 4\}$, running all on the same machine, a Xeon Server, having 4 cores, Intel i5 Xeon E3-1230V3 @ 3.30 GHz, main memory 32 GBytes DDR3 @ 2400 Mhz.

For each instance of `SubSetSum`, $n \in \{2, 3, \ldots, 20\}$ and each tool configuration, 3 runs were considered. In each case the user time and system time were recorded, and the average total time for these three runs was considered.

Table 1 shows the statistics after 3 runs. Columns have the following meaning: n value; the number of compartments resulted from division at the end of computation (2^n of type Main); average time needed by Flame serial version, by kPWorkbench, by Flame parallel version using 2, 3 or 4 processors. All the times are given in seconds and were measured by `/usr/bin/time -v`, in order to have the same metric for all the tools.

Tools configuration. Because the execution time would have been increased by FLAME saving to disk all the intermediary configurations, we have chosen to output the same amount of information with each tool (chosen rules and new configurations) and save only the last configuration file in XML format for the FLAME simulation.

Comparing our case study with previous experiments assessing FLAME and kPWorkbench performance [2,13], this is the first time when FLAME is not saving large XML files after each iteration. This modification, realised in order to have equal conditions, is explaining why the FLAME simulator is obtaining better time in this case study, compared to kPWorkbench, although in previous experiments it has been different. Also, another important difference is the type of the model, previous experiments did not use division and this could result in different execution times.

As in the previous experiments only the serial version of FLAME was employed, we lack of other results to compare with, in order to address the question: why is the time obtained in the parallel version much higher than the serial version? One explanation could be that model chosen does not have very complex processing functions, so the time needed for communication between processors is increasing the total time needed, without benefiting from the parallelism. Another explanation could be some tweaking settings of FLAME or Open MPI, which could be better configured, in order to get the best performance for the parallel implementation.

Also, in Table 1 we have provided the number of compartments for each n as a *rough* estimator of the space used: with a larger n the number of rules and also of object types for the compartment increases. So, a larger number of compartments comes also with more rules and more object types to be stored.

In order to have a better visualisation of the experimental results, the data from Table 1 have been represented in Fig. 3. The left plot shows the average time versus the number of compartments, the right plot displays for the horizontal axis the logarithmic scale of its left counterpart.

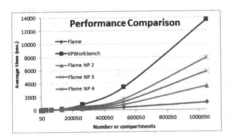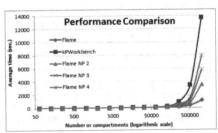

Fig. 3. Comparative simulation results for kPWorkbench, FLAME serial and parallel versions, with NP 2, 3 and 4

Unfortunately, at the time of writing this paper, there are neither public available tools for conversion from kP-Lingua specifications to FLAME GPU, nor from FLAME models to FLAME GPU. This is the reason why FLAME GPU models were not considered in the evaluation, although we have studied this possibility. However, as reported in a previous article [13], where a pulse generator model was translated manually to FLAME GPU, better execution time is expected for GPU version, but the construction of the model is much more tedious compared to the FLAME version.

7   Conclusions and Further Work

This paper presents recent efforts towards modelling of kernel P systems with structural rules in two agent based simulation environments, known as FLAME and FLAME GPU. In this context, we have extended the module of kPWorkbench for automated generation of FLAME models from kP-Lingua specifications to consider kP systems with division and dissolution rules. We also provided an overview of the differences between FLAME and its GPU version, and outlined the main issues that should be taken into account for a model transformation.

Finally, we have conducted experiments to compare the performances of FLAME, serial and parallel versions, with respect to kPWorkbench, for a kernel P system with division rules.

As future work, we will tackle the automated translation from either kP–Lingua specifications or their FLAME counterparts models to FLAME GPU specifications, based on the main ideas presented here. Also we will address alternative MPI implementations and realise performance comparisons about the application of division and dissolution rules on more complex examples.

Acknowledgements. The work of RL, IN and LM was supported by a grant of the Romanian National Authority for Scientific Research, CNCS-UEFISCDI (project number: PNII-ID-PCE-2011-3-0688).

A   Appendix

Algorithm 1. Transforming a kP Systems into Flame algorithm

1: **procedure** ADDTRANSITION(startState, stopState, strategy, guard)
  ▷ *procedure adding the appropriate transition strategy to the current agent stack given as parameter and FLAME function applying rules conforming to execution strategy*
  ▷ *guard is an optional parameter that represents the transition guard*
2:    **if** strategy is Sequence **then**
3:        agentTransitions.Push(startState, stopState, SequenceFunction, guard)
            ▷ *FLAME function SequenceFunction applies rules in sequentially mode*
4:    **else if** strategy is Choice **then**
5:        agentTransitions.Push(startState, stopState, ChoiceFunction, guard)
            ▷ *FLAME function ChoiceFunction applies rules in choice mode*
6:    **else if** strategy is ArbitraryParallel **then**
7:        agentTransitions.Push(startState, stopState, ArbitraryParallelFunction, guard)
            ▷ *FLAME function ArbitraryParallelFunction applies rules in arbitrary parallel mode*
8:    **else if** strategy is MaximalParallel **then**
9:        agentTransitions.Push(startState, stopState, MaximalParallelFunction, guard)
            ▷ *FLAME function MaximalParallelFunction applies rules in maximal parallel mode*
10:    **end if**
11: **end procedure**
12:
    ▷ *main algorithm for traforming a kP system into Flame*
13:
14: agentsStates.Clear()
15: agentsTransitions.Clear()
    ▷ *empty state and transition stacks of agents*
16: **foreach** membrane in kPSystem **do**
    ▷ *for each membrane of kP system build corresponding agent, consisting of states and transitions*
17:    agentStates.Clear()
18:    agentTransitions.Clear()
        ▷ *empty state and transition stacks of agent that is built for the current membrane*
19:    agentStates.Push(startState)
        ▷ *adding the initial state of the X machine*
20:    agentStates.Push(initializationState)
        ▷ *adding initialization state*
21:    agentTransitions.Push(startState, initializationState, IsNotPreviousApplyStructureRule)
        ▷ *adding transition between the initial and initialization states; this transition performs objects allocation on rules and other initializations; if the agent is active, no rule of structure has been applied in the previous iteration*
22:    agentTransitions.Push(startState, endState, IsPreviousApplyStructureRule)
        ▷ *adding transition between the initial and end state; if the agent is inactive, a rule of structure has been applied in the previous iteration*
23:    **foreach** strategy in membrane **do**
        ▷ *for each strategy of the current membrane the corresponding states and transitions are built*
24:        previousState = agentStates.Top()
            ▷ *the last state is stored in a temporary variable*
25:        **if** is first strategy and strategy.hasNext() **then**
            ▷ *when the strategy is the first of several, state and transition corresponding to the execution strategy are added*
26:            agentStates.Push(strategy.Name)
27:            AddTransition(previousState, strategy.Name, strategy)
28:        **else**
29:            **if** not strategy.hasNext() **then**
                ▷ *if it is the last strategy, the transition corresponding to the execution strategy is added*
30:                AddTransition(previousState, completedExecutionState, strategy)
31:            **else**

Algorithm 1. Transforming a kP Systems into Flame algorithm (continued)

32:     agentStates.Push(strategy.Name)
      ▷ *add corresponding state of the current strategy*
33:     **if** strategy.Previous() is Sequence **then**
      ▷ *verify that previous strategy is of sequence type*
34:       AddTransition(previousState, strategy.Name, strategy, IsApplyAllRules)
        ▷ *add transition from preceding strategy state to the current strategy state.*
        The guard is active if all the rules have been applied in the previous strategy
        transition.
35:     agentTransitions.Push(previousState,completedExecutionState,IsNotApplyAllRules)
       ▷ *add transition from preceding strategy state to state in which all strategies*
       were finalized. The guard is active if not all rules have been applied in the
       previous strategy transition
36:     **else**
37:       AddTransition(previousState, strategy.Name, strategy)
        ▷ *add transition from preceding strategy state to the current strategy state*
38:       agentTransitions.Push(previousState,
       completedExecutionState, IsApplyStructureRule)
        ▷ *add transition from preceding state strategy to state in which all strategies*
        were finalized. The guard is active when the structural rule has been applied
        on the previous strategy transition
39:     **end if**
40:    **end if**
41:   **end if**
42: **end for**
43: agentStates.Push(completedExecutionState)
   ▷ *adding state in which all strategies were finalized*
44: agentStates.Push(PrepareTheNewMembranes)
   ▷ *adding state in which id(s) is required for newly created membrane(s)*
45: agentTransitions.Push(completedExecutionState, PrepareTheNewMembranes,
46: IsApplyStructureRule)
   ▷ *add the transition to the prepare the new membranes state on which id(s) is required for*
   newly created membrane(s), if the structure rule has been applied. The request is made
   through messages to the instance manager, agent that allocate new IDs for new agents
   of current type.
47: agentStates.Push(CreateNewMembrane)
   ▷ *adding state in which IDs are received through messages from instance manager agent*
   and the new agents are created
48: agentTransitions.Push(PrepareTheNewMembranes, CreateNewMembrane)
   ▷ *on this transition the new agents are created with the new received ids*
49: agentStates.Push(applyChangesState)
   ▷ *adding state in which changes produced by the applied rules are committed*
50: agentTransitions.Push(completedExecutionState, applyChangesState, IsNotApplyStructureRule)
   ▷ *add transition to the apply changes state where changes produced by rules are applied, if*
   has not been applied any structure rule
51: agentTransitions.Push(applyChangesState, receiveState)
   ▷ *adding transition on which changes produced by the applied rules are committed*
52: agentStates.Push(receiveState)
   ▷ *add state that receives objects sent by applying the communication rules in other membranes*
53: agentTransitions.Push(receiveState, endState)
   ▷ *add transition to the end state that receives objects sent by applying the communication*
   rules in other membranes
54: agentStates.Push(endState)
   ▷ *add the final state*
55: agentsStates.PushAll(agentStates.Content())
   ▷ *add the contents of the stack that holds the current agent states to the stack that holds*
   the states of all agents
56: agentsTransitions.PushAll(agentStates.Content())
   ▷ *add the contents of the stack that holds the current agent transitions to the stack that*
   holds the transitions of all agents
57: **end for**

References

1. Bai, H., Rolfe, M.D., Jia, W., Coakley, S., Poole, R.K., Green, J., Holcombe, M.: Agent-based modeling of oxygen-responsive transcription factors in Escherichia coli. PLoS Comput. Biol. **10**(4), e1003595 (2014)
2. Bakir, M.E., Konur, S., Gheorghe, M., Niculescu, I., Ipate, F.: High performance simulations of kernel P systems. In: 2014 IEEE International Conference on High Performance Computing and Communications, 6th IEEE International Symposium on Cyberspace Safety and Security, 11th IEEE International Conference on Embedded Software and Systems, HPCC/CSS/ICESS, Paris, France, 20–22 August 2014, pp. 409–412. IEEE (2014)
3. Ciobanu, G., Wenyuan, G.: P systems running on a cluster of computers. In: Martín-Vide, C., Mauri, G., Păun, G., Rozenberg, G., Salomaa, A. (eds.) WMC 2003. LNCS, vol. 2933, pp. 123–139. Springer, Heidelberg (2004). doi:10.1007/978-3-540-24619-0_9
4. Diez Dolinski, L., Núñez Hervás, R., Cruz Echeandía, M., Ortega, A.: Distributed simulation of P systems by means of map-reduce: first steps with Hadoop and P-Lingua. In: Cabestany, J., Rojas, I., Joya, G. (eds.) IWANN 2011. LNCS, vol. 6691, pp. 457–464. Springer, Heidelberg (2011). doi:10.1007/978-3-642-21501-8_57
5. García-Quismondo, M.: Modelling and simulation of real-life phenomena in membrane computing. Ph.D. thesis, University of Seville, November 2013
6. Gheorghe, M., Ipate, F., Dragomir, C., Mierla, L., Valencia-Cabrera, L., García-Quismondo, M., Pérez-Jiménez, M.J.: Kernel P Systems - Version I. In: Eleventh Brainstorming Week on Membrane Computing (11BWMC), pp. 97–124, August 2013
7. Gheorghe, M., Ipate, F., Mierla, L., Konur, S., kPWorkbench: a software framework for kernel P systems. In: Macías-Ramos, L.F., Păun, G., Riscos-Núñez, A., Valencia-Cabrera, L. (eds.) Thirteenth Brainstorming Week on Membrane Computing, WBMC, Sevilla, Spain, 2–6 February 2015, pp. 179–194. Fenix Editora (2015)
8. Gheorghe, M., Konur, S., Ipate, F., Mierla, L., Bakir, M.E., Stannett, M.: An integrated model checking toolset for kernel P systems. In: Rozenberg, G., Salomaa, A., Sempere, J.M., Zandron, C. (eds.) CMC 2015. LNCS, vol. 9504, pp. 153–170. Springer, Heidelberg (2015). doi:10.1007/978-3-319-28475-0_11
9. Gutiérrez, A., Fernández, L., Arroyo, F., Martínez, V.: Design of a hardware architecture based on microcontrollers for the implementation of membrane systems. In: Eighth International Symposium on Symbolic and Numeric Algorithms for Scientific Computing, SYNASC 2006, pp. 350–353 (2006)
10. Ipate, F., Bălănescu, T., Kefalas, P., Holcombe, M., Eleftherakis, G.: A new model of communicating stream X-machine systems. Rom. J. Inf. Sci. Technol. **6**(1), 165–184 (2003)
11. Ipate, F., Lefticaru, R., Mierlă, L., Cabrera, L.V., Han, H., Zhang, G., Dragomir, C., Jiménez, M.J.P., Gheorghe, M.: Kernal P systems: applications and implementations. In: Yin, Z., Pan, L., Fang, X. (eds.) Proceedings of The Eighth International Conference on Bio Inspired Computing: Theories and Applications (BIC-TA), pp. 1081–1089. Springer, Heidelberg (2013)
12. Kirk, D.B., Hwu, W.W.: Programming massively parallel processors: a hands-on approach, 1st edn. Morgan Kaufmann Publishers Inc., San Francisco (2010)

13. Konur, S., Kiran, M., Gheorghe, M., Burkitt, M., IpateF.: Agent-based high-performance simulation of biological systems on the GPU. In: 17th IEEE International Conference on High Performance Computing and Communications, HPCC, 7th IEEE International Symposium on Cyberspace Safety and Security, CSS, and 12th IEEE International Conference on Embedded Software and Systems, ICESS, New York, NY, USA, 24–26 August 2015, pp. 84–89. IEEE (2015)
14. Macías-Ramos, L.F.: Developing efficient simulators for cell machines. Ph.D. thesis, University of Seville, February 2016
15. Martínez-del-Amor, M.Á.: Accelerating membrane systems simulators using high performance computing with GPU. Ph.D. thesis, University of Seville, May 2013
16. Martínez-del-Amor, M.A., García-Quismondo, M., Macías-Ramos, L.F., Valencia-Cabrera, L., Riscos-Núóez, A., Pérez-Jiménez, M.J.: Simulating P systems on GPU devices: a survey. Fundam. Inform. **136**(3), 269–284 (2015)
17. Martínez-del-Amor, M.A., Macías-Ramos, L.F., Valencia-Cabrera, L., Riscos-Núñez, A., Pérez-Jiménez, M.J.: Accelerated simulation of P systems on the GPU: a survey. In: Pan, L., Păun, G., Pérez-Jiménez, M.J., Song, T. (eds.) BIC-TA 2014. CCIS, vol. 472, pp. 308–312. Springer, Heidelberg (2014). doi:10.1007/978-3-662-45049-9_50
18. Munshi, A., Gaster, B.R., Mattson, T.G., Fung, J., Ginsburg, D.: OpenCL Programming Guide, 1st edn. Addison-Wesley, Boston (2011)
19. Nickolls, J., Buck, I., Garland, M., Skadron, K.: Scalable parallel programming with CUDA. Queue **6**(2), 40–53 (2008)
20. Niculescu, I., Gheorghe, M., Ipate, F., Stefanescu, A.: From kernel P Systems to X-machines and FLAME. J. Automata Lang. Comb. **19**(1–4), 239–250 (2014)
21. Owens, J.D., Houston, M., Luebke, D., Green, S., Stone, J.E., Phillips, J.C.: GPU Computing. Proc. IEEE **96**(5), 879–899 (2008)
22. Păun, G.: Computing with membranes. J. Comput. Syst. Sci. **61**(1), 108–143 (2000)
23. Petreska, B., Teuscher, C.: A reconfigurable hardware membrane system. In: Martín-Vide, C., Mauri, G., Păun, G., Rozenberg, G., Salomaa, A. (eds.) WMC 2003. LNCS, vol. 2933, pp. 269–285. Springer, Heidelberg (2004). doi:10.1007/978-3-540-24619-0_20
24. Richmond, P., Walker, D.C., Coakley, S., Romano, D.M.: High performance cellular level agent-based simulation with FLAME for the GPU. Brief. Bioinform. **11**(3), 334–347 (2010)
25. Takizawa, H., Koyama, K., Sato, K., Komatsu, K., Kobayashi, H.: CheCL: transparent checkpointing and process migration of openCL applications. In: IEEE International on Parallel Distributed Processing Symposium (IPDPS), pp. 864–876 (2011)
26. Wang, L., Tao, J., Ranjan, R., Marten, H., Streit, A., Chen, J., Chen, D.: G-Hadoop: MapReduce across distributed data centers for data-intensive computing. Future Gener. Comput. Syst. **29**(3), 739–750 (2013). Special Section: Recent Developments in High Performance Computing and Security
27. The P-Lingua Website. http://www.p-lingua.org/
28. kPWorkbench Home Page. http://kpworkbench.org/
29. FLAME website. http://www.flame.ac.uk/
30. FLAME GPU website. http://www.flamegpu.com/
31. The Message Passing Interface (MPI) standard. http://www.mcs.anl.gov/research/projects/mpi/

32. The NVIDIA Website. http://www.nvidia.com/content/global/global.php
33. OpenCL standard webpage. http://www.khronos.org/opencl
34. The Sevilla HPC Server. http://www.gcn.us.es/gpucomputing/
35. The Open MPI project. https://www.open-mpi.org/

Shallow Non-confluent P Systems

Alberto Leporati, Luca Manzoni, Giancarlo Mauri, Antonio E. Porreca,
and Claudio Zandron[(✉)]

Dipartimento di Informatica, Sistemistica e Comunicazione,
Università degli Studi di Milano-Bicocca, Viale Sarca 336/14, 20126 Milano, Italy
{leporati,luca.manzoni,mauri,porreca,zandron}@disco.unimib.it

Abstract. We prove that non-confluent (i.e., strongly nondeterministic) P systems with active membranes working in polynomial time are able to simulate polynomial-space nondeterministic Turing machines, and thus to solve all **PSPACE** problems. Unlike the confluent case, this result holds for shallow P systems. In particular, depth 1 (i.e., only one membrane nesting level and using elementary membrane division only) already suffices, and neither dissolution nor send-in communication rules are needed.

1 Introduction

Families of *confluent* recogniser P systems with active membranes [9] are known to characterise **PSPACE** in polynomial time [13,14]. In this kind of P systems the computations can be locally nondeterministic, but the final result (acceptance or rejection) must be consistent across all computations. This result seems to require that the membrane nesting depth of each P system in the family depends on the length of the input (the published results show that a *linear* depth suffices [13]); furthermore, all known algorithms employ non-elementary membrane division (i.e., division of membranes containing further membranes, resulting in the replication of whole subtrees of the membrane structure).

More recently, it has been proved [2] that when only elementary division (i.e., division for membranes not containing further membranes) is available, the power of P systems decreases to $\mathbf{P}^{\#\mathbf{P}}$, the class of problems solved in polynomial time by deterministic Turing machines with an oracle for a counting problem [8]; this class is conjectured to be strictly smaller than **PSPACE**. More specifically, P systems of depth 1 (consisting of an outermost membrane containing only elementary membranes) already characterise $\mathbf{P}^{\#\mathbf{P}}$ [3], and thus increasing the depth without also allowing non-elementary division does not increase the computing power. P systems of depth 0, where there exists only one membrane and division is unavailable, are known to characterise **P** [3,15].

Fewer results are known for non-confluent P systems, where the computations need not agree on the result, and the overall behaviour is accepting if and

This work was partially supported by Fondo d'Ateneo (FA) 2015 of Università degli Studi di Milano-Bicocca: "Complessità computazionale e applicazioni crittografiche di modelli di calcolo bioispirati".

A. Leporati et al. (Eds.): CMC 2016, LNCS 10105, pp. 307–316, 2017.
DOI: 10.1007/978-3-319-54072-6_19

only if there exists an accepting computation (i.e., a strongly nondeterministic behaviour analogous to Turing machines). Clearly, all lower bounds of confluent P systems hold for non-confluent ones. The only other published result concerning non-confluent recogniser P systems with active membranes, to the authors' best knowledge, is a characterisation of **NP** by means of polynomial-time non-confluent P systems with active membranes without any kind of membrane division [11].

Membrane division in confluent P systems is commonly used to simulate the effect of nondeterminism, by exploring in parallel all possible nondeterministic choices and combining the results by disjunction [15], threshold or majority [3], or alternation of conjunctions and disjunctions [13], depending on which rules are available and the depth of the membrane structure. It is then natural to ask whether these results can be somehow improved by employing actual nondeterminism, i.e., by exploiting non-confluence in addition to membrane division.

In this paper we prove that this is indeed the case, since the lower bound **PSPACE** can actually be reached by "shallow" (small-depth) polynomial-time non-confluent P systems: specifically, depth 1, and thus division only for elementary membranes, already suffice for reaching **PSPACE**. Furthermore, the P systems employed can be *monodirectional* [1,4], i.e., without using send-in communication rules. Monodirectionality is known to decrease the power of confluent P systems; for instance, polynomial-time monodirectional confluent P systems of depth 1 characterise $\mathbf{P}_{\|}^{\mathbf{NP}}$ (the class of problems solved in polynomial time with parallel queries to an **NP** oracle, conjectured to be smaller than $\mathbf{P}^{\#\mathbf{P}}$), and $\mathbf{P}^{\mathbf{NP}}$ (the class where the oracle queries are not restricted to be parallel, which is probably smaller than **PSPACE**) if the depth is unbounded [4].

2   Basic Notions

In this paper we use P systems with active membranes [9] using only object evolution rules $[a \to w]_h^\alpha$, send-out communication rules $[a]_h^\alpha \to [\ ]_h^\beta \, b$ and elementary membrane division rules $[a]_h^\alpha \to [b]_h^\beta \, [c]_h^\gamma$.

The *depth* of a P system is defined as the depth of its membrane structure when considered as a rooted tree, i.e., as the length of the longest path from the outermost membrane to an elementary membrane.

In particular, we are dealing with *recogniser P systems* Π [10], whose alphabet includes the distinguished result objects yes and no; exactly one result object must be sent out from the outermost membrane to signal acceptance or rejection, and only at the last computation step. If all possible computations of Π agree on the result, the P system is said to be *confluent*. In this paper, however, we only deal with the more general *non-confluent* recogniser P systems, where different computations need not agree on the result, and the final result is acceptance if and only if *at least one* computation is accepting.

A decision problem, or language $L \subseteq \Sigma^*$, is solved by a *family* of P systems $\boldsymbol{\Pi} = \{\Pi_x : x \in \Sigma^*\}$, where Π_x accepts if and only if $x \in L$. In that case, we say that $L(\Pi) = L$. As usual, we require a uniformity condition [6] on families of P systems:

Definition 1. *A family of P systems $\Pi = \{\Pi_x : x \in \Sigma^\star\}$ is* (polynomial-time) *uniform if the mapping $x \mapsto \Pi_x$ can be computed by two polynomial-time deterministic Turing machines E and F as follows:*

- *$F(1^n) = \Pi_n$, where n is the length of the input x and Π_n is a common P system for all inputs of length n, with a distinguished input membrane.*
- *$E(x) = w_x$, where w_x is a multiset encoding the specific input x.*
- *Finally, Π_x is simply Π_n with w_x added to its input membrane.*

The family Π is said to be (polynomial-time) *semi-uniform if there exists a single deterministic polynomial-time Turing machine H such that $H(x) = \Pi_x$ for each $x \in \Sigma^\star$.*

The class of decision problems solved by uniform families of non-confluent P systems with active membranes working in polynomial time is denoted by the symbol $\mathbf{NPMC}_{\mathcal{AM}}$. The corresponding class for families of P systems with depth-1 membrane structures using only object evolution, send-out communication and elementary membrane division rules is denoted by $\mathbf{NPMC}_{\mathcal{AM}(\text{depth-1},-i,-d,-ne)}$, where $-i$, $-d$, and $-ne$ denote the lack of send-in, dissolution, and non-elementary division rules, respectively. For the complexity classes defined in terms of Turing machines, such as $\mathbf{NP}$, $\mathbf{P}_{\|}^{\mathbf{NP}}$, $\mathbf{P}^{\mathbf{NP}}$, $\mathbf{P}^{\#\mathbf{P}}$, and $\mathbf{PSPACE}$ we refer the reader to Papadimitriou's book [8].

3 Simulating Nondeterministic Turing Machines

Let N be a nondeterministic Turing machine working in polynomial space $p(n)$. Let Σ be the tape alphabet of N, and let Q be its set of states. Without loss of generality, we assume that N has a unique accepting configuration, consisting of a unique accepting state, an entirely blank tape, and the tape head located on the leftmost position. We can assume that all computations of N halt within exponential time $t(n) = |\Sigma|^{p(n)} \times |Q| \times p(n)$.

Suppose that string x is an input for N, and let $m = p(|x|) + 3$. A configuration $\mathcal{C}$ of N can be encoded as a delimited string $\$a_1 \cdots a_{k-1}qa_k \cdots a_{p(n)}\$$ of length m over the alphabet $\Sigma \cup Q \cup \{\$\}$. This denotes that the tape of N contains the string $a_1 \cdots a_{k-1}a_k \cdots a_{p(n)}$, that the machine is in state q, and that the tape head is located on the k-th tape cell.

Deciding whether N accepts an input x is equivalent to deciding whether the unique final accepting configuration $\mathcal{C}'$ is reachable from the initial configuration $\mathcal{C}$ on input x within $t(|x|)$ steps. Let $\mathcal{C}_1$ and $\mathcal{C}_2$ be configurations of N, let $\mathcal{C}_1 \to \mathcal{C}_2$ denote that $\mathcal{C}_2$ is reachable from $\mathcal{C}_1$ via a single computation step, and let $\mathcal{C}_1 \to^t \mathcal{C}_2$ denote reachability within t steps. Then, we have

$$\mathcal{C}_1 \to^1 \mathcal{C}_2 \qquad \text{iff} \quad \mathcal{C}_1 = \mathcal{C}_2 \text{ or } \mathcal{C}_1 \to \mathcal{C}_2$$

$$\mathcal{C}_1 \to^t \mathcal{C}_2 \text{ with } t > 1 \qquad \text{iff} \quad \text{there exists } \mathcal{C} \text{ such that } \mathcal{C}_1 \to^{\lceil t/2 \rceil} \mathcal{C} \to^{\lfloor t/2 \rfloor} \mathcal{C}_2$$

The Turing machine N on input x of length n is simulated by a P system Π_x, whose initial configuration is

$$
\left[\begin{array}{c}
\left[\begin{array}{c}
a_{1,1} \quad \cdots \quad a_{m,m} \\
b_{1,m+1} \quad \cdots \quad b_{m,2m} \\
d_{\lceil \log t(n) \rceil}
\end{array}\right]_h \\
\mathsf{yes}_{2 \times \lceil \log t(n) \rceil + r(n) + 2}
\end{array}\right]_k^0
\right]^0
\tag{1}
$$

Here the string $a_1 \cdots a_m$ encodes the initial configuration of N on input x, that is, $a_1 \cdots a_m = \$q_0 x \sqcup^{p(n)-n}\$$ with $\sqcup$ denoting a blank cell and q_0 the initial state of N; these symbols need a further subscript in Π_x in order to keep track of their position within the string. Analogously, the string $b_1 \cdots b_m$ encodes the unique accepting configuration of N, that is, $b_1 \cdots b_m = \$q_{\mathsf{yes}} \sqcup^{p(n)}\$$, where q_{yes} is the accepting state. In this case, the symbols are subscripted with $m+1, \ldots, 2m$ as if the P system stored a single string $a_1 \cdots a_m b_1 \cdots b_m$; this will prove useful in a later phase of the simulation. The other objects do not encode information about N, but play an auxiliary role in the simulation; in particular, the function $r(n)$, appearing in the subscript of the object yes, will be defined later.

For the whole first phase of the computation of Π_x (including the initial configuration) the membranes with label h maintain, as an invariant, a configuration of the form

$$
\left[\begin{array}{c}
x_{1,1} \quad \cdots \quad x_{m,m} \\
y_{1,m+1} \quad \cdots \quad y_{m,2m} \\
d_t
\end{array}\right]_h^\alpha
\tag{2}
$$

where $1 \le t \le \lceil \log t(n) \rceil$, the charge α is either 0 or $+$, and $x_{1,1} \cdots x_{m,m}$ and $y_{1,m+1} \cdots y_{m,2m}$ are multisets respectively encoding the strings $x_1 \cdots x_m$ and $y_1 \cdots y_m$, which in turn encode two configurations $\mathcal{C}_1$ and $\mathcal{C}_2$ of N as described above. This invariant is restored every two steps of the first phase of the computation of Π_x.

The purpose of this membrane, for $t > 1$, is to guess a computation path of length at most 2^t from $\mathcal{C}_1$ to $\mathcal{C}_2$; computation paths from $\mathcal{C}_1 \to \cdots \to \mathcal{C}_2$ shorter than 2^t are padded to length 2^t by repeating some intermediate configurations (recall that $\mathcal{C} \to^1 \mathcal{C}$ for all $\mathcal{C}$). If $t = 0$, the membrane checks whether the configuration $\mathcal{C}_2$ is reachable by N in one step from $\mathcal{C}_1$; if it is the case, then it outputs an object yes, and otherwise an object no after exactly $2t + r(n) + 1$ computation steps.

Let us describe recursively the behaviour of the membrane. If $t > 0$, then the problem of guessing a computation $\mathcal{C}_1 \to^{2^t} \mathcal{C}_2$ is divided into the two subproblems of guessing a computation $\mathcal{C}_1 \to^{2^{t-1}} \mathcal{C}$ and a computation $\mathcal{C} \to^{2^{t-1}} \mathcal{C}_2$, where $\mathcal{C}$ is a nondeterministically guessed mid-point. This mid-point is guessed by rewriting each object σ_i of the multiset $x_{1,1} \cdots x_{m,m}$ into a primed version σ'_i of itself, together with an object τ_i'', where τ is a nondeterministically chosen symbol of the alphabet of the configurations of N:

$$[\sigma_i \rightarrow \sigma_i' \, \tau_i'']_h^\alpha \qquad \text{for } \alpha \in \{0, +\}, \sigma, \tau \in \Sigma \cup Q \cup \{\$\} \text{ and } 1 \leq i \leq m \qquad (3)$$

Notice that the P system guesses an arbitrary string as a configuration $\mathcal{C}$; the string might even be an invalid encoding (e.g., with multiple symbols denoting the state of N); the validity of the configuration will be checked later. Simultaneously, the objects of the target configuration $y_{1,m+1} \cdots y_{m,2m}$ are primed:

$$[\sigma_i \rightarrow \sigma_i']_h^\alpha \qquad \text{for } \alpha \in \{0, +\}, \sigma \in \Sigma \cup Q \cup \{\$\} \text{ and } m+1 \leq i \leq 2m \qquad (4)$$

While the objects encoding the configurations of N are thus rewritten, the membrane is divided by d_t into two membranes differing only in their charge:

$$[d_t]_h^\alpha \rightarrow [d_t']_h^+ \, [d_t']_h^0 \qquad \text{for } \alpha \in \{0, +\} \text{ and } 1 \leq t \leq \lceil \log t(n) \rceil$$

Hence, the original membrane h leads to the following configuration:

$$\begin{array}{|ccc|}^+ \\ x_{1,1}' & \cdots & x_{m,m}' \\ z_{1,1}'' & \cdots & z_{m,m}'' \\ y_{1,m+1}' & \cdots & y_{m,2m}' \\ & d_t' & \\ \end{array}_h \quad \begin{array}{|ccc|}^0 \\ x_{1,1}' & \cdots & x_{m,m}' \\ z_{1,1}'' & \cdots & z_{m,m}'' \\ y_{1,m+1}' & \cdots & y_{m,2m}' \\ & d_t' & \\ \end{array}_h$$

where the objects $z_{i,i}''$ represent the mid-point configuration $\mathcal{C}$ guessed by the membrane. Now configuration $\mathcal{C}$ becomes the target configuration in the left membrane, having charge $+$. This requires eliminating all primes, deleting the objects $y_{1,m+1}' \cdots y_{m,2m}'$ and adjusting the subscripts of $z_{1,1}'' \cdots z_{m,m}''$; this is performed by the following rules:

$$\begin{array}{ll} [\sigma_i' \rightarrow \sigma_i]_h^+ & \text{for } \sigma \in \Sigma \cup Q \cup \{\$\} \text{ and } 1 \leq i \leq m \\ [\sigma_i' \rightarrow \epsilon]_h^+ & \text{for } \sigma \in \Sigma \cup Q \cup \{\$\} \text{ and } m+1 \leq i \leq 2m \\ [\sigma_i'' \rightarrow \sigma_{i+m}]_h^+ & \text{for } \sigma \in \Sigma \cup Q \cup \{\$\} \text{ and } 1 \leq i \leq m \end{array}$$

On the other hand, the configuration $\mathcal{C}$ becomes the source configuration in the right membrane (with charge 0), where the objects $x_{1,1}' \cdots x_{m,m}'$ must be deleted:

$$\begin{array}{ll} [\sigma_i' \rightarrow \epsilon]_h^0 & \text{for } \sigma \in \Sigma \cup Q \cup \{\$\} \text{ and } 1 \leq i \leq m \\ [\sigma_i' \rightarrow \sigma_i]_h^0 & \text{for } \sigma \in \Sigma \cup Q \cup \{\$\} \text{ and } m+1 \leq i \leq 2m \\ [\sigma_i'' \rightarrow \sigma_i]_h^0 & \text{for } \sigma \in \Sigma \cup Q \cup \{\$\} \text{ and } 1 \leq i \leq m \end{array}$$

Finally, the object d'_t is rewritten into d_{t-1} inside both membranes:

$$[d'_t \rightarrow d_{t-1}]^\alpha_h \qquad \text{for } \alpha \in \{0, +\} \text{ and } 1 \le t \le \lceil \log t(n) \rceil$$

Hence, the P system reaches the configuration

$$\left[\begin{array}{ccc} x_{1,1} & \cdots & x_{m,m} \\ z_{1,m+1} & \cdots & z_{m,2m} \\ & d_{t-1} & \end{array} \right]^+_h \qquad \left[\begin{array}{ccc} z_{1,1} & \cdots & z_{m,m} \\ y_{1,m+1} & \cdots & y_{m,2m} \\ & d_{t-1} & \end{array} \right]^0_h$$

with two membranes having a configuration of the form (2). This restores the associated invariant.

After $2 \times \lceil \log t(n) \rceil$ steps (twice the initial subscript of the object d_t), all membranes with label h simultaneously reach a configuration of the form

$$\left[\begin{array}{ccc} x_{1,1} & \cdots & x_{m,m} \\ y_{1,m+1} & \cdots & y_{m,2m} \\ & d_0 & \end{array} \right]^\alpha_h$$

for some $\alpha \in \{0, +\}$ and $x_1, \ldots, x_m, y_1, \ldots, y_m \in \Sigma \cup Q \cup \{\$\}$. The last phase of the simulation is triggered by objects d_0 being sent out and changing the charge of the membranes to $-$:

$$[d_0]^\alpha_h \rightarrow [\ ]^-_h \# \qquad \text{for } \alpha \in \{0, +\} \tag{5}$$

While rule (5) is applied, the charge of the membrane is still 0 or $+$, and the rules of type (3) and (4) are still enabled; thus, each membrane h reaches a configuration of the form

$$\left[\begin{array}{ccc} x'_{1,1} & \cdots & x'_{m,m} \\ z''_{1,1} & \cdots & z''_{m,m} \\ y'_{1,m+1} & \cdots & y'_{m,2m} \end{array} \right]^-_h$$

When the charge of a membrane with label h is $-$, the objects of the form τ''_i (which have been just produced, but are actually not needed in this phase) are deleted:

$$[\tau''_i \rightarrow \epsilon]^-_h \qquad \text{for } \tau \in \Sigma \cup Q \cup \{\$\} \text{ and } 1 \le i \le m$$

The remaining objects σ_i' are rewritten into a "tilded" version. This allows us to re-use the charges 0 and $+$ in the next phase of the computation (which will make use of a simulation from [3]) without creating conflicts with previous rules.

$$[\sigma_i' \rightarrow \tilde{\sigma}_i]_h^- \qquad \text{for } \sigma \in \Sigma \cup Q \cup \{\$\} \text{ and } 1 \leq i \leq 2m$$

This leads to the configuration

$$\left[\begin{array}{ccc} \tilde{x}_{1,1} & \cdots & \tilde{x}_{m,m} \\ \tilde{y}_{1,m+1} & \cdots & \tilde{y}_{m,2m} \end{array} \right]_h^- \tag{6}$$

Each membrane h now contains what can be considered as a string of length $2m$, consisting of the concatenation of two (possibly malformed) encodings of configurations of N.

From [3] we know that a single membrane is able to efficiently simulate a polynomial-time *deterministic* Turing machine (as long as there is no communication with adjacent membranes) if the tape is encoded as in configuration (6). The idea is to simulate a larger number of charges (referred to as *extended charges*) by encoding them in the subscripts of each object; the subscripts are kept synchronised by multiple sequential updates of the actual charges $\{+, 0, -\}$. The extended charges are employed in order to store pairs (q, i) of state and tape head position of the simulated Turing machine. A transition such as $\delta(q, a) = (q', a', +1)$ is then implemented as a rule of the form $[a_i]_h^{(q,i)} \rightarrow [a_i']_h^{(q',i+1)}$, which is actually carried out in multiple steps using standard charges, object evolution and send-out communication rules.

In our particular case, each membrane h can simulate a Turing machine that checks whether the content of such membrane consists of two valid consecutive configurations of N, or two identical valid configurations of N. We can assume, without loss of generality, that such Turing machine halts exactly in polynomial time $r(n)$ for all strings of length n; the result is given by outputting yes or no from the membrane.

After $2 \times \lceil \log t(n) \rceil + r(n)$ steps, a total of $2^{\lceil \log t(n) \rceil}$ instances of yes and no reach the outermost membrane k. If there is at least one instance of no, then there existed an instance of membrane h containing either an invalid configuration, or two non-consecutive configurations; this means that the P system Π_x guessed a malformed computation of N. In that case, it sends out any of the objects no as the final result of the computation:

$$[\text{no}]_k^0 \rightarrow [\,]_k^- \text{ no}$$

If there is no instance of no inside k, then all membranes h contained valid consecutive configurations (or pairs of identical valid configurations). Since the initial membrane h contained the initial and final configurations of N on input x, this means that Π_x guessed a legitimate accepting computation of N. In that case, all objects yes sent out from the elementary membranes h are ignored, and instead the timed object yes_t, which already appears in the initial configuration (1), produces the output of the P system. This object counts down for the entire duration of the simulation:

$$[\mathsf{yes}_t \to \mathsf{yes}_{t-1}]_k^0 \qquad \text{for } 1 \leq t \leq 2 \times \lceil \log t(n) \rceil + r(n) + 2$$

If at time $2 \times \lceil \log t(n) \rceil + r(n) + 2$ membrane k still has charge 0, then the P system has not rejected, and it can send out yes_0 as yes, as the result:

$$[\mathsf{yes}_0]_k^0 \to [\ ]_k^- \mathsf{yes}$$

In both cases Π_x halts by sending out a result at the last computation step.

The P system Π_x has thus an accepting computation if and only if there exists a computation path from the initial configuration of N on input x to its accepting computation, that is, if and only if N accepts.

Notice that the mapping $x \mapsto \Pi_x$ is uniform, since all rules of Π_x only depend on the *length* of the input, and not on the input itself. Furthermore, the initial membrane structure is the same for all Π_x. The only portion of the initial configuration that depends on the actual input x is the content of membrane h, which is chosen as the input of the P system. The mapping $x \mapsto \Pi_x$ can also be computed in polynomial time: the encoding of the input simply consists in adding subscripts to the input symbols of x, and the rules are easy to compute, since they all range over sets independent of the input, or over sets of natural numbers depending on the input length, and never require sophisticated computation.

Theorem 1. *Let N be a nondeterministic Turing machine working in polynomial space. Then, there exists a uniform family $\boldsymbol{\Pi}$ of non-confluent P systems of depth 1, using only object evolution, send-out and elementary division rules, and working in polynomial time such that $L(N) = L(\boldsymbol{\Pi})$.* □

Since arbitrary polynomial-space Turing machines can be simulated, the whole class they characterise is solved by shallow non-confluent P systems with a limited range of rules:

Corollary 1. $\boldsymbol{PSPACE} \subseteq \mathbf{NPMC}_{\mathcal{AM}(\text{depth-1},-\text{i},-\text{d},-\text{ne})}.$ □

4   Conclusions

The results obtained in this paper show that, even with depth-1 membrane structures and monodirectional communication, non-confluent P systems with active membranes are already able to solve **PSPACE**-complete problems in polynomial time, and are thus conjecturally stronger than confluent ones with the same restrictions (and even those with only one of such restrictions).

This result is a first step towards a characterisation of the power of polynomial-time non-confluent P systems with active membranes. If **PSPACE** turned out to also be an upper bound, although it has been conjectured that it might not be so [14], this would show that non-confluence subsumes both nesting depth beyond 1 and bidirectionality. In that case, it would be interesting to find other parameters (such as unusual combinations of admissible rules) which can be "tuned" in order to obtain complexity classes between **NP** and **PSPACE**.

We also conjecture that an algorithm similar to the one provided here for P systems with active membranes can also be implemented for tissue-like P systems using either cell division [12] or cell separation rules [7], since they seem to share several features and limitations of cell-like P systems of depth 1 [5].

References

1. Alhazov, A., Freund, R.: On the efficiency of P systems with active membranes and two polarizations. In: Mauri, G., Păun, G., Pérez-Jiménez, M.J., Rozenberg, G., Salomaa, A. (eds.) WMC 2004. LNCS, vol. 3365, pp. 146–160. Springer, Heidelberg (2005). doi:10.1007/978-3-540-31837-8_8

2. Leporati, A., Manzoni, L., Mauri, G., Porreca, A.E., Zandron, C.: Simulating elementary active membranes. In: Gheorghe, M., Rozenberg, G., Salomaa, A., Sosík, P., Zandron, C. (eds.) CMC 2014. LNCS, vol. 8961, pp. 284–299. Springer, Heidelberg (2014). doi:10.1007/978-3-319-14370-5_18

3. Leporati, A., Manzoni, L., Mauri, G., Porreca, A.E., Zandron, C.: Membrane division, oracles, and the counting hierarchy. Fundam. Informaticae **138**(1–2), 97–111 (2015)

4. Leporati, A., Manzoni, L., Mauri, G., Porreca, A.E., Zandron, C.: Monodirectional P systems. In: Macìas-Ramos, L.F., Păun, G., Riscos-Núñez, A., Valencia-Cabrera, L. (eds.) Proceedings of the 13th Brainstorming Week on Membrane Computing, pp. 207–226. Fénix Editora (2015)

5. Leporati, A., Manzoni, L., Mauri, G., Porreca, A.E., Zandron, C.: Tissue P systems can be simulated efficiently with counting oracles. In: Rozenberg, G., Salomaa, A., Sempere, J.M., Zandron, C. (eds.) CMC 2015. LNCS, vol. 9504, pp. 251–261. Springer, Heidelberg (2015). doi:10.1007/978-3-319-28475-0_17

6. Murphy, N., Woods, D.: The computational power of membrane systems under tight uniformity conditions. Nat. Comput. **10**(1), 613–632 (2011)

7. Pan, L., Pérez-Jiménez, M.J.: Computational complexity of tissue-like P systems. J. Complex. **26**(3), 296–315 (2010)

8. Papadimitriou, C.H.: Computational Complexity. Addison-Wesley, Boston (1993)

9. Păun, G.: P systems with active membranes: attacking NP-complete problems. J. Autom. Lang. Comb. **6**(1), 75–90 (2001)

10. Pérez-Jiménez, M.J., Romero-Jiménez, A., Sancho-Caparrini, F.: Complexity classes in models of cellular computing with membranes. Nat. Comput. **2**(3), 265–284 (2003)

11. Porreca, A.E., Mauri, G., Zandron, C.: Non-confluence in divisionless P systems with active membranes. Theor. Comput. Sci. **411**(6), 878–887 (2010)

12. Păun, G., Pérez-Jiménez, M.J., Riscos Núñez, A.: Tissue P systems with cell division. Int. J. Comput. Commun. Control **3**(3), 295–303 (2008)

13. Sosík, P.: The computational power of cell division in P systems: beating down parallel computers? Nat. Comput. **2**(3), 287–298 (2003)

14. Sosík, P., Rodríguez-Patón, A.: Membrane computing and complexity theory: a characterization of PSPACE. J. Comput. Syst. Sci. **73**(1), 137–152 (2007)
15. Zandron, C., Ferretti, C., Mauri, G.: Solving NP-complete problems using P systems with active membranes. In: Antoniou, I., Calude, C.S., Dinneen, M.J. (eds.) UMC'2K. DISCMATH, pp. 289–301. Springer, Heidelberg (2001). doi:10.1007/978-1-4471-0313-4_21

Revising the Membrane Computing Model for Byzantine Agreement

Radu Nicolescu[✉]

Department of Computer Science, University of Auckland,
Private Bag, 92019 Auckland, New Zealand
r.nicolescu@auckland.ac.nz

Abstract. We refine our earlier version of P systems with complex symbols. The new version, called cP systems, enables the creation and manipulation of high-level data structures which are typical in high-level languages, such as: relations (graphs), associative arrays, lists, trees. We assess these capabilities by attempting a revised version of our previously best solution for the Byzantine agreement problem – a famous problem in distributed algorithms, with non-trivial data structures and algorithms. In contrast to our previous solutions, which use a greater than exponential number of symbols and rules, the new solution uses a *fixed sized* alphabet and ruleset, independent of the problem size. The new ruleset follows closely the conceptual description of the algorithm. This revised framework opens the way to further extensions, which may bring P systems closer to the conceptual Actor model.

Keywords: Distributed algorithms · Byzantine agreement · EIG trees · Membrane computing · P systems · cP systems · Inter-cell parallelism · Intra-cell parallelism · Prolog terms and unification · Complex symbols · Cells with subcells · Generic rules · Synchronous and asynchronous models · Actor model

1 Introduction

We refine our earlier version of P systems with complex symbols. The new version, called cP systems, enables the creation and manipulation of high-level data structures which are typical in high-level languages, such as: relations (graphs), associative arrays, lists, trees.

We assess these capabilities by attempting a revised version of our previously best solution for the Byzantine agreement problem, a famous problem in distributed algorithms, with non-trivial data structures and algorithms. In contrast to our previous solution, which uses a greater than exponential number of symbols and rules, the new solution uses a *fixed sized* alphabet and ruleset, independent of the problem size. The new ruleset follows closely the conceptual description of the algorithm.

Section 2 introduces high-level data structures in cP systems. Sections 3, 4, and 5 discuss the Byzantine algorithm and its classical implementation based on

© Springer International Publishing AG 2017
A. Leporati et al. (Eds.): CMC 2016, LNCS 10105, pp. 317–339, 2017.
DOI: 10.1007/978-3-319-54072-6_20

EIG trees; this material is reproduced or adapted from our earlier papers [7,8] The remaining sections discuss our newly revised solution.

2   Data Structures in cP Systems

We assume that the reader is familiar with the membrane extensions collectively known as *complex symbols*, proposed by Nicolescu et al. [17,19–21]. However, to ensure some degree of self-containment, our revised extensions, called cP systems, are reviewed in Appendix A. The reader is encouraged to check the main changes from our earlier versions, including: a simplified definition for complex symbols (subcells) and a standard set of complexity measures.

In this section we sketch the design of high-level data structures, similar to the data structures used in high-level pseudocode or high-level languages: numbers, relations, functions, associative arrays, lists, trees, together with alternative more readable notations. These data structures are critical in our model of the Byzantine algorithm.

Natural Numbers. Natural numbers can be represented via *multisets* containing repeated occurrences of the *same* atom. For example, considering that 1 represents an ad-hoc unary digit, the following complex symbols can be used to describe the contents of a virtual integer *variable* a: $a() = a(\lambda)$ — the value of a is 0; $a(1^3)$ — the value of a is 3. For concise expressions, we may alias these number representations by their corresponding numbers, e.g. $a() \equiv a(0), b(1^3) \equiv b(3)$. Nicolescu et al. [19–21] show how the basic arithmetic operations can be efficiently modelled by P systems with complex symbols.

Lists. Using complex symbols, list $[u, v, w]$ can be represented as the term $\gamma(u\ \gamma(v\ \gamma(w\ \gamma())))$, where the ad-hoc atom γ represents the list constructor *cons* and $\gamma()$ the empty list. Hiding the less relevant representation choices, we may alias this list by the more expressive equivalent notation $\gamma(u\,|\,v\,|\,w)$ – or by $\gamma(u\,|\,\gamma(v\,|\,w))$ – where operator $|$ separates the head and the tail of the list.

Trees. Consider the *binary tree* $z(a, (b), (c, (d), (e)))$, i.e. z points to a root node which has: (i) the value a; (ii) a left node with value b; and (iii) a right node with value c, left leaf d, and right leaf e. Using complex symbols, tree z can be represented as $z(a\ \phi(b)\ \psi(c\ \phi(d)\ \psi(e)))$, where ad-hoc atoms ϕ, ψ introduce left subtrees, right subtrees (respectively).

Relations and Functions. Consider the *binary relation* r, defined by: $r = \{(a,b),\ (b,c),\ (a,d),\ (d,c)\}$ (which has a diamond-shaped graph). Using complex symbols, relation r can be represented as a *multiset* with four r terms, $\{r(\kappa(a)\ \upsilon(b)),\ r(\kappa(b)\ \upsilon(c)),\ r(\kappa(a)\ \upsilon(d)),\ r(\kappa(d)\ \upsilon(c))\}$, where ad-hoc atoms κ and υ introduce *domain* and *codomain* values (respectively). Hiding the less relevant representation choices, we may alias the items of this multiset by a more expressive notation such as: $\{(a \overset{r}{\rightleftarrows} b),\ (b \overset{r}{\rightleftarrows} c),\ (a \overset{r}{\rightleftarrows} d),\ (d \overset{r}{\rightleftarrows} c)\}$.

If the relation is a *functional relation*, then we can emphasise this by using another operator, such as "mapsto". For example, the functional relation

$f = \{(a,b),\ (b,c),\ (d,c)\}$ can be represented by multiset $\{f(\kappa(a)\,\upsilon(b)),$ $f(\kappa(b)\,\upsilon(c)),\ f(\kappa(d)\,\upsilon(c))\}$ or by the more suggestive notation: $\{(a \overset{f}{\mapsto} b),\ (b \overset{f}{\mapsto} c),$ $(d \overset{f}{\mapsto} c)\}$. To highlight the actual mapping value, instead of $(a \overset{f}{\mapsto} b)$, we may also use the succinct abbreviation $f[a] = b$.

In this context, the $\rightleftarrows$ and $\mapsto$ operators are considered to have a high associative priority, so the enclosing parentheses are mostly required for increasing the readability (e.g. in text).

Associative Arrays. Associative arrays can be considered as particular cases of functional relations. Consider the *associative array* x, with the following key-value mappings: $\{1 \mapsto a,\ 1^3 \mapsto c,\ 1^7 \mapsto g\}$. Using complex symbols, array x can be represented as a multiset with three terms, $\{x(\kappa(1)\,\upsilon(a)),\ x(\kappa(1^3)\,\upsilon(c)),$ $x(\kappa(1^7)\,\upsilon(g))\}$, where ad-hoc atoms κ and υ introduce keys and values (respectively). Hiding the less relevant representation choices, we may alias the items of this multiset by the more expressive notation $\{1 \overset{x}{\mapsto} a,\ 1^3 \overset{x}{\mapsto} c,\ 1^7 \overset{x}{\mapsto} g\}$.

3   Byzantine Agreement

The Byzantine agreement problem was first proposed by Pease *et al.* in 1980 [22] and further elaborated in Lamport *et al.*'s seminal paper [12]. This problem addresses a fundamental issue in complex systems: correctly functioning processes must be able to overcome their possible differences and achieve a consensus, despite arbitrarily faulty processes that can give conflicting information to different parts of the system.

The Byzantine agreement has become one of the most studied problems in distributed algorithms—some even consider it the "crown jewel" of distributed algorithms. Lynch covers several versions of this problem and their solutions, including a complete description of the classical algorithm, based on Exponential Information Gathering (EIG) trees as a data structure [13].

Recent years have seen revived interest in this problem and its solutions, to achieve higher performance or stronger resilience, in a wide variety of contexts [1, 3, 4, 14], including, for example, solutions for quantum computers [2].

To the best of our knowledge, except our previous work on Byzantine agreement problem [7–11], no other complete solutions for P systems has been published. In the context of P systems, this problem was briefly mentioned, without solutions [5, 6]. Our solution was based on the classical EIG-based algorithm, where each EIG node was implemented by a distinct cell.

In this paper, we provide a newly revised P solution for the Byzantine agreement problem, based on EIG trees, for N processes connected in a complete graph. Each process is modelled by the combination of $N + 1$ cells: one "main" cell, which evaluates the EIG tree, plus one "firewall" cell for each duplex link (including one for itself). The new main cell uses a *fixed* number of states and high-level rules: 9 states and 16 rules for the main cell, and 5 states and 7 rules for the firewall cell; these high-level rules closely map the EIG algorithm description. In contrast, our previous best solution [8] used $\mathcal{O}(L)$ states and $\mathcal{O}(N!)$ symbols and rules (i.e. factorial complexity), where L is the number of messaging rounds (where $L = \lceil (N-1)/3 \rceil$).

4   EIG Trees

We assume that the reader is familiar with the basic terminology and notations: functions, relations, graphs, nodes (vertices), arcs, directed graphs, dags, trees, alphabets, strings and multisets [18]. Given two sets, A, B, a subset f of their cartesian product, $f \subseteq A \times B$, is a *functional relation* if $\forall (x, y_1), (x, y_2) \in f \Rightarrow y_1 = y_2$. Obviously, any function $f : A \to B$ can be viewed a functional relation, $\{(x, f(x)) \mid x \in A\}$, and, vice-versa, any functional relation can be viewed as a function.

We now recall a few basic concepts from combinatorial enumerations. The *integer range* from m to n is denoted by $[m, n]$, i.e. $[m, n] = \{m, m+1, \ldots, n\}$, if $m \leq n$, and $[m, n] = \emptyset$, if $m > n$. The set of *permutations* of n of length m is denoted by $P(n, m)$, i.e. $P(n, m) = \{\pi : [1, m] \to [1, n] \mid \pi \text{ is injective}\}$. A permutation π is represented by the sequence of its values, i.e. $\pi = (\pi_1, \pi_2, \ldots, \pi_m)$, and we will often abbreviate this further as the sequence $\pi = \pi_1.\pi_2 \ldots \pi_m$. The sole element of $P(n, 0)$ is denoted by $()$, or by λ, if the context removes any possible ambiguity. Given a subrange $[p, q]$ of $[1, m]$, we define a *subpermutation* $\pi(p : q) \in P(n, q-p+1)$ by $\pi(p : q) = (\pi_p, \pi_{p+1}, \ldots, \pi_q)$. The *image* of a permutation π, denoted by $\mathrm{Im}(\pi)$, is the set of its values, i.e. $\mathrm{Im}(\pi) = \{\pi_1, \pi_2, \ldots, \pi_m\}$. The *concatenation* of two permutations is denoted by $\odot$, i.e. given $\pi \in P(n, m)$ and $\tau \in P(n, k)$, such that $\mathrm{Im}(\pi) \cap \mathrm{Im}(\tau) = \emptyset$, $\pi \odot \tau = (\pi_1, \pi_2, \ldots, \pi_m, \tau_1, \tau_2, \ldots, \tau_k) \in P(n, m+k)$.

An *Exponential Information Gathering* (EIG) tree $T_{N,L}$, $N \geq L \geq 0$, is a labelled rooted tree of height L that is defined recursively as follows. The tree $T_{N,0}$ is a rooted tree with just one node, its root, labelled λ. For $L \geq 1$, $T_{N,L}$ is a rooted tree with $1 + N|T_{N-1,L-1}|$ nodes (where $|T|$ is the size of tree T), root λ, having N subtrees, where each subtree is isomorphic with $T_{N-1,L-1}$ and each node, except the root, is labelled by an element of $[1, N]$ that is *different* from any ancestor node (and also different from any left sibling node, if we want to display it like an ordered tree). Note that, $T_{N,L-1}$ is isomorphic and identically labelled with the tree obtained from $T_{N,L}$ by deleting all its leaves.

It is straightforward to see that there is a bijective correspondence between the permutations of $P(N, L)$ and the sequences (concatenations) of labels on all paths from root to the leaves of $T_{N,L}$. Thus, each node σ in an EIG tree $T_{N,L}$ is uniquely identified by a permutation $\pi_\sigma \in P(N, l)$, where $l \in [0, L]$ is also σ's depth, and, vice-versa, each such permutation π has a corresponding node σ_π. We will further use this node-permutation identification, while referring to nodes.

Given EIG tree $T_{N,L}$, an attribute is a function $\aleph : T_{N,L} \to V$, for some value set V; alternatively, $\aleph$ can be given as a functional subset of $\{\pi \in P(N, t) \mid t \in [0, L]\} \times V$. The classical EIG-based Byzantine algorithm uses two attributes: (i) a top-down attribute *val*, here called α; and (ii) a bottom-up attribute *newval*, here called β.

Figure 1 illustrates three isomorphic EIG trees, (a) $T_{4,2}^2$, (b) $T_{4,2}^3$, (c) $T_{4,2}^4$. As we will see next, theses are the EIG trees built by non-faulty processes 2, 3, 4 (respectively) in our sample scenario 5.1, where process 1 is Byzantine-faulty (so its own internal structure is irrelevant).

Consider EIG tree Fig. 1b, for process 3, $T_{4,2}^3$. Level 0 corresponds to permutation set $\{\lambda\}$. Level 1 corresponds to permutation set $\{(1), (2), (3), (4)\}$. Level 2 corresponds to permutation set $\{(1,2), (1,3), (1,4), (2,1), (2,3), (2,4), (3,1), (3,2), (3,4), (4,1), (4,2), (4,3)\}$. This tree is decorated with two attributes, α and β. Using the alternate notation for permutations (to avoid embedded parentheses), attribute α corresponds to the functional relation $\{(\lambda, 1), (1,0), (2,0), (3,1), (4,1), (1.2,0), (1.3,0), (1.4,1), (2.1,0), (2.3,0), (2.4,0), (3.1,0), (3.2,1), (3.4,1), (4.1,1), (4.2,1), (4.3,1)\}$.

5   The EIG-Based Byzantine Agreement Algorithm

Each process starts with its *own* initial decision choice. At the end, all non-faulty processes must take the same final decision, even if the faulty processes attempt to disrupt the agreement, accidentally or intentionally.

The classical EIG-based algorithm solves the Byzantine agreement problem in the *binary decision* case (true $= 1$, false $= 0$), for N *processes*, connected in a *complete graph* (where edges indicate *reliable duplex communication lines*), provided that $N \geq 3F + 1$, where F is the maximum number of faulty processes. This is a *synchronous* algorithm; celebrated results (see for example [13]) show that the Byzantine agreement is *not* possible if $N \leq 3F$, in the *asynchronous* case or when the communication links are *not* reliable.

Without providing a complete description, we provide a sketch of the classical algorithm, *reformulated* on the basis of the theoretical framework introduced in Sect. 4. For a more complete and verbose description of this algorithm, including correctness and complexity proofs, we refer the reader to Lynch [13].

Each non-faulty process, h, has its own copy of an EIG tree, $T_{N,L}^h$, where $L = F + 1$. This tree is decorated with two attributes, $\alpha^h, \beta^h : \{\pi \in P(N,t) \mid t \in [0, L]\} \rightarrow \{0, 1, \texttt{null}\}$, where $\texttt{null}$ designates undefined items (not yet evaluated). Attributes α^h and β^h are also known as val_h and $newval_h$ [13], or *top-down* and *bottom-up* [9]. As their alternative names suggest, α^h is first evaluated, in a top-down tree traversal, in increasing level order; next, β^h is evaluated, in a bottom-up traversal, in decreasing level order.

The algorithm works in two phases. Its *first phase* is a *messaging* phase which completes the evaluation of the top-down attribute α^h. Initially, $\alpha^h(\lambda) = v^h$, the initial choice of process h; all the other α^h and β^h values are still undefined. Next, there are L messaging rounds. At round $t \in [1, L]$, h broadcasts to all processes (including self), a reversibly encoded message which identifies its α^h values at level $t - 1$ and their EIG destinations. Here, we encode all these via the set $\{(\pi \odot h, \alpha^h(\pi)) \mid \pi \in P(N, t-1), h \notin \text{Im}(\pi)\}$. All other non-faulty processes broadcast messages, in a similar way. More compact encodings are possible, but we don't follow this issue here.

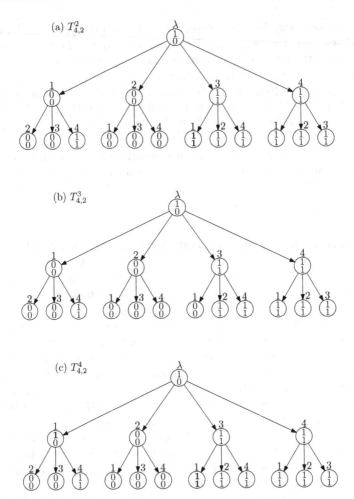

Fig. 1. Three sample EIG trees, $T^h_{4,2}$, $h \in \{2, 3, 4\}$, completed with two attributes, α and β. The node labels appear besides the node blob. Each node blob contains its two attribute values: the top-down α value at the top, and the bottom-up β value at the bottom.

Process h decodes and processes the messages that it receives. From process f, $f \in [1, N]$, process h receives the set $\{(\pi \odot f, \alpha^f(\pi)) \mid \pi \in P(N, t - 1)\}$. Each item $(\pi \odot f, \alpha^f(\pi))$ is used to assign further α^h values, to the next level down the EIG tree, by setting $\alpha^h(\pi \odot f) = \alpha^f(\pi)$.

As this formula suggests, it is indeed *critical* that h "knows" the origin f of each received message and that this origin mark cannot be faked by faulty processes. Wrong or missing values are replaced by the value of a predefined default parameter, $v_0 \in \{0, 1\}$. Thus, there are L messaging rounds and, after the last round, all nodes are decorated with values of attribute α. In fact, only the last level α values are actually needed, to start the next phase, a practical implementation can choose to discard the other α values.

Then, the algorithm switches to its *second phase*, the evaluation of the bottom-up attribute β^h. First, for leaves, $\beta^h(\pi) = \alpha^h(\pi), \pi \in P(N, L)$.

Next, given β^h values for level $t \in [1, L]$, each β^h value for the next level up, $\beta^h(\pi), \pi \in P(N, t-1)$, is evaluated on the basis of the β^h values of node π's children, i.e. on the multiset $\{\beta^h(\pi \odot f) \mid f \in [1, N] \setminus \mathrm{Im}(\pi)\}$, using a local majority voting scheme: $\beta^h(\pi) = 0$, if a strict majority of the above multiset values are 0; or, $\beta^h(\pi) = 1$, if a strict majority of the above multiset values are 1; or, $\beta^h(\pi) = v_0$ (the same default parameter mentioned above), if there is a tie.

At the end, the β^h value for the EIG root, $\beta^h(\lambda)$, is process h's final decision. All non-faulty processes will simultaneously reach the same final decision; any decision taken by faulty nodes is not relevant.

Example 5.1 (Sample Byzantine Scenario). Consider a Byzantine scenario with $N = 4$ and $F = 1$, thus $L = 2$. Assume that processes 1, 2, 3 and 4 start with initial choices 0, 0, 1, and 1, respectively. Further, assume that process 1 is faulty. Figure 2 shows sample messages which could be exchanged in this scenario and Fig. 1 shows the corresponding EIG trees, for non-faulty processes 2, 3, 4.

Each of the non-faulty processes, 1, 2 and 3, broadcasts identical messages to each of the four processes. The faulty process 1 sends conflicting messages. In our scenario, $x = 0$, in the message sent to 1, 2 and 3, but $x = 1$, in the message sent to 4. Also, $y = 1$, in the message sent to 1, 2 and 4, but $y = 0$, in the message sent to 3. White spaces are placeholders indicating potential messages which are not created, because they would have contained duplicated process numbers (1.1, 2.2, 3.3, 4.4). The second phase is not detailed here, except the common final decisions (the question mark indicates an irrelevant value).

The second phase is illustrated in Fig. 1, for all non-faulty processes 2, 3, 4. All three EIG tress are shown completed all attribute values. Consider the EIG tree (b) owned by process 3, $T^3_{4,2}$. The α^3 values are filled from messages received in the two messaging rounds, as indicated in Fig. 2.

The β^3 values are evaluated as required by the algorithm, by a local majority voting scheme. The evaluation of $\beta^3(\lambda)$ reaches a tie, on multiset $\{0, 0, 1, 1\}$, which has two 0's and two 1's; this tie is broken using the default value, here we assume $v_0 = 0$. Thus, $\beta^3(\lambda) = 0$ is the final decision of process 3, which is different from its initial choice, $\alpha^3(\lambda) = 1$.

A similar argument shows that all other non-faulty processes, 2 and 4, end with the same final decision, 0, thereby achieving the required agreement, despite starting with different initial choices and the conflicting messages sent by faulty process 1. Briefly, the Byzantine-faulty process may sometimes affect the outcome (between 0 and 1), but cannot affect the consensus: all non-faulty processes will take the same final decision.

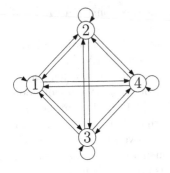

Process	1	2	3	4
Initial choice	0	0	1	1
Faulty	Yes	No	No	No
Round 1 messages	$(1, x)$	$(2, 0)$	$(3, 1)$	$(4, 1)$
Round 2 messages	$(2.1, 0)$ $(3.1, y)$ $(4.1, 1)$	$(1.2, 0)$ $(3.2, 1)$ $(4.2, 1)$	$(1.3, 0)$ $(2.3, 0)$ $(4.3, 1)$	$(1.4, 1)$ $(2.4, 0)$ $(3.4, 1)$
Final decision	?	0	0	0

Fig. 2. A sample Byzantine scenario, $N = 4$, $F = 1$, where process 1 is Byzantine faulty. Process 1 sends out syntactically correct but different messages to the non-faulty processes: $x = 0, y = 1$ to process 2; $x = 0, y = 0$ to process 3; $x = 1, y = 1$ to process 4. As shown in Fig. 1, non-faulty processes 2, 3, 4 build different EIG trees, but they still reach the same final decision.

6   Revised Byzantine Agreement Solution

Each non-faulty node (process) is modelled by a subsystem which combines $N + 1$ cells: one "main" cell, plus one "firewall" cell for each process (including one for itself). The EIG tree evaluation functionality is localized into the main cell. The main cells communicate only via their associated firewall cells. Figure 3 illustrates the communication digraph for the particular case $N = 4$. The whole subsystem corresponding to a faulty process (1 in our example), may be replaced by any arbitrary entity.

The system evolves along 9 states, for the main cells, and 5 states, for the firewall cells. Figure 4 gives a bird's eye view of this process, for the particular case $N = 4$. Both kind of cells start in state S_0. In state S_0, main cells, μ_i, build the root of their EIG trees.

The *first* (*messaging*) phase is covered by L repetitions of the state cycle S_1, S_2, S_3, S_4. In state S_1, main cells, μ_i, broadcast their outgoing θ' messages to their local firewalls, ν_{ij}. In state S_2, local firewalls, ν_{ij}, forward isomorphic messages θ'' to their partners firewalls, ν_{ji}. In state S_3, local firewalls, ν_{ij}, forward isomorphic messages θ' to their main cells, μ_i. In state S_4, main cells, μ_i, use incoming θ' messages to build the next level of their EIG trees. The messaging phase ends after L messaging rounds, when all cells, μ_i and ν_{ij}, enter state S_5. State S_5 is the end state for the firewall cells, ν_{ij}.

In state S_5, all main cells, μ_i, have computed all top-down attributes, α, and start the *second* phase, i.e. the bottom-up evaluation of attributes β. This second phase ends after L repetitions of the state cycle S_6, S_7, S_8, when all main cells, μ_i, enter state S_9. Each bottom-up cycle computes a new level of the β

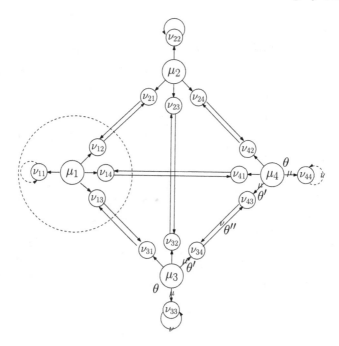

Fig. 3. A sample Byzantine problem, $N = 4$, modelled as a cP system digraph with N subsystems, N main cells (μ_i) and N^2 firewall cells (ν_{ij}), $i, j \in [1, N]$. The dashed blob delimits the subsystem of a possibly faulty process (here 1).

attributes. At the end, the final decision value is given by the β attribute of the EIG root.

7   Initial Configurations

Figure 5 lists the initial multiset for the main cell μ_i, i.e. for process $i \in \{1, 2, \dots, n\}$. Process IDs are encapsulated in ι (*iota*) sub-subcells. Subcell $\bar{\mu}$ contains the ID of the current process, i, i.e. $\iota(1^i)$. Subcell $\bar{\pi}$ contains the set of all process IDs, i.e. $\{1, 2, \dots, n\}$, given as the multiset $\{\iota(1^1), \iota(1^2), \dots \iota(1^n)\}$. Subcell $\bar{\ell}$ represents l, the maximum number of levels for the EIG tree; this is computed as $l = \lceil (n - 1)/3 \rceil$. Subcells $\bar{\delta}$ contain the two admissible decision values, here t (true=1) and f (false=0). Subcell $\bar{\alpha}$ contains $v_i \in \{t, f\}$, process i's initial choice. Subcell $\bar{v}_0$ contains $v_0 \in \{t, f\}$, i.e. the default value, known by all processes. All these initial symbols will be immutable.

Figure 6 lists the initial multiset for the firewall cell ν_{ij} (serving μ_i) to its partner firewall cell ν_{ji} (serving μ_j), for $i, j \in \{1, 2, \dots, n\}$. Subcell $\bar{\mu}$ contains the ID of the current process, here $\iota(1^i)$. Subcell $\bar{\nu}$ contains the ID of the other linked process, here $\iota(1^j)$. As in main cell μ_i, subcell $\bar{\ell}$ represents l, the maximum number of levels for the EIG tree. All these initial symbols will be immutable.

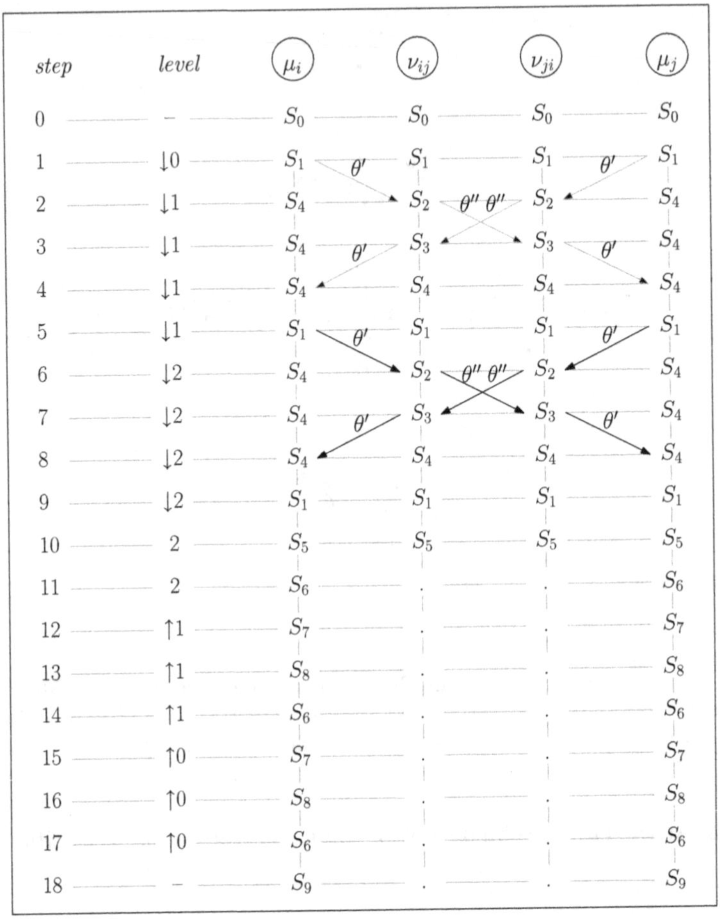

Fig. 4. State and interaction chart. Here: (i) μ_i, μ_j are the main cells of two non-faulty processes, i, j; (ii) ν_{ij}, ν_{ji} are firewall cells at the end of the communication link between i and j.

$$\{\ \bar{\pi}(\iota(1^1)\ \iota(1^2)\ \ldots\ \iota(1^n)),\ \bar{\mu}(\iota(1^i)),\ \bar{\ell}(1^l),\ \bar{\delta}(t),\ \bar{\delta}(f),\ \bar{\alpha}(v_i),\ \bar{v}_0(v_0)\ \}$$

Fig. 5. Initial multiset for the main cell μ_i, i.e. for process $i \in \{1, 2, \ldots, n\}$.

$$\{\ \bar{\mu}(\iota(1^i)),\ \bar{\nu}(\iota(1^j)),\ \bar{\ell}(1^l)\ \}$$

Fig. 6. Initial multiset for the firewall cell ν_{ij} (serving μ_i) to its partner firewall cell ν_{ji} (serving μ_j), for $i, j \in \{1, 2, \ldots, n\}$.

8   Rules for Messaging Phase

Sending Messages. Figure 7 lists the ruleset which completes the initialisation of main cell μ_i and then sends out expected round messages, exiting to state S_5 at the end of the messaging phase. Subcell ℓ gives the current level in the EIG tree. Subcell θ represents a node in the EIG tree during the top-down messaging phase. Sub-subcells θ/ℓ, θ/α, θ/π, and θ/ρ respectively indicate the node level, its top-down α value, its associated permutation (i.e. EIG branch), and the set of all process numbers appearing in π (i.e. $\mathrm{Im}(\pi)$). Subcell θ' represents an outgoing message and has sub-subcells isomorphic to θ (except that it does not have a ρ sub-subcell).

Technically, subcell θ/π is a list of process IDs and subcell θ/ρ is the corresponding set of process IDs; both are initially empty. For example, the EIG branch 3.1 with top-down attribute $\alpha = 0$ is represented by subcell $\theta(\ell(2)\ \pi(\iota(1)\,|\,\iota(3))\ \rho(\iota(1)\,\iota(3))\ \alpha(0))$. Conceptually, the information hold by subcells θ/ℓ and θ/ρ is redundant, as it can be computed from π; however, their presence simplifies and speeds up the overall evolution.

Rule (0) constructs a zero current level and the root of the EIG tree. Rule (1) exists to state S_5 when all required messaging rounds (tree levels) have been completed. Rule (2) sends out messages θ', based on values from node θ. The outgoing messages already indicate their destination: the included level is already increased by one and the current process id is prepended to the branch permutation. Rule (3) increments the current level.

S_0	$\rightarrow_{\min\otimes\min}$	$S_1\ \ell(0)\ \theta(\ell(0)\ \pi(|)\ \rho()\ \alpha(V))$ $\|\ \bar{\alpha}(V)$	(0)
S_1	$\rightarrow_{\min\otimes\min}$	S_5 $\|\ \bar{\ell}(L)$ $\|\ \ell(L)$	(1)
S_1	$\rightarrow_{\max\otimes\min}$	$S_2\ \theta'(\ell(L1)\ \pi(X|P)\ \alpha(V))\ \downarrow_\mu$ $\|\ \bar{\mu}(X)$ $\|\ \ell(L)$ $\|\ \theta(\ell(L)\ \pi(P)\ \alpha(V)\ \rho(\_))$ $\neg\ \theta(\ell(L)\ \pi(P)\ \alpha(\_)\ \rho(XQ'))$	(2)
$S_1\ \ell(L)$	$\rightarrow_{\min\otimes\min}$	$S_4\ \ell(L1)$	(3)

Fig. 7. Ruleset which completes the initialisation of the main cells and then (repeatedly) sends out expected round messages, exiting to state S_5 at the end of the messaging phase.

Firewall. Figure 8 lists the ruleset of the firewall cell ν_{ij}. During the messaging phase, its states are exactly synchronised to the states of its main cell, μ_i. Messages θ' are received or assumed to be received from its main cell, μ_i, and are forwarded as θ'' to its partner firewall cell, ν_{ji} (associated to main cell μ_j). Messages θ'' are assumed to be received from the partner firewall cell, ν_{ji}; θ'' are forwarded to the main cel, μ_i, as θ' – but *only if* the permutation head properly identifies the other process (so the sender's identity cannot be faked by Sybil attacks). No other messages can reach the main cell (this explains why these cells are called "firewall").

Subcell ℓ gives the current "reverse" level in the EIG tree – which is decremented from maximum to zero (instead of being incremented the other way). Rule (0) constructs this "reverse" current level. At the end of the messaging phase, rule(1) exits to end state S_5. Rule (2) decrements the current level. Rule (3) transforms incoming message θ' into an isomorphic θ'' and forwards it to its partner firewall, ν_{ji}. Rule (4) transforms incoming message θ'' into an isomorphic θ' and forwards it to its main cell, μ_i, provided that the sender is properly recorded as the permutation head. Rules (5) and (6) keep the synchronisation with main cell, μ_i.

$$
\begin{array}{lll}
S_0 & \rightarrow_{\min\otimes\min} & S_1\ \ell(L)\ \|\ \bar{\ell}(L) \quad\quad\quad (0)\\
S_1\ \ell() & \rightarrow_{\min\otimes\min} & S_5 \quad\quad\quad\quad\quad\quad\quad\quad\ (1)\\
S_1\ \ell(L1) & \rightarrow_{\min\otimes\min} & S_2\ \ell(L) \quad\quad\quad\quad\quad\ \ (2)\\
S_2\ \theta'(T) & \rightarrow_{\max\otimes\min} & S_3\ \theta''(T)\downarrow_\nu \quad\quad\quad\ \ (3)\\
S_3\ \theta''(\pi(Y|P)\ T') & \rightarrow_{\max\otimes\min} & S_4\ \theta'(\pi(Y|P)\ T')\uparrow_\mu\ \|\ \nu(Y)\ (4)\\
S_3 & \rightarrow_{\min\otimes\min} & S_4 \quad\quad\quad\quad\quad\quad\quad\quad\ (5)\\
S_4 & \rightarrow_{\min\otimes\min} & S_1 \quad\quad\quad\quad\quad\quad\quad\quad\ (6)\\
\end{array}
$$

Fig. 8. Ruleset of the firewall cell.

Receiving Messages. Figure 9 lists the ruleset which receives incoming messages and records these in a new level down in the EIG tree. Note that, after passing the firewall, all these incoming messages have a *correct sender* Y. Rule (1) records the α attributes of the incoming message θ', whose level and branch permutation match existing nodes. For missing or unmatched (malformed) messages, rule (2) assumes the default value v_0. Rules (3) and (4) delete all previous level θ nodes and incoming θ' messages (not strictly necessary, but keeps the cells clean).

For example, with reference to Figs. 1 and 2, consider that process 3 receives from process 1 the second level message $\theta'(\ell(2)\ \pi(\iota(1)\,|\,\iota(3))\ \alpha(0))$. At this stage, process 2 already is in state S_4 and has the following subcells: $\bar{\pi}(\iota(1)\ldots)$, $\ell(2)$,

$$S_4 \quad \rightarrow_{\text{max}\otimes\text{min}} \quad S_1 \; \theta(\ell(L1) \; \pi(Y|P) \; \rho(YQ) \; \alpha(V)) \quad\quad (1)$$
$$\| \; \bar{\delta}(V)$$
$$\| \; \ell(L1)$$
$$\| \; \theta(\ell(L) \; \pi(P) \; \rho(Q) \; \alpha(\_))$$
$$\neg \; \theta(\ell(L) \; \pi(P) \; \rho(YQ') \; \alpha(\_))$$
$$\| \; \theta'(\ell(L1) \; \pi(Y|P) \; \alpha(V))$$

$$S_4 \quad \rightarrow_{\text{max}\otimes\text{min}} \quad S_1 \; \theta(\ell(L1) \; \pi(Y|P) \; \rho(YQ) \; \alpha(V)) \quad\quad (2)$$
$$\| \; \bar{v}_0(V)$$
$$\| \; \ell(L1)$$
$$\| \; \theta(\ell(L) \; \pi(P) \; \rho(Q) \; \alpha(\_))$$
$$\neg \; \theta(\ell(L) \; \pi(P) \; \rho(YQ') \; \alpha(\_))$$
$$\neg \; \theta'(\ell(L1) \; \pi(Y|P) \; \alpha(\_))$$

$$S_4 \; \theta(r(L) \; \_) \quad \rightarrow_{\text{max}\otimes\text{min}} \quad S_1 \quad\quad (3)$$
$$\| \; \ell(L1)$$

$$S_4 \; \theta'(\_) \quad \rightarrow_{\text{max}\otimes\text{min}} \quad S_1 \quad\quad (4)$$

Fig. 9. Ruleset to receive a set of messages and record these in a new level down in the EIG tree.

$\bar{\delta}(0)$, $\bar{\delta}(1)$, $\ell(2)$, $\theta(\ell(1) \; \pi(\iota(3)\,|) \; \rho(\iota(3)) \; \alpha(1))$. Then, rule (4) selects the target state S_1 and creates new subcell $\theta(\ell(2) \; \pi(\iota(1)\,|\,\iota(3)) \; \rho(\iota(1)\,\iota(3)) \; \alpha(0))$ – for EIG branch 3.1 and top-down value 0.

9   Rules for Second Phase

Figure 10 lists the ruleset which iteratively evaluates the bottom-up β attributes for main cell μ_i. Subcell τ represents a node in the EIG tree during the bottom-up evaluation phase (we could have reused the already existing θ's, but it seems cleaner this way). Sub-subcells τ/ℓ and τ/π have the same meaning as for θ's. Sub-subcell τ/β contains the value of the bottom-up β attribute. Subcell ω stores the final decision (in agreement with all non-faulty processes).

Rule (1) determines β for the leaves of the EIG tree. Rule (2) fires after the β evaluation has reached the EIG root and records the final decision. Rule (3) decrements the EIG level. Rule (4) cancels all pairs of opposite τ/β's, i.e. containing t vs. f. If any t remains, rule (5) decides for t. If any f remains, rule (6) decides for f. Otherwise, rule (7) decides for the default value v_0. Finally, rule (7) deletes all previously existing τ's (again, not necessary, but keeps cells clean).

$$S_5 \; \theta(\ell(L) \; \pi(P) \; \rho(\_) \; \alpha(V)) \qquad \longrightarrow_{\texttt{max} \otimes \texttt{min}} \qquad S_6 \; \tau(\ell(L) \; \pi(P) \; \beta(V)) \qquad (1)$$
$$\| \; \ell(L)$$

$$S_6 \; \ell() \qquad \longrightarrow_{\texttt{min} \otimes \texttt{min}} \qquad S_9 \; \omega(V) \qquad (2)$$
$$\| \; \tau(r() \; \pi() \; \beta(V))$$

$$S_6 \; \ell(L1) \qquad \longrightarrow_{\texttt{min} \otimes \texttt{min}} \qquad S_7 \; \ell(L) \qquad (3)$$

$$S_7 \; \tau(\ell(L1) \; \pi(Y|P) \; \beta(t))$$
$$\tau(\ell(L1) \; \pi(Y|P) \; \beta(f)) \qquad \longrightarrow_{\texttt{max} \otimes \texttt{max}} \qquad S_8 \qquad (4)$$
$$\| \; \ell(L)$$

$$S_7 \; \tau(\ell(L1) \; \pi(Y|P) \; \beta(t)) \qquad \longrightarrow_{\texttt{min} \otimes \texttt{min}} \qquad S_8 \; \tau(\ell(L) \; \pi(P) \; \beta(t)) \qquad (5)$$
$$\| \; \ell(L)$$

$$S_7 \; \tau(\ell(L1) \; \pi(Y|P) \; \beta(f)) \qquad \longrightarrow_{\texttt{min} \otimes \texttt{min}} \qquad S_8 \; \tau(\ell(L) \; \pi(P) \; \beta(f)) \qquad (6)$$
$$\| \; \ell(L)$$

$$S_7 \qquad \longrightarrow_{\texttt{max} \otimes \texttt{min}} \qquad S_8 \; \tau(\ell(L) \; \pi(P) \; \beta(V)) \qquad (7)$$
$$\| \; \bar{v}_0(V)$$
$$\| \; \ell(L)$$
$$\neg \; \tau(\ell(L) \; \pi(P) \; \beta(\_))$$

$$S_8 \; \tau(\_) \qquad \longrightarrow_{\texttt{max} \otimes \texttt{min}} \qquad S_6 \qquad (8)$$

Fig. 10. Ruleset which evaluates the bottom-up attribute β.

10 Static Complexity

Figure 11 summarizes the main differences between the previous best solution [7,8] and the current solution. In contrast to the previous solution, this new solution, based on complex symbols and generic rules, uses a small and *fixed* size set of objects, states and rules. The high-level rules map naturally to the main steps of the algorithm described in Sects. 4 and 5. In fact, this high-level ruleset compares favourably even with the semi-formal description of these sections,

Complexity measure	Previous version	Current version
Cells per process	$3N + 1$	$N + 1$
Atomic symbols	$O(N!)$	16
States	$O(L)$	$9 + 5$
Rules	$O(N!)$	$16 + 7$

Fig. 11. Summary of complexity measures (where $L = \lceil (N - 1)/3 \rceil$).

because: (i) it is fully formal; (ii) it is directly executable; and (iii) it seems succinter.

11   Conclusions and Open Problems

We have refined our earlier version of P systems with complex symbols. The new version, called cP systems, enables the creation and manipulation of high-level data structures which are typical in high-level languages, such as: relations (graphs), associative arrays, lists. We leveraged these capabilities to present a revised succint version of our previously best solution for the Byzantine agreement problem. In contrast to the previous solution, which uses a super-exponential number of symbols and rules, the new solution uses a *fixed sized* alphabet and ruleset, independent of the problem size, and the ruleset follows closely the conceptual description of the algorithm.

Like other versions of P systems, our cP systems are formal models which can become directly executable, if properly supported by tools. Further research should address this issue, best by formalising the cP semantics.

Dinneen et al. [7,8] also mention an open problem which is still unsolved. Even if their numbers have been substantially reduced, our solution still requires N^2 additional firewalls cells, one of each side of each communication channel. These firewalls are not conceptually required, as – with a few extensions – each node could decide which symbols it should accept and when. Further research is needed on this. Besides increasing the speed, a proper solution could more generally bring P systems closer to the Actor model.

Acknowledgments. We are deeply indebted to the co-authors of our former studies on the Byzantine agreement and to the anonymous reviewers, for their most valuable comments and suggestions.

A   Appendix. cP Systems: P Systems with Complex Symbols

We present the details of our complex-symbols framework, slightly revised from our earlier papers [16,17].

A.1   Complex Symbols as Subcells

Complex symbols play the roles of cellular micro-compartments or substructures, such as organelles, vesicles or cytoophidium assemblies ("snakes"), which are embedded in cells or travel between cells, but without having the full processing power of a complete cell. In our proposal, *complex symbols* represent nested data compartments which have no own processing power: they are acted upon by the rules of their enclosing cells.

Technically, our *complex symbols*, also called *subcells*, are similar to Prolog-like *first-order terms*, recursively built from *multisets* of atoms and variables.

Atoms are typically denoted by lower case letters (or, occasionally, digits), such as a, b, c, 1. *Variables* are typically denoted by uppercase letters, such as X, Y, Z. For improved readability, we also consider *anonymous variables*, which are denoted by underscores ("_"). Each underscore occurrence represents a *new* unnamed variable and indicates that something, in which we are not interested, must fill that slot.

Terms are either (i) simple atoms, or (ii) atoms (called *functors*), followed by one or more parenthesized *multisets* (called *arguments*) of other symbols (terms or variables), e.g. $a(b^2X), a(X^2c(Y)), a(b^2)(c(Z))$. Functors that are followed by more than one parenthesized argument are called *curried* (by analogy to functional programming) and, as we see later, are useful to precisely described deep "micro-surgical" changes which only affect inner nested symbols, without directly touching their enclosing outer symbols. Terms that do *not* contain variables are called *ground*, e.g.:

- Ground terms: a, $a(\lambda)$, $a(b)$, $a(bc)$, $a(b^2c)$, $a(b(c))$, $a(bc(\lambda))$, $a(b(c)d(e))$, $a(b(c)d(e))$, $a(b(c)d(e(\lambda)))$, $a(bc^2d)$; or, a curried form: $a(b^2)(c(d)e^3)$.
- Terms which are not ground: $a(X)$, $a(bX)$, $a(b(X))$, $a(XY)$, $a(X^2)$, $a(XdY)$, $a(Xc())$, $a(b(X)d(e))$, $a(b(c)d(Y))$, $a(b(X)d(e(Y)))$, $a(b(X^2)d(e(Xf^2)))$; or, a curried form: $a(b(X))(d(Y)e^3)$; also, using anonymous variables: $a(b\_)$, $a(X\_)$, $a(b(X)d(e(\_)))$.

Note that we may abbreviate the expression of complex symbols by removing inner λ's as explicit references to the empty multiset, e.g. $a(\lambda) = a()$.

Complex symbols (subcells, terms) can be formally defined by the following grammar:

```
<term>        ::= <atom> | <functor> ( '(' <argument> ')' )+
<functor>     ::= <atom>
<argument>    ::= λ | ( <term-or-var> )+
<term-or-var> ::= <term> | <variable>
```

Natural Numbers. Natural numbers can be represented via *bags* containing repeated occurrences of the *same* atom. For example, considering that 1 represents an ad-hoc unary digit, then the following complex symbols can be used to describe the contents of a virtual integer *variable* a: $a() = a(\lambda)$ — the value of a is 0; $a(1^3)$ — the value of a is 3. For concise expressions, we may alias these number representations by their corresponding numbers, e.g. $a() \equiv a(0), b(1^3) \equiv b(3)$. Nicolescu et al. [19–21] show how arithmetic operations can be efficiently modelled by P systems with complex symbols.

Lists. Using complex symbols, the list $[u, v, w]$ can be represented as $\gamma(u\ \gamma(v\ \gamma(w\ \gamma())))$, where the ad-hoc atom γ represents the list constructor *cons* and $\gamma()$ the empty list. Hiding the less relevant representation choices, we may alias this list by the more expressive notation $\gamma[u, v, w]$.

Trees. Consider the binary tree $z = (a, (b), (c, (d), (e)))$, i.e. z points to a root node which has: (i) the value a; (ii) a left node with value b; and (iii) a right node with value c, left leaf d, and right leaf e. Using complex symbols, tree y can be represented as $z(a\ \phi(b)\ \psi(c\ \phi(d)\ \psi(e)))$, where ad-hoc atoms ϕ, ψ introduce left subtrees, right subtrees (respectively).

Associative Arrays. Consider the associative array $\{1 \mapsto a,\ 1^3 \mapsto c,\ 1^7 \mapsto g\}$, where the "mapsto" operator, $\mapsto$, indicates key-value mappings. Using complex symbols, this array can be represented as a multiset with three items, $\{\,\mu(\kappa(1)\,\upsilon(a)),\ \mu(\kappa(1^3)\,\upsilon(c)),\ \mu(\kappa(1^7)\,\upsilon(g))\,\}$, where ad-hoc atoms μ, κ, υ introduce mappings, keys, values (respectively). Hiding the less relevant representation choices, we may alias the items of this multiset by the more expressive notation $\{\,(1 \overset{\mu}{\mapsto} a),\ (1^3 \overset{\mu}{\mapsto} c),\ (1^7 \overset{\mu}{\mapsto} g)\,\} \equiv \{\,1 \overset{\mu}{\mapsto} a,\ 1^3 \overset{\mu}{\mapsto} c,\ 1^7 \overset{\mu}{\mapsto} g\,\}$. In this context, the "mapsto" operator, $\mapsto$, is considered to have a high associative priority, so the enclosing parentheses are mostly required for increasing the readability (e.g. in text). If we are not interested in the actual mapping value, instead of $(a \overset{\mu}{\mapsto} \_)$, we refer to this term by the succinct abbreviation $x[a]$.

Unification. All terms (ground or not) can be (asymmetrically) *matched* against *ground* terms, using an ad-hoc version of *pattern matching*, more precisely, a *one-way first-order syntactic unification*, where an atom can only match another copy of itself, and a variable can match any bag of ground terms (including the empty bag, λ). This may create a combinatorial *non-determinism*, when a combination of two or more variables are matched against the same bag, in which case an arbitrary matching is chosen. For example:

- Matching $a(b(X)fY) = a(b(cd(e))f^2g)$ deterministically creates a single set of unifiers: $X, Y = cd(e), fg$.
- Matching $a(XY^2) = a(de^2f)$ deterministically creates a single set of unifiers: $X, Y = df, e$.
- Matching $a(XY) = a(df)$ non-deterministically creates one of the following four sets of unifiers: $X, Y = \lambda, df$; $X, Y = df, \lambda$; $X, Y = d, f$; $X, Y = f, d$.

Performance Note. If the rules avoid any matching non-determinism, then this proposal should not affect the performance of P simulators running on existing machines. Assuming that bags are already taken care of, e.g. via hash-tables, our proposed unification probably adds an almost linear factor. Let us recall that, in similar contexts (no occurs check needed), Prolog unification algorithms can run in $O(ng(n))$ steps, where g is the inverse Ackermann function. Our conjecture must be proven though, as the novel presence of multisets may affect the performance.

A.2   Generic Rules

Rules use *states* and are applied top-down, in the so-called *weak priority* order. Rules may contain *any* kind of terms, ground and not-ground. In *concrete* models, *cells* can only contain *ground* terms. *Cells* which contain *unground* terms can only be used to define *abstract* models, i.e. high-level patterns which characterise families of similar concrete models.

Pattern Matching. Rules are matched against cell contents using the above discussed *pattern matching*, which involves the rule's left-hand side, promoters and inhibitors. Moreover, the matching is *valid* only if, after substituting variables by their values, the rule's right-hand side contains ground terms only (so *no* free variables are injected in the cell or sent to its neighbours), as illustrated by the following sample scenario:

– The cell's *current content* includes the *ground term*:
  $n(a\,\phi(b\,\phi(c)\,\psi(d))\,\psi(e))$
– The following *rewriting rule* is considered:
  $n(X\,\phi(Y\,\phi(Y_1)\,\psi(Y_2))\,\psi(Z)) \rightarrow v(X)\,n(Y\,\phi(Y_2)\,\psi(Y_1))\,v(Z)$
– Our pattern matching determines the following *unifiers*:
  $X = a,\, Y = b,\, Y_1 = c,\, Y_2 = d,\, Z = e.$
– This is a *valid* matching and, after *substitutions*, the rule's *right-hand* side gives the *new content*:
  $v(a)\,n(b\,\phi(d)\,\psi(c))\,v(e).$

Generic Rules Format. We consider rules of the following *generic* format (we call this format generic, because it actually defines templates involving variables):

$$
\begin{aligned}
&current\text{-}state\ \ symbols\ldots\ \rightarrow_\alpha\ target\text{-}state\ (immediate\text{-}symbols)!\ldots\\
&\qquad\qquad\qquad\qquad (in\text{-}symbols)\ldots\ \ (out\text{-}symbols)_\delta\ldots\\
&\qquad\qquad\qquad\qquad \mid promoters\ldots\ \neg\ inhibitors\ldots
\end{aligned}
$$

Where:

– All *symbols*, including *states*, *promoters* and *inhibitors*, are *multisets of terms*, possibly containing *variables* (which can be *matched* as previously described).
– Parentheses can be used to clarify the association of symbols, but otherwise have no own meaning.
– Subscript $\alpha \in \{\texttt{min}, \texttt{max}\} \times \{\texttt{min}, \texttt{max}\}$, indicates a combined *instantiation* and *rewriting* mode, as further discussed in the example below.
– *Out-symbols* are sent, at the end of the step, to the cell's structural neighbours. These symbols are enclosed in round parentheses which further indicate their destinations, above abbreviated as δ. The most usual scenarios include:

- (a) $\downarrow_i$ indicates that a is sent to child i (unicast);
- (a) $\uparrow_i$ indicates that a is sent to parent i (unicast);
- (a) $\downarrow_\forall$ indicates that a is sent to all children (broadcast);
- (a) $\uparrow_\forall$ indicates that a is sent to all parents (broadcast);
- (a) $\updownarrow_\forall$ indicates that a is sent to all neighbours (broadcast).

  All symbols sent via one *generic rule* to the same destination form one single *message* and they travel together as one single block (even if the generic rule has multiple instantiations).

- Both *immediate-symbols* and *in-symbols* remain in the current cell, but there is a subtle difference:

- *in-symbols* become available after the end of the current step only, as in traditional P systems (we can imagine that these are sent via an ad-hoc *loopback* channel);
- *immediate-symbols* become immediately available (i) to the current rule, if it uses the max instantiation mode, and (ii) always, to the succeeding rules (in weak priority order).

Immediate symbols can substantially improve the runtime performance, which could be required for two main reasons: (i) to achieve parity with best traditional algorithms, and (ii) to ensure correctness when proper timing is logically critical. However, they are seldom required and not used in the systems presented in this paper.

Example. To explain our combined instantiation and rewriting mode, let us consider a cell, σ, containing three counter-like complex symbols, $c(1^2)$, $c(1^2)$, $c(1^3)$, and the four possible instantiation$\otimes$rewriting modes of the following "decrementing" rule:

$$(\rho_\alpha)\ S_1\ c(1\,X) \to_\alpha S_2\ c(X), \text{where } \alpha \in \{\text{min,max}\} \times \{\text{min,max}\}.$$

1. m If $\alpha = $ min$\otimes$min, rule $\rho_{\text{min}\otimes\text{min}}$ nondeterministically generates and applies (in the min mode) *one* of the following two rule instances:

$$(\rho_1')\quad S_1\ c(1^2) \to_{\text{min}} S_2\ c(1)\quad \text{or}$$
$$(\rho_1'')\quad S_1\ c(1^3) \to_{\text{min}} S_2\ c(1^2).$$

Using (ρ_1'), cell σ ends with counters $c(1)$, $c(1^2)$, $c(1^3)$. Using (ρ_1''), cell σ ends with counters $c(1^2)$, $c(1^2)$, $c(1^2)$.

2. If $\alpha = $ max$\otimes$min, rule $\rho_{\text{max}\otimes\text{min}}$ first generates and then applies (in the min mode) the following *two* rule instances:

$$(\rho_2')\quad S_1\ c(1^2) \to_{\text{min}} S_2\ c(1)\quad \text{and}$$
$$(\rho_2'')\quad S_1\ c(1^3) \to_{\text{min}} S_2\ c(1^2).$$

Using (ρ_2') and (ρ_2''), cell σ ends with counters $c(1)$, $c(1^2)$, $c(1^2)$.

3. If $\alpha = $ min$\otimes$max, rule $\rho_{\text{min}\otimes\text{max}}$ nondeterministically generates and applies (in the max mode) *one* of the following rule instances:

$$(\rho_3')\quad S_1\ c(1^2) \to_{\text{max}} S_2\ c(1)\quad \text{or}$$
$$(\rho_3'')\quad S_1\ c(1^3) \to_{\text{max}} S_2\ c(1^2).$$

Using (ρ_3'), cell σ ends with counters $c(1)$, $c(1)$, $c(1^3)$. Using (ρ_3''), cell σ ends with counters $c(1^2)$, $c(1^2)$, $c(1^2)$.

4. If $\alpha = \texttt{max}\otimes\texttt{max}$, rule $\rho_{\texttt{min}\otimes\texttt{max}}$ first generates and then applies (in the $\texttt{max}$ mode) the following *two* rule instances:

$$(\rho_4')\quad S_1\ c(1^2)\ \rightarrow_{\texttt{max}}\ S_2\ c(1)\quad \text{and}$$
$$(\rho_4'')\quad S_1\ c(1^3)\ \rightarrow_{\texttt{max}}\ S_2\ c(1^2).$$

Using (ρ_4') and (ρ_4''), cell σ ends with counters $c(1)$, $c(1)$, $c(1^2)$.

The interpretation of $\texttt{min}\otimes\texttt{min}$, $\texttt{min}\otimes\texttt{max}$ and $\texttt{max}\otimes\texttt{max}$ modes is straightforward. While other interpretations could be considered, the mode $\texttt{max}\otimes\texttt{min}$ indicates that the generic rule is instantiated as *many* times as possible, without *superfluous* instances (i.e. without duplicates or instances which are not applicable) and each one of the instantiated rules is applied *once*, if possible.

If a rule does not contain any non-ground term, then it has only one possible instantiation: itself. Thus, in this case, the instantiation is an *idempotent* transformation, and the modes $\texttt{min}\otimes\texttt{min}$, $\texttt{min}\otimes\texttt{max}$, $\texttt{max}\otimes\texttt{min}$, $\texttt{max}\otimes\texttt{max}$ fall back onto traditional modes $\texttt{min}$, $\texttt{max}$, $\texttt{min}$, $\texttt{max}$, respectively.

Special Cases. Simple scenarios involving generic rules are sometimes semantically equivalent to loop-based sets of non-generic rules. For example, consider the rule

$$S_1\ a(x(I)\ y(J))\ \rightarrow_{\texttt{max}\otimes\texttt{min}}\ S_2\ b(I)\ c(J),$$

where the cell's contents guarantee that I and J only match integers in ranges $[1, n]$ and $[1, m]$, respectively. Under these assumptions, this rule is equivalent to the following set of non-generic rules:

$$S_1\ a_{i,j}\ \rightarrow_{\texttt{min}}\ S_2\ b_i\ c_j,\ \forall i \in [1, n], j \in [1, m].$$

However, unification is a much more powerful concept, which cannot be generally reduced to simple loops.

Micro-Surgery: Operations that Only Affect Inner Nested Symbols. Such operations improve both the crispness and the efficiency of the rules. Consider a cell that contains symbols $o(abpq), r$ and a naive rule which attempts to change the inner b to a d, if an inner p and a top–level r are also present:

$$S_1\ o(bR)\ \rightarrow_{\texttt{min}\otimes\texttt{min}}\ S_2\ o(dR)\ \mid\ o(p_-)\ r.$$

Unless we change the "standard" application rules, this rule fails, because symbol p is locked as a promoter and cannot be changed at the same time (not even by copy/paste from the left-hand side R to the right-hand side R). We solve this problem without changing the standard application rules, by adding an access path to the inner symbols needed. The *access path* is a slash delimited list of outer symbols, in nesting order, which opens an inner bag for usual rewriting operations; these outer symbols on the path are not themselves touched. For example, this modified rule solves the problem by opening the contents of o for processing:

$$S_1\ o/b\ \rightarrow_{\texttt{min}\otimes\texttt{min}}\ S_2\ o/d\ \mid\ o/p\ r.$$

This extension helps even more when we want to localise the changes to inner symbols of a specific outer symbol. For example, consider a similar operation that needs to be applied on the innermost contents of symbol $o(i,j)(abpq)$, identified by its coordinates i, j.

$$S_1 \; o(x(i) \, y(j))/b \; \to_{\min \otimes \min} \; S_2 \; o(x(i) \, y(j))/d \; \mid \; o(x(i) \, y(j))/p \; r.$$

If all or most symbols involved share the same path, then the path could qualify the whole rule; existing top-level symbols could be qualified by usual path conventions, e.g. in our case, r could be explicitly qualified by either of / or ../:

$$o(x(i) \, y(j)) :: S_1 \; b \; \to_{\min \otimes \min} \; S_2 \; d \; \mid \; p \; ../r.$$

Note that the usual rulesets are just a special case of this extension, when all rules are by default qualified with the root path /.

Note. For all modes, the instantiations are *conceptually* created when rules are tested for applicability and are also *ephemeral*, i.e. they disappear at the end of the step. P system implementations are encouraged to directly apply high-level generic rules, if this is more efficient (it usually is); they may, but need not, start by transforming high-level rules into low-level rules, by way of instantiations.

Benefits. This type of generic rules allow (i) a reasonably fast parsing and processing of subcomponents, and (ii) algorithm descriptions with *fixed size alphabets* and *fixed sized rulesets*, independent of the size of the problem and number of cells in the system (often *impossible* with only atomic symbols).

Synchronous vs Asynchronous. In our models, we do not make any *syntactic* difference between the synchronous and asynchronous scenarios; this is strictly a *runtime* assumption [15]. Any model is able to run on both the synchronous and asynchronous runtime "engines", albeit the results may differ.

In the *synchronous* scenario of traditional P systems, all rules in a step take together exactly *one* time unit and then all message exchanges (including loopback messages for in-symbols) are performed at the end of the step, in *zero* time (i.e. instantaneously). Alternatively, but logically equivalent, we here consider that rules in a step are performed in *zero* time (i.e. instantaneously) and then all message exchanges are performed in exactly *one* time unit. We prefer the second interpretation, because it allows us to interpret synchronous runs as special cases of asynchronous runs.

In the *asynchronous* scenario, we still consider that rules in a step are performed in *zero* time (i.e. instantaneously), but then, to arrive at its destination, each message may take *any* finite real time in the $(0, 1]$ interval (i.e. travelling times are typically scaled to the travel time of the slowest message). Additionally, unless otherwise specified, we also assume that messages traveling on the same directed arc follow a *FIFO* rule, i.e. no fast message can overtake a slow progressing one. This definition closely emulates the standard definition used for asynchronous distributed algorithms [13]. Clearly, the asynchronous model is highly non-deterministic, but most useful algorithms manage to remain confluent.

In both scenarios, we need to cater for a particularity of P systems, where a cell may remain active after completing its current step and then will automatically start a new step, without necessarily receiving any new message. In contrast, in classical distributed models, nodes may only become active after receiving a new message, so there is no self-activation without messaging. We can solve this issue by (i) assuminging a hidden self-activation message that cells can post themselves at the end of the step and (ii) postulating that such self-addressed messages will arrive not later than any other messages coming from other cells.

Obviously, any algorithm that works correctly in the asynchronous mode will also work correctly in the synchronous mode, but the converse is *not* generally true: extra care may be needed to transform a correct synchronous algorithm into a correct asynchronous one; there are also general control layers, such as *synchronisers*, that can attempt to run a synchronous algorithm on an existing asynchronous runtime, but this does not always work [13].

Complexity Measures. We consider a set of basic complexity measures similar to the ones used in the traditional *distributed algorithms* field.

- *Time complexity*: the supremum over all possible running times (which, although not perfect, is the most usual definition for the asynchronous time complexity).
- *Message complexity*: the number of exchanged messages.
- *Atomic complexity*: the number of atoms summed over all exchanged messages (analogous to the traditional bit complexity).

References

1. Abd-El-Malek, M., Ganger, G.R., Goodson, G.R., Reiter, M.K., Wylie, J.J.: Fault-scalable Byzantine fault-tolerant services. In: Herbert, A., Birman, K.P. (eds.) SOSP, pp. 59–74. ACM (2005)
2. Ben-Or, M., Hassidim, A.: Fast quantum Byzantine agreement. In: Gabow, H.N., Fagin, R. (eds.) STOC, pp. 481–485. ACM (2005)
3. Cachin, C., Kursawe, K., Shoup, V.: Random oracles in constantinople: practical asynchronous Byzantine agreement using cryptography. J. Cryptol. **18**(3), 219–246 (2005)
4. Castro, M., Liskov, B.: Practical Byzantine fault tolerance and proactive recovery. ACM Trans. Comput. Syst. **20**(4), 398–461 (2002)
5. Ciobanu, G.: Distributed algorithms over communicating membrane systems. Biosystems **70**(2), 123–133 (2003)
6. Ciobanu, G., Desai, R., Kumar, A.: Membrane systems and distributed computing. In: PĂun, G., Rozenberg, G., Salomaa, A., Zandron, C. (eds.) WMC 2002. LNCS, vol. 2597, pp. 187–202. Springer, Heidelberg (2003). doi:10.1007/3-540-36490-0_12
7. Dinneen, M.J., Kim, Y.-B., Nicolescu, R.: A faster P solution for the Byzantine agreement problem. In: Gheorghe, M., Hinze, T., Păun, G., Rozenberg, G., Salomaa, A. (eds.) CMC 2010. LNCS, vol. 6501, pp. 175–197. Springer, Heidelberg (2010). doi:10.1007/978-3-642-18123-8_15

8. Dinneen, M.J., Kim, Y.B., Nicolescu, R.: A faster P solution for the Byzantine agreement problem. Report CDMTCS-388, Centre for Discrete Mathematics and Theoretical Computer Science, The University of Auckland, Auckland, New Zealand, July 2010. http://www.cs.auckland.ac.nz/CDMTCS/researchreports/388-DKN.pdf

9. Dinneen, M.J., Kim, Y.B., Nicolescu, R.: P systems and the Byzantine agreement. J. Logic Algebraic Program. **79**, 334–349 (2010)

10. Dinneen, M.J., Kim, Y.B., Nicolescu, R.: P systems and the Byzantine agreement. Report CDMTCS-375, Centre for Discrete Mathematics and Theoretical Computer Science, The University of Auckland, Auckland, New Zealand, January 2010. http://www.cs.auckland.ac.nz/CDMTCS//researchreports/375Byzantine.pdf

11. Dinneen, M.J., Kim, Y.B., Nicolescu, R.: A faster P solution for the Byzantine agreement problem. In: Gheorghe, M., Păun, G., Hinze, T. (eds.) Eleventh International Conference on Membrane Computing (CMC11), 24–27 August 2010, Friedrich Schiller University, Jena, Germany, pp. 167–192. Pro Business GmbH, Berlin (2015)

12. Lamport, L., Shostak, R.E., Pease, M.C.: The Byzantine generals problem. ACM Trans. Program. Lang. Syst. **4**(3), 382–401 (1982)

13. Lynch, N.A.: Distributed Algorithms. Morgan Kaufmann Publishers Inc., San Francisco (1996)

14. Martin, J.P., Alvisi, L.: Fast Byzantine consensus. IEEE Trans. Dependable Sec. Comput. **3**(3), 202–215 (2006)

15. Nicolescu, R.: Parallel and distributed algorithms in P systems. In: Gheorghe, M., Păun, G., Rozenberg, G., Salomaa, A., Verlan, S. (eds.) CMC 2011. LNCS, vol. 7184, pp. 35–50. Springer, Heidelberg (2012). doi:10.1007/978-3-642-28024-5_4

16. Nicolescu, R.: Parallel thinning with complex objects and actors. In: Gheorghe, M., Rozenberg, G., Salomaa, A., Sosík, P., Zandron, C. (eds.) CMC 2014. LNCS, vol. 8961, pp. 330–354. Springer, Heidelberg (2014). doi:10.1007/978-3-319-14370-5_21

17. Nicolescu, R.: Structured grid algorithms modelled with complex objects. In: Rozenberg, G., Salomaa, A., Sempere, J.M., Zandron, C. (eds.) CMC 2015. LNCS, vol. 9504, pp. 321–337. Springer, Heidelberg (2015). doi:10.1007/978-3-319-28475-0_22

18. Nicolescu, R., Dinneen, M.J., Kim, Y.B.: Towards structured modelling with hyperdag P systems. Int. J. Comput. Commun. Control **2**, 209–222 (2010)

19. Nicolescu, R., Ipate, F., Wu, H.: Programming P systems with complex objects. In: Alhazov, A., Cojocaru, S., Gheorghe, M., Rogozhin, Y., Rozenberg, G., Salomaa, A. (eds.) CMC 2013. LNCS, vol. 8340, pp. 280–300. Springer, Heidelberg (2014). doi:10.1007/978-3-642-54239-8_20

20. Nicolescu, R., Ipate, F., Wu, H.: Towards high-level P systems programming using complex objects. In: Alhazov, A., Cojocaru, S., Gheorghe, M., Rogozhin, Y. (eds.) Proceedings of the 14th International Conference on Membrane Computing, CMC14, Chişinău, Moldova, 20–23 August 2013, pp. 255–276. Institute of Mathematics and Computer Science, Academy of Sciences of Moldova, Chişinău (2013)

21. Nicolescu, R., Wu, H.: Complex objects for complex applications. Rom. J. Inf. Sci. Technol. **17**(1), 46–62 (2014)

22. Pease, M.C., Shostak, R.E., Lamport, L.: Reaching agreement in the presence of faults. J. ACM **27**(2), 228–234 (1980)

23. Păun, G., Rozenberg, G., Salomaa, A. (eds.): The Oxford Handbook of Membrane Computing. Oxford University Press, Inc., New York (2010)

Rewriting P Systems with Flat-Splicing Rules

Linqiang Pan[1], Bosheng Song[1(✉)], and K.G. Subramanian[2]

[1] Key Laboratory of Image Information Processing and Intelligent Control
of Education Ministry of China, School of Automation,
Huazhong University of Science and Technology, Wuhan 430074, Hubei, China
lqpan@mail.hust.edu.cn, boshengsong@hust.edu.cn
[2] Department of Mathematics, Madras Christian College, Tambaram,
Chennai 600059, India
kgsmani1948@gmail.com

Abstract. Rewriting P systems, as language generating devices, are one of the earliest classes of P systems with structured strings as objects and the rewriting rules as evolution rules. Flat splicing is an operation on strings, inspired by a splicing operation on circular strings. In this work, we consider a variant of rewriting P systems with only regular or linear rewriting rules and alphabetic flat splicing rules, and the language generative power of rewriting P systems with flat splicing rules in comparison with flat splicing systems and Chomsky hierarchy is investigated.

Keywords: Bio-inspired computing · Membrane computing · P system · Flat splicing · Chomsky hierarchy

1 Introduction

Membrane computing, which was motivated by the organization and functioning of living cells, has grown to a great extent in breadth and depth, at least at the theoretical level, since its introduction around the year 2000 [14,15]. The novel computing device in this area, known broadly as *P system*, has become a versatile framework in many application problems as well [3,4,18,19,21,22]. Among different varieties of P systems, the *rewriting P system* considered as a language generating device, is one of the earliest P system models introduced by Păun [14] with structured strings as objects and rewriting rules as in formal language theory, in order to deal with symbolic computations.

The language generation power of rewriting P systems has been investigated, several variants with different additional features have been introduced into such kind of P systems. For instance, deadlock state [2], variable thickness [5], combining Chomsky rules and contextual rules [9], using one-sided contextual rules and erasing contextual rules [10], using global rules [12], using partially parallel rewriting rules [13]. It is shown that several of the above mentioned variants of rewriting P systems can generate any recursively enumerable languages.

On the other hand, in the area of DNA computing, Head [6] introduced a novel operation on strings, called *splicing*, while modelling the recombinant

© Springer International Publishing AG 2017
A. Leporati et al. (Eds.): CMC 2016, LNCS 10105, pp. 340–351, 2017.
DOI: 10.1007/978-3-319-54072-6_21

behaviour of DNA strings. Inspired by the splicing operation on circular strings [7], Berstel et al. [1] consider an operation on strings called *flat splicing* which "cuts" a string $u = x\alpha\beta y$ between α and β and inserts in u, a string $v = \gamma z \delta$ between α and β as dictated by a flat splicing rule of the form $(\alpha|\gamma - \delta|\beta)$. In particular, when $\alpha, \beta, \gamma, \delta$ are letters of an alphabet or the empty word, the rule is called an *alphabetic flat splicing rule*.

In this work, we consider a variant of rewriting P systems with only regular or linear rewriting rules and alphabetic flat splicing rules, besides the initial words in the regions being only symbols from the alphabet of the system. The language generative power of these rewriting P systems with alphabetic flat splicing rules in comparison with flat splicing systems is investigated. Moreover, the family of languages generated by these rewriting P systems with alphabetic flat splicing rules are also compared with the language families in Chomsky hierarchy. Specifically, we prove that the family of context-free languages is included in the family of languages generated by rewriting P systems with alphabetic flat splicing rules, having two membranes, a priority relation on the regular rules and initial strings in the regions having length at least one. A preliminary version of this work appears in [11].

2   Preliminaries

We refer to [20] for concepts and results related to formal grammars and languages and to [14,15,17] for P systems.

An *alphabet* V is a finite and nonempty set of symbols and a *word* (also called a linear word) w is a finite sequence of symbols belonging to V. The set of all words over V is denoted by V^* which includes the empty word λ (with no symbols) and $V^+ = V^* - \{\lambda\}$. The *length* $|w|$ of a word w is the number of symbols in w counting repetitions.

We denote the families of languages generated by *context-sensitive, context-free, linear* or *regular grammars* of the Chomsky hierarchy by CSL, CFL, LIN, respectively [20]. The family of finite languages is denoted by FIN.

We recall the notion of *flat splicing* on words, which was considered by Berstel et al. [1]. A flat splicing rule r is of the form $(\alpha|\gamma - \delta|\beta)$, where $\alpha, \beta, \gamma, \delta$ are words over the alphabet V. The words $\alpha, \beta, \gamma, \delta$ are called the *handles* of the rule. When all the four handles of the rule r are letters in V or the empty word, the flat splicing rule r is called *alphabetic*.

For two words $x = u\alpha\beta v$, $y = \gamma w \delta$, $u, v, w \in V^*$, an application of the flat splicing rule $r = (\alpha|\gamma - \delta|\beta)$ to the pair (x, y) yields the word $z = u\alpha\gamma w\delta\beta v$ and we write $(x, y) \vdash_r z$. In other words, an application of the rule r inserts the second word y between α and β in the first word x yielding the word z. When $\alpha = \beta = \gamma = \delta = \lambda$, the flat splicing rule is simply $(\lambda|\lambda - \lambda|\lambda)$ and an application of this kind of rule allows insertion of any word y into any other word x and the insertion can be done anywhere in x.

A *flat splicing system* (*FSS*) [1] is a triple $\mathcal{S} = (\Sigma, I, R)$, where Σ is an alphabet, I, called initial set, is a set of words over Σ and R is a finite set of flat splicing rules. The FSS S is respectively called finite, regular or context-free according to the I is a finite set, a regular set or a context-free language. The language L generated by S is the smallest language containing I and such that for any two words $u, v \in L$ and any rule $r \in R$, if the rule r is applicable to the pair (u, v) and if the word w is obtained on applying the rule r to the pair (u, v), that is, if $(u, v) \vdash_r w$, then w is also in L. When all the flat splicing rules are alphabetic, the FSS is called an *alphabetic flat splicing system* ($AFSS$). The families of languages generated by FSS and $AFSS$ are respectively denoted by $\mathcal{L}(FSS, X)$ and $\mathcal{L}(AFSS, X)$ for $X = FIN, REG$ or CF according as the initial set is finite, regular or CF.

We illustrate an alphabetic flat splicing system and its work with an example.

Example 1. Consider the alphabetic flat splicing system $S_1 = (\{a, b, c\}, \{ac, b\}, R_1)$, where

$$R_1 = \{r_1 = (a|a - c|c), r_2 = (b|b - \lambda|\lambda), r_3 = (a|b - \lambda|c).\}$$

Application of the rule r_2 to the pair of words (b, b) inserts (the second) b to the right of (the first b) yielding b^2. Likewise applying the rule r_2 to the pair (b, b^2) or (b^2, b) yields b^3. Note that an application of r_2 to the pair (b^2, b) can insert b to the right of b^2 or between the two b's. Thus proceeding like this, the words generated will be of the form b^n, $n \geq 1$. In a similar manner, applying the rule r_1 to the pair (ac, ac) will yield $a^2 c^2$ and continuing this we obtain words of the form $a^n c^n$, $n \geq 1$. On the other hand, using the rule r_3 to the pairs of the form $(a^n c^n, b^m)$, $n, m \geq 1$, yields the word $a^n b^m c^n$. The language generated by S_1 is

$$L(S_1) = \{b^n | n \geq 1\} \cup \{a^n c^n | n \geq 1\} \cup \{a^n b^m c^n \mid n, m \geq 1\}.$$

It has been shown in [1] that alphabetic flat splicing rules and context-free initial sets can produce only context-free languages.

Theorem 1. [1] *The language generated by an alphabetic flat splicing system with context-free initial set is context-free.*

Insertion/deletion systems have been investigated in the context of study on models in DNA computing (see, for example, [16], Chap. 6) and a number of language theoretical results have been established. In particular, insertion systems have close similarity with flat splicing systems as pointed out in [1]. But it has been shown in [1] that these two systems generate incomparable families of languages. We now recall insertion systems as described in [1].

An insertion system $\gamma = (\Sigma, I, R)$, where Σ is a nonempty alphabet, I, called the initial set, is a finite nonempty set of words over Σ and R is a finite nonempty set of rules, called *insertion rules*, of the form $(u|\beta|v)$, where u, β, v are words over Σ. Given a word w of the form $w = xuvy$, an application of the rule $(u|\beta|v)$ generates the word $w' = xu\beta vy$. The language generated by the system γ is the set of words over Σ obtained by repeated application of the insertion rules, starting with the words in the initial set I. The family of languages generated by insertion systems is denoted by $L(ins)$. An insertion system is alphabetic if the contexts u, v of the rules $(u|\beta|v)$ have length at most 1. The family of languages generated by insertion systems as defined above, is denoted by $\mathcal{L}(ins)$ and by $\mathcal{L}(ains)$ when the insertion systems are alphabetic.

The following results on (alphabetic) insertion systems and flat splicing systems are known [1].

Theorem 2. (*i*) *The families of languages generated by flat splicing systems and insertion systems are incomparable.*

(*ii*) *Alphabetic insertion systems always generate context-free languages.*

3   A Rewriting P System with Linear Rewriting Rules and Alphabetic Flat Splicing Rules

We now introduce a cell-like rewriting P system with internal output computing languages of structured strings. The regions of the P system can have regular or linear rewriting rules and/or alphabetic flat splicing rules and initial objects in the regions are only symbols from an alphabet.

Definition 1. *A rewriting P system with linear rules and/or alphabetic flat splicing rules of degree $m \geq 1$ ($RP_m(LIN/AFSR)$) is*

$$\Pi = (V, T, \mu, F_1, \cdots, F_m, R_1, \cdots, R_m, i_o),$$

where

(*i*) V *is the total alphabet of the system;*

(*ii*) $T \subset V$ *is the terminal alphabet;*

(*iii*) μ *is the membrane structure consisting of m membranes labelled in a one-to-one way with $1, \ldots, m$;*

(*iv*) $F_1, \ldots, F_m$ *are finite subsets of V associated with the m regions of μ (the elements of $F_i, 1 \leq i \leq m$, are called initial symbols);*

(*v*) $R_1, \ldots, R_m$ *are finite sets of rules associated with the m regions of μ;*

(*vi*) i_o *is the label of an elementary membrane of μ, called the output membrane.*

A rule in a region can be a linear rewriting rule of the form $A \to \alpha B \beta$ or $A \to \gamma$, $A, B \in V - T$, $\alpha, \beta, \gamma \in T^*$ or an alphabetic flat splicing rule as described earlier. The rules have attached targets *here, out, in* (in general, *here* is omitted). A linear rule in a region rewrites a string in the region as in a Chomsky grammar while an alphabetic flat splicing rule in a region is applied to a pair of strings in the region. If the rewriting rules in the regions are only regular rules of the form $A \to \alpha B$ or $A \to \gamma$, $A, B \in V - T$, $\alpha, \gamma \in T^*$, then we denote the system as $RP_m(REG/AFSR)$.

A computation in a $RP_m(LIN/AFSR)$ is defined in a way similar to a string rewriting P system [14,15]. A computation starts from an initial configuration defined by the membrane structure with the initial symbols, if any, in the m regions. The rules in a region are used in a nondeterministic maximally parallel manner which means that the strings to evolve and the rules to be applied to them are chosen in a nondeterministic manner, but all strings in all the regions which can evolve at a given step should do it. On the other hand, the application of a linear rule to a string in a region or an alphabetic flat splicing rule to a pair of strings in a region, is sequential in the sense that only one rule is applied to a string or a pair of strings, resulting in an evolved string which is placed in the region indicated by the target associated with the rule used. The target *here* means that the evolved string remains in the same region, *out* means that the evolved string exits the current membrane (if the rule was applied in the skin membrane, then it can exit the system such that strings leaving the system are "lost" in the environment), and *in* means that the string is sent to one of the directly lower membranes, nondeterministically chosen if there exist several of them (if no internal membrane exists, then a rule with the target indication *in* cannot be used).

A computation is successful only if it stops reaching a configuration where no rule can be applied to the existing strings. The result of a halting computation consists of strings is composed only of symbols from T placed in the output membrane in the halting configuration. The set of all such strings computed (also called generated) by the system Π is denoted by $L(\Pi)$.

The family of all languages $L(\Pi)$ generated by systems Π as above, with at most m membranes, with linear rules and/or flat splicing rules is denoted by $\mathcal{L}(RP_m(LIN/AFSR))$. If the rewriting rules are regular the corresponding family is denoted by $\mathcal{L}(RP_m(REG/AFSR))$.

In order to illustrate the definition of $RP_m(REG/AFSR)$, we give the following example.

Example 2. Consider the $RP_2(REG/AFSR)$

$$\Pi_1 = (\{S_1, S_2, A, B_1, B_2, B_3, a, b, c, d\}, \{a, b, c, d\}, [_1 [_2]_2]_1, \{S_1, S_2\}, \emptyset, R_1, R_2, 2),$$

where R_1 consists of the regular rewriting rules

$$S_1 \to B_1, S_1 \to cB_2, S_1 \to acB_3, S_2 \to xyA,$$

$$B_1 \to acB_1, B_2 \to acB_2, B_3 \to acB_3, A \to dbA$$

and the alphabetic flat splicing rules

$$(\lambda|x - A|B_1), (\lambda|x - A|B_2), (\lambda|x - A|B_3),$$

with all the three alphabetic flat splicing rules having target indication "*in*" while R_2 consists of the following regular rewriting rules:

$$A \to \lambda, B_1 \to \lambda, B_2 \to \lambda, B_2 \to d, B_3 \to d.$$

Computation in Π_1 takes place as follows: The region 1 has axiom strings S_1, S_2 while region 2 has none initially. One of the three rules $S_1 \to B_1, S_1 \to cB_2, S_1 \to acB_3$ in region 1 could be applied to the axiom string S_1 initially.

If we start with applying the rewriting rule $S_1 \to B_1$ to the axiom string S_1 and follow it by the application of the rule $B_1 \to acB_1$, for certain times, say n times ($n \geq 1$), then this yields the string $(ac)^n B_1$. Simultaneously, in region 1, the axiom string S_2 yields the string $xy(db)^n A$ (for the same n) by the application of the rule $S_2 \to xyA$ followed by the application of the rule $A \to dbA$ for n times. If at this stage the alphabetic flat splicing rule $(\lambda|x - A|B_1)$ in region 1, with target indication "in" is applied to the pair $((ac)^n B_1, xy(db)^n A)$, then the string $(ac)^n xy(db)^n AB_1$ is generated and is sent to region 2, where the application of the rules $A \to \lambda, B_1 \to \lambda$ erase the symbols A, B_1 thereby yielding the string $(ac)^n xy(db)^n$.

Likewise, if we start with applying the rewriting rule $S_1 \to cB_2$ to the axiom string S_1 in region 1 and follow it by the application of the rule $B_2 \to acB_2$, for certain times, say n times ($n \geq 1$), then this yields the string $c(ac)^n B_2$. Again the alphabetic flat splicing rule $(\lambda|x - A|B_2)$ in region 1, with target indication "in" can be applied to the pair $(c(ac)^n B_2, xy(db)^n A)$, then the string $c(ac)^n xy(db)^n AB_2$ is generated and is sent to region 2, where the application of the rule $A \to \lambda$, and either $B_2 \to \lambda$ or $B_2 \to d$ erase the symbol A and either erase B_2 or replace it by d thereby yielding the string $c(ac)^n xy(db)^n$ or $c(ac)^n xy(db)^n d$. Generation of strings of the form $(ac)^n xy(db)^n d$ is similar with the computation in region 1 starting with applying the rule $S_1 \to acB_3$ to the axiom string S_1 and following it by the application of the rule $B_3 \to acB_3$ certain number of times, so that the alphabetic flat splicing rule $(\lambda|x - A|B_3)$ applied to the pair $(ac(ac)^n B_3, xy(db)^n A)$ will yield and send the string $ac(ac)^n xy(db)^n AB_3$ to region 2, where A is erased and B_3 is replaced by d. Thus the language L generated by Π_1 is $L = L(\Pi_1) = M \cup cM \cup cMd \cup acMd$, where $M = \{(ac)^n xy(db)^n | n \geq 0\}$.

Remark 1. The language L in Example 2 is in fact considered in [1] and an alphabetic flat splicing system with six rules is given generating a language P which contains L. It has also been shown that P cannot be generated by an insertion system, by providing an argument that is based on the words in L.

We now examine the generative power of the rewriting P systems with regular and/or flat splicing rules.

Theorem 3. (i) $\mathcal{L}(RP_1(REG/AFSR)) - \mathcal{L}(FSS, FIN) \neq \emptyset$;
   (ii) $\mathcal{L}(RP_1(REG/AFSR)) - \mathcal{L}(ins) \neq \emptyset$.

Proof. The language $L_1 = \{xa^n y | n \geq 0\}$ over the alphabet $\{x, a, y\}$ is not in the family $\mathcal{L}(FSS, FIN)$ as shown in [1]. But clearly, it is in $RP_1(REG/AFSR)$ since we can have a $RP_1(REG/AFSR)$ with only one membrane containing regular rules $S \to xA, A \to aA, A \to y$ with the initial symbol S generating L_1. In fact we do not need any alphabetic splicing rules in the membrane. This proves statement (i).

In order to prove statement (ii), we note that a language P (as mentioned in the Remark 1) is shown in [1] to be not $\mathcal{L}(ins)$. Although P is not explicitly described, it is noted in [1] that P is generated from the initial words xy, a, b, c, d by the following six flat splicing rules:

$$(c|x - y|\lambda), (\lambda|c - y|d), (a|c - d|\lambda), (\lambda|a - d|b), (c|a - b|\lambda), (\lambda|c - b|d).$$

But the language P is in $RP_1(REG/AFSR)$ since we can have a $RP_1(REG/AFSR)$ with only membrane containing initial symbols S, a, b, c, d, a regular rule $S \to xy$ and the six alphabetic flat splicing rules mentioned above. In fact, these alphabetic splicing rules alone are shown in [1] to generate P, but their initial set has xy (a string of length more than 1) and so we have included the rule $S \to xy$ in the membrane to generate xy. Note that by definition, the initial objects in the regions of the P system can be only symbols (of length 1). This proves statement (ii). □

Theorem 4. (i) $REG \subset \mathcal{L}(RP_1(REG/AFSR)) \subset \mathcal{L}(RP_2(REG/AFSR))$;
(ii) $\mathcal{L}(RP_2(REG/AFSR)) - \mathcal{L}(FSS, REG) \neq \emptyset$;
(iii) $\mathcal{L}(RP_2(REG/AFSR))$ *contains a context-sensitive language which is not context-free. As a consequence,* $\mathcal{L}(RP_2(REG/AFSR)) - CSL \neq \emptyset$.

Proof. The inclusion $REG \subseteq \mathcal{L}(RP_1(REG/AFSR))$ is straightforward as the regular rules generating a regular language can be taken as the rules in the only one membrane of a corresponding $RP_1(REG/AFSR)$ (with no alphabetic flat splicing rule in the region) and the start symbol of the grammar is the initial object in the membrane. The proper inclusion in statement (i) follows by noting that the language P in the proof of statement (ii) of Theorem 3 is in $\mathcal{L}(RP_1(REG/AFSR))$ but is a non-regular language. In fact the non-regular context-free language $L = M \cup cM \cup cMd \cup acMd$, where $M = \{(ac)^n xy(db)^n | n \geq 0\}$ is a subset of P and contains all the words in P having exactly one x and one y, which implies P is also non-regular.

In order to prove statement (ii), we note that the inclusion $\mathcal{L}(RP_1(REG/AFSR)) \subseteq \mathcal{L}(RP_2(REG/AFSR))$ holds by definition while the proper inclusion is seen by considering the non-regular context-free language $L_2 = \{xa^n b^n y | n \geq 1\}$ over the alphabet $\{x, y, a, b\}$. In fact, the following $RP_2(REG/AFSR)$, Π_2, generates L:

$$\Pi_2 = (\{S_1, S_2, A, B, x, y, a, b\}, \{x, y, a, b\}, [_1 [_2]_2]_1, \{S_1, S_2\}, \emptyset, R_1, R_2, 2),$$

where R_1 consists of the regular rules $S_1 \to xA, A \to aA, S_2 \to B, B \to bB$ and the alphabetic flat splicing rule $(a|\lambda - B|A)$ with target *in*. R_2 consists of the regular rules $A \to a, B \to \lambda$.

In fact, in region 1, the initial symbols S_1, S_2 respectively generate $xa^n A$ and $b^n B$ (for the same $n \geq 1$) and if at this stage, the alphabetic flat splicing rule is applied to the pair $(xa^n S_1, b^n B)$, then the string $xa^n Ab^n B$ is generated and is sent to region 2. Here in region 2, the application of the rules $A \to a, B \to \lambda$ yields the string $xa^n b^n y$.

But the language L_2 cannot be generated by any $RP_1(REG/AFSR)$ with only one membrane. In fact, regular rules alone are not enough as the language is non-regular while alphabetic flat splicing rules alone are not enough which can be shown by an argument similar to the one given in [1] in proving that the language $\{xa^ny|n \geq 0\}$ is not a flat splicing language. On the other hand, if we assume that the only membrane has some regular rules and some flat splicing rules that can generate the words xa^nb^ny, then strings with some powers of a or powers of b cannot be inserted independently between x and y. The only possibility is to insert between x and y for some string having the form a^nb^n with suitable nonterminals, if any, in between. Since the nonterminals are to be erased ultimately, the only membrane should have rules which will lead to terminal strings of the required form. But this would mean that strings (without the symbols x, y) not in the language will be generated. This shows only one membrane is not enough.

In order to prove statement (iii), consider the language

$$L_3 = \{c^p \mid p \geq 1\} \cup \{a^nb^n \mid n \geq 1\} \cup \{a^nb^nc^{n+m} \mid n, m \geq 1\},$$

which is context-sensitive and not context-free. The following $RP_2(REG/AFSR)$ generates the language L_3:

$$(\{S_1, S_2, S_3, a, b, c\}, \{a, b, c\}, [_1 [_2]_2]_1, \{S_1, S_2\}, \{S_3\}, R_1, R_2, 2),$$

where R_1 consists of the regular rules $S_1 \rightarrow aS_1, S_2 \rightarrow bS_2$ and an alphabetic flat splicing rule $(a|b - S_2|S_1), in$ while R_2 consists of the regular rules $S_1 \rightarrow \lambda, S_2 \rightarrow \lambda, S_3 \rightarrow \lambda, S_3 \rightarrow cS_3$ and an alphabetic flat splicing rule $(S_2|c - S_3|S_1), in$.

The computation takes place as follows: In region 1, S_1, S_2 generate the strings a^nS_1 and b^nS_2, while at the same time in region 2, S_3 generates c^nS_3. At this point if the alphabetic flat splicing in region 1 takes place on the pair (a^nS_1, b^nS_2), then the string generated is $a^nb^nS_2S_1$ which is sent to region 2. Here application of the regular rule $S_3 \rightarrow cS_3$ could take place, say m times, so that the string generated is $c^{n+m}S_3$ $(m \geq 1)$. If at this point, the alphabetic flat splicing rule is applied on the pair $(a^nb^nS_2S_1, c^{n+m}S_3)$, the string generated is $a^nb^nS_2c^{n+m}S_3S_1$. At the same time, prior to applying the flat splicing rules, if the erasing rules are applied, strings of the form c^p, a^nb^n will be generated. Thus the language generated is L_3.

Theorem 5. $\mathcal{L}(RP_1(LIN/AFSR)) \subset \mathcal{L}(RP_2(LIN/AFSR))$.

Proof. The inclusion holds by definition. In order to prove proper inclusion, consider the language $L_4 = \{a^nb^nc^n \mid n \geq 1\}$, which is context-sensitive and not context-free. The following $RP_2(LIN/AFSR)$ generates the language L_4:

$$(\{S_1, S_2, a, b, c\}, \{a, b, c\}, [_1 [_2]_2]_1, \{S_1, S_2\}, \emptyset, R_1, R_2, 2),$$

where R_1 consists of the linear rules $S_1 \rightarrow aS_1c, S_2 \rightarrow bS_2$ and an alphabetic flat splicing rule $(a|b - S_2|S_1), in$, while R_2 consists of the rules $S_1 \rightarrow \lambda, S_2 \rightarrow \lambda$. The computation takes place as follows: In region 1, S_1, S_2 generate the strings $a^nS_1c^n$ and b^nS_2 for the same n. At this point if the alphabetic flat splicing in region 1 is applied on the pair $(a^nS_1c^n, b^nS_2)$, then the string generated is

$a^n b^n S_2 S_1 c^n$ which is sent to region 2. Here application of the rules $S_1 \to \lambda, S_2 \to \lambda$ erases the nonterminals, thus yielding the string $a^n b^n c^n$.

On the other hand, one membrane is not enough to generate L_4 since $AFSS$ rules alone cannot generate the non-CF language due to Theorem 1, while linear rules alone are also not enough. So if both types of rules are included in the only membrane to generate L_4, then the nonterminals of the linear rules are to be erased or replaced by terminal strings finally. But this will lead to strings not in L_4.

4 $RP_m(REG/AFSR)$ with Extended Initial Objects

In rewriting P systems [14] generating languages, the initial objects in the membranes can be strings of finite languages. This means that strings of length more than one can be the initial objects unlike the objects in $RP_m(LIN/AFSR)$ or $RP_m(REG/AFSR)$ considered here so far, where the initial objects are symbols from the alphabet.

Instead of recalling the formal details of the definition of a rewriting P system [14], we illustrate with an example of a rewriting P system having regular rules in its regions and computing a context-free language. Note that the system works in maximal parallelism manner, but at the level of a membrane the rewriting by a rule is sequential and the rewritten string moves to the membrane indicated by the target.

Example 3. Consider the rewriting P system of degree 2 with regular rewriting rules, given by $(V, T, \mu, L_1, L_2, R_1, R_2, 2)$, where the total alphabet $V = \{A, B, a, b\}$, the terminal alphabet $T = \{a, b\}$, the membrane structure $\mu = [_1 [_2]_2]_1$. The sets of initial strings in the membranes are given by $L_1 = \emptyset, L_2 = \{AB\}$. The sets R_1, R_2 with regular rules with associated targets (*here*, *in* or *out*) are given by

$$R_1 = \{B \to bB(in)\}, R_2 = \{A \to aA(out), A \to a(here), B \to b(here)\}.$$

Computation in this P system will take place as follows: Only the membrane 2 has an initial string AB (of length 2) which will evolve by the sequential application of a rule in region 2. If the rule $A \to aA(out)$ is applied to AB, the generated string aAB is sent to region 1, where the application of the rule $B \to bB(in)$ generates $aAbB$ which is sent back to region 2. The process can repeat or terminate by the application of the rules $A \to a(here), B \to b(here)$ yielding words of the form $a^n b^n, n \geq 1$. The language generated is a non-regular context-free language $\{a^n b^n \mid n \geq 1\}$. An application of the rule $B \to b$ followed by the application of the rule $A \to aA(out)$ will send the string to region 1 where it will get stuck. Note that if in region 2, the initial string is allowed to have length not more than 1, this language cannot be generated with regular rules and two membranes.

We now allow in our definition of $RP_m(REG/AFSR)$ initial objects to have length more than 1 but continue to refer to such a system by $RP_m(REG/AFSR)$

itself. A priority relation $>$ on the rules is a well-known notion used in P systems. If a region has rules r_1, r_2 with $r_1 > r_2$, then if both the rules could be applied to strings in that region, only r_1 is applied. We denote such a system with a priority relation on the regular rules in the regions and initial strings in the regions having length one or more by $RP_m(REG/AFSR, pri)$. The corresponding family of languages is denoted by $\mathcal{L}(RP_m(REG/AFSR, pri))$.

Theorem 6. $CFL \subset \mathcal{L}(RP_2(REG/AFSR, pri))$.

Proof. Let L (without the empty word) be a context-free language and $G = (N, \Sigma, P, S)$ be a context-free grammar in Chomsky normal form with P consisting of n rules of the form $A \to BC$ or $A \to a$ generating L. The members of N are the nonterminals and those of T are terminals of G with $S \in N$ as the start symbol. We construct a $RP_2(REG/AFSS, pri)$ Π_3 to generate L. $\Pi_3 = (V, T, [_1 [_2]_2]_2, L_1, L_2, (R_1, >), R_2, 2)$, where $V = N \cup \Sigma \cup \{F_i, E, E' \mid F_i, E, E' \notin N, 1 \le i \le n\}, T = \Sigma$, such that with each rule $r_i, 1 \le i \le n$, a distinct symbol F_i is associated. We set

$$L_1 = \{SE, F_j BC, F_k a \mid r_j : A \to BC \in P, r_k : A \to a \in P,$$

$$F_j, F_k \text{ are associated with rules } r_j, r_k\},$$

$$L_2 = \emptyset,$$

$$R_1 = \{(A|F_j - C|\alpha), (A|F_k - a|\alpha) \mid r_j : A \to BC, r_k : A \to a,$$

$$A, B, C \in N, a \in \Sigma, \alpha \in V - \{F_i | 1 \le i \le n\}\} \cup \{(E|E' - \lambda|\lambda)(in)\},$$

$$R_2 = \{X \to \lambda \mid X \in N \cup \{F_i, E, E' \mid 1 \le i \le n\}\}.$$

As usual, we omit mentioning the target *"here"*. The priority relation $>$ on the rules of R_1 is defined as follows: $r > (E|E' - \lambda|\lambda)$ for each rule r in $R_1 - \{(E|E' - \lambda|\lambda)\}$. The construction is very close to a similar result in [8].

It can be seen that a derivation in the context-free grammar G starting from S and leading to a word in L can be simulated by Π_3 as follows: The computation starts with the initial string SE in membrane 1 and the result of rewriting by a rule of the form $A \to BC$ is captured by inserting $F_j BC$ (F_j being the associated symbol) to the immediate right of the symbol A in the currently generated word. Likewise, corresponding to the application of the rule $A \to a$, the word $F_k a$ (F_k being the associated symbol) is inserted again to the immediate right of A. Due to the priority, only when no other rule could be applied, the rule $(E|E' - \lambda|\lambda)$ could be applied which will send the current word to the membrane 2. Here all the nonterminals (symbols not in Σ) are erased and the resulting terminal word is collected in the language, thus generating the context-free language L.

Finally, we note that in Theorem 4, a $RP_2(REG/AFSR)$ is shown to generate a context-sensitive language which is not context-free. This shows that the inclusion is proper.

5   Conclusions and Discussions

In this work, we have considered rewriting P systems with simple rewriting rules and flat splicing rules with a sequential application of rules to an object in a membrane, and the language generative power of such P systems has been investigated. It may be of interest to examine the power of parallel application of rules as in L systems with similar simple rewriting rules.

The language generative power of rewriting P systems with regular rules and flat splicing rules in comparison with flat splicing systems has been investigated in Sect. 3. It is of interest to investigate whether rewriting P systems with regular rules and flat splicing rules can generate any recursively enumerable language.

The priority relation has been considered in rewriting P systems in Sect. 4, which ensures that the context-free grammar is simulated correctly. It remains open whether the result in Theorem 6 still holds if the priority relation is removed.

Acknowledgements. The work of L. Pan and B. Song was supported by National Natural Science Foundation of China (61320106005, 61602192 and 61033003), Ph.D. Programs Foundation of Ministry of Education of China (20120142130008), China Postdoctoral Science Foundation (2016M600592), the Innovation Scientists and Technicians Troop Construction Projects of Henan Province (154200510012). K.G. Subramanian acknowledges support from the Emeritus Fellowship of University Grants Commission, India for the period 2016-17.

References

1. Berstel, J., Boasson, L., Fagnot, I.: Splicing systems and the Chomsky hierarchy. Theoret. Comput. Sci. **436**, 2–22 (2012)
2. Besozzi, D., Ferretti, C., Mauri, G., Zandron, C.: Parallel rewriting P systems with deadlock. In: Hagiya, M., Ohuchi, A. (eds.) DNA 2002. LNCS, vol. 2568, pp. 302–314. Springer, Heidelberg (2003). doi:10.1007/3-540-36440-4_27
3. Ciobanu, G., Pérez-Jiménez, M.J., Păun, G.: Applications of Membrane Computing. Springer, Berlin (2006)
4. Colomer, A.M., Margalida, A., Valencia-Cabrera, L., Palau, A.: Application of a computational model for complex fluvial ecosystems: the population dynamics of zebra mussel Dreissena polymorpha as a case study. Ecol. Complex. **20**, 116–126 (2014)
5. Freund, R., Martín-Vide, C., Păun, Gh.: From regulated rewriting to computing with membranes: collapsing hierarchies. Theoret. Comput. Sci. **312**(2–3), 143–188 (2004)
6. Head, T.: Formal language theory and DNA: an analysis of the generative capacity of specific recombinant behaviours. Bull. Math. Biol. **49**, 735–759 (1987)
7. Head, T.: Circular suggestions for DNA computing. In: Carbone, A., et al. (eds.) Pattern Formation in Biology, Vision and Dynamics, pp. 325–335. World Scientific, Singapore (2000)
8. Krassovitskiy, A.: On the power of small size insertion P systems. Int. J. Comput. Commun. **VI**, 266–277 (2001)

9. Krishna, S.N., Lakshmanan, K., Rama, R.: Hybrid P systems. Rom. J. Inf. Sci. Technol. **4**, 111–123 (2001)
10. Krishna, S.N., Lakshmanan, K., Rama, R.: On the power of P systems with contextual rules. Fundam. Inform. **49**, 167–178 (2002)
11. Pan, L., Song, B., Subramanian, K.G.: Rewriting P systems with flat-splicing rules. In: Proceedings of 17th International Conference on Membrane Computing, Milano, pp. 249–259 (2016)
12. Păun, A.: P systems with global rules. Theoret. Comput. Syst. **35**(5), 471–481 (2002)
13. Păun, A.: On P systems with partial parallel rewriting. Rom. J. Inf. Sci. Technol. **4**, 203–210 (2001)
14. Păun, Gh.: Computing with membranes. J. Comput. Syst. Sci. **61**, 108–143 (2000)
15. Păun, Gh.: Computing with Membranes: An Introduction. Springer, Berlin (2002)
16. Păun, Gh., Rozenberg, G., Salomaa, A.: DNA Computing-New Computing Paradigms. Texts in Theoretical Computer Science. An EATCS Series. Springer, New York (1998)
17. Păun, Gh., Rozenberg, G., Salomaa, A.: The Oxford Handbook of Membrane Computing. Oxford University Press, New York (2010)
18. Peng, H., Wang, J., Pérez-Jiménez, M.J., Riscos-Núñez, A.: An unsupervised learning algorithm for membrane computing. Inf. Sci. **304**, 80–91 (2015)
19. Peng, H., Wang, J., Pérez-Jiménez, M.J., Wang, H., Shao, J., Wang, T.: Fuzzy reasoning spiking neural P system for fault diagnosis. Inf. Sci. **235**, 106–116 (2013)
20. Rozenberg, G., Salomaa, A. (eds.): Handbook of Formal Languages, vol. 1-3. Springer, Berlin (1997)
21. Zhang, G., Gheorghe, M., Pan, L., Pérez-Jiménez, M.J.: Evolutionary membrane computing: a comprehensive survey and new results. Inf. Sci. **279**, 528–551 (2014)
22. Zhang, G., Rong, H., Neri, F., Pérez-Jiménez, M.J.: An optimization spiking neural P system for approximately solving combinatorial optimization problems. Int. J. Neural Syst. **24**(5), 1–16 (2014)

A View of P Systems from Information Theory

José M. Sempere[(✉)]

Departamento de Sistemas Informáticos y Computación,
Universidad Politécnica de Valencia, Valencia, Spain
jsempere@dsic.upv.es

Abstract. In this work we propose new view of P systems by using the framework of Information Theory. Given a cell-like P system with communication and evolution rules, we analyze the amount of information that it holds as the result of symbol movements across the membranes. Under this approach, we propose new definitions and results related to the information of P systems and their entropy. In addition, we propose a new working manner for P systems based only in the entropy evolution during the computation time.

Keywords: Communication P systems · Information theory · Entropy

1 Introduction

P systems were introduced as a computational model inspired by the information and biochemical product processing of living cells through the use of membrane communication. In most of the works about P systems, information is represented as multisets of symbols/objects which can interact and evolve according to predefined rules. From the beginning, the most important component of the system has been the kind of rules that it holds. There have been different proposals to define the rules of the system such as evolution rules, communication rules, active rules to create/dissolve membrane structures, active rules with polarization, and so on and so forth [13].

Here, we pay attention to the following fact: the rules of a P system produce/consume new symbols in different regions of the system. So, they can be considered information regulators that act over a region, which can be considered information senders and receivers in a pure communication system. Hence, the behavior of the P system can be analyzed from the Information Theory point of view. In this context, the main concept to be defined and applied is the concept of *entropy*. From the definition of entropy, we can analyze any P system through the characterization of the information at every region according to its membrane structure and rules.

Furthermore, if we consider the P system as a metaphor of a living system, then, by applying thermodynamic laws, the system will tend to increase

Work partially supported by the Spanish Ministry of Economy and Competitiveness under EXPLORA Research Project SAF2013-49788-EXP.

A. Leporati et al. (Eds.): CMC 2016, LNCS 10105, pp. 352–362, 2017.
DOI: 10.1007/978-3-319-54072-6_22

its entropy. Hence, we can establish a new working manner of any P system that selects the rules and its application number as a function of incrementing the entropy. This new way of working is named *entropic manner* and will be explained in more detail.

The structure of this work is as follows: First, we give the basic definitions needed in this work and related to Information Theory, multisets and P systems. Then, we establish different entropy definitions for the structure and ingredients of some P systems. We overview some algorithmic ways to calculate the entropies of the system, and we consider probabilistic/stochastic and non-probabilistic/non-stochastic systems. In the next section, we define P systems working in an entropic way and we overview the application of rules under this approach. Finally, we propose some additional research topics related to this approach and we report work in progress.

2   Basic Concepts

We will introduce basic concepts related to multisets, Information Theory and P systems. We suggest to the reader the references [12,13] to introduce membrane computing, and the books [5,15] to introduce Information Theory. We will provide some definitions from multiset theory as exposed in [17].

Information Theory. We can suggest to the reader the books [5,15] and the classical work by C.E. Shannon [16] in order to have a full view of Information Theory.

An *information source* is defined by the tuple (S, P), where S is an alphabet (random variables) and P is a probability distribution over S. A cornerstone of Information Theory is the concept of *entropy* which is attached to information sources. The entropy of an information source I, with an alphabet S and probability distribution $P : S \to [0, 1]$ is defined as

$$H(I) = - \sum_{a \in S} P(a) \cdot \log_2 P(a)$$

Observe that we are working with trivial codes where the alphabet of an information source is its encoding. We have fixed the base 2 for the logarithmic functions, so the information entropy is described in bits. The change from a binary base to a different one can be easily carried out in a logarithm base change. In addition, we can consider the conditional and joint entropies of two random variables X and Y, respectively $H(X \mid Y)$ and $H(X, Y)$, by using the appropriate probability distributions.

Given, two probability distributions p and q over S, the *relative entropy* or *Kullback-Leibler distance* is defined by

$$D(p \parallel q) = \sum_{a \in S} p(a) \cdot \log_2 \frac{p(a)}{q(a)}$$

and, for two random variables X and Y, with a joint probability distribution $p(x, y)$, the *mutual information* $I(X, Y)$ is defined as

$$I(X, Y) = \sum_{x \in X} \sum_{y \in Y} p(x, y) \cdot \log_2 \frac{p(x, y)}{p(x) \cdot p(y)}$$

Observe that the mutual information is the relative entropy between the joint distribution and the product distribution. The following relations between mutual information and entropies hold

- $I(X, Y) = H(X) + H(Y) - H(X, Y)$,
- $I(X, Y) = H(X) - H(X \mid Y) = H(Y) - H(Y \mid X)$.

Multisets and P Systems. Let D be a set. A multiset over D is a pair $\langle D, f \rangle$ where $f : D \longrightarrow \mathbb{N}$ is a function. If $A = \langle D, f \rangle$ and $B = \langle D, g \rangle$ are two multisets then the removal of multiset B from A, denoted by $A \ominus B$, is the multiset $C = \langle D, h \rangle$ where, for all $a \in D$, $h(a) = max(f(a) - g(a), 0)$, and their sum, denoted by $A \oplus B$, is the multiset $C = \langle D, h \rangle$, where for all $a \in D$, $h(a) = f(a) + g(a)$. We will say that $A = B$ if the multiset $(A \ominus B) \oplus (B \ominus A)$ is empty that is $\forall a \in D$, $f(a) = 0$.

The size of any multiset M is the number of elements that it contains and will be denoted by $|M|$. In the following, we will represent multisets by using strings over the alphabet induced by D. Hence, for every alphabet $D = \{a_1, a_2, \cdots, a_n\}$ and for every string $x \in D^*$, we will use the well known Parikh vector defined by $\Psi_D(x) = (|x|_{a_1}, |x|_{a_2}, \ldots, |x|_{a_n})$ where $|x|_{a_i}$ is the number of occurrences of the symbol a_i in x. Observe that, in this case, the length of the string is the size of the multiset that it defines. Finally, for any multiset denoted by the string x, $alph(x)$ denotes the set D that defines the multiset x.

A *cell-like* P system of degree m with *communication* rules is a construct

$$\Pi = (V, \mu, w_1, \cdots, w_m, R_1, \cdots, R_m, i_0),$$

where:

- V is an alphabet (the *objects*)
- μ is a membrane structure consisting of m membranes
- w_i, $1 \leq i \leq m$, is a string representing a multiset over V associated to the region i
- R_i, $1 \leq i \leq m$, is a finite set of rules of the form (u, v) with $u \neq \lambda$ and $v \neq \lambda$ (evolution rules), $(u, out; v, in)$ with $u \neq \lambda$ and $v \neq \lambda$ (antiport rule) and (x, out) or (x, in) with $x \neq \lambda$ (symport rule). The strings u, v and x are defined over the alphabet V, and λ denotes the empty string.
- i_0 is a number between 1 and m and it specifies the *output* membrane of Π (in the case that it equals to ∞ the output is read outside the system).

Observe that, in the previous definition, we have omitted an output alphabet, a catalyst alphabet and dissolution rules. In addition, we have omitted priorities in the rule sets and other communication rules with explicit address. The main reason is that we want to establish a preliminary analysis with the most simple P systems. We have relaxed the definition of P systems by using standard symbol-object ingredients together with antiport (symport) rules. Furthermore, we have not fixed a working manner of the system. The main reason is that all the definitions and results that we propose in this work are valid for any of the working modes proposed in the literature [13].

Given a P system $\Pi = (V, \mu, w_1, \cdots, w_m, (R_1, \rho_1), \cdots, (R_m, \rho_m), i_0)$, a *configuration* of Π at time t will be denoted by $(\mu, w_1^t, w_2^t, \cdots w_m^t)$ where w_i^t is the multiset of objects that region i holds at time t. Obviously, for every region i $w_i^0 = w_i$ (the initial configuration). A *computation* is defined as a (finite) sequence of configurations $C_0, C_1, \cdots, C_p$ where every configuration follows from the previous one by applying the rules over the multisets in a predefined (maximal, minimal, sequential, etc.) manner. Observe that, given that the system has no creation nor dissolution rules, it is no necessary to include μ in the configuration.

Given that a P system is a non-deterministic computational device, it is quite useful the use of computation trees instead of computation sequences. A computation tree is defined by a set of nodes (configurations) with the following conditions: First, the root is the initial configuration of the system and every son of an internal node is defined by the application of rules over the multiset of every region. Given that the system is non-deterministic then every son of an internal node is defined by one possible combination of rule applications over the configuration that it defines. Figure 1 shows a graphical view of this definition.

$$(\mu, w_1^0, ..., w_{i_0}^0, ..., w_m^0) \quad \text{Initial configuration}$$

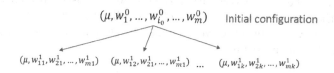

Fig. 1. A computation tree of a P system

An important concept to define entropies for P system is to establish whether the objects are produced in a stochastic/probabilistic manner or not. For the former, the probabilistic distribution is carried out by the definition of stochastic/probabilistic P systems such as Dynamical Probabilistic P systems (DPP) [14] or Population Dynamics P Systems (PDP) [4], together with their simulation algorithms [2, 10, 11].

3   The Entropy of a P System

We will define the entropy of a P system by analyzing how the multisets at every region evolve according to the rules of the system. First, we define the entropy of the multisets of the regions and, then, the entropy of a P system. In order to carry out a rigorous analysis, we need to distinguish whether the P system is a probabilistic/stochastic one or not. In the following, we discuss both cases.

The Non-probabilistic/Non-stochastic Case. We consider that every multiset at every region in the P system is defined by the application of rules in a pure non-deterministic non-probabilistic/non-stochastic case. Hence, the multisets at every region during the computation reflect, in an isolated way, the information production that can be considered to calculate the entropy. We will introduce a definition of entropy that is related to every multiset without any probabilistic information source.

Definition 1 (self-referred entropy of a multiset). *Let us consider a multiset $A = \langle D, f \rangle$ represented by x. The self-referred entropy of x is defined as*

$$H_s(x) = -\sum_{a \in D} fr(a) \cdot log_2 fr(a)$$

where $fr(a) = \frac{|x|_a}{|x|}$.

Observe that, in the previous definition, the probability distribution has been substituted by the frequency of appearance of every object at the region $(fr(a))$.

In the following, we analyze the evolution of self-referred entropies according to the computations of the system.

Definition 2. *Let Π be a P system of degree m and $c_t = (\mu, w_1^t, \cdots, w_m^t)$ be a configuration of the system during a computation at time t. Then*

1. *The absolute entropy of Π at time t is $H_{abs}^t(\Pi) = \sum_{1 \leq i \leq m} H_s(w_i^t)$*
2. *The maximal entropy of Π at time t is $H_{max}^t(\Pi) = max\{H_s(w_1^t), \cdots, H_s(w_m^t)\}$*
3. *The minimal entropy of Π at time t is $H_{min}^t(\Pi) = min\{H_s(w_1^t), \cdots, H_s(w_m^t)\}$*
4. *The average entropy of Π at time t is $H_{avg}^t(\Pi) = \frac{H_{abs}^t(\Pi)}{m}$*
5. *The holistic entropy of Π at time t is $H_{hol}^t(\Pi) = H_s(w_1^t w_2^t \cdots w_m^t)$*

Property 1. The following relation holds

$$H_{min}^t(\Pi) \leq H_{avg}^t(\Pi) \leq H_{max}^t(\Pi) \leq H_{abs}^t(\Pi) \leq H_{hol}^t(\Pi)$$

Proof. Trivial from the definitions.

The question about the computation of the entropy of a P system is completely based on the calculation of the different multisets at every region, according to the rules that affect to that region. Hence, at time t the multiset w_i^t will evolve, in the next transition, to the multiset $w_i^t \ominus left(R, i) \oplus right(R, i)$, where $left(R, i)$ is a multiset based on the left hand side of the rules that affect to the region i, and $right(R, i)$ is a multiset based on the right hand side of the rules that affect to the region i. Hence, the way to calculate the different entropies defined before is carried out by the following execution scheme:

1. Calculate the following configuration of the system according to its working manner (minimal, maximal, sequential, etc.)
2. For every multiset w_i^{t+1} calculate $H_s(w_i^{t+1})$.
3. Calculate the different entropies based on the self-referred entropies of the system.

The Probabilistic/Stochastic Case. In this case, we assume that every rule in the system has a *kinetic (stochastic)* real value that influences the application of the rules and the way to obtain the new configurations during the computation time. The main systems that have been proposed to calculate the configurations in a probabilistic/stochastic manner have been Dynamical Probabilistic P systems (DPP) [14], including the τ-DPP systems [3], or Population Dynamics P Systems (PDP) [4]. In both cases, there are simulation algorithms that manage the configurations evolution in order to produce the desired stochastic/probabilistic effect [1,2,8–11].

In this case, the definition of entropy should be based on the appearance probabilities of every symbol at every region. Here, the symbol probabilities come from different probabilities sources according to rules at (different) regions that produce the same symbol with different probabilities.

For example, let us consider the P system of Fig. 2. There are three regions and the object b can be produced at region 1 by using the rule r_1 at region 2 or the rule r_2 at region 3. While the rule r_1 is applied at every computation step (it has probability 1.0 to be applied), the rule r_2 should compete with rule r_3 to be applied (if we suppose a uniform distribution of kinetic constants). So, the object 'b' at region 1 has probability 1.0 or probability 0.5 depending on the rule that has produced it.

We evaluate every symbol at every region by establishing where it was created in order to reflect this situation. Then, given a P system Π, let us suppose that, at region i, the object 'a' can be produced by the set of rules R_a^i, with cardinality $|R_a^i|$. This set is easily deduced by the set of rules at every region adjacent to region i. We propose a naive approximation to the probability of symbol 'a' at region i, and computation time t, as follows

$$P_i^t(a) = \frac{\sum_{r \in R_a^i} Pr^{t-1}(r)}{|R_a^i|}$$

where $Pr^{t-1}(r)$ is the probability of applying the rule r at time $t-1$ that is calculated in a stochastic/probabilistic way as referred above.

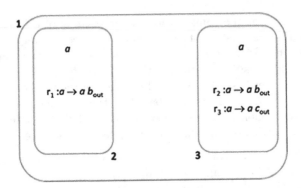

Fig. 2. A P system with competing rules

Now, we can reformulate the entropy of any multiset that reflects the stochastic/approximation approach.

Definition 3 (entropy of a multiset at time t). *Let Π be a P system and let x be a multiset at time t located at region i. The entropy of x at time t is defined as*

$$H^t(x) = - \sum_{a \in alph(x)} |x|_a \cdot P_i^t(a) \cdot log_2 P_i^t(a).$$

If we substitute at Definition 2, the entropy $H_s(w_i^t)$ by $H^t(w_i^t)$ then we have the corresponding entropies of the P system into a stochastic/probabilistic approach. Additionally, we can calculate the entropy of the system by executing the following scheme:

1. Calculate the following configuration of the system and the probabilities of the rules according to a pre-defined algorithm [1,2,8–11].
2. For every multiset w_i^{t+1} calculate $H^{t+1}(w_i^{t+1})$.
3. Calculate the different entropies of the system based on the entropies at time $t+1$.

Trivially, the relation of Property 1 holds for the definition of entropies under the probabilistic/stochastic approach.

Relative Entropy and Mutual Information Between Adjacent Regions. We will use the mutual information in order to analyze how every multiset at a given region influences the entropy variation for the multisets at its adjacent regions. Let Π be a P system and R_i and R_j two adjacent regions according to its membrane structure, then we propose the following relatives entropies of the random variables W_i^t and W_j^t that reflects the contents of regions R_i and R_j at time t:

1. The mutual information $I(W_i^t, W_j^t)$ reflects the information that is only explained by observing the two regions simultaneously at every computation step

2. The relative entropy $D(P(W_i^t|W_j^{t-1}), P(W_i^t) \cdot P(W_j^{t-1}))$ that measures the causality information effects of one region over the other with respect to their behavior as independent regions.

Observe, that we can generalize the random variables in order to consider the set of regions adjacent to a given one. Hence, we can define the random variable $W_{i_1,i_2,\cdots,i_p}^t$ that takes into account the contents of the regions $R_{i_1}, R_{i_2}, \cdots, R_{i_p}$ which are adjacent to the region R_i at computation time t.

In addition, we can use the computation time to study the information effects of the contents of a given region R_i, at time t, over a non-adjacent region R_k in computation time $t + p$ with $p > 1$.

The scheme to calculate the previous information metrics is based again on the algorithms to calculate the multisets at every region and the estimation of conditional and joint probability distribution.

4 P Systems with Entropic Transitions

The transition modes of a P system has been classically one of the hot topics in membrane computing [7]. In this section we are going to propose a new working manner based on the informational aspects of the system. Furthermore, we can redefine the *confluence* of P systems computation based on this working manner. The following definition introduces this aspect.

Definition 4 (entropic confluence). *Let* $\Pi = (V, \mu, w_1, \cdots, w_m, (R_1, \rho_1), \cdots, (R_m, \rho_m), i_0)$ *be a P system of degree* m. *We will say that* Π *is*

1. *entropic confluent if, for every pair of halting configurations* $(\mu, w_1^t, \cdots, w_{i_0}^t, \cdots, w_m^t)$ *and* $(\mu, w_1^q, \cdots, w_{i_0}^q, \cdots, w_m^q)$, $H_s(w_{i_0}^t) = H_s(w_{i_0}^q)$
2. *complete entropic confluent if, for every pair of halting configurations* $(\mu, w_1^t, \cdots, w_m^t)$ *and* $(\mu, w_1^q, \cdots, w_m^q)$, $\forall i, 1 \leq i \leq m$, $H_s(w_i^t) = H_s(w_i^q)$
3. *absolute entropic confluent if, for every pair of halting configurations* $(\mu, w_1^t, \cdots, w_m^t)$ *and* $(\mu, w_1^q, \cdots, w_m^q)$, $\sum_{1 \leq i \leq m} H_s(w_i^t) = \sum_{1 \leq i \leq m} H_s(w_i^q)$
4. *maximal entropic confluent if, for every pair of halting configurations* $(\mu, w_1^t, \cdots, w_m^t)$ *and* $(\mu, w_1^q, \cdots, w_m^q)$, $max\{H_s(w_1^t), \cdots, H_s(w_m^t)\} = max\{H_s(w_1^q), \cdots, H_s(w_m^q)\}$
5. *minimal entropic confluent if, for every pair of halting configurations* $(\mu, w_1^t, \cdots, w_m^t)$ *and* $(\mu, w_1^q, \cdots, w_m^q)$, $min\{H_s(w_1^t), \cdots, H_s(w_m^t)\} = min\{H_s(w_1^q), \cdots, H_s(w_m^q)\}$
6. *average entropic confluent if, for every pair of halting configurations* $(\mu, w_1^t, \cdots, w_m^t)$ *and* $(\mu, w_1^q, \cdots, w_m^q)$, $\frac{\sum_{1 \leq i \leq m} H_s(w_i^t)}{m} = \frac{\sum_{1 \leq i \leq m} H_s(w_i^q)}{m}$
7. *holistic entropic confluent if, for every pair of halting configurations* $(\mu, w_1^t, \cdots, w_m^t)$ *and* $(\mu, w_1^q, \cdots, w_m^q)$, $H_s(w_1^t \cdots w_m^t) = H_s(w_1^q \cdots w_m^q)$

Observe that some definitions of entropic confluence implies some other ones. For example, if the system is complete entropic confluent then it is entropic confluent and absolute entropic confluent. An absolute entropic confluent system is average entropic confluent, and so on a so forth.

Entropic Behavior. Inspired by thermodynamics, and as a consequence of the second law of thermodynamics, the *Principle of Maximum Entropy* arises: *"Closed systems evolve to an equilibrium state characterized by a maximum of entropy"*. Hence, we can consider a different working manner for P systems based on the growth of the entropy.

Given a P system, we say that the system applies a (maximal, absolute, minimal, average, holistic) *entropic transition* if it applies only the set of rules that increases the (defined) entropies of the system.

Observe that the set of rules that must be applied at every computation step is based in the multisets of objects that every region contains and it can be different at every computation step. In order to illustrate this fact, let us see the following example: Let $r_1 : a \rightarrow aa$ and $r_2 : ab \rightarrow aabb$ be two rules of the same region in a P system. If we consider the multiset $aabb$, then the entropic transition will be carried out by applying rule r_2 instead of r_1, here we obtain the new multiset $aaaabbbb$ which has a maximum self-referred entropy (observe that this maximum is achieved with a uniform distribution of objects). If the multiset is abb then the rule to be applied in order to increase the self-referred entropy is r_1 instead of r_2 and it produces the new multiset $aabb$ (again, we obtain an uniform distribution of objects).

Definition 5. *A P system works in a (maximal, absolute, minimal, average, holistic) entropic manner if at every computation step it only applies (maximal, absolute, minimal, average, holistic) entropic transitions.*

Observe that the simulation of a P system working in any entropic manner, can be a difficult task to be simulated, given that the search of the set of rules needed at every computation step is not a trivial task. In some cases, it can be considered a Multiobjective Optimization Problem with conflicts, given that different functions must be maximized (the entropies functionals at every region), and the increase of entropy at one region could decrease the entropy at an adjacent region (by using symport or antiport rules). Here, some entropy optimization problems can be proved to be $\mathcal{NP}$-optimization ones [6].

Another aspect that must be explored with respect to P systems working in an entropic manner, is the halting criterion. Observe that in our proposal, if no rule increments the entropy of the system, then no rule can be applied at a given time and, accordingly to the usual criterion, the system halts. Obviously, under this point of view the sets of natural numbers and languages that P systems recognize, accept or generate should be defined within this new approach.

5   Conclusion, Further Research and Future Works

In this work we have proposed the Information Theory as a framework to study P systems under a new view. We think that this approach opens new and exciting topics that should be studied in the near time. Among other questions we can point out, the following ones:

1. How does the operational mode (i.e. maximal or minimal parallelism, sequential, etc.) affect to entropy?
2. What is the relationship between confluence and entropic confluence?
3. What is the definition of the entropy of a P system, if the external output is defined?

With respect to the last question, if we consider any P system with a network structure (tissue-like P systems, Spiking Neural P systems, ...) then the entropy should be calculated by taking the output sequence as a pure communication channel. Here, the output alphabet, the time between outputs (specially, in the case of SN P systems) and the definition of randomness are essential aspects that should be considered in order to explore new aspects of this approach.

All these aspects will be studied in the near future and some of them are actually work in progress.

References

1. Besozzi, D., Cazzaniga, P., Pescini, D., Mauri, G.: A multivolume approach to stochastic modeling with membrane systems. In: Condon, A., et al. (eds.) Algorithmic Bioprocesses, pp. 519–542. Springer, Heidelberg (2009)
2. Cardona, M., Colomer, M.A., Margalida, A., Palau, A., Pérez-Hurtado, I., Pérez-Jiménez, M.J., Sanuy, D.: A computational modeling of real ecosistems based on P systems. Nat. Comput. **10**(1), 39–53 (2011)
3. Cazzaniga, P., Pescini, D., Besozzi, D., Mauri, G.: Tau leaping stochastic simulation method in P systems. In: Hoogeboom, H.J., Păun, G., Rozenberg, G., Salomaa, A. (eds.) WMC 2006. LNCS, vol. 4361, pp. 298–313. Springer, Heidelberg (2006). doi:10.1007/11963516_19
4. Colomer, M.A., Martínez-del-Amor, M.A., Pérez-Hurtado, I., Pérez-Jiménez, M.J., Riscos-Núñez, A.: A uniform framework for modeling based on P systems. In: IEEE Fifth International Conference on Bio-inspired Computing: Theories and Applications (BIC-TA 2010), vol. 1, pp. 616–621 (2010)
5. Cover, T.M., Thomas, J.A.: Elements of Information Theory. Wiley, Hoboken (1991)
6. Fleszar, K., Glaßer, C., Lipp, F., Reitwießner, C., Witek, M.: The complexity of solving multiobjective optimization problems and its relation to multivalued functions. Electronic Colloquium on Computational Complexity (ECCC), Report No. 53 (2011)
7. Freund, R., Ibarra, O.H., Păun, A., Sosìk, P., Yen, H.: Catalytic P Systems. In: Păun, G., Rozenberg, G., Salomaa, A. (eds.) The Oxford Handbook of Membrane Computing. Oxford University Press, Oxford (2010)
8. Gillespie, D.T.: Exact stochastic simulation of coupled chemical reactions. J. Phys. Chem. **81**(25), 2340–2361 (1977)
9. Gillespie, D.T.: Stochastic simulation of chemical kinetics. Annu. Rev. Phys. Chem. **58**, 35–55 (2007)
10. Martínez del Amor, M.A., Pérez-Hurtado, I., Pérez-Jiménez, M.J., Riscos-Núñez, A., Colomer, M.A.: A new simulation algorithm for multienvironment probabilistic P systems. In: IEEE Fifth International Conference on Bio-inspired Computing: Theories and Applications (BIC-TA 2010), vol. 1, pp. 59–68 (2010)

11. Martínez-del-Amor, M.A., et al.: DCBA: simulating population dynamics P systems with proportional object distribution. In: Csuhaj-Varjú, E., Gheorghe, M., Rozenberg, G., Salomaa, A., Vaszil, G. (eds.) CMC 2012. LNCS, vol. 7762, pp. 257–276. Springer, Heidelberg (2013). doi:10.1007/978-3-642-36751-9_18

12. Păun, G.: Membrane Computing: An Introduction. Springer, Heidelberg (2002)

13. Păun, G., Rozenberg, G., Salomaa, A. (eds.): The Oxford Handbook of Membrane Computing. Oxford University Press, Oxford (2010)

14. Pescini, D., Besozzi, D., Mauri, G., Zandron, C.: Dynamical probabilistic P systems. Int. J. Found. Comput. Sci. **17**(1), 183–204 (2006)

15. Roman, S.: Introduction to Coding and Information Theory. Springer, New York (1997)

16. Shannon, C.E.: A mathematical theory of communication. Bell Syst. Tech. J. **27**, 379–423 (1948). 623–656

17. Syropoulos, A.: Mathematics of Multisets. In: [2], pp. 347–358

Author Index

Adorna, Henry N.   190
Alhazov, Artiom   51, 67, 83
Aman, Bogdan   51, 103

Bakir, Mehmet Emin   119
Barbuti, Roberto   28
Battyányi, Péter   136
Belingheri, Omar   67
Bove, Pasquale   28

Cabarle, Francis George C.   190
Cavaliere, Matteo   3
Ceterchi, Rodica   233
Cienciala, Luděk   151
Ciencialová, Lucie   151
Ciobanu, Gabriel   103, 165

Farinelli, Alessandro   177
Franco, Giuditta   177
Freund, Rudolf   51, 67, 83

Gapuz, Katrina B.   190
Gazdag, Zsolt   209
Gheorghe, Marian   119, 233

Hatnik, Uwe   251
Hernandez, Nestine Hope S.   190
Hinze, Thomas   16, 251

Ipate, Florentin   233
Isawasan, Pradeep   272
Ivanov, Sergiu   51, 67

Juayong, Richelle Ann B.   190

Kolonits, Gábor   209
Konur, Savas   119, 233

Lefticaru, Raluca   286
Leporati, Alberto   307

Macías-Ramos, Luis F.   286
Manzoni, Luca   307
Mauri, Giancarlo   307
Mendoza, Ephraim D.   190
Mierlă, Laurenţiu   286
Milazzo, Paolo   28
Muniyandi, Ravie Chandren   272

Nicolescu, Radu   317
Niculescu, Ionuţ Mihai   286

Pan, Linqiang   340
Pardini, Giovanni   28
Porreca, Antonio E.   67, 307

Rizzi, Romeo   177

Sanchez, Alvaro   3
Sempere, José M.   352
Song, Bosheng   340
Sosík, Petr   151
Stannett, Mike   119
Subramanian, K.G.   272, 340

Todoran, Eneia Nicolae   165

Vaszil, György   136
Venkat, Ibrahim   272
Verlan, Sergey   83

Weber, Lea Louise   251

Zandron, Claudio   67, 307

Printed in the United States
By Bookmasters